FROM SHIBE PARK TO CONNIE MACK STADIUM

Great Games In Philadelphia's Lost Ballpark

Edited by
GREGORY H. WOLF

Associate Editors
LEN LEVIN, BILL NOWLIN, AND CARL RIECHERS

Society for American Baseball Research, Inc.
Phoenix, AZ

From Shibe Park to Connie Mack Stadium: Great Games in Philadelphia's Lost Ballpark
Copyright © 2022 Society for American Baseball Research, Inc.
Edited by Gregory H. Wolf
Associate Editors: Len Levin, Bill Nowlin, and Carl Riechers

Back Cover photo:
Shibe Park (National Baseball Hall of Fame, Cooperstown, New York)

ISBN 978-1-970159-86-8
(Ebook ISBN 978-1-970159-85-1)
Library of Congress Control Number (LCCN) 2022917181
Book design: David Peng

Unless otherwise noted, all photos are in the public domain.

Society for American Baseball Research
Cronkite School at ASU
555 N. Central Ave. #416
Phoenix, AZ 85004
Phone: (602) 496-1460
Web: www.sabr.org
Facebook: Society for American Baseball Research
Twitter: @SABR

TABLE OF CONTENTS

SHIBE PARK TO CONNIE MACK STADIUM: AN INTRODUCTION

By Gregory H. Wolf

"Never before in the history of baseball in this city has the opening of the championship season been awaited with such manifest destiny," declared the *Philadelphia Inquirer* on April 12, 1909.[1] On that day, the Philadelphia Athletics inaugurated baseball's first steel and concrete ballpark, ushering in a new era. An architectural marvel, Shibe Park boasted an ornate Beaux Arts tower at its main entrance at the intersection of 21st Street and Lehigh Avenue, an exterior adorned with arched windows and friezes that evoked French palaces, a double-decked grandstand, and a seating capacity of 23,000. On Opening Day, the ballpark was filled with more than 35,000 spectators, including 12,000 standing-room customers. "Smashing all records for attendance and creating a brand-new epoch in the history of the national pastime," opined the *Inquirer*, "the greatest crowd that has ever witnessed a baseball game stormed Shibe Park."[2] Ban Johnson, president of the American League, praised the park as "the greatest place of its character in the world,"[3] while Philadelphia Mayor John E. Reyburn, who threw out the ceremonial first pitch, declared it "the finest baseball stadium in the country."[4]

From Shibe Park to Connie Mack Stadium: Great Games in Philadelphia's Lost Ballpark evokes memories and the exciting history of the celebrated ballpark through stories of about 100 games played there and several feature essays. Originally named after Benjamin Shibe, the sporting-goods magnate who owned a 50 percent stake in the AL charter member Athletics from 1901, Shibe Park was the home of the A's from 1909 until their relocation to Kansas City after the 1954 season, as well as the Philadelphia Phillies from 1938 until the ballpark's closure at the end of the 1970 season. In 1953 Shibe Park was renamed Connie Mack Stadium in honor of the baseball icon who had managed the Athletics for their first 50 seasons and co-owned the club since its inception, and beginning 1913 as a full partner with "Uncle Ben" Shibe.

Shibe Park/Connie Mack Stadium hosted big-league baseball for 62 seasons and more than 6,000 games, including in excess of 3,500 games by the A's and 2,500 by the Phillies. It was the home for some of the best – and worst – teams in history. The games included in this volume reflect every decade in the ballpark's history, from the inaugural game on April 12, 1909, to the last, on October 1, 1970, as well as the A's final home game in the City of Brotherly Love, on September 19, 1954, and the Phillies' debut in their new home in an Independence Day doubleheader in 1938, ending their run of five-plus decades in the pillbox Baker Bowl, which was located just blocks from Shibe Park.

Unlike its contemporaries, such as Forbes Field in Pittsburgh and Griffith Stadium in Washington, Shibe Park was never a primary home of a Negro League team, though Negro League teams occasionally played there. In addition to an insightful feature essay exploring the history of Negro League baseball at the ballpark, we've included a story about the Cleveland Buckeyes' victory over the Homestead Grays on September 20, 1945, to capture the Negro League title, and another about Game Three of the 1947 Negro League World Series featuring the New York Cubans and the Buckeyes on September 24, 1947, both of which took place at Shibe Park.

Shibe Park hosted 20 World Series games involving the A's or Phillies, and you can read about each one of them in this volume. Connie Mack's first dynasty, led by his $100,000 infield – Stuffy McInnis, Eddie Collins, Jack Barry, and Home Run Baker – captured four pennants and three championships in a five-year stretch (1910-1914), before Mack dismantled it for financial reasons. The Tall Tactician's second dynasty took the A's last pennants, winning three straight and two championships (1929-1931). Those teams, led by Hall of Famers Lefty Grove, Mickey Cochrane, Jimmy Foxx, and Al Simmons, met their demise as the Great Depression's grip on Mack and the county tightened. Mack and the A's never fully recovered: The A's managed only four winning seasons in their last 22

In 1913 the Athletics (96-57) won their third World Series in four seasons.

years in the ballpark (1933-1954) and only two first-division finishes.

The Phillies, whose origins extend back to 1883 when they were known as the Quakers, played in Shibe Park/Connie Mack Stadium for 33 seasons (from mid-1938 through 1970). Among the big-leagues' most uncompetitive teams since World War I, the Phillies captured a surprising pennant in 1950. Aptly named the Whiz Kids, a group of young players, including Robin Roberts, Richie Ashburn, Del Ennis, and Curt Simmons, led the Phillies to their first pennant since 1915 and just their third winning season since they traded Pete Alexander after the 1917 season. The Phillies' two games against the Yankees in the 1950 fall classic were the last World Series (and postseason) games in the history of Shibe Park. The Phillies seemed destined to capture the pennant in 1964, holding a 6½-game lead over the Cincinnati Reds with 12 games to go. Their monumental collapse, known as the "Phold" is also presented – perhaps painfully for some readers – in this volume.

Some of the games of this volume have historical significance, like Jackie Robinson's 1947 debut in Shibe Park as a member of the Brooklyn Dodgers; the first night game in the ballpark, in 1939; the first night All-Star Game, in 1943; and the park's last home opener, in 1970. Other games recall significant or milestone feats, including

Babe Ruth becoming the first player to hit three home runs in the ballpark (1930), Al Simmons becoming the first Athletic to achieve the feat (1932), and Lou Gehrig's four-home-run game (1932). You can read about longtime A's slugger Jimmie Foxx belting his 500h home run in Shibe Park in 1940, but as a member of the Boston Red Sox, and his teammate Ted Williams deciding to play in a season-ending doubleheader with a .400 batting average on the line. Andy Seminick was the first member of the Phillies to whack a trifecta in Shibe (1949), while teammate Del Wilber once belted three 'taters which accounted for all three runs in a Phillies shutout victory in 1951. We also present some wild and improbable comebacks and some high-octane slugfests.

For those who want pitching, *From Shibe Park to Connie Mack Stadium: Great Games in Philadelphia's Lost Ballpark* contains some of the greatest mound feats at the park's six-plus-decade history. We've included all nine no-hitters, four of which were by Athletics pitchers. Hall of Famer Chief Bender tossed the first (1910), while Bill Stoneman of the expansion Montreal Expos tossed the last (1969). Sandy Koufax of the Los Angeles Dodgers authored the most famous one (1964), the third of his four no-nos; while the A's Dick Fowler tossed the most improbable one (1945), in his first start in almost three years

after serving for 30 months in the Canadian Army in World War II. Other no-nos are from players whose memories and accomplishments this book helps preserve, such as Joe Bush, Sam Jones, Howard Ehmke, Bill McCann, and George Culver. Mike McCormick's unofficial five-inning no-hitter is included, too. Additional games recount marathon pitching or dominant performances by hurlers like Jack Coombs, Eddie Plank, Claude Passeau, Jim Bunning, and Bob Gibson. We have the bizarre, too, such Allen Travers' complete-game, 24-2 loss in 1912 on a day when the Detroit team went on strike, forcing a group of amateurs to take the field; and also the A's Jack Nabors losing his final game of the 1916 season to finish with a 1-20 record

From Shibe Park to Connie Mack Stadium: Great Games in Philadelphia's Lost Ballpark is the result of the tireless work of dozens of members of the Society for American Baseball Research. SABR members researched and wrote all of the essays in this volume. These uncompensated volunteers are united by their shared interest in baseball history and a resolute commitment to preserving its history. Without their unwavering dedication, this volume would not have been possible.

I am indebted to the associate editors and extend to them my sincerest appreciation. Bill Nowlin, the second reader, fact-checker Carl Riechers, and copy editor Len Levin read all the essays and made numerous corrections to language, style, and content. Their attention to detail has been invaluable. It has been a pleasure to once again work on a book project with such professionals. What a team we have!

I thank all of the authors for their contributions, meticulous research, cooperation through the revising and editing process, and finally their patience. It was a long journey from the day the book was launched to its completion, and we've finally reached our destination. We did it! Please refer to the list of contributors at the end of the book for more information.

This book would not have been possible without the generous support of the staff and Board of Directors of SABR, SABR Publications Director Cecilia Tan, and designer David Peng.

We express our thanks and gratitude to a number of folks who helped procure photos for this book. Thanks to Matthew J. Richards, vice president and general manager of sales, and Andy Krause, sport product manager at Getty Images, for their invaluable assistance.

And finally, I wish to thank my wife, Margaret, and daughter, Gabriela, for their support of and endless patience with my baseball pursuits.

We invite you to sit back, relax for a few minutes, and enjoy reading about the great games and the exciting history of Shibe Park/Connie Mack Stadium.

Gregory H. Wolf
December 1, 2022

NOTES

1   "American Leaguers Will Get Going in New Play Ground by Battling Boston's Team – With Bright Day Record-Breaking Crowd Will Storm the Big Gates," *Philadelphia Inquirer*, April 12, 1909: 10.

2   Greatest Baseball Crowd at Shibe Park Sees Athletics Win Opening Game," *Philadelphia Inquirer*, April 13, 1909: 1.

3   "Praise And Admiration Heard Everywhere," *Philadelphia Inquirer*, April 13, 1909: 13.

4   "Praise And Admiration Heard Everywhere."

SHIBE PARK /
CONNIE MACK STADIUM

By James Lincoln Ray

Shibe Park, later known as Connie Mack Stadium, goes back to the Philadelphia Athletics, its original occupant, and their owner Benjamin Franklin Shibe. When Shibe in 1901 took charge of the new team, one of eight clubs in the brand-new American League, he could not have foreseen that the Athletics would become so popular so quickly.

Philadelphia already had a major-league team, the National League's Phillies, who remain the nation's oldest continuous same-name, same-city sports franchise. Founded in 1883, the Phillies certainly weren't breaking any attendance records. However, the American League Athletics caught on quickly with Philadelphia fans. In just its second season the team won the American League pennant. The Phillies, by comparison, didn't win their first pennant until 1915, and their second until 1950 – one of the longest droughts in professional sports. The 1901 A's attracted more than 206,000 fans to their 9,500-seat home field, Columbia Park, at 29th Street and Columbia Avenue in the North Philadelphia neighborhood known as Brewery-town. Theirs was the highest attendance in the American League, and nearly four times that of the Phillies who played in the Philadelphia Baseball Grounds, known after 1913 as the Baker Bowl.

When the Athletics won their second pennant, in 1905, attendance had grown to more than 550,000. By 1907 it had exploded to 625,000. The team often had to barricade the gates and turn away thousands. Ben Shibe thought that if he built a new park with greater seating capacity, Philadelphia fans would fill the place up.

Shibe found the ideal location for his planned stadium, on Lehigh Avenue between 20th and 21st Streets, just five blocks west of the Phillies' home, soon-to-be called the Baker Bowl. He liked the site because the land was cheap and it was easily accessible by public transportation. Trolley cars ran east-west along Lehigh Avenue, and north-south along nearby Broad (14th) Street, aptly named because it was by far the widest street in the city, as well as the longest straight street in the United States, and both the Pennsylvania and Reading Railroads had stations close by. The land was cheap because the Philadelphia Hospital for Contagious Diseases, called the "Smallpox Hospital," was on Lehigh Avenue a block west of Shibe's site. Shibe used inside information that the hospital was about to be closed down and acted quickly to buy up the entire block, totaling 5.75 acres, for $67,500. He used associates to purchase many small parcels of land in order not to arouse

Fans gather on rooftops on 20th Street across from Shibe Park to watch the 1913 World Series.

suspicion of his intentions that might lead some owner to hold out for an exorbitant amount.

Shibe wanted more than a stadium. He wanted an edifice of the latest technology, and hired a remarkable company, William Steele and Sons, to construct it. Steele had built some of the city's most important structures, including the highly acclaimed Witherspoon Building, the city's first steel and concrete skyscraper, in 1895-97. The firm also designed and built the first cement-mixer truck, which revolutionized the industry. Steele broke ground on Shibe Park in April 1908 and completed the project in less than a year. Five hundred tons of steel and several thousand cubic yards of reinforced concrete were used in the construction.

The original stadium layout had a double-decked grandstand that ran from first base, wrapped around home plate, and continued down the line to third base. A grandstand roof protected fans from the elements, and metal folding chairs replaced common bleacher seats on both levels. The price of admission for lower-level seats was $1, and for upper deck seats was 50 cents.

An additional 13,000 pavilion bleacher seats extended along the foul lines from first and third base to the foul poles. Shibe priced these seats at 25 cents because, as the *Evening Telegraph* reported, those "who live by the sweat of their brow should have as good a chance of seeing the game as the man who never rolled up his sleeves to earn a dollar."[1] Pleased with the egalitarian design, the *Telegraph* proclaimed that Shibe had created a stadium "for the masses as well as the classes."[2]

In addition to the 23,000 seats, there were two standing-room sections, one in the outfield grass and the other in the wide aisles behind the pavilion bleachers. They could accommodate 17,000 more patrons.

The rectangular shape of the city block resulted in imbalanced dimensions for the field. The block was 40 feet shorter east-west than north-south.

With home plate located in the southwest corner of the block, the right-field foul pole was 340 feet and the left-field pole 378 feet from home plate. Center field was enormous. At its deepest, the two perpendicular outfield walls met and formed a right angle 515 feet from home plate.

The exterior of the stadium was more French palace than ballpark. Outside the grandstand, an ornate brick façade had huge arched windows separated by Ionic pilasters, decorative friezes with baseball motifs, and gabled dormer windows on the upper deck's copper-trimmed green-slate mansard roof. Figurative sculptures in terra cotta of Shibe and co-owner/manager Connie Mack peered out over the main entrances. Other entrances were decorated with the letter "A" carved in Old English script. Above the 21st Street entrance was one of the team's stores. There was a restaurant for patrons on the ground level that faced both Lehigh and 21st Streets.

The iconic feature of the exterior was the domed tower at the corner of 21st and Lehigh. It contained offices for Shibe's sons, Jack and Tom, who managed the team's business operations. A domed cupola topped off the tower and housed Connie Mack's "Oval Office."

Upon completion, Shibe Park received rave reviews. "A palace for fans, the most beautiful and capacious baseball structure in the world," said one Philadelphia newspaper.[3] "Shibe Park is the greatest place of its character in the world," said another.[4] Mayor John E. Reyburn called the new facility a "pride to the city." When he first saw the park, pioneer player George Wright said: "It is the most remarkable sight I have ever witnessed."[5]

Monday, April 12, 1909, was Opening Day. By 9 A.M. the ticket line wrapped around the entire city block as baseball fans eagerly waited to see their team in its new baseball palace. As the crowd inevitably became impatient and rowdy, nervous ushers closed the gates to the entrances, turning the fans outside into a howling mob of thousands pressed against the locked barricades.[6]

Eventually, the weight and pressure of the mass of humanity forced one of the gates open and hundreds poured in without paying. About 7,000 rooters watched the game from the outfield, standing seven-deep and held back by a rope stretched across the entire expanse of the outfield. Another 6,000 fans looked in from rooftops around the block. "It seemed as if all of Philadelphia was there," wrote the *Public Ledger*. Mayor Reyburn threw out the first ball a few minutes before the 3:00 P.M. start.

Future Hall of Famer Eddie Plank pitched a wonderful game as the A's defeated the Boston Red Sox, 8-1. The *Philadelphia Evening Bulletin* reported, "It was a great day for Philadelphia in the baseball world, it was a great day for the fans, a most profitable one for the owners of Shibe Park, and a grand start for the Athletics. The attendance will probably go on the record as the largest in the history of baseball."[7] Plank's catcher was 38-year-old backup Doc Powers, who was a physician and very popular around the league. He became ill in the seventh inning but finished the game. He died of complications from peritonitis two weeks later.

The Athletics enjoyed immediate success in their new home. Although they finished in second place in 1909, they won the American League pennant the next season, and went on to hammer the Chicago Cubs in the World Series in five games. The team repeated as world champions in 1911 and then again in 1913, each time beating the New York Giants.

The A's performance encouraged Shibe to expand the park. He added a new unroofed bleacher section across left field, and also added roof structures to cover the open pavilions down the first-base and third-base lines.

But the record crowds Shibe and Connie Mack hoped for didn't come. Despite the expanded seating, and another pennant-winning team, attendance dropped sharply in 1914 to 346,000, from a high of 674,915 in 1909 Besides the

Shibe Park during Game Two of the 1910 World Series between the Philadelphia Athletics and Chicago Cubs. The A's exploded for six runs in the seventh inning to win, 9-3.

lowered revenues, the Athletics faced increasing competition for players from the upstart Federal League, which began play in 1914 and induced American and National League stars to jump to the new league. Among them, pitchers Chief Bender and Eddie Plank signed with Federal League teams in December 1914.

Connie Mack decided that it would be better to sell his remaining stars for much-needed cash rather than risk losing them for nothing to the new league. Among those disposed of by Mack were future Hall of Famers Eddie Collins, Frank "Home Run" Baker, and Herb Pennock. By the middle of the 1915 season, the team that later became known as Connie Mack's First Dynasty had been completely dismantled.

The talent drain led to seven straight last-place finishes and years of anemic attendance figures. Between 1915 and 1921 attendance averaged about 226,000 fans a year, less than a third of what the team had drawn during its heady days. Mack slowly rebuilt his team with new talent and attendance increased. This encouraged Shibe's sons Jack and Tom, who shared control with Mack after their father's death in 1922, to upgrade the park again. This time they replaced the open left-field bleachers with a double-decked roofed terrace, installed a 750-seat mezzanine area, raised the original grandstand roof, and installed a press box and 3,500 more seats beneath it.

By 1929 the A's were once again on top of the baseball world. Behind the feats of future Hall of Famers Jimmie Foxx, Lefty Grove, Mickey Cochrane, and Al Simmons, the A's ran away with the American League, finishing 104-46, a full 18 games ahead of the Yankees. They crushed the Chicago Cubs in the World Series. The success of the 1929 team led to banner year at Shibe Park: 839,176 passed through the gates, about 30,000 fewer than the record attendance in 1925. When the Athletics repeated as World Series winners in 1930, and won a third straight pennant in 1931, writers began referring to the team as Connie Mack's Second Dynasty. The future for the team, its fans, and Shibe Park looked as promising and full of hope as a clear spring morning.

By 1932 the full effects of the Great Depression hit Philadelphia. The team drew less than 300,000 fans three times within four seasons (1933-1936), and hitting a low of 233,173 in 1935. Facing financial pressures and dim income prospects, Mack once again sold off his star players, and once again the team fell into the American League cellar. Fans stopped coming to the park. A terrible team and a worse economy were not a good recipe for drawing the working class to the ballpark. The Depression also led to the end of a great Shibe Park tradition that forever damaged the relationship between the A's and their neighborhood fans.

From the time Shibe Park opened in 1909 through the end of Mack's Second Dynasty, homeowners on 20th Street had a clear view of the ballpark's playing field. They could watch games from their top-floor windows and their rooftops. Some said that the views from 20th Street compared favorably with many of the seats inside the park. Enterprising homeowners constructed bleachers on their roofs and sold tickets. During the 1929 World Series, almost 3,000 people watched from the makeshift bleachers. Two more World Series further lined the pockets of these homeowners.

As long as the Athletics were drawing big crowds, Mack and the Shibes tolerated the situation. But when attendance continued to decline after the selloff of the Second Dynasty, and when the team learned that strapped homeowners who could no longer fill their rooftop bleachers were pilfering customers from Shibe Park's ticket line, Jack Shibe decided that enough was enough. In the winter of 1934-1935, the team built a 22-foot-high corrugated metal extension wall on top of the outfield wall. The extension made the right field wall 50 feet high and blocked the view of the field from the 20th Street rooftops.[8] Fans labeled the wall the spite fence or Connie Mack's Spite Wall, even though Jack Shibe had spearheaded the project.

The wall didn't just spite fans, it also infuriated some players who figured they were going to lose home runs. Outfielders also despised the hulking structure because its rippled corrugated facing caused baseballs to carom unpredictably.

Angry residents sued to have the fence taken down. Mack hired a tough young attorney named Richardson Dilworth, who won the case and the Spite Wall stayed. Dilworth later became a two-term mayor of Philadelphia.

In the middle of the 1938 season, the Phillies abandoned crumbling Baker Bowl and became tenants of the Athletics at Shibe Park. Despite resistance from neighbors, Mack installed eight 146-foot light towers. The first night game in the American League was played at Shibe Park on May 16, 1939. The A's lost to the Cleveland Indians, 8-3.

After World War II, Mack tried to expand the seating capacity again, this time to 50,000. There was a problem with the design, however; the rear wall would protrude past the right-field fence, hanging 15 feet above the sidewalk of North 20th Street and forming a covered arcade walkway. The proposal galvanized the 20th Street neighbors against Mack, and this time his legal team lost.

Although the A's would never field a legitimate contender after the 1932 dismantling (though they were in a crowded race in 1948), the ballpark's other tenant, the Phillies, had been stockpiling young talent after World War II and had a remarkable season in 1950. They dramatically defeated the Brooklyn Dodgers on the last day of the season and captured the National League pennant, the last in the history of the ballpark. They were swept in the World Series by the Yankees.

After the 1950 season, the 87-year-old Mack retired after managing the Athletics for 50 years, the longest managerial tenure in baseball history. In a last effort to revitalize the team, Mack's children changed the name of Shibe Park to Connie Mack Stadium before the 1953 season. It didn't help at the box office. In 1954 the A's drew just over 300,000 fans, less than one-half the Phillies' attendance and not nearly enough to support a two-family business (the Macks and the Shibes). It was clear to all that Philadelphia would no longer support two baseball teams. Heavily in debt to the banks, in August 1954 the owners sold the franchise to Chicago businessman Arnold Johnson for $3.375 million. Johnson moved the team to Kansas City for the 1955 season.

Phillies owner Bob Carpenter purchased Connie Mack Stadium for $1.675 million and made immediate changes. When the ballpark opened for the 1955 season, large billboards covered the outfield walls advertising Goldenberg's Peanut Chews, Plachter Cadillac, Alpo dog food, and Coca-Cola. Carpenter installed a new straight-across fence that covered the awkward square corner in center field and lessened the distance to center field to 447 feet. In 1956 he purchased a 50-foot-high outfield scoreboard similar to the one in Yankee Stadium. It was topped by a ten-foot-high Ballantine Beer sign, and was capped with a distinctive Longines clock.

After Connie Mack died in February 1956, sculptor Harry Rosin created a statue of "Mr. Baseball." It was unveiled on April 16, 1957, across Lehigh Avenue in Reyburn Park (rededicated as Connie Mack Plaza) as part of the Opening Day ceremonies.

The final game at Connie Mack Stadium was played on October 1, 1970, with the Phillies defeating the Montreal Expos, 2-1, in ten innings. Souvenir hunters began dismantling the stadium while the game was still in progress. They pulled up chairs, signs, gates, and the sod from the field. A postgame ceremony was canceled because of the mayhem. Over a headline that said, "Wrecking Crew of 31,822 Breaks Up the Old Ball Park," the *Philadelphia Inquirer* wrote, "Fans ripped up their seats and ransacked the dugouts. They tore off railing[s] and billboards. A gigantic old rain tarp was torn to shreds and both the infield and outfield were ruined."[9] A shameful end to a once-beautiful ballpark.

Over its 62 seasons, Shibe Park drew more than 47 million fans. The 1964 Phillies drew the highest single-season attendance, 1,425,891. The Athletics' best-attended season was 1948, when they last were in contention for a pennant, and drew 945,076 fans. The A's and the Phillies won a total of eight pennants in the ballpark. The Athletics played in seven World Series during their tenure at the stadium, and clinched three of their five championships at Shibe Park.

Other great baseball moments at Shibe Park include the 1943 and 1952 All-Star Games; the first American League night game, in 1939; four no-hitters by A's pitchers; and three historic performances by opposing players.

The first of those occurred on June 3, 1932, when the Yankees' Lou Gehrig hit four home runs. He narrowly missed a fifth homer when Al Simmons made a great running catch at the wall in center field. The second historic feat came on September 28, 1941, the last day of the season. The Red Sox were in town for a season-ending doubleheader. The matchup meant nothing in the standings, but it did mean a lot in the record books. Ted Williams entered the day with a .3995 batting average, which would have officially been rounded up to .400 had he decided not to play.

But Williams played, went 6-for-8 in the doubleheader, and finished the season at .406.

The third outstanding performance involved the Phillies. Sandy Koufax pitched a no-hitter against them on June 4, 1964 (Los Angeles Dodgers 3, Phillies, 0). Koufax faced the minimum 27 batters and struck out 12. Only a walk to Richie Allen on a full count in the fourth inning kept it from being a perfect game. Allen was thrown out trying to steal second base.

Events at Shibe Park/Connie Mack Stadium were not limited to Athletics and Phillies games. The park hosted its first Negro League game in 1919, and served as a neutral site for the 1945 Negro League series in which the Cleveland Buckeyes defeated the Homestead Grays. The Negro League Philadelphia Stars played home games at Shibe Park in the 1940s, and often drew crowds of more than 10,000.

The National Football League's Philadelphia Eagles moved to Shibe Park in 1940 and played their home games there through the 1957 season. During that tenure, the Eagles won the 1948 and 1949 NFL titles. The 1948 title game was played in a blizzard. Several championship boxing matches were also held at the park, the most famous of which was between Benny Leonard and Johnny Kilbane in 1917.

Events at Shibe were not always sports-related. In 1940 Republican presidential candidate Wendell Willkie came to Shibe for a speech and political rally. Four years later, Franklin Delano Roosevelt made one of his few 1944 public appearances at 21st and Lehigh. In 1948 Progressive Party candidate Henry A. Wallace made his acceptance speech there. The Ringling Brothers Circus set up shop at Shibe in 1955, and evangelist Billy Graham had many successful events there. A rodeo came to the park in 1962, but the animals destroyed the turf and weren't invited back.

Less than a year after the final baseball game, two brothers sneaked into the park and started a fire that grew into a five-alarm blaze. The fire burned through most of the original upper deck, collapsing the roof. The intense heat twisted and exposed the steel beams and left them grasping out finger-like. The ballpark remained in this condition for four years until October 1975, when a judge issued an order that it be demolished. The famous corner tower and its domed cupola was the last section of the ballpark demolished, on July 13, 1976.

In 1991 Deliverance Evangelistic Church built a church on the site. A historical marker for the ballpark was erected by the Philadelphia Historical Commission on November 9, 1997.

This biography is included in the book *The Year of the Blue Snow: The 1964 Philadelphia Phillies* (SABR, 2013), edited by Mel Marmer and Bill Nowlin.

SOURCES

Fitzpatrick, Frank. "Bad Playoff Weather Dogged the Eagles of Old," *Philadelphia Inquirer*, January 19, 2003.

Karsch, Carl G. "Five Generations of Builders," www.ushistory.org/carpentershall.

Kuklick, Bruce. *To Everything a Season: Shibe Park and Urban Philadelphia* (Princeton, New Jersey: Princeton University Press, 1991).

Macht, Norman L., *Connie Mack and the Early Years of Baseball* (Lincoln: University of Nebraska Press, 2007).

Westcott, Rich. *Philadelphia's Old Ballparks* (Philadelphia: Temple University Press, 1996).

"30,000 in New Shibe Park," *New York Times*, April 12, 1909.

Philadelphia Public Ledger, April 12, 1909.

Philadelphia Evening Bulletin, April 12, 1909.

Philadelphia Inquirer, April 13, 1909.

Baseball-Reference.com.

BaseballAlmanac.com.

Retrosheet.org.

www.philadelphiaathletics.org.

www.ballparktour.com

NOTES

1   Rich Westcott, *Philadelphia's Old Ballparks* (Philadelphia: Temple University Press, 1996), 105.

2   Westcott, 105.

3   *Philadelphia Public Ledger*, April 12, 1909.

4   Westcott, 109.

5   Westcott, 109.

6   *Philadelphia Public Ledger,* April 13, 1909.

7   The official paid attendance was 30,162. An additional 5,000 fans either sneaked in or had free passes to attend. Several thousand more sat on the rooftops of the homes on 20th Street, and another 30,000 crowded the streets outside the stadium.

8   Ballparksofbaseball.com https://www.ballparksofbaseball.com/ballparks/shibe-park/

9   *Philadelphia Inquirer*, October 2, 1970, 1.

Sunday Baseball comes to Shibe Park ~ Very Late

By Alan Cohen

"You see, Mr. Gaffney, in 1794, when this law was passed, the communities were very small, consisting of little towns and villages where they had cock-fighting, dog-fighting, and other sports and games which no doubt did create a noise which disturbed the entire community. But conditions have changed since that time and I don't believe they had any baseball games in 1794. You see we must view this subject in a sensible light.

– Judge Frank Smith comments to Philadelphia City Solicitor Joseph Gaffney at a hearing in Philadelphia, August 19, 1926[1]

Dating back to the nineteenth century, cities and towns were uncomfortable with baseball being played on what was, and is, to most Americans, the Sabbath, a day for rest and prayer. Laws impacted play in both the major leagues and the minor leagues. Battles over Sunday baseball continued into the twentieth century and many of us can still remember that when we were growing up, there was little if any Sunday night baseball, and that Pennsylvania law dictated that no inning could commence after 7:00 P.M. on Sundays.

During the early days of Organized baseball, several major-league teams would venture to remote beach locations for Sunday games. Philadelphia was no exception.

The Philadelphia Athletics of the American Association ventured to Gloucester Point in New Jersey to play on Sundays for three seasons after the Gloucester City Council approved the games on May 19, 1888.[2] Of course, this met with some opposition. These words appeared in the *Harrisburg Independent* on June 27, 1888: "Sunday baseball and Sunday beer go hand in hand, the one being necessary to invigorate the other and both being of the character of a defilement of a day which all laws, divine and human, demand shall be kept holy."[3] By July 1888 there was talk of impeaching the mayor of Gloucester for failing to enforce laws against beer and baseball. Boats would ferry fans to the resort where not only was there a ballgame, but an opportunity to buy beer. As noted in the *Philadelphia Inquirer*, "Every Sunday evening, the ferry boats landing at Christian and South streets emit hundreds of drunken, quarreling, swearing discordant men and women, who create disturbances and street fights and generally wind up by obtaining a rest in the station house cells."[4] On September 1, 1889,

Frank Fennelly, then playing with the Athletics, hit the 32nd of his 34 major-league homers at Gloucester Point.

Sunday-play bans in most major-league cities continued into the twentieth century. Only six of the 16 major-league teams played Sunday home games in 1902. During the first two decades of the twentieth century, one by one, the bans were lifted.

During the First World War, Connie Mack offered a suggestion that Shibe Park be used for Sunday games to benefit the war effort. The idea was to open the ballpark on Sundays for the 20,000 servicemen stationed in Philadelphia and have games between enlisted men and professional teams.[5] But the idea met with opposition from the clergy. Reverend James M.S. Isenberg said, "I think it is a poor way to teach our young men to violate the Lord's day when we believe our cause is right."[6] Nothing came of the effort and Sunday baseball did not come to Philadelphia in 1918.

However, in 1918, Washington hosted Sunday baseball for the first time, and in 1919 the three New York teams followed suit. The last two states holding out against Sunday baseball were those cradles of democracy, Massachusetts and Pennsylvania.

In Philadelphia, the Athletics decided to rail against the state's Blue Laws, enacted on April 22, 1794, and the first Sunday game was played at Shibe Park on August 22, 1926. Lefty Grove pitched the Athletics to a 3-2 win over the White Sox.

On August 19, the Thursday before the game, the pros and cons of Sunday baseball were argued at a hearing after Connie Mack sought an injunction preventing any interference by the authorities, including Mayor Freeland Kendrick. During the hearing, Charles G. Gartling, the Athletics' counsel, argued that the police had no right to enter the grounds and break up a game. He maintained that the only recourse of the police would be to arrest the players the next day and fine them $4. A contrary view was expressed by Philadelphia City Solicitor Joseph P. Gaffney. Gaffney maintained that professional baseball games on Sunday constituted a breach of peace, and thus could be stopped by the police.[7]

Among those who gave testimony was Connie Mack. An impressive figure on the witness stand, he said that at the Sunday games he had witnessed in other cities, fans were better dressed and better behaved than crowds on other days. Hearing that, Gaffney came up with a hypothetical situation. "Suppose in the ninth inning, two men were out, three were on base, the home team two runs behind, and the batter hits a home run. Would the crowd lose his control and respect for Sunday?" Mack responded, "I can see the crowd just rising quietly and leaving." The courtroom broke into laughter and the judge had to use his gavel.[8]

The injunction was issued by Judge Frank Smith, who held that "baseball does not tend to immorality or the corruption of youth" and added that baseball took a person "out into the open, who might otherwise spend his time to his own disadvantage."[9] The game was played in somewhat intemperate weather, but Mack was pleased that the fans had the opportunity to witness the event. He said, "The most severe critics and opponents of Sunday baseball, at the game, would, I am sure, be satisfied that the club gave everything it had for the enjoyment of a large number of people and, as a result, their feelings toward Sunday baseball would be changed. I wish all those who oppose Sunday baseball could have been here today. They would see that we are not causing a lessening in Church attendance."[10]

As with much of the debate concerning Sunday baseball, there was some levity displayed in the reporting. This notice appeared in the *Philadelphia Inquirer* on August 21, 1926: "(On August 20) Members of the Germantown Boys Club were guests of Cornelius McGillicuddy, that wicked advocate of Sunday baseball. The loud rooting disturbed the peace of an organ grinder with a monkey, who was working the east side of Twentieth Street between Lehigh and Somerset."[11]

On Sunday, August 22, more than 12,000 fans braved the elements and saw the Athletics defeat the White Sox, 3-2, in 1 hour and 45 minutes. Rain had intermittently pelted Philadelphia for the week leading up to the game and most observers were surprised that the game was played at all. As noted by James C. Isaminger in the *Philadelphia Inquirer*, the game "was played under distressing weather conditions and started in an exasperating drizzle that threated at any minute to turn into such a fury of a storm as to quickly chase the players off the field. There was some luck left for the wicked Sunday exploiters of baseball for the ominous downpour never came, and rain stopped entirely by the middle of the game to be renewed later in the form of a scotch mist."[12] (In weather jargon, scotch mist is a light, steady drizzle.)

Injunction or not, the opponents of Sunday baseball in Philadelphia were not about to allow Sunday baseball to continue without a court battle. The game on August 22 was the only Sunday game scheduled and played in Philadelphia that season. Mayor Kendrick and City Solicitor Joseph Gaffney were openly opposed to Sunday baseball and noted that Judge Smith's ruling came in a preliminary hearing. No arrests were made on Sunday because a Pennsylvania law enacted in 1705 made it illegal to arrest people on Sunday except for felony or breach of peace. The city officials vowed to seek a reversal of Judge Smith's ruling and the clergy was adamant. Reverend William B. Forney of the Philadelphia Sabbath Association said, "Sunday's game was the most outrageous thing put on in any civilized community. The crowds yelled and screamed enough to disgust any one. I was ashamed that such an exhibition could be held on the Sabbath."[13]

The matter did wind up in the courts. On October 28 the Dauphin County Court ruled that professional Sunday baseball constituted "worldly entertainment" and was therefore illegal. On June 25, 1927, the Pennsylvania Supreme Court, in a 5-to-2 decision upheld the ruling that professional baseball is a business and worldly entertainment and, as such, was in violation of the Blue Laws of 1794. Thus, Sunday baseball remained banned in Pennsylvania.[14]

After a referendum in 1928, the ban in Boston was lifted in 1929, leaving the three Pennsylvania teams as the only teams without Sunday baseball.

But the Blue Laws were not uniformly applied in Pennsylvania. Minor-league baseball was played on Sunday in various locations, but the courts would not allow Sunday baseball at the major-league level. In Philadelphia on Sunday June 14, 1931, the Penn Athletic Club hosted the Englewood (New Jersey) Athletic Club in a game at the Baker Bowl, the Phillies ballpark. It was a poorly played affair with seemingly as many errors as hits as the hosts won 14-12.[15]

Sunday baseball became an economic necessity, especially for the Athletics. During the court hearing in 1926, the Athletics president, John R. Shibe, had testified that the team could make an additional $20,000 per game on Sundays. Although they had been in the World Series from 1929 through 1931, their attendance slipped as the Depression worsened. It declined from 839,176 in 1929 to 721,636 in 1930 and 627,464 in 1931. In 1933, attendance was down to 297,138.

In 1931 a bill allowing Sunday baseball was introduced in the state legislature by South Philadelphia's Stephen C. Denning, but the opposition remained strong. Despite the extraordinary measure of bringing one pro-Sunday-ball legislator, who had been ill, to the pivotal vote by ambulance, the measure failed to pass.

Connie Mack maintained that his Athletics, despite winning pennants from 1929 through 1931, were losing potential revenue by the absence of Sunday baseball, necessitating the selling of Al Simmons, Jimmy Dykes, and Mule Haas to the Chicago White Sox for $100,000 after the 1932 season.

But the forces against the 1794 Blue Laws had picked up momentum, and the bills enabling Sunday baseball and other types of recreation moved forward. No fewer than six anti-Blue Laws bills were introduced in the early '30s. Rallies supporting the measures included a large gathering at the Elks Club, meeting at the behest of the Association for the Encouragement and Regulation of Sunday Sports and featuring Philadelphia Councilman W. W. Roper.

At the rally, James J. Walsh, managing secretary of the Market Street Merchants Association, tried to strike a conciliatory tone. He said, "Our country is getting diminishing returns from its youth, diminishing returns from its home life, diminishing returns from its laws, while restrictive and prohibitive legislation, or the demand for it, is ever mounting. The Blue Laws of Pennsylvania should be revised – and by such a revision we do not by any means intend a 'wide-open city.' A good baseball game on Sunday is not a crime; a good musical concert certainly should not be disallowed."[16]

A public hearing on a bill sponsored by state Representative Louis Schwartz of Philadelphia was scheduled for January 31. This bill, limited in scope, allowed for the playing of baseball and other outdoor sports (excluding boxing, wrestling, hunting, and fishing) on Sundays between 2:00 P.M. and 6:00 P.M. The bill called for referendums to sanction these activities. Proponents of the legislation (including Roper, Walsh, Adolph Hirschburg of the American Federation of Labor, Edward A. Kelly, and Connie Mack) were heard as were opponents led by Reverend W.D. Forney of the Lords Day Alliance.[17] Mack testified that it had been his experience that in seven American League cities, Sunday games were played with no disorder. He said, "If I felt for a moment that Sunday baseball

was going to be detrimental to morals of people of Philadelphia, our gates would never open."[18]

Councilman W.W. Roper's testimony was compelling. He said, "The Pennsylvania Blue Laws of 1794 undoubtedly reflected the spirit of those times. Conditions today are totally different from what they were 150 years ago. Regulations designed for the primitive society of the eighteenth century cannot be inflicted upon us in this age without injury to the health and welfare of our people. Respect for law is somewhat like respect for an individual. Neither is given gratuitously – they must both be earned. And respect for law can only be earned through its appeal to the sense of justice. Today, a large majority of the people demand the right to enjoy orderly healthful recreation on their day of rest."[19]

Dr. Robert Bagnell of the State Council of Churches countered by saying, "We are opposed to any effort to lessen the sanctity of the day or open it to the inroads of commercialism. Don't let the camel get his nose under the tent. Once the camel gets inside the tent, Sunday motion pictures will follow."[20]

The legislation was passed in the Pennsylvania House of Representatives, but was stalled in the Senate. Indeed, the bill was voted down on March 14. But proponents did not give up the fight. The bill was reconsidered in the Senate and amendments were added, the key one being a call for a statewide referendum the following November, killing the idea of Sunday baseball for 1933. On April 11, 1933, the amended bill was passed. After much deliberation, and at the urging of Connie Mack, Governor Gifford Pinchot signed the bill into law on April 25.[21]

"While the spectators uncorked some healthy American rooting, it was an orderly crowd, and not one untoward event marked the first game under the law sponsored by Representative Louis Schwartz, who watched the game from a box."

– *Philadelphia Inquirer*, April 8, 1934[22]

In November of 1933, Philadelphia and Pittsburgh said "yes" to allowing Sunday baseball. The first legal Sunday baseball game in Philadelphia was played on April 8, 1934, as the Phillies took on the Athletics in an exhibition game at Shibe Park. A week later the teams opposed each other at the Baker Bowl. The Athletics hosted Washington in the first legal regular-season Sunday game on April 22. Before the game, as 20,306 spectators looked on, Connie Mack gave a silver loving cup to Representative Schwartz for his role in passing the enabling legislation.[23] One week later, the Pittsburgh Pirates hosted Cincinnati and the Philadelphia Phillies hosted the Dodgers in the first National League Sunday games in those cities.

SOURCES

For further reading on the subject of Sunday baseball, the author recommends:

Bevis, Charlie. *Sunday Baseball: The Major Leagues' Struggle to Play Baseball on the Lord's Day, 1876-1934* (Jefferson, North Carolina: McFarland and Company, 2003).

DeMotte, Charles. *Bat, Ball, and Bible: Baseball and Sunday Observance in New York* (Washington: Potomac Books, 2013).

NOTES

1   "Court Will Decide if Sunday Baseball Is Breach of Peace," *Philadelphia Inquirer*, August 20, 1926: 7.

2   "Sunday Baseball Games at Gloucester," *New York Tribune*, May 20, 1888: 2.

3   *Harrisburg* (Pennsylvania) *Independent*, June 27, 1888: 1.

4   "Still Defying the Law," *Philadelphia Inquirer*, July 2, 1888: 5.

5   "Sunday Baseball in Quaker City?" *Reading Times*, May 1, 1918: 11.

6   "Church Opposes Sunday Games," *Harrisburg Telegraph*, May 3, 1918: 18.

7   "Court Will Decide if Sunday Baseball Is Breach of Peace," *Philadelphia Inquirer*, August 20, 1926: 1.

8   "Court Will Decide if Sunday Baseball Is Breach of Peace," *Philadelphia Inquirer*, August 20, 1926: 7.

9   "Court Restrains Police from Stopping Sunday Ball Game," Sunday *News* (Lancaster, Pennsylvania), August 22, 1926: 2.

10 "First Sunday Major league Ball Game in Phila. Goes Over with a Bang," *Boston Herald*, August 23, 1926: 6.

11 "Macaroons," *Philadelphia Inquirer*, August 21, 1926: 10.

12 James C. Isaminger, "Grove Hurls Mackmen to Victory in First Sunday Major Game Played Here," *Philadelphia Inquirer*, August 23, 1926: 16.

13 "Mayor to Continue Sunday Ball Fight," *Philadelphia Inquirer*, August 24, 1926: 2.

14 "Shibe Inspects Jersey Site for Sunday Games," *Philadelphia Inquirer*, March 29, 1931: 6.

15 "Pennacs Biff Out Win Over Englewood Rival in Phillies' Park Fuss," *Philadelphia Inquirer*, June 15, 1931: 13.

16 "Blue Law Foes Mass to Voice Protest," *Philadelphia Inquirer*, January 31, 1933: 12.

17 John M. Cummings, "Early Report Scheduled on Sunday Sport," *Philadelphia Inquirer*, January 31, 1933: 1.

18 Cummings, "Committee Votes for Legalization of Sunday Sport," *Philadelphia Inquirer*, February 1, 1933: 1, 6, 7.

19 "Committee Votes for Legalization of Sunday Sport."

20 "Committee Votes for Legalization of Sunday Sport."

21 "Pinchot Approves Sunday Baseball Ballot by People," *Wilkes-Barre* (Pennsylvania) *Record*, April 26, 1933: 1.

22 Isaminger, "Haslin and Allen Lead Phil Parade in Series Starter," *Philadelphia Inquirer*, April 9, 1934: 13.

23 Isaminger, "Infield Miscue, Schulte Clout, Send Down A's," *Philadelphia Inquirer*, April 23, 1934: 15.

When Satch and Josh and Jackie and Willie Came to Town: Negro League Baseball at Shibe Park

By Alan Cohen

Black ballplayers first set foot on the field at Shibe Park at the end of the 1919 season when the Bacharach Giants of Atlantic City, New Jersey faced off against the Hilldale club of Philadelphia on September 8.[1] The Bacharachs, behind the pitching of Dick "Cannonball" Redding, won the game 10-0.[2] It was the ninth meeting of the season between the two clubs. Each team had won four of the prior eight games. By winning, the Bacharachs laid claim to the title of eastern champions of America, a distinction that was mythical at best. There was, at that point, no formally recognized Negro League in baseball.

The Negro National League was formed the following season and the Eastern Colored League came into existence three years later. The first Negro League game at Shibe Park, between the Kansas City Monarchs and Hilldale, took place on October 8, 1925. It was the fifth game of the Negro League World Series. The Monarchs had won the pennant in the Negro National League and Hilldale had prevailed in the Eastern Colored League. On October 8, Hilldale defeated the Monarchs. Rube Curry hurled scattered eight hits for the winners, who went up four games to one in the best of nine Series.[3] Two days later,

back at Shibe Park, Hilldale won, 5-2, to win the Series in six games.

Shibe Park did not become a regular venue for Negro League ball until World War II. The Philadelphia Stars, beginning in 1934, were an integral part of the Negro National League, but their games were played at the 44th and Parkside Ballpark.

After a 17-year absence, Negro League baseball returned to Shibe Park during the 1942 Negro League World Series and did so with the two top players in the Negro Leagues, Satchel Paige of the Monarchs and Josh Gibson of the Homestead Grays.

The fifth game of the Negro League World Series between the Homestead Grays and the Kansas City Monarchs was played at Shibe Park on September 29, 1942. The Monarchs had won the first three games of the Series and the fourth was ruled a "no-contest" after it was discovered that the Homestead Grays, in winning, had used ineligible players in the game. The Monarchs needed only one more win to clinch the title. Eight players from that game have made it to the Hall of Fame.

The Monarchs were led by star pitcher Satchel Paige[4] and won the game 9-5 in front of 14,029 spectators. The Grays took a 5-2 lead after three innings. Paige entered the game with two on and two out in the fourth inning and the Grays did not score again. Paige allowed no hits while striking out seven and walking two over the game's remaining 5⅓ innings. Why hadn't Paige started the game? He was late after being arrested for speeding through Lancaster, Pennsylvania, en route from Pittsburgh.[5]

The Monarchs scored in the first inning when Bill Simms tripled and came home on a single by Newt Allen. The Grays tallied three runs in the bottom of the first inning. With two out, Howard Easterling walked, advanced to third on a two-base error and scored on an infield hit by Buck Leonard. Josh Gibson, who had reached on the error, scored along with Leonard on a double by Ray Brown. The Monarchs got one of the runs back in the third inning. Willard Brown reached on an error, went station to station on a single by Joe Greene and a bunt by Buck O'Neil, and scored when a grounder by Bonnie Serrell was misplayed. After the Grays scored a pair in the bottom of the third to take a 5-2 lead, the Monarchs got back into the game when Greene launched a two-run homer off John Wright in the fourth inning. They took the lead with a pair in the seventh and blew the game open with three in the eighth. Wright was the losing pitcher.[6]

With both the Phillies and Athletics using Shibe Park, there were few open dates, and there was a concern as to how many people of color would attend games on a weeknight in a predominantly White part of the city. During the years when the Stars played at Shibe Park, most of their home games were still played at Parkside. Shibe Park was used primarily on Monday and Tuesday nights. Quite often, the opposition was provided by the Kansas City Monarchs and Homestead Grays, and doubleheaders were common.

The first Philadelphia Stars appearance at Shibe Park occurred on June 21, 1943. The Monarchs' Paige was matched up against Barney

Brown of the Stars. Brown was backed up by a lineup that featured slugging first baseman Jim West, along with Henry Spearman, player-manager Homer Curry, Henry Kimbro, and outfielder Felton Snow. Pitchers Bill Byrd and Bob Clark were also available.[7] The Stars won the game, 8-5, in front of 24,165 fans, which would be the biggest turnout ever to see Negro League ball at Shibe Park. Hitting stars for Philadelphia as they came from behind to win were Homer Curry with three hits, including a double, and center fielder Gene Benson with three singles.[8] Benson played with the Stars from 1938 through 1948.

A September 8, 1943, encounter matched the Monarchs and the Homestead Grays. It was Paige vs. Gibson, the slugging catcher of the Grays. The Grays won the game 12-2 in front of 12,198 spectators. The only Monarchs runs came on a two-run homer by Willard Brown in the fourth inning off John Wright, who was otherwise flawless in the complete-game victory.[9] It was the third homer in as many 1943 appearances at Shibe Park for Brown, whose talents were recognized by the Hall of Fame in 2006.

In a doubleheader on July 18, 1944, the Homestead Grays played the Baltimore Elite Giants in the opener and the Philadelphia Stars in the nightcap. In the opener, Josh Gibson homered in an 11-4 Grays win. It was his first homer in three visits to Shibe Park and he would go on to hit home runs in each of the big-league parks he played in. Roy Campanella of Baltimore had three hits in a losing cause. In the nightcap, the game was halted by curfew after 11 innings with the score tied 4-4. The attendance for the doubleheader was a season's high 15,072.[10]

There was a three-team event on August 28, 1944. In the first game, the Philadelphia Stars faced the Birmingham Black Barons, and in the nightcap the winner of the first game faced Paige's Monarchs. The doubleheader drew 13,136 fans, and they saw Birmingham win the opener 6-3. The Barons jumped off to the early lead when

Lorenzo "Piper" Davis slammed a three-run homer and Earl Bumpus scattered nine hits in winning the game for Birmingham. In the second game, Paige and Hilton Smith combined to shut out the Barons 10-0. Paige pitched four innings, allowing only one hit. The hitting star for the Monarchs was Bonnie Serrell, who had four hits, including a first-inning homer, and became the first Negro League player to hit for the cycle at Shibe Park.[11]

On May 21, 1945, the Stars played the Grays in a Negro National League game at Shibe Park. With 10,021 fans looking on, the Grays won the game 7-1 as pitcher Roy Welmaker scattered eight hits and 19-year-old Dave Hoskins had three hits, including a triple.[12] Seven years later, Hoskins broke the color barrier in the Texas League.

On June 18, 1945, the Kansas City Monarchs were back in town. Satchel Paige was still the big drawing card, but readers of the *Philadelphia Inquirer* learned that the Monarchs also featured a rookie shortstop who had played his college ball at UCLA: Jackie Robinson. The Stars, in a fairly one-sided game, defeated the Monarchs 5-1. A Monday night crowd of 10,412 watched the Stars get to Paige for five runs and seven hits over four innings, the key blows being a double by Frankie Austin and a triple by Marvin Williams. The Monarchs' leading hitter was Robinson. He had a single and a double in his Shibe Park debut.[13]

Negro League baseball was also entertainment and on Wednesday, July 11, 1945, the Cincinnati Clowns came to town with their assortment of players short and tall. There were two games that night. In the opener the Stars played the Newark Eagles to begin the second half of the Negro National League season. Pitching for the Stars was Roy Partlow, and he was matched up against the Eagles' youngster Don Newcombe. Although Newcombe was the winning pitcher in the 5-3 contest, Partlow struck out 10 Eagles. During the intermission the crowd of 11,408 was entertained by the antics of baseball clown Circus Eddie

Hamman. After the intermission, the Stars went on to defeat the Clowns 9-1.[14]

The fourth game of the 1945 Negro League World Series was played at Shibe Park on September 20, 1945. The Homestead Grays, appearing in their eighth consecutive Series, took on the Cleveland Buckeyes. It was the Buckeyes' first-ever appearance at Shibe Park. They were led by their center fielder, Sam Jethroe, who had led the league in batting in 1945. Having won the first three games of the Series, the Buckeyes closed things out on September 20. With Frank Carswell on the mound and Jethroe leading the offensive onslaught with three hits, the Buckeyes won 5-0, as an estimated 5,000 fans looked on, to break the Grays' grasp on the Negro League title. The team, which called both Pittsburgh and Washington home, had won the Series in 1943 and 1944.[15] After winning the game the Buckeyes took a bit of a break and came out on the field to play the Philadelphia Stars, winning 4-1 with seldom-used John Brown besting Roy Partlow.[16]

Negro League baseball returned to Shibe Park in 1946. Josh Gibson tripled during Homestead's 5-2 win over the Stars in front of 10,751 fans on May 13. Ted Radcliffe was known as "Double-Duty," and showed why in the game. Homestead's second-string catcher, at age 43, came on in relief of pitcher Wilmer Fields with two runs in, two men on base, two out, and the tying run at the plate in the form of Homer Curry. With a 3-and-2 count, Radcliffe was summoned into the game and struck out Curry for the final out of the game.[17]

The Stars hosted the New York Black Yankees and Newark Eagles on May 31, 1946, and the 11,990 fans witnessed three homers. In the opener, Wes Dennis homered for the Stars and pitcher Barney Brown scattered six hits in the 7-2 win. In the nightcap, the Eagles, with Larry Doby and Johnny Davis providing long balls, won 9-2, with Leon Day taking care of the pitching duties.[18]

On August 12, 1946, in a first for the Negro Leagues, the Cincinnati Clowns traveled by air from Birmingham, Alabama, to Philadelphia to take on the Stars in the second game of a doubleheader at Shibe Park. In the first game, the Stars hosted the Newark Eagles. The Eagles won 6-2 as their keystone combination of Larry Doby and Monte Irvin each had an RBI double. In the nightcap, the game was stopped by curfew after nine innings with the score tied 7-7.[19] Newark was back on September 3 to play in the nightcap of the final Negro League doubleheader of the season at Shibe Park. The Stars beat the Eagles 12-7. Three of the Eagles' 13 hits, including a double and homer, were struck by Doby.[20]

On May 26, 1947, Doby stopped by with the Newark Eagles, and he began his 1947 season at Shibe Park the same way he had ended 1946. His eighth-inning three-run homer off Bill Byrd was the margin of victory as Newark defeated the Baltimore Elite Giants 3-2. In the second game that night, the Stars and New York Black Yankees were tied 2-2 when play was halted after the 12th inning.[21] By the end of the season, Doby was with the Cleveland Indians, and he came back to Shibe Park on many occasions. He had five major-league homers there, the first coming on July 15, 1948.

On June 16, 1947, a crowd of 7,189 saw the New York Cubans defeat Baltimore in the opener, 3-1, and the Stars defeat the Grays 7-2 in the nightcap, with pitcher Eugene Smith homering and 21-year-old Harry Simpson going 3-for-3 with a double and a triple.[22] On June 23 the Eagles were back in town and Larry Doby had two hits as the Eagles defeated the Cubans, 7-4, with three runs in the 11th inning. The Stars fell to Baltimore's Bill Byrd, 3-1.[23]

On July 7 the Stars hosted the Monarchs. Kansas City, with Connie Johnson pitching and Hank Thompson homering, defeated the Stars 13-8 in a game that was stopped after six innings to allow the Monarchs to catch a train. Stars

highlights included a homer by Mahlon Duckett and Bill Cash becoming the first Negro League player to have two homers in the same game at Shibe Park.[24]

On August 18 the opening game of a doubleheader featured the New York Cubans and Baltimore Elite Giants. Luis Tiant of the Cubans pitched nine innings as his team won 9-2. Joe Black took the loss for Baltimore. The Cubans' attack included three hits from Minnie Miñoso. Junior Gilliam went 1-for-4 for Baltimore.[25]

Another Negro League World Series game was held at Shibe Park in 1947. The New York Cubans faced the Cleveland Buckeyes. Rafael Noble was the hitting star as the Cubans won on September 24 to take a 2-1 lead in the Series. His grand slam in the fifth inning off Eugene Bremmer (the first grand slam ever hit at a Negro League game at Shibe Park) powered his team to a 7-0 lead. and Dave Barnhill, except for a glitch in the eighth inning, overpowered the Buckeyes in pitching the complete-game win. The crowd was only 1,739.[26] Attendance for the entire season at Shibe Park was down dramatically from 1946. For nine dates, the total was 50,211. The Cubans won the Series in five games. It was the next to last Negro League World Series.

In 1948 the Stars continued to appear at Shibe Park and there were still some talented players around who would in the coming years make it to the big leagues. Harry Simpson spent the season with the Stars, Monte Irvin with the Newark Eagles, Minnie Miñoso with the New York Cubans, and Luke Easter with the Homestead Grays. Each would be in Organized Baseball the next season, Irvin going to the Giants and Simpson, Miñoso, and Easter signing with the Cleveland Indians.

On August 9, 1948, Shibe Park witnessed an exhibition of greatness by Miñoso. The New York Cubans star homered and tripled in a 4-1 win. Miñoso, early in his major-league career, was traded from the Indians to the Chicago White

Sox. Two of his major-league homers came at Shibe Park, the first on August 1, 1951.

The 1948 season was the last season for the Negro National League. In 1949, ten teams, including the Stars, were in the Negro American League. The Birmingham Black Barons, who had played in the last Negro League World Series, in 1948, losing to the Homestead Grays, had not visited Shibe Park in 1948, but they were in town on July 6, 1949, losing to the Baltimore Elite Giants 11-8. Birmingham's lineup included a player who would go on to the best major-league career of the players who played Negro League ball at Shibe Park.

Center fielder Willie Mays was two months past his 18th birthday when he first played at Shibe Park. Two weeks before the Barons next returned to Shibe Park in 1950, Mays, who was batting .340 for the Barons, had been sold to the Giants. On July 12, 1950, Mays was at Trenton.[27] He made his major-league debut at Shibe Park on May 25, 1951, and, won the 1951 National League Rookie of the Year Award. Over the course of his career, he hit 18 homers at Shibe Park. The Elite Giants also fielded two future big leaguers. Junior Gilliam and Joe Black signed with the Dodgers after the 1950 season. Black was the National League Rookie of the Year in 1952, going 15-4 with 15 saves. One year later, Gilliam joined the Dodgers and won the 1953 Rookie of the Year Award.

The Philadelphia Stars played through 1952 and appeared several times each year at Shibe Park, often hosting the Indianapolis Clowns. After the Stars folded, Shibe Park, renamed Connie Mack Stadium in 1953, continued to host exhibitions featuring the Clowns. The players in those years bore little resemblance to the great black players who had graced Shibe Park in the days when the legends of the Negro Leagues displayed their remarkable talent.

SOURCES

In addition to the sources cited in the Notes, the author also found these articles helpful:

"Gibson Homer Ace: Slammed One 514 Feet," *Philadelphia Inquirer*, July 30, 1944: 2S.

"Satchel Paige Faces Grays Here Tonight," *Philadelphia Inquirer*, September 29, 1942: 26.

"Play First Game in Cleveland Thursday; Grays are Favorites," *Pittsburgh Courier*, September 15, 1945: 12.

Scheffer, William J. "15,000 See Grays Lose to Kansas [*sic*]," *Philadelphia Inquirer*, September 30, 1942: 35, 38.

Smith, Wendell. "Smitty's Sports Spurts: Statistics Show How Kansas City Walloped Grays in World Series," *Pittsburgh Courier*, October 10, 1942: 17.

NOTES

1   "Negro Nines Play on Shibe Grounds," *Evening Public Ledger* (Philadelphia, Pennsylvania), September 8, 1919: 17.

2   "Bacharach Giants Crush Hilldale," *Philadelphia Inquirer*, September 9, 1919: 14 and "Bacharachs Win the Championship," *Chicago Defender*, September 20, 1919: 11.

3   "Hilldale Defeats Kansas City Foes," *Philadelphia Inquirer*, October 9, 1925: 27.

4   "Negro Series at Shibe Park: Homestead to Meet Kansas City Under Lights Sept. 29," *Chester* (Pennsylvania) *Times*, September 18, 1942: 15.

5   Associated Press, "Kansas City Takes Negro Baseball Title," *Ottawa Citizen*, September 30, 1942: 20.

6   William J. Scheffer, "15,000 See Grays Lose to Kansas," *Philadelphia Inquirer*, September 30, 1942: 35, 38.

7   "Paige to Hurl for Monarchs Against Phila. Stars Tonight," *Philadelphia Inquirer*, June 21, 1943: 22.

8   William J. Scheffer, "Phila. Stars Win Before 24,165," t*Philadelphia Inquirer*, June 22, 1943: 24.

9   Scheffer, "12,198 See Monarchs, Paige Lose," *Philadelphia Inquirer*, September 9, 1943: 25.

10 "Josh Gibson Gets His Shibe Park Home Run," *Allentown* (Pennsylvania) *Morning Call,* July 19, 1944: 10.

11 "Paige Yields 1 Hit in Four Innings," *Philadelphia Inquirer*, August 29, 1944: 19.

12 Scheffer, "Grays Jar Stars Before 10,021," *Philadelphia Inquirer,* May 22, 1945: 21.

13 Scheffer, "Phila Stars Beat Kansas City, 5-1: Chase Paige in Fourth Before 10,412, Ricks Scatters Seven Hits," *Philadelphia Inquirer*, June 19, 1945: 17.

14 Scheffer, "11,408 See Stars Split Twin-Bill," *Philadelphia Inquirer*, July 12, 1945: 20.

15 "Cleveland Rules Baseball World," *Pittsburgh Courier*, September 29, 1945: 12.

16 Scheffer, "Buckeyes Blank Grays, Win Title," *Philadelphia Inquirer*, September 21, 1945: 24.

17 "Grays Beat Stars, 5-2, Under Arcs," *Philadelphia Inquirer*, May 14, 1946: 24.

18 Scheffer, "Phila. Stars Split Before 11,990," *Philadelphia Inquirer*, June 1, 1946: 17.

19 Scheffer, "Stars Beaten by Newark, Tie Clowns," *Philadelphia Inquirer*, August 13, 1946: 25.

20 "Stars Win 12-7; Baltimore Victor," *Philadelphia Inquirer*, September 4, 1946: 37.

21 Scheffer, "Eagles Win, 3-2; Stars Tied, 2-2," *Philadelphia Inquirer*, May 27, 1947: 32.

22 "Stars, Cubans Victors in Negro League," *Philadelphia Inquirer*, June 17, 1947: 25.

23 Scheffer, "Giants, Eagles Win Contests," *Philadelphia Inquirer*, June 24, 1947: 25.

24 Scheffer, "Monarchs Beat Stars; Rain Halts 2d," *Philadelphia Inquirer*, July 8, 1947: 22.

25 Scheffer, "Stars Victors in 9th, 4-3; Cubans Win," *Philadelphia Inquirer*, August 19, 1947: 25.

26 "Cubans Win 9-4, Take Series Lead," *Philadelphia Inquirer*, September 25, 1947: 24.

27 "Barons, Monarchs Play Phila. Stars Here," *Philadelphia Inquirer*, July 9, 1950: 12S.

Shibe Park Opens to Celebration and Sorrow

April 12, 1909
Philadelphia Athletics 8, Boston Red Sox 1

By Bob LeMoine

Philadelphia resident George McFadden was there bright and early. There would be 6,055 games played in the history of Shibe Park (renamed Connie Mack Stadium decades later), and no one knows how many games Mr. McFadden attended. His claim to fame is that he was the first fan to enter the sparkling new and innovative steel and concrete park. He was the only one in line at 7 A.M.; by 8:30 there were 200 lined up behind him, and crammed trains and streetcars were still dropping people off. Soon Lehigh Avenue and 21st Street were lined with fans, a good day for the roving peanut vendors. Officially, 30,162 entered that day, but the *Philadelphia Inquirer* estimated another 5,000 "gained admission either by invitation, by scaling the high walls or pressing into the grounds when the gates were rushed by the surging crowds."[1] The immense crowd entered just after noon through the 16 turnstiles. McFadden didn't scale any walls, but plunked down his 25 cents, turning down a $25 offer for his spot. He was the first to experience what the *Inquirer* dubbed "the turning of a fresh and scintillating page in the annals of the horsehide sphere."[2]

The gates were closed at 3 P.M., shutting out hordes of people still standing in line. It was the good fortune of some to own a home on 20th Street or Somerset Street, where they heard knocking at their doors as disgruntled fans offered them $2 to $5 to let them watch the game from their roofs. Some found a cheaper way by clambering up trees and telegraph poles. Others hurled rocks at the ballpark windows, breaking a few before being chased off by the police. After the pregame ceremonies of bands and anthems, umpire Tim Hurst called "Play ball!" and a new era began. Tommy Connolly also umpired this historic opener. Fans stood behind a rope in the outfield, creating ground-rule-double territory.

In 1908 Boston (75-79-1) and Philadelphia (68-85-4) finished fifth and sixth respectively in the American League. Fred Lake had taken over as Red Sox manager with 40 games to go in 1908, finishing a respectable 22-17. Connie Mack was in his ninth year as manager of the Athletics and had 41 more to go in his Hall of Fame career. Mack sent his veteran ace Eddie Plank to the hill. Plank had suffered a down year in 1908 (14-16 2.17 ERA) after winning 20-plus games in five of the six previous seasons. Boston had traded its ace pitcher, 42-year-old Cy Young, to Cleveland in the offseason for Jack Ryan and Charlie Chech. For this game, Lake turned to Frank Arellanes, with four wins to his name in his rookie campaign in 1908.

A paragon of consistency, Gettysburg Eddie Plank won 284 games during his 14 years with the A's (1901-1914), including at least 20 seven times. A crucial member of five pennant winners and three World Series winners, Plank posted a 1.32 ERA in 54⅔ World Series innings despite his 2-5 record.

Boston went out one-two-three in the top of the first. With one out in the bottom of the inning, Simon Nicholls beat out a slow roller to the mound. Eddie Collins, who 30 years later would be included in the Baseball Hall of Fame's first induction ceremony, singled over second base. Danny Murphy singled to right to score Nicholls, the first run in the ballpark's history, to the roar of the crowd. An inspired Collins raced for home but was nailed on strong throws by Doc Gessler in right and relay man Heinie Wagner, who fired the ball to catcher Bill Carrigan. During the inning, the carriage gate in center field was forced open by the crowd, and police had to corral 1,000 people rushing in. The A's led, 1-0 after one, and the teams were scoreless in the second, noted for Boston third baseman Harry Lord catching Doc Powers' popup in a sea of scattering musicians.

With two out in the bottom of the third, Collins lined a single to left, then scooted to third on Murphy's double to center. Harry Davis

singled to right, scoring both.[3] Boston had a great opportunity in the fourth. Lord smashed the ball to right and would have had a triple were it not for a fan snagging the ball over the rope. Chick Stahl reached when Stuffy McInnis dropped his popup, and a walk to Gessler loaded the bases with no one out. But Tris Speaker fouled out, Wagner popped out, and Jack Thoney grounded out. Then the Red Sox ran themselves out of the fifth inning when with two out Lord was thrown out trying to stretch a hit into a double, "a foolish play at best," wrote Tim Murnane in the Boston Globe.[4]

In the bottom of the fifth, Nicholls doubled into the crowd in left field. He moved to third on Collins's groundout and scored on Murphy's single past Wagner at short. The Athletics now led, 4-0.

Boston countered with a run in the top of the sixth. Gessler drew a one-out walk. Speaker popped up to third. Wagner's single to right sent Gessler to third. Thoney doubled into the crowd in right, scoring Gessler. Carrigan's high fly to right was tracked down by Murphy, so Boston couldn't chip any more off its deficit, now 4-1. It would not be a shutout for Plank that day. Historically, he ranks fifth all time with 69 shutouts.[5] Considering the way the game is played in the twenty-first century, his place will be secure for all time.

The Athletics added a run in the seventh. Topsy Hartsel singled to center and when Nicholls followed with another, Lake pulled Arellanes, who had surrendered 11 hits and four runs. Jack Ryan came in from the bullpen and walked Collins to load the bases. Murphy's groundball to Chick Stahl at first forced Hartsel at home. With the bases still loaded, Ryan plunked Harry Davis to force in Nicholls, the A's fifth run. But Ryan avoided further damage as Amos Strunk tapped in front of the plate, where Carrigan scooped up the ball and forced Collins at home. The A's now led, 5-1, after seven innings.

The Athletics made sure they sent their Opening Day crowd home happy, scoring three more runs in the bottom of the eighth. Powers reached on shortstop Wagner's error. Plank fouled out to Carrigan, but Hartsel's grounder caromed off third baseman Lord's knee and into left field. Ryan walked Nicholls and Collins, the latter pass scoring Powers. Murphy launched a drive down the left-field line to score two more and blow the game open, 8-1.

Boston had a spark in the ninth. With Thoney on second, Carrigan reached on Nicholls' error. Babe Danzig, pinch-hitting for Ryan, was hit by Plank. The bases were loaded, but Amby McConnell popped out and Lord struck out, the ball disappearing into Powers' mitt as the A's won the opening game at Shibe Park, 8-1. Murphy (4-for-5) and Nicholls (3-for-4) were the hitting stars of the day. The A's put runners on base in six of their eight innings while for Boston, according to Murnane, the game was "like a glass of champagne with the bubbles all burst."[6]

As he celebrated that first on the new diamond, no one knew catcher Doc Powers was standing on a baseball field for the last time. No one knew the agonizing pain he was likely experiencing. The *Philadelphia Inquirer* made only brief mention of Powers having a "seizure" in the seventh inning, but staying in the game.[7]

Powers died two weeks later, on April 26, at the age of 38. SABR researcher Robert D. Warrington has written an excellent analysis of this incident in the Fall 2014 *Baseball Research Journal*, which goes beyond the scope of this article.[8] A quick Web search today for Doc Powers will return several erroneous books and websites that have disseminated misinformation regarding Powers' demise: that sandwiches he ate that day caused food poisoning, or that he crashed into a wall attempting to catch a foul ball.[9] Neither is based on historical evidence. The cause of death was reported as intussusception, which the Mayo Clinic defines as "a serious condition in which part of the intestine slides into an adjacent part of the intestine."[10] Neither a bad sandwich nor a banging into a wall would have contributed to this condition, which Powers, sadly, a physician who didn't seek treatment for himself, must have noticed.

Just as thousands crammed into Shibe Park on Opening Day to welcome the new ballpark, so too on April 29 thousands crammed into St. Elizabeth's Church, to say goodbye to their popular catcher. Fans who had watched from the rooftops now were crowded outside the church's entrance. A year later, Connie Mack organized a charity game on "Doc Powers Day" at Shibe Park to raise money for Powers' family. "The park will be a great aid to the city," Mayor John E. Reyburn said on Opening Day. It was indeed, for the place dubbed "the World's Greatest Ball Park" was already at the heart of the Philadelphia community, a place for cheers and tears.[11]

No doubt George McFadden experienced some of both.

SOURCES

"Great Crowds at Opening Games in American League," *Boston Herald*, April 13, 1909: 1, 9.

"Local Fans Do Not Forget the Late Dr. Powers," *Philadelphia Inquirer*, July 1, 1910: 1.

"Unusual Tribute Paid to Memory of Dr. Powers," *Philadelphia Inquirer*, April 30, 1909: 1.

"When Gates Are Closed Thousands Climb Upon Surrounding Rooftops," *Philadelphia Inquirer*, April 13, 1909: 10.

The author also consulted baseball-reference.com and retrosheet.org.

NOTES

1   "Greatest Baseball Crowd at Shibe Park Sees Athletics Win Opening Game, 8-1," *Philadelphia Inquirer*, April 13, 1909: 1.

2   "Greatest Baseball Crowd at Shibe Park Sees Athletics Win Opening Game, 8-1."

3   Tim Murnane's account in the *Boston Globe* records Collins scoring on Murphy's double.

4   T.H. Murnane, "Red Sox Run Second Best," *Boston Globe*, April 13, 1909: 1.

5   Only Walter Johnson, Pete Alexander, Christy Mathewson, and Cy Young have more shutouts.

6   Murnane: 1.

7   Murnane: 10. The account read: "The only thing that occurred to cast a shadow over the joy of the fans was the seizure of 'Doc' Powers with acute gastritis in the seventh inning. The redoubtable catcher, however, refused to abandon his post behind the plate, and though suffering intense agony, pluckily stuck to it until the end of the game. On the verge of collapse, he was taken to the Northwest General Hospital."

8   Robert D. Warrington, "A Ballpark Opens and a Player Dies: The Converging Fates of Shibe Park and 'Doc' Powers," *Baseball Research Journal*, Fall 2014. The article is available on the SABR website: sabr.org/research/ballpark-opens-and-ballplayer-dies-converging-fates-shibe-park-and-doc-powers Retrieved May 19, 2018.

9   The "sandwich theory" was circulated by sportswriters at the time. While newspaper reports mention Powers catching foul balls twice during the game, neither was reported as something likely to have caused internal injuries.

10 "Intussusception." Mayo Clinic Diseases & Conditions. mayoclinic.org/diseases-conditions/intussusception/symptoms-causes/syc-20351452 Retrieved May 19, 2018. "This 'telescoping' often blocks food or fluid from passing through. Intussusception also cuts off the blood supply to the part of the intestine that's affected, which can lead to a tear in the bowel (perforation), infection and death of bowel tissue."

11 "Praise and Admiration Heard on Every Hand," *Philadelphia Inquirer*, April 13, 1909: 10.

CHARLES BENDER TOSSES FIRST NO-HITTER
IN SHIBE PARK HISTORY

May 12, 1910
Philadelphia Athletics 5, Cleveland Naps 0

By Gregory H. Wolf

"Bender's control, his absolute mastery over the batters and his speed were almost ideal," gushed the *Philadelphia Inquirer* about Charles Bender's no-hitter, the first in the history of Shibe Park.[1] Cleveland Naps batters were "Benderized and hypnotized" by the Athletics hurler, opined the *Cleveland Plain Dealer*, noting in the racially insensitive parlance of the era that Bender "sunk his tomahawk deep into the Naps.[2]

After finishing in second place in 1909, owner-manager Connie Mack's A's exploded out of the gate in 1910, winning 12 of their first 16 games as they prepared for a four-game set against the second-place Naps (12-6) in the City of Brotherly Love. The first two scheduled contests had not produced a winner: In the opener the A's Cy Morgan battled Addie Joss to a 1-1, 12-inning tie and the second game was rained out. Right-hander Jack Coombs warmed up for the first-place club, ready to make his third start of the season. Just as home-plate umpire Bill Dinneen called for the batterymates, the Tall Tactician, made a sudden and unexpected switch, according to the *Cleveland Press*, and announced Bender as his starter.[3]

A 26-year-old right-hander, Bender had the reputation of a cerebral, unflappable hurler. He won 17 games and logged 270 innings as a 19-year-old rookie in 1903 and notched 18 more victories for the AL pennant winners in 1905, highlighted by an overpowering four-hit shutout against Iron Man Joe McGinnity and the New York Giants in Game Two of the World Series. Entering the '10 season with a stellar 102-71 career slate, Bender's success was set against the backdrop of the fierce racial prejudice and discrimination he endured on and off the baseball field because of his Native American ancestry. Charles Albert Bender's mother was part Ojibwa and his father German-American. The young Bender lived on the White Earth Reservation in northern Minnesota, and was later educated in boarding schools, including the Carlisle Indian School in Carlisle, Pennsylvania, which legendary athlete Jim Thorpe had also attended. Bender despised the moniker Chief, and was known for his calm demeanor on the mound despite taunts and violent references to his heritage. Sportswriters typically reduced him to a caricature of Native American culture, a fierce warrior with a tomahawk and headdress.

Coming off an 18-8 campaign with a 1.66 ERA, the stout 6-foot-2, 185-pound Bender began the 1910 season on a roll, tossing four consecutive complete-game victories. He looked

Charles Albert "Chief" Bender fashioned a Hall of Fame career with the A's, going 193-102 in 12 seasons with the club (1903-1914), and helped the A's to three World Series titles and five pennants.

to extend that streak on a cool Tuesday afternoon with temperatures in the 50s against the Naps, whose name derived from hitter extraordinaire Nap Lajoie, who had also managed the club until yielding to Deacon McGuire in the middle of the 1909 season. The Naps' leadoff batter, rookie Jack Graney, lined a "low and savage drive," according to the *Plain Dealer*, that looked as if it would fall in for a hit until center fielder Rube Oldring rushed in and made a shoestring catch.[4] Oldring's snare turned out to be the play of the game as the Naps didn't sniff at another hit all afternoon. The only other cause for excitement occurred in the sixth when right fielder Danny Murphy sprinted to the concrete wall separating the bleachers from the playing field in foul territory to corral Bris Lord's popup, and then jumped over the wall and up three rows of seats before he could catch his balance.[5] Bender's solitary blemish was a fourth-inning walk to Terry Turner, who was immediately erased attempting to steal.

While Bender mowed down the Naps, the A's faced 24-year-old southpaw Fred Link (2-1), who burst on the scene after winning 20 or more games in three of his first four seasons in the minors. He debuted by tossing a 10-inning complete-game four-hitter to beat the Detroit Tigers on April 15 and was coming off an 11-inning, three-hit victory against the St. Louis Browns in his last start. In the second inning, Murphy belted a double down the left-field line. Moments later, he was caught a "mile off second" when Link made a quick toss to shortstop Turner, whose muff enabled Murphy to reach third.[6] That play epitomized the afternoon for Link and the Naps. Normally a good-fielding team (finishing with the AL's second highest fielding percentage, behind the A's), the Naps committed four costly blunders in this contest. Jack Barry's roller to left drove in Murphy for what proved to be the only run the A's needed with Bender on the rubber.

In the fourth, Home Run Baker beat out an infield hit to Lajoie at second base. Link's quick toss to first seemingly caught Baker napping, but his throw sailed and Baker advanced a station. After Harry Davis's sacrifice bunt, Murphy's "wicked smash," which third baseman Bill Bradley "partly batted down," accounted for the second run.[7] It was almost déjà vu in the sixth when the fleet-footed Baker beat out an infield down the first-base line and reached second when Link, covering first, couldn't hold on to first baseman George Stovall's throw. Davis's single plated Baker for a 3-0 lead.

A capable hitter who knocked in 16 runs on 25 hits in 1910, Bender singled in the seventh and scored the A's fourth and final run, on Topsy Hartsel's triple.

Breezing through the ninth, Bender retired Lord on a line drive to Hartsel in left field, then fanned Bradley. Elmer Flick, pinch-hitting for Link, popped a "dinky little foul" to catcher Ira Thomas to end the game in 1 hour and 36 minutes.[8]

Bender faced the minimum 27 batters and fanned four en route to the first no-hitter in the history of Shibe Park, baseball's first steel and concrete stadium, which opened at the beginning of the previous season; and the first no-no by an A's pitcher in Philadelphia. It was the second in A's history, following Weldon Henley's no-hitter against the St. Louis browns on July 22, 1905.

In his next start, Bender tossed a four-hit shutout against the Chicago White Sox in what unfolded as a career year. He won a personal-best 23 games, completed 25 of 28 starts, and posted a career-low 1.58 ERA in 250 innings. He teamed with Coombs, who emerged as baseball's best hurler (31-9), to form a staggering duo that led the A's to their first of four pennants in a five-year stretch that included World Series titles in 1910, 1911, and 1913. Bender went on to win 212 games (127 losses) in his 16-year career and was elected to the Baseball Hall of Fame in 1953.

SOURCES

In addition to the sources cited in the Notes, the author accessed Retrosheet.org, Baseball-Reference.com, and SABR.org.

NOTES

1   "Naps Were Helpless Before Big Injun," *Philadelphia Inquirer*," May 13, 1910: 10.

2   "Even Lajoie Cannot Make Hit Off the Great Chieftain," *Cleveland Plain Dealer*," May 13, 1910: 10.

3   "Big Chief Bender Kept Base Paths Looking as Bare as Abandoned Trail," *Cleveland Press*, May 12, 1910: 12.

4   "Even Lajoie Cannot Make Hit Off the Great Chieftain."

5   "Even Lajoie Cannot Make Hit Off the Great Chieftain."

6   "Even Lajoie Cannot Make Hit Off the Great Chieftain."

7   "Even Lajoie Cannot Make Hit Off the Great Chieftain."

8   "Even Lajoie Cannot Make Hit Off the Great Chieftain."

PHILADELPHIA NATIVE DANNY MURPHY CYCLES BUT ATHLETICS FALL TO BROWNS

August 25, 1910
St. Louis Browns 9, Philadelphia Athletics 6

By Mike Huber

The league-leading Philadelphia Athletics saw their six-game win streak snapped at the hands of the "meek and lowly trailing Browns of St. Louis"[1] in a Thursday afternoon game at Shibe Park, the first game in a three-game series. The Browns entered the game with a record of 34-77; this meant that they were 43 games under .500 and 44 games behind the 79-34 Athletics. Not only had the Athletics won six in a row, but they earned victories in 10 of their last 11 contests (and they were on their way to finishing August with a 22-7 mark), while the Browns came to Philadelphia having lost seven in a row and 9 of their previous 11 games. In head-to-head matchups prior to this game, Philadelphia had prevailed in five straight meetings, outscoring St. Louis 25-9. Yet on this day, the Browns persevered. According to the *St. Louis Star and Times*, "Connie Mack sent eighteen of his tried and trusty gladiators in against them; all proved absolutely harmless."[2] The only exception for the home team came from right fielder Danny Murphy, who went 5-for-5 at the plate and hit for the cycle in the losing effort.

St. Louis jumped on Philadelphia starter Eddie Plank for a run in the first inning and then added two more in the third.[3] Then, in the fifth inning, the crowd watched a bit of entertainment,

courtesy of Browns manager Jack O'Connor. Cy Morgan had taken over the pitching duties for Philadelphia in the fourth inning. With a 3-0 lead, George Stone was on third base and Pat Newnam stood at second. With two outs, Bobby Wallace stroked a hard grounder that ricocheted off pitcher Morgan's leg and rolled toward shortstop Jack Barry. Stone scored easily and O'Connor, standing in the third-base coaching box, waved Newnam home. Barry scooped up the ball and fired home to catcher Ira Thomas, who, in home-plate umpire Tommy Connolly's opinion, tagged Newnam before he touched the plate. Instead of appealing to the umpire, O'Connor "ran towards the plate and yelled, 'Did he touch you? He didn't, did he?'"[4] The sports pages of the *St. Louis Post-Dispatch* reported, "the crowd let out a roar at O'Connor's odd way of objecting to a decision, and even Umpire Connolly was forced to smile at Jack's remark."[5] Two more runs had scored, increasing the lead to 5-0. The Browns added a sixth run in the top of the sixth inning, and that was all for Morgan. He was replaced by Jimmy Dygert, who pitched the seventh.

Philadelphia finally put up some tallies in the seventh inning. The Athletics plated five runs off Browns starter Fred Link, who could get only two outs in the inning. Bill Bailey came on in relief to get the final out. Chief Bender, one of Mack's pitchers, had pitched a nine-inning complete game the day before and had picked up his 21st victory, so he was unavailable to toe the rubber, but Mack used him as a pinch-hitter for Dygert. Bender bashed a two-run double, to raise his batting average to .286.

St. Louis answered with a run in the eighth and two more in the ninth. Philadelphia tried to rally in the bottom of the ninth, as Mack sent in his ace pitcher, Jack Coombs, as a pinch-hitter. Coombs, who had pitched a 10-inning complete game two days earlier and was scheduled to pitch against these Browns the next day, struck out. The Athletics did get one run across on Murphy's solo home run to complete the cycle, but they lost the game, 9-6.

As stated earlier, the lone bright spot for the Athletics was the hitting of Murphy. According to the *Philadelphia Inquirer*, "Above all the fuss and feathers, the hitting of one Daniel Murphy stuck out like a sore thumb on a player piano's mitts."[6] Murphy was home-grown, born in Philadelphia in the centennial anniversary year of the nation (August 11, 1876). He was perfect at the plate, collecting five hits and extending his hitting streak to eight games, which was tied for second-longest of the season (Murphy put together a 10-game hitting streak from June 7 to 18).

Murphy tied a team record for the 1910 season by totaling 11 bases in one game. But in only one inning (the seventh) were any of his teammates on base when he got a hit. He finished the game with a lone run batted in, from his solo home run. He did raise his batting average eight points and his slugging percentage 21 points, to .463.

The top of the Browns' lineup set the pace. Frank Truesdale, Stone, and Newnam each collected three hits against the Athletics hurlers. Truesdale and Stone each doubled and Newnam tripled in the game. Interestingly, Bailey was awarded the win, his third of the season against

13 losses. Link had pitched 6⅔ innings for St. Louis and left with the lead, but he did not get the victory.

Philadelphia skipper Connie Mack, the Tall Tactician, set a season record when he "sent in every one of his six pitchers in an effort to stem the tide of defeat."[7] It was to no avail, as the *Philadelphia Inquirer* reported; "[b]y lamming our pitchers all over the lot and jumping on our team like a lot of abysmal brutes, this gang of Jack O'Connor's piled up a six-run lead on us in six innings."[8] The hometown paper pulled no punches on its pitching staff, writing, "As for our pitchers, they performed consistently throughout. They started bad and they were bad all the way."[9] Plank's record dropped to 14-8.

The *St. Louis Post-Dispatch* tried to blame the Athletics loss on superstition. For example, "the Athletics have won only one game on a Thursday since last June."[10] As a second reason, the Athletics had been nearing the .700 winning percentage mark, and it seemed that every time they came close, they would lose. That plateau had become a Sisyphus-type scenario for the Mackmen. They came into this contest with a record of 79-34, giving them a win percentage of .699, but it was "too much of a hoodoo to get over."[11]

Murphy was the second of three players in the 1910 season to hit for the cycle. On July 3 Pittsburgh's Chief Wilson accomplished the feat at the expense of the Cincinnati Reds, and on October 6, during the last week of the regular season, Bill Collins of the Boston Doves recorded a natural cycle (by hitting a single, double, triple, and home run in that order) as Boston[12] crushed the Philadelphia Phillies, 20-7. Murphy's cycle was the first for the Athletics since the inaugural season for the American League (1901), when Philadelphians Harry Davis (July 10) and Nap Lajoie (July 30) each hit for the cycle.

In addition to Murphy's cycle, another exciting event occurred with ties to the American League. The newly installed lights at White Sox Park (later renamed Comiskey Park) "received their first real tryout"[13] when a lacrosse game between the Illinois Athletic Club and the Calumet Lacrosse team was played under one million candlepower of light, "which constitutes a portion of the light plant that will give Chicago night baseball in the near future."[14] That future took close to 30 years to arrive, as the first night game at Comiskey Park took place on August 14, 1939. Four years earlier, on May 24, 1935, the Reds and Phillies played the first night game in major-league history.

The August 25 loss brought Philadelphia's record to 79-35. With 37 games left to play in the season, the Athletics needed only 21 victories to reach the century mark. The *Evening Journal* (Wilmington, Delaware) ran an article the day after this game, proclaiming, "The Athletics are going to win the world's pennant."[15] The story quoted Ed Bang of the *Cleveland News* as saying, "By drawing comparisons, I firmly believe that the Athletics will prove themselves masters of the Cubs, Pirates, or whoever may win the National League flag. The one big reason why the Athletics should win the world's championship is that the Cubs are not the great machine they were two, three and four years back. They have been going; the Athletics have been coming."[16]

Philadelphia won 23 of those 37 games to finish the season at 102-48. (The Athletics tied Cleveland in an 11-inning scoreless game on September 21.) They then beat the Cubs in the World Series, making Mr. Bang's prediction come true. Danny Murphy, a .300 batter during the regular season, "batted .400, lashing eight hits, including three doubles and the only home run of the series, and drove in nine runs as the Athletics crushed the Cubs 4-1 for Mack's first World Series win."[17]

SOURCES

In addition to the sources mentioned in the Notes, the author consulted Baseball-Reference.com and Retrosheet.org.

Regarding the decision to give Bailey the win instead of Link, the author consulted SABR's Records Committee who shared "All the Record Books Are Wrong," by John Thorn, the official historian for Major League Baseball (Ourgame.Mlblogs.Com/All-the-Record-Books-Are-Wrong-340d12173b88 – accessed July 2018). Thorn writes, "Scoring rules governing won and lost decisions by a pitcher did not become official until 1950. It was decided that all pitching decisions during the period 1920-1949 shall stand as they are in the official records, but that for the period 1876-1919 the 1950 ruling shall be in effect. The reason for this was that since 1920 the official scorer did exist, and he had the explicit authority to award the victory based on common practice, which was very close to the rule adopted in 1950. In the pre-1920 period, however, there was no official scoring rule or common practice for wins by a pitcher and for many years no official scorer." Therefore, today's practices of awarding the victory to a pitcher who had the lead after pitching at least five innings did not always apply.

NOTES

1   "League Leaders Fear Our Browns," *St. Louis Star and Times*, August 26, 1910: 7.

2   "League Leaders Fear Our Browns."

3   Play-by-play for this game is not available, and the newspaper accounts do not explain how the runs were scored.

4   "Browns Play Smart Ball in Defeating Mack's Men," *St. Louis Post-Dispatch*, August 26, 1910: 7.

5   "Browns Play Smart Ball in Defeating Mack's Men."

6   Jim Nasium, "Mackies' Pitchers Get Bamboozled," *Philadelphia Inquirer*, August 26, 1910: 10.

7   *St. Louis Post-Dispatch.*

8   Jim Nasium.

9   Jim Nasium.

10   "Browns Play Smart Ball in Defeating Mack's Men."

11   "Browns Play Smart Ball in Defeating Mack's Men."

12   In 1906, the National League's Boston Beaneaters changed their name to the Doves, which lasted four seasons. In 1911, the team was called the Boston Rustlers, and in 1912 they became the Boston Braves.

13   "Commy Shows That Night Baseball Is Possible," *St. Louis Post-Dispatch*, August 26, 1910: 7.

14   "Commy Shows That Night Baseball Is Possible."

15   "Cubs Not So Strong; Athletics Stronger," *Evening Journal* (Wilmington, Delaware), August 26, 1910: 10.

16   "Cubs Not So Strong; Athletics Stronger."

17   Doug Skipper, "Danny Murphy," sabr.org/bioproj/person/ef6684c3. Accessed June 2018.

COOMBS FANS 14 IN FOUR-HIT SHUTOUT

August 26, 1910
Philadelphia Athletics 6, St. Louis Browns 0

By Gregory H. Wolf

Jack Coombs was in the midst of one of the most spectacular seasons in baseball history as he took the mound against the lowly St. Louis Browns. After posting a pedestrian 35-35 record in his first four seasons, the 27-year-old right-hander for the Philadelphia A's was leading the majors with 22 wins (against just seven loses) and eight shutouts, one of which was a monumental 16-inning, three-hit, scoreless tie with 18 strike-outs against the Chicago White Sox on August 4. "Jawn," as Philadelphia newspapers like to call him, had also completed 26 of 28 starts and was coming off consecutive 10-inning complete-game victories, yielding just one run in each, in a span of six days.

Coombs' emergence as the circuit's best hurler had propelled skipper (and owner) Connie Mack's squad to the best record (79-35) in the major leagues. With a 12-game lead over the second-place Boston Red Sox, it was a forgone conclusion that the Athletics would capture their first pennant since 1905 and the second in franchise history as a charter member of the AL. The Brownies, on the other hand, had baseball's worst record (35-77) and had been riding a seven-game losing streak before beating the A's in the first game of the three-game set the day before by exploding for 15 hits in a 9-6 thrashing, the most runs the A's had surrendered in more than two months. First-year skipper Jack O'Connor sent 29-year-old right-hander Barney Pelty to the mound. In his eighth season, all with the Browns, Pelty was 4-9 with an 82-91 career slate.

The Friday afternoon game at Shibe Park, the A's state-of-the-art steel-and-concrete ballpark (baseball's first), which had opened to inaugurate the 1909 season, was played under what sportswriter Jim Nasium of the *Philadelphia Inquirer* described as "lowering skies" and "leaden atmosphere" with temperatures in the 70s. He further noted that such conditions created a "proper setting to render pitchers with plenty of smoke."[1]

After two scoreless frames, the Browns mounted the first scoring chance when Bobby Wallace led off the third by drawing Coombs' first and only free pass of the game, stole second, and moved to third when catcher Jack Lapp's throw sailed into the outfield. Flashing his speed and knee-buckling curveball, once described as dropping several feet at the plate without moving its lateral direction,[2] Coombs fanned Jim Stephens and Pelty and then dispatched Frank Truesdale on an infield grounder to end the frame. The

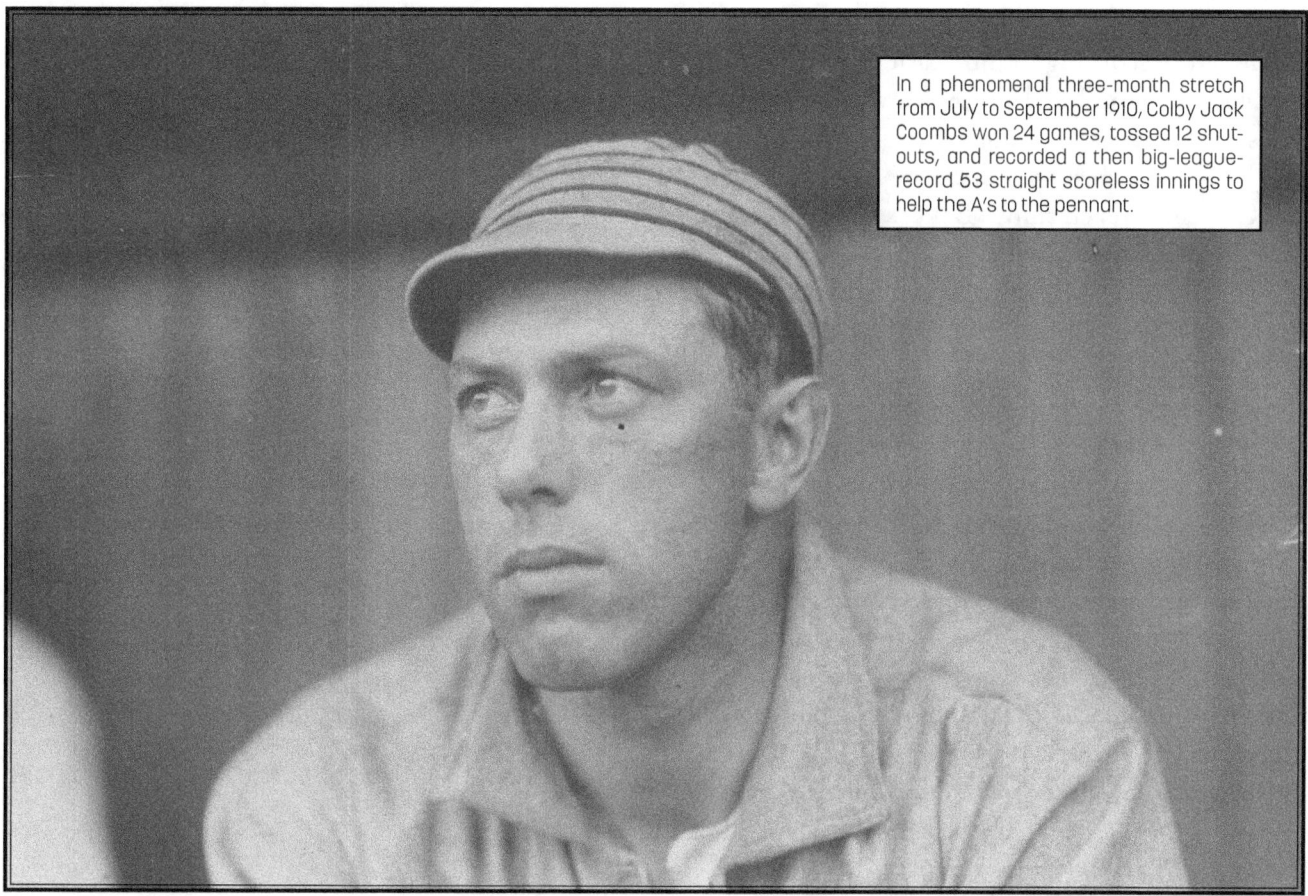

In a phenomenal three-month stretch from July to September 1910, Colby Jack Coombs won 24 games, tossed 12 shutouts, and recorded a then big-league-record 53 straight scoreless innings to help the A's to the pennant.

Browns reached as far as second on only one other occasion, in the sixth when Stephens led off with a single and moved up a station on Pelty's sacrifice, but Coombs again reared back and punched out the next two batters to quash the scoring chance. Coombs, opined the *St. Louis Post-Dispatch*, "fooled O'Connors' pets in a wholesale manner."[3]

The contest unfolded as a pitchers' duel with Pelty matching zeroes with Coombs through the first five frames while the twirlers yielded only four total hits (three off Pelty). The double shutout ended in the sixth when the A's Frank "Home Run" Baker led off with a triple to left-center and then sprinted home when center fielder Danny Hoffman's return throw sailed over Wallace's head at short. Ben Houser followed with single and it looked as though Pelty might be on the ropes when Lapps laced a two-out single, but Coombs' popup to right ended the threat.

The A's, who eventually led the AL in 1910 with a team batting average of .266 and ranked second with 4.3 runs per game (just behind the Detroit Tigers' 4.4), put on an exhibition of Deadball Era offensive tactics in the seventh. Bris Lord led off with a double and moved up a station when Rube Oldring, who entered the game leading the club with a .325 batting average, beat out a bunt to third. Eddie Collins's single brought Lord home and the floodgates were open. After Baker's sacrifice moved both runners into scoring position, Oldring aggressively ran home on Houser's grounder to second and scored standing up, according to the *Inquirer*. Danny Murphy's sacrifice fly driving in Collins accounted for the third and final run of the frame to make it 4-0.

The A's tacked on two more runs in the eighth. With Lord on second via a fielder's choice and a stolen base, Collins hit a two-out single to Hoffman, whose bad day in center field continued. According to Jim Nasium, the former A's flychaser, who had led the AL with 46 stolen bases for the pennant-winning team in 1905, "let [the ball] ooze through," enabling Lord to score and Collins to reach third.[4] Baker's single to right scored Collins to make it 6-0.

Through eight innings, Coombs had yielded just three hits and had fanned 13, including two in five different innings, and had registered at least one punchout in every frame thus far. George Stone eked out a seeing-eye infield single with one out, but Coombs retired Pat Newnam on a fly to right fielder Danny Murphy, who registered the only two outfield putouts for the A's the entire game. Colby Jack put an emphatic exclamation point on his masterpiece by registering his 14th strikeout of the afternoon, whiffing Art Griggs to end the game in exactly two hours. "Coombs was the whole show," gushed the *St. Louis Star*.[5]

Coombs continued to befuddle hitters for the rest of the season with his heater and curveball, which F.C. Lane wrote in *Baseball Magazine* said "actually shortened [his arm] by the stiffening of the cords at the elbow."[6] Coombs won his next six starts, giving him nine consecutive victories, and ultimately won 10 straight decisions, during which he pitched four shutouts and logged 53 consecutive scoreless innings. He finished the season by leading the big leagues with 31 wins (9 losses) and 13 shutouts, and ranking second in ERA (1.30), just behind Big Ed Walsh of the Chicago White Sox. He capped off the campaign by tossing three complete-game victories in the World Series against the Chicago Cubs, helping the Mackmen to their first title.

SOURCES

In addition to the sources cited in the Notes, the author accessed Retrosheet.org, Baseball-Reference.com, SABR.org, and *The Sporting News* archive via Paper of Record.

NOTES

1 Jim Nasium, "In Beating Browns Coombs Sets Record," *Philadelphia Inquirer*, August 27, 1910: 10.

2 Malachi Kittredge in the *National Game*, quoted from Bill James and Rob Neyer, *The Neyer/James Guide to Pitchers* (New York: Fireside, 2004), 171.

3 "Coombs Pitches Pennant Ball Against O'Connorites," *St. Louis Post-Dispatch*, August 27, 1910: 6.

4 Jim Nasium.

5 J. Coombs Fans Fourteen Browns," *St. Louis Star*, August 27, 1910: 10.

6 F.C. Lane, *Baseball Magazine*, November 1913, quoted from Bill James and Rob Neyer, *The Neyer/James Guide to Pitchers* (New York: Fireside, 2004), 171.

Bender Baffles Bruins in Fall Classic Opener

October 17, 1910
Philadelphia Athletics 4, Chicago Cubs 1

Game One of the World Series

By Gregory H. Wolf

Skipper Connie Mack was tired of waiting. Eleven days after his Philadelphia Athletics (102-48) played their last regular-season game, they finally took the field for Game One of the World Series.[1] The delay was caused by the National League, which had concluded its regular season just two days earlier with the juggernaut Chicago Cubs (104-50) capturing their fourth pennant in five seasons. Frank Chance's squad was a nominal favorite to win its third title in that span, despite losing the coin toss to determine which team would enjoy home-field advantage.[2]

The City of Brotherly Love was baseball-mad about the Athletics, who became first team to eclipse the century mark in victories in the 10-year history of the American League. On a warm and sunny Monday afternoon with temperatures in the low 70s, Shibe Park, baseball's first steel and concrete ballpark, was packed with an overflowing crowd of 26,891 spectators, more than three times the A's regular-season (and the major-league highest) game average of 7,550.[3] The carnival-like atmosphere at the intersection at 21st Street and Lehigh Avenue had begun the night before with hundreds of fans camping out for a chance to buy a general-admission ticket. The *Philadelphia Inquirer* reported that the throng was 7,000 strong by

7 A.M. on the day of the game and grew to more than 20,000 people.[4] Rowhouse rooftops along 20th Street and Somerset Street across from the ballpark had been converted into makeshift viewing stands despite orders from the Bureau of Building Inspectors forbidding it.[5]

The Athletics and Cubs were evenly matched, balanced teams each of which led its league in ERA and came within a handful of runs in pacing its circuit in runs scored. The Cubs' advantage was their World Series experience: They fielded essentially the same team that had won a major-league record 622 games over the previous six seasons (still the record as of 2022). Chance took a gamble on his starting pitcher. Instead of his ace, Mordecai "Three Finger" Brown (25-14, 1.86 ERA), he called on right-hander Orval Overall, known for his "oxlike strength," gushed Windy City sportswriter Harry Daniel.[6] Overall had won just 12 games in an injury-plagued campaign; however, he was 82-38 since his acquisition in mid-1906 and even better in the World Series, in which he was 3-0 and sported a stellar 1.12 ERA in 48⅓ innings.

There was considerable speculation about whom Mack would send to the mound in Game One. Many figured the Tall Tactician would

After graduating from the Carlisle Indian School in 1902, Charles Albert Bender played semipro baseball in Harrisburg, where Connie Mack signed him that summer. The following season he debuted as an 18-year-old for the A's and won 17 games.

go with Jack Coombs, who burst on the scene with one of the greatest seasons in AL history, leading the league with 31 wins and 13 shutouts. However, two of the few remaining players from the A's 1905 pennant winners warmed up prior to the game: Eddie Plank and Charles Albert "Chief" Bender.

Mack chose right-handed Bender against the Cubs' righty-heavy lineup. The 26-year-old Native American, who hated the racist monikers the press gave him, boasted a 125-76 slate, including 23-5 with a 1.58 ERA in 1910, but hadn't pitched since he won his final start on September 7. With the pennant effectively wrapped up in mid-August, Mack had given his cerebral hurler time to overcome some nagging injuries. Bender, however, was far from idle. He had scouted the Cubs during their series against the Phillies in Philadelphia

in mid-September. None of the A's were rusty, though, as Mack's troops played a three-game series (October 11-13) against Jimmy McAleer's All-Stars, a barnstorming team consisting of AL stalwarts.[7] Bender had two more advantages: He was the only A's player with a World Series victory, having tossed a four-hit shutout in Game Two against the New York Giants in 1905; and he was the only A's pitcher to have beaten the Cubs. The two teams had played an exhibition game the previous October and Bender blanked the Cubs and Overall on two hits.[8]

Scheduled to start at 2 P.M., the game was delayed by 14 minutes as Chance and Mack wrangled with the four-man umpiring crew about the ground rules. Both managers objected to still and movie cameramen on the field behind home plate; they were dispatched to the grandstand. More disconcerting were the thousands of spectators standing in right field and left field cordoned off by rope, the first time that was required since Shibe Park opened in 1909.[9]

Armed with various noisemakers, the crowd was "wild with enthusiasm" when Bender took the mound, reported Chicago sportswriter Harry Daniel.[10] Leadoff hitter Jimmy Sheckard sent Bender's first pitch sailing over the left-field bleachers, but it was a foul. It was also the hardest hit ball off Bender the entire afternoon. Three pitches later, Bender fanned Sheckard. The Cubs' most dangerous hitter, Frank "Wildfire" Schulte, whose 10 home runs tied Fred Beck of the Boston Braves for the NL lead, followed with a single, but was caught stealing. Solly Hofman was retired on a grounder. The A's managed one single against Overall in the first, and, like Schulte, Eddie Collins was caught stealing.

After Bender set down the Cubs in order in the second, Frank "Home Run" Baker led off with a smash to left field that "pulled up in the crowd" for a ground-rule double, and moved to third on Harry Davis's sacrifice.[11] Danny Murphy's single drove Baker home. With two out and Murphy on third and Ira Thomas on first via a walk, Bender hit a "vicious" chopper to second baseman Heinie Zimmerman, who had replaced Johnny Evers, sidelined with an ankle injury.[12] (No slouch at the plate, Bender had batted .269 and knocked in 16 runs in 1910.) The ball "bounded out of his hands" and into center field, plating Murphy.[13] No error was given to Zimmerman, who "should have cleanly made the assist," argued sportswriter Fred J. Hewitt.[14]

The A's tacked on another run in the third when Bris Lord led off with a deep shot into the crowd in right-center field for a ground-rule double. Collins sacrificed him to third, then Baker singled to left to make it 3-0.

The A's three runs were more than Bender needed as he delivered "one of the most marvelous exhibitions of pitching in the history of baseball,"

gushed Daniel.[15] He baffled the Cubs with his array of fastballs, curveballs, and his nickel curves (proto-sliders). His delivery was mesmerizing, too. "[H]is long, wiry arm would swing through the air," explained Daniel. "Twice it would circle around like a great revolving wheel. Then his left leg would go up and the arm of steel would flash around with a dazzling side-arm movement."[16] Through eight innings Bender faced the minimum 24 batters. Schulte walked in the fourth, but was again gunned down trying to steal second on another bullet from catcher Ira Thomas.

"Wild and weak" through three innings, Overall was replaced by spot starter Harry McIntire.[17] Sportswriters from around the country suggested the next day that Chance had thrown in the towel with this decision instead of calling on Brown, King Cole (20-4), or Ed Reulbach. However, the 31-year-old right-hander McIntire mystified the A's with a confusing underhand motion and kept the Cubs in the game. He held the A's hitless from the fourth inning through the seventh, yielding only walks to Amos Strunk in the fifth and Thomas in the seventh.

The A's added an insurance run in the eighth. After Eddie Collins drew a two-out walk, McIntire tossed nervously over to first, hoping to pick him off rather than face the dangerous Baker at the plate. Coming off an AL-record 81 swipes in 1910, Collins was finally caught napping, but McIntire's toss flew past first base and Collins reached third. Baker smashed a line drive "splintering the right field fence," which dropped into the crowd for his second ground-rule double and resulted in another run.[18]

Bender suffered some bad luck in the ninth, but kept his cool and remained the "very embodiment of confidence," opined the *Inquirer*.[19] Joe Tinker received a second chance when Thomas muffed his popup behind the plate by grounding the next pitch past second, then took second when center fielder Strunk fumbled the ball. It was the Cubs' first hit since the first inning.

Johnny Kling followed with another single to plate Tinker (unearned run), then gave way to pinch-runner John Kane, who advanced a station on pinch-hitter Gene Beaumont's grounder. After Sheckard fanned, Schulte drew a walk to bring the tying run to the plate. With the count 1-and-2, Hofman grounded to Baker, who stepped on third for the final out, ending the game in 1 hour and 54 minutes and securing the A's victory.

Home Run Baker was the batting hero of the game, collecting three of the A's seven hits and driving in two runs, but this game was about Bender. Praised for his "phenomenal speed, accurate control, and magnificent head work,"[20]

Bender went the distance for the 26th time in 29 starts of the season, fanned eight and walked two in an overpowering victory that "turned much baseball calculation topsy-turvy," wrote Chicago's *Inter Ocean*.[21] The A's emerged as the new Series favorites.

SOURCES

In addition to the sources cited in the Notes, the author accessed Retrosheet.org, Baseball-Reference.com, and SABR.org.

NOTES

1 The A's played their final game on October 6; the final day of the regular season in the AL was October 8.

2 A's owner Ben Shibe won the coin toss from Cubs owner Charles Webb Murphy several days before the beginning of the World Series; however, it was not without controversy, as Tom Swift explains. AL President Ban Johnson flipped the coin, which had apparently rolled off a table. Under the rules the two owners had agreed upon, the flip should have been nullified. Tom Swift, *Chief Bender's Burden: The Silent Struggle of a Baseball Star* (Lincoln: Bison Books, 2010), 144.

3 "Local Weather Report from U.S. Weather Bureau," *Philadelphia Inquirer*, October 18, 1910: 2.

4 "Doors Are Opened Early for Vast Bleacher Throng," *Philadelphia Inquirer*, October 18, 1910: 13.

5 "Spectacle of Brilliant Crowd Rarely Equaled at Any Event," *Philadelphia Inquirer*, October 18, 1919: 13.

6 Harry Daniel, "Indian's Wonderful Pitching for Athletics Costs the Cubs the First Game of the World Series," (Chicago) *Inter Ocean*, October 18, 1910: 1.

7 The McAleer All-Stars had some of the biggest names in the AL, including Ty Cobb, Tris Speaker, and Walter Johnson. See "All Stars Here to Battle With Mackies," *Philadelphia Inquirer*, October 12, 1910: 10; Jim Nasium, "Pick of A.L. Teams Clean Up Mackies," *Philadelphia Inquirer*, October 12, 1910: 10.

8 Ring Lardner, "Redskin Tames Overall's Cubs," *Chicago Tribune*, October 20, 1909: 12.

9 "Spectacle of Brilliant Crowd Rarely Equaled at Any Event."

10 Daniel: 1.

11 Frank J. Hewitt, "Bender Invincible and Cubs Lose First," (Chicago) *Inter Ocean*, October 18, 1910: 2.

12 Daniel: 2.

13 "Story in Detail of Victory Over Cubs of Chicago," *Philadelphia Inquirer*, October 18, 1910: 12.

14 Hewitt.

15 Daniel: 2.

16 Daniel: 2.

17 Daniel: 1.

18 Hewitt.

19 The Old Sport, "Frank Baker's Timely Hits Big Factor in Mackmen's Victory," *Philadelphia Inquirer*, October 18, 1910: 1

20 Daniel: 1.

21 Daniel: 1.

Jack Coombs, Eddie Collins Lead Athletics Over Cubs

October 18, 1910
Philadelphia Athletics 9, Chicago Cubs 3

Game Two of the World Series

By Mike Lynch

After Philadelphia defeated the Chicago Cubs 4-1 in Game One of the 1910 World Series behind the three-hit pitching of Chief Bender and bat of Frank "Home Run" Baker, Athletics founder and manager Connie Mack gave the ball to staff ace Jack Coombs. After four pedestrian years in which the Iowa-born right-hander went 35-35 with a 2.45 ERA, Coombs came into his own in 1910, going 31-9 with a 1.30 ERA, tossed a league-best 13 shutouts, and didn't allow a home run in 353 innings.[1]

Cubs skipper and first baseman Frank Chance turned to his own ace, Mordecai "Three Finger" Brown, a versatile veteran righty who not only paced the Cubs in wins with 25, but tied Cincinnati Reds hurler Harry Gaspar for the National League lead in saves with seven.[2] Brown also paced the circuit in complete games, shutouts, and WHIP, and with his 34th birthday only a day away, he thought there was no way he could lose.[3]

The Tuesday game drew 24,597 fans to Shibe Park a day after almost 27,000 watched the first tilt. One scribe was perplexed by the drop-off, considering it was a perfect day for baseball and that an Athletics victory in Game One all but ensured that more Philadelphians would show up for the second contest.[4] But a failure by the city's police force to uphold an order issued before the first game prohibiting fans from watching from rooftops across from the park emboldened more people to do just that for Game Two.[5]

Coombs was shaky in the first and walked leadoff man Jimmy Sheckard on four pitches. Frank Schulte forced Sheckard at second on a grounder to Eddie Collins, but Solly Hofman walked on six pitches, the last two of which nearly hit him, and Chance singled to third after almost being plunked himself. Heinie Zimmerman plated the first run on a fly ball to Amos Strunk, and Hofman and Chance advanced to third and second, respectively. Coombs continued to be wild and almost hit Harry Steinfeldt with his second pitch, but the Cubs third baseman helped the A's hurler by whiffing at a ball over his head to end the threat.

Brown struck out Strunk to start the bottom half of the first and got an assist from catcher

In 1910 Jack Coombs had one of the most dominant seasons in baseball history, leading the major leagues with 31 wins and 13 shutouts. He tossed three complete-game victories in six days to propel the A's to the World Series title over the Chicago Cubs in five games.

Johnny Kling, who scooped the third strike from the dirt and fired to Chance for the out. Bris Lord grounded to third for an easy out before Collins fisted a single over Zimmerman's head, then stole second after a cat-and-mouse game in which Brown threw to first three times before throwing two waste pitches to Baker. Collins made it to second easily on Brown's third delivery to Baker, but the third sacker grounded back to the mound to end the inning.

Coombs was much sharper in the second, but ran into some bad luck when first baseman Harry Davis dropped Baker's throw after the third baseman snared a grounder by Joe Tinker to lead off the frame. The pitcher's luck quickly turned, however, when Kling shot a line drive right to Collins, who threw to Davis to double up Tinker. Brown grounded to Collins for the third out.

Brown retired Davis on a fly ball to Hofman before walking Danny Murphy on four pitches. Tinker made a nice play on a grounder by Jack Barry, fielding the ball at second, stepping on the bag, and throwing to first to complete the double play and end the inning. The third started with a second free pass to Sheckard and a Schulte sacrifice bunt that would have been the first out had Davis not dropped Coombs's throw and committed his second miscue in as many innings.

With runners at first and second, Hofman popped his bunt to Davis, who held on this time, and Coombs fanned Chance after catcher Ira Thomas saved a wild pitch by stopping a low curveball with his bare hand. Zimmerman lined the first pitch he saw to Lord in left field and the game went to the bottom of the third with the Cubs clinging to a 1-0 lead.

Philadelphia took a 2-1 lead in the bottom of the third, thanks in part to a comedy of errors by Steinfeldt and perfectly placed hits by Strunk and Collins. Thomas led off with a slow roller to third that Steinfeldt tried to barehand but missed for his first error. Coombs whiffed for the first out, then Strunk expertly bunted between the mound and first base, and though Brown was able to reach the ball he couldn't hold on and all were safe. Lord grounded to Zimmerman, who threw to Tinker to force Strunk at second with Thomas advancing to third on the play.

Brown was careful with Collins and tossed him four straight curves, three of which were balls, before firing a fastball over for strike two. His next fast one caught too much of the plate and Collins served it between Steinfeldt and the third-base bag for a double. Thomas scored easily and Lord followed him home when Steinfeldt missed Sheckard's throw from left. Baker grounded to Zimmerman and the inning was over.

Coombs and Brown traded goose eggs in the fourth, the only blemishes being Tinker's hit off Coombs and hits by Barry and Thomas off Brown. Coombs almost did himself in when he made consecutive errors on bunts by Brown and Sheckard to lead off the fifth, bobbling Brown's until he was safe and falling down while attempting to field Sheckard's. A third bunt, this one by Schulte, went to Davis for an out, but the runners moved to second and third with Hofman and Chance due up.

Three more errant curves and an inside fastball loaded the bases for Chance, but Brown foolishly tried to tag up on a short fly ball to Murphy in right and Murphy's perfect throw nailed the hurler at the plate to retire the side. The A's manufactured their third run in the bottom of the fifth. Lord poled a one-out single before being erased by a fielder's choice that put Collins on first.

Again, Brown tried to get the better of the American League's stolen-base champ by throwing three wide ones to Baker, but Collins refused to budge until Brown's fourth pitch when he swiped his second base of the game.[6] Baker walked and Davis atoned for his errors with a run-scoring single before Murphy grounded out to end the inning.

Both teams threatened in the sixth but neither scored. The Cubs put a man on second to no avail;

the A's had runners at first and third with one out before Brown worked out of the jam with help from Strunk, who tried to bunt Thomas home and failed miserably. "It looked like a large joke to see Strunk trying to squeeze Thomas home from third," opined the *Chicago Tribune*. "... Strunk bunted as if he never tried it before."[7]

The game went to the seventh with Philadelphia still up 3-1 and that's when they stepped on the throttle, but not before Chicago made things interesting. Sheckard followed a Brown strikeout with a shot into the right-field crowd for a double, and Hofman followed a fly out by Schulte with a walk. Chance singled to center and scored Sheckard to cut the lead to 3-2, but that was as close as the Cubs would get.

Collins started the bottom of the inning with a free pass and moved to third on Baker's single to right. Davis doubled into the left-field crowd to score Collins, and Murphy did the same to plate Baker and Davis, prompting Chance to order Lew Richie to warm up. Barry sacrificed Murphy to third and the move paid off when Thomas followed with a run-scoring single to boost Philadelphia's lead to 7-2.

Coombs grounded to first for the second out, but Strunk's double scored Thomas, and Sheckard's failure to hold on to Lord's line drive to left plated Strunk. Lord was thrown out trying to steal second with Collins at the plate, but when the smoke cleared, the score stood at 9-2 in Philadelphia's favor.

The Cubs continued to fight, loading the bases in the eighth and scoring a run in the ninth when Zimmerman knocked in Hofman with a two-bagger, but Coombs wrapped groundouts around a walk to Tinker to end the game and send the Athletics to Chicago with a two-game lead.

SOURCES

In addition to the sources cited in the Notes, the author accessed Retrosheet.org, Baseball-Reference.com, and SABR.org.

NOTES

1   On the surface a 2.45 ERA is much more impressive than "pedestrian," but Coombs's career ERA+ prior to 1910 was only 5 percent better than league average.

2   The save rule wasn't adopted until 1969 and saves were retroactively calculated by researchers for every season that came before. It's because of them that we know Brown and Gaspar had seven each.

3   "Sidelights on the Second Battle," *Chicago Tribune*, October 19, 1910: 21.

4   "Sidelights on the Second Battle."

5   "Sidelights on the Second Battle."

6   Collins led the American League with 81 stolen bases in 1910, finishing with 16 more than the 1909 leader, Ty Cobb.

7   "Sidelights on the Second Battle."

Frank Baker's Pair of Homers Helps Athletics Clinch Second Straight Pennant

September 26, 1911
Philadelphia Athletics 11, Detroit Tigers 5

By Mike Lynch

Heading into the 1911 season, the Philadelphia Athletics were a near unanimous choice to capture their second straight American League pennant and fourth in 11 years despite boasting one of the youngest lineups in the circuit. Their average age was a hair younger than 27 with a core that featured 20-year-old Stuffy McInnis at first base, 24-year-olds Eddie Collins and Jack Barry at second base and shortstop, respectively, 25-year-old Frank "Home Run" Baker at third, and 22-year-old reserve outfielder Amos Strunk.

The Detroit Tigers, on the other hand, were said to have felt the "effects of time" in 1910 when they finished in third place after having copped three straight pennants from 1907 through 1909.[1] John B. Foster of the *New York Evening Telegram* blamed Detroit's slide in the standings in 1910 on "snarling and petty fault finding on the part of the players," especially Ty Cobb, whom he called a "spoiled baby."[2]

But when the Tigers defeated the Athletics, 9-8, on May 19, 1911, they pushed their record to 27-5, and it looked as though they would cruise to another pennant. The next closest team, the Chicago White Sox, was already 9½ games back and the Athletics sat in fifth place with a 12-game deficit. According to the *Philadelphia Inquirer*, the Tigers benefited from "striking splendid weather" during spring training and "started off as though they meant to make a runaway race of it."[3]

Indeed, the Tigers won 21 of their first 23 games and capped off their run with a 10-0 drubbing of the New York Highlanders on May 9. Led by Cobb, Sam Crawford, Donie Bush, and pitcher George Mullin, Detroit was scoring more than six runs a game while allowing fewer than three. Only one pitching staff was stingier – the Pittsburgh Pirates were allowing 2.85 runs to that point – and the next most potent offense, belonging to the Philadelphia Phillies, was a full run behind.

But the race was far too early to call and the early fates of both squads proved to be a fluke. After a 13-15 start, Philadelphia went 52-20 and passed the Tigers atop the standings on August 7, then spent the next seven weeks building on their lead, which stood at 10½ games on September 25.

The *Inquirer* blamed lousy weather for the Athletics' slow start and reported that magnate and skipper Connie Mack had "never encountered such adverse weather conditions for a spring training trip, and as a result it was not until the championship season was well under way that the Athletics began to round into first-class playing shape."[4]

At 95-46, all the Athletics had to do to cop their second straight flag was beat the 85-57 Tigers, which was easier said than done. The Tigers had just beaten the Athletics in the first game of a two-game set on Monday and they were the only team with a winning record against Philadelphia, having won 12 of 21 contests.

For Tuesday's game Mack called on 28-year-old right-hander Jack Coombs, who was leading the league with 26 wins. Of his 12 losses, four had come against Detroit. Hughie Jennings countered with 27-year-old righty Ed Willett, who had struggled to a 13-12 record and an ERA in the mid-3's after averaging 17 wins and a 2.33 ERA over the previous three seasons.[5] The Virginia native had faced Philadelphia twice out of the bullpen and surrendered 10 runs in seven innings before his first start against them.

Neither team scored in the first and Coombs got out of the second with another zero on the scoreboard, but Willett wasn't so lucky. Athletics cleanup hitter Frank Baker led off the bottom of the second with his ninth homer of the season to stake Philadelphia to a 1-0 lead. "Frank Baker busted open the action of the fray," wrote Jim Nasium of the *Philadelphia Inquirer*, "and slapped one of Willetts' [sic] shoots on the snoot and lifted it far over the right field wall close to the foul line for the first run of the game."[6]

Danny Murphy walked and all hands were safe when first baseman Del Gainer fumbled Willett's throw on a bunt by Claud Derrick. Barry's force out sent Murphy to third and he and Barry scored on a double to right-center by catcher Jack Lapp. Willett worked out of the jam thanks in part to Bush, who hauled in Coombs' short fly and doubled up Lapp at second to keep the score at 3-0.

Perhaps buoyed by Bush's play, the Tigers tied the score, 3-3, in the top of the third. Baker tossed

Hall of Fame third baseman Frank "Home Run" Baker was one of the Deadball Era's great sluggers, pacing the AL in round-trippers in four straight seasons (1911-1914) and RBIs two times as the offensive focal point of Connie Mack's first dynasty.

wildly to Derrick on Willett's grounder to lead off the inning, Bush singled to right, and Cobb beat out a chopper in front of the plate to load the bases with nobody out. Crawford plated Willett on a force out at second, Jim Delahanty knocked in Bush with a sacrifice fly to right, and Crawford tied the score when he crossed the plate on a two-bagger by Delos Drake. Coombs ended the frame and averted tragedy after walking Gainer when he speared a liner by George Moriarty that was heading for his face.[7]

Willett immediately killed Detroit's momentum when the Athletics scored two in the bottom of the third. "Then the champs came in and proceeded without further monkey business to put the finishing touches on Mr. Willetts," wrote Jim Nasium.[8] The Tigers hurler retired Bris Lord to begin the inning, but a Rube Oldring hit followed by a triple to left-center field by Collins untied the score. Baker drove in his second run of the game with a double to left and it looked as if the inning would get out of hand when Murphy singled to put runners at first and third with only one out. But Bush made another sensational play on Derrick's grounder and turned an inning-ending double play.

Coombs continued to put up zeroes and the 5-3 cushion held until the bottom of the sixth when Philadelphia scored another run, this time against relief pitcher Ralph Works, who entered the game the fourth. Singles by Lapp and Coombs put runners on first and second, and a wild pitch advanced Lapp to third. He came home on a force out at second by Lord and Philadelphia's lead grew to 6-3.

The onslaught continued in the seventh when Collins walked, then scored on Derrick's three-bagger to put the Athletics up 7-3. Philadelphia effectively put the game on ice in the bottom of the eighth when four more runs came home. "The eighth inning was a series of disastrous events for Mr. Works," Jim Nasium reported. "Coombs started the stuff with one down by slamming a two-base whack to the corner of the latitude then Works splashed the ball into the palpitating gizzard of Bris Lord."[9]

Both runners scored on a double down the left-field line by Oldring to push the lead to 9-3, then Baker slammed his second four-bagger of the contest and became the first player to hit two home runs in one game at Shibe Park.[10] That was all the runs the Athletics would score, but it was more than enough. The Tigers rallied for two runs in the top of the ninth when Cobb singled with two outs and Crawford followed with a two-run homer off Coombs. But the hurler rebounded and fanned Delahanty to win the game, 11-5, and the Athletics clinched their second straight American League pennant.

"There was no doubting the Athletics' intentions of winning the game yesterday," waxed the *Philadelphia Inquirer*. "They gave both Willetts and Works one of the worst grillings to which a pair of visiting slabmen have been subjected at Shibe Park this season. Singles, doubles, triples and home runs were smashed out with such regularity that the 10,000 odd fans were kept continually yelling themselves hoarse over the terrific exhibition of clubbing on the part of the Mackies."[11]

SOURCES

In addition to the sources cited in the Notes, the author accessed Retrosheet.org, Baseball-Reference.com, and SABR.org.

NOTES

1 John. B. Foster, "Athletics to Run Their Race in 1911 Against the Field," *Owensboro* (Kentucky) *Messenger*, April 2, 1911: 9.

2 Foster.

3 The Old Sport, "Athletics Win Championship From Detroit," *Philadelphia Inquirer*, September 27, 1911: 1.

4 "Athletics Win Championship From Detroit."

5 Willett finished the season with a 3.66 ERA, but it's difficult to know what his exact ERA was going into the September 26 game because neither Baseball-Reference.com nor Retrosheet.org has complete earned-runs data for game logs and daily splits.

6 Jim Nasium, "This Is the Game Which Decided It," *Philadelphia Inquirer*, September 27, 1911: 10.

7 "Athletics Again Are Champions of American League," *Detroit Free Press*, September 27, 1911: 11.

8 "Athletics Again Are Champions of American League."

9 "Athletics Again Are Champions of American League."

10 Baker accomplished the feat again on June 26, 1914, against the Washington Senators in the second game of a doubleheader.

11 "Athletics Win Championship From Detroit."

BAKER'S BASH KNOTS WORLD SERIES

October 16, 1911
Philadelphia Athletics 3, New York Giants 1

Game Two of the World Series

By Matt Albertson

The World Series returned to Philadelphia for the second year in a row in 1911, and 26,286 baseball fans swarmed a wet Shibe Park on October 16, 1911, for Game Two of the 1911 World Series between the New York Giants (99-54) and Philadelphia Athletics (101-50). Despite their losing Game One, 2-1, at the Polo Grounds, the *Evening Bulletin* reported that the Athletics were favored 6 to 5 to win Game Two.[1]

The starting pitchers for the game were Rube Marquard for the Giants and Eddie Plank for the Athletics. Marquard had been purchased by the New York Giants in 1908 from the Indianapolis Indians for a record $11,000, leading many to dub him the "$11,000 Beauty." Marquard struggled in his first two full seasons in the big leagues, and compiled a 9-17 record with a 3.14 ERA. He struck out 161 and walked 113. He was then dubbed the "$11,000 Lemon." But Marquard turned doubters into believers in 1911 when he went 24-7 in 45 games with a 2.50 ERA, striking out 237 and walking 106. Marquard pitched 16 more seasons for the Giants, Dodgers, Reds, and Braves before retiring in 1925 at age 38. His career record was 201-177 and he had a 3.08 ERA in 536 games with 1,593 strikeouts and 858 walks. He was elected to the Baseball Hall of Fame in 1971.

Philadelphia Athletics owner-manager Connie Mack signed 25-year-old Eddie Plank to a contract in 1901. Plank was enrolled at Gettysburg Academy and played for the Gettysburg College baseball team. He joined the Athletics in Baltimore in May 1901 and at the end of the season, he had a 17-13 record in 33 games with a 3.31 ERA. In 1911 Plank went 23-8 with a 2.10 ERA at age 35. He retired after the 1917 season at age 41 after 17 seasons in the major leagues and finished with a 326-194 record and a 2.35 ERA.

The *Evening Bulletin* noted that "seats for the game were as rare as aeroplane visits to the moon."[2] Female fans began to enter the park at 11 A.M. and made their way to the right-field bleachers. New York fans, fearing limited seating, arrived en masse at noon while droves of fans rushed on-field police officers and found standing room all around the outfield. Athletics President John Shibe stationed several men around the ballpark to gather foul balls. He even secured an injunction against 20th street property owners for failing to secure proper permits in an attempt to prevent the sale of seats on top of row houses, but it did not matter. Many fans who did not have tickets to the game were still able to buy tickets for a rooftop bleacher seat. Factories in the neighborhood shut down at noon, allowing workers to watch the game from factory windows.[3] A constant buzz was in the air prior to first pitch and even caused one overexcited man to be taken out of the grounds on a stretcher to the Woman's Homeopathic Hospital.[4]

A hush overcame the crowd as Plank delivered the first pitch of the game at 2:02 P.M. and subsequently struck out Giants leadoff man Josh Devore looking, to the delight of the local fans. Larry Doyle was up next and he sent a long fly to Athletics left fielder Bris Lord. Fred Snodgrass was hit by a pitch on a two-strike count and became the Giants' first baserunner. But Red Murray lined out to second baseman Eddie Collins to conclude the top half of the first inning.

In the Athletics' half, leadoff man Lord knocked a 2-and-1 pitch to right field and took second on Murray's error. Rube Oldring's sacrifice advanced Lord to third. With Collins at bat, Marquard unleashed a wild pitch that allowed Lord to score the first run of the game. Collins singled past Giants third baseman Buck Herzog but Marquard gathered himself as he struck out Frank Baker and got Danny Murphy to fly out to left field to end the inning.

Fred Merkle led off the second for the Giants and grounded out to third base. Herzog smashed a 1-and-2 pitch over third baseman Oldring's head for a double and advanced to third on Art Fletcher's groundball to Collins. Catcher Chief Meyers, a Native American who was the Giants' best hitter in 1911, drove Merkle in with a single to left field, tying the game, 1-1. Plank then struck out Marquard to end the inning.

Only two men reached base between the bottom of the second inning and top of the sixth — the A's Jack Barry got to second base in the second inning on an error by left fielder Devore, and the Giants' Snodgrass singled in the top of the third. Otherwise the 36-year old Plank and the 24-year-old Marquard mowed down the opposing batters with few balls leaving the infield. The Athletics

finally broke the stalemate in the bottom of the sixth inning. Marquard retired Lord and Oldring on fly balls. With two out and none on, Eddie Collins slashed a double down the left-field line. Frank Baker stepped to the plate next.

Giants manager John McGraw, an expert at the mental game, had chided Baker from the dugout while the Athletics were in the field in an attempt to break Baker's concentration. "You're a quitter," the New York manager cried. "[Hughie] Jennings and the whole Detroit club told us so."[5] It was a reference to a game earlier in the year when Detroit's Ty Cobb spiked Baker sliding into third base. Baker was mild-mannered and McGraw sought to leverage this alleged weakness, despite the fact that Baker slashed .334/.379/.508 and led the league with 11 home runs in 1911.

Before the game, McGraw had told Marquard to stay away from the strike zone when he pitched to Baker. Marquard struck out Baker on three straight curveballs in the first inning and got him out on a weak grounder to second base in the fourth. But in the sixth, the pitcher ignored McGraw's advice when Baker refused to offer at a nibbling breaking ball outside the zone. "...I had one strike on him and he had refused to bite on another outcurve which was a little too wide," Marquard said in an article under his byline in the New York Times. "I thought to cross him by sending in a fast high straight ball the kind that I know he liked. Meyers had called for a curve, but I could not see it [due to the sun], and signaled a high fast ball,"[6] Marquard suggested that Collins had relayed the signal to Baker from second base. Baker sent Marquard's fastball over the right-field wall, and the Athletics led 3-1.

According to Connie Mack biographer Norman Macht, "Delirium erupted within Shibe Park, in the windows and along the rooftops of Twentieth Street, and downtown on Broad Street, where the action was being recreated. ... The howling, stomping, whistling, and cheering had begun at 3:20 and went on for a full five minutes.

Fans sitting behind the visitors' dugout banged on its tin roof with canes and bottles and feet."[7]

Marquard was pulled after the seventh inning and replaced by 23-year-old Doc Crandall, who set down the Athletics without a hit in the eighth. Marquard had surrendered only four hits but Baker's blast proved fatal to the Giants. The Series was now tied. The Athletics' Plank pitched a complete game and surrendered five hits, struck out eight, and allowed only one run. The game was a true pitchers' duel but Baker's home run stole the headlines and was a catalyst for his future identity as Home Run Baker.

SOURCES

In addition to the sources cited in the Notes, the author accessed Retrosheet.org, Baseball-Reference.com, Newspapers.com, and SABR.org.

NOTES

1   "Plank Opposes Marquard in Second Great Struggle of World's Series Contest," *Philadelphia Evening Bulletin*, October 16, 1911.

2   Plank Opposes Marquard in Second Great Struggle of World's Series Contest."

3   Plank Opposes Marquard in Second Great Struggle of World's Series Contest."

4   "Fan Overcome by Excitement," *Philadelphia Evening Bulletin*, October 16, 1911.

5   Lew Friedman, *Connie Mack's First Dynasty: The Philadelphia Athletics, 1910-1914* (Jefferson, North Carolina: McFarland & Company, 2017), 83.

6   Rube Marquard, "Giants Beaten by Home Run Hit," *New York Times*, October 17, 1911.

7   Norman Macht, *Connie Mack and the Early Years of Baseball* (Lincoln: University of Nebraska Press, 2007), 525.

"WHAT'S THE MATTER WITH BAKER? HE'S ALL RIGHT."

October 24, 1911
Philadelphia Athletics 4, New York Giants 2

Game Four of the World Series

By Bob LeMoine

The Philadelphia Athletics were on Cloud Nine as they pulled out a come-from-behind victory in 11 innings over the New York Giants in Game Three of the 1911 World Series and led the Series two games to one. As they took the field on October 24, they had been soaring for an entire week, thanks to lousy weather in Philadelphia. Their soaring was figurative, of course, compared with those who were really in the clouds. Orville Wright was at Kill Devil Hill, North Carolina, that day, breaking a world's record by maintaining his aeroplane in the air for 9 minutes and 45 seconds.[1] A's fans, however, were fascinated more with the soaring home runs off the bat of Frank Baker, who inherited the name for which he would forever be known: Home Run Baker. He was the league leader with 11 home runs in 1911, but this Series cemented his fame for all time.

It all began as a feud between Baker and the Giants' Fred Snodgrass. Baker earlier in the season had an incident with Detroit's Ty Cobb in which the Georgia Peach slid hard into third and spiked Baker on the arm. Giants manager John McGraw thought Baker looked weak, so he encouraged his team to play a rougher brand of ball. Snodgrass went hard into Baker in Game One of the Series, gashing his arm. Baker won

Game Two with a decisive home run, and then, as the Giants held a 1-0 lead in the ninth inning of Game Three, he smashed another home run to force a tie. The game went into extra innings and Snodgrass again slid spikes up at Baker, trying to take third on a passed ball. The A's prevailed and Baker said, "Yes, Snodgrass spiked me intentionally. He acted like a swell-headed busher. You can use those very words, too."[2]

The *Philadelphia Inquirer* dubbed Snodgrass the "Spiking Kid," and the crowd voiced their disapproval at his arrival at Shibe Park. For his part, Baker was treated like royalty, as banners were flown on the houses outside the ballpark, and the name Home Run Baker would stick forever after. The crowd anxiously awaited every Baker at-bat, waiting for him to launch another round-tripper. "The fans shouted his name continuously and his vicious drives invariably brought the fans to their feet in a stampede of enthusiasm," the *Philadelphia Inquirer* noted.[3]

The crowd of 24,355 was also shivering on that chilly October day which "caused fans and fanettes to turn out in wraps and blankets that made the crowd assume the appearance of football cohorts," wrote the *Inquirer*.[4] While the grandstand and bleachers were mostly filled, there were plenty of open seats in the outfield. One group of filled seats was in the first row of the upper pavilion which belonged to a group dubbed the "50 Tourists," guests of the *Inquirer*. They made their presence felt. "Armed with megaphones, cow bells, tom-toms and other earsplitting devices" they made a "bedlam of noise" and created their own impromptu song to their hero:

What's the matter with Baker? He's all right!
What's the matter with Baker? He's all right!
He slammed the ball right over the fence;
He only did it in self-defense!
What's the matter with Baker? He's all right![5]

Two Hall of Fame managers, McGraw and Connie Mack, sent two of the greatest pitchers of all time to the mound. McGraw went with his ace, Christy Mathewson, who at 26-13 had the National League's best ERA at 1.99. Chief Bender was 17-5 with a 2.16 ERA for the Athletics. The two legends had faced each other six years earlier in Game Five of the 1905 World Series, when Matty outdueled Chief, 2-0, for his third shutout of the Series. This year, Mathewson had squeaked out a win over Bender in Game One, a 2-1 classic, despite Bender's 11 strikeouts. The Christian Gentleman (another of Mathewson's sobriquets) was brought back for Game Three and went the distance for McGraw in an 11-inning loss as the defense around him faltered. That was a week ago, as a stretch of bad weather postponed the series for five consecutive days. "With a week's rest Mathewson went into the game brimful of confidence," wrote the *New York Times*.[6]

The Giants jumped on the board quickly. Leadoff batter Josh Devore beat out a hit back to the mound that glanced off Bender's meat hand. Larry Doyle launched a triple as center fielder Rube Oldring slipped in the mud and the ball rolled to the fence. Devore scored. Snodgrass, hearing "yells of derision," lofted a fly ball to left that scored Doyle and gave the Giants a 2-0 first-inning lead.[7]

Mathewson allowed a hit in the bottom of the first but struck out the side, so no damage was done. In the second he allowed Danny Murphy a leadoff double. Murphy was caught napping at second and Mathewson picked him off, but his throw was wild and Murphy took third. Mack must have accepted the fact that his A's would not have many chances like this against Mathewson, so he tried some trickery; with Jack Barry at the plate, Mack put the squeeze play in motion. But Barry missed the bunt and Murphy was a dead duck at home. Barry then reached on a bunt down the third-base line that Mathewson and Buck Herzog hoped would roll foul. Ira Thomas popped up to end the inning, filled with a flurry of activity, but the A's had nothing to show for it.

The game remained 2-0 into the bottom of the fourth. Home Run Baker led off with a double to left-center. Murphy followed with another double to left-center, and Baker scored. Murphy scored on a double into the right-field corner by Davis that "singed the ozone" in the words of the *Inquirer*.[8] Mathewson was perplexed and there was a conference at the mound with the entire infield as action began in the New York bullpen. "Matty was plainly nettled."[9] Davis scored on a sacrifice fly by Thomas. The A's scored three in the inning and now led, 3-2.

In the top of the fifth, the Giants' Chief Meyers doubled but was thrown out when he tried to advance on a wild pitch, "on an eye lash decision at the sack," wrote the *Inquirer*.[10] In the bottom of the inning after two were out, Eddie Collins singled and scored "like a scared rabbit" on Baker's double to deep center. The A's led, 4-2.[11]

The Giants' Larry Doyle had egg on his face in the top of the sixth after he walked. After Snodgrass struck out, Red Murray hit a high pop foul toward third. Doyle was running with the pitch and became the victim of the A's trickery. Barry at shortstop went through the motions of fielding a groundball and Collins covered second, playing along. Doyle fell for the bluff despite McGraw and others yelling at him from the dugout. Oblivious to where the ball really was, Doyle arrived at second, only to see it land in Baker's glove, and he was easily doubled off first. Ridiculing his reputation as a smart player, the *Inquirer* wisecracked that the "superior illumination of the belfry of which we have heard so much was not in evidence, unless it was furnished by Barry and Collins."[12] Fans mockingly cheered Doyle "who walked into the trap as if blindfolded." Doyle's teammates smirked, and an anxious McGraw was seen biting his finger.[13]

Bender would allow the Giants only three hits and no runs from the sixth inning on. He faced trouble in the eighth. Devore singled and Snodgrass reached on an error, but with two outs Murray popped up to the catcher to leave two on base. Matty was pinch-hit for in the eighth, so eight-year veteran Hooks Wiltse came in to pitch a scoreless eighth. Fred Merkle, who had been struck out three times by Bender, led off the Giants ninth with a double. He made it to third on a groundout, but Art Fletcher popped out and Myers grounded out. The Athletics won, 4-2, and now had a commanding three-games-to-one advantage in the series.

Bender scattered seven hits, giving up two in an inning only in the first, while striking out four. Mathewson was certainly not his legendary self that day, allowing 10 hits, described as "juicy swats" by the *Inquirer*, with six of them being doubles: two each by Murphy and Baker."[14] The two Hall of Fame pitchers and Wiltse threw a total of 202 pitches in the game: Mathewson 84, Bender 106, and Wiltse 12.[15]

Baker, Bender, and the A's were indeed "all right," and on their way back to New York for Game Five.

SOURCES

In addition to the sources cited in the Notes, the author accessed Retrosheet.org and Baseball-Reference.com.

NOTES

1   "Wright Maintains New Soarer Nine Minutes in the Air," *Philadelphia Inquirer,* October 25, 1911: 1.

2   C. Starr Mathews, "'I'll Cut You Down,'" *Baltimore Sun,* October 19, 1911: 10.

3   "Athletics' Bats Win Against Pitching of Mathewson," *Philadelphia Inquirer,* October 25, 1911: 10.

4   "Athletics' Bats Win Against Pitching of Mathewson": 11.

5   "Famous Fifty Elect Matty to Down and Outers," *Philadelphia Inquirer,* October 25, 1911: 10.

6   "Three Straight for Athletics," *New York Times,* October 25, 1911: 1.

7   "Three Straight for Athletics": 10.

8   "Athletics' Bats": 10.

9   "Three Straight for Athletics": 2.

10 "Play by Play Briefly Told of Macks' Great Victory," *Philadelphia Inquirer,* October 25, 1911: 10.

11 "Three Straight for Athletics": 10.

12 "Athletics' Bats Win Against Pitching of Mathewson": 10.

13 "Three Straight for Athletics": 10.

14 "Athletics' Bats Win Against Pitching of Mathewson": 10.

15 "Record of the Pitchers," *New York Times,* October 25, 1911: 3.

Bender Tosses Four-Hitter as Mackmen Crush Giants to Capture Second Straight Championship

October 26, 1911
Philadelphia Athletics 13, New York Giants 2

Game Six of the World Series

By Gregory H. Wolf

"The old White Elephant stands above the great throbbing world of baseball," gushed sportswriter Jim Nasium following the Philadelphia Athletics crushing 13-2 victory over the New York Giants in Game Six of the 1911 World Series to capture their second consecutive title.[1] "The Athletics were positively savage the with the bat," opined scribe Thomas S. Rice, by setting a new Series record for the most runs scored in a game and the largest margin of victory.[2] The "real hero of the Series," wrote the *Brooklyn Eagle*, was not the A's offense, but rather their pitcher Chief Bender, who tossed his second complete-game victory in three days.[3] Bender exhibited "cool and calculating leadership" and "never lost his head," wrote the *New York Tribune*,[4] while the *New York Times* praised him as "one of the greatest slabmen of his time" and a "cool, brainy, unshakable flinger."[5]

Skipper Connie Mack's high-scoring A's (101-50) were heavily favored going into the Series, but the first five games were hardscrabble affairs,

each won by one or two runs and featuring a total of just 25 runs scored. Manager John McGraw's Giants (99-54) squeaked out their second one-run victory in Game Five at the Polo Grounds, sending the teams back to Philadelphia on the latest day a World Series Game had ever been played (a record that stood until 1981). The fall classic was in its 13th day, prolonged by six consecutive days of rain between Games Three and Four.

Mystery surrounded the skippers' choices for starting pitchers. McGraw, who had relied on only his stars Christy Mathewson (26-13) and Rube Marquard (24-7) thus far, chose Red Ames among the four who warmed up (Ames, Doc Crandall, Hooks Wiltse, and Marquard). The curveballing Ames, coming off an 11-10 campaign to push his record to 95-71 in his nine-year career, had made his first Series appearance the day before, tossing four scoreless frames. After Jack Coombs (28-12) severely injured his groin in Game Five and was lost for the remainder of the Series, Mack needed to be strategic and sent his three other primary regular-season starters to warm up. Mack surprised everyone by choosing Bender over Eddie Plank (23-8), who had started only Game Two 10 days earlier, though had taken the loss in relief in Game Five, and Cy Morgan (15-7), who hadn't pitched since October 5.

The 27-year-old Bender had long proved to be a big-game pitcher, as well as one of the Tall Tactician's favorites. He had a 142-81 slate in nine seasons, including 17-5 in 1911, and had excelled in the World Series, where he owned a 1.54 ERA in 52⅔ innings, having completed all six of his starts. He had lost the Series opener to Mathewson, 2-1, tossing 137 pitches and fanning 11, then handed Big Six his second Series defeat in Game Four, 4-2.[6] "They say the Chief isn't good for a quick comeback," quipped the *New York Sun*, echoing an oft-repeated critique of Bender's durability that revealed as much about the racism Bender faced as reality.[7]

Shibe Park drew a less-than-capacity crowd of 20,485 spectators, almost 6,000 fewer than for Game Two, on a clear, cool, autumnal Thursday afternoon with temperatures in the 50s.[8] About a half-hour before the 2 P.M. start time, fans from the overcrowded bleachers were permitted onto the field, where they were cordoned off by rope in left field and right field.[9]

The "baseball maddened crowd was stunned" in the first inning, wrote the *Inquirer*, when Larry Doyle lined a one-out hit off the right-field fence, just missing a home run, and the ball fell into the crowd for a ground-rule double.[10] Two batters later, Red Murray hit a routine fly ball that should have ended the frame, but Danny Murphy made a "scholastic muff" enabling Doyle to score.[11] Murphy was struggling. His flub attempting to catch a foul ball enabled the Giants to score the game-winning run in the 10th inning the day before, but he would emerge as an offensive hero in this game.

The A's tied the game in the third on Bris Lord's one-out double scoring Ira Thomas, who had led off with a walk. It was the first of the A's 13 unanswered runs, highlighted by two big innings. The Mackmen blew it open in the fourth with consecutive singles by Home Run Baker and Murphy. Graybeard Harry Davis, forced into action because of 20-year-old emerging star Stuffy McInnis's season-ending hit-by-pitch injury on September 25, grounded to second baseman Doyle, who hesitated, looked home and then to first base before firing to the catcher, but Baker scored easily. Though no error was given, the Giants committed two on the next batter leading Jim Nasium to quip that their defense played like "a bunch of trolley leaguers on a barn storming tour through the mustache-cup belt."[12] It began when Ames fielded Jack Barry's routine sacrifice bunt. His throw to first bounced off Barry's head and into right field, and Murphy scored. Retrieving the orb, Murray heaved it wildly over shortstop Art Fletcher's head and into the wall along the left-field foul line, enabling Davis and Barry to score and give the A's a 5-1 lead. The comedy of errors "broke the Giants nerve and defense," quipped the *Inquirer*.[13] Wiltse replaced Ames to start the fifth. The A's padded their lead in the sixth on Murphy's leadoff double "over [Fred] Snodgrass's head" and Barry's sacrifice fly.[14]

The baseball world wondered when the A's offense would explode. Mack's squad had led the majors by scoring 5.7 runs per game and posting a composite .296 batting average, featuring five starters who batted at least .310, led by Eddie Collins (.365), Baker (.334), and Murphy (.329). The wait ended in the seventh when the A's "riddled [the Giants] with a fusillade of ringing hits," noted the *Times*, scoring a then-World Series record seven runs in an inning.[15] After Bender flied out, the next eight batters reached base, "overwhelming the Giants, scoring runs galore, swatting balls to every corner of the lot," wrote the *Inquirer*.[16] After Lord and Rube Oldring singled, Fred Merkle muffed Ames's throw on Collins's sacrifice bunt, resulting in the first run. Baker, Murphy, and Davis all connected for RBI singles. Barry doubled to plate another, finally mercifully sending Wiltse to the showers. Marquard came on in relief, but his second pitch to Thomas crossed up catcher Chief Meyers, "dented the screen in the grandstand," and Davis and Barry scored the final two runs of the inning. "The hollowness of the one-sided victory," opined the *Tribune*, "took much of the enthusiasm out of the crowd."[17] With the outcome of the game and Series secure after seven innings, spectators began to leave Shibe Park.

Bender should have had a shutout in the game. The A's led the majors with the fewest errors and the highest fielding percentage, but were uncharacteristically sloppy. The 6-foot-2 right-hander yielded only four hits, yet pitched with men on in every inning except the fourth when he retired the side on three pitches. Barry, who had led all big-league shortstops with a .944 fielding average, committed three errors (in the second, seventh, and eighth). Despite the miscues, the Giants had two men on base only once. In the fifth, Meyers singled with two outs and Doc Crandall, pinch-hitting for Ames, drew a free pass. With the 23rd pitch of his most taxing inning, Bender retired Josh Devore on "a high, fast drop," according to the *Inquirer*, which caught him looking on a 3-and-2 count.[18] The A's fifth and final error led to the second Giants tally, and like the first it was unearned. With one out in the ninth, Herzog's single to center caught Oldring "loafing."[19] Oldring fumbled the ball, allowing Herzog to reach second. He advanced another station on Bender's wild pitch, then tallied the Series' final run on Fletcher's groundout. In a remarkable gesture of sportsmanship that reflected the Athletics' close-knit bonds, Harry Davis motioned to McInnis on the bench to take his place. In his last season as a player, Davis had agreed months earlier to become the manager of the Cleveland Naps in 1912. In a conclusion befitting the A's championship season, McInnis recorded the last out, receiving Baker's throw on Art Wilson's grounder to end the game in 2 hours and 12 minutes.

The A's captured their second straight championship in a Series that was more competitive than the final game suggested. The biggest difference in the Series was that the A's trio of pitchers – Coombs, Bender, and Plank – logged every inning and limited the Giants to a .175 batting average on 33 hits. Bender needed just 102 pitches (74 strikes) to complete Game Six. Had there been an MVP award, he would have earned it: three complete games and a 1.04 ERA in 26 innings. The star on offense was Home Run Baker, who produced a Series-most seven runs, nine hits, and five runs batted in (tied with Davis), and belted two of the Series' three round-trippers.

SOURCES

In addition to the sources cited in the Notes, the author accessed Retrosheet.org, Baseball-Reference.com, SABR.org, and the following newspaper articles:

Bulger, Bozeman. "Hitting's the Main Thing in Baseball, and That's Why Athletics Won Title," (New York) *Evening World,* October 27, 1911: 22.

"Coombs Badly Injured," *Philadelphia Inquirer*, October 27, 1911: 8.

Mathewson, Christy. "Mathewson Gives Praise to Macks," *Philadelphia Inquirer,* October 27, 1911: 10.

NOTES

1   Jim Nasium, "Macks Make Every One of the 13 Hits Count a Run," *Philadelphia Inquirer*, October 27, 1911: 10.

2   Thomas S. Rice, "Remarkable Series Ended with Slaughter of the Giants," *Brooklyn Eagle*, October 27, 1911: 25. The A's 13 runs remained the World Series record until the New York Yankees pounded the New York Giants 18-4 in Game Two of the 1936 fall classic, which also set a new record for the largest margin of victory in a World Series. The A's 13 runs were matched by the Giants in Game Three in 1921 in their defeat of the Yankees, 13-5; and by the Yankees in Game Four in 1932, defeating the Chicago Cubs, 13-6. The A's 11-run margin of victory was tied by the St. Louis Cardinals in Game Seven in 1935 when they beat the Detroit Tigers, 11-0.

3   Rice.

4   "Athletics Capture the World Series Title," *New York Tribune*, October 27, 1911: 1.

5   "Athletics Are the Champions," *New York Times*, October 27, 1911: 1.

6   Bender's total of 137 pitches is from "Bender Pitched 102 Balls to Giants," *Philadelphia Inquirer*, October 27, 1911: 10.

7   "Athletics Rout the Giants," (New York) *Sun*, October 27, 1911: 1. Bender averaged 25 starts and 21 complete games among his 31 appearances from 1903 to 1911. He suffered poor health and arm miseries most of his career, yet Mack recognized his value and gave him extra time between starts.

8   "Yesterday's Local Weather Report," *Philadelphia Inquirer*, October 27, 1913: 2.

9   "Athletics Capture the World Series Title."

10 "Macks Bat Out Victory; Scoring Runs with Ease," *Philadelphia Inquirer*, October 27, 191: 1.

11 "Turning Point Was the Fourth Inning," *Philadelphia Inquirer*, October 27, 1911: 1.

12 Jim Nasium.

13 "Turning Point Was the Fourth Inning."

14 "Athletics Rout the Giants."

15 "Athletics Are the Champions."

16 "Macks Bat Out Victory; Scoring Runs with Ease."

17 "Athletics Capture the World Series Title."

18 "Bender Pitched 102 Balls to Giants."

19 Jim Nasium.

TIGERS GO ON STRIKE, AMATEURS TAKE THE FIELD

May 18, 1912
Philadelphia Athletics 24, Detroit Tigers 2

By J.G. Preston

The most unusual major-league team ever to take the field wore the uniforms of the Detroit Tigers on May 18, 1912, at Shibe Park. Six of the men who started the game never played another major-league game; a seventh played in one other major-league game but never played in any other professional game. The first baseman was 41 years old and had not played in a major-league game in seven years, while the catcher was 48 years old. The pitcher, who had never pitched a game before (and would never pitch one again), gave up more runs than any pitcher has in a major-league game since 1894.

This ragtag lineup was employed because the Tigers' regular players went on strike, refusing to play because of what they considered an unjust suspension of teammate Ty Cobb by American League President Ban Johnson. It's a situation that hasn't happened in major-league baseball before or since. What took place that day was, in the view of one observer, "the greatest farce in the baseball line that has ever been unloaded upon the public since the inception of the game."[1]

The story of this game begins three days earlier, when the Tigers played the final game of a series in New York against the Highlanders (the team now known as the Yankees) at Hilltop Park. In the top of the fourth inning,[2] Cobb went into the stands and attacked a fan (later identified as Claude Lucker) who was heckling him, although heckling may be too mild a word. Here's how the incident was described in the next day's *New York Times*:

> "For three days a group of fans have been sitting behind the Detroit bench, enjoying an uninvited monologue for Cobb's discomfort. What they have been saying to the Georgia Peach has no place in a family newspaper or even one that circulates in barber shops only. The conversation yesterday got as rough as No. 2 sandpaper and Cobb hurdled into the ring. ... Cobb's execution was rapid and effective. ... Jabs bounded off the spectator's face like a golf ball from a rock."[3]

Umpire Silk O'Loughlin ejected Cobb, and the fan was tossed from the ballpark.

Here's how Cobb was quoted in the next day's *Detroit Free Press*; to what degree this resembles what he actually said is impossible to know: "I think the provocation was sufficient to justify my action, no matter how much I may regret the encounter. No self-respecting man could endure such insults, especially after repeatedly warning his persecutor. I tried to find a representative of the New York club with sufficient authority to have the man ejected, but could not locate one, so I was exasperated beyond all endurance finally and struck the fellow." Among other things, Cobb reportedly took umbrage at being called a "half-negro."[4]

Johnson happened to be at the game and was asked if Cobb would be suspended. "I don't know until I hear the facts, but I can't see any justification for a player climbing up in the stand and fighting a spectator," he said.[5] The next morning, May 16, Johnson announced that Cobb was suspended indefinitely, without having spoken to Cobb, which drew this reported response from Cobb: "I should at least have an opportunity to state my case. I feel a great injustice has been done."[6] Cobb justified his actions, saying, "No man with a right to the title would stand for the things I was called. They are unprintable, and if President Johnson would allow them to be used without knocking the man down who said them, he is not a man."[7]

The Tigers' scheduled game against the Athletics at Shibe Park on May 16 was rained out, and they played without Cobb on May 17, but all of Cobb's teammates signed a telegram that was sent to Johnson that day. "Feeling Mr. Cobb is being done injustice by your action in suspending him, we, the undersigned, refuse to play another game after today until such action is adjusted to our satisfaction," the telegram read. "He was fully justified in his action. ... We want him reinstated for tomorrow's game, May 18, or there will be no game. If players cannot have protection, we must protect ourselves."[8] There was talk of the team going on a barnstorming tour, perhaps even traveling to Japan.[9]

The threat of a strike put Tigers President Frank Navin in a tough position. While he was reportedly "heart and soul in sympathy" with his players,[10] he faced a possible $5,000-a-day fine (the equivalent of about $131,000 in 2020[11]) from the league for forfeiting a game, and potentially the loss of his franchise. As a result, Tigers manager Hughie Jennings was determined to field a team – any team – on May 18 when his real players left the field after Cobb was told he could not play that day.

Two of the players came from his own staff. James "Deacon" McGuire, a 48-year-old former catcher who had played in at least one big-league game in 25 previous seasons, went behind the plate, and 41-year-old Joe Sugden, whose last major-league appearance was in 1905 (although he had played in the minors since then), was assigned to first base. Both have been described in different accounts as coaches or scouts for the Tigers; they probably served in both roles.

There are varying accounts of how the rest of the team was put together. Here's how it was told in the next day's New York Times:

> "Through the stands was carried the rumor that Jennings wanted volunteers. By the dozens, amateurs, semi-professionals, and college athletes left their seats and swarmed around the Detroit bench trying to look like real ball players. Jennings sorted over the bunch and picked out six likely-looking young men."[12]

But perhaps Jennings already had a lead on who would fill in for him. "I have in mind ten or twelve good players in this city," he was quoted as saying the morning of the game. "If the regular players refuse to take part in the game, I will put these local men in uniform and line them up against the Athletics."[13]

While it wasn't reported at the time, in later years the story became that the replacement players had been assembled by Aloysius Travers, a junior at Philadelphia's St. Joseph's College. Here's what Travers told a New York Times reporter on the 50th anniversary of the game in 1962:

"It was about two hours before the game that I was asked by a local sports writer[14] to get up a team. Connie Mack [the A's manager and co-owner] and everybody needed our help to save the Detroit franchise. I was an assistant baseball manager for St. Joseph's College and I knew a lot of kids. I hurried down to 23rd Street and Columbia Avenue and picked up the boys. We were told that all we had to do was to get dressed and make an appearance. It was all arranged with Connie Mack. The game would be called off if the players struck, but they had to have twelve men in uniform to avoid the fine and losing the franchise."[15]

As it turned out, with a crowd estimated in various reports at anywhere from 15,000 to 20,000 on hand for a Saturday afternoon game, Mack couldn't resist playing the game and keeping the ticket revenue, strike or no strike.

Travers could have seemed a logical candidate to find possible replacement players, since with his role on the St. Joseph's baseball team he might have had connections to some reasonably qualified players. St. Joseph's had defeated the A's in an exhibition game the day before the American League's 1912 season opened. But none of the men who played for the Tigers on May 18 had played in that exhibition,[16] and no evidence has been found that any of the Tigers' replacement players aside from Travers ever attended St. Joseph's.

One possible indication that Travers helped organize the Tigers' replacement players that day is that manager Jennings batted him third in the lineup, perhaps a sign that he was under the impression that Travers was the best of the crew he assembled. Otherwise there would seem to be little reason for Jennings to even choose Travers to be on the field, let alone batting third. There's never been any published indication that Travers had ever played the game at any kind of competitive level.

Not only was Travers in the lineup, he was the Tigers' pitcher ... and by his own admission, he had never pitched before. "I was to play right field," Travers told a *Philadelphia Inquirer* reporter in 1964, "but I learned that whoever pitched would get $50. So I volunteered to pitch."[17]

One New York Times story referred to Travers as "manager and former star pitcher of St. Joseph's College team,"[18] but another story in the same issue said Travers "could do little but float the ball up to the plate,"[19] and yet another account of the game said Travers "could scarcely throw."[20] In the 1962 *New York Times* interview, Travers said, "The only pitch I knew how to throw was the slow curve. I had a beautiful slow ball." He claimed to have thrown only one fastball in the game, in the first inning to future Hall of Famer Frank "Home Run" Baker. According to Travers, Baker hit the ball over the right-field fence but foul, and catcher McGuire came to the mound to tell him, "Son, if you value your life, no more of them fast balls."[21]

Travers was one of eight men who would make his only major-league appearance in this game for the Tigers. Among them was 18-year-old center fielder Bill Leinhauser, who not only took Cobb's place in center field but also wore Cobb's uniform and used his glove. "I still recall the thrill of meeting Ty Cobb at the bench and shaking his hand," Leinhauser told a *Philadelphia Daily News* reporter in 1972. "None of us ever thought the Tigers would carry out their threat of a strike. [Jennings] wanted us to be on hand just in case. He didn't want to take any chances."[22]

(Both Travers and Leinhauser went on to have interesting lives, although neither played professional baseball again. Travers was ordained a Jesuit priest in 1926, making him the only former major leaguer to enter the priesthood. He returned to St. Joseph's College as dean of men in 1935, then taught Spanish and religion at St. Joseph's Preparatory School, his alma mater, from 1943 until his death in 1968.[23] Leinhauser served in World War I before spending 41 years in the

Philadelphia police department, retiring as the head of the North Central Detective Division.[24]

The team that took the field for the Tigers "did not have the appearance of pennant contenders in a Class A league and they looked as though they knew it and were nervous about it," according to one report.[25] Another observer was more blunt: "Few of those in the lineup could play, and those that could were too frightened to do anything."[26]

Aside from McGuire and Sugden, only two other men who played for the Tigers that day ever appeared in another major-league game. One was manager Jennings, who had a long major-league career in the 1890s and early 1900s; at age 43, he put himself in to bat for Travers in the ninth inning and struck out.[27]

The other was a man who played one other major-league game, also under unusual circumstances. Billy Maharg, 31 years old, just 5-feet-4½-inches tall and best known in the Philadelphia area as a boxer, started the game at third base and batted second. It's been reported that Maharg took a bad-hop groundball in the face during the game and lost several teeth as a result. None of the contemporaneous reports on the game include that, but it may well be true, as Maharg was lifted for a pinch-hitter after three innings, having fielded three balls in the third, including the final out.

Four years later Maharg again appeared in a major-league game, after becoming an assistant trainer-gofer for the Phillies in 1916. In the final game of the season, manager Pat Moran used Maharg as a pinch-hitter and let him finish the game in right field. But Maharg is most remembered today for an interview he gave to a Philadelphia reporter in September 1920, in which he said several White Sox players had agreed to lose the 1919 World Series in exchange for a $100,000 payoff from gamblers.[28]

When the game got underway, the defending World Series champion Athletics quickly took control. Pitcher Jack Coombs retired the Tigers

in order in the first inning, and then his teammates gave him all the runs he would need in the bottom of the frame. Harl Maggert led off with a walk and went to second on Amos Strunk's bunt single. Eddie Collins also bunted and beat it out for a hit, but when Maggert tried to score, Sugden threw him out at the plate. Baker grounded out, Strunk scoring from third and Collins moving to third. Danny Murphy walked and stole second, and when McGuire's throw went into center field, Collins came home. Stuffy McInnis then singled to score Murphy and make it 3-0.

As expected, the replacement Tigers struggled to generate any offense. Coombs retired the first eight men to face him before right fielder Hap Ward[29] walked in the third, but he was thrown out trying to steal to end the inning. The A's scored three runs in their half of the third to take a 6-0 lead, when McInnis hit a ball through Vincent Maney[30] at short with the bases loaded that went for a triple.

At this point some in the crowd grew restless. "At the end of the third inning there was a rush by a couple of thousand bleacherites, who demanded their money back," according to one report. "When this was refused nearly all returned to their seats."[31]

Carroll "Boardwalk" Brown took the mound for the A's to start the fourth inning and allowed the Tigers their first hit of the day, a triple by Ed Irwin,[32] pinch-hitting for Maharg. A Philadelphia native with nearly a decade of professional playing experience, Irwin had actually worn a major-league uniform previously; he had played in an exhibition game for the Phillies on April 21 and may have appeared on their roster during the regular season, but he had not played in a regular-season game with them and was no longer their property at the time of this game, which was his first – and last – in the major leagues.[33]

Irwin was the only one of the one-game major leaguers to get a hit that day ... and he got two of them, as he smacked another triple in the ninth, leaving him with a career slugging percentage of 2.000. The other two Tigers hits in the game came in the fifth inning. Sugden and McGuire, the major-league veterans in the lineup, had consecutive singles off Brown with one out, and Maney was hit by a pitch[34] to load the bases. A's catcher Jack Lapp threw to first in an attempt to pick off Maney, but the throw was wild, allowing Sugden and McGuire to score the only two Tigers runs of the day, making the score 6-2, Philadelphia.

The A's added to their lead with an eight-run outburst in the fifth, including a two-run double when Ward fell down fielding Strunk's fly ball. (Earlier, in the second inning, Ward had made an outstanding catch of a ball hit by Jack Barry, the best play of the day by one of the replacements.) Four more runs scored in the sixth, four in the seventh, and two in the eighth to make the final score 24-2. Fortunately for all concerned, the A's didn't have to bat in the bottom of the ninth. The game ended after a crisp 1 hour and 45 minutes.

The 24 runs Travers allowed are the most given up by a pitcher in any major-league game since Philadelphia scored 29 runs against Jack Wadsworth of Louisville in a National League game on August 17, 1894.[35]

The A's made 24 outs in the game, but six of them were made on the bases. In addition to Maggert being thrown out at home in the first inning, McInnis made the final out of the inning when he stole second base and was caught in a rundown when he walked off the bag; Lapp was thrown out trying to stretch a single into a double in the second; Murphy was thrown out trying to stretch a triple into a home run in the fifth; Strunk lined into a double play in the seventh; and Barry was caught stealing third in the eighth.

Travers retired only 18 of the 52 batters to face him while giving up 16 singles, four doubles and six triples. (Amazingly, no one hit a home run off him). He walked seven and actually struck out one: pitcher Brown in the fourth. (Brown made up for it with a run-scoring single in the fifth and

an RBI triple in the sixth.) Only one Philadelphia batter reached base on an error, but the official box score for the game shows that the Tigers committed seven errors, two of them by McGuire.

Collins led the A's, with five hits (all singles, at least three of them bunts) in six at-bats and four runs, and was credited with five of the A's 10 stolen bases. Murphy, who singled, tripled, and walked three times, also scored four runs. McInnis and Strunk each had four hits; McInnis and Barry had four RBIs. Of the 11 Athletics who played, only starting pitcher Coombs, who flied out in his only at-bat, did not have at least one hit, score at least one run, and drive in at least one.

The Tigers struck out 15 times in the game, 14 of them by the men who were playing in their only major-league game. (Second baseman Jim McGarr fanned in all four of his at-bats.[36]) Seven of those strikeouts were recorded over the final three innings by 18-year-old Herb Pennock, who was making only his second major-league appearance. Pennock also had an RBI double for his first big-league hit. Pennock went on to win 241 games in the majors, most of them after being traded to the Yankees, and was elected to the Hall of Fame.

Fortunately for the Tigers, the strike was a one-day affair. There was no game scheduled on May 19, because of Pennsylvania's ban on Sunday baseball, and a scheduled game at Philadelphia on May 20 was postponed. (Mack said, "The Athletics are not desirous of winning games from scrub teams, and for that reason the game ... has been called off."[37]) During a meeting with team President Navin on May 20, Cobb urged his teammates to take the field for their game the next day at Washington while he awaited a ruling on his suspension from league President Johnson. The players refused, but later in a second meeting with Navin agreed to return, after Navin told them that he would see that Cobb's suspension was adjusted as soon as possible, that he would pay any fines the league levied against the players, and that steps would be taken to protect players from abuse by fans.[38]

On May 25 Johnson announced that Cobb would be fined $50 and would be eligible to return to action the next day, concluding what was a 10-day suspension, during which Cobb missed six games. Johnson said the league would increase the police force at all ballparks, but added, "[S]ure and swift punishment will be meted out to those who in disregard of discipline and of obligations to their club and league assume to act as judge and avenger of real or fancied wrongs while on duty."[39]

SOURCES

Newspaper articles were accessed via Newspapers.com and GenealogyBank.com. *Sporting Life* was accessed through the digital collection of the LA84 Foundation (digital.la84.org/digital/collection/p17103coll17). The box score was found on Retrosheet.org. The play-by-play of the first eight innings of the game is in the *Detroit Times* of May 18, 1912. Thanks to Bill Francis of the National Baseball Hall of Fame Library for providing materials, and to David Smith of Retrosheet for his assistance in confirming the play-by-play of the game.

NOTES

1   "Tigers Quit Field, Cobb Is Suspended," *Philadelphia Inquirer*, May 19, 1912: 17.

2   Accounts differ as to exactly when this incident took place. The *New York Times* says it happened with one out and Detroit pitcher Ed Willett at bat, while the *Detroit Free Press* and *Sporting Life* both say it happened before the inning began. In any event Cobb was apparently neither at bat nor in the field when he went into the stands.

3   "Cobb Whips Hilltop Fan for Insults," *New York Times*, May 16, 1912: 12.

4   "Cobb Is Vindicated by Those Nearest to Scene of Fray," *Detroit Free Press*, May 16, 1912: 11.

5   "Tigers Slug Warhop, Ty Slugs a Spectator," *New York Sun*, May 16, 1912: 10.

6   "Ty Cobb Suspended," *New York Times*, May 17, 1912: 11.

7   "Cobb Says He Would Slug Insulter Again," *New York Evening World*, May 17, 1912: 22.

8   "Ball Players Threaten Strike if 'Ty' Cobb Is Not Reinstated," *New York Evening World*, May 17, 1912: 1.

9   "Tigers Walk Off Field on Strike; Spectators Cheer," *St. Louis Post-Dispatch*, May 18, 1912: 1.

10   "Tigers Demand Ty Cobb's Reinstatement," *Detroit Times*, May 17, 1912: 1.

11   bls.gov/data/inflation_calculator.htm.

12   "Detroit Team Out on Strike," *New York Times*, May 19, 1912: 1.

13   "Can't Make Them Play, Says Jennings," *Detroit Times*, May 18, 1912: 9. In *The Tiger Wore Spikes: An Informal Biography of Ty Cobb*, a 1956 book by John McCallum, Arthur "Bugs" Baer claimed Jennings picked his players at the Aldine Hotel, which is indeed where the Tigers were staying. "I lit out for the Aldine Hotel in time to run into a parade of 700 semipros all anxious to fill Ty Cobb's shoes. All 700 of us walked single file past Jennings and he tapped the ones he wanted and that was his team. The first nine he picked got 50 smackers each. Then he picked a couple more for emergency who got $25 just for sitting on the bench. I got tapped to sit on the bench." Quoted in Jerome Holtzman, "Replacement Team in Cobb's Day Lacked Something: Quality," *Chicago Tribune*, January 24, 1995: 39. No published accounts of this game indicated there were players on the bench who did not get into the game, but it's possible. Far less likely is that 700 men appeared before Jennings.

14 Syndicated sports columnist Red Smith wrote the story of Philadelphia sportswriter John Nolan asking Travers to bring "his gang" to the park that day as possible replacement players on several occasions, such as "Cobb and a Certain Baseball Strike," *Providence* (Rhode Island) *Sunday Journal*, January 10, 1960: S-2, and "He Kept Right on Pitching for St. Joseph's," *Philadelphia Inquirer*, April 25, 1968: 39.

15 Howard M. Tuckner, "'Hero' Recalls 1912 Baseball Strike," *New York Times*, May 19, 1962: 20.

16 A box score and brief account of the exhibition game appeared in the *Philadelphia Inquirer* on April 11, 1912: 10 ("Mackies Ease Up, St. Joseph's Wins").

17 Edward G. Olson, "Two Sandlotters Who Helped Save a Franchise," *Philadelphia Inquirer*, July 26, 1964: 15. The 1912 *New York Times* story cited above, as well as other reports from the game, said each of the Tigers' replacement players would receive $50. No contemporaneous account has been found stating that the pitcher would be paid more than the other players. Travers had told a different story two years before this interview, when in 1962 he told the *New York Times*, "The pitcher was going to get $25 and the rest $10 each." Tuckner.

18 "Detroit Team Out on Strike."

19 "Substitute Detroit Game," *New York Times*, May 19, 1912: 37.

20 "Tigers on Strike; Macks Win, 24-2," *Chicago Tribune*, May 19, 1912: 7.

21 Tuckner.

22 Ed Conrad, "Sixty Years Ago: Tiger Strike Carried Out, but the Show Goes On," *Philadelphia Daily News*, April 8, 1972: 27.

23 "Father Travers Dies; Pitched 'Big Game,'" *Philadelphia Inquirer*, April 22, 1968: 18.

24 Dwight Ott, "William C. Leinhauser, 84," *Philadelphia Inquirer*, April 16, 1978: 40.

25 "Tigers Quit Field, Cobb Is Suspended."

26 "Almost a Record Score," *Washington Post*, May 19, 1912: Sporting Section 1.

27 This was Jennings's last major-league plate appearance, but not his last major-league game as a player. In the final game of the 1918 season – a game that saw, among other things, Ty Cobb pitch two innings and make his only major-league appearance at third base, outfielder Bobby Veach make his only major-league pitching appearance, and catcher Oscar Stanage make his only major-league appearance at shortstop – the 49-year-old Jennings played the final inning at first base. retrosheet.org/boxesetc/1918/B09022DET1918.htm.

28 Much more about Maharg's connection to the 1919 World Series is included in Bill Lamb's definitive biography of Maharg in the SABR Baseball Biography Project, sabr.org/bioproj/person/60bd890e. Lamb also debunks the oft-repeated claim that Maharg's actual last name was Graham and that he used Maharg ("Graham" spelled backward) as a pseudonym.

29 The obituary for the man believed to be Hap Ward does not mention that he played in this game, but makes the claim that "[d]uring his high school years in Philadelphia, he played baseball on Connie Mack's Athletics team under the name of 'Mike Murphy.'" "Former Athlete J. Ward," *Camden* (New Jersey) *Courier-Post*, September 15, 1979: 32. The only Mike Murphy who ever played in a regular-season game for the A's did so in 1916, when Ward was 31. It's possible Ward/"Murphy" was with the A's on some sort of tryout basis in his teen years, which would have been in the early 1900s, without ever getting into a regular-season game.

30 The identity of the Tigers' shortstop in this game has long been confused. Contemporaneously published box scores listed his last name as Meeney (*Detroit Times*), Meaney (*New York Times* and *Detroit Free Press*) and Meany (*Philadelphia Inquirer*). Some sources through the years have identified the man as Pat Meaney, a veteran minor-league outfielder and Philadelphia native who would have been 40 years old at the time of this game. In fact, *The Minor League Register* (Durham, North Carolina: Baseball America, Inc., 1994) includes this game in Meaney's career record. Vince Maney was working at a Philadelphia iron works and playing semipro ball at the time of this game. Researcher Bill Dougherty (like Maney, a native of Batavia, New York) determined that Maney was the Detroit shortstop in this game and apparently found a letter Maney wrote to his brother describing his play. Bill Kauffman, *Poetry Night at the Ballpark and Other Scenes from an Alternative America: Writings 1986-2014* (Eugene, Oregon: Front Porch Republic Books, 2015), 5. In the letter Maney said he was paid $15. It's possible Maney attempted to play under a pseudonym. While the *New York Times* box score shows the shortstop as Meaney, the front-page story in the same issue says, "'Joe' Harrigan, who has a reputation in Southwark, was sent out to plug the gap at shortstop." "Detroit Team Out on

Strike." Likewise, the lineup that appeared in the St. Louis Post-Dispatch story of May 18 showed "Harrigan" as the shortstop ("Tigers Walk Off Field on Strike; Spectators Cheer"), but the box score that appeared in the next day's edition listed the shortstop as "Meaney."

31 "Substitute Detroit Game," *New York Times*, May 19, 1912: 37. Ticket prices for the game ranged from 25 cents to $1, according to an ad on page 10 of the May 18 Philadelphia Inquirer.

32 Irwin's full name was William Edward Irwin. Bill Lamb writes, in his biography of Irwin for the SABR Biography Project, that Irwin was known during his lifetime as Bill, but modern reference works identify him as Ed. At times his last name was mistakenly spelled in reference works as Irvin. sabr.org/bioproj/person/27d493d1.

33 Bill Lamb, "Ed Irwin," SABR Biography Project.

34 The play-by-play in the *Detroit Times* of May 18, 1912, shows Maney walked, but the Retrosheet box score shows Maney with a hit-by-pitch and two strikeouts. Retrosheet founder David Smith says a scorebook from a Philadelphia sportswriter "is clear" that Maney was hit by a pitch in the fifth inning. Email correspondence with the author, May 21, 2019. Maney's official stat line in Baseball-Reference.com shows him with two strikeouts, a walk and a hit-by-pitch – in three plate appearances, which can't be correct.

35 "The Colonels Again Go Under," *Philadelphia Inquirer*, August 18, 1894: 3. Wadsworth finished his major-league career with a 6-38 record, allowing 393 runs in 367⅔ innings. The all-time major-league record for most runs allowed by a pitcher in a game is held by Dave Rowe, normally an outfielder, who gave up 35 runs pitching for Cleveland against Chicago in a National League game on July 24, 1882, when pitchers were still required to throw underhand. For an account of that game, see "Base-Ball Games," *Chicago Tribune*, July 25, 1882: 7.

36 McGarr's brief obituary does not mention that he played major-league baseball, but says he "is in the Baseball Hall of Fame." *Fort Lauderdale* (Florida) *News*, July 23, 1981: 4B. McGarr was the last man alive who played in this game.

37 "American League Likely to Expel Striking Players," *Philadelphia Inquirer*, May 20, 1912: 11.

38 "Tigers Strike Is Settled Through Navin's Efforts," *Detroit Times*, May 20, 1912: 1; "Tigers Team Agrees to Play When Navin Offers Aid to Cobb," *New York Evening World*, May 20, 1912: 1.

39 "Cobb Case Concluded," *Sporting Life*, June 1, 1912: 1.

HALL OF FAME PITCHERS' DUEL IN MARATHON

September 27, 1912
Washington Senators 5, Philadelphia Athletics 4
(19 Innings)

By J.G. Preston

Eddie Plank won 326 games in the major leagues – and a game in which he pitched 16 scoreless innings wasn't one of them. That stretch of shutout pitching came in a game that went 19 innings and lasted more than four hours before the Athletics' Hall of Fame lefty lost to another Hall of Famer, Washington's Walter Johnson.

The late-season contest matched the teams battling for second place behind the Boston Red Sox, who had already clinched the American League pennant. Washington's starting pitcher was Bob Groom, who had won his previous nine starts, pitching complete games in all of them, to improve his record to 23-12. Plank took the mound with a record of 26-5, ranking third in the major leagues in wins behind Johnson and Boston's Joe Wood.

The Senators started the game intent on extending Groom's winning streak and increasing their 1½-game lead over the A's. With one out in the top of the first, Eddie Foster singled and Clyde Milan followed with a bunt single, with Foster taking second. Both runners advanced on a groundout by Chick Gandil, and Foster then came home on Plank's wild pitch.[1]

Plank was shakier in the second inning. Howie Shanks led off with a double. George McBride laid down a bunt, and when A's third baseman Frank "Home Run" Baker muffed catcher Ben Egan's throw to third, there were runners on the corners. Rip Williams singled to score Shanks, McBride stopping at second, and both runners moved up on Groom's sacrifice. Danny Moeller then hit a groundball to A's shortstop Jack Barry, and when McBride beat Barry's throw home, it was 3-0, Washington. Foster followed with a single to score Williams and send Moeller to third.

But Plank got out of the inning, even as manager Connie Mack had a substitute warming up, when Milan grounded to Baker, whose throw home retired Moeller after a rundown, and Gandil flied out. And over the next six innings, Plank allowed just one hit, a single by Gandil in the fifth.

Plank's pitching was accompanied by a torrent of invective from Senators manager Clark Griffith and coach Germany Schaefer from the coaches' boxes. They "kept up a continuous stream of remarks to the twirler," according to a report in the *Washington Times*. "Some of these remarks were hardly polite."[2] And they were probably easy to hear, since the *Washington Herald* reported there were fewer than 500 people in the stands for the game.[3] "Griffith and Schaefer kept up a constant cross-fire of remarks," wrote

William O. Weart in *The Sporting News,* "but the more they chattered, the harder Plank stuck to his work."[4]

Meanwhile, the A's kept putting runners on base, but couldn't bring any of them home. They loaded the bases with one out in the second, but Baker got a bad jump trying to score on a long fly ball by Jack Lapp, batting for Egan, and was thrown out at home. The A's got three hits in a row in the fifth, but Lapp, who got the first of them, was picked off second and the A's never got a runner as far as third. Then Philadelphia loaded the bases with no one out in the sixth before Barry lined into a double play and Lapp grounded out.

The A's finally got on the board in the seventh, when Plank and Harl Maggert singled, Eddie Collins walked, and Plank came home on Baker's groundout. But it was still 4-1, Washington, going into the ninth.

It looked as though the Senators would add to their lead in the ninth. Williams led off with a double and went to third on Groom's sacrifice. But right fielder Eddie Murphy caught Moeller's line drive and threw out Williams trying to score.

Groom took a three-run lead into the bottom of the ninth ... and couldn't hold it. Murphy opened the inning with a single off Groom's glove. After Maggert flied out, Collins reached on an infield hit and Baker slammed a pitch to right that hit the wall, missing a home run by just a few feet. Murphy scored but Collins was held at third. Stuffy McInnis followed with a groundout to McBride at short, scoring Collins, to bring the A's within one run with two out. Rube Oldring followed with a hot shot to third that got by Foster for the A's 16th hit off Groom, and Baker came home to tie the game. (This was Oldring's first game in more than three weeks; Mack had suspended him without pay, supposedly for the rest of the season, for being out of condition, but with second place on the line, Mack brought him back for this game.[5])

The game stayed tied for the next nine innings, as Plank found himself dueling with Johnson. The A's and Senators were supposed to play a doubleheader on this day, with Johnson scheduled to pitch the second game, but with Groom struggling, Johnson entered the game to start the bottom of the 10th. Just the day before he had pitched 2⅔ innings in relief. The 24-year-old had already won 31 games in 1912 and was on his way to leading the American League in strikeouts and earned-run average.

Johnson pitched his way out of jam after jam as the game proceeded through extra innings. In the 11th inning Maggert got to third with one out but was thrown out at the plate trying to score on a short passed ball. Collins tripled with two out in the 13th, bringing McInnis to the plate. "Naturally [Senators third baseman] Foster played deep, for [McInnis] hits hard in that direction, so that when a slow swinging bunt came down his way it looked as if the game was over," J. Ed Grillo wrote in the *Washington Evening Star.* "Foster, however, came in at full speed, grabbed the ball with one hand and without steadying himself made the throw to first and got his man. It was one of the fastest plays ever made by a third baseman."[6]

In the 14th Lapp doubled with two out, but Plank, given a chance to win his own game, struck out. Then in the 16th, Baker led off with a single, after which McInnis got a base hit to right. Even though his run would not matter, McInnis tried to stretch the hit to a double and was thrown out at second, with Baker stopping at third. Johnson then fanned Oldring and Barry to end the inning.

The visitors had a few scoring chances of their own in extra innings, but Plank kept them off the board. The Senators had runners on second and third with one out in the 14th, but Johnson struck out and, after Moeller walked to load the bases, Foster flied out. McBride led off the 16th with a double but was doubled up after a lineout by Williams. Then in the 18th, McBride beat out a bunt with two out, and when he took off to steal, Lapp threw wildly into right field. McBride tried to come all the way around to score, but Murphy's throw home just beat him to end the inning.

Plank took the mound at the start of the 19th having held the Senators scoreless for the previous 16 innings, but the Senators would score the winning run without hitting a ball out of the infield. Williams led off with a walk, and when Johnson laid down a bunt, Plank overran the ball and Johnson was safe at first. Moeller then hit one back to Plank, who threw to third to force out Williams. Foster – the 74th batter to face Plank in the game – hit a groundball to short, and Barry threw to Collins at second to force out Moeller for the second out, but when Collins threw to first ("foolishly," according to the *Washington Post's* Joe S. Jackson, as he had "practically no chance" to retire Foster), his throw bounced off McInnis's body and Johnson came home with the tiebreaking run

The Big Train then retired the A's in order in the bottom of the inning to wrap up his 32nd win; he would pitch a complete game in a win against the New York Highlanders six days later to finish the season with a record of 33-12. For Plank, the appearance would be his last of the season, as he finished with a record of 26-6. He allowed 13 hits over 19 innings, while his teammates piled up 24 hits plus six walks, but left 19 men on base and couldn't find a way to win the game.

SOURCES

Game accounts were found at Newspapers.com. *The Sporting News* was accessed via PaperOfRecord.com.

NOTES

1   Joe S. Jackson, "Nationals Win Game in Nineteenth Inning," *Washington Post*, September 28, 1912: 8. This is the source of all play-by-play information unless otherwise noted. Milan's hit being a bunt is noted in William Peet, "New A.L. Record When Nationals Trim Athletics in 19 Innings," *Washington Herald*, September 28, 1912: 10.

2   "Senator," "Nineteen Innings to Decide Game," *Washington Times*, September 28, 1912: 14.

3   Peet.

4   William O. Weart, "Spoil Quaker Fans," *The Sporting News*, Oct. 3, 1912: 1.

5   Peet; Bill Bishop, "Rube Oldring," SABR Baseball Biography Project, sabr.org/bioproj/person/71f1da1c.

6   J. Ed Grillo, "Second Place Now Seems Assured for Nationals," *Evening Star* (Washington), September 28, 1912: 9.

Mackmen Clinch Pennant, then Put on Offensive Clinic

September 23, 1913
Philadelphia Athletics 21, Detroit Tigers 8

By Lawrence Knorr

As the 1913 regular season neared its end on Tuesday, September 23, the Philadelphia Athletics under Connie Mack had clinched the pennant behind a stellar 1-0 shutout performance by Eddie Plank the afternoon before. Plank's gem was the second game of a doubleheader following a 4-0 shutout by Bullet Joe Bush earlier in the day. Hughie Jennings's Tigers, the victims of both defeats, fell to 32½ games out in sixth place in the American League. For Mack's men, it was their third pennant in four seasons. For Jennings, it was now four years since the Tigers' last pennant and two since their last strong season (second place in 1911).

Detroit's team, while not competitive in 1913, featured a 26-year-old center fielder named Ty Cobb who was about to win his seventh straight American League batting title. Also in the lineup was Sam Crawford, who led the league in triples and hit .317 while playing right field or first base.

The Athletics of 1913 featured the famous "$100,000 infield," Home Run Baker at third base, Jack Barry at shortstop, Eddie Collins at second base, and Stuffy McInnis at first base. Future Hall of Famers Eddie Plank and Chief Bender were the aces of the pitching staff,

helped by a great season from Boardwalk Brown and contributions from Bullet Joe Bush and Byron Houck.

After the doubleheader sweep, fans flocked to Connie Mack's office at Shibe Park and hung around to wish the team well in the World Series. Mack suggested that he would be giving his regulars three days off but not until the Washington series. He planned to have them all back at Shibe Park for the final series against the New York Yankees as a tuneup for the likely encounter with John McGraw's New York Giants.[1]

Hughie Jennings tapped 20-year-old rookie Lefty Williams to take the hill against the Athletics on Tuesday, the 23rd, which was the final game of the series. Williams was 1-0 at the time, having beaten the Washington Senators 4-2 in his first major-league start, on September 17. He would later be known for his performance in the 1919 World Series as a member of the Black Sox. Though acquitted by a jury, Williams was among the players banned from baseball by Commissioner Kenesaw M. Landis after the 1920 season.[2]

With the pennant in the bag, Mack started 19-year-old Herb Pennock, who had pitched mostly in relief for two seasons. Pennock would go on to win 241 games and land in the Hall of

A's owner-manager Connie Mack with player-coach Ira Thomas, who platooned as catcher on the 1910-1911 World Series championship teams. A longtime A's pitching coach and scout, Thomas played a pivotal role in Mack's second dynasty (1929-1931).

Fame mostly for his work with the Yankees of the 1920s.[3]

The game did not begin well for the teen Pennock. After retiring the Tigers' leadoff hitter, shortstop Donie Bush, shortly after 2:00 P.M. before 4,000 Philadelphia fans, Pennock walked second baseman Paddy Baumann and then served up a shot over the right-field fence by Sam Crawford. The Tigers led 2-0.

Pennock was back at it in the second inning. With two out, third baseman Baldy Louden and pitcher Lefty Williams walked. Bush followed with a single, scoring Louden. Baumann's double scored Williams and Bush. Crawford capped the inning with a triple that added another run, Baumann crossing the plate. The Tigers led 6-0. It was beginning to look like a blowout for the Tigers, the A's bats quiet so far as if the players were disinterested since winning the pennant.

The A's awakened against Williams in the second. Stuffy McInnis, Jimmy Walsh, and Jack Barry knocked consecutive singles, McInnis scoring on Barry's hit. Wally Schang was plunked by a Williams offering, loading the bases. Pitcher Pennock made the first out, popping up to catcher Frank Gibson. Right fielder Eddie Murphy then stepped in and launched one of Williams's offerings on a line to center, over Cobb's head. This cleared the bases as Murphy slid into third with a triple. The score was now 6-4, but the fun was only beginning.

Left fielder Rube Oldring singled Murphy home. Second baseman Eddie Collins followed with a single, Oldring heading to third. With men on the corners, Home Run Baker served a Williams offering to right, scoring Oldring. The speedy Collins tried to score from first, but was cut down at the plate for the second out, the score tied 6-6.

McInniss gave the A's the lead with a hit that scored Baker. After Walsh walked, Barry singled in McInnis and Walsh. Schang then drove in the 10th run of the inning, his single driving Barry home. Pennock made his second and the final out of the inning. The A's now led 10-6 on a 10-spot in the second. It was a season high for runs in an inning for Philadelphia. It was also the end of Williams's outing. His line for the day was two innings pitched, 10 earned runs allowed on 11 hits.

Though the Tigers tallied another run in the third inning, the A's pressed on the accelerator, scoring in every inning the rest of the way: two in the third, one in the fourth, two in the fifth, one in the sixth, three in the seventh, and two in the eighth. The 11 additional runs were all charged to Ralph Comstock, who gave up 14 hits in his six innings.

The final score was 21-8. For the Athletics, the $100,000 infield scored 10 runs and knocked in nine on a total of 12 hits. Barry led with five RBIs followed by Murphy's four. Overall, the team ripped 25 hits, walked five times, and were hit by pitches twice. Young Herb Pennock went the distance, earning his second win of the season. He yielded 13 hits, walked five, and was charged with eight earned runs.

The limping Tigers had one bright spot in the game. Sam Crawford nearly hit for the cycle, needing only a single in his final two at-bats. It was not to be.

After this game the A's cruised to the finish line with a 2-8 record over the final 10 games. They went on to defeat the New York Giants in five games in a memorable World Series, Eddie Plank defeating Christy Mathewson in the final game to clinch another championship for Connie Mack.[4]

SOURCES

In addition to the sources cited in the Notes, the author accessed Retrosheet.org and Baseball-Reference.com.

NOTES

1   Jim Nasium, "Athletics Are Champions for Fifth Season," *Philadelphia Inquirer*, September 23, 1913: 1, 12.

2   Jacob Pomrenke, "Lefty Williams," SABR BioProject, sabr.org/bioproj/person/0998b35f.

3   Frank Vaccaro, "Herb Pennock," SABR BioProject, sabr.org/bioproj/person/612bb457.

4   Lawrence Knorr, *Gettysburg Eddie: The Story of Eddie Plank* (Mechanicsburg, Pennsylvania: Sunbury Press, Inc., 2018), 291-292.

"BIG SIX" OUTDUELS "GETTYSBURG EDDIE" IN EXTRA-INNING CLASSIC

October 8, 1913
New York Giants 3, Philadelphia Athletics 0

Game Two of the World Series

By Gregory H. Wolf

It was the "most wonderful pitchers' battle ever in a World Series," gushed sportswriter Bozeman Bulger about the epic battle between Christy Mathewson and Eddie Plank.[1] Syndicated columnist Hugh Fullerton praised the hurling duel as "a wonderful game, tense in situations, magnificent with the courage and nerve displayed by these two veteran pitchers."[2] The future Hall of Famers engaged in a scoreless contest through nine innings, before "Big Six" "practically single handed, fought the foe into submission," opined the *New York Tribune*, knocking in the game's first run in the 10th inning to lead the New York Giants to a 3-0 victory over the Philadelphia Athletics.[3]

Skipper John McGraw's reigning three-time NL champion Giants (101-51) looked like "forlorn hope," quipped the *Tribune*, as they prepared for Game Two of the World Series.[4] Initially favored to win the title, they had lost the opener at the Polo Grounds, 6-4, and faced with a depleted lineup the team with the best home record in baseball. First baseman Fred Merkle injured his ankle in Game One and was replaced by center

fielder Fred Snodgrass, who was "lame enough to be in bed," hobbled by a charley horse and barely able to run.[5] Utilityman Tillie Shafer was shifted to center even though he had made only 11 career starts in that position. If that wasn't bad enough, catcher Chief Meyers, who led the team in batting (.312) and slugging (.410), suffered a seriously sliced right hand on a throw from Buck Herzog during warm-ups and missed the rest of the Series.[6] Larry McLean, a 6-foot-5 behemoth, donned the tools of ignorance for his 25th start of the season since his acquisition on August 6 from the St. Louis Cardinals. Skipper Connie Mack's A's (96-57), a remarkably healthy club all season long, were ready to unleash the majors' highest-scoring offense in pursuit of their third title in four seasons.

It was a cloudy, sunless Wednesday afternoon with temperatures in the mid-60s in the City of Brotherly Love.[7] Morning rain and mist cast doubts on whether the game would be played. Nonetheless a throng of 7,000 fans had gathered by 7 A.M. at the box office at Shibe Park, located at the intersection of 21st street and Lehigh,

Game Two of the 1913 World Series at Shibe Park. New York Giants ace Christy Mathewson, on the mound, dueled Eddie Plank through nine scoreless innings. The Giants scored three in the 10th off Gettysburg Eddie to give Big Six a shutout.

for a chance to purchase tickets. By order of the National Commission, baseball's governing body, spectators would not be permitted to stand cordoned off in the outfield as they were in 1911. In addition to the capacity crowd of 20,563 at the ballpark, another five thousand sat atop the makeshift viewing stands on rowhouse rooftops along 20th Street and Somerset Street.

Neither McGraw nor Mack revealed his starting pitcher prior to the game and sent several to warm up, but both went with their longtime aces.[8] The NL's greatest hurler, with 337 wins in his 13 full seasons, the 32-year-old right-handed Mathewson was coming off another spectacular season (25-11, league-best 2.06 ERA). At 37 years of age, the southpaw Plank (18-10) was the oldest pitcher in the majors. Though not a star in Matty's class, "Steady Eddie" had won 269 games in his 13-year career, easily the most in AL history. Mathewson and Plank had a long history together. They had first encountered one another

as Pennsylvania college stars in 1899, for Bucknell and Gettysburg, respectively. In Game One of the 1905 World Series, Mathewson beat Plank, tossing the first of his three shutouts to help the Giants to their last title.

The game got underway at 2 P.M. after a brief ceremony presenting the Washington Senators Walter Johnson the Chalmers Award and a new automobile as AL MVP. Herzog led off by sending Plank's fourth pitch into shallow left field, but second baseman Eddie Collins raced back to snare the Texas Leaguer, setting the tone for the kind of defensive struggle the game would become.[9] Through the first eight innings, Plank surrendered only three hits. He began the game "with a whizzing burst of speed, slowed and began to cross them up with curves and added his cross-fire," wrote Fullerton.[10] His biggest threat came in the third when Snodgrass hit a one-out liner past third base and hobbled to first on what should have been a double. Mathewson followed with a single to center field and then moved to second on Rube Oldring's ill-advised attempt to nab Snodgrass at third. Writhing in pain, Snodgrass was replaced by pinch-runner Hooks Wiltse. Plank fielded Herzog's tapper and threw home to catch Wiltse in a rundown while Mathewson and Herzog reached third and second, respectively. Larry Doyle flied meekly to center. The game's defensive highlight occurred in the top of the eighth when right fielder Eddie Murphy made a "spectacular catch," according to the *Philadelphia Inquirer.* At full speed, Murphy "plunged face forward" to snare Mathewson's liner inches from the ground, then somersaulted to a stop.[11]

The Giants were in trouble in the first inning when Doyle made a "schoolboy's fumble" on Murphy's routine leadoff grounder to second.[12] Oldring fouled a bunt, then singled to left, and both runners moved up a station on Collins's bunt. To the plate strolled Home Run Baker, baseball's most potent long-ball threat. The three-time reigning major-league leader in round-trippers, Baker had blasted a home run the day before at the Polo Grounds. This time he struck out on three pitches.[13] Three innings later, Baker hit a one-out bounder that "touched Doyle's fingertips," reported the *New York Sun,* and caromed into right for scratch hit.[14] With two outs, Amos Strunk drew a walk on seven pitches, Mathewson's only free pass of the game, but Jack Barry grounded out. The A's threatened again when Collins and Baker connected for consecutive two-out singles in the eighth. Mathewson called his infielders to the mound, then dispatched Stuffy McInnis on an easy grounder to third that Herzog fielded for a force out of Collins.

The ninth inning demonstrated why these two teams had dominated their leagues in recent seasons. Beginning to show the "wear and tear of the grind," opined the *Sun,* Plank surrendered a one-out single to Art Fletcher and then walked George Burns on four pitches.[15] He extinguished the threat by retiring Shafer and Red Murray on

a total of six pitches, prompting a loud outburst from skipper McGraw, who was coaching first base, for their failure to take pitches.[16]

In the bottom of the frame, Mathewson was at his best: "daring, confident, and with magnificent control," cooed the *New York Times.*[17] Not to be overlooked was Wiltse, who had replaced Snodgrass after running for him. A pitcher with 135 career victories thus far in his 10-year career, Wiltse had been a little-used reliever in 1913, but was known as one of the best fielders at his position. He made his big-league debut at first base in three games at the end of the season. After Strunk led off with a single, Barry bunted past Mathewson. Doyle charged and in a "reckless manner," according to the *Tribune,* threw wildly past Wiltse even though he had no chance at the out.[18] In the first of three tactical mistakes by the A's in the inning, third-base coach Harry Davis held up the speedy Strunk at third as Wiltse retrieved the ball and threw home, enabling Barry to advance to second. Needing just a long fly to win the game, Mack permitted the next two batters to come to the plate, even though he had two capable pinch-hitters, Danny Murphy and Wally Schang. The Tall Tactician was subsequently roundly criticized in the press for these conservative decisions. Batting .227, Jack Lapp grounded to Wiltse who fired a bullet to erase a sliding Strunk on a close call at home plate. Plank, a .105 hitter, also grounded to Wiltse, whose throw home caught Barry in a rundown. With batters on second and third and needing a single to win it, Eddie Murphy grounded back to Mathewson who tossed to his road roommate Wiltse to end a dramatic inning. The Philadelphia crowd showed its respects with a "spontaneous outburst" of applause.[19]

Back on the mound in the 10th, Plank yielded a leadoff single to McLean, who was then replaced by pinch-runner Eddie Grant. After Wiltse sacrificed, Mathews hit "savagely to deep center" to drive in the game's first run.[20] Herzog followed with a grounder to Eddie Collins. Going for a double play, the anchor of the A's vaunted $100,000 infield threw wildly, hitting Mathewson in the shoulder, enabling runners to advance to second and third.[21] After Plank hit Doyle on the arm to load the bags, the infield moved in to set up a play at the plate. The plan backfired when Fletcher chopped a grounder over Barry's head at shortstop to plate two more runs. Plank fanned Burns and retired Shafter on his 25th pitch of the inning and 137th of the game.[22]

Mathewson emerged as "master, king, emperor and ruler of all baseball pitchers," gushed the *Tribune*, by retiring Oldring, Collins, and Baker in order in the 10th.[23] Fittingly, Wiltse was involved in Mathewson's 104th and final pitch.[24] Playing with an infielder's glove instead of a first baseman's mitt, Wiltse knocked down Baker's liner. It rolled to Doyle, who threw back to Wiltse covering the bag for the out, ending the game in 2 hours and 22 minutes.

SOURCES

In addition to the sources cited in the Notes, the author accessed Retrosheet.org, Baseball-Reference.com, SABR.org, and the following newspaper articles:

"Eddie Plank Invincible Until That Rally in Glorious Tenth," *New York Tribune*, October 9, 1913: 10.

"How the Giants Got Their Runs in Thrilling Tenth," *New York Sun*, October 9, 1913: 4.

"How the Giants Won," *New York Times*, October 9, 1913: 2.

Nasium, Jim. "Old Masters' Battle on Diamond Was One of Brains and Brawn," *Philadelphia Inquirer*, October 9, 1913: 10.

Rice, Grantland. "Big Six vs. Plank and 3 to 0 Score," (Baltimore) *Sun*, October 9, 1913: 9.

"Took Chance on Plank and Lost by Failure to Score," *Philadelphia Inquirer*, October 9, 1913: 10.

NOTES

1   Bozeman Bulger, "Matty's Own Hit Wins After Remarkable Ten Inning Pitching Duel," *New York Evening World*, October 9, 1913: 1.

2   Hugh Fullerton, "Defeat Hit Mack Hard," *New York Times*, October 9, 1913: 3.

3   "Matty Baffles Athletics by the Wizardry of His Fadeaway," *New York Tribune*, October 9, 1913: 1.

4   "Matty Baffles Athletics by the Wizardry of His Fadeaway."

5   "Matty Baffles Athletics by the Wizardry of His Fadeaway."

6   "Matty Baffles Athletics by the Wizardry of His Fadeaway."

7   "Yesterday's Local Weather Report," *Philadelphia Inquirer*, October 9, 1913: 2.

8   Jeff Tesreau (22-13) and Al Demaree (13-4) warmed up for the Giants, as did Mathewson. Boardwalk Brown (17-11) and Plank warmed up for the A's.

9   The fourth pitch is from "Matty Pitched but 104 Balls in Beating Macks," *Philadelphia Inquirer*, October 9, 1913: 11.

10 Fullerton.

11 "'Big Six' Handed Plank Hard Bump in Second Game," *Philadelphia Inquirer*, October 9, 1913: 1.

12 "Matty Pitched but 104 Balls in Beating Macks."

13 "Matty Pitched but 104 Balls in Beating Macks."

14 "Mathewson Reigns; Giants Even Series," *New York Sun*, October 9, 1913: 4.

15 "Mathewson Reigns; Giants Even Series."

16 "Matty Pitched but 104 Balls in Beating Macks."

17 "Matty Blanks Athletics; Wins Game with Hit," *New York Times*, October 9, 1913: 1.

18 "Matty Baffles Athletics by the Wizardry of His Fadeaway."

19 "Matty Baffles Athletics by the Wizardry of His Fadeaway."

20 "Matty Pitched but 104 Balls in Beating Macks."

21 "Matty Pitched but 104 Balls in Beating Macks."

22 Pitch counts from "Matty Pitched but 104 Balls in Beating Macks," *Philadelphia Inquirer*. According to the *Inquirer*, Plank threw 84 strikes and 53 balls.

23 "Matty Baffles Athletics by the Wizardry of His Fadeaway."

24 Pitch counts from "Matty Pitched but 104 Balls in Beating Macks." According to the *Inquirer*, Mathewson threw 81 strikes and 23 balls.

"THE MIGHTY SHOUT OF VICTORY"

October 10, 1913
Philadelphia Athletics 6, New York Giants 5

Game Four of the World Series

By John G. Zinn

No matter how much the residents around Shibe Park loved the Athletics, their proximity to the ballpark was a mixed blessing the night before the fourth game of the 1913 World Series. Not long after Philadelphia won the third game in New York and took a two-games-to-one lead, fans started gathering outside the ticket windows. Around midnight an estimated 2,000 people were not only waiting, they were helping themselves to the residents' doormats, eggs, milk, and newspapers. By 10:00 A.M., the crowd had become a "howling mob" of 8,000, waiting impatiently for 4,000 bleacher seats to go on sale. Not surprisingly, fights broke out over places in line.[1] When the ticket windows finally opened, the lucky purchasers rushed inside, making "a sound similar to that of a cattle stampede." The less fortunate had to turn to the same put-upon local residents, who more than made up for their losses by raising the price for a rooftop view from 50 cents to a dollar.[2]

Regardless of whether they were inside or outside the ballpark, the fans speculated about the identity of the A's starting pitcher especially when Connie Mack kept everyone guessing by having all his pitchers "strung out in a row and warming up" just 15 minutes before game time.[3] While the "dopesters and fans" thought Mack would save

Chief Bender for Saturday or Monday, the Tall Tactician had other ideas. "Just a few minutes before game time," Bender appeared in front of the grandstand, ready to take the mound.[4] No such deception was practiced by John McGraw, who called on his "last pitching hope," Al Demaree, to make his first World Series appearance.[5]

The game began with three "closely fought" innings that saw Philadelphia take a 1-0 lead.[6] Stuffy McInnis got things going in the A's second with a hit that fell safely primarily because the injured Fred Snodgrass couldn't reach it. After Amos Strunk grounded out on a bunt, Jack Barry hit a foul that Fred Merkle, playing on "a bandaged ankle," got his hands on, but couldn't hold. The missed opportunity cost the Giants when Barry's double drove in the game's first run.[7] According to the *Philadelphia Evening Bulletin*, Barry reached second in spite of "Rough-neck Merkle," who "threw both arms around Barry," an infraction missed by all four umpires.[8] There was no more scoring and after three innings Philadelphia led 1-0.

The A's resumed the attack in the bottom of the fourth when with one out Strunk hit one "wickedly" toward third. Giants third baseman Buck Herzog "threw himself at the ball," but had no play at first. Barry then singled Strunk to third

Charles Albert Bender on the mound in Game Four of the 1913 World Series against the New York Giants. Considered a poised, unflappable pitcher in high-pressure situations, Bender went 6-4 with a 2.44 ERA in 85 World Series innings. (Photo: public domain)

and advanced to second on the throw.[9] Next up was rookie catcher Wally Schang, who, although he had hit a home run the day before, "had evidently not impressed McGraw" since he had Demaree pitch to Schang even though Bender was up next.[10] After "awful lunges at [two] slow balls," Schang hit the third one beyond the "superhuman efforts" of Larry Doyle and Art Fletcher, driving in two runs.[11] After Schang went to second on the throw and advanced to third on a passed ball, Bender hit a grounder toward first. Merkle couldn't come up with it, Schang scored and the Giants first baseman was charged with an error.[12] The star-crossed Merkle received some sympathy from the Philadelphia newspapers, especially the *Evening Bulletin*, which claimed Merkle couldn't have fielded the ball "if he had had seven gloves and a lot more hands."[13] Trailing 4-0, the Giants understandably "looked disheartened when they came to the bench."[14]

Disheartened or not, McGraw's men rallied when Red Murray walked and Larry McLean "hit a vicious grounder back of second base."

Eddie Collins "made a sensational attempt to get the ball," but "accidentally kicked" it into left field, sending Murray to third. Looking for speed on the bases, McGraw inserted Claude Cooper as a pinch-runner for McLean.[15] After Merkle struck out, Harry McCormick, the "king of the pinch hitters," batted for Demaree.[16] Before pitching, Bender, with remarkable foresight, moved his left fielder, Rube Oldring in 10 to 15 feet. McCormick hit a 2-and-1 pitch "on a dead line, low and hard into left," but Oldring charged in with "his hands cupped at his shoe tops" and made a run-saving catch. Bender celebrated his "sheer wizardry" by jolting "an imaginary uppercut into the air." Desperate to salvage something, the Giants tried a double steal, but Cooper was thrown out, keeping the Giants scoreless.[17]

Rube Marquard took over for Demaree in the fifth and after getting two quick outs walked Strunk and gave up a double to Barry. Once again the Giants had the opportunity to walk Schang and pitch to Bender; once again, they chose not to; and once again, the rookie catcher singled in two runs. With a Philadelphia victory seeming almost certain, the *Inquirer* declared that "the saddest sight of all was a certain crumpled up man on the Giants bench." Although McGraw's teams had won five pennants, the almost certain loss of three straight World Series left him "huddled in a suffering heap." Marquard allowed no more scoring and both sides went out quickly in the sixth.[18]

Although many Philadelphia fans doubtless thought the game and the Series were over, the Giants suddenly came from behind "like a long lean thoroughbred reserving his speed for the stretch."[19] It began innocently in the Giants seventh when George Burns tried to get out of the way of a pitch, but the ball hit his bat, it rolled to shortstop, and he reached first. It didn't seem significant when Tillie Shafer popped out to Collins, but Murray got a new life when Schang dropped his foul tip and Red singled to left. Catcher Art Wilson, who had come into the game with Marquard, struck out, but Burns and Murray pulled a double steal. Once again, the Giants were lucky as Burns would have been out, but Frank Baker dropped the throw from Schang.[20] Both missed opportunities proved costly when on a two-strike pitch, Bender "lobbed up a semi-speedy one right where Merkle loves them."[21] Bad ankle or not, the Giants first baseman hit a "long sharp drive to left center" which in spite of Oldring's "desperate effort," took "one high bound" into the stands for a home run that got the Giants back in the game.[22] Perhaps stunned by the blow, the A's went out on just seven pitches in the bottom of the seventh.

If the Giants needed proof that the game was turning in their favor, it came in the eighth when Herzog, who was up to then hitless in the Series, "surprised himself, the crowd and Chief Bender" by getting a hit.[23] Larry Doyle followed with a potential double-play ball to Collins, but the second baseman slipped and was only able to force Herzog. Fletcher quickly resumed the assault with a "wicked line" drive off Bender's pitching arm. The A's pitcher recovered the ball and threw "wild and hard" to second, but fortunately Barry, "by a great effort," caught it and forced Doyle for the second out. It was, to put it mildly, "decidedly timely" because Burns ripped a double to right, followed by Shafer's triple that incredibly and improbably brought the Giants to within one run of tying a game that seemed lost.[24] The crowd, which had been so gleeful earlier, was now "stunned with fear," when it wasn't shivering "with palpitation."[25] Fortunately for Philadelphia, Murray, with the tying run a mere 90 feet away, "lunged at the first ball" and grounded out to second.[26]

By this point Bender was "in evident distress" and the batboys worked him over with towels like a prizefighter preparing for the final round.[27] Marquard again shut down the A's in the eighth and the Giants came to bat in the ninth before "a timid quiet crowd."[28] Doc Crandall pinch-hit for Wilson, but grounded out to Collins, bringing up Merkle. Any Giants fan hoping for a repeat performance was quickly disappointed when he flied out to right field on the first pitch as Philadelphia fans "gave vent to a big gasp of relief."[29] The Giants put their last hope on Eddie Grant, who hit for Marquard. With the count full, Grant "lunged forward with might and main," but hit a foul fly "straight up in the air" which Schang caught easily.[30] With Philadelphia now up three games to one, the *New York Tribune* predicted that the Giants chances were "about as good as a plugged nickel in the Waldorf."[31] The sentiment was shared by the Philadelphia fans, who let out "a shout that echoed and re-echoed around the concrete confines of Shibe Park and rolled away in reverberation for squares. It was the mighty shout of victory."[32]

SOURCES

In addition to the sources cited in the Notes, the author relied on Baseball-reference.com and Retrosheet.org.

NOTES

1 "Overflow Crowd Fights for View," *Philadelphia Inquirer*, October 11, 1913: 13.

2 Bozeman Bulger, "Giants' Shortstop Fined for Row with the Umpire Over Decision on Shafer," *New York Evening World*, October 10, 1913: 2.

3 Bozeman Bulger, "Athletics Win Fourth, Hitting Demaree and Marquard with Ease," *New York Evening World*, October 10, 1913: 1.

4 "Victory Today Will Win Championship and Head Off Criticism," *Philadelphia Inquirer*, October 11, 1913: 12.

5 "Athletics Win Again, Choking Off Giant Rally," *New York Times*, October 11, 1913: 1.

6 D.L. Reeves, "Athletics Bats Again Triumph," *Philadelphia Public Ledger*, October 11, 1913: 1.

7 "How the Game Was Played," *Philadelphia Inquirer*, October 11, 1913: 13.

8 "How the Game Was Played"; "Bender Toyed with Giants," *Philadelphia Evening Bulletin*, October 11, 1913.

9 "How the Game Was Played."

10 "Athletics Win Again and Now Loom Up as Baseball Champions of the World," *New York Tribune*, October 11, 1913: 6.

11 Reeves: 12; "How the Game Was Played."

12 "How the Game Was Played."

13 "How the Game Was Played"; "Bender Toyed with Giants."

14 "How the Game Was Played."

15 "How the Game Was Played."

16 "Breaks of the Game Were with Athletics," *New York Tribune*, October 11, 1913: 6.

17 "Bender Again Beats Giants," *Philadelphia Inquirer*, October 11, 1913: 12; "How the Game Was Played."

18 "Bender Again Beats Giants"; "How the Game Was Played."

19 Reeves: 1.

20 Reeves: 12; "How the Game Was Played."

21 Hugh Fullerton, "Luck Big Factor," *New York Times*, October 11, 1913: 3.

22 "How the Game Was Played"; "Breaks of the Game Were with Athletics." Balls hit into the stands on a bounce were home runs until 1930 in the American League and 1931 in the National, baseballhall.org/discover/inside-pitch/ al-lopez-hits-last-bounce-home-run.

23 "How the Game Was Played."

24 "How the Game Was Played."

25 Reeves: 12; "Bender Again Beats Giants."

26 "How the Game Was Played."

27 "Housetops Remain a Haven for the Fans," *New York Tribune*, October 11, 1913: 6.

28 Reeves: 1.

29 "How the Game Was Played."

30 "How the Game Was Played."

31 "Athletics Win Again and Now Loom Up as Baseball Champions of the World."

32 Reeves: 1.

RUDOLPH OUTPITCHES BENDER IN WORLD SERIES OPENER

October 9, 1914
Boston Braves 7, Philadelphia Athletics 1

Game One of the World Series

By Mark S. Sternman

The upstart Boston Braves surprised the defending World Series champion Philadelphia Athletics in Game One as postseason novice Dick Rudolph easily outpitched the seasoned veteran Chief Bender, 7-1. It was the first time in a Series game that Philadelphia manager Connie Mack – with four prior World Series under his belt – had to remove his starter for ineffectiveness rather than injury.[1] Rudolph's gem, delivered on a day when his wife gave birth to a girl, heralded a Series in which Braves pitching and dominating defense stopped Athletics hitting, showing that the unique pressures of the fall classic could not cool Boston manager George Stallings' hot squad.

One would have thought that the more experienced Philadelphia team would show more patience at the plate, defensive grace with its $100,000 infield, and moxie on the bases. In fact, the opposite transpired in all three categories, both in Game One and throughout the World Series. "The beating was perhaps the worst that has ever been handed to an opponent in the opening game of a postseason series between major league clubs," Tim Murnane wrote in the *Boston Daily Globe*.[2]

The trio of Boston starters all used the aggressiveness of the Athletics against them. No one did so more effectively than Rudolph, who, after Game One, observed, "I found out what makes the Athletics such a hitting team. They're all what we call free swingers."[3]

One sportswriter gushed that Rudolph "pitched one of the most remarkable games in the history of the sport. ... He used a slow ball, a curve, his spitter, and not once during the game did the Athletics really threaten him."[4]

In addition to Rudolph's off-speed stuff, his "slow, deceptive delivery ... proved the Mackmen's undoing, for they are notoriously weak on this service, and Rudolph was at his best in this respect today."[5]

By failing to make Rudolph, who threw fewer than ten pitches in both the eighth and ninth innings, and the other Braves starters work, Philadelphia never forced Boston to turn to its questionable pitching depth, allowing Game Two starter Bill James to relieve Lefty Tyler in extra innings in Game Three and Rudolph to pitch Game Four on regular rest. With runners on the corners and none out in the second inning, for

A's players prior to Game One of the 1914 World Series at Shibe Park. After winning the pennant by 8½ games, the A's (99-53-6) lost four straight to the Boston Braves.

instance, "Barry helped Rudolph out immensely by fanning on a ball about a foot outside."[6]

With multiple baserunners in each of the first two frames, Game One began auspiciously for the Athletics. After Bender retired the Braves in order in the first, Eddie Murphy singled. Rube Oldring then bunted. Hank Gowdy "ran down to retrieve it and with little time to spare, shot it toward first base high in the air. By a wonderful jump, Schmidt speared the ball and got down on the bag in time to retire the sprinting Oldring."[7]

Rudolph then walked Collins to put runners on first and second for Frank Baker. Rather than take a strike following the free pass, Baker hit the first pitch toward "the right field grandstand seats, which Schmidt … mitted for the second out. Murphy tried to edge up to third … but Schmidt's bounding throw reached Deal in time … to tag out Eddie and end the promising inning in a cloud of gloom."[8]

"Schmidt's great throw and Deal's swift stab probably decided the game."[9]

The promising start fizzled with a single play that evinced several themes that would run throughout the Series: poor situational hitting

and blundering baserunning by Philadelphia, and sharp pitching and sparkling defense by the Boston infield, including repeated fine plays by its unheralded corner players.

The Braves had timely hitting, too, especially from Gowdy, the surprising batting star of the 1914 World Series. Thanks to Gowdy, the Braves took a lead that they would not relinquish in the top of the second. Gowdy drove in Possum Whitted, who had walked, with a double, and Rabbit Maranville scored Gowdy with a single. The Athletics came back with a Stuffy McInnis walk and an Amos Strunk single. McInnis scored on an error by Herbie Moran in left, and Strunk went to third.

Philadelphia had the tying run on third with no out. But Jack Barry struck out, the first of eight K's for Rudolph, and Wally Schang hit to Johnny Evers, who "scooped up the ball and shot it to Gowdy, nailing Strunk at the plate by a very narrow margin."[10] Rudolph then sealed the squander by getting Bender to force Schang.

The Athletics ran into another out in the fourth inning, when Strunk tried to stretch a single, but "was cut down at second on Connolly's sharp relay into Maranville. Strunk probably would have made the midway sack had he not lost his stride in rounding first base."[11]

In his brief appearances in the 1914 Series, Strunk would struggle on the basepaths and in the field before giving way to injury. He made two hits in his first two trips to the plate, but failed in his final five opportunities. His successor, Jimmy Walsh, also fared poorly in center field and running the bases.

Boston got far better play from its key substitute. Over the next three games, the Braves, minus injured slugger Red Smith, who spent the Series in a Brooklyn hospital laid up with a broken leg, would barely exceed their run total from this first contest, but the fine fielding of Maranville remained constant throughout the quartet: "Barry smote a Texas Leaguer in the fifth inning. Connolly could not reach it, and Deal lacked the leg locomotion to get near it. Maranville almost dropped out of a cloud and with his back to the ball, he nailed it."[12]

The Braves broke open a 3-1 run game with a trio of runs in the sixth inning, when Bender was knocked from the box. With runners on first and second with one out, Whitted delivered the key blow, a two-run triple, when he "connected squarely with one of Bender's fast straight ones and it was going even faster and straighter toward the score-board in far centre field after Whitted had given it his special slugging treatment."[13]

Charlie Deal ended the four-run sixth inning by hitting into his third double play of the game.

Forced into service because of the Smith mishap, the unheralded Deal made up for his lackluster bat with his glove in both the first and final frames of the game.[14] In the latter case, a Philadelphia paper noted, "No third baseman could have handled McInnis' solid crack in the ninth better than did Deal, who pulled the ball down with his bare hand."[15]

Deal later made the Series-clinching play on McInnis to end Game Four.

In a Series marred by runners giving up outs on the basepaths at inopportune times, the Braves had the opener's most daring baserunning play, too, when the slow-footed pair of Butch Schmidt and Hank Gowdy pulled off a double steal in the eighth to make the final score 7-1. "Collins caught Lapp's short throw, but in returning the ball Eddie threw high and Schmidt slid under Lapp."[16]

Stallings may have called the play to send a message that the Braves would not back down even up by a big score, or he may have simply wanted to avoid having Deal, in the box with Gowdy on first and Schmidt on third, hit into his fourth double play of the game.

With better starting pitching for Philadelphia, the runs would not come so easily for Boston for the rest of the Series, but the ultimate results would remain the same.

This article is included in *The Miracle Braves of 1914: Boston's Original Worst-to-First World Series Champions* (SABR, 2014), edited by Bill Nowlin.

NOTES

1 The Boston captain did point, however, to a physical affliction affecting Bender, writing that Chief "has had to have his arm treated with electricity after every game he pitched during the season and for several days afterwards to put life into it." John J. Evers, "Hank Gowdy and Rudolph Heroes," *Boston Post*, October 10, 1914: 11.

2 T.H. Murnane, "Game Is Braves' 7 to 1," *Boston Daily Globe*, October 10, 1914: 1.

3 "Dick Rudolph's a Modest Hero," *Philadelphia Bulletin*, October 10, 1914: 9.

4 Hugh S. Fullerton, "Connie's Machine Is Good As Ever, Says Fullerton," [Philadelphia] *Evening Ledger*, October 10, 1914: 2.

5 "Braves Win First Game, 7 to 1," *Boston Daily Advertiser*, October 10, 1914: 1.

6 Eddie Collins, "Eddie Collins Says Mackmen Have No Excuses," [Philadelphia] *Evening Ledger*, October 10, 1914, p. 2. After Game Four, Collins also complained, "We never attempted to find out anything about Rudolph. By this I mean whether it would be more to our advantage, say, to wait him out, or if bunting would upset him." Eddie Collins, "Pitchers Made Us 'Look Bad,' Says Collins," [Philadelphia] *Evening Ledger*, October 14, 1914:2.

7 Paul H. Shannon, "No Excuses Left for Mack's Men," *Boston Post*, October 10, 1914: 11.

8 "Hank Gowdy Swung at a 100 P.C. Mark," *Philadelphia Inquirer*, October 10, 1914: 11.

9 R.E. McMillin, "Athletics Smashed by Braves 7 to 1," *Boston Journal*, October 10, 1914: 10.

10 "Two Important Plays in the Game," *Boston Post*, October 10, 1914: 13.

11 "Hank Gowdy Swung at a 100 P.C. Mark," *Philadelphia Inquirer*, October 10, 1914: 11.

12 "Mackmen's Defeat Decisive – But Remember They Came back in '11," *Philadelphia Bulletin*, October 10, 1914: 8.

13 Walter E. Hapgood, "Braves Win Opening Game of World Series," *Boston Herald*, October 10, 1914: 8.

14 "Tyler places great confidence in Deal. 'He is the dark horse,' the crack pitcher averred. 'I look for him to do great things. He's steady and calm and nervy, and while he is not as strong at the bat as Smith, he's no laggard with the stick,' " in "Smith's Loss Fails to Depress Braves," *Philadelphia Bulletin*, October 7, 1914: 17.

15 "Stallings' Braves Defeat Athletics; Knock out Bender," *Philadelphia Inquirer*, October 10, 1914: 1.

16 On the play, "Gowdy kept going for third and Lapp's throw beat him to the bag," in "Stallings' Braves Defeat Athletics; Knock out Bender," *Philadelphia Inquirer*, October 10, 1914: 11.

BILL JAMES OUTDUELS EDDIE PLANK

October 10, 1914
Boston Braves 1, Philadelphia Athletics 0

Game Two of the World Series

By Mark S. Sternman

On an unusually warm October day in Philadelphia in front of more than 20,000 fortunate fans, the Boston Braves moved halfway toward winning the World Series for the first time with a dramatic 1-0 whitewashing of the Philadelphia Americans behind the brilliant two-hit pitching of Bill James, the unlikely ninth-inning offensive outburst of substitute third baseman Charlie Deal, and the defensive wizardry of Rabbit Maranville. The game represented a pitching duel for the ages featuring the veteran Eddie Plank and the youngster James.

By their actions and their inactions, both George Stallings and Connie Mack made the ninth inning a particularly memorable one. In fact, the World Series gamesmanship had begun even before the Series. Deal was replacing Red Smith, who had broken his ankle in the last game of the regular season. Mack commented that he regretted the injury to Smith "as he wanted the Athletics to meet the Braves at their best," words that would appear in a different light after Deal's heroics.[1]

The "bats of the Boston visitors, which had been so efficacious against the speed and curves of Chief Bender," had remained quiet as the scoreless game made its way to the final frame.[2] Ever superstitious, Boston manager Stallings sought to spark his team by turning to a human good-luck charm in reserve outfielder Josh Devore,[3] who replaced Game One winner Dick Rudolph on the first-base coaching lines in the ninth inning. By cause or by coincidence, Devore worked his magic quickly after Maranville grounded to Barry, his opposite number at short.

Deal lifted a fly to deep right-center field. "It was a long ball, but would not have been a difficult catch."[4] Amos Strunk, who "has always been classed with Tris Speaker for his ability in going back for balls,"[5] broke in but misjudged and/or lost the ball in the sun, which "shone brilliantly upon the soft greens of the in and outfields."[6] By the time Strunk had reversed direction and retrieved the smash, Deal had reached second safely with his first safety of the postseason (he would get just one more hit in the Series) and Boston's only extra-base hit of the game.

Wally Schang had Deal in trouble immediately, caught far off second base after a Plank pitch, but when Schang fired the ball to Jack Barry covering second, Deal daringly lit off for third and took the bag. "Barry did not throw to Frank Baker. He drew his arm back, but the throw never came. … Deal was directly in line with

Baker and the throw might have hit the runner in the back and ended the chances of the Athletics right there."[7]

Now, with no score, one out, and Deal on third base, Stallings faced a decision on his pitcher, James. Stallings had had both James and Lefty Tyler warm up before the game, but in a surprise to fans, who had expected to see Tyler perform,"[8] chose right-hander James to start Game Two. (Mack also had Plank take batting practice before Game One but had gone instead with Chief Bender, his usual opening-game hurler.) Should he dispatch a pinch-hitter to bat for James, and perhaps get the first run of the game across the plate? But James, who was "working a fast one and quick-breaker spitter on the Athletics" in pitching to the minimum 24 hitters through the first eight frames, so Stallings let Seattle Bill bat for himself against Gettysburg Eddie.[9] One can understand this decision given "the one game contributed by long Bill James was the most perfect piece of twirling skill seen in a world's series in many a day."[10]

To no avail. For the fourth straight time, Plank struck out his opposite number, which left Leslie Mann to face the southpaw with two down and Deal still on third in a game that had gone scoreless for its first 50 outs.

But Gettysburg Eddie faltered in the end. He forced Mann to go the other way, and the Bostonian "whacked a short safe one-shot that fleet, game Eddie Collins could not reach though he leaped four feet into the air and landed in a shapeless heap on the outfield turf."[11] The single plated Deal with what turned out to be the only run of the ballgame.

Plank ended up hurling 129, 132, or 149 pitches in and out of trouble all day.[12] "Inning after inning the Braves got runners on the bases, and, just as they were about to strike their telling blow, gray-eyed Plank, still cunning and wily in the evening of his baseball career, suddenly would pull himself together and halt the Boston uprising."[13]

In his syndicated column, Ty Cobb credited Stallings' platoon system, one originally devised by Mack, for the run, writing, "(T)hat game was won by Stallings' shrewd shifts. He put Mann and Ted Cather into his batting order in place of Moran and Joe Connolly, to get two right-handed batters against a southpaw, and how well it worked the result showed."[14]

Having given the Athletics a pep talk before the game, Cobb hardly counted as an impartial observer but he still credited the Braves for heady play.

James, who had pitched unerringly after walking Eddie Murphy to start the game, struggled to hold the lead in the ninth, sandwiching walks to Jack Barry (on four pitches) and pinch-hitter Jimmy Walsh around a strikeout of Wally Schang. With the tying run on second and the winning run on first, James induced a hot shot through the box by Murphy that looked as if it would get through and tie the game.

But Johnny Evers had moved Maranville just to the right of the second-base bag, so Rabbit made three great plays in one by receiving the ball, brushing off the lumbering Walsh (Maranville "bounded away from Walsh like a rubber ball"[15]), and firing the pill to Butch Schmidt at first to turn a dazzling short-to-first double play, the game's only twin killing and the only double play Murphy hit into in all of 1914. It ended the game and the Shibe Park season. "Maranville's utterly impossible double play [saved] the whole show."[16]

Maranville had more than made up for dropping Stuffy McInnis' foul fly for a one-out error in the eighth inning, a miscue that could have been a major one so late in a scoreless duel but that James mitigated by inducing Stuffy to sky to Deal at third.

In addition to the ninth-inning dramatics, each team threatened to score throughout the game although James did retire 15 Athletics in a row after walking Murphy in the bottom of the first.

Plank, by contrast, saw Bostonians reach base frequently, but pitched in a pinch by stranding Braves in scoring position in the first, second, fourth, and sixth. Schang ended the third by throwing out Johnny Evers trying to swipe second "by such a distance that the long chinned Trojan seemed to be standing still."[17] Boston went down in order only in the seventh.

Deal's dash for third in the ninth capped off a game that featured audacious but often overly-aggressive baserunning. The other successful swipes included Deal stealing second in the top of the second with two outs,[18] and Barry stealing second during Schang's ninth-inning fan.

In addition to Schang gunning down Evers, James picked off Murphy pitcher-to-first-to-shortstop in the first, Hank Gowdy threw out Schang trying to take third on a pitch of the dirt after Wally had broken up James's 15-in-a-row run with a sixth-inning two-bagger down the left-field line,[19] and James picked off another batter – Collins this time – after Eddie had reached on an infield single to second with two outs in the seventh.

The final two baserunning mistakes for the Americans had similar outcomes but resulted in different reactions. Some, including Schang himself, thought Schang safe at third – postgame photographic evidence seemed to indicate that he had taken the bag – but umpire Bill Byron ruled otherwise.[20] The *Boston Evening American* credited Gowdy with "pegg[ing] him out, assisted somewhat by a perfectly splendid and stouthearted tagging stunt by our old acquaintance, slight Charlie [Deal]."[21]

Byron's decision made Plank's grounder to short an inning-ender rather than an RBI that would have scored Schang and given the Philadelphians a critical 1-0 lead. In his column, Cobb implied that Byron, a National League umpire, might have exhibited bias in his call. No such controversy resulted from the Collins play, in which James caught Eddie napping as the latter hung his head after failing to retreat safely back to first.

Evers saw this as swift and divine retribution by the baseball gods. Having thought that his snap throw had in fact beaten Collins to first base, Evers after the safe call "threw his hands over his head, and everyone knew what he meant."[22]

Amazingly, Schang and Collins, the only two Athletics with base hits, both ended up making outs on the bases before a fellow Philadelphian could complete his turn at bat. Whether the Athletics took the Braves too lightly or failed to focus on the game with Federal League riches lingering in the minds of many ballplayers remains unclear; indisputably, however, in Game Two Boston played like a confident veteran bunch while the Mackmen made multiple mistakes, an odd state of affairs given that Philadelphia played Game Two, its fourth World Series in five years, in the friendly confines of Shibe Park.

The Braves did enjoy, however, a loyal and vocal fan base that made the trip from Boston to Philadelphia to cheer on the visitors and visit invective on the home team. The Royal Rooters, who had hassled Honus Wagner and his Pittsburgh comrades in 1903, stayed true to their city. Former Boston Mayor John Fitzgerald, known then as Honey Fitz and later as the grandfather of President John F. Kennedy, said "in the most courteous manner [that] Plank was one hundred years old, had a glass arm and was blind of one eye."[23]

Taking two in Philadelphia left the brash Bostonians feel that their miraculous run would continue. Stallings told his equipment manager to pack the road uniforms of the Braves and take them home rather than leave them at Shibe Park. Stallings said, "We won't be coming back. It'll be all over after the two games in Boston."[24]

Lest readers today accuse writers from yesteryear of spinning yarns in the afterglow of victory, Stallings' players made similar statements at the time. Gowdy hardly hedged: "We're out for four straight and it looks all the more and more that we were going to get them."

Herbie Moran, who did not even play in Game Two, predicted flatly: "The Braves will win four straight."[25]

Like the Chicago Cubs from 1906 to 1910, the only other team that then had reached the World Series with the same frequency as the Athletics, but had dropped off the pace due to age, the loss of Evers, and the lure of the Federal League, the end of this great Philadelphia squad seemed suddenly near.

Damon Runyon observed at the time, "The star of the American League seems to be slowly sinking."[26] Norman Macht wrote nearly a century after the game, "Nobody spoke in the home clubhouse after the game. Plank stood on a stool, head in his hands, while the others silently showered, dressed, and left."[27]

One could hardly fault Plank, at least, for his efforts in defeat.[28] He "pitched those nine exciting, thrilling innings just like the old master that he is. … Hats off to Ancient Edward, like his rival, Matty, as great, or greater, in defeat as ever he was in victory."[29]

Newspaper reporters invoked Christy Mathewson when summarizing the efforts of both the losing and winning hurlers. "James … twirled a quality of baseball that would have been a credit to a Mathewson, a Johnson or a Rudolph."[30]

In his own newspaper article, Manager Stallings paid tribute to his winning pitcher, writing of James: "To him, almost alone, belongs the verdict."[31]

The last words belonged to the National League's Chalmers Award winner in 1914, Johnny Evers, who, after all, had a better view of the game than any sportswriter or historian. Though viewed today as a fierce partisan rather than a dispassionate observer, Evers astutely and evenly summed up the compelling contest, stating, "Bill James pitched wonderful ball, but he had little on that old veteran Plank."[32]

This article is included in *The Miracle Braves of 1914: Boston's Original Worst-to-First World Series Champions* (SABR, 2014), edited by Bill Nowlin.

NOTES

1   J.R. Cary, "Charles Deal, The Man Who Made Good in the Pinch," *Baseball Magazine*, February 1915, 54. Massachusetts Governor David Walsh said after the game, "If I were Mr. Deal tonight I should not swap places with anybody on earth."

2   *Boston Evening Record*, October 11, 1914: 2.

3   Devore "considers himself a lucky fellow. Devore was turned over to Cincinnati by McGraw last year. Cincinnati sent him to the Phillies, and from here he went to Boston. ... He believes he is lucky because he was born on Friday the thirteenth." In "Punch Your Head' Stallings to Mack," *Philadelphia Bulletin*, October 8, 1914: 17.

4   John I. Taylor, *Boston Globe*, October 11, 1914: 9. Taylor was the former owner of the Red Sox.

5   "World's Series Echoes," *Sporting Life*, October 17, 1914: 3.

6   *Boston Evening Record*, October 11, 1914: 1. The sun had affected flies earlier in the game as well: "Baker flew to Whitted, who lost the ball in the sun, but finally spotted it again and made a fine catch after a long run." J.C. O'Leary, *Boston Globe*, October 10 (evening edition), 1914: 1. A little more than 15 years later, Chicago Cubs center fielder Hack Wilson would more famously lose a fly in the Shibe Park sun, a misplay that would help the Athletics win Game Four of their World Series 10-8 and eventually the Series in five games.

7   Damon Runyon, *Boston Evening American*, October 11, 1914: 3 of special World's Series section. In a newspaper column after the game, Barry himself wrote, "I didn't throw the ball because I couldn't. Schang's throw to me was perfect, but the ball slipped out of my hand and popped up on the top of my fingers and I couldn't throw it." Jack Barry, "Ball Slipped from Barry's Hand while Deal Was Stealing Third," *Philadelphia Bulletin*, October 12, 1914: 12.

8   *Boston Evening Record*, October 11, 1914: 1.

9   *Boston Evening Record*, October 11, 1914: 1.

10 John J. Ward, *Baseball Magazine*, February 1915: 33.

11 Nick Flatley, *Boston Evening American*, October 11, 1914, page 2 of a special World's Series section.

12 Newspaper accounts of the game use the higher figures; a history uses the lower one. T.H. Murnane in the *Boston Globe* had 149, and the *Philadelphia Inquirer* had 132. Norman L. Macht had 129 in *Connie Mack and the Early Years of Baseball*. Both papers agree that James threw just 92 pitches. The *Philadelphia Inquirer* had James at 76 pitches through eight innings, with innings three through eight at no more than ten pitches per frame. James threw 16 pitches in the pressure-packed ninth, 13 more than he had thrown in his most stressful inning to that point, the second.

13 *New York Times*, October 11, 1914.

14 *Boston Evening American*, October 11, 1914, page 1 of the special World's Series section.

15 *New York Times*, October 11, 1914.

16 William A. Phelon, *Baseball Magazine*, February 1915: 12.

17 Damon Runyon, *Boston Evening American*, October 11, 1914, page 3 of the special World's Series section.

18 "Happenings by three seem to follow that Deal boy. In the first game he walloped into three (double) plays, and yesterday he three times forces runners again before he landed that long fly that Strunk misjudged." "Braves Again Victors, Athletics' Falter in Field with Bats Silenced," *Philadelphia Inquirer*, October 11, 1914: sports section 3.

19 "Wally Schang suddenly broke the monotony of hitless Athletics' frames by driving a two-base hit past third, making second by sliding on his stomach and beating by a scant fraction of an inch a beautiful throw-in by Cather from deep left corner." Ed McGrath, *Boston Post*, October 11, 1914: 11.

20 "Photographs of the play also show Schang on the base with Deal still waiting for the ball." Hugh S. Fullerton, "Mack Keeps Men Secluded before Game in Boston," [Philadelphia] *Evening Ledger*, October 12, 1914: 2.

21 Nick Flatley, *Boston Evening American*, October 11, 1914, page 2, special World's Series section. "'It's all over and there's no use of complaining,' said Schang, 'but Deal hasn't touched me yet on that play. I made a hook slide and caught the outside of the bag with my foot. Deal's gloved hand swept around quickly but he never touched me. Byron called the play so quickly that he said I was out before the play was finished.'" "Mack and Braves Each Make a Tally Early in the Game," Philadelphia Bulletin, October 12, 1914: 2. According to Retrosheet, Lord Byron was umpiring first base, not third base, in Game Two.

22 John J. Hallahan, *Boston Herald*, October 11, 1914: 2.

23 F.J. McIsaac, *Boston Evening American*, October 11, 1914: page 4, special World's Series section.

24 Harold Kaese, *The Boston Braves* (Boston: Northeastern University Press, 2004), 163.

25 Nick Flatley, *Boston Evening American*, October 11, 1914: page 4, special World's Series section.

26 Damon Runyon, *Boston Evening American*, October 11, 1914: page 3, special World's Series section.

27 Norman L. Macht, *Connie Mack and the Early Years of Baseball* (Lincoln: University of Nebraska Press, 2007), 642.

28 This was the last but hardly the first time when Plank lacked run support in the World Series: "Eddie Plank suffered his fourth shutout in world's series battles." "Braves Again Victors, Athletics' Falter in Field with Bats Silenced," *Philadelphia Inquirer*, October 11, 1914: sports section p. 1.

29 Nick Flatley, *Boston Evening American*, October 11, 1914: page 2, special World's Series section.

30 Walter E. Hapgood, *Boston Herald*, October 11, 1914, 1.

31 George Stallings, *Boston Evening American*, October 11, 1914: page 4, special World's Series section.

32 C.P. Stack, *Baseball Magazine*, February 1915, 73.

BULLET JOE BUSH FIRES NO-HITTER

August 26, 1916
Philadelphia Athletics 5, Cleveland Indians 0

By Gregory H. Wolf

"Such a brand of revenge was never seen before," gushed sportswriter Harry P. Edwards in the *Cleveland Plain Dealer*.[1] In the game after getting knocked out of the box, yielding six hits and five runs (though just two earned) in a three-inning start resulting in his 20th loss of the season, Philadelphia Athletics right-hander Bullet Joe Bush held the Cleveland Indians hitless, retiring the final 27 batters he faced.

Athletics owner-manager Connie Mack had little to be excited about in 1916. The days of winning four pennants and three World Series titles in a five-year span (1910-1914) seemed like an eternity ago. Rapidly rising player salaries and lower revenues forced the Tall Tactician to sell his star players, among them Eddie Collins and Home Run Baker, and had lost others to the upstart Federal League, like hurlers Chief Bender and Eddie Plank. The A's plummeted to the worst record (43-109) in the big leagues in 1915 and it was even more dismal thus far in 1916 as they prepared to play the final contest of a four-game series against the Indians. Mack's club once again had the worst slate (25-91) in the majors and had endured an unimaginably futile 4-56 stretch. Indians skipper Lee Fohl had transformed the Tribe from a seventh-place team in '15 into a

pennant contender, who trailed the front-running Boston Red Sox by 6½ games.

One of the few bright spots for Mack was 23-year-old "speed demon hurler" Joe Bush.[2] The 5-foot-9, 175-pound Minnesotan debuted for the Mackmen as a teenager in 1912, and produced a 15-6 slate as a swingman for the world champions the next season, a role he occupied again for the pennant winners in 1914, going 17-13. Lauded by the *Philadelphia Inquirer* for his "great curve and blinding speed," Bush was emerging as one of the most effective and durable hurlers in the junior circuit, despite his 13-20 record thus far in '16, ranking third in complete games (21 in 27 starts) and fourth in strikeouts (128).[3] His mound opponent was 26-year-old right-hander Stan Coveleski (14-10), who had had a cup of coffee with the A's in 1912 but was now with the Indians in his first full season.

The demise of the Athletics dynasty was followed by an implosion of attendance at Shibe Park, the steel-and-concrete ballpark that opened in 1909. The A's averaged only 2,427 spectators per contest in 1916, the second lowest figure in the majors. Attendance for this game isn't available; however, given that it was a Saturday afternoon game on a warm, late summer afternoon when Sunday baseball in the City of Brotherly Love was still banned, those who did venture out to the north side of the city witnessed a historical game.

If only he could have taken back one pitch. No doubt Bush must have had such thoughts after this game, maybe for the rest of his life. He walked the first batter of the game, Jack Graney, and then proceeded to retire the next 27 batters. The first was Terry Turner, whose sacrifice moved Graney up a station. The Indians were a "meek and lowly lot" thereafter, gushed the *Inquirer*.[4] Edwards wrote admiringly that "Bush simply had everything, control, speed and curves" and added that his "change of pace was amazing. The break of his fastball was marvelous."[5] The *Inquirer* likewise extolled Bush's "bewildering change-of-pace," which the paper opined "stood Lee Fohl's hard-hitting bunch on their heads."[6]

Bush did not yield the semblance of a hit. The *Plain Dealer* noted that "not even a close decision" nor "a brilliant play had to be made."[7] The only tense moment occurred in the fifth inning when catcher Val Picinich grabbed Chick Gandil's bunt in front of home plate but "threw wild" to first, erasing the runner "by a fraction of a stride," according to the *Inquirer*.[8] Just 19 years old, Picinich was one month removed from playing semipro ball and was making only his 15th big-league start as a catcher.

Coveleski, who eventually went on to a Hall of Fame career, winning 20 or more games five times and posting 215 lifetime victories, had a tough day and was plagued by some shoddy defense. In the second inning, Wally Schang hit a fly ball to right-center field, which right fielder Braggo Roth should have caught; however, he thought center fielder Tris Speaker would take the ball, and suddenly stopped.[9] The ball dropped between the two flychasers and Schang raced to third. Two batters later, Stuffy McInnis "skimmed a roller between" shortstop Bill Wambsganss' feet to drive in the game's first run.[10]

The Athletics loaded the bases with no outs in the next frame, yet came away with just a solitary run. After Jimmy Walsh led off with a single and was forced by Amos Strunk, Schang connected on what the *Plain Dealer* described as a "freak hit," a tailor-made double-play bouncer back to the mound, but the ball "took a peculiar bound" and Coveleski had no play at either first or second.[11] Nap Lajoie's free pass filled the bags and then McInnis squeezed home Strunk on a bunt to first.

Coveleski came undone in the fifth, yielding three straight extra-base knocks. Picinich led off with a double and moved to third on a passed ball. Bush, who eventually transformed into an adept hitter, batting .253 in his career, belted an RBI double. Whitey Witt followed with a triple to plate Bush, and subsequently scored on Walsh's sacrifice bunt to make it 5-0. Fritz Coumbe replaced Coveleski to start the sixth and hurled three frames of scoreless relief.

Bush took the mound in the ninth three outs from his first no-hitter and the third in franchise history. Weldon Henley tossed the first, on July 22, 1905, against the St. Louis Browns, at League Park, where the Athletics played before Shibe Park opened in 1909. Chief Bender tossed the second (and first in Shibe Park), on May 12, 1910, against the Cleveland Naps. With heightened excitement, and undoubtedly adrenaline-induced nervousness, Bush had a three-ball count on the first two hitters, Steve O'Neill and Bob Coleman, pinch-hitting for Coumbe, before striking each out. Bush completed his no-no by inducing Graney, the Indians' only baserunner of the game, to up to McInnis at first to end the game in 1 hour and 39 minutes.[12]

As the final out was recorded, an estimated 500 fans poured onto the field to congratulate the young hurler, who, newspapers noted entered "baseball's mythical Hall of Fame," a much-used euphemism for monumental accomplishments, such as a no-hitter.[13] Hundreds of fans were still waiting at the park to catch a glimpse of Bush as he went home.

In a commanding effort, Bush fanned seven and induced 12 popups (eight of those to the outfield) and eight grounders. Nonetheless, Bush's no-hitter couldn't disguise the fact that the A's were a terrible ballclub en route to arguably the worst season in post-1900 big-league history, finishing with a 36-117 record and (as of 2021) a major-league record-low .235 winning percentage. Bush struggled, too, after his gem, losing his next four starts, plagued by wildness (16 earned runs and 20 walks in 31⅓ innings) before tossing his eighth shutout in his final start of the season to finish with 15 wins and a big-league-most 24 losses. Bush went on to win 196 games in his career (184 losses), including 26 victories for the pennant-winning New York Yankees in 1922, and played on three World Series champions (Athletics in 1913, Boston Red Sox in 1918, and Yankees in 1923). He never threw another no-hitter, though he hurled three one-hit shutouts.

SOURCES

In addition to the sources cited in the Notes, the author accessed Retrosheet.org, Baseball-Reference.com, SABR.org, and *The Sporting News* archive via Paper of Record.

NOTES

1   Henry P. Edwards, "Indians Blanked When Joe Bush Pitches No-Hit Game for Mackmen," (Cleveland) *Plain Dealer*, August 27, 1916: III, 1.

2   Edwards.

3   "Bush Ascends to No-Hit Pedestal," *Philadelphia Inquirer*, August 27, 1916: 53.

4   "Bush Ascends to No-Hit Pedestal."

5   Edwards.

6   "Bush Ascends to No-Hit Pedestal."

7   Edwards.

8   "Bush Ascends to No-Hit Pedestal."

9   Edwards.

10   Edwards.

11   Edwards.

12   Game time from "Bush Ascends to No-Hit Pedestal."

13   "Bush Ascends to No-Hit Pedestal."

Jack Nabors Finishes Season with a 1-20 Record

September 28, 1916
Washington Senators 4, Philadelphia Athletics 1

By J. G. Preston

The 1916 Philadelphia Athletics were the worst major-league team of the twentieth century. And the unfortunate man who bore the brunt of their badness was pitcher Herman John "Jack" Nabors.

Just two years earlier, the A's had won 99 games for the best record in baseball. But facing financial pressure from the Federal League, owner-manager Connie Mack either sold his star players or let them go to the Feds rather than meet their salary demands. Hall of Famers Eddie Collins, Eddie Plank, Chief Bender, and Frank "Home Run" Baker were all elsewhere when the 1915 season began; Jack Barry, Eddie Murphy, Bob Shawkey, and Herb Pennock were sold or waived in midseason. The gutted A's finished 1915 with a record of 43-109, 56 games worse than the year before

It got worse in 1916.

After splitting a doubleheader with the Yankees on May 30, 1916, the A's had a record of 14-22 and weren't even in last place. (They were a half-game ahead of the St. Louis Browns.) But the Yankees swept a twin bill from the A's the next day, starting a remarkable stretch that saw the A's go 5-58 through August 8. On September 27 they lost their 114th game of the season, breaking the twentieth-century record for losses set by the 1904 Senators.

The next day Jack Nabors took the mound.

Nabors had made a remarkable rise to the major leagues the year before, when Mack purchased him from the Newnan (Georgia) Cowetas of the Class D Georgia-Alabama League. Nabors had gained national attention on June 15, 1915, when he pitched a 13-inning no-hitter against Talladega (Alabama). He didn't walk anyone, either; two men reached on errors, preventing him from a perfect game.[1] He also pitched a 15-inning shutout against Anniston (Alabama) in which he allowed only three hits.[2]

Nabors had a 12-1 record when Mack purchased him in July after what *Sporting Life* termed "a spirited bidding contest."[3] Of course, Mack may not have had perfect information about his new acquisition. An item in *Sporting Life* in July 1915 claimed Nabors was "but 20 years of age," but he was actually dominating Class D competition at the age of 27.[4]

It didn't go well for Nabors when he reached Philadelphia. He allowed eight runs in his first start and nine in his second, and he finished the season with an 0-5 mark. But with the A's, as noted, rather short on talent, Nabors was still with the team in 1916, and he was the Opening Day starter against the defending World Series champion Red Sox, pitching four shutout innings before being relieved. He finally broke through with a victory in his third start of the season, on April 22, pitching a complete game in a 6-2 win over Boston; both runs against him were unearned. (Fielding was an issue for the 1916 A's. They committed 314 errors in 154 games, leading to 191 unearned runs, nearly one-fourth of all the runs they allowed.)

But after that, given little support by his teammates (in addition to their defensive woes, the A's averaged less than three runs a game), Nabors saw the losses pile up, despite some fine performances along the way. He lost two games in which he did not allow an earned run, and three others in which he allowed only one. On June 24 he took a one-hitter into the ninth inning against the Red Sox, only to lose. He took a 1-19 record to the mound against the Washington Senators on September 28.

The A's took a 1-0 lead in the third inning when Thomas Healy singled, went to second on a bunt by Lee King, and scored from second on a wild pitch by Bert Gallia.[5] Meanwhile, Nabors held the Senators scoreless on four hits through five innings.[6] But Washington tied the game when Nabors' defense let him down in the sixth. Joe Leonard singled with one out, and after Eddie Foster flied out, Mike Menosky hit a groundball to Roy Grover at second base for what should have been the third out. But Grover fumbled it, and his throw to second to try to retire Leonard was too late. Elmer Smith followed with a single to score Leonard.[7]

Washington broke the tie in the seventh inning. Howie Shanks and Ray Morgan opened the inning with singles, moved up a base on a sacrifice bunt by John Henry and scored on a sacrifice fly by Gallia.[8] (Morgan's hit, a line drive through the legs of third baseman Healy, who was playing in anticipating a bunt, led to some comedy

from Senators third-base coach and noted baseball clown Nick Altrock. "After that Nick did some fancy ducking and imitating of Healey [sic] until the inning closed," according to the *Washington Evening Star*.[9]) Nabors held the Senators scoreless in the eighth inning before being removed for a pinch-hitter; reliever Rube Bressler allowed two runs in the ninth to make the final score 4-1, Washington.

The loss was Nabors' 20th of the season (something not noted in the newspaper accounts of the game) and his 19th straight, still the major-league record for most consecutive losses in a season. This despite the fact that he allowed only two runs in eight innings. "It was one of Nabors' best exhibitions," according to the *Philadelphia Inquirer*, "for he forgot to pass a man [in other words, he didn't walk anyone], eliminated wild pitches from his repertoire and in general behaved with all the skill and cunning a regular moundsman uses in his daily labors."[10]

This would be Nabors' final start of the season, although he pitched twice more in relief, including in the final game of the season, in which he worked the final four innings to earn a save by modern standards as the A's knocked off the pennant-winning Red Sox and their 23-game winner Babe Ruth. With a final record of 1-20, Nabors still holds the major-league record for most losses in a season by a pitcher with no more than one win. (His 1916 teammate Tom Sheehan ranks second in that category with a 1-16 mark, a record equaled by Mike Parrott of the Mariners in 1980 and Anthony Young of the Mets in 1993.)

Nabors appeared in only two more major-league games before the A's traded him to Indianapolis of the American Association in April 1917, leaving him with a career record of 1-25. The rest of his life did not go well; after serving in the US Army in 1918, he came down with a severe case of the flu during the influenza pandemic in the winter of 1918-19 and was never well after that. He died of tuberculosis in 1923, only 35 years old.[11]

And as for the 1916 A's? They finished the season with a record of 36-117. After the schedule expanded to 162 games, both the 1962 Mets (120) and 2003 Tigers (119) lost more games, but the A's had the lowest winning percentage of any twentieth-century team.

SOURCES

Accounts of this game in the *Philadelphia Inquirer*, *Washington Post*, *Washington Evening Star* and *Washington Times* were accessed via Newspapers. com. *Sporting Life* was accessed through the LA84 Foundation's Digital Library Collections (digital.la84. org/digital/collection/p17103coll17). Stephen V. Rice has a fine accounting of Jack Nabors' 1916 season in his biography of Nabors in the Society for American Baseball Research's Baseball Biography Project (sabr.org/bioproj/person/d10f6d3d).

NOTES

1 "A New Pitching Record," *Sporting Life*, June 26, 1915: 10.

2 "A World's Record Pitcher," *Sporting Life*, July 17, 1915: 8.

3 "Mack Lands Minor League Marvel," *Sporting Life*, July 31, 1915: 3.

4 "A World's Record Pitcher," *Sporting Life*, July 17, 1915: 8.

5 Stanley T. Millikin, "Gallia Is Strong Throughout; Nabors Weakens Late in Game," *Washington Post*, September 29, 1916: 8.

6 Box score with the number of hits per inning in the *Philadelphia Inquirer*, September 29, 1916: 14.

7 "Griffs Wide Awake," *Evening Star* (Washington), September 29, 1916: 18. The box score of this game on Retrosheet.org shows that none of the runs allowed by Nabors were unearned, but this run clearly was. On the other hand, the box score in the *Washington Post* shows that Nabors allow no earned runs, and the run he allowed in the seventh clearly was.

8 Millikin. The Retrosheet box score shows Gallia with a sacrifice hit, not a sacrifice fly, but the *Washington Post* and *Washington Times* game stories say Gallia hit a fly ball to center fielder Amos Strunk, and the box scores in the *Post*, the *Washington Times* and the *Evening Star* all show Gallia with a sacrifice fly.

9 "Rice Shows Swat Form," *Evening Star*, September 29, 1916: 18.

10 "Tainted Fielding Lost Nabors Game," *Philadelphia Inquirer*, September 29, 1916: 14.

11 Stephen V. Rice, "Jack Nabors," SABR Baseball Biography Project, sabr.org/bioproj/person/d10f6d3d.

Four Late-Game Comebacks Result in Dizzying Victory

May 20, 1918
Philadelphia Athletics 5, Detroit Tigers 4 (14 Innings)

By Paul E. Doutrich

The 1918 season did not start well for either the Philadelphia Athletics or the Detroit Tigers. After a month the two teams found themselves at the bottom of the American League standings. On May 20 they met for the first time to play a four-game series.[1] For the A's, the games provided an opportunity to put some distance between themselves and the cellar-dwelling Tigers. For Detroit it was a chance to trade places in the standings with Philadelphia. As added incentive, Detroit manager Hughie Jennings promised his players that if they won three of the four games, he would buy them each a straw hat.[2]

The game began well for the Athletics. Playing in front of hometown fans Connie Mack's crew put a run on the board in the bottom first inning. More specifically, Manny Kopp put a run up for the Athletics. Batting second, he smacked a pitch over Detroit's right fielder, Harry Heilmann, that rolled to the wall. Gliding into third with a triple, the speedy Kopp scored when Donie Bush, the Tigers shortstop, hopped his relay throw past third baseman Ossie Vitt. Bush, known for his defensive prowess, was acknowledged to be among the best shortstops in baseball but on this day, he began the game with a rare run-scoring error.

Neither team scored again until Harry Heilmann came to the plate in the Detroit fifth inning. To that point Athletics pitcher Elmer Myers had kept the Tigers hitless. Heilmann changed that by drilling a pitch into the left-field stands. It was his first home run of the season. He would hit four more before military service prematurely ended his season. With the American participation in World War I rapidly expanding, the government decreed that as of July 1 all men employed in nonessential occupations must either work in war-related jobs or be eligible for the military draft. Ballplayers were deemed nonessential. The edict was challenged but on July 19 the "work-or-fight" policy was upheld. As did several other players, including A's shortstop Red Shannon, Heilmann immediately enlisted in the US Navy. Many other players chose to find jobs in war industries after the season ended.[3] Babe Ruth, for instance, worked at a Bethlehem Steel plant in Lebanon, Pennsylvania. Of course, Heilmann was not thinking about future circumstances as he rounded the bases that day in Philadelphia. He had just tied the game.

The next inning Detroit added another run. Ty Cobb worked Meyers for a two-out walk. Cobb stole second and went to third on a wild pitch.

Bobby Veach, the Tigers' left fielder and cleanup hitter, followed Cobb to the plate. Veach, Cobb, and Heilmann, comprised arguably the best-hitting outfield in baseball. Veach was the RBI man of the trio. Two of the previous three years he had led the American League in RBIs and he was on his way to topping the league again in 1918. A gregarious, mild-mannered player, Veach did not fit Cobb's image of a competitor even though he was one of the more feared power hitters in the American League. This time up he banged a Myers pitch off the knee of Philadelphia's first baseman, George Burns, driving in Cobb with the go-ahead run.

Through the next three innings Myers dominated Tigers hitters. Meanwhile, the Athletics unsuccessfully pecked away at Detroit's pitcher, George Dauss. Dubbed "Hooks" because he had such a good curveball, Dauss was a crafty pitcher who, despite giving up base hits, was able to keep Philadelphia off the scoreboard after the first inning.

The Athletics came to the plate in the bottom of the ninth still down a run. Burns led off with a single. Third baseman Larry Gardner, one of the few college graduates playing in the major leagues then, followed with a bunt single and shortstop Shannon walked, loading the bases with no one out. Philadelphia manager Connie Mack chose to pull Joe Dugan in favor of Rube Oldring. In the 1920s Jumpin' Joe became the regular third baseman on the legendary Murderers' Row Yankees teams, but in 1918 he was a sub-200 hitter who had yet to establish himself. His replacement bounced one back to Dauss who forced Burns at the plate. Next up was Wicky McAvoy, the A's catcher, who dropped a Texas Leaguer into left. Gardner scampered home with the tying run but Shannon, unsure whether the ball would be caught, was forced at third. Dauss then got Myers to end the inning.

The Tigers retook the lead in the top of the 10th on a muffed infield fly. Bush led off with a groundball that shortstop Shannon booted. Ossie Vitt sacrificed Bush to second and Ty Cobb smacked a sharp line drive off Myers, sending Bush to third. With runners on the corners, the A's intentionally walked the dangerous Veach and instead pitched to Heilmann. The strategy appeared to work. The Tigers right fielder popped one to Claude Davidson, who had replaced Dugan at second base. Perhaps Davidson simply misplayed the ball or perhaps he was trying to set up a double play and forgot about the infield-fly rule. Regardless, he let the ball drop. Bush took advantage of the mistake and streaked home with the go-ahead run.

Again, three outs away from a defeat, the A's fought back. Right fielder Charlie Jamieson, a converted pitcher whose speed made him an excellent leadoff hitter, walked to start the 10th. Kopp sacrificed him to second and he scored on center fielder Tillie Walker's single.

After a scoreless 11th inning, the Tigers got another run in the top of the 12th. With one out, singles by Vitt and Cobb put the go-ahead run on second base. As they had in the ninth, Mack and company chose to issue an intentional pass to the Tigers hard-hitting left fielder Bobby Veach and pitch to Heilmann. Again, the strategy backfired. Heilmann pounded a fly ball to Kopp in left field, enabling Vitt to score easily.

For the third time the Athletics found themselves at the brink of defeat and for the third time they avoided it. This time with a bit of controversy. With one out in the bottom of the inning, Walker and Burns singled. Next, Gardner hit a tailor-made double-play ball back to Dauss on the mound. Dauss fired to Vitt at third who pegged one across the diamond to Lee Dressen at first, apparently getting Gardner by a couple of steps, according to the Tigers.[4] Umpire Brick Owens, who "couldn't bear to see Gardner perish on the last end of a double play," disagreed.[5] Instead, he called Gardiner safe. One batter later, Burns trotted home with the tying run on Shannon's single.

The closest thing to a threat either team offered in the 13th was a long fly ball off the bat of Detroit's Ossie Vitt that Kopp hauled in just in front of the left-field wall. The Tigers again went quietly in the 14th. The Athletics did not.

As evening shadows began to stretch across Shibe Park, Manny Kopp opened the inning with a walk. One out later he stole second. Pitching carefully to Burns, who already had four hits, Dauss plunked him on the thigh. Gardner then shot a single to right that filled the bases. With one out, Red Shannon came to the plate with a chance to be a hero. Instead he popped up to Young at second. As light-hitting Claude Davidson approached the plate, it appeared that Detroit might escape the threat. Dauss's first two pitches were both strikes. Then on the third pitch Kopp took things into his own hands. As Dauss went into his windup the fleet-footed left fielder broke for the plate. The pitch came in low and outside, enabling Kopp's "feet-first slide (to) beat the pitch to the plate."[6] So ended "the wildest, weirdest and most nerve-racking battle seen this year."[7]

Of the 4,500 spectators still in Shibe Park, none was more excited than the usually composed Connie Mack. Commented a sportswriter, "It was the first time in history we have seen Connie Mack leave the players' bench to grasp one of his athletes by the hand and slap him on the back for winning a ball game."[8]

SOURCES

In addition to the sources cited in the Notes, the author accessed Retrosheet.org, Baseball-Reference.com, and SABR.org.

NOTES

1   Only two games of the four-game series were played. Tuesday's game was rained out and made up on July 6. Thursday's game was also rained out and made up on July 23, in a six-game series.

2   Harry Bullion, "Told About Tigers," *Detroit Free Press*, May 21, 1918: 11.

3   The War Department allowed the major leagues until September 1 to complete the regular season before players would be drafted.

4   Harry Bullion, "Kopp Steals Home to Win Long Battle," *Detroit Free Press*, May 21, 1918: 11.

5   Bullion, "Kopp Steals Home to Win Long Battle."

6   Jim Nasium, "Mannie Kopp Stealing Home with Two Out in the 14th Wins for Mackmen," *Philadelphia Inquirer*, May 21, 1918: 12.

7   Robert W. Maxwell, "Jackson and Others Who Sought Deferred Classification Ordered to Report for Army Duty at Once," *Philadelphia Evening Public Ledger*, May 21, 1918: 12.

8   Jim Nasium.

SHAWKEY FANS 15 AND WINS 20TH

September 27, 1919
New York Yankees 9, Philadelphia Athletics 2
(Second Game of a Doubleheader)

By Kevin Larkin

Before the Yankees-Athletics doubleheader on September 27, 1919, New York pitcher Bob Shawkey had won 20 games in a season once. In 1916, his first full season with the Yankees, the man known as Sailor won a league-leading 24 games. Shawkey was 24-14 and retrospectively had a league-leading eight saves.

Entering the doubleheader, the third-place Yankees (77-59, .566) led the fourth-place Detroit Tigers (78-60, .565) by one percentage point. With just three games left on the schedule, the Yankees trailed the second-place Cleveland Indians by 5½ games. The woeful Athletics were in last place with a record of 36-101.

Shortstop Roger Peckinpaugh, batting .307, and Frank "Home Run" Baker (10 round-trippers) led the Yankees offense. The Boston Red Sox trailed the first-place Chicago White Sox by 20 games, but Babe Ruth was making a mockery of the home-run race in his last season before being traded to the Yankees.

In the first game of the twin bill, 35-year-old veteran hurler Jack Quinn pitched the Yankees to a 4-1 victory, allowing 10 hits, walking two, and striking out six. Second baseman Del Pratt led the offense with a home run and single, and three runs batted in.

The Athletics had been in last place in the American League since 1915 after owner-manager Connie Mack sold off most of his star players following the stunning upset loss to Boston's "Miracle Braves" in the 1914 World Series. Philadelphia did not escape the AL cellar until 1922.

The Yankees' pitcher for the second game, right-hander Shawkey, 28, broke into the major leagues in 1913 with the Athletics. In June of 1915 Mack sold him to the Yankees for $3,000.

Athletics pitcher Pat Martin, 25 years old, was making just his second major-league start. In fact, Martin would make just five more starts in the major leagues, as his career ended on June 6, 1920 in a game won by the Yankees, 12-6, with Martin not figuring in the decision.

Shawkey had picked up his 19th victory three days before, on September 24, pitching all 13 innings and beating Waite Hoyt and the Red Sox, 2-1. In his start before that, he gave up seven runs in 5⅓ innings in relief of Hank Thormahlen in an 11-2 loss to the Chicago White Sox.

With just one game to go after the doubleheader, the Yankees hoped to hold off the Tigers and retain their third-place finish for a larger share of postseason money.[1]

The Yankees made their intentions known immediately. Right fielder Sammy Vick led off the game with a single and Roger Peckinpaugh walked. Vick went to third on Baker's force-play grounder. First baseman Wally Pipp popped out but Del Pratt walked, loading the bases, and Duffy Lewis's single scored Vick. Center fielder Chick Fewster slammed a bases-clearing triple, and the Yankees led 4-0. Catcher Muddy Ruel's popout to second baseman Jimmy Dykes ended the inning.

The Athletics got a run in the second inning when Shawkey walked Dykes and Art Ewoldt and Ewoldt scored on a single by A's catcher Lena Styles.

After a scoreless third inning, New York added a run when Fewster singled to left-center field, Shawkey sent him to third with a single to left field, and Fewster scored on Vick's fly ball to Amos Strunk in right field.

The teams were scoreless for the next 4½ innings, until the top of the ninth inning, when four more Yankee baserunners crossed the plate with two outs. Peckinpaugh walked. Baker's single to center and Wally Pipp's bunt single loaded the bases. Del Pratt singled to center field and Philadelphia center fielder Frank Welch made a bad throw trying to pick off a runner. When the dust had cleared, all four Yankees, including Pratt, had scored.[2]

Down 9-1 going into the home half of the ninth, the Athletics got a run. With two outs, Charlie High pinch-hit for Al Wingo and reached first on Peckinpaugh's error. High stole second and third, and came home on Ivy Griffin's single. Amos Strunk's groundout to second ended the game. Shawkey had held the Athletics to seven hits and struck out 15 batters.

Sportswriters credited the Yankees' sweep to the nearly unhittable pitching of Quinn and Shawkey. Wrote one Philadelphia scribe, "Through the paraspinous pitching by Jack and Bob[3] and more or less clouting on the part of their associates in the enterprise, the Yankees beat our Athletics in two ballgames, the score being 4 to 1 and 9 to 2."[4] The double victory over the disheartened Athletics gave New York a half-game lead over Detroit in the race for third place in the American League, and the New York sportswriters took a more sanguine view: "The team of Mack was helpless before Bob and he registered 15 strikeouts, the record for the season."[5]

Philadelphia Inquirer sportswriter Edgar Forrest Wolfe, who wrote under the playful name Jim Nasium, waxed almost poetic about Shawkey's strikeouts. "During the progress of that record battle yesterday another record of eleven years standing had a minor squeak from being kicked totally out of the succulent statistics as Shawkey came within one record for strikeouts in the American League set by Rube Waddell against the Athletics in 1908 by Rube Waddell," he wrote.[6]

Before his 15-strikeout performance, Shawkey had never reached double figures in strikeouts. and after this 15-strikeout game would reach double figures in strikeouts two more times, the first time on July 18, 1922, against the Detroit Tigers (10 strikeouts) and on July 5, 1926, against the Athletics (10 whiffs again).

Shawkey won 20 or more games four times in his career: 1916 (24-14), 1919 (20-11), 1920 (20-13), and 1922 (20-12). He pitched for the Yankees from 1915 to 1927, when he retired.

Shawkey's feat was not the only thing that made the headlines in baseball on September 27, 1919. The Red Sox' Babe Ruth hit his major-league record-breaking 29th home run of the season in a loss to the Washington Senators at Griffith Stadium.

SOURCES

Besides the sources cited in the Notes, the author consulted the Baseball-Reference.com and Retrosheet.org websites.

NOTES

1   "Mackmen Defeated Twice by Yankees," *New York Times*, September 28, 1919: 117.

2   "Mackmen Defeated Twice By Yankees."

3   At this long remove, one can only assume that some Philadelphia sportswriters sought a little self-amusement while covering the woebegone team. "Paraspinous" and "paraspinal" are medical terms meaning adjacent to the spine. *Merriam-Webster.com Medical Dictionary*, merriam-webster.com/medical/paraspinal. Accessed September 13, 2020.

4   Jim Nasium, "Shawkey Fans 15, Macks Losing Two," *Philadelphia Inquirer*, September 28, 1919: 20.

5   "Mackmen Defeated Twice by Yankees."

6   Jim Nasium.

Baseballs and Bullets Fly as Meusel Hits for his Second Career Cycle

July 3, 1922
New York Yankees 12, Philadelphia Athletics 1

By Mike Huber

On the eve of Independence Day 1922, the New York Yankees exploded with 17 hits in a fireworks hitting display against the Philadelphia Athletics. Bob Meusel hit for the cycle, and Babe Ruth and Everett Scott each homered as well, leading the Bronx Bombers to a 12-1 victory at Philadelphia's Shibe Park. Harry Newman of the *New York Daily News* labeled the offensive outburst, "Swatting, men, swatting!"[1]

The season was about half-finished as the two teams settled in to play the fourth game in a six-game series. New York owned a 42-32 mark while holding down second place in the American League. Last-place Philadelphia had a record of 27-39. The Yankees had taken the first three games of the series, outscoring the Athletics 20-8 in that stretch.

On this Monday afternoon, before a crowd of about 13,000, Athletics manager Connie Mack sent second-year pitcher Jim Sullivan to the mound. Sullivan's career could be defined by the 1922 season. He pitched in two games in late 1921, starting (and completing) both, but suffered two defeats by allowing 13 runs in 17 innings pitched (although only six runs were earned). The right-hander pitched in 20 games in 1922, but this was one of only two starts. He was sold by the

Athletics to Portland of the Pacific Coast League on August 19, after building another 0-2 record with a 5.44 earned-run average.[2]

Yankees skipper Miller Huggins countered with Carl Mays, who was making his 16th start of the season. This was his fifth start against the Athletics in 1922, and Mays had been perfect, pitching four complete games, including an 11-inning contest, and winning all four. Entering this game, according to the *New York Times*, "Carl Mays was in fine trim with his submarine pitching."[3]

The Yankees wasted no time in getting to Sullivan. Whitey Witt led off the top of the first with a single to right. He advanced to second on a sacrifice bunt by Mike McNally. That brought Ruth, who had led the league in runs batted in for the last three seasons, to the plate. With a count of two balls and a strike, Ruth "clicked off a towering infield fly."[4] Philadelphia first baseman Joe Hauser settled under it but the ball "bounded out of his hands into those of [shortstop Chick] Galloway"[5] for an out instead of an error. On the play, Witt advanced to third base.

Batting cleanup for New York was 25-year-old right fielder Bob Meusel. He brought into the game a four-game hitting streak and a batting average of .321. He drove one of Sullivan's deliveries into center field for an RBI single. Then, with Wally Pipp batting, Meusel attempted to steal second and was thrown out.

In the second inning, New York put together three singles and a sacrifice to plate two more tallies. Pipp started the inning with a single to left. Aaron Ward sacrificed him to second base. Scott smacked a single to center. Pipp raced around third and headed home. Philadelphia's Beauty McGowan fielded the hit and fired toward the infield, but third baseman Jimmy Dykes couldn't handle the throw. Pipp scored and Scott ended up on third base. Fred Hofmann followed with a single into left field, and Scott scored an unearned run, upping the New York advantage to 3-0.

In the fifth, "young Sullivan was given a pounding."[6] Witt drew a one-out walk. McNally singled to right, sending Witt to third. Ruth dribbled a ball in front of the plate and catcher Cy Perkins threw him out at first, but now New York had runners on second and third. Meusel "cracked the ball against the scoreboard in centre field for three bases."[7] Pipp singled in Meusel for the third run of the inning.

Meanwhile, Mays was mowing down the A's. Through the first four innings, he had faced only two above the minimum, yielding a one-out walk in the first and a two-out single in the third, though neither runner advanced. In the bottom of the fifth, Dykes cracked a two-out double to right field, but he was stranded when Heinie Scheer, pinch-hitting for Sullivan, grounded out to Mays on the mound.

In the seventh, with one down and Charlie Eckert now pitching for the A's, Ruth "considered 13 a lucky number, when he crowned the ball for a circuit drive to bring his total up to the jinx figure."[8] The ball landed in the left-field bleachers for a home run. The shot tied him for third in the American League, behind the Browns' Ken Williams (20) and the Athletics' Tillie Walker (17). (Cardinals star Rogers Hornsby led the senior

circuit with 18 home runs.) After the game, Ruth told reporters that he "will soon pass those other home run clubbers who are now leading him."[9] Ruth had now hit five round-trippers in his last four games. Not to be outdone, Meusel followed Ruth with a home run drive "into the same place."[10] The score was now 8-0, in favor of the visitors.

The Yankees were not done yet. According to the *Philadelphia Inquirer*, "a five-hit bombardment in the eighth round scored four more runs and the home team was licked to a frazzle."[11] Scott homered, becoming the third New Yorker to make a "wallop to the harassed left field stand."[12] He had hit only one home run in all of the 1921 season, and this was already his second "circuit smash"[13] of the 1922 campaign.[14] Hofmann singled but was forced out by Mays. Witt singled, but he was forced out by McNally, with Mays going to third. Ruth then joined the club, hitting a single to center, plating Mays. Meusel drove a double to left. His two-bagger just missed being another home run, and both McNally and Ruth crossed the plate. Left fielder Walker chased the drive to the left-field bleacher wall and "made a stab for the pill as it sailed over his head,"[15] preventing it from going into the stands. With the double, Meusel had hit for the cycle and had extended the Yankees' lead to 12-0.

With two outs in the bottom of the eighth, Hauser "lifted the ball over the fence,"[16] breaking up the shutout. It was his second round-tripper of the season. The Athletics had a runner (McGowan) on in the ninth, but he got only as far as second base. The game ended with the score 12-1.

Mays was masterful. The Athletics' bats were "helpless before the underhand pegger and all they could get was half a dozen scattered hits."[17] He walked two and struck out two. The Yankees won their fourth straight game over the Mackmen.

This was second time in his career that Meusel had hit for the cycle, collecting a home run, triple, double, and single in a game. His first feat was accomplished on May 7, 1921, against the Washington Senators (also an away game). Meusel became just the third batter since 1901 to accomplish this rare event twice (after the Pittsburgh Pirates' Fred Clarke and St. Louis Browns' George Sisler).

In 1922 four batters hit for the cycle: Ross Youngs (New York Giants, April 29), Jimmy Johnston (Brooklyn Robins, May 25), Ray Schalk (Chicago White Sox, June 27), and Meusel. Six seasons later, on July 26, 1928, Meusel became the first player in the modern era to hit for the cycle three times. John Reilly of the Cincinnati Reds also hit for the cycle three times – September 12, 1883, September 19, 1883, and August 6, 1890. Since Meusel's trifecta, Babe Herman and Adrian Beltre have each hit for the cycle three times.

Regarding the Yankees, Bert Daniels was the first player in franchise history to hit for the cycle (July 25, 1912). The next three cycles by a Yankees player were all accomplished by Meusel.

POSTSCRIPT

The Yankees' batters were not the only ones who provided fireworks and excitement. In the fourth inning, there was a different kind of blast. The *New York Herald* chronicled that "one of the most popular of the local gunmen inadvertently dropped his automatic out of the upper tier of the grand stand. It fell into the dugout and was discharged. Fortunately it fell into the home team's dugout and missed all of the players."[18] Amazingly, even with the scrambling in the Philadelphia dugout when the pistol fired, as players rushed to "crawl through cracks and knotholes to points of safety,"[19] no one was injured. The *Herald* story incredibly explained that "an automatic would have to be aimed by an expert to hit any of them."[20] A local policeman reportedly told the gunman "to be more careful in the future. [Additionally,] it is believed that the Philadelphia Gunmen's Association will suspend him for ten days for bringing undue notoriety to the profession."[21]

SOURCES

In addition to the sources mentioned in the Notes, the author consulted Baseball-Reference.com, MLB.com, SABR.org and Retrosheet.org.

NOTES

1   Harry Newman, "Ruth's Homer No. 13 Features Swat Jamboree," *New York Daily News*, July 4, 1922: 16.

2   Sullivan played part of one more season in the majors, 1923, in which he made three September appearances for the Cleveland Indians, pitching a total of five innings. He accrued one more loss, giving him a career record of 0-5 with a 5.52 ERA.

3   "Yanks Overwhelm Athletics by 12-1," *New York Times*, July 4, 1922: 14.

4   "Philadelphia Gunman Does a Faux Pas in Shibe Park," *New York Herald*, July 4, 1922: 11.

5   "Yanks Bump Macks; Take Another, 12-1," *Philadelphia Inquirer*, July 4, 1922: 10.

6   "Yanks Bump Macks; Take Another, 12-1,"

7   *New York Times.*

8   "The Home Run Contest," *Baltimore Sun*, July 4, 1922: 8.

9   Newman. Ruth ended the season with 35 home runs, fourth best in the majors, but he did not catch those ahead of him. St. Louis Cardinals slugger Rogers Hornsby led all major leaguers with 42, followed by Ken Williams (39), Tillie Walker (37), and then Ruth.

10   *New York Times.*

11   *Philadelphia Inquirer.*

12   *New York Herald.*

13   *New York Times.*

14   In eight seasons with the Boston Red Sox (1914 through 1921), Everett Scott hit seven home runs in 1,096 games. He was traded to the Yankees on December 20, 1921, and finished 1922 with three home runs. In his 13-year career, Scott hit 20 home runs in 1,654 games.

15   *New York Herald.*

16   *Philadelphia Inquirer.*

17   Newman.

18   *New York Herald.*

19   *New York Herald.*

20   *New York Herald.*

21   *New York Herald.*

A's Eddie Rommel Wins 27th Game for 65-Win Team

September 30, 1922
Philadelphia Athletics 7, Washington Senators 4
(Second Game of a Doubleheader)

By Don Zminda

In a career that included 13 seasons as a major-league pitcher and 22 more as an American League umpire, Eddie Rommel proved himself to be both accomplished and unconventional. As a pitcher with the Philadelphia Athletics, Rommel was an early master of an unconventional pitch – the knuckleball – and the winner of 171 games. In the 54 years that the team played in Philadelphia (1901-54), only Hall of Famers Eddie Plank (284 wins), Lefty Grove (195), and Chief Bender (193) won more games for the A's franchise. As an American League umpire from 1938 to 1959, Rommel worked in two World Series and six All-Star Games. He was unconventional as an ump as well. On April 18, 1956, at Washington's Griffith Stadium, Rommel – umpiring at third base in a game between the hometown Senators and the New York Yankees – became the first major-league umpire to work a game while wearing eyeglasses. He continued to wear glasses through the end of his umpiring career, though only in night games in which he was working the bases.

Rommel's best season as a player came in 1922. Fifty years before another Philadelphia

pitcher, Steve Carlton, amazed the baseball world by winning 27 games for a Phillies club that won only 59 games all year, Rommel posted a major-league-best 27 wins for a seventh-place A's team with a 65-89 record. Rommel also led the American League in games pitched that year with 51, and ranked in the league's top five in innings pitched (fourth, 294.0), complete games (tied for fifth, 22), and games finished in relief (tied for fifth, 16). There were no Cy Young Awards in 1922, but in the American League Most Valuable Player voting, Rommel finished second behind George Sisler of the St. Louis Browns, who batted .420 that year.

Typically for Rommel, he finished the 1922 season in unconventional fashion. Due to post-ponements, the Athletics ended the year with three consecutive home doubleheaders against the Washington Senators. Rommel worked a game – and got a decision – on each of the three days. On Thursday, September 28, Rommel started game one for the A's, but was lifted after allowing five hits, five runs, and two homers in the first inning. He took his 13th loss of the year in

The main entrance of Shibe Park was an octagonal Beaux Arts tower, which housed team offices.

the 9-6 Senators victory. On Friday, September 29, Rommel entered game one in the 12th inning with the score tied, 2-2. He allowed a run on a homer by rookie Pete Lapan, but wound up as the winning pitcher when the A's scored two runs in the bottom half of the inning.

Pennsylvania law prohibited Sunday baseball in 1922, so the Athletics finished the year with a Saturday twin bill against the Senators. Rommel's victory on Friday was his 26th of the year, tying him with Joe Bush of the Yankees for the major-league lead in pitcher wins. Another victory would give Rommel the outright lead in wins. After Washington took Saturday's first game, 7-3, A's manager Connie Mack selected Rommel to start game two. His opponent was left-hander Ray Francis, who – like Rommel – had started one of the games on Thursday. Francis had lasted only

1⅔ innings in Thursday's second game, allowing seven hits and 10 runs (six earned) in a 12-5 defeat that dropped his season record to 7-17.

The Washington lineup that Rommel faced on Saturday featured three Hall of Famers – Bucky Harris, Sam Rice, and Goose Goslin (though Harris would be enshrined as a manager). Washington's starters also included two of the better players of the era, first baseman Joe Judge and shortstop Roger Peckinpaugh; like Harris, Rice, and Goslin, both Judge and Peckinpaugh would be regular starters for the Senators teams that would win American League pennants in 1924-25. The Athletics' lineup in Saturday's second game featured no players who would be enshrined in Cooperstown, but it included several players of note along with Rommel. Like Rommel, right fielder Bing Miller and third baseman Jimmy

Dykes would last long enough to become contributing members of the A's AL championship clubs of 1929-31. Cy Perkins, a reserve catcher for the 1929-30 champions, would have a 17-year major-league career. Thirty-five-year-old left fielder Tillie Walker was nearing the finish of a 13-year career that would end the next year, but he was enjoying his greatest season. Walker entered the game with a career-high 36 home runs, second in the American League behind Ken Williams of the Browns (39). Neither the Senators nor A's would use a substitute in Saturday's season finale.

The Senators established a pattern in the early innings of the game, getting two hits in each of the first three frames but failing to score a run. Rommel drove in the game's first run with a single to center in the bottom of the third. The A's then broke the game open with four runs on five hits an inning later; a bases-loaded triple by Dykes was the key blow.

Washington finally got on the board with single runs in the fifth and sixth innings, but despite getting two hits in six of the first seven innings, those were the Senators' only runs until the eighth. The A's, meanwhile, scored again in the bottom of the fifth on Walker's 37th and final home run of the season. At the time, Walker's total was the fifth-highest home-run total by a player in a single season, topped only by Babe Ruth (59 homers in 1921, 54 in 1920), Rogers Hornsby (42 in 1922), and Ken Williams (39 in 1922). Though he is largely forgotten today, Walker ranked in the all-time top 10 in career home runs (tied for seventh with 118) when his major-league career ended after the 1923 season.

The Senators scored twice in the eighth inning to get within two runs (6-4), but the A's scored a run of their own in the bottom half, and Rommel closed out Philadelphia's 7-4 victory an inning later. Remarkably, he had allowed a total of 17 hits in the game, but no more than two in any inning except for Washington's three-hit eighth.

Rommel's career would last for another decade, and he would earn fame for yet another game in which he took home a victory despite allowing a high number of hits. On July 10, 1932, the A's – still prohibited from playing home games on Sundays – traveled to Cleveland to play a single road game in the midst of a homestand. Mack had brought along only two pitchers, and when starter Lew Krausse allowed three runs in the first inning, Rommel entered the game in the bottom of the second. As in the season-ending game in 1922, Rommel had pitched on each of the previous two days (two innings on Friday, three on Saturday) … and as in 1922, he proceeded to allow a high number of hits. Did he ever: The game lasted 18 innings, and Rommel, who worked the final 17, allowed a staggering 29 hits and 14 runs (13 earned) before the A's finally prevailed, 18-17. The 29 hits allowed are still the major-league record for hits allowed by a pitcher in a single game since 1900.

That 1932 game was the 171st and final victory of Eddie Rommel's career. It was also the fifth time in a major-league career which included exactly 501 games pitched that Rommel allowed at least 15 hits in a game. Remarkably, he was the winning pitcher in each of those five games.

SOURCES

Deale, Tim. "Eddie Rommel." SABR BioProject biography, sabr.org/bioproj/person/333594e9; accessed August 18, 2018.

"Mackmen Wind Up with Even Split," *Philadelphia Inquirer*, October 1, 1922.

Neyer, Rob. "Eddie Rommel" chapter from Bill James and Rob Neyer, *The Neyer/James Guide to Pitchers* (New York: Fireside, 2004), 75-80.

Baseball-Reference.com/boxes/PHA/PHA192209302.shtml

Retrosheet.org/boxesetc/1922/B09302PHA1922.htm

Statspass.com

ALL SMILES:
SAD SAM JONES TOSSES NO-HITTER

September 4, 1923
New York Yankees 2, Philadelphia Athletics 0

By Gregory H. Wolf

Skipper Miller Huggins's Yankees had rolled over competition all season long and were cruising to their third straight pennant. Owners of the best record in baseball (81-43), the Yankees were 13 games ahead of the second-place Cleveland Indians and shut down opponents with a staff that eventually led the league in team ERA (3.62). Blessed with five legitimate aces, including Bullet Joe Bush, Bob Shawkey, Herb Pennock, and Waite Hoyt, Hug called on 30-year-old right-hander Sad Sam Jones to take the mound in the third game of a four-game series against the Philadelphia Athletics at Shibe Park.

Jones had emerged on the national stage five years earlier, winning 16 games in his first full season and helping the Boston Red Sox capture the pennant and 1918 World Series. Since then his career had been defined by inconsistencies. After two down seasons, he won 23 for the Red Sox in 1921, and was then shipped along with Bush and Everett Scott to the Yankees in a blockbuster trade for four players and $100,000. Jones split his 26 decisions in 1922, posted a staff-high 3.67 ERA and was relegated to bullpen duty in the Yankees' loss to the New York Giants in the World Series.

A rubber-armed hurler, Jones got out to a hot start in '23, posting a 14-6 record by the end of July. "Jones is the stylist among American League pitchers," gushed longtime nemesis Ty Cobb. "He has the ideal delivery. He is free, pitches with the slightest effort. Jones has everything in his assortment of foolers, a good fast ball, fast breaking curves and a fine change of pace."[1] Overwork may have contributed to Jones's poor August, during which his ERA bloated to 5.72 while opponents batted .327. His start against the seventh-place A's (52-70) was undoubtedly an audition for a start in the fall classic. To oppose Sad Sam, Connie Mack, the A's owner-skipper since the founding of the AL in 1901, sent Bob Hasty, a 27-year-old right-hander, whose 12-12 slate improved his career numbers to 27-47.

A beautiful late summer day with temperatures in the 80s drew 5,000 spectators to Shibe Park for a Tuesday afternoon of the national pastime. Hasty entered the game with the AL's fourth highest ERA (4.58); however, his performance would have been the story of the game had his teammates mustered any offense again Jones. The robust 6-foot-3, 210-pound Georgian held the Yankees to just seven hits, three of which came in the fateful third. Fred Hofmann led off with a walk and moved to third on Scott's single. Jones's infield tapper moved Scott up a station. Former A's center fielder Whitey Witt spanked a single to deep center to drive in what proved to be the game's only runs, as Hofmann and Scott easily scored. After Joe Dugan popped up, Babe Ruth (leading the majors at the time with a .393 batting average and pacing the AL with 32 home runs) singled, and it appeared as through the vaunted Yankee sluggers might blow the game open, but third baseman Sammy Hale made what the *New York Times* described as a "classy stop" on Wally Pipp's sharp grounder to third base to end the threat.[2] Hasty otherwise kept the Bronx Bombers off balance, surrendering just one extra-base hit, a leadoff double by Bob Meusel in the fourth.

In a career that spanned 22 seasons (1914-1935), 647 appearances, including 487 starts, 229 wins, and 36 shutouts, Jones pitched to contact and relied on a baffling delivery and changing speeds to confuse hitters instead of brute power. He also occasionally struggled with control, so it was no big deal when he issued a one-out walk to Chick Galloway in the first. Jones set down the next 21 batters.

With one out in the bottom of the eighth, Frank Welch smashed a "scorching grounder right plumb into Scott's chest," reported sportswriter Jack Farrell of the *New York Daily News*.[3] According to the *Philadelphia Inquirer*, the hard-hit ball bounced out of the shortstop's hand first, then hit his chest; though Scott scooped up the ball, his throw to first was late and Welch was safe.[4] "Samuel was visibly nervous at this break of luck," continued Farrell, and for good reason.[5] The scoreboard at the ballpark displayed neither hits nor errors. "The ball might have been given as a hit or tabulated as an error," opined the *Philadelphia Inquirer*.[6] Unaware of the official scoring, Jones induced Jimmy Dykes to hit a grounder forcing Welch at second and then ended the frame on Cy Perkins's fly out to

center field. When the pitcher returned to the dugout between innings, "he displayed a broad grim," recounted Farrell, when he discovered that Welch's smash had been ruled an error to keep his no-hitter intact.[7]

"[F]ame beckoned its clammy hand to Jones," wrote the *Inquirer* in the poetic parlance of the time, as Jones took the mound in the bottom of the ninth, three outs from what newspapers called the hall of fame, a mythical Valhalla of baseball eternity.[8] He retired Beauty McGowan, pinch-hitting for Hasty, on a roller to keystone sacker Aaron Ward, then dispatched Wid Matthews on another grounder, this time to short. To the plate stepped Galloway, who hoped to end Jones's quest to become just the second Yankee to hurl a no-hitter, joining George Mogridge, who tossed one against the Boston Red Sox at Fenway Park on April 24, 1917. Galloway, shunning written or unwritten baseball codes, tried to catch Jumping Joe Dugan napping and bunted down the third-base side. But Dugan was ready for a tricky play, charged the bunt, and "just managed to throw out the runner by a step," noted the *Times*, which added that "Jones had a close call."[9] The game was completed in 1 hour and 23 minutes.[10]

"There was no wild demonstration by the Yankee players," reported the *Daily News*.[11] For the fans, however, it was a different story, and many of them ran onto the field to congratulate the hurler.[12] Jones made his way to the dugout, where the 5-foot-5, 130-pound Huggins shook his hand and offered a few words of praise as did his teammates, and even some of the A's players.

The *Inquirer* gushed that Jones's no-hitter "capsheafs a career for the season that has raised Jones from the depths to a pinnacle of success."[13] Jones faced 29 batters, walked one and did not register a strikeout. The only strikeout victim of the game was Babe Ruth.

Jones's no-hitter augured a productive final month of the season for the Ohio native. In his next outing, six days later, Jones faced only 31 batters, tossing a two-hitter to beat the Red Sox, 8-1, at Yankee Stadium. Sad Sam won five of six decisions with a 2.20 ERA in September to conclude the season with a team-best 21 wins (along with a 3.63 ERA and 8 losses), and joined Bush (19-15), Hoyt (17-9), Pennock (19-6), and Shawkey (16-11) by logging well in excess of 200 innings.[14]

SOURCES

In addition to the sources cited in the Notes, the author accessed Retrosheet.org, Baseball-Reference.com, Newspapers.com, and SABR.org.

NOTES

1   "Sam Jones in Hall of Fame," *Reading* (Pennsylvania) *Times*, September 5, 1923: 6.

2   "Sam Jones Pitches No-Hit, No-Run Game," *New York Times*, September 5, 1923: 11.

3   Jack Farrell, "Athletics Get but Two Men to First," (New York) *Daily News*, September 5, 1923: 22.

4   "Jones Hurls No-Hit Game Against Macks," *Philadelphia Inquirer*, September 5, 1923: 20.

5   Farrell.

6   "Jones Hurls No-Hit Game Against Macks."

7   Farrell

8   Farrell.

9   "Sam Jones Pitches No-Hit, No-Run Game."

10 Farrell.

11 Farrell.

12 "Jones Hurls No-Hit Game Against Macks."

13 "Jones Hurls No-Hit Game Against Macks."

14 The five Yankee starters, Bush (275⅔), Hoyt (238⅔), Pennock (238⅓), Shawkey (258⅔), and Jones (243), combined to start 143 of the team's 152 games, completed 97 of them, and logged an astonishing 1,254⅓ innings (90.8 percent of the team's total). So much for relievers.

Ehmke's No-Hitter Saved by Baserunning Blunder and Official Scorer's Change of Heart

September 7, 1923
Boston Red Sox 4, Philadelphia Athletics 0

By Gregory H. Wolf

Howard Ehmke "devastated the Mackmen like a lanky cyclone," gushed the *Philadelphia Inquirer* after the Red Sox hurler's no-hitter against the Athletics, adding "[He was] unquestionably in the fettle in which heroic deeds are born."[1] The *Boston Globe* described the submariner Ehmke's gem as a "classy curving performance," but noted that it was a "tainted no-hit, no-run game," which included a baserunning blunder nullifying a double and a scoring change.[2]

A late-season matchup between the AL's two worst teams does not conjure up the fairy-tale setting for great baseball feats. A decade earlier, however, the Athletics and Red Sox ruled the junior circuit, capturing the pennant for eight of nine straight seasons (1910-1918), with the Red Sox winning four World Series titles and the Athletics three. And then they sold off their stars: Owner-skipper Connie Mack jettisoned Eddie Collins and Home Run Baker, among many; and Red Sox owner Harry Frazee famously sold Babe Ruth. Since those notorious transactions, the teams resided in the league's cellar. En route to their ninth straight losing season, Mack's A's

had been a feel-good story of the 1923 season. Above .500 on July 9, they had since slumped, having lost 36 of 52 games to fall into seventh place (53-72). The offensively challenged A's had scored just 37 runs in the previous 15 games and had been held hitless by Sad Sam Jones of the New York Yankees three days earlier, on September 4. First-year manager Frank Chance's Red Sox, whose club finished in last place in 1922 to break the A's seven-year hold on that dubious rank, were once again pulling up the rear (48-75).

The bright spot on each of these miserable clubs was its ace starting pitcher. The A's Eddie Rommel, who had led the big leagues with 27 wins in 1922, had beaten the Red Sox, 6-2, a day earlier in the opening contest of the series. Therefore, Mack called 6-foot-6, 180-pound right-hander William Jennings Bryan Harriss, known by the appropriate moniker Slim. The AL leader with 20 losses a year earlier, the 25-year-old Harriss was 8-14 (4.09 ERA) to push his career slate to 37-64. Banished to the bullpen about three weeks earlier because of his infectiveness, Harriss had tossed

13⅓ innings of scoreless relief to earn another starting nod.

Toeing the rubber for the Red Sox was Howard Ehmke, known for his unique side-arm, almost underhand delivery. The *Boston Herald* cooed that the 6-foot-3 gangly hurler had a "wonderful cross-fire delivery which seemed to come from some place in the vicinity of the shortfield, instead of the pitching peak."[3] He had been acquired in the offseason in a trade with the Detroit Tigers, with whom he had established a reputation as a steady workhorse, averaging 16 wins and 248 innings per season (1919-1922). However, he clashed mightily with player-manager Ty Cobb, who levied accusations that he was indifferent, disinterested, and lacked the mental toughness to be a winner, and finally cast off his hurler.[4] Enjoying what the *Herald* praised as a "brilliant season," Ehmke got off to a hot start in his first year with the Red Sox (12-5), but had struggled over the last two months, losing 10 of 14 decisions with a dismal 5.40 ERA to fall back under .500 (91-92) in his career.[5]

On a pleasant late summer afternoon with temperatures in the high 70s in the City of Brotherly Love, a small crowd of 2,000 patrons ventured to Shibe Park, baseball's first steel-and-concrete ballpark, located at the intersections of 21st Street and Lehigh on the north side of the city.[6]

The lowest-scoring team in the league, averaging 3.8 runs per game, the Red Sox struck first. Val Picinich laced a one-out single to center and moved up a station on Dick Reichle's sacrifice bunt, and then another when Harriss balked trying to catch him napping at the keystone bag.[7] Ira Flagstead's single drove in the first run.

With the way Ehmke twirled on this Friday afternoon, a single tally would have sufficed. Harriss pitched well until the eighth when the "Red Sox broke out with renewed fury," observed the *Herald*.[8] Flagstead led off with his third hit of the game, a single to left. The club's biggest offensive threat, Joe Harris, who entered the game batting .344, singled. Howie Shanks spanked a double over center fielder Wid Matthews's head to drive in the Red Sox' second run. On "Mack's wig-wagged orders," Harriss walked Mike Menosky to load the bases.[9] Norm McMillian hit a routine grounder to short. Harris "should have been an easy out" at home plate, the *Herald* asserted, but Chick Galloway allowed the ball to get through for an error and both Harris and Shanks scored to give the Red Sox a 4-0 lead.

Ehmke came out blazing, retiring the first 12 batters he faced. A contact pitcher, Ehmke had surrendered just over a hit per inning in his career thus far. Devoid of overpowering stuff, he often struggled with his control while trying to find the proper release point in his bewildering delivery, with the ball leaving his hand just inches above the ground. Joe Hauser coaxed a walk from Ehmke to begin the fifth and was forced by Bing Miller's grounder. Frank Welch hit into an inning-ending double play.

Ehmke's no-hitter was preserved by a base-running "Merkle" blunder with two out in the sixth inning. To the plate stepped Slim Harriss, whose "feebleness with the bat is a baseball jest," according to the *Globe*.[10] Entering the game with four hits in 53 at-bats, the string bean twirler bashed one over Menosky's head in left field. According to the *Herald*, the ball "rolled all the way" to the bleacher wall,[11] while the *Globe* reported that the smash "struck the scoreboard on the bound."[12] In any case, it was a clean hit and Harriss "ran like a scared rabbit," quipped the *Globe*, to second base.[13] Menosky relayed the ball to McMillan, who quickly rifled the ball to a clamoring Joe Harris at first. Harris pointed to the bag, claiming the inexperienced baserunner had missed it. Umpire Red Ormsby agreed, called Harriss out, and the no-hitter was intact.

After breezing through the seventh, retiring the side on three popups, Ehmke once again had Lady Luck on his side. With two outs, Frank

Welch, who entered the game batting a robust .303, belted a blooper to left field. According to the *Globe*, the ball "was at Menosky's knees" and the charging flychaser fumbled it.[14] The official scorer immediately ruled it a hit; the *Philadelphia Inquirer* called it a "snap verdict."[15] The no-hitter was over. The next batter, Jimmy Dykes, grounded to force Welch and the inning was over.

But hold on. The official scorer later amended his decision and ruled an error on Mensoky, though it is unclear exactly when this ruling was made. According to the *Globe*, he consulted with the players involved, suggesting that the discussion took place immediately after the game.[16] But the *Inquirer* noted, "[I]nstantly, however, he decided that his first decision was awry" and changed the ruling.[17]

In the ninth, Ehmke retired Heinie Scheer, Beauty McGowan, pinch-hitting for Harriss, and then Matthews to end the game in 1 hour and 34 minutes.

Ineptitude on the basepaths and scoring change aside, Ehmke was credited with a no-hitter and there are no asterisks following his accomplishments. He faced 28 batters, striking out one and walking one. It was the first Red Sox no-hitter since Dutch Leonard held the Tigers hitless on June 3, 1918. For the A's, it was the second time in four games that they had failed to connect for a hit.

In his next start, four days later at Yankee Stadium, Ehmke yielded a "puzzling grounder" to Whitey Witt, the first Yankees batter of the game.[18] Third baseman Howie Shanks "fumbled the ball" and did not attempt to throw to first. The official scorer, New York sportswriter Fred Lieb, ruled the play a hit.[19] Ehmke did not allow another hit the entire game, and won 3-0. Lieb's decision was controversial, to say the least. "I thought it was an error all the way," said Witt.[20] As memorable as these two games were, his final start of the season was one of the worst in big-league history: he surrendered a whopping 21 hits and 17 runs (16 earned), and walked four in a sobering 24-4 loss to the Yankees at Fenway Park. He finished the season with a 20-17 slate, 28 complete games, and a 3.78 ERA in 316⅔ innings.

SOURCES

In addition to the sources cited in the Notes, the author accessed Retrosheet.org, Baseball-Reference.com, SABR.org, and *The Sporting News* archive via Paper of Record.

NOTES

1 "Ehmke Hurls No-Hit Game Against Macks," *Philadelphia Inquirer*, September 8, 1923: 18.

2 "Ehmke Blanks Macks Without a Safe Drive," *Boston Globe*, September 8, 1923: 8.

3 "Ehmke Walks in as Jones Leaves Hall of Fame Door Open," *Boston Herald*, September 8, 1923: 6.

4 See Gregory H. Wolf, "Howard Ehmke," SABR Bio-Project, sabr.org/bioproj/person/753ebff0.

5 "Ehmke Walks in as Jones Leaves Hall of Fame Door Open."

6 Weather from "Yesterday's Local Weather Report," *Philadelphia Inquirer*," September 8, 1923: 2. Estimated attendance from "Ehmke Walks in as Jones Leaves Hall of Fame Door Open."

7 Neither Baseball-Reference.com nor Retrosheet. org has a play-by-play summary for this game. Individual plays have been found in various newspapers and cited where applicable.

8 "Ehmke Walks in as Jones Leaves Hall of Fame Door Open."

9 "Ehmke Walks in as Jones Leaves Hall of Fame Door Open."

10 "Ehmke Blanks Macks Without a Safe Drive."

11 "Ehmke Walks in as Jones Leaves Hall of Fame Door Open."

12 "Ehmke Blanks Macks Without a Safe Drive."

13 "Ehmke Blanks Macks Without a Safe Drive."

14 "Ehmke Blanks Macks Without a Safe Drive."

15 "Ehmke Hurls No-Hit Game Against Macks."

16 "Ehmke Blanks Macks Without a Safe Drive."

17 "Ehmke Hurls No-Hit Game Against Macks."

18 "Ehmke Held Yanks to 1 Hit," *Fitchburg* (Massachusetts) *Sentinel*, September 12, 1923: 8.

19 The Sporting News, September 20, 1923: 1.

20 John McKeon, "Howard Ehmke Lost His Shot at Immortality to a Controversial Scorer's Decision," *Die Hard*, March 1995: 22.

ATHLETICS OVERCOME 12-RUN DEFICIT

June 15, 1925
Philadelphia Athletics 17, Cleveland Indians 15

By Joseph Wancho

From 1910 through 1914, Philadelphia won four of five pennants in the American League. Included in this stretch were three World Series championships (1910, 1911, and 1913). But after losing to the Boston Braves in the 1914 fall classic, the Athletics fortunes' plummeted as they occupied the cellar of the junior circuit from 1915 to 1921. It was an incredible run of futility for the A's, but skipper Connie Mack was slowly bringing the team around to the caliber of the championship teams.

Conversely, the Cleveland Indians flew one solitary flag over Dunn Field. The Tribe polished off Brooklyn in seven games in the 1920 World Series. Although they remained competitive, the Indians could not claim a second pennant in the ensuing years. They slipped to a sixth-place finish in 1924. It was the first time the Indians had finished in the second division of the AL since 1916.

Philadelphia held a 1½-game lead over Washington in the American League standings when Cleveland arrived at Shibe Park for a four-game set beginning on June 14, 1925. The Indians were tied for fourth place with St. Louis, nine games off the pace.

Behind the pitching of right-hander Benn Karr, the Tribe blanked the A's, 3-0, on a five-hitter in the opener. Coupled with the Senators' 9-8 win over St. Louis, the Athletics lead shrank to a mere half-game over the Nats.

For the second game of the series, Cleveland manager Tris Speaker sent southpaw Jake Miller to the hill. In his first full season, Miller took the ball with a 3-3 record and an ERA of 2.25. Mack countered with right-hander Eddie Rommel. The Baltimore native toed the pitching rubber at Shibe Park with a 9-4 record and a rather robust ERA of 4.73.

After a scoreless first inning, Cleveland jumped on Rommel for four tallies in the top of the second inning. The first run crossed the plate on a base hit by Ray Knode. Rommel threw a wild pitch with the bases full of Indians, allowing Freddy Spurgeon to score from third base. In Spurgeon's haste to score, he collided with plate umpire Brick Owens. The impact sent Owens sprawling. He was subsequently carried off the diamond and was delivered to a hospital for treatment. X-rays revealed that Owens had a torn muscle in his back, near his pelvis, and it was not believed to be serious. Bill Dinneen, who was umpiring at first base, took over for Owens behind the plate.

Mack had seen enough and lifted Rommel from the game in favor of Stan Baumgartner. A single by Charlie Jamieson and a double by Cliff Lee tallied the next two runs for Cleveland. Rommel's day was in the books. It was a short outing, as he went 1⅓ innings, and he was charged with four earned runs.

The A's scored a run in the bottom of the second inning when Jim Poole doubled and scored on a Chick Galloway single. But Cleveland came right back in the top of the third. Joe Sewell and Glenn Myatt each blasted a solo home run off A's reliever Fred Heimach to increase the Indians' advantage to 6-1. Myatt's homer left the yard, bounding over the right-field fence and onto Twentieth Avenue. Sewell's round-tripper was just that, of the inside-the-park variety. Again the Athletics scored a run in the bottom of the inning, but the Indians' lead was growing at 6-2 after three innings.

The middle innings were no better for the Athletics. Heimach surrendered two more runs in the top of the fourth on a triple by Lee and a double by Speaker. Heimach was replaced by Art Stokes. Cleveland reached Stokes for four runs in the fifth inning. The big hit was a two-run single by Jamieson.

After the Indians scored two more in the top of the sixth, they led Philadelphia, 14-2. The A's scored their third run in the home half of the sixth inning, to make the score look more like that of a football game, 14-3. The teams exchanged runs in the seventh inning, and it was 15-4.

The Tribe did not score a run in the eighth inning for the first time since the first. Miller was still on the mound as the bottom of the inning commenced. He was not having that great a day, but his offense was certainly carrying the day to this point as he walked four, struck out one, and gave up 10 hits. The Athletics stranded eight baserunners through seven innings.

Miller began the eighth inning by walking Galloway. Tom Glass flied out to right field and Max Bishop walked. Jimmy Dykes cleared the bases with a triple to cut the lead to 15-6. Speaker

pulled Miller from the game. By Speece emerged from the Cleveland bullpen.

But the relief pitcher was anything but, as he could not record an out. Instead, Speece gave up consecutive singles to Bill Lamar, Al Simmons, Frank Welch, and Charlie Berry. Southpaw Carl Yowell entered the game for Cleveland. The Indians lead was sliced to 15-9, and once again a pitcher from Cleveland's relief corps did not record an out. Yowell walked Poole to load the bases. Galloway followed with a single to left field and both Welch and Berry scored to make it 15-11. Yowell was given the hook by Speaker and George Uhle entered the game.

Sammy Hale, pinch-hitting for the pitcher, Glass, singled off Uhle to score Poole and send Galloway to third base. Hale promptly stole second base. Bishop singled to center field to plate both Galloway and Hale. The score was now 15-14.

Dykes grounded out to the shortstop, forcing Bishop at second base. Walter French entered the game to run for Dykes. But now there were two down. Uhle walked Lamar. Simmons came to the plate and unloaded a three-run shot over the roof in left field. That concluded the scoring for the Athletics, who crossed the dish 13 times in the inning to take a 17-15 lead. The *Philadelphia Inquirer* wrote, "As Al circled the bases … the din could be heard for blocks. It made madcaps of a big proportion of the 8,000, who jumped to their feet and shrieked and made wild gestures of joy. Scores sailed their straw skimmers down to the playing field."[1]

Rube Walberg entered the game to pitch the ninth inning. He closed the door on the Tribe to complete one of the most improbable comebacks in major-league history. Cleveland twice led by 12 runs, and the Athletics tied the record for biggest comeback in a major-league game. It had previously been accomplished by the Detroit Tigers on June 18, 1911. The Tigers trailed the Chicago White Sox, 13-1, heading into the bottom of the fifth inning at Bennett Park. Detroit scored five runs in the eighth and three more runs in the ninth to pull out the win.

For the Athletics, Tom Glass picked up his first win of the season. Uhle (7-5) took the loss. Jamieson had five hits for the Indians, while Sewell and Knode each had four. Lamar had four hits for the A's and Simmons and Galloway each drove in three runs.

With the win the A's now led Washington, which was idle, by a full game. But Washington eventually won the pennant. Philadelphia finished in second place, 8½ games back. The Indians finished in sixth place, 27½ games behind the Senators.

SOURCES

In addition to the sources cited in the Notes, the author accessed Retrosheet.org, Baseball-Reference.com, and SABR.org.

NOTES

1   James C. Isaminger, "Athletics Wonderful Finish Enables Them to Gain on Senators in American Race," *Philadelphia Inquirer*, June 16, 1925: 13.

VIOLENT VICISSITUDES

July 10, 1926
Philadelphia Athletics 17, Chicago White Sox 14

By Ken Carrano

Philadelphia is not known the to be coolest place to summer in, and the summer of 1926 was no exception. Temperatures had been rising steadily after a rainy fourth of July and reached 94 degrees on July 9 with a forecast for even warmer weather on July 10.[1] The weather was having a tragic effect on the city. The death toll from the heat wave had reached six people on the 10th as the Athletics faced the Chicago White Sox in the third game of a four-game series. The A's had entered the series a half-game behind the White Sox in second place behind the New York Yankees, but after two one-run victories the A's had passed the White Sox and were 7½ games behind the Yankees.

Starting for the White Sox on this steamy day was Ted Blankenship, who came into the game with a 10-7 record after shutting out the Cleveland Indians on July 6. Opposing Blankenship was future Hall of Fame pitcher Lefty Grove who had last pitched on July 5, when he beat the Yankees in game one of a doubleheader and got a three-inning save in game two. Grove's record coming into the game was only 9-8, but his ERA was a microscopic 1.81. He would go on to lead the American League in ERA in 1926 with a mark of 2.51, but this game did not help. Perhaps because

of the heat, this was one of the worst efforts of the year for both pitchers.

There would be no scoring in the game until the fourth inning but the A's had some chances early. In the first inning, one-out singles had runners on the corners for Bill Lamar. Walt French tried to score on Lamar's fly ball to center, but Johnny Mostil cut him down at the plate to keep the game scoreless. The A's had two runners on in the third as well, but Lamar struck out to end that frame. The third inning was the last to have no runs scored until the ninth, leading to what sportswriter James C. Isaminger described in the *Philadelphia Inquirer* as "an afternoon of violent changing vicissitudes."[2]

The fun started for Philadelphia in the bottom of the fourth. Four consecutive singles by Jimmy Dykes, Jim Poole, Mickey Cochrane (one RBI), and Chick Galloway (two RBIs) made the score 3-0 before the first out was recorded. Grove recorded the first out with a sacrifice, and then Max Bishop plated Galloway with the fifth single of the inning. After a popout, Al Simmons took a different path to scoring runs this inning with a home run, and the A's had a commanding 6-0 lead. The heat of the day finally got to Grove in the top of the fifth, as a walk, singles by Bill

Barrett and Willie Kamm, and a groundout by Johnny Grabowski cut the deficit to 6-2. After a groundout, doubles by Mostil and Bill Hunnefield brought the White Sox back two runs closer at 6-4.

Sloppy Thurston, who had pinch-hit for Blankenship in the top of the fifth, took the hill for the White Sox in the bottom of the inning but didn't stay long. Dykes led off the inning again, this time with a double. Poole moved Dykes to third with a groundout, and Cochrane's triple brought him home. When Galloway's single scored Cochrane, White Sox manager Eddie Collins decided that Thurston had seen enough action for the day, and brought in Sarge Connally to shut down the rally, which he did, but only after allowing a single to pinch-hitter Sammy Hale that scored Galloway and at 9-4 restored most of the A's lead.

The White Sox got all of those runs back in the top of the sixth without a hit. Bibb Falk's grounder was booted by Dykes, and Earl Sheely drew a base on balls from Sam Gray, who had relieved Grove to start the inning. Barrett followed with a slow roller to Galloway, whose wild throw to right field allowed both runners to score and Barrett to get to third, where he scored on another grounder to Galloway, making it a 9-7 game.

On this day, no lead or comeback was safe. The A's upped their lead to 11-7 in the bottom of the sixth but ran themselves out of a potential big inning. After a leadoff groundout, Dykes walked and Poole doubled, and after Cochrane was walked intentionally, the bases were loaded. The light-hitting Galloway (who entered the game averaging .218) atoned for his earlier error with a single to right that scored Dykes and Poole. Cochrane decided to test Barrett's arm by trying for third, and Barrett passed the test by throwing him out. Galloway, with the play in front of him, went for second and was thrown out as well, making it an unusual right field-to third base-to shortstop double play that also scored

two runs. Galloway's five RBIs in the game were a career high.

The White Sox had spent the last couple of innings getting themselves off the deck and did so again in the seventh. Mostil and Hunnefield led off the inning with singles and both scored on Falk's double that also ended Gray's afternoon. Joe Pate replaced Gray and allowed a double to Kamm that cut the A's lead to 11-10. In the bottom of the inning, Connally did what the 30,000 in attendance must have thought was impossible by retiring the A's without allowing a run, setting up the pivotal eighth inning.

Collins selected White Sox pitcher Ted Lyons to pinch-hit for Connally to lead off the eighth. Lyons was one of the better hitting pitchers in baseball, but he struck out to open the inning.[3] Mostil followed with a single and Collins singled to put the tying and lead runs aboard. Falk put the White Sox in the lead with his sixth home run of 1926, giving him five RBIs for the game.[4] Sheely followed with another home run and the White Sox now led, 14-11. The vicissitudes were not done yet, though.

Even though Lyons pinch-hit for the pitcher in the top of the eighth, Collins selected Red Faber to pitch the bottom of the inning. Faber hadn't pitched since a complete-game 7-2 win over the Detroit Tigers on July 4, but was not right on this day. Lamar led off with a double, and after Dykes grounded out, Poole hit a ball to Kamm, who tried and failed to get Lamar at the plate. Cy Perkins walked, putting the tying runs on base for Joe Hauser, whose double tied the game, 14-14, and ended Faber's day earlier than Collins expected. Milt Steengrafe relieved Faber, but the relief was all for the A's as he walked Bishop and hit French to load the bases. Simmons's double to left put the A's back in front, 16-14. Next Steengrafe walked Lamar and hit Dykes to push French home with the Athletics' 17th and final run of the afternoon. Poole popped up to short to end the inning, but the damage was done.

The White Sox tried to rally one more time, against the fifth Athletics pitcher of the game, Rube Walberg, and had the tying run at the plate after Kamm and Harris singled two put two runners on with one out, but neither Mostil nor Hunnefield could be the hero, and the game ended 17-14. The 17 runs were the most the A's scored in a game in 1926, matching a 17-15 affair against the Cleveland Indians in 1925. The 17 runs were also the most the White Sox allowed in a game in 1926; it was only the third time since 1908 that they scored 14 runs and lost.[5] After an off day, the White Sox avoided a series sweep on July 12 by beating the A's 8-6, with Blankenship recovering from his beating to earn a 3⅔-inning save for Lyons, his only save in 1926 and the last of his career.

SOURCES

In addition to the sources cited in the Notes, the author accessed Retrosheet.org, Baseball-Reference.com, SABR's BioProject via SABR.org, *The Sporting News* archive via Paper of Record, the *New York Times* archives, and the *Chicago Tribune* and *Philadelphia Inquirer* via newspapers.com.

NOTES

1 Historical weather data provided by the Franklin Institute, ffi.edu.

2 James C. Isaminger, "Athletics Capture Weird Contest From Eddie Collins' Crew," *Philadelphia Inquirer*, July 11, 1926: 43.

3 In the years Lyons was active (1923-1942), only Red Ruffing (503), Bob Smith (409), and Bucky Walters (386) had more hits that Lyons' 364.

4 Falk won the White Sox triple crown in 1926 with 8 home runs, 108 RBIs, and a .345 batting average.

5 The White Sox lost 16-15 decisions to the Tigers on June 18, 1911, and June 2, 1925.

THE MULE'S HOME RUN ENDS MARATHON

August 22, 1928
Philadelphia Athletics 6, Cleveland Indians 5
(17 Innings)

By Joseph Wancho

The climate in the American League was changing. From 1921 to 1927, the New York Yankees claimed five pennants and two world championships. Only the Washington Senators (1924-25) were able to break the Yankees' stranglehold on the league.

The Yankee roster had names that rolled off the tongue and were familiar to baseball fans across the land. Babe Ruth, Lou Gehrig, Tony Lazzeri, Joe Dugan, Mark Koenig, Bob Meusel, Earle Combs, Herb Pennock, Urban Shocker, Waite Hoyt. They were a formidable bunch and one of the greatest monikers in all of sports was bestowed upon them: Murderer's Row.

But as the Yankees were seemingly headed toward their third consecutive pennant in 1928, they couldn't help but notice that a new foe was gaining ground. The Philadelphia Athletics, or the Mackmen as they were known in honor of their owner-manager, Connie Mack, were building quite a club of their own. The Athletics had not been a prominent team in the AL since the Deadball Era. The A's, under the direction of the venerable Mack, won six pennants and three world championships between 1902 and 1914.

As Mack sold off stars, they hit rock bottom, finishing in the basement of the AL from 1915 to 1921. Then they began their return to prominence. They slowly made their way up through the division, finishing in the top half from 1925 to 1927, and now they were brandishing their own household names: Mickey Cochrane, Jimmie Foxx, Al Simmons, Sammy Hale, Bing Miller, Lefty Grove, Rube Walberg, Eddie Rommel, Jack Quinn.

The end of August was rapidly approaching with just over two-thirds of the 1928 schedule in the books. The race for the AL pennant was between two teams, New York and Philadelphia. Thus far, they had hooked up 18 times and the New Yorkers won 13 games, which might partially explain the 5½-game lead the Yankees held over the Athletics.

Cleveland was in Philadelphia beginning August 21 for a four-game set at Shibe Park. The Indians, who only two years before had finished in second place, were now considered an also-ran in the AL. At the start of the series in Philadelphia, Cleveland was in fourth place, a whopping 25½ games in back of the Yankees.

In the opener, the A's clubbed the Indians, 12-4. A six-run first followed by three more over the next two innings was more than enough for Jack Quinn to win his 16th game of the season.

The second game featured a matchup between Cleveland's George Uhle (11-16, 3.98 ERA) and Philadelphia's George Earnshaw (5-6, 4.51 ERA). Uhle led the AL in wins 1923 and 1926, but he was not pitching as well currently. Uhle had a five-game losing skid from July 23 to August 7, and had just broken the streak with a five-hit, complete-game win over Boston on August 14.

Earnshaw was in his rookie season after pitching for four-plus seasons with Baltimore of the International League. In that time, Earnshaw made 126 starts and posted a 78-48 record with a 4.01 ERA.

For the first six innings, there was little excitement for the estimated crowd of 6,000. The Athletics scored the only run of the game in the bottom of the second. Foxx reached first base via a single, but was he erased on a force-play grounder by Miller. Mule Haas followed with a double to left field, and Miller scored when Indians left fielder Sam Langford threw wildly to the infield.

Cleveland knotted the score at 1-1 in the top of the seventh inning. Then the Indians' bats came alive in the top of the eighth when they put a four-spot on the board. The uprising began when Luther Harvel singled to left field. Luke Sewell followed with a bunt to the pitcher; Earnshaw's throw to first baseman Ossie Orwoll was dropped and everyone was safe. Uhle followed with another bunt for a single and the bases were loaded. Langford laced a single to center field to plate Harvel and Sewell. Carl Lind laid down yet another bunt, although this time Cochrane pounced on the ball and threw him out, but the runners moved up a base. Joe Sewell doubled home Uhle and Langford and the Indians were out in front, 5-1.

Philadelphia was down, but the A's were certainly not out. Max Bishop led off the bottom of the eighth with a single. After Orwoll flied out, Cochrane doubled to right field and Bishop took third. After a Simmons fly out, Foxx singled

home Bishop and Cochrane. Walks to Miller and Haas loaded the bases and ended the day for Uhle. He was replaced by John Miljus. The young right-hander was known to throw a slow ball to keep batters off balance.

Mack went to his bench as well and sent Eddie Collins to pinch-hit for shortstop Joe Boley. The old pro Collins showed 'em how it's done and bounced one of Miljus's slow balls past the pitcher's mound for a single that scored Foxx. Walt French batted for Earnshaw and flied to left for the third out.

The score was now 5-4 in favor of Cleveland. But they could not extend their lead in the top of the ninth against Rommel, who replaced Earnshaw on the mound. The A's were down to their last at-bats, and the situation looked promising when Bishop led off with a single to right field. Orwoll sacrificed him to second base. Cochrane walked but Simmons fouled out. With two down, Foxx hit to short, and when Joe Sewell's throw soared over first baseman Ed Morgan's head, Bishop raced home with the tying run.

To extra innings the game went, and each team had opportunities to get the all-important one run across the plate.

In the bottom of the 10th with two outs, Rommel and Bishop singled. But Orwoll grounded into a force play to end the threat. In the top of the 11th, Joe Sewell led off with a single and went to second when center fielder Haas fumbled the ball. Sewell took third base when Johnny Hodapp sacrificed him over. Homer Summa followed and grounded to first base. Orwoll scooped up the grounder and fired home. Sewell was coming home all the way and was tagged out in a rundown.

And on it went as both Miljus and Rommel pitched splendidly in relief. Mule Haas stepped into the batter's box leading off the home half of the 17th inning. He got a hold of a pitch from Miljus and sent it out onto 20th Street for a game-ending home run. It was his fifth of the year.

Surprisingly, the game took just 3:15 to play. Rommel (9-4) got the win while Miljus (5-9) was tagged with the loss.

The Athletics would have to wait another year to make it to the postseason. Although they finished strong, they fell short to the Yankees by 2½ games. New York won 16 of the 22 games between the two teams. New York went on to sweep the St. Louis Cardinals in the World Series.

The Athletics won the AL pennant three years in a row (1929-1931). In 1929 they defeated the Chicago Cubs and in 1930 they topped the Cardinals for back-to-back World Series championships. The Cardinals got even the following year, beating Philadelphia in seven games.

It was the last year the franchise would make it to the fall classic until 1972, when the team had relocated to Oakland from Kansas City.

SOURCES

The author accessed Baseball-Reference.com for box scores/information and other data, as well as Retrosheet.org.

The author also used game stories in the *Philadelphia Inquirer* and the *Cleveland Plain Dealer.*

GROVE AND UHLE BATTLE INTO EXTRA INNINGS

June 3, 1929
Philadelphia Athletics 3, Detroit Tigers 2
(13 Innings)

By Brian M. Frank

Something had to give as the league-leading Philadelphia Athletics and their ace, Lefty Grove, took on undefeated hurler George Uhle and the Detroit Tigers. The streaking Athletics had won five games in a row and 16 of 17, to open up a 5½-game lead atop the American League standings, with a 30-9 record. Grove was having another outstanding season, coming into the game with a 7-1 record and a 2.34 ERA.

The Tigers, on the other hand, were 24-22, and in fourth place. However, George Uhle had been dominating. He'd won every one of his starts, going 9-0 with a 1.86 ERA.[1] Two games before, he'd thrown an eye-popping 20 innings to defeat the Chicago White Sox. In order to earn his 10th consecutive victory he'd have to beat Grove and the high-flying A's.

Even though Detroit was struggling, and had dropped the first two games of the series, Athletics manager Connie Mack had a favorable opinion of the Tigers and their ability to turn their fortunes around. Mack told the *Detroit Free Press*, "I believe now that it is the club that we will have to beat if we win the pennant."[2]

The much anticipated third game of the series began as expected, as Grove "throttled the Tiger side in order at the outset."[3] In the Athletics half of the inning, Uhle "started like a mowing machine working on a field of grass" as he struck out the first two hitters he faced and retired the side in order.[4]

The first hit of the game came in the second inning, when A's cleanup hitter Al Simmons, who was batting .357, "birched a single to right."[5] After taking second on a passed ball, Simmons was sacrificed to third, and Uhle faced his first big test of the afternoon, as 21-year-old Jimmie Foxx strode to the plate with a runner at third and one down. Foxx was having a terrific season, entering the game with a .422 batting average and 9 home runs. However, Uhle fanned the slugger on an inside curve and got Bing Miller to fly out to left field to get out of the inning.

Grove didn't allow a baserunner until the fourth inning, when his "complete mastery over the Tigers" was finally solved.[6] After Roy Johnson struck out on three pitches, Harry Rice doubled to left field and Charlie Gehringer singled to bring home the game's first run. However, Foxx cut the throw to the plate, fired the ball to second and Max Bishop slapped the tag on Gehringer for the second out. Grove got out of the inning by inducing Harry Heilmann to ground out to short.

A poor throw by Uhle in the fifth inning proved to be costly. Miller led the inning off with a single and Jimmy Dykes attempted to advance him by dropping down a bunt. Uhle fielded the ball and fired a low throw to second that shortstop Heinie Schuble was unable to handle. Both runners were safe and Uhle was charged with an error. The *Detroit Free Press* wrote that the "misplay could have been converted into an out had not Schuble failed to handle cleanly a ball that bounded perfectly into his hands."[7] Grove sacrificed the runners up a base. Max Bishop then grounded out to second and Miller raced home with the A's first run. Mule Haas continued the rally with a single to center "just out of Rice's reach" to give Philadelphia its first lead of the game, 2-1.[8] Because of Uhle's error, both runs were unearned.

The Tigers scratched out a run off Grove in the seventh to tie the score. Charlie Gehringer drew a one-out walk and went to third on Heilmann's single to left. Dale Alexander "chopped a high bounder'" shortstop Jimmy Dykes fielded it and fired a "smoking throw" to get the runner at first.[9] But Gehringer crossed the plate to knot the score, 2-2.

The teams remained deadlocked as the game moved into extra innings, with both pitchers able to buckle down and work out of jams when necessary. The *Free Press* wrote that "Uhle was in trouble more consistently than Grove, yet he was the master when it came to getting out of it unscathed."[10] Uhle was also aided by a terrific catch by right fielder Harry Heilmann in the 10th inning. With two down and runners at the corners, Heilmann "saved the game from ending when he made a brilliant catch of (Sammy) Hale's liner."[11]

Both teams threatened to score in the 11th, but failed to bring a run home. Grove walked a pair of batters in the Tigers half of the frame, but Gehringer lined into an inning-ending double play to bail him out. Dykes singled with two

down in Philadelphia's half of the inning. Grove followed that up with a single, and after center fielder Harry Rice bobbled the ball, the runners ended up at second and third. However, Max Bishop grounded one to second base to end the inning and send the game to the 12th.

The A's finally broke through in the 13th. Jimmie Foxx "rattled the numerals on the scoreboard" for a double to lead off the bottom of the inning, his third hit of the day, raising his average to .425.[12] After Foxx was sacrificed to third, Uhle gave Dykes an intentional pass to put runners at the corners with one down. Connie Mack then sent 42-year-old Eddie Collins to the plate to pinch hit for Grove. Uhle "decided to take no chances on the vintage emergency man" and walked Collins to load the bases.[13]

Max Bishop, known for having a keen batting eye, stepped to the plate with the bases loaded and one out. Bishop was hitting just .238 at the start of the game, but because he had more walks (49) than hits (34), his on-base percentage was .435. Due to his penchant for drawing walks, the *Philadelphia Inquirer* wrote, "In such a situation, Bishop was perhaps the most dangerous man in the east for Uhle to confront."[14]

The first two pitches in the critical at-bat did not portend well for Uhle, as they were both balls. He then delivered strike one, followed by ball three. Bishop watched Uhle's next pitch go past for strike two, to make the count full. He then took another pitch, which home-plate umpire George Hildebrand judged as low. The bases-loaded walk allowed Foxx to trot home with the winning run, as Uhle "went through a pantomime that registered dissent over the umpire's decision."[15]

The walk brought home the first run Uhle had allowed since the fifth inning, and the first earned run he allowed in the game. The *Philadelphia Inquirer* wrote that it was "a freakish finale to a rousing battle and it gave the 15,000 spectators an idea of how highly important a base on balls can sometimes loom in these humming days with constant flurries of home runs in every park."[16]

The game had lived up to its billing, with both pitchers performing masterfully. Lefty Grove threw 13 innings, allowing two runs on four hits, while striking out seven and walking five. He earned his eighth win against one loss, lowered his ERA to 2.20, and helped lead the A's to their 17th win in 18 games.

George Uhle surely deserved a better fate after allowing three runs, just one earned, in 12⅓ innings, but his throwing error in the fifth and the bases-loaded walk in the 13th proved to be his undoing. The right-hander allowed 11 hits in the game while walking six (three intentionally) and striking out six. He took his first loss of the season after nine victories. Harry Bullion in the *Detroit Free Press* commented, "Uhle should have won today and continued indefinitely to compile his triumphs, but fate stepped in and precluded that."[17]

In such a superbly pitched game, perhaps it was fitting that the contest was decided by a single full-count pitch that had to be judged either a ball or strike by the home-plate umpire, rather than a ringing double off the wall or a long home run. The *Philadelphia Inquirer*'s James Isaminger wrote, "No majestic drive over the wall or into the stands, no booming crash against the fence beat Uhle, but just a meek and colorless base on balls, which under the conditions leaped into tremendous importance. …"[18] A game that had been dominated by two pitching aces ultimately came down to a single pitched ball in the 13th inning.

SOURCES

In addition to the sources cited in the Notes, the author consulted Baseball-Reference.com.

NOTES

1   Baseball-Reference has Uhle's ERA as 1.86. Retrosheet has it at 1.96. The difference stems from his start on May 29 against the St. Louis Browns, when Baseball-Reference charges him with four earned runs, while Retrosheet charges him with five.

2   "Connie Mack Avers Tigers Team to Beat," *Detroit Free Press*, June 4, 1929: 22.

3   James Isaminger, "Pass to Max Bishop With Winning Tally Brings Foxx Across," *Philadelphia Inquirer*, June 4, 1929: 22.

4   Isaminger.

5   Isaminger.

6   Harry Bullion, "Unearned Tallies Win for Mackmen," *Detroit Free Press*, June 4, 1929: 24.

7   Bullion, 21.

8   Bullion, 24.

9   Isaminger.

10 Bullion, 21.

11 Isaminger.

12 Bullion, 21.

13 Isaminger.

14 Isaminger.

15 Isaminger.

16 Isaminger.

17 Bullion, 21.

18 Isaminger.

FOXX AND GROVE LEAD RESURGENT A'S TO ROUT

July 25, 1929
Philadelphia Athletics 21, Cleveland Indians 3

By Jack Zerby

Connie Mack's Philadelphia A's hadn't won an American League pennant since 1914. But the team was beginning to contend again after finishing in eighth place for seven straight seasons from 1915 through 1921. Beginning with the 1922 season, the 66-year-old Mack, the only manager the A's had ever had since the franchise debuted as an original member of the league in 1901, had been steadily rebuilding his team with ever-improving finishes as Philadelphia went through 1929 spring training in Fort Myers, Florida.[1]

The 1928 club had finished second, a scant 2½ games behind the New York Yankees.[2] Mack, though, was "dubious about the prospects of his team" as the A's returned north, telling Philadelphia sportswriters that "if the boys can be made to hustle the way they were hustling the end of last season, I think that something might yet be done, so far they have not been."[3]

Al Simmons's health was a major concern. Simmons had helped get the rebuild going, debuting with the A's in 1924. He hit .308 as a rookie and never lower than .341 through the 1928 season.[4] But the "black-visaged concocter of swats ... had a slight recurrence of rheumatism late in the exhibition season," and had been advised by his doctor not to play for at least two weeks.[5]

Simmons was so discouraged that he "threatened to pack up and go to Milwaukee and take to the North Woods for the season," but he reconsidered after a visit by Mack and club vice president John Shibe. "[They] have always treated me royally. I will wait and see how things stand a little later," Simmons said.[6]

Philadelphia opened with a 13-4 win at Washington on April 17 without Simmons. But thoughts of the North Woods proved premature and Mack was likely pleased to have his slugger back in the lineup as a pinch-hitter by the A's' fifth game, on April 23. Then, after May 17, when the A's won to stand a comfortable 15-8 with a half-game lead, they hustled to 10 more straight wins to increase the lead to four games. By the close of play on July 24, they were firmly in control with a lead of 10 games.[7]

Fully recovered from the rheumatism that had delayed his 1929 start, Simmons was back in left field and having another prodigious season through July 24, hitting .361 with 22 home runs and 93 RBIs. But two other pieces of the A's rebuild, first baseman Jimmie Foxx (.388 with 20 home runs and 77 RBIs through July 24) and starting pitcher Lefty Grove (16-2 in 22 starts with a 1.95 ERA), were easing Mack's preseason

Jimmie Foxx belted at least 30 home runs in 12 straight seasons (1929-1940), leading the AL four times. In 1940 he became just the second player with 500 career home runs, retiring with 534 in 1945.

concerns as well. Both had debuted for Mack in 1925 and were in their fifth major-league season. Foxx, though, had been a teenage prodigy, reaching the majors at age 17.[8] Grove, 29, had spent five years prepping in the minors and was already in his 10th season of Organized Baseball in 1929.[9]

A recorded 5,000 fans and threatening skies greeted the fourth-place Cleveland Indians as they visited Shibe Park for the final game of a midweek series on Thursday afternoon, July 25. The Indians had managed to win the second game of a Tuesday doubleheader against the torrid A's, but this time Philadelphia, led by Foxx and Grove, made sure to a avoid a series split.

Veteran *Philadelphia Inquirer* sportswriter James C. Isaminger[10] wrapped it up nicely in his game story lead, showing off his penchant for history in classic late-1920s style: "Athletic bats made a river of blood run at Shibe Park yesterday afternoon when the league leaders slashed, hacked, and poleaxed Cleveland to fine bits and made a second Austerlitz of the afternoon by winning 21-3."[11] Throwing in everything but allusion to a baseball game with a football score, the scribe described the romp as "the limit in worstings" and a "real debacle," opining that "never did the Indians have a chance to win after the amplifiers announced the batteries."[12]

Grove started for the A's and, given the outcome, Cleveland surprisingly had a short-lived lead, scratching out a run in the top of the first inning on a one-out single by Lew Fonseca. The Athletics came back with vengeance in their first against Indians right-hander Johnny Miljus (6-7, 4.90) with a varied attack featuring a leadoff bunt single by Max Bishop, a pair of walks, appropriately scattered singles that kept the merry-go-round moving, Grove's own two-run double, a bases-loaded triple steal that scored Bing Miller, a Cleveland throwing error, a "synthetic" bad-hop inside-the-park home run by Mule Haas, and Foxx's 21st home run, which scored Simmons ahead of him.

Eight runs behind and with still only two outs in the Philadelphia first inning, Cleveland got a ray of hope when "rain descended so hard that [home-plate] Umpire [Dick] Nallin called time and the players ran for cover."[13]

But "after a wait of more than twenty minutes, the rain died down to a Scotch mist and there was a peek of sun" after a 35-minute rain delay.[14] Victims of a vicious onslaught but still game, Cleveland finally got out of the first inning without further damage, then nicked Grove's tightened arm for a run in the top of the second when Ed Morgan singled home Luke Sewell, who had doubled with one out. The A's rudely retaliated with five more runs in their second and third innings, with Foxx's two-run homer in the third – his second of the day and 22nd of the season, tying him with Simmons for the team lead – the biggest blow. Sewell scored a small-ball run for Cleveland in the fourth, but the A's matched it in their half.

It was 15-3 Philadelphia after four innings. Cleveland was done, but the A's weren't. Buoyed by his big lead and turning his thoughts to hitting, Grove "lofted a high homer over the right field wall, scoring three more runs" in the Philadelphia fifth as the home club tacked on five more tallies.[15] After Grove retired the Indians in the sixth, Mack gave him a rest; Eddie Rommel pitched the final three innings and the A's scored a run, their 21st, for him in their final at-bat. Grove's outing hadn't been anything to write home about – over six innings, he gave up three runs on eight hits and walked five, and his ERA went from 1.95 to 2.03 in the process – but he did what he needed to with a sizable lead and got his 17th win of the season.

Grove's three-run home run was the only four-bagger he hit in 1929. With his double, he had five RBIs. With Foxx's four driven home, the duo still accounted for fewer than half the Philadelphia runs. Simmons had only one of the A's 25 hits – his average dropped two points to .359 – but he scored three runs and drove in a pair.

The win pushed Philadelphia's lead to 10½ games over the Yankees. That increased to 18 as the A's rolled to a 104-46 record and the 1929 American League pennant.

The inevitable clinch came with a 5-0 win over the White Sox at Shibe Park on September 14. The A's had clearly absorbed Mack's finely tuned remarks through the press back in April when he questioned their hustle. With the season-long resolve reflected by 103 other wins and no losing streak longer than four games, the July 25 romp over Cleveland was just one more piece of evidence[16] that the team Mack had put together for 1929 was fully capable of meeting his expectations. Now he re-addressed them, quietly as always and again through the press, in the wake of the pennant-sealing victory: "I feel my boys have worked hard and deserve every credit for standing by and playing such consistent ball all through the season." And this time he acknowledged the Philadelphia faithful as well: "I am also delighted to know how pleased Philadelphia fans must feel. Without their encouragement we could not have done this."[17]

And he had to have been even happier a month later when the A's capped the 1929 season with a near-sweep World Series victory over the Chicago Cubs at Shibe Park, winning Game Five with a hustling ninth-inning, come-from-behind rally.

SOURCES

In addition to the sources cited in the Notes I used the Baseball-Reference.com and Retrosheet for the box scores noted below, team and player pages, and day-by-day logs.

baseball-reference.com/boxes/PHA/PHA192907250.shtml

retrosheet.org/boxesetc/1929/B07250PHA1929.htm

NOTES

1   Spring Training Sites – American League entry, Baseball Alamanac.com, accessed February 12, 2019.

2   The 1927 A's had also finished second, but 19 games behind the legendary "Murderers' Row" Yankees.

3   "Connie Mark Far From Satisfied with Showing of His Players," *Philadelphia Inquirer*, April 1, 1929: 18.

4   Granted, both major leagues were on the cusp of the explosive offensive production that culminated in 1930 and 1931, but Simmons's average of .354 with 191 hits and 111 RBIs over his first five seasons (1924-1928) is remarkable.

5   "Al Simmons, Again Ailing, Is Lost to Mackmen for Indefinite Period," *Philadelphia Inquirer*, April 10, 1929: 18.

6   "Al Simmons, Again Ailing, Is Lost to Mackmen for Indefinite Period."

7   The A's played .711 baseball (42-17) from May 28 through July 24. The Yankees were in second place, 10 games behind; Cleveland was a game over .500 at 46-45, 20½ games back in fourth place.

8   On the recommendation of his old third-base stalwart Frank "Home Run" Baker, managing in 1924 at Easton in the Eastern Shore League, Mack had signed Foxx, still a high-schooler, in 1924. "Jimmy Foxx," John Bennett, SABR Baseball Biography Project, sabr.org, accessed February 5, 2019.

9   Grove, who ultimately won an even 300 games in the majors, was developed by the International League Baltimore Orioles and won 111 minor-league games from 1920 through 1924. Mack acquired Grove's contract from Baltimore for $100,600 in October 1924.

10   Isaminger first covered sports in Philadelphia in 1905, and moved from the Philadelphia North American to the Inquirer in 1925. He received the J.G. Taylor Spink Award from the National Baseball Hall of Fame in 1974. James Isaminger entry, Baseball Hall.org., accessed February 7, 2019.

11   James C. Isaminger, "Athletics Slaughter Cleveland, 21-3," Philadelphia Inquirer, July 26, 1929: 18. The Austerlitz reference is to the Battle of Austerlitz, fought on December 2, 1805, in Moravia, now a part of the Czech Republic. It is considered one of Napoleon's greatest military victories. Austerlitz entry, Britannica.com, accessed February 7, 2019.

12   Isaminger.

13   Isaminger.

14   Isaminger.

15   Isaminger.

16   The 21 runs Philadelphia scored on July 25 weren't even the club's biggest output in 1929. On May 1, they had lit up the Red Sox at Fenway Park, 24-6, scoring 10 runs in the sixth inning. Grove was also the starter and winner in that one.

17   "Connie as Happy as Schoolboy Over Winning of Pennant," *Philadelphia Inquirer*, September 15, 1929: 1.

THE MISSISSIPPI MUDCAT SHUTS DOWN THE MACKMEN

October 11, 1929
Chicago Cubs 3, Philadelphia Athletics 1

Game Three of the World Series

By Gregory H. Wolf

Guy Bush "pitched one of his finest games," gushed sportswriter Irving Vaughn, following the hurler's resounding 3-1 victory over the seemingly invincible Philadelphia Athletics. "[He] curved them into complete silence."[1] "The Cubs' victory started and ended with Guy Bush," emphatically stated A's beat writer Stan Baumgartner, as Bush recorded the NL's first win in the fall classic in 11 games.[2]

Skipper Joe McCarthy's Cubs (98-54) were reeling after the A's (104-46) ambushed them at Wrigley Field in the first two games of the World Series. In what had been expected to be an evenly matched series featuring baseball's two highest-scoring teams,[3] the Cubs were outscored 12-4, fanned 26 times, and played uncharacteristically poor defense.

Marse Joe's decision to call on right-hander Guy Bush for the pivotal Game Three in Philadelphia was controversial. Called the Mississippi Mudcat, Bush was known as much for his pitching as he was for his appearance and personality. "He has the sideburns of an adagio dancer and his hair is so slick it looks like enamel," quipped sportswriter Jimmy Powers;[4] while Baumgartner described him as a "tall, lanky, dark-skinned rebel with the courage of a Robert E Lee and the heart of a Patrick Henry."[5] Not overpowering like Cubs Charlie Root or Pat Malone, 18-game winner Bush was a rubber-armed hurler who had appeared in an NL-best 50 games in '29, including 30 starts, and logged 270⅔ innings, third-most in the circuit. Despite his accomplishments, he was considered the Cubs' "big problem in the pre-series dope," opined *Chicago Tribune* sportswriter Edward Burns.[6] After starting the season with a 16-1 record, Bush struggled the last five weeks, losing all four of his decisions and posting a 7.74 ERA in 43 innings. His two-inning relief outing in Game One, in which he surrendered three hits and two unearned runs, didn't inspire confidence either.

The Tall Tactician, A's owner-skipper Connie Mack had another trick up his sleeve. Presiding over the big league's best staff (its 3.44 ERA and 4.1 runs per game were easily baseball's best), Mack had already surprised the Cubs by starting 35-year-old, seven-game winner Howard Ehmke in the opener. The submariner responded by fanning a World Series-record 13 batters. Either Lefty Rube Walberg (18-11) or 45-year-old ageless wonder Jack Quinn was expected to start Game Three; however, Mack called in George Earnshaw, who had started Game Two just two days earlier and was knocked out after 4⅔ innings, yielding eight hits and three runs. Big George, a 6-foot-4, 210-pound behemoth, led the majors with 24 wins in 1929 and Mack was confident the hard-throwing right-hander could neutralize the Cubs' right-handed-heavy lineup.

The City of Brotherly Love braced for record crowds at Shibe Park, hosting its first World Series since 1914, but the turnout was smaller than anticipated on a cloudy Friday afternoon with temperatures in the 60s. The paid attendance was 29,921, but *Philadelphia Inquirer* sportswriter George Dixon noted "scores of empty seats."[7] Even the newly erected viewing stands on row houses on 20th Street from Lehigh to Somerset drew little attention. Unlike at Wrigley Field, Shibe Park seemed devoid of festivities, with no bunting along the stands and no bands or dignitaries, though baseball comedians Al Schacht and Nick Altrock performed before the game. John Drebinger lamented in the *New York Times* that it "the most silent world's series in the history of the great fall classic."[8]

Earnshaw came out smoking. Through five innings he fanned seven, the same amount he had punched out in Game Two, thus already exceeding his average of 5.27 strikeouts per nine innings, which ranked second in the AL. He yielded only two hits, both by Hack Wilson, and escaped a jam on the first one. Wilson, who had smashed 39 home runs and led the NL with 159 RBIs, led off the second with a long shot that Vaughn of the *Tribune* thought "looked like a sure run" over center fielder Mule Haas's head.[9] The ball rolled to the wall, but Wilson held up at third. With one out, Wilson broke for home, but Riggs Stephenson grounded to Max Bishop, and his throw home easily erased Wilson, who wasn't able

to slide because Stephenson's bat inadvertently landed on the third-base line.[10]

Unlike Earnshaw, Bush was hit freely, bent, but didn't break. In the first four innings, he yielded six hits and walked one, and another reached via an error, but the Mississippi Mudcat was tight in the pinches and stranded all eight baserunners. Even when the Cubs recorded an out, something bad happened. After first baseman Charlie Grimm retired leadoff hitter Max Bishop on a popup, he was subsequently struck in the mouth by the ball as it went around the horn.[11] Bush escaped his first jam, in the second, when Jimmy Dykes and Joe Boley singled with two outs. With two strikes on Earnshaw, Dykes attempted to steal home. Catcher Zack Taylor dropped the ball as Dykes crossed the plate, but home-plate umpire Charlie Moran had already called strike three on Earnhart, prompting a loud protest by Dykes.[12]

Bush was tested again in the third inning after Haas and Mickey Cochrane singled with one out with Al Simmons and Jimmie Foxx due to bat. With Sheriff Blake warming up in the Cubs bullpen, Bush went to an 3-and-0 count on Simmons. Bucketfoot Al, who hit 34 home runs, batted .365, and led the AL with 157 RBIs, popped up to third. Foxx, the 21-year-old slugger, who emerged as a star with 33 round-trippers, sent an easy grounder to shortstop Woody English who fumbled it to load the bases. On his 24th pitch of the inning, Bush retired Bing Miller on an outfield fly.[13] "That was pitching, pitching that requires skill and courage," opined sportswriter Don Maxwell.[14]

The vaunted A's offense finally broke through in the fifth when Cochrane led off with a bounder to short and beat the throw to first. Bush retired the slugging Simmons-Foxx duo, but Cochrane advanced to second and then scored on Miller's single.

Bush's antics at the plate in the sixth helped wake up the Cubs' sputtering offense. According

Aerial view of Shibe Park during the 1929 World Series. The park was located in North Philadelphia, about four miles from the historical center of the city. (Photo via Getty Images)

to the *Philadelphia Inquirer*, Bush toyed with Earnshaw, "deliberately jutting his head out over the plate."[15] Earnshaw's bugaboo was his control (he led the AL with 125 free passes in '29) and he walked Bush, who had just 10 walks in 397 plate appearances thus far in his career. Earnshaw "should have dusted him off and had every right to do so," continued the *Inquirer*. After Norm McMillan popped up to Cochrane on a bunt attempt, reliable Jimmy Dykes fumbled Woody English's potential inning-ending double-play grounder. The Cubs' fortunes turned on hits by NL MVP Rogers Hornsby (39-149-.380) and Kiki Cuyler, both mired in 1-for-10 slumps with six strikeouts each. The *Tribune* described them as the "goatiest goats that ever amazed the baseball world with unexpected inefficiency."[16] Hornsby singled to left to tie the game. After Wilson's infield grounder moved up the runners, Cuyler singled over Earnshaw's head to put the

Cubs in the lead, 3-1. On his 28th pitch of the inning, Big George retired Stephenson to retire the Cubs.[17]

The Cubs had a man in scoring position in two of the final three innings, but Earnshaw clamped down the threat. With two outs in the eighth, Hornsby smacked a two-out double and Wilson drew Earnshaw's second and last walk of the game; Stephenson (17-110-.362) doubled to lead off the ninth, but failed to advance. With his 130th pitch of the game, Earnshaw fanned Bush, his 10th strikeout. It was also the Cubs 36th strikeout of the World Series, easily the most ever through three games, and just nine away from the then-Series record.

Staked to a 3-1 lead, Bush pitched his best ball in six weeks. After a one-two-three sixth, Bush once again faced Simmons and Foxx with men in scoring position, and once again held the dangerous sluggers hitless. After Bishop led off with a single and Cochrane smacked a one-out single, Simmons connected for a hard smash to deep center field, which looked as though it was "heading for the stands," wrote the *Inquirer's* James Isaminger.[18] Wilson raced back to snare the ball, but both runners advanced. Needing a single to tie the game, Foxx topped one in front of the plate. Taylor easily grabbed it and threw him out to end the threat.

Bush retired the last six batters he faced to end the game in 2 hours and 9 minutes. The first victory by the NL team in the World Series since the St. Louis Cardinals defeated the New York Yankees in Game Seven in 1926, Bush's victory rekindled the Cubs' title hopes. In the biggest win of his career, Bush tossed 140 pitches (85 strikes), scattered nine hits, fanned four, and walked two.[19]

SOURCES

In addition to the sources cited in the Notes, the author accessed Retrosheet.org, Baseball-Reference.com, SABR.org, and *The Sporting News* archive via Paper of Record.

NOTES

1   Irving Vaughan, "Bush Pitches Cubs to 3-1 Victory," *Chicago Tribune*, October 12, 1929: 1.

2   Stan Baumgartner, "Victory Began and Ended with Bush as Teammates Lagged," *Philadelphia Inquirer*, October 12, 1929: 18.

3   Highest-scoring teams based on runs per game. The Cubs averaged 6.3 runs per game; the A's 6.0. The Detroit Tigers also averaged 6.0 runs per game.

4   Jimmy Powers, "Guy Bush Has Gobs of What It Takes," *New York Daily News*, October 12, 1929: 28.

5   Baumgartner.

6   Edward Burns, "Hear That Din? It's from the Cubs' Dressing Room," *Chicago Tribune*, October 12, 1929: 23.

7   George Dixon, "Shibe Park Battle Stirs No Whoopee From Polite Fans," *Philadelphia Inquirer*, October 12, 1929: 1.

8   John Drebinger, "Cubs Triumph, 3-1, In 3d Series Game Before 30,000 Fans," *New York Times*, October 12, 1929: 1.

9   Vaughan.

10 Vaughan.

11 Drebinger.

12 Drebinger.

13 Pitch counts from "Number of Balls Pitched Per Inning," *Philadelphia Inquirer*, October 12, 1929: 19.

14 Don Maxwell, "Here's Chance AT Last! Pick a Cub Hero," *Chicago Tribune*, October 12, 1929: 23.

15 "Footnotes of the A's-Cubs Battle," *Philadelphia Inquirer*, October 12, 1929: 18.

16 "Kai and Raja Awake from Strikeout Nap," *Chicago Tribune*, October 12, 1929: 23.

17 Pitch counts from "Number of Balls Pitched Per Inning."

18 James C. Isaminger, "Cubs Beat A's, 3-1' Bush Outsmarts Macks in Pinches," *Philadelphia Inquirer*, October 12, 1929: 1, 18.

19 Pitch counts from "Number of Balls Pitched Per Inning," *Philadelphia Inquirer*, October 12, 1929: 19.

A's Stage Historic World Series Comeback with 10-Run Inning

October 12, 1929
Philadelphia Athletics 10, Chicago Cubs 8

Game Four of the World Series

By Scott Ferkovich

The Chicago Cubs' Hack Wilson jogged out to his position in center field to start the home half of the seventh inning. Turning toward the diamond, he again took note of the late afternoon sun, which had descended to a point almost directly above Shibe Park's double-decked grandstand behind home plate. The dazzling orb's slanting rays were now aimed straight into his eyes. It had already made trouble for Wilson. Two innings earlier, in this fourth game of the 1929 World Series against the Philadelphia Athletics, he had dropped a fly ball after losing it in the October brightness. But he made a spectacular running, leaping grab of a deep fly off the bat of Joe Boley, the next batter. To many observers, it was one of the finest catches they'd ever seen in a World Series. Then, in the sixth, he had trouble with another ball because of the sun, but was able to corral it.

Luckily for the Cubs, Wilson's struggles had not resulted in any damage. Their starting pitcher, Charlie Root, winner of 19 games in 1929, was cruising, having allowed only three hits. Chicago's vaunted offense, meanwhile, had taken an 8-0 lead. It simply was not the Athletics' day.

Nine more outs was all Root needed. Nine more outs, and the Series would be tied at two games apiece. Just two days ago, the Series had seemed all but over, the Athletics having won the first two contests at Wrigley Field, including a 13-strikeout gem by seldom-used journeyman Howard Ehmke. Chicago took Game Three, however, in a hostile Shibe Park, behind Guy Bush's tough pitching. Now, the momentum seemingly had shifted back to manager Joe McCarthy's Cubs. They had 22-game-winner Pat Malone ready for Game Five, and the final two would be back at Wrigley, where Chicago had been nearly unbeatable that summer, at 52-25. Only the Athletics, at 57-16, had had a better home record in the majors in 1929.

Al Simmons, Philadelphia's slugging left fielder, led off the seventh. On Root's third offering, "Bucketfoot Al" hit a home run to left that cleared the roof. The shutout was lost, and the home crowd finally had something to cheer about. Root took a new ball from home plate umpire Roy Van Graflan.

Jimmie Foxx singled, and Bing Miller hit a fly ball to center. The staggering Wilson lost it in the sun, and it fell in for a single, with Foxx taking second. Singles by Jimmy Dykes and Boley scored Foxx and Miller to make it 8-3.

With runners on first and third and nobody out, George Burns pinch hit for pitcher Eddie Rommel. He was quickly dispatched on a pop fly to shortstop Woody English, the runners holding.

Max Bishop, who had hit only .232 during the regular season but had also led the league with 128 walks, singled to left, scoring Dykes, sending Boley to third. Suddenly, the Cubs lead had been cut in half. McCarthy headed to the mound, took the ball from a frustrated Root, and waved in lefty Art Nehf from the bullpen to face the left-handed-hitting Mule Haas.

In center field, Wilson adjusted his cap and dark sunglasses, the better to peer in against the blinding beams of the sun. At 29, Wilson had led the National League in home runs three of the previous four seasons. Born in the steel mill town of Ellwood City, Pennsylvania, he was the illegitimate son of an alcoholic steelworker and a teenage mother who died when he was seven.

Wilson didn't appear athletic at 5 feet 6 inches tall, 190 pounds, with an 18-inch neck, spindly lower legs, and size 5 1/2 feet that only a ballerina could love. Yet he could hit a baseball a mile. He began his big-league career with the New York Giants. But manager John McGraw, the dinosaur disciple of small ball, wasn't won over by the top-heavy Wilson, despite his .295 average in a limited role in his rookie year of 1924. The Giants traded him to the Toledo Mud Hens in August of 1925. Following that season, the Cubs, in an unnoticed transaction, acquired Wilson in the Rule 5 draft.

Wilson and Jazz-Age Chicago were partners in perfect pitch. In awe of his clouts onto Waveland Avenue, Wrigley Field's denizens cheered him in the afternoon, and then toasted him late into the night as he made the rounds of the Windy City's numerous speakeasies. In 1930, his *annus mirabilis*, Wilson whacked 56 home runs, and established a major-league single-season record with 191 RBIs, one of baseball's most enduring numbers. 1931 was Wilson's *annus horribilis*, with only 13 home runs and 61 RBIs; within three years his career was finished, the fall precipitated by alcohol and riotous living. He gained induction into Cooperstown in 1979, 31 years after his death. But on the late afternoon of October 2, 1929, at the corner of 21st and Lehigh in the City of Brotherly Love, Hack Wilson was about to engage in combat one too many times with Hyperion the sun-god, and end up getting burned.

One out, runners on first and third, 8-4 in favor of Chicago. Mule Haas, who had hit 16 home runs in 1929, sent Nehf's first fastball on a line toward center field. Wilson drifted back. Despite his sunglasses, he again lost the ball in the glare. It soared over his head and rolled to the fence. The desperate outfielder ran the ball down, Boley and Bishop scoring. Haas, defying his nickname, sprinted like lightning around the bases. Wilson heaved a late throw in, and Haas slid into the home dish in a cloud of dust. Safe, declared Van Graflan.

The Cubs had blinked, and the score was suddenly Chicago 8, Philadelphia 7, with only one out.

The 36-year-old Nehf, winner of 184 games over 15 seasons, walked Mickey Cochrane. McCarthy, for the second time in the inning, marched out to the mound, and Nehf, for the final time in his big-league career, marched off of it.

Enter pitcher John Frederick "Sheriff" Blake, who failed to lay down the law. Al Simmons, back in the saddle for the second time that inning, singled to left. Foxx did the same, scoring Cochrane to tie it. McCarthy yanked the badge off Blake and tried his luck with Pat Malone, who plunked Bing Miller with his first pitch. Jimmy Dykes doubled, driving in two more to put the Athletics up by a deuce.

The Shibe Park crowd was delirious with delight. Strikeouts by Boley and Burns brought the frame to an end, but the book had already been written.

Athletics manager Connie Mack brought in Lefty Grove, winner of 20 in 1929, to start the eighth. He fanned four of the six batters he faced. At 3:42 pm, Rogers Hornsby flied to left for the final out of the game. Wilson was left on one knee in the on-deck circle.

What had looked like a 2-2 Series tie had suddenly become a three-games-to-one Athletics lead. Chicago never recovered. They lost the Series the following day in equally heartbreaking fashion, when Philadelphia scored three runs in the bottom of the ninth to wipe out a 2-0 Cubs lead.

Declared Mack to his men after Game Four, "I'd just like to be able to express to you the things I feel. But I can't. I'll have to let it go at that." To reporters he gushed, "I've never seen anything like that rally. There is nothing in baseball history to compare it with. It was the greatest display of punch and fighting ability I've ever seen on a field."[1]

In the dejected Cubs clubhouse, McCarthy mumbled, "You can't beat the sun, can you?"[2] Then, in an effort to deflect blame from his star center fielder, he pointed out, "The poor kid simply lost the ball in the sun, and he didn't put the sun there."[3]

Ed Burns of the *Chicago Tribune* wrote, "The greatest debacle, the most terrific flop in the history of the World Series. We've been looking at our score book for an hour now, thinking there must have been some horrible mistake, but ten she is folks."[4]

"Couldn't see the balls," Wilson clarified.[5] "I'm a big chump, and nobody's going to tell me different."[6]

Wilson and his four-year-old son Bobby departed the park together in a taxi. "The devil with them, Daddy," he remarked. "We'll get them next year."[7]

SOURCES

Chastain, Bill. *Hack's 191: Hack Wilson and His Incredible 1930 Season* (Guilford, Connecticut: Lyons Press, 2012).

Kashatus, Bill. *Connie Mack's '29 Triumph* (Jefferson, North Carolina: McFarland), 1999.

NOTES

1   Roberts Ehrgott, *Mr. Wrigley's Ball Club: Chicago and the Cubs During the Jazz Age* (Lincoln: University of Nebraska Press, 2013), 200.

2   Ehrgott, 201.

3   Clifton Blue Parker, *Fouled Away: The Baseball Tragedy of Hack Wilson* (Jefferson, North Carolina: McFarland, 2000), 85.

4   Ehrgott, 201.

5   Ehrgott, 201.

6   Parker, 85.

7   Parker, 85.

MILLER'S WALK-OFF HIT
GIVES MACKMEN THE TITLE

October 14, 1929
Philadelphia Athletics 3, Chicago Cubs 2

Game Five of the World Series

By Gregory H. Wolf

It was another dramatic victory or staggering collapse, depending on perspective. After exploding for a World Series-record 10 runs in the seventh inning to win Game Four, the Philadelphia Athletics scored all of their runs in the ninth inning in Game Five to defeat the Chicago Cubs, 3-2, and capture their first championship since 1913 on Bing Miller's thrilling game-ending double. "We outplayed and outlucked the Cubs," gushed Connie Mack, A's owner-manager. "No team in the world could have beaten us in this series."[1] The unsung hero of the game, however, was reliever Rube Walberg, whose spectacular performance was "one of the best examples of rescue pitching ever seen in a World's Series," submitted Philadelphia sportswriter James C. Isaminger.[2]

The Tall Tactician had seemingly pulled all the right strings thus far in the fall classic against the Cubs (98-54), and this game was no different. Most pundits expected staff ace Lefty Grove, coming off his third straight season with at least 20 victories, to get the start with the title on the line. Surprisingly, he had made only two

relief appearances thus far, tossing 4⅓ scoreless innings in Game Two and two in Game Four. However, Grove hadn't been feeling "well enough to pitch at least nine innings," revealed Mack after the A's victory. "His pitching fingers have been sore."[3] Instead Mack stunned everyone by calling on Howard Ehmke again. The 35-year-old submariner had neutralized the Cubs' right-handed-heavy lineup, which had led the majors in scoring (6.3 runs per game) by fanning a World Series-record 13 in the Game One victory.

Cubs skipper Joe McCarthy called on big Pat Malone to keep the Cubs' championship hopes alive and shift the series back to the Windy City, where anything could happen. The big 26-year-old, 6-foot, 200-pound right-hander from Altoona, Pennsylvania, was arguably the NL's best pitcher in 1929. After going 18-13 as a rookie, the hard-throwing Malone led the league with 22 victories, five shutouts, and 166 strikeouts, while his 5.6 strikeouts per nine innings paced the majors. He had been bombed in Game Two, yielding six runs (three earned) in 3⅔ innings and was collared with the loss. He was well rested, despite pitching two-thirds of an inning of relief in Game Four.

On a cloudy gray afternoon with temperatures in the 60s, Shibe Park, baseball's first steel-and concrete ballpark, was filled with 29,921 spectators, including President Herbert Hoover.

Ehmke, who had made only eight starts in the '29 regular season, wasn't as sharp as in his Game One masterpiece. He yielded a hit in each of the first three innings and then got in a jam in the fourth after retiring the Cubs' two most dangerous hitters, Rogers Hornsby and Hack Wilson. Following Kiki Cuyler's double and Riggs Stephenson's walk, Charlie Grimm and Zack Taylor connected for consecutive RBI singles to give the Cubs a 2-0 lead and knock Ehmke out of the game.

With the Cubs threatening to blow the game open, Mack called on Rube Walberg to put out the fire. The 32-year-old southpaw was one of Mack's "Big Three" hurlers, along with Grove and George Earnshaw (24-8), on a staff that led the majors in ERA (3.44). Wahlberg (18-11) had paced the staff with 20 complete games, but had made only one shaky relief appearance thus far in the World Series. In Game Four he tossed one inning, permitted two inherited runners to score, and was charged with an unearned run.

Walberg "lost no time rescuing the sliding Athletics," gushed Isaminger in the *Philadelphia Inquirer*.[4] He quickly ended the frame by fanning Malone, the first of 10 straight Cubs he dispatched. In the seventh he retired the side on three pitches. Philadelphia sportswriter S.O. Grauley wrote Walberg was "pitching his arm off an using his head like a [Christy] Mathewson," making a lofty comparison to "Big Six," whose three straight shutouts in the 1905 World Series were the gold standard to measure postseason success.[5]

While Walberg held the Cubs to just two hits in 5⅓ scoreless innings to keep the Athletics in

An overlooked player on a team filled with superstars, versatile flychaser Bing Miller was a star in his own right, batting .311 in his 16-year big-league career. A clutch hitter, Miller doubled in Game Five of the 1929 World Series to give the A's the title in walk-off fashion. (Photo by *Sporting News* and Rogers Photo Archive via Getty Images)

the game, Malone was tossing a "masterpiece," wrote Isaminger.[6] Through eight innings he had "tied the Mack clouters into a state of helplessness," extolled Cubs beat writer Irving Vaughan.[7] Malone had faced just 26 batters, yielding two hits, walking one, and benefiting from two double plays. In the fifth Jimmie Foxx reached on Hornsby's error at second and moved up a station on Miller's single, but Malone set down Jimmy Dykes and Joe Boley on popups.

Clinging to a precarious 2-0 lead, Malone punched out Walter French, pinch-hitting for Walberg to start the ninth. Hal Carlson (11-5 with a dismal 5.16 ERA) was warming up in the Cubs bullpen,[8] but his services didn't appear necessary with Malone "hurling fireballs with speed that dazzled the Mackian forces."[9] Quipped Philadelphia sportswriter John M. McCullough about the fans at Shibe Park, "the faint-hearted were toiling up the aisles towards the exits, apparently suffering from acute dyspepsia."[10]

Those hopeless fans who left the park missed what is surely one of the most exciting and dramatic conclusions to any World Series. The vaunted A's offense which had scored an AL-most 6.0 runs per game (tied with the Detroit Tigers) "suddenly turned on [Malone] and plastered his trappings," reported Isaminger.[11] Max Bishop, 3-for-20 in the Series thus far, singled to left to initiate a "current of heart pulsing and sturdy base blows,' wrote Isaminger, which "lifted [the A's] from the gutter to the purple raiment of the anointed."[12]

To the plate stepped Mule Haas, mired in a 4-for-20 slump but one of the heroes of Game Four. His inside-the-park home run, which center fielder Hack Wilson lost in the sun, accounted for three runs in the A's seventh-inning explosion. No slouch at the plate, Haas had batted .313 in the regular season and his 16 round-trippers ranked third on the club behind Al Simmons (34) and Foxx (33). Haas sent Malone's first pitch to deep right field. "There was a strange silence as Cuyler

backed against the fence as if he was going to catch the ball," noted Vaughan.[13] With one swing, the game was tied.

The rough-and-tumble Malone was livid. According to Grauley, he stomped to the plate and barked at his batterymate Zack Taylor about the pitch call.[14] Malone returned to the mound where he was surrounded by his infielders, who offered words of encouragement and also discussed strategy with Mickey Cochrane, Simmons, and Foxx due up.

The inspirational leader of the Athletics, Cochrane battled Malone for six pitches, grounding out to second. Simmons, who had finished second in the AL with a .365 batting average, belted Malone's second pitch off the scoreboard in right field for a double. Not wanting to take any chances, Malone intentionally walked the 21-year-old Foxx, who had emerged as one of baseball's most dangerous sluggers.

Bing Miller dropped the three bats he was swinging in the on-deck circle and dug in at the plate with the chance to be a hero. Historians can be forgiven for overlooking Miller on a team filled with superstars and Hall of Famers. A solid if unspectacular contributor, the 34-year-old Miller was coming off a season in which he batted .331, a few ticks higher than his then career .322 mark in nine seasons. Malone's first pitch sailed high, followed by two straight over the plate, but Miller didn't move his bat. "I took two strikes to wait for the ball I wanted," said Miller.[15] On Malone's 22nd pitch of the inning and 112th of the game,[16] Miller "drove [the ball] on a low, sweeping line" to right center, reported sportswriter John Drebinger.[17] As Miller raced to second, Simmons easily scored the Series-winning run and ended the game in 1 hour and 42 minutes.

Pandemonium reigned as the A's players celebrated near the mound and fans poured onto the field. "Paper by the ton had swirled through the stands and out onto the field," reported McCullough.[18]

It was a stunning yet not unexpected victory for the 104-46 Athletics, who were heavy favorites entering the World Series. The electrifying late-game rallies lent the A's an air of invincibility while the Cubs' stunning, soul-crushing collapses contributed to what would emerge as a reputation for flopping on the biggest stage in baseball and losses their next four World Series (1932, 1935, 1938, and 1945). The A's pitching staff thoroughly dominated the Cubs hitters, limiting them to just 17 runs (12 earned), a .249 batting average, and just one home run. They also struck out a then World Series record 50 batters.

Connie Mack became the first big-league manager to win four World Series championships. It was his first since his Deadball Era dynasty anchored by the "$100,000 infield" captured four pennants and three titles in a five-year span (1910-1914).[19] This new dynasty, which would win three straight pennants, and another championship in 1930, would stake its claim as one of the best teams in baseball history.

SOURCES

In addition to the sources cited in the Notes, the author accessed Retrosheet.org, Baseball-Reference.com, SABR.org, and *The Sporting News* archive via Paper of Record.

Grauley, S.O. "What Happened to Every Pitched Ball as Athletics Slew Chicago Bruins," *Philadelphia Inquirer*, October 14, 1929: 24.

NOTES

1   Stan Baumgartner, "Connie in Tears, Hugs and Dances with Happy 'Boys,'" *Philadelphia Inquirer*, October 14, 1929: 1.

2   James C. Isaminger, "Macks Win Games and Series; Hoover Is Thrilled as Hectic Rally in 9th Beat Cubs, 3-2," *Philadelphia Inquirer*, October 14, 1929: 1.

3   Baumgartner.

4   Isaminger.

5   S.O. Grauley, "Walberg Comes in to Make Cubs Lay Their Maces Down," *Philadelphia Inquirer*, October 14, 1929: 23.

6   Isaminger.

7   Irving Vaughan, "Macks Wins, 3-2; They're World Champions," *Chicago Tribune*, October 15, 1929: 31.

8   John M. McCullough, "Pandemonium Grips Hopeless Fans as A's Crash Through," *Philadelphia Inquirer*, October 15, 1929: 1.

9   Grauley.

10 McCullough.

11 Isaminger.

12 Isaminger.

13 Vaughan.

14 Grauley.

15 Baumgartner.

16 Isaminger.

17 John Drebinger, "Athletics Win Title; 3 Run Rally in Ninth Beats Cubs, 3-2," *New York Times*, October 15, 1929: 1.

18 McCullough.

19 The $100,000 infield refers to Stuffy McInnis, Eddie Collins, Jack Barry, and Home Run Baker.

BABE RUTH FIRST TO HIT THREE HOME RUNS
IN A GAME AT SHIBE PARK

May 21, 1930
Philadelphia Athletics 15, New York Yankees 7
(First Game of a Doubleheader)

By J.G. Preston

Babe Ruth made history on May 21, 1930, when, in the first game of a doubleheader, he became the first player to hit three home runs in a game at Shibe Park.[1] Oddly enough, that's not the primary reason why Babe is remembered for this game. Instead, he is incorrectly remembered, thanks to erroneous information in at least two of his major biographies, for something he *didn't* do that day.

The Babe's big day began in the top of the first inning, when, with one out and Lyn Lary on first base, he hit a ball over the right-field wall against George Earnshaw. Home run number two came his next time up, in the third inning. With one out, Earle Combs on second base and Lary on first, Ruth hit another homer to right, this one going ever farther. James C. Isaminger described it in the next day's *Philadelphia Inquirer*:

"He drove the ball over the wall, Twentieth street, a dwelling and all, the pill finally falling down in the second street from the park for the longest circuit crack that eyes in the press box ever envisaged."[2]

William E. Brandt of the *New York Times* was likewise impressed: "The ball soared across the first row of houses across the street from the right-field wall, diving into the back yard of a house facing on the next street."[3]

The Yankees increased their lead to 6-0 in the fourth inning on another home run, this one off the bat of third baseman Ben Chapman, an inside-the-park blow that eluded A's left fielder Al Simmons. Yankee right-hander Red Ruffing, who had been acquired from the Red Sox just two weeks earlier, held the A's to two singles over the first three innings, but the home team got on the board in the bottom of the fifth, when Joe Boley singled in one run and a second scored on an error by New York second baseman Tony Lazzeri.

Earnshaw was removed for a pinch-hitter during that fourth-inning rally, and his replacement, 46-year-old Jack Quinn, held the Yankees scoreless over the next three innings. Ruth batted once during that time, in the fifth inning, and again hit a fly ball to right, but this time it stayed in the park and was caught by Bing Miller. Meanwhile, Jimmie Foxx knocked Ruffing out of the box with a two-run homer in the bottom of the fourth to cut the Yankees' lead to 6-4.

Then, in the bottom of the eighth, the A's exploded. Yankees pitcher Roy Sherid, who relieved Ruffing in the fifth, walked Simmons leading off. Foxx tripled to score Simmons, and when Miller walked, manager Bob Shawkey called on Hank Johnson to take the mound. The A's immediately tied the game when Wally Schang hit into a fielder's choice, Foxx scoring, and it was 6-6.

Boley singled Schang to second, and both runners advanced on a wild pitch. That brought Quinn to the plate, but with the count 2-and-2, A's captain Eddie Collins, running the team in the absence of manager Connie Mack, who had an infected tooth,[4] called on Spencer Harris to take Quinn's place at the plate, and Harris walked to load the bases.

Max Bishop followed with a groundball to Lary at short, and when Lary's throw to the plate in an attempt to get a force out was wild, Schang scored to put the A's in front, 7-6. Mule Haas then bunted, and when Boley was called safe on the throw home, Yankees catcher Bill Dickey threw the ball against home plate ("in a childish display of temper," according to one account[5]); the ball rolled to the A's dugout, allowing Harris to score as well, and home-plate umpire Dick Nallin ejected Dickey. It got worse for the Yankees from there: an RBI single by Jimmy Dykes, a sacrifice fly by Simmons, and run-scoring singles by Miller and pinch-hitter Cy Perkins made it 13-6, A's.

But the Babe wasn't done yet. In the top of the eighth, with one out and the bases empty, Ruth hit another home run to right, this one off Lefty Grove, for his first-ever regular-season three-homer game. (He had hit three home runs in both Game Four of the 1926 World Series and Game Four of the 1928 World Series.) The crowd of more than 32,000 rewarded the Bambino with "one of the greatest ovations ever tendered any national pastimer at Shibe Park," according to

Tom Ryan of the *Camden* (New Jersey) *Evening Courier*. "Even Bing Miller's prize-winning world's series hit, which drove home the deciding run in the final game of [the 1929] world series with the Cubs, did not draw more applause ... than the Babe's third homer."

That made the score 13-7 in favor of Philadelphia. Simmons drove in two with a double in the bottom of the eighth to make it 15-7, which was the final score. Ruth was denied a chance to try for a major-league-record-tying fourth homer; he was on deck when Lary popped out to end the game.

The story of Ruth's three home runs was embellished in 1975, when University of Notre Dame history professor Marshall Smelser published his biography of Ruth, *The Life That Ruth Built*. Here's how Smelser tells the story of that day:

"For the first time in a regular season game he hit three home runs in one game. ... And he still had one more time at bat on a day when he was as hot as hydrogen fusion. Nobody had hit *four* in one game since Ed Delahanty did it in 1896. When Ruth came up in the ninth he faced the right-handed spitball pitcher Jack Quinn. Outraging reason, Ruth decided to bat right-handed against a right-hander. He took two called strikes in this unfamiliar batter's box, then crossed over to bat left-handed – and struck out. ... It was his dumbest hour."[6]

Smelser's book is not footnoted, and it's not at all clear where he got this story. But it quickly falls apart under inspection. Ruth did not strike out in the game, nor did he come to bat after hitting his third home run; he did not bat in the ninth inning, nor did Quinn pitch in the ninth. Ruth *did* face Quinn in the game: in the fifth inning, when he flied out.

None of the accounts of the game in the *Philadelphia Inquirer*, *New York Times* or *The Sporting News* mention Ruth attempting to bat right-handed at any point in the game, something you think might have caught their writers' attention. In fact, there is no evidence this allegation ever appeared in print anywhere before Smelser's book was published. Perhaps Smelser heard the tale from one of the many former teammates of Ruth he interviewed.

But Smelser's book is still considered one of the most significant biographies of Ruth, and as a result the yarn about Ruth batting right-handed also appears in Leigh Montville's best-selling 2006 bio, *The Big Bam*.[7] And as this was written in 2019, the claim that Ruth swung right-handed after hitting three home runs still appeared on several online baseball history sites, including Baseball-Reference.com, TodayInBaseballHistory.com and NationalPastime.com.

In the second game of the May 21 doubleheader, Ruth was held to a single in a 4-1 A's win. But he repeated his three-homer performance the next day at Shibe – only it took him two games to do it. He hit two homers in the first game of the doubleheader and another in the nightcap.

SOURCES

Full play-by-play of this game is on Retrosheet.org. Newspaper accounts of the game were accessed via Newspapers.com, the *New York Times* digital archive and PaperOfRecord.hypernet.ca (for *The Sporting News*).

NOTES

1 There were 20 later occasions on which a player hit three or more homers in a game at Shibe Park (or under its later name, Connie Mack Stadium), including Ruth's teammate Lou Gehrig the day after Ruth did it. Gehrig (1932) and Pat Seerey of the White Sox (1948) each hit four home runs in a game at Shibe. baseball-reference.com/tiny/XLxuF.

2 James C. Isaminger, "Ruth Slams 3 Homers in First, But 9-Run Rally Wins Battle," *Philadelphia Inquirer*, May 22, 1930: 18.

3 William E. Brandt, "3 Homers by Ruth Fail to Save Yanks," *New York Times*, May 22, 1930: 21.

4 Tom Ryan, "Athletics and Yankees Renew Hostilities Today at Shibe Park in Second Double-header," *Camden* (New Jersey) *Evening Courier*, May 22, 1930: 22.

5 Ryan.

6 Marshall Smelser, *The Life That Ruth Built: A Biography* (Lincoln: University of Nebraska Press, 1993): 422.

7 Leigh Montville, *The Big Bam: The Life and Times of Babe Ruth* (New York: Doubleday, 2006): 312.

Simmons' Sixth RBI Plates Reliever Grove for Marathon Win

September 4, 1930
Philadelphia Athletics 8, Boston Red Sox 7
(15 Innings)

By Gordon Gattie

The Philadelphia Athletics and Boston Red Sox were heading in different directions as September arrived. The 90-45 Athletics were leading the American League by 6½ games, while the Red Sox were struggling in the basement with a 44-86 record. The Athletics had won the 1929 AL pennant by a whopping 18 games over the New York Yankees, and defeated the Chicago Cubs in five games to win their first World Series since 1913. The 1929 World Series ended with a Game Five ninth-inning three-run rally culminating with a Series-ending double by Bing Miller that scored Al Simmons from second base.[1]

Philadelphia was guided by Connie Mack, now managing in his 33rd season (including his first three with the Pittsburgh Pirates). The Athletics enjoyed a glory period during the late 1920s, with future Hall of Famers Lefty Grove, Al Simmons, Mickey Cochrane, and Jimmie Foxx complemented by solid players like second baseman Max Bishop, veteran outfielder Jimmy Dykes, and late-blooming pitcher George Earnshaw. From 1929 to 1931 the Philadelphia Athletics' dynasty rivaled classic Yankees teams from the 1920s, 1930s, and 1950s; the 1970s Oakland Athletics, and early twentieth-century Chicago Cubs.[2] The Athletics won two World Series titles, three pennants, and over 100 games each season during the three-year stretch. Each season from 1927 to 1932, Philadelphia won at least 91 games and finished first or second. Expectations were high for the 1930 Athletics as the "great pitching trio of Grove, Earnshaw and [Rube] Walberg remains the most powerful pitching trio in the two majors."[3] Entering September, the Athletics were poised to repeat as AL champions.[4]

Boston fans faced challenging times in the late 1920s: From 1925 through 1929 the Red Sox finished last, never attaining a winning percentage above .400. They were led by pitchers Milt Gaston and Danny MacFayden, and outfielders Earl Webb and Tom Oliver. Boston projected to finish last again in 1930, potentially double-digit games behind seventh-place Washington.[5] Matching expectations, the Red Sox were unable to escape the cellar after losing a July 20 doubleheader, and endured a 14-game losing streak in May and another 11-game stretch in late July/early August.[6]

On September 3 Philadelphia pounded the Red Sox 11-4 in the first of a four-game series. Grove tossed six innings for his 23rd win and Jack Quinn pitched three scoreless frames for his sixth save. Foxx delivered his 33rd clout while newcomer Jimmy Moore plated four runs in his Athletics debut during the 16-hit barrage.[7] Boston scored four runs off Grove in the sixth inning after spotting Philadelphia a 5-0 lead, but couldn't keep pace.[8] The loss was Boston's fifth consecutive defeat and followed a Labor Day doubleheader loss to Washington.[9]

Swingman Bill Shores started for Philadelphia; he had won his last five decisions, including a shutout and three other complete games in which he allowed two runs or less. He had struggled early in the season, losing his rotation spot after surrendering six runs without registering an out in a May start against New York.[10] Shores rebounded over the summer, building a 10-3 record with a 4.37 ERA over 123⅔ innings entering the game. He experienced control problems, walking 54 batters while striking out only 33 during his 25 appearances. Shores mostly threw curveballs and fastballs as a youngster, and then added a knuckleball as his career ended.[11]

His mound opponent was the veteran MacFayden, now a regular on Boston's staff. He pitched solidly though he received little run support. MacFayden threw four shutouts in 1929, and recorded a 3.62 ERA (117 ERA+), but was 10-18 as Boston finished last in the standings and run production. Through August he had a 9-12 record and 4.25 ERA in 28 starts and 224⅔ innings. He relied mainly on his curveball, learning how to change speeds and windups over his remaining 13 big-league years.[12]

Shores quickly retired the first three Red Sox on two foul pop flies and a lineout. MacFayden struggled from the onset, walking Athletics leadoff hitter Bishop and allowing a bunt single to Dykes. After Cochrane advanced both runners with a sacrifice, Simmons opened the scoring

with a two-run double to left field. Both teams went scoreless over the next two frames. After three innings, Philadelphia led 2-0.

Boston's bats awakened in the fourth inning; after two infield outs, Webb doubled to center. Shore's control problems surfaced, as he walked Bobby Reeves and Phil Todt to load the bases. Shore plunked Hal Rhyne, and the Red Sox were on the board. Johnnie Heving hit into a fielder's choice, limiting Boston to one run. In the bottom half, MacFayden apparently settled down, allowing a lone double and three infield groundouts.

In the fifth, Shores couldn't shake his wildness, walking MacFayden and Oliver. After his fourth walk, Mack replaced him with reliever Roy Mahaffey. Russ Scarritt laid down a bunt, but Mahaffey's attempt to throw out the lead runner failed and the bases were loaded.[13] Bill Regan tied the game on a sacrifice fly scoring MacFayden, then Webb singled home Oliver to give Boston its first lead, 3-2. Mahaffey fouled out and Todt walked but Rhyne's fielder's choice ended the inning. In the bottom of the fifth, MacFayden turned wild, walking Bishop and Cochrane around a sacrifice bunt. Simmons's single to center plated Bishop, Al's third RBI, and Philadelphia regained the lead when Foxx's fly scored Cochrane. Miller grounded out to strand runners at the corners.

Boston catcher Heving greeted the returning Mahaffey with a sixth-inning leadoff double; with Oliver batting, Heving stole third base, the fourth and final steal of his career. Oliver's sacrifice fly drove Heving home with the tying run. The Athletics threatened in the bottom half after two singles and a sacrifice placed runners at second and third with one out, but Bishop struck out and Dykes grounded out. The scoreboard read 4-4 after six innings.

Even though he pitched six innings the previous day, Grove replaced Mahaffey on the hill in the seventh and proceeded to establish a tone by striking out Regan and retiring Webb and Reeves on groundballs. Grove and MacFayden were extremely effective over the last three innings of regulation, with a single and two walks the total offensive output from both ballclubs. They entered extra innings knotted 4-4.

With one out in the Red Sox 10th, Reeves blasted a homer into the left-field stands,[14] giving Boston a 5-4 lead. Grove retired Todt and Rhyne to prevent further damage. Foxx grounded out to start the bottom half, then Miller evened the score again by smacking a MacFayden curveball into the lower deck. Moore singled but was erased on a double play.

Over the next three innings, both teams missed winning opportunities. In the 11th, MacFayden walked two hitters with two outs, but Simmons grounded out. In the next inning, Boston's Regan tripled with one out but an inning-ending double play – with Foxx's foot possibly pulled off the bag[15] – squashed the threat. In the 13th inning, Grove got into trouble when Bill Sweeney's double and Rhyne's single placed runners at the corners with no outs. Heving hit a groundball to Athletics shortstop Joe Boley who threw to Bishop, forcing Rhyne out at second base; Sweeney dashed for home but was thrown out at the plate.[16]

Oliver started the 14th for the Red Sox by singling to center and moved to second when Scarritt sacrificed. Regan singled Oliver home and Boston regained the lead, 6-5. A groundout advanced Regan to second, then he scored on Otis Miller's single, giving the Red Sox at 7-5 their first two-run lead. Sweeney's single and a Philadelphia error placed two more runners in scoring position, but Rhyne grounded out, squelching the rally.

After losing his last nine decisions to Philadelphia going back to 1928, MacFayden finally could taste victory over Philadelphia. But Cochrane started the bottom half by hitting a double to right field; Simmons followed with his 33rd homer into the left-field seats and the teams were deadlocked yet again. MacFayden was replaced by Ed Durham, who retired the next three Philadelphia hitters.

In the 15th inning, Grove retired the Red Sox in order. Boley started the Athletics' half with a fly out, Grove singled, and Bishop flied out, so another inning looked inevitable. However, Dykes singled and Cochrane walked to load the bases for their cleanup hitter. Over three hours after the first pitch, Simmons crushed a Durham pitch off the center-field wall to score Grove and give Philadelphia the 8-7 victory.[17] Simmons starred with four hits and six RBIs while Grove earned his 24th win after delivering nine innings on zero days' rest.

The Athletics clinched the AL pennant on September 18 after a 14-10 slugfest victory with Grove earning his ninth save.[18] Philadelphia defeated the St. Louis Cardinals in six games to repeat as World Series champions. Grove led the AL with 28 wins, 9 saves, a 2.54 ERA, and 209 strikeouts, while Simmons paced the junior circuit with a .381 batting average and 152 runs.

SOURCES

Besides the sources cited in the Notes, the author consulted Baseball-Almanac.com, Baseball-Reference.com, Retrosheet.org, and the following:

James, Bill. *The New Bill James Historical Abstract* (New York: The Free Press, 2001).

James, Bill, and Jim Henzler. *Win Shares* (Morton Grove, Illinois: STATS, Inc., 2002).

Thorn, John, and Pete Palmer, et al. *Total Baseball: The Official Encyclopedia of Major League Baseball* (New York: Viking Press, 2004).

NOTES

1   Jimmy Keenan, "The 1929 Mack Attack," in *The National Pastime: From Swampoodle to South Philly* (Phoenix: Society for American Baseball Research, 2013, Expanded E-Edition).

2   Rob Neyer and Eddie Epstein, *Baseball Dynasties: The Greatest Teams of All Time* (New York: W.W. Norton & Company, 2000): 112-131.

3   Fred Lieb, "Athletics and Cubs Are Favored to Repeat as Pennant Winners," *The Sporting News*, April 17, 1930: 5.

4   George Kirksey, "Major League Pennant Races Seemed Ended with Athletics and Cubs," *Republican and Herald* (Pottsville, Pennsylvania), September 5, 1930: 11.

5   Lieb: 5.

6   "Red Sox Display Real Form in Second Game," *Boston Globe*, August 4, 1930: 6.

7   James C. Isaminger, "Young Moore Steals Show as A's Flog Hub Hose to Increase Lead," *Philadelphia Inquirer*, September 4, 1930: 14.

8   "Red Sox Cannon Fodder in Athletics 11-4 Win," *Boston Globe*, September 4, 1930: 14.

9   "Senators 5½ Games Behind the Athletics," *Boston Globe*, September 3, 1930: 20.

10 Gregory H. Wolf, "Bill Shores," SABR Biography Project, sabr.org/bioproj/person/edbc7b2f.

11 Bill James and Rob Neyer, *The Neyer/James Guide to Pitchers* (New York: Fireside Books, 2004), 384.

12 James and Neyer, 287.

13 "Al Simmons' Hitting Wins for the Champions," *Boston Globe*, September 5, 1930: 29.

14 James C. Isaminger, "Simmons Saves Tilt with Homer, Wins It with Ringing Single," *Philadelphia Inquirer*, September 5, 1930: 20.

15 "Al Simmons' Hitting Wins for the Champions."

16 James C. Isaminger, "Simmons Saves Tilt with Homer, Wins It with Ringing Single."

17 Associated Press, "Lefty Chalks 24th Victory by Nosing Out Boston in 15th," *Reading* (Pennsylvania) *Times*, September 5, 1930: 21.

18 James C. Isaminger, "Macks Score 5 Runs In 7th to Win and Hold Championship," *Philadelphia Inquirer*, September 19, 1930: 22.

GROVE OUTDUELS GRIMES

October 1, 1930
Philadelphia Athletics 5, St. Louis Cardinals 2

Game One of the World Series

By Brian M. Frank

To win their second consecutive World Series, the Philadelphia Athletics would have to beat a red-hot St. Louis Cardinals team in the 1930 Series. After being in fourth place, 12 games behind the league-leading Brooklyn Dodgers on the morning of August 9, the Cardinals won 39 of their final 49 games to storm their way to a National League pennant. The Athletics, meanwhile, won 102 games, finishing eight games ahead of the second-place Washington Senators in the American League.

Just as he'd done in the 1929 World Series, Connie Mack didn't name a starting pitcher in the lead-up to Game One. While many presumed Mack would give the ball to Lefty Grove, others thought he might try to surprise the Cardinals by tapping someone else for the job. St. Louis manager Gabby Street, on the other hand, named Burleigh Grimes, the 37-year-old spitballer, as the Cardinals starter before the Series started.

The Cardinals' fantastic finish made them extremely confident heading into the Series. Gabby Street boasted, "Mack is a great leader and he has a good team, but I have a better one. And ballplayers are the ones who win ballgames. I can't see how we can lose."[1] The most outspoken Cardinal was Grimes, who seemed to take pleasure in disparaging the Athletics lineup, saying, "They talk about (Al) Simmons and (Mickey) Cochrane and (Jimmie) Foxx, but they're not so tough. I'd a whole lot rather pitch against them than against the Phillie sluggers."[2] The hurler declared, "If I can't handle this team, I'm ready for the old man's home."[3] Grimes also made it clear that he relished the opportunity to pitch against Lefty Grove, boasting, "If he uses Grove, we'll beat him as sure as the moon looks down and then what is Mack going to do?"[4]

The Athletics were a determined bunch, though not as brash as the contemptuous Grimes. Connie Mack merely said that "the spirit of my players is wonderful and everybody in the squad is confident we will win our fifth title."[5] But showing more diplomacy than Grimes or Street, Mack added, "We expect no easy sailing and realize, every one of us, that we face a foe that will not crumble easily. We can win only by playing our best game."[6]

As most suspected, and as Grimes hoped, Mack sent Grove to the mound to start Game One. The fireballer had led the American League in wins (28), ERA (2.54), and strikeouts (209). It would be Grove's first World Series start after appearing in a pair of games in relief the season before. Grimes, on the other hand, had joined the Cardinals during the season after struggling with the Boston Braves. He seemed rejuvenated when he moved to St. Louis, going 13-6 with a 3.01 ERA with the Cardinals. He'd made three World Series starts in his career, a full decade earlier with the Brooklyn Robins.

With President Herbert Hoover on hand for the festivities, and "weather better suited to football than the summer sport of the nation," Grove's first pitch was ruled outside, and the 1930 World Series was underway.[7] Grove started the game strong, retiring the first six hitters he faced, three of them on strikeouts.

Grimes, meanwhile, began the game just as colorfully as his interviews had been all week. In the first inning he knocked down Mickey Cochrane with a pitch near his head, triggering a verbal sparring match between the two that continued throughout the game.

In the second inning, Jimmie Foxx lined a ball that banged off the right-field wall. As Ray Blades went to grab it, he "dropped it like a hot coal after picking it up," and Foxx was able to scoot into third on what the official scorer ruled a triple.[8] After the game, Gabby Street commented that Blades dropped the ball because he "got his hands in the spit. You know, Grimes put a lot of moist on the ball."[9] Bing Miller then launched a fly ball to Blades, which brought Foxx across the plate with the first run of the Series.

The Cardinals responded in the third. After Gus Mancuso blooped a single to right, Charlie Gelbert "knifed a dainty single between (Max) Bishop and Foxx" to put men at first and second with nobody out.[10] Grimes was next to bat. He "bluffed to bunt toward third and then deftly turned his bat and bunted on the other side of Grove. The pitcher had started toward third and when he tried to shift to the other side he slipped and fell."[11] Foxx fielded the ball, but Grimes crossed first safely to load the bases with nobody out. The next batter, Taylor Douthit hit a fly ball

to center field that brought Mancuso home as Gelbert raced to third. Sparky Adams, followed with a sacrifice fly, and the Cardinals took the lead, 2-1. After Frankie Frisch beat out an infield single, Grove was able to get Jim Bottomley to pop out foul to Foxx, ending the inning without any further damage.

In the fourth inning, AL batting champion Simmons, connected with a ball "so squarely that the pill traveled as if shot out of a gun" and "kept on until it sped over the board bearing the names of the players and vanished into Twentieth Street."[12] The home run knotted the score at 2-2.

With one out in Philadelphia's half of the sixth, Max Bishop worked Grimes for a walk. Jimmy Dykes then drove a ball to deep left-center field that looked as though it might leave the ballpark, "but at the last instant it took a nose dive and crashed against the wall."[13] Shortstop Charlie Gelbert appeared to have a play at the plate on Bishop, but, for whatever reason, he held the ball momentarily before relaying it home, allowing Bishop to score standing up, and the Athletics took the lead, 3-2.

Throughout it all, the fans at Shibe Park continued to show their displeasure with Burleigh Grimes. Sportswriter James L. Kilgallen reported: "How they booed him! They got on him early and by the sixth inning his every appearance was greeted with a Bronx cheer."[14]

In the seventh, Grimes "replied to jeers" from the crowd by singling with one down, but then the Athletics defense took over.[15] Douthit hit a grounder between short and third, and shortstop Joe Boley made "a lateral dive" to stop the ball, and "while still on the ground" he fired the ball to Bishop at second to force out Grimes.[16] Connie Mack called it the turning point of the game, and said the play was "one of the greatest I have seen in my long baseball career. It was remarkable."[17] Boley's acrobatic play looked even bigger when the next batter, Sparky Adams, singled. With two on and two out, Frankie Frisch hit a line

Hall of Famer and 300-game winner Lefty Grove led the AL in wins four times, ERA five times, and strikeouts seven times in his nine seasons with the A's (1925-1933). In 1931 he was named AL MVP after he posted a 31-4 slate while leading the A's to their third straight pennant. (Photo via Getty Images)

drive to left field that looked as if it might tie the game, but second baseman Max Bishop made a terrific leaping catch. Frisch later said that if the ball "had only been over his head or a foot or so to his right or left, it would have been an entirely different ballgame. It would have tied the score and probably put us ahead."[18]

Mule Haas tripled down the right-field line in the Athletics' seventh. He scored on a "stunning specimen of the squeeze play engineered in the most scientific manner by Boley."[19] Philadelphia added an insurance run in the eighth when Cochrane got his revenge on Grimes for knocking him down in the first. He lined a pitch over the right-field wall, to make the score 5-2. As Cochrane rounded the bases, "Grimes looked like a man who had just read the stock market quotations."[20]

Grove retired the Cardinals in order in the ninth, making his first World Series start a complete-game win. He allowed nine hits, striking out five and walking one. The outspoken Grimes allowed just five hits and three walks. However, all five hits were for extra bases – two home runs, two triples, and a double. A disgusted Grimes complained after the game, "Who ever heard of a team getting five runs on five hits?"[21]

Grimes remained impertinent after the loss, saying, "In a short series like this, a club gets a certain number of breaks. The A's got all the breaks against me. Under the law of averages, they can't expect another break in the whole series."[22] Gabby Street echoed his hurler's sentiments: "Listen, if that's the best they've got we'll beat them. We'll beat Grove the next time. Five hits, five runs. Why, man, you've got to be the luckiest team in the world to win like that!"[23]

In contrast to Grimes' bombast, the Athletics continued to have a quiet confidence about them. When asked after the win what he thought about the Cardinals, Grove responded, "Tell you more about it when the series is over."[24]

SOURCES

In addition to the sources cited in the Notes, the author consulted Baseball-Reference.com.

NOTES

1 J. Roy Stockton, "Mack Is Silent but He Is Expected to Start Grove Against Grimes in Opener," *St. Louis Post-Dispatch*, September 30, 1930: 1B.

2 Stockton.

3 James L. Kilgallen (International News Service), "Burleigh Anxious to Defeat Rivals' Greatest Pitcher," *St. Louis Star*, September 30, 1930: 18.

4 Stan Baumgartner, "Frisch Looks for Four Straight Wins Over A's if Grove Hurls in First Game Against Grimes," *Philadelphia Inquirer*, September 30, 1930: 1. "'Nothing to Give Out,' Mack's Only Reply to Queries About His Starting Pitcher," *St. Louis Post-Dispatch*, September 30, 1930: 1.

5 James C. Isaminger, "Earnshaw Favorite as Pitching Choice in First Contest," *Philadelphia Inquirer*, October 1, 1930: 22.

6 Isaminger, "Earnshaw Favorite as Pitching Choice in First Contest."

7 J. Roy Stockton, "Grimes Yields Only 5 Hits; Cochrane and Simmons Get Homers; Grove Is Effective," *St. Louis Post-Dispatch*, October 1, 1930: 2B.

8 James C. Isaminger, "Cochrane, Simmons Rap Circuit Clouts; Foxx Begins Hitting," *Philadelphia Inquirer*, October 2, 1930: 16.

9 James L. Kilgallen, "Burleigh Loafed on Bases and Let A's Bunt in Pinch," *St. Louis Star*, October 2, 1930: 16.

10 Isaminger, "Cochrane, Simmons Rap Circuit Clouts; Foxx Begins Hitting.""

11 Stockton, "Grimes Yields Only 5 Hits."

12 Isaminger, "Cochrane, Simmons Rap Circuit Clouts."

13 Stan Baumgartner, "Cards Got Nine Hits to Macks' Five, but Blows Were Feeble," *Philadelphia Inquirer*, October 2, 1930: 16.

14 James L. Kilgallen, "Burleigh Loafed on Bases."

15 Stockton, "Grimes Yields Only 5 Hits."

16 Isaminger, "Cochrane, Simmons Rap Circuit Clouts."

17 Kilgallen, "Burleigh Loafed on Bases."

18 Stan Baumgartner, "Snappy Series Singles from Shibe Park as Macks Shuffled Cards in Starter," *Philadelphia Inquirer*, October 2, 1930: 18.

19 Isaminger, "Cochrane, Simmons Rap Circuit Clouts."

20 Baumgartner, "Snappy Series Singles."

21 Kilgallen, "Burleigh Loafed on Bases."

22 Kilgallen, "Burleigh Loafed on Bases."

23 "Cards Stormy Over Defeat by 'Lucky' A's," *Chicago Tribune*, October 2, 1930: 21.

24 Baumgartner, "Snappy Series Singles."

EARNSHAW QUIETS THE CARDINALS

October 2, 1930
Philadelphia Athletics 6, St. Louis Cardinals 1

Game Two of the World Series

By James Forr

These St. Louis Cardinals were a gang of swaggering roughnecks who deferred to no one, not even the defending world champions. Their preening and trash-talking started even before the World Series began and continued during and after their 5-2 loss in the opener. In Game Two Philadelphia turned to a tall, well-bred gentleman from the leafy New York suburbs to shut them up.

Manager Gabby Street's Redbirds were so unfazed following their Game One defeat that it was almost obnoxious. They couldn't come through with the big hit against the great Lefty Grove, but that didn't shake their confidence one bit. "We thought we were the better club and now we know it," insisted Street.[1] "They used their best and perhaps their one good pitcher and they had to have all the breaks to win."[2] Many managers may feel that way after a loss but few are bold enough to say it, and the Athletics took notice.

There was a sliver of truth in his comments, though. Outside of Grove, the Athletics had no great pitchers, just a stable of solid, steady workhorses. One of them was literate Swarthmore College product George Earnshaw, the Game Two starter, fresh off his second consecutive 20-win season.

Opposing him was Flint Rhem, who earned headlines three weeks earlier when he went AWOL from the team, and then swore with a straight face he been taken hostage by armed bandits who forced him to consume large quantities of alcohol. No one believed him. After all, persuading Rhem to drink did not typically require kidnapping, guns, or any form of persuasion at all, really. But although he may have been a bad liar, Rhem was a fine pitcher who went 12-8 in 1930 and had won 20 games for the Cardinals during their World Series run in 1926.

It was a sunny, breezy afternoon and quite chilly, albeit slightly warmer than the previous day, when the weather forced fans to break out their overcoats. A sellout crowd of 32,295 packed Shibe Park, with perhaps another 2,000 fans watching from the rooftops beyond right field.[3]

Earnshaw retired the first two batters of the game before Frankie Frisch laced a double down the left-field line. It was Frisch's 43rd hit in World Series competition, breaking a record set by the White Sox' Eddie Collins in 1919. The Cardinals stranded him at second when Jim Bottomley flied out to center.

Rhem had nothing and was fooling no one, and that became apparent right away. Max Bishop led off the bottom of the first with a fly ball that Taylor Douthit tracked down in deep right-center. Third baseman Sparky Adams then made a brilliant play to retire Jimmy Dykes on a sharply hit grounder that was headed down the line. At that point the miracles ceased.

The Cardinals' plan was to work over Philadelphia's most dangerous hitters with breaking pitches low in the strike zone.[4] Rhem didn't follow that script with Mickey Cochrane, although it isn't clear exactly what he did. The *Washington Post's* Shirley Povich described the 2-and-2 pitch to Cochrane as a fastball off the end of the bat. J. Roy Stockton of the *St. Louis Post-Dispatch* saw it as a curveball in on the handle. But regardless of where the pitch was, or what it was, it ended up out on 20th Street beyond the right-field wall, Cochrane's second home run in as many days. After Al Simmons followed with a single, Jimmie Foxx scorched a double to left-center field, which scored a sliding Simmons ahead of the throw and gave Philadelphia a 2-0 lead.

With one out in the second, Cardinals rookie George Watkins cut the margin in half with a solo shot of his own. Next, Gus Mancuso reached on an infield single and Charlie Gelbert followed with a bad-hop base hit that shot over the head of second baseman Bishop, sending Mancuso to third. "That's the first break the Cardinals have had in the Series," mused one writer to his colleagues in the press box.[5] But Earnshaw escaped trouble by striking out Rhem and setting down Douthit on a little looper to Bishop. St. Louis barely laid a hand on Earnshaw the rest of the afternoon.

The A's opened up on Rhem again in the third. He retired the first two men easily but then second baseman Frisch misplayed a routine grounder from Cochrane, which proved to be Rhem's undoing. Simmons followed with a laser to right field. Watkins broke late and tried for a shoestring catch but the ball skipped past him

and rolled to the wall. Cochrane came home and Simmons ended up with a double.

Rhem fell behind on the next hitter, Foxx, three balls and no strikes, before dropping in a curve for a 3-and-1 count. Surprisingly, this is when Street decided to order an intentional walk. Rhem shook his head and stomped around the mound, but complied. Bing Miller hammered the next pitch into left field for a single. Rhem, sensing that Chick Hafey's throw to the plate would be late, tried to cut it off but the ball caromed off his glove and toward the backstop. Simmons scored to make it 4-1, and the runners moved up to second and third on Rhem's error. The Cardinals avoided further damage when Mule Haas lined out sharply to Douthit.

Philadelphia finally pummeled the beleaguered Rhem into submission in the fourth. Joe Boley opened with a single off shortstop Gelbert's glove. After Earnshaw struck out, Bishop coaxed a four-pitch walk – one of seven bases on balls he drew in the series. Then Dykes, one of the hitting stars of the 1929 World Series, blasted a double to deep center field, scoring Boley and Bishop, making it 6-1, and ending the day for Rhem.

The rest of the afternoon was almost entirely uneventful. The crowd "found it difficult to stifle a yawn," quipped John Drebinger in the *New York Times*.[6] Earnshaw allowed just two hits over the final seven innings. Jim Lindsey and Syl Johnson were no less impressive for the Cardinals, combining for 4⅔ innings of no-hit relief. One of the few remaining lively moments came during the seventh-inning stretch when a band taunted the Cardinals and tickled the fans with an appropriately anguished version of "The St. Louis Blues."

Athletics manager Connie Mack had relief pitchers warming briefly on a couple of occasions, once in the seventh after a leadoff walk and again in the eighth after a leadoff single, but Earnshaw smothered those threats effortlessly. In the ninth he checkmated the Cardinals by retiring Hafey on a grounder and then striking out Watkins and Mancuso. Earnshaw took the ball from his catcher, Cochrane, leaped over the foul line, and bounded into the dugout, a brilliant day of work behind him. He scattered six hits, walked one, and fanned eight.

Dykes couldn't resist getting in a shot at the Cardinals after the game. "They can't complain about the breaks beating them today," he crowed. "I don't think the Cardinals would have scored another run off Earnshaw if the game would have lasted 24 hours."[7] Mack was more diplomatic, but echoed the general point. "He [was] fast and his control was good. And when Earnshaw is in that mood, he's just about unbeatable."[8] He was unbeatable for the rest of the Series, too, surrendering only two runs in 25 innings over three starts.

Sid Keener, the sports editor of the *St. Louis Star*, was among those who were critical of Street's

decision-making in Game Two. He wondered why the St. Louis manager didn't lift Rhem for a pinch-hitter when the Cardinals had the tying run at third in the second inning. Beyond that, he questioned the decision to start Rhem in the first place when Bill Hallahan, who led the staff in starts and wins, was rested and ready to go. Street seemed insulted by the criticism. "I thought Rhem was the one who would win for us. Beyond that I have nothing to say," he snapped.[9]

The defeated Cardinals moped around the clubhouse for a few moments until Frisch, bat in hand, jumped up on an equipment trunk and shouted, "Is there a man here who thinks we're licked?" Combative Game One starter Burleigh Grimes responded, "Hell, no!" and his suddenly re-energized teammates joined in the shouting.[10]

In truth, St. Louis had good reason to despair. They had been dominated in the first two games,

Aerial view of Shibe Park for the opening game of the 1930 World Series. After posting a 102-52 regular season record, the A's beat the St. Cardinals in six games to claim their second straight title. (Photo via Getty Images)

their number four and five hitters, Bottomley and Hafey, were a combined 1-for-16, and no team had ever rallied from a 2-0 deficit to win a best-of-seven World Series. Nonetheless, the Series was headed west for the next three games, Hallahan would be on the mound in Game Three, and the Cardinals' reservoir of confidence was bottomless. "Enjoy yourselves until we get back,"[11] Frisch sneered at the A's fans as the Cardinals' team buses prepared to pull away. Indeed, St. Louis would not go down easily.

SOURCES

In addition to the newspaper sources cited in the Notes, the author used Baseball-Reference.com and Retrosheet.org.

The author also reviewed the following sources for play-by-play and other information:

"Gossip of Second Game," *The Sporting News*, October 9, 1930: 6.

Isaminger, James C., and John M. McCullough. "A's Topple Cards 6-1 for Second of Series; Earnshaw Fans 8," *Philadelphia Inquirer*, October 3, 1930: 1.

Macht, Norman. *Connie Mack: The Turbulent and Triumphant Years* (Lincoln: University of Nebraska Press, 2012), 592.

Baumgartner, Stan. "Snappy Series Singles from Shibe Park as Macks Shuffled Cards in Second," *Philadelphia Inquirer*, October 3, 1930: 26.

NOTES

1   Harry T. Brundidge, "'We Thought We Were the Better Club, Now We Know It,' Says Gabby," *St. Louis Star*, October 2, 1930: 1.

2   J. Roy Stockton, "Grimes Yields Only Five Hits; Cochrane and Simmons Get Homers; Grove Is Effective," *St. Louis Post-Dispatch*, October 1, 1930: 2B.

3   Shirley L. Povich, "Cardinal Guns Are Muffled by Earnshaw," *Washington Post*, October 3, 1930: 1.

4   Sid Keener, "A's Big Three Knock Gabby's Plans Sky High," *St. Louis Star*, October 3, 1930: 1.

5   J. Roy Stockton, "Rhem Batted from the Box; Watkins Knocks a Home Run, Cochrane Gets His Second One," *St. Louis Post-Dispatch*, October 2, 1930: 3C.

6   John Drebinger, "Athletics Win Again from Cardinals, 6-1," *New York Times*, October 3, 1930: 1.

7   William Hennigan, "Mack Praises Pitching of Earnshaw," *Washington Post*, October 3, 1930: 19.

8   Hennigan.

9   Sid Keener, "Sid Keener's Column," *St. Louis Star*, October 3, 1930: 22.

10 Harry T. Brundidge, "Rhem's Failure Victory for Drys, Says Teammate," *St. Louis Star*, October 3, 1930: 1.

11 Herman Wecke, "Redbirds Think Hallahan's Speed Will Check Athletics," *St. Louis Post Dispatch*, October 3, 1930: 2B.

Earnshaw's Complete-Game Gem on One-Day Rest Gives Athletics Second Straight Championship

October 8, 1930
Philadelphia Athletics 7, St. Louis Cardinals 1

Game Six of the World Series

By Gregory H. Wolf

George Earnshaw "gave an exhibition of pitching mastery that has been seldom equaled in [the] world series," declared St. Louis sportswriter John E. Wray.[1] Pitching on one day's rest, the Philadelphia Athletics hurler tossed a complete game to win Game Six and capture the club's second straight title. Lauded as the "the lion-hearted leviathan of the peak" by A's beat writer James Isaminger, Earnshaw extended his Series scoreless streak to 23⅓ innings before yielding a ninth-inning tally in the resounding 7-1 victory over the Cardinals.[2]

In his 50th year of baseball, owner-skipper Connie Mack's A's (102-52) ran away with the pennant, which sportswriter Grantland Rice considered a "wonder" given that the Tall Tactician "had only two dependable pitchers all year."[3] Those two – Earnshaw and Lefty Grove – proved to be an unconquerable combination. In the "Year of the Hitter," pitching decided the Series. Grove won the Series opener, 5-2, followed by Earnshaw's 6-1 victory in the second contest. After the Cardinals won a pair in the Gateway City, Earnshaw held the Redbirds scoreless on two hits through

seven innings in Game Five before yielding to a pinch-hitter. Grove tossed two innings of relief and picked up the win on Jimmie Foxx's dramatic two-run ninth-inning home run.

On the train ride from St. Louis back to the City of Brotherly Love, Mack approached Earnshaw and Grove about starting Game Six. Both hurlers volunteered to pitch. Grove (28-5) was baseball's best pitcher, having paced the majors in wins, ERA (2.54 in 291 innings), and strikeouts (209); he was probably also baseball's best closer – if there had been such a designation at the time – relieving 18 times among his big-league-most 50 appearances. Mack decided to go with Earnshaw and keep his ace ready in the bullpen with the option to start Game Seven, if needed. "In all my years in baseball," said Mack, "I have never seen two pitchers more willing to work at all times than this master right-hander and this king of left-handers."[4]

Grove's dominance during the A's dynasty has cast a shadow on Earnshaw, a hulking, 6-foot-4, 210-pound behemoth affectionately called Moose. In just his second full season in the majors, the

The heart and soul of Connie Mack's second dynasty, Hall of Famer Mickey Cochrane batted .321 in his nine seasons with the Athletics (1925-1933). (Photo Reproduction by Transcendental Graphics/Getty Images)

30-year-old hurler followed his 24-win campaign with a 22-13 slate, led the majors with 39 starts, and trailed only Grove in appearances (49) and strikeouts (193); his 4.44 ERA in 296 innings was below the major-league average (4.83), but he struggled with control, issuing a league-most 139 walks.

On a pleasant Wednesday afternoon with overcast skies and temperature in the 60s, Shibe Park was once again filled to capacity with 32,295 spectators.[5] Several thousand more were sitting atop the row houses on 20th Street behind right field. Al Schacht and Nick Altock provided the crowd with pregame entertainment and baseball shenanigans.

Earnshaw "blazed through the Red Bird flock" in the first, wrote Philadelphia sportswriter S.O. Grauley, fanning two of the three batters he faced.[6] Grove was already in the bullpen and stayed warm throughout the game.[7] Skipper Gabby Street's Cardinals (92-62) had led the NL with 1,004 runs while each member of their starting lineup batted at least .300, but the offensive juggernaut had scored just 11 runs in the first five Series games. Typically disciplined at the plate, the Cardinals were "swinging at everything" since the first game, an anonymous umpire told St. Louis sportswriter Sid Keener.[8] Consequently, Earnshaw kept "his fastballs high on the outside and his curves low on the inside," noted the arbiter, and the Cardinals failed to adjust.

The Cardinals staff finished second in the NL in team ERA (4.39), yet lacked a bona fide ace, like Grove or Earnshaw. Their best hope was hard-throwing 27-year-old right-hander Bill Hallahan, who emerged in his first full season in the majors to lead the staff in practically every category, including wins (15) and innings (237⅓), while also pacing the NL with 177 punchouts. Wild Bill also led the league in walks (126). In Game Three he blanked the A's despite yielding seven hits and five walks.

After Jimmy Dykes drew a one-out walk in the bottom of the first, Mickey Cochrane lined a screeching shot to first base. According to Keener, Jim Bottomley leaped and "connected with the ball."[9] "Just for a moment it looked like Sunny Jim had a perfect double play" to end the inning, wrote Keener, but Bottomley couldn't corral the ball, which flew into right field, through George Watkins' legs for an error, and rolled to the wall. Dykes scored and Cochrane might have, reported Isaminger, but was held at third by coach Eddie Collins.[10] The "ball game was lost" on Cochrane's double, lamented Keener.[11] After Al Simmons fanned, Foxx walked. Mired in a 1-for-18 slump, Bing Miller blasted a double to the scoreboard to plate Cochrane.

Earnshaw systematically dismantled the Cardinals, yielding just three hits and a walk through eight scoreless frames. His "speed was as blinding, his control excellent and his curve broke fast enough to befuddle the Missourians," gushed Grauley.[12] His effectiveness notwithstanding, Earnshaw was in excruciating pain, suffering from a deep stone bruise on his foot that he had aggregated in Game Five. According to the *Philadelphia Inquirer*, Earnshaw removed his shoe each inning so that the trainer could massage his foot.[13] The foot agony didn't bother his reflexes. In both the sixth and seventh innings, he snared bullets back to the mound, robbing what might have been hits from Andy High and Frankie Frisch, respectively. "Big George acted like a man who had snared a couple of hand grenades and was trying to be nonchalant about it," quipped A's beat writer George H. Dixon.[14]

While Earnshaw mowed down the Redbirds, the A's vaunted offense, which trailed only the New York Yankees in scoring, kept swinging for the fences. Hallahan, who was pitching on three days' rest, labored through the second, hitting Max Bishop with a pitch and walking Dykes, but escaped the jam. Nonetheless, he was removed from the game because a blister on the tip of his middle finger burst.[15] "I had a little swelling of the finger before the game," Hallahan admitted later.[16]

Al Simmons, who had led the AL with a .381 batting average while rapping 36 home runs and driving in 165 runs, led off the Athletics' third inning with a towering blast into the upper deck in left field off reliever Syl Johnson to give the A's a 3-0 lead. Isaminger described the shot as the "crack of doom to the Cardinals' hopes of winning the game."[17]

Bucketfoot Al's long ball did, in fact, silence the crowd after its momentary eruption of euphoria wore off. Newspapers described the Philadelphia crowd as subdued. While Isaminger wrote that the spectators "sat through most [of the game] without one situation where there was uneasiness,"[18] syndicated scribe Westbrook Pegler declared that there was "no suspense at any time," and that the game "petered out instead of rising to a climax."[19]

In the fourth with Bishop on via a walk, Dykes connected for a "bristling drive that screamed on a line straight into the left field stands," wrote Isaminger, extending the A's lead to 5-0. The dependable third baseman, who had entered the game mired in a 2-for-16 slump and was coming off two rough defensive games, was the hitting hero of this game, reaching base all four times on two hits and two walks, scoring twice, and knocking in two runs.

Emerging as baseball's most feared slugger after Babe Ruth, Foxx (.335-37-156) doubled to open the fifth. The A's reverted to "scientific baseball," wrote Isaminger, as Miller executed a sacrifice bunt followed by Mule Haas's deep fly out to drive in Foxx.[20]

The A's scored their seventh unanswered run in the sixth off Jim Lindsey, who relieved Johnson to start the frame. Bishop walked and moved to third on Dykes' doubles, and scored on Cochrane's sacrifice fly.

Earnshaw took the mound in the ninth riding a streak of 22⅔ scoreless innings since yielding a one-out home run to Watkins in the second inning of Game Two. High led off with a single, followed by Watkins' walk to bring the slumping heart of the Cardinals batting order to the plate. Frisch, who had scored 121 runs and knocked in 114 while batting .346, hit a screeching liner directly at Foxx who doubled up Watkins. The Fordham Flash concluded the Series without scoring or driving in a run. Chick Hafey (.336-26-107) connected for a double to left, driving in High. Bottomley (.304-15-97), whom St. Louis sportswriters derided as the biggest flop of the series for his dreadful 1-for-22 performance, walked. On his 24th pitch of the inning and 124th of the game, Earnshaw retired Jimmie Wilson on a fly ball to right field to end the game in 1 hour and 46 minutes.[21]

Earnshaw's three-start performance was hailed as one of the best in the history of the World Series, even though he didn't win three games as eight pitchers before him had done.[22] His complete-game five-hitter with six punchouts and three walks pushed his Series totals to a 0.72 ERA in 25 innings, while surrendering just 13 hits and walking 7 while fanning 19. Grauley praised Eanshaw's performance as the greatest World Series pitching since Christy Mathewson set the standard by pitching three shutouts for the New York Giants in 1905.[23]

The World Series in the Year of the Hitter, when big-teams produced a record .296 batting average and established new scoring records, unfolded as a showcase of pitchers. The A's managed only seven hits in Game Six, but they all went for extra bases. In the Series, the A's outscored the Cardinals 21-12; both teams batted well below their regular-season average (the A's .197 down from .294 and the Cardinals .200, a far cry from their .314 average).

POSTSCRIPT

The A's and Cardinals met for a rematch in 1931. While Mack fielded practically the same team, Street's club was infused with some new talent, including the exciting catalyst Pepper Martin and rookie pitcher Paul Derringer. The final result shocked many and signaled the end of a dynasty.

SOURCES

In addition to the sources cited in the Notes, the author accessed Retrosheet.org, Baseball-Reference.com, SABR.org, *The Sporting News* archive via Paper of Record, and the following:

Haley, Martin. "Pitched Brilliantly in 3 Games, Winning Two and Sharing Honors in Third," *St. Louis Globe-Democrat*, October 9, 1930: 20.

Stockton, J. Roy. "Cardinal Southpaw Looked Better Than Ever at Start; Redbirds Fought All the Way," *St. Louis Post-Dispatch*, October 9, 1930: 28.

NOTES

1   John E. Wray, "Wray's Column," *St. Louis Post-Dispatch*, October 9, 1930: 28.

2   James C. Isaminger, "Fifth Diadem Jauntily Atop Connie's Head," *Philadelphia Inquirer*, October 9, 1930: 1, 20.

3   Grantland Rice, "The Sport Light," Philadelphia Inquirer, October 9, 1930: 21.

4   Connie Mack, "Connie Mack Proud of Fighting Aides; Praises Earnshaw," *Philadelphia Inquirer*, October 9, 1930: 21.

5   "Yesterday's Local Weather Report," *Philadelphia Inquirer*, October 9, 1930: 2.

6   S.O. Grauley, "George's Iron-Man Feat Just Short of Great Matty's Mark," *Philadelphia Inquirer*, October 9, 1930: 22.

7   Babe Ruth, "Grove Pitches Nine Innings in 'Bullpen,'" *St. Louis Post-Dispatch*, October 9, 1930: 28.

8   Sid Keener, "Sid Keener's Column," *St. Louis Star and Times*, October 9, 1930: 18.

9   Sid Keener, "Frisch, Bottomley and Hafey Drove in 1 Run in Series," *St. Louis Star and Times*, October 9, 1930: 18.

10   Isaminger.

11   Keener, "Frisch, Bottomley and Hafey Drove in 1 Run in Series."

12   Grauley.

13   Walter S. Cahill, "Footnotes of A's-Cards Battle," *Philadelphia Inquirer*, October 9, 1930: 20.

14   George H. Dixon, "Macks Collect 7 Runs on 7 Hits to End Series," *Philadelphia Inquirer*, October 9, 1930: 1.

15   Stan Baumgartner, "Blister on Finger Forced Removal of Wild Bill Hallahan," *Philadelphia Inquirer*, October 9, 1930: 22.

16   Baumgartner.

17   Isaminger.

18   Isaminger.

19   Westbrook Pegler, "Calm Follows Storm in Final of Fall Classic," *St. Louis Globe-Democrat*, October 9, 1930: 20.

20   Isaminger.

21   Pitch count from Grauley. Earnshaw threw 124 pitches, of which 88 were strikes and 36 balls.

22   Those eight pitchers are Bill Dinneen (Boston Red Sox, 1903, 3-1 in 4 starts, 2.06 ERA in 35 innings), Deacon Phillippe (Pittsburgh Pirates, 1903, 3-2 in 5 starts, 3.07 ERA in 44 innings), Christy Mathewson (New York Giants, 1905, 3-0 with three straight shutouts), Babe Adams (Pittsburgh Pirates, 1909, 3-0 in 3 starts, 1.33 ERA in 27 innings), Jack Coombs (Philadelphia Athletics, 1910, 3-0 in 3 starts, 3.33 ERA in 27 innings), Smoky Joe Wood (Boston Red Sox, 1912, 3-1 in 4 games, 3 starts, and 4.50 ERA in 22 innings), Red Faber (Chicago White Sox, 1917, 3-1 in 4 games, 3 starts, 2.33 ERA in 27 innings), and in the best-of-nine 1920 World Series Stan Coveleski (Cleveland Indians, 3-0 in 3 starts, and 0.67 in 27 innings). Several other pitchers with at least three starts in the one World Series should be mentioned, though they did not win three games: George Mullin, Detroit Tigers, 1909 (2-1 in 4 games, 3 starts with 2.25 ERA in 32 innings); Chief Bender, Philadelphia Athletics, 1911 (2-1 in 3 starts, 1.04 ERA in 26 innings); Mathewson in 1911 (1-2 in 3 starts, 2.00 ERA in 27 innings), Lefty Tyler (Chicago Cubs, 1918, 1-1 in 3 starts, 1.17 ERA in 23 innings), Walter Johnson (Washington Senators, 1925, 2-1 in 3 starts with 2.08 ERA in 26 innings). The 1921 best-of-nine World Series featured four outstanding pitching performances: The New York Giants' Phil Douglas (2-1 in 3 starts with 2.08 ERA in 26 innings) and Art Nehf (1-2 in 3 starts with 1.38 ERA in 26 innings) and the New York Yankees' Waite Hoyt (2-1 in 3 starts, 0.00 ERA with 2 unearned runs in 27 innings) and Carl Mays (1-2 in 3 starts, 1.73 ERA in 26 innings),.

23   Grauley.

A's Clinch AL Pennant Without Fanfare

September 15, 1931
Philadelphia Athletics 14, Cleveland Indians 3

By Harry Schoger

The Philadelphia Athletics had a veritable lock on first place. A win today, Tuesday, September 15, would produce their 99th victory of the season, a goal reached only five times before in franchise history. The second-place Washington Senators were mathematically still in the hunt. An A's win coupled with a Senators loss would seal the pennant for the Philadelphians, their third in a row. They would tie with the New York Yankees for the American League record. John McGraw had won four straight (1921-24) with the National League New York Giants.

By dint of his seemingly insurmountable lead, owner-manager Connie Mack, widely known as Mr. Mack, had already begun shuffling his juggernaut lineup to give his regulars some rest and his backup players some experience and/or preparedness for the World Series. Stars Jimmie Foxx, Mickey Cochrane, Max Bishop, Bing Miller, and Mule Haas all enjoyed a well-deserved rest for the day. In spite of the A's star-studded lineup, the Yankees still dominated the AL statistically in most offensive categories. It was the A's formidable mound corps that gave them their margin over the vaunted New Yorkers.

The opponents for the day were the fourth-place Cleveland Indians, who had only one pennant in team history. They won in 1920 under the leadership of their player-manager, peerless Tris Speaker, commonly known as the Grey Eagle for his prowess in covering center-field territory.

Philadelphia had been beset for several days with an unseasonal heat wave. At 85 degrees, this day constituted a modest break in the swelter.[1] A relatively sparse crowd, as few as 1,500, filed into venerable Shibe Park.[2] The game was the 10th of a 19-game homestand. It was also the third game of a four-game final series with the Indians. The day before, the two opponents had split a doubleheader.

Mack bestowed the honor of pitching the potential pennant-winning game on veteran Eddie Rommel, an illustrious veteran who had toiled for only the Athletics in his 12-year career. He had pitched two innings in relief the previous day. In his prime he had led the American League in wins twice, with 27 in 1922 and 21 in 1925. He was right-handed and the first major-league hurler to master and employ the knuckleball. His 27 victories in 1922 remain as of 2022 the major-league record for knuckleballers.

Rommel's receiver for the day was a 28-year-old rookie named Joe Palmisano, whose entire career consisted of 19 games in the current season. He was replacing starter Mickey Cochrane, who was slated to be interviewed by the legendary Grantland Rice on the radio at 9:30 P.M.

Mel Harder, a 21-year-old hurler, was the starter on the mound for the Indians. In spite of his youth, Harder was a mainstay in the Cleveland pitching rotation. His batterymate was Luke Sewell, an 11-year veteran, who was the backbone of the Cleveland catching corps.

Eric McNair, a utility infielder, replaced Max Bishop at second base and in his usual leadoff spot in the lineup. Bishop was arguably the best leadoff man in the major leagues.[3] The outfield was shuffled to give Mule Haas and Bing Miller some rest. League-leading batter Al "Bucketfoot" Simmons was shifted from his normal post in left-field to center. Twenty-year-old rookie Lou Finney, making only his second start, was installed in left field. Jimmy Moore took over right-field duties. At first base replacing Jimmie Foxx was Phil Todt, who had been claimed from the Red Sox on waivers in February.

The first inning set the tone for the day. Odell Hale led off for the Indians with a triple to right field. Bruce Connatser popped out to shortstop. Dick Porter flied out to Finney in short left field. The rookie threw out Hale at the plate, snuffing out the early scoring opportunity.

In the bottom half of the inning, McNair led off with a ground single to the shortstop, Ed Montague. Finney singled. Montague made a throwing error that allowed McNair to score and Finney to take third. Jimmy Moore doubled to left to drive in Finney. Simmons grounded out to short, allowing Moore to advance to third. Phil Todt singled to drive in Moore, ending the A's scoring. Jimmy Dykes grounded to second and Todt was out on a fielder's choice. Dib Williams singled to right field and Dykes stopped at second. Palmisano grounded to the shortstop, who threw out Williams for the force, stranding two runners.

In the top of the second, Earl Averill, leading off, hit a homer, his 30th, to deep right, breaking the ice for the Indians and reducing the margin to two runs.

In the bottom of the second, the A's canceled out the Indians' run and added a second to the margin. Both runs were unearned because of a second throwing error by Montague.

The Indians failed to score in their half of the third. The A's added two more runs on the strength of a two-out triple by Finney. It spelled the end of Harder's day's work. He was relieved by Oral Hildebrand, who retired the final A's batter on a fly ball to left field. In 2⅔ innings Harder yielded 10 hits and seven runs, of which two were unearned, walked one, struck out one and hit one batsman.

The game proceeded in much the same vein for its duration. When the smoke finally cleared, the A's second string had outscored the Indians 14-3. Rommel, 6-5, threw a complete game, yielding nine hits, including one home run, two triples, and one double. He and his defense stranded six Indians runners. Cleveland had 17 total bases but managed only three runs. The A's had 21 total bases and produced 14 runs with the help of three Cleveland errors. The loss dropped Harder's record to 13-13. Time of the game: 1:44.

The Philadelphia offensive output was truly a team effort. Everyone got into the act. The entire lineup, including Rommel, hit safely and produced at least one RBI. Only Rommel failed to score. Dib Williams had five singles in five at-bats. Perhaps the treat for the A's fans was the play of rookie Lou Finney in his second start. In five plate appearances and four at-bats he collected three hits, a triple and two singles, drove in two runs and was hit by a pitched ball. In the outfield he was errorless, made seven putouts and had the only outfield assist of the day.

The Philadelphians had beaten the Indians for the 17th time in the season while losing four to them. The crowd left the ballpark with little fervor or fanfare. There was no celebration.[4] The scoreboard indicated Washington was leading the St. Louis Browns in the fourth inning. Besides, ultimately winning the pennant was a foregone conclusion. There was no need for excitement.

Shibe Park was empty an hour after the game. At 6:15 P.M. news arrived that the St. Louis Browns had turned the tables on the Senators and won in the bottom of the ninth.[5] The entire country soon knew the Mackmen had won the American League pennant. Mr. Mack had beaten his own record by taking his ninth AL flag. By the end of the regular season the Senators stumbled along the way and were overtaken by the Yankees for second place, 13½ games behind the Athletics.

The A's, who had won the 1930 World Series from the Cardinals in six games, had a rematch with St. Louis in the 1931 fall classic. Their opponents enjoyed sweet revenge in a seven-game Series. It was the high-water mark for the Athletics. They would never win another pennant in the City of Brotherly Love.

SOURCES

In addition to the sources cited in the Notes, the author consulted Baseball-Reference.com, Retrosheet.org, Baseball-Almanac.com and the following:

"'Fine,' Mildly Enthuses Connie, Hoping That Ninth Flag Will Not Be Macks' Last," *Philadelphia Inquirer*, September 16, 1931.

NOTES

1   "Yesterday's Local Weather Report" and "Cooler Weather Due; Showers Promised" *Philadelphia Inquirer*, September 16, 1931: 1, 2.

2   "Macks Annex Pennant Again, Upset Indians," *San Bernardino County* (California) *Sun*, September 16, 1931: 14.

3   Bill Nowlin, "Max Bishop," SABR Biography Project, sabr.org/bioproj/person/ab12ea82.

4   "Philadelphia Accepts Feat Without Cheering," *Lansing* (Michigan) *State Journal*, September 16, 1931: 13.

5   James Isaminger, "A's Take Third Pennant and Equal League Record," *Philadelphia Inquirer*, September 16, 1931: 1.

CARDINALS TAG GROVE EARLY; GRIMES GRINDS

October 5, 1931
St. Louis Cardinals 5, Philadelphia Athletics 2

Game Three of the World Series

By Doug Feldmann

When the 1931 World Series opened at Sportsman's Park in St. Louis on October 1st, it appeared to be a mere continuation of the regular season. The Philadelphia A's star pitcher, Robert Moses "Lefty" Grove, rebounded from an early 2-0 deficit to cruise to a 6-2 win for Connie Mack's team. Grove had outdone himself in 1931, improving upon a career year in 1930 in which he posted a 28-5 record and a 2.54 earned-run average. In '31, Grove sailed to a 31-4 mark and a minuscule 2.06 ERA. With a fastball so rapid he could "throw a lambchop past a wolf," as one witness asserted,[1] Grove struck out 175 batters, leading the American League for the seventh straight season (a streak beginning in his rookie year of 1925). His ERA had been the lowest in the circuit in each of the past four. Grove had lost only twice since the first week of June.

After Grove's Game One victory, the resolute Cardinals rebounded in Game Two with a 2-0 shutout from Bill Hallahan, as center fielder Pepper Martin began a personal vendetta against A's stalwart catcher Mickey Cochrane. In going 5-for-7 in the Series' first two games, Martin had also swiped three bases.

As the battle shifted east to Shibe Park for Game Three, Grove was summoned to the mound once again by Mack while St. Louis manager Gabby Street handed the ball to right-hander Burleigh Grimes. Grimes, in his 16th major-league season, was one of 17 veteran pitchers permitted to continue throwing a spitball when the pitch was banned in 1920. Grimes was looking to avenge himself against Grove; he had lost twice to the southpaw in the 1930 World Series between the A's and Cardinals.

The weather for Game Three "couldn't have been better had it been made to order for a mid-July afternoon," the *Philadelphia Inquirer* noted.[2] The temperature climbed to 84 degrees near game time, 11 degrees above normal in the city for early October. The festivities were launched – literally – by President Herbert Hoover throwing out the first ball from his box seat; his errant fling sailed over the head of Cochrane deflecting off the shin of third-base umpire Dick Nallin, standing nearby. (After Grove fired a strike on the first pitch to the Cardinals' Sparky Adams to start the game, home-plate umpire Dolly Stark went over and gave Hoover the ball as a replacement for his original toss.)

Both teams went down in order in the first inning, but the Cardinals pounced on Grove in the second. "That sinister word called 'depression' that has worried economic authorities for some time hit baseball yesterday," wrote James Isaminger in the *Philadelphia Inquirer*. "It hit the best team in baseball anyway."[3] A lead-off walk to Jim Bottomley preceded singles by Martin and Jimmie Wilson. Charley Gelbert followed with a run-scoring liner to Bing Miller in right for a 2-0 St. Louis lead.

Two more Cardinals tallies came in the fourth, with the big blow coming from Grimes himself – a two-out single to right-center that scored Martin and Chick Hafey, increasing the advantage to 4-0 as the Cardinals were "screaming and tearing around like birds of prey," noted Isaminger's colleague at the *Inquirer*, John McCullough.[4]

Aside from his momentous offensive blow, Grimes was even more impressive on the mound. Threatening to become the first pitcher to ever fire a no-hitter in a World Series game, he entered the A's eighth maintaining the 4-0 lead.

At that juncture, it appeared the bats of the Mighty Macks had awakened. Jimmie Foxx walked to start the inning, and Miller followed with the A's first hit of the day – a scorching single to center that nearly carried Grimes with it to the outfield. But the spitballer righted himself to get Jimmy Dykes to pop to third, Dib Williams to fly to left, and Doc Cramer – batting for Grove, who had now permitted 23 hits in his two series starts – to line a shot that was snared by Frankie Frisch at second, quelling the rally as quickly as it had begun.

Roy Mahaffey took over on the Philadelphia mound in the top of the ninth. Bottomley stroked a double that sent George Watkins home from second base. Watkins had pinch-run for Wally Roettger after Roettger reached first on a force play.

Grimes ("wearing a two-day growth of beard," noted J. Roy Stockton of the *St. Louis Post-Dispatch*[5]) continued his scoreless domination into the ninth as Max Bishop tapped to Bottomley unassisted at first and Mule Haas grounded out

to Grimes. But on the latter play, the pitcher attempted to field the hot grounder barehanded and injured the index finger on his pitching hand. "There was a long conference on the mound before Burleigh decided to carry on," Stockton wrote.[6] After Cochrane walked and was replaced by pinch-runner Eric McNair, Al Simmons connected for an opposite-field home run over the wall in right, plating a pair of runs to narrow the gap to 5-2. "It seemed the injury impaired his control," wrote Stockton, "or at least, that was an explanation of the pass to Cochrane and the homer by Simmons."[7]

More trouble loomed, as next up was the intimidating Foxx – having taken his place alongside the New York Yankees' Babe Ruth and Lou Gehrig as one of the most feared sluggers in the game. But a pair of whistling fastballs and a final spitter flew past the flailing slugger, as Stark hollered and raised his right arm three times. The strikeout sealed the contest and a two-games-to-one lead in the Series for St. Louis in a game that took 2 hours and 10 minutes in front of 32,295 spectators.

Martin had taken a break from his basestealing rampage on the afternoon but nonetheless posted two more hits, giving him seven in three games. In addition to Grimes, other hitting stars on the day for the Cardinals were Wilson (3-for-4 and an RBI) and Bottomley and Roettger (a double for each). But it was the two-hit pitching performance crafted by Grimes against the powerful Philadelphia lineup that truly stole the show, one of the finest World Series performances on the mound to that time as he gained revenge for his two defeats against Grove the previous autumn. "To be frank," Isaminger concluded, "the A's never looked sourer in a World's Series."[8]

Sitting amid Isaminger, McCullough, and Stockton in the crowded Shibe Park press box was the Yankees' star Ruth, trying to cheer on the American League representative. In pulling for the A's, the Babe had "doffed the uniform of the Yanks for the more somber garb of a journalist. Mr. Ruth pushed his broad shoulders into the throng struggling to get out of the arena of disaster yesterday. Said Mr. Ruth, 'They gotta start hittin' 'em.'"[9]

SOURCES

In addition to the sources listed in the Notes, the author consulted Baseball-Reference.com, Retrosheet.org, and SABR.org.

NOTES

1 Ken Burns' *Baseball* series, PBS Television.

2 *Philadelphia Inquirer*, October 6, 1931.

3 James Isaminger, "Hoover Sees Grimes Beat Athletics, 5-2, as Cards Lash Grove," *Philadelphia Inquirer*, October 6, 1931.

4 John McCullough, "St. Louis Ace Allows Macks Only Two Hits," *Philadelphia Inquirer*, October 6, 1931.

5 J. Roy Stockton, "Cards Beat Athletics, 5-2; Lead in Series," *St. Louis Post-Dispatch*, October 5, 1931.

6 Stockton.

7 Stockton.

8 Isaminger.

9 McCullough.

EARNSHAW THROWS TWO-HIT SHUTOUT TO EVEN FALL CLASSIC

October 6, 1931
Philadelphia Athletics 3, St. Louis Cardinals 0

Game Four of the World Series

By Don Zminda

Three games into the 1931 World Series, the Philadelphia Athletics' championship run was in jeopardy. Winners of three consecutive American League pennants from 1929 to 1931, the A's had defeated the Chicago Cubs, four games to one, in the 1929 World Series, and then topped the St. Louis Cardinals in six games in 1930. Facing the Cardinals again in 1931, the Athletics were looking to become the first major-league team to win the World Series in three consecutive seasons. But after the A's had taken Game One in St. Louis, 6-2, behind 31-game winner Lefty Grove, the Cardinals had responded with a 2-0 victory in Game Two (behind Bill Hallahan) and a 5-2 victory when the Series moved to Philadelphia for Game Three, with Burleigh Grimes defeating Grove.

A's manager Connie Mack turned to George Earnshaw in an attempt to avoid falling behind three games to one. In six previous World Series starts, the big (6-foot-4, 210-pound) right-hander known as "Moose" had posted a stellar 1.54 ERA … and he had been particularly good against the Cardinals. In the 1930 Series, Earnshaw had started three times against St. Louis, allowing only two runs in 25 innings (0.72 ERA) and working 22 consecutive scoreless innings from the third inning of Game Two through the eighth inning of Game Six. The A's had won all three of Earnshaw's 1930 World Series starts, including the clinching 7-1 victory in Game Six. Though he had lost Game Two of the 1931 Series to Hallahan, Earnshaw permitted only two runs in eight innings. His pitching log for four World Series starts against the Cardinals: a 2-1 record (the A's had won three of the four games), a 1.09 ERA (four earned runs in 33 innings), and a .164 opponents' batting average (19-for-116). "We'd heard about Lefty Grove, how hard he could throw," Cardinals pitcher Burleigh Grimes told Donald Honig. "But I'll tell you, the guy we thought threw the hardest was Earnshaw. Big George Earnshaw."[1]

The Cardinals' hitting star thus far in the series was center fielder Pepper Martin, a player who had recorded only 14 major-league at-bats prior to the 1931 season. In the loss to Grove in Game One, Martin had gone 3-for-4 and stolen a base. In the Cardinals' 2-0 Game Two victory against Earnshaw, Martin had scored both of their runs. In the second inning, Martin had doubled, stolen third ("catching the Athletics' battery flatfooted," according to James C. Isaminger of the *Philadelphia Inquirer*) and then raced home on Jimmie Wilson's fly ball. In the seventh, wrote Isaminger, "Martin put on a real display of dazzling baseball … and had the crowd spellbound." After leading off the half-inning with a single, he stole second, took third on an infield out, and scored on Charley Gelbert's squeeze bunt to the mound. According to Isaminger, "George threw poorly to [A's catcher Mickey] Cochrane, who was pulled slightly out of position."[2] Martin continued to torment the Athletics in St. Louis's Game Three victory, going 2-for-4 and scoring two of the Cardinals' five runs.

Martin and Earnshaw offered quite a contrast. According to *The Sporting News*' Bill Dooly, Earnshaw's father was "a shipping prince, owner of a line of freighters that carried the Earnshaw house flag over the briny deep to the farthest corners of the world." When he first broke into baseball after attending Swarthmore College, wrote Dooly, "Baseball was just a lark to Earnshaw. …"[3] Martin, meanwhile, seemed like the perfect symbol of the Great Depression that brought hard times to many Americans in the 1930s. Baseball Hall of Fame historian Lee Allen wrote that the 5-foot-8 Martin had "worked as a newsboy … as a grease monkey in a filling station, as a tinsmith's helper, and as a diver for lost golf balls in a municipal course." After turning to baseball, Allen wrote, Martin "would ride the rods to various spring-training camps, pocketing the expense checks that the Cardinals sent him."[4]

Game Four of the 1931 World Series featured the second battle between the hobo and the man whose October 1930 *Sporting News* profile included a photo montage entitled "Born with Silver Spoon in Mouth – Arm of Gold." Earnshaw's mound opponent was right-hander Syl Johnson. The A's got to Johnson quickly; Max Bishop led

off the bottom of the first with a single, advanced to second on a Mule Haas sacrifice bunt, moved to third on Mickey Cochrane's groundout, and scored on a double by Al Simmons. Meanwhile Earnshaw did not allow a hit until Martin singled with one out in the fifth. Martin stole second – his fourth steal of the Series, and his third off Earnshaw – an out later, but Earnshaw struck out Charley Gelbert to end the inning. "Catcher Cochrane was anointed the goat [of the Series] for letting the Wild Horse [Martin] run wild," wrote Warren Corbett, "but Martin said neither Grove nor Earnshaw knew how to hold baserunners because they didn't allow many runners."[5]

It was still 1-0 with two out in the bottom of the sixth when Jimmie Foxx hit a long home run to left field; *Spalding's Base Ball Guide* described the homer a "a prodigious fly over the left field stands, one of the longest hits to that region in the history of the grounds."[6] Bing Miller, the next hitter, doubled to right center, and Jimmy Dykes followed with a single to left to make it 3-0. A single by Dib Williams advanced Dykes to second and finished Johnson, but Cardinals reliever Jim Lindsey struck out Earnshaw to end the inning.

Meanwhile Earnshaw was totally shutting down the Cardinals … except for Martin, whose double leading off the eighth was St. Louis's second and final hit of the game. St. Louis failed to capitalize, and Earnshaw retired the last six Cardinals to complete his two-hit shutout in 1 hour and 58 minutes. He struck out eight, walked one and faced only 30 hitters. The next morning's *Philadelphia Inquirer* included a pitch-by-pitch summary of the game; the author counted 102 pitches from Earnshaw, 74 of them strikes.

Earnshaw's performance earned praise from all sides. "Earnshaw was superlative," said Cardinals manager Gabby Street. "I am glad [Burleigh] Grimes pitched yesterday. Had the two boys faced each other the game might have been going yet. He was as perfect as he was in the final tilt last year."[7] In a bylined article, A's manager Connie

Mack wrote that "I have been watching World's Series since they started … but I do not recall one pitcher who looked as good as George Earnshaw. … It was the most amazing display of heart and skill I have ever seen in a vital game in the years I have been in baseball."[8] In another bylined piece, New York Giants manager John McGraw wrote: "Earnshaw pitched one of the steadiest games I ever saw. In fact he is one of the best world series pitchers the game has ever known. In his cool steadiness he sometimes reminds me of [Christy] Mathewson. Instead of being disturbed, Earnshaw seems to pitch better in a world series game than in the regular season."[9]

However, Earnshaw's victory only knotted the Series at two wins apiece, and McGraw gave the Cardinals the pitching edge going forward, praising "the sound judgment of Gabby Street in holding back [Bill] Hallahan for the next game."[10] And the Cardinals seemed the hungrier team. "If we lose the series," Earnshaw had said on the morning of Game One, "it will be because our enthusiasm – our drive for more honors – is a bit jaded. … Take my case for instance. After what I did last year anything I do in the future will be an anti-climax. I haven't the same ambition and enthusiasm to pitch this year that I had last. The additional money – the two thousand dollars that represents the difference between the winner's and loser's share of the World's Series – I can honestly say does not kindle enthusiasm."[11]

Ultimately the Series would go the seven-game limit, with Earnshaw facing Burleigh Grimes in the finale at St. Louis's Sportsman's Park. Earnshaw pitched respectably, giving up four runs (three earned) and only four hits in seven innings, but the Cardinals prevailed, 4-2. Neither Earnshaw nor Connie Mack's Philadelphia Athletics ever returned to the World Series.

SOURCES

In addition to the sources cited in the Notes, the author consulted:

Baumgartner, Stan. "Bunts and Pop Flies as Macks Tied Series," *Philadelphia Inquirer*, October 7, 1931: 14.

Grauley, S. O. "Can't Make Meal on 'Pepper' Alone and Earnshaw Proves It," *Philadelphia Inquirer*, October 7, 1931: 12.

Grauley, S. O. "Pitch by Pitch Dissection Here Reveals Earnshaw's Hill Genius and Shows How Redbirds Joyous Note Was Stilled," *Philadelphia Inquirer*, October 7, 1931: 13.

Isaminger, James B., editor. *Reach Official American League Base Ball Guide for 1932* (New York: A.J. Reach, Wright & Ditson, Inc.), 81-106.

Keener, Sid. "Sid Keener's Column," *St. Louis Star and Times*, October 7, 1931: 10.

McCullough, John M. "Yes, Indeed. Very Pleasant Day, Despite That Martin Person, Sole Fly in the A's Ointment." *Philadelphia Inquirer*, October 7, 1931: 6.

Stockton, J. Roy. "Athletics Beat Cards, 3-0, and Tie Series," *St. Louis Post-Dispatch*, October 6, 1931: 13.

Wiegand, Harold J. "Earnshaw's Speed and Macks' Rally Crush Cards, 3-0," *Philadelphia Inquirer*, October 7, 1931" 1.

baseball-reference.com/postseason/1931_WS.shtml

retrosheet.org/boxesetc/1931/B10060PHA1931.htm

NOTES

1 Donald Honig, *The Man in the Dugout* (Lincoln: University of Nebraska Press, 1977), 46.

2 James C. Isaminger, "A's Defeated, 2-0; Hallahan, Martin Put Cards in Race," *Philadelphia Inquirer*, October 3, 1931: 1.

3 Bill Dooly, "Earnshaw, World Series Hero, Is Scion of Wealthy New York Family and First Pitched as a Diversion," *The Sporting News*, October 16, 1930: 5.

4 Lee Allen, *The National League Story: The Official History* (New York: Hill & Wang, 1961), 204-05.

5 Warren Corbett, "George Earnshaw," SABR Bioproject Biography, sabr.org/bioproj/person/4cd6c79e.

6 John B. Foster, editor, *Spalding's Offical Base Ball Guide 1932*, 23.

7 Stan Baumgartner, "Redbirds Loud in Praise of Robust Home Run by Foxx," *Philadelphia Inquirer*, October 7, 1931: 13.

8 Connie Mack, "Best Hurling I Ever Saw in World's Series – Connie," *Philadelphia Inquirer*, October 7, 1931: 1.

9 John J. McGraw, "Cards Now Have Pitching Edge, Says M'Graw," *St. Louis Post-Dispatch*, October 6, 1931: 14.

10 McGraw.

11 Stan Baumgartner, "Ambition to Achieve Win Born in Earnshaw After Connie Has Say," *Philadelphia Inquirer*, October 7, 1931: 7.

WILD BILL AND THE WILD HORSE OF THE OSAGE LEAD THE CARDINALS CHARGE

October 7, 1931
St. Louis Cardinals 5, Philadelphia Athletics 1

Game Five of the World Series

By Gregory H. Wolf

"There were just seven wonders of the world before this world series broke out and today there are nine," gushed sportswriter Grantland Rice after the St. Louis Cardinals rode the exploits of Wild Bill and the Wild Horse of the Osage to a convincing 5-1 victory over the Philadelphia Athletics to take a three-games-to-two lead in the fall classic.[1] Scribes lavished praise on the Redbirds' two unexpected stars. En route to his second complete-game victory of the Series, Bill Hallahan's "steel left arm stilled the power and might of the House of Mack," opined S.O. Grauley of the *Philadelphia Inquirer*.[2] Pronounced an "irrepresble madcap" and "one-man show" by Cardinals beat writer J. Roy Stockton,[3] Pepper Martin continued his torrid hitting and "waved his bat dramatically to pound the Athletics into submission," quipped James Isaminger of the *Inquirer*, knocking in four runs and tying a World Series record with his 12th hit.[4]

Meeting for the second straight season on baseball's biggest stage, owner-manager Connie Mack's A's "had been expected to trample over these red-breasted Cardinals with ease," observed John Drebinger of the *New York Times*.[5] However, the A's (107-45) thunderous bats went silent after a victory in Game One; the team collected just 15 hits and five runs in the next three contests, endangering their quest for a third straight title and their claim to one of the greatest dynasties in baseball history, Lacking the big names and slugging stars of their opponents, Cardinals skipper Gabby Street's rough-and-tumble lot (101-53) relied on speed and defense, and no one exemplified that better than Pepper Martin, described by sportswriter John M. McCullough as a "leather-faced, grinning, steel-muscled, fast-as-light hero" and a "swashbuckling pirate in dirt-grimed pants."[6] The 27-year-old from Osage County, Oklahoma, in his first full season in the big leagues, displaced five-year starter Taylor Douthit in center field and sparked the club with his energized play. His feats thus far in the Series cast him into the national spotlight. He scored the only two runs and swiped two bags in the Cardinals shutout in Game Two; scored two more in another victory in Game Three; and after four games had 9 hits in 14 at-bats.

The A's pitching staff, featuring 31-game winner Lefty Grove and two other 20-game winners, George Earnshaw and Rube Walberg, was the envy of baseball; however, the Cardinals' unheralded staff produced a slightly lower team ERA (3.45 to 3.47), but without the headline-grabbing names. Its ace was 28-year-old Hallahan, a pugnosed hard thrower, whose moniker derived from his control problems. In his second full season as a starter, Wild Bill tied for the NL lead with 19 wins, but also paced the circuit in both strikeouts and walks for the second straight season. The A's were well acquainted with the Binghamton, New York, native. In three starts against them in the World Series in the last two seasons, Hallahan had blanked them twice in St. Louis, including a sparkling three-hitter five days earlier; but he had been pummeled in two ineffective frames in the Game Six clincher in '30 in the City of Brotherly Love.

On a warm, 80-degree Wednesday afternoon following a late-morning thunderstorm, Shibe Park was filled to capacity, with 32,295 spectators expecting to see Walberg on the mound for the home team after Grove and Earnshaw had started the first four contests. But the Tall Tactician made one of his "copyrighted pitching upsets," noted Isaminger, and surprisingly sent Waite Hoyt to the mound.[7] A one-time star with the New York Yankees, who had excelled in the World Series, posting a 6-3 slate and a minuscule 1.62 ERA in 77⅔ innings, Hoyt's glory days were well behind him. Mack acquired him in a midseason waiver transaction from the Detroit Tigers, after which he produced a 10-5 slate, pushing his career record to 189-131.

The Cardinals came out swinging. Sparky Adams led off with a shot down the left-field line. It "would have been a double for a man with sound limbs," opined Stockton, but Adams, suffering from a badly sprained ankle, stopped at first and was replaced by pinch-runner Andy High.[8] Two batters later, NL MVP Frankie Frisch slashed

a single to center field and raced to second when Mule Haas made an ill-advised throw to nab High at third. Street's strategy to move Martin from his customary sixth spot to cleanup paid immediate dividends as Pepper sent a fly to left field to drive in High.

The Cardinals squandered leadoff hits in the second and fourth. In the latter, Martin beat out a drag bunt to first and moved to third on Jim Bottomley's one-out hit. Wilson followed with a screeching liner right at second baseman Max Bishop, who doubled Sunny Jim off first.

In a tense pitchers' duel, the Redbirds broke through in the sixth when Frisch hit a bullet that ricocheted off third baseman Jimmy Dykes' outstretched glove, according to Stockton, and rolled down the foul line as Frisch pulled into second.[9] Martin, who hit seven home runs and drove in 75 runs in '31, followed with a prodigious two-run blast into the upper deck of the left-field stands.

The Cardinals' three-run lead looked secure the way Hallahan "silenced the big guns" in the A's lineup, wrote Stockton.[10] Through six innings, Wild Bill had yielded just two hits, both to Al "Bucketfoot" Simmons, who captured his second straight AL batting crown (.390). His first safely was a prodigious blast off the scoreboard to lead off the second. Two batters later Bing Miller hit a high bounder to shortstop Charley Gelbert, who fired to first for an easy out. Attempting to catch the Redbirds napping and kick-start the A's moribund offense, Simmons rounded third at full speed, but Bottomley alertly threw home to erase Al in an inning-ending twin killing at the plate. Though Sunny Jim had struggled at the plate thus far in the series (2-for-14), he atoned with his defensive prowess, which he exhibited again in the fifth. Simmons's second hit caromed off Hallahan's leg into left field and Jimmie Foxx walked. Bottomley then made successive plays at least 180 feet apart, lauded Rice, by catching Miller's bunt popup and then racing into foul territory to snare Dykes' fly, potentially saving a run in a 1-0 game.[11]

It was a different story in the last three frames as the A's chipped at Hallahan for seven hits, yet failed to connect in the clutch. With one out in the seventh, Simmons notched his third hit, which was followed by Foxx's smash off Hallahan, deflecting just out of Frisch's reach. Miller hit a looping grounder to High at third base. "Simmons could have been thrown out at the plate," opined Stockton, but High tried for an inning-ending double play.[12] His throw to Frisch forced Foxx, but the relay throw to first was late, and the A's had finally scored a run. Dykes followed with a single off High's glove to bring the potential go-ahead run to the plate, but Dib Williams popped up.

The Cardinals answered in the eighth against Rube Walberg, the anticipated starter for the game, now in his second inning of relief of Hoyt. George Watkins walked with one out, stole second base, and then scored on Martin's third hit and fourth RBI of the game, making it 4-1. It was also Martin's record-tying 12th hit of the World Series, equaling the mark of Buck Herzog (1912) and Shoeless Joe Jackson (1919), both in eight-game Series, and Sam Rice (1925).

Hallahan stopped another A's surge in the eighth that began with two successive scratch hits with two outs. He had no play on Jimmy Moore's high bounder near the plate; Mickey Cochrane followed with a tricky grounder, which, according to Stockton, bounced off Bottomley's glove.[13] Hallahan's tormenter, representing the tying run, came to the plate, but Simmons grounded softly for a force at third, crushing the A's hopes.

A relentless, scrappy team, the Cardinals bunched together three singles, resulting in another run in the ninth off knuckleballer Eddie Rommel for a 5-1 lead.

Wild Bill was back on the mound in the ninth, just three outs away from victory in the pivotal fifth game of a tied series. Foxx, who had belted 30 home runs (the third of 12 consecutive years he reached that plateau), surprised everyone by bunting. Catcher Jimmie Wilson, who, opined sportswriter Herman Wecke of the *Post-Dispatch*, had clearly "outplayed" counterpart Cochrane in the Series thus far,[14] lost track of the ball, apparently thinking that it had bounced over his head.[15] Following two groundball force outs, Williams hit a short blooper to center, just out of Martin's reach. Hallahan fanned pinch-hitter Joe Boley to end the game in 1 hour and 56 minutes.

Hallahan threw 124 pitches (36 balls) to fashion his second complete-game victory in the Series, while fanning four and walking one.[16] The star of the show, however, was Martin, the 5-foot-8 power coil and catalyst, who had thoroughly confounded A's pitchers and rocketed to national stardom and catapulted the Redbirds to the precipice of a title. Widely anticipated to capture their third straight championship, the A's lost in a "startling turn of events," submitted Drebinger, as the Series moved to St. Louis.[17]

SOURCES

In addition to the sources cited in the Notes, the author accessed Retrosheet.org, Baseball-Reference.com, Newspapers.com, and SABR.org.

"The Game, Play-by-Play," *St. Louis Post-Dispatch*, October 7, 1931: 1B.

NOTES

1   Grantland Rice, "Pepper Martin's Baseball Magic Makes A's Dizzy," (Minneapolis) *Star Tribune*, October 8, 1931: 1.

2   S.O. Grauley, "'Pepper' – Red Hot, 'Wild Bill' – Cool, Macks – Luke Warm," *Philadelphia Inquirer*, October 8, 1931: 18.

3   J. Roy Stockton, "'Pepper' Martin, World Series Sensation, Tells How He Does It," *St. Louis Post-Dispatch*, October 8, 1931: 1B.

4   James C. Isaminger, "Hallahan on Hill, Martin With Ash, Too Much For A's," *Philadelphia Inquirer*, October 8, 1931: 1.

5   John Drebinger, "34,000 See Cardinals Defeat Athletics in Fifth Game of World's Series," *New York Times*, October 8, 1931: 32.

6   John M. McCullough, "A's Defeated, 5-1, By Pepper Martin as Cards Get 5th," *Philadelphia Inquirer*, October 8, 1931: 1.

7   Isaminger.

8   J. Roy Stockton, "Hallahan Victor Over the Athletics for Second Time; Simmons Gets Team's Score," *St. Louis Post-Dispatch*, October 7, 1931: 18.

9   J. Roy Stockton, "Hallahan Victor Over the Athletics for Second Time."

10 J. Roy Stockton, "Hallahan Victor Over the Athletics for Second Time."

11 Rice.

12 J. Roy Stockton, "Hallahan Victor Over the Athletics for Second Time."

13 J. Roy Stockton, "Hallahan Victor Over the Athletics for Second Time."

14 Herman Wecke, "Earnshaw Likely to be Mack's Pitcher; High to Play Third," *St. Louis Post-Dispatch*, October 8, 1931: 1B.

15 J. Roy Stockton, "Hallahan Victor Over the Athletics for Second Time."

16 "Pitched Balls," *Philadelphia Inquirer*, October 10, 1931: 18.

17 Drebinger.

Lou Gehrig Hits Four Home Runs, Tony Lazzeri Hits for Cycle in Yankees Romp

June 3, 1932
New York Yankees 20, Philadelphia Athletics 13

By Mike Huber

It was a game of excess, played on a Friday afternoon in Philadelphia's Shibe Park. Two teams combined for 104 plate appearances, 77 total bases, and 17 runners left on base. The first-place Yankees were playing the fourth game of a six-game series against the Athletics, who occupied fourth place in the American League, 5 games behind New York. The 5,000 fans at the game saw 33 runs, 36 hits, 9 home runs, 5 triples, 14 walks, 12 strike-outs, and 5 errors.

On any other day, Yankees third baseman Tony Lazzeri would have owned the newspaper sports-page headlines. But on this day he was overshadowed by four different baseball events. On a day when Lazzeri hit for a natural cycle (single, double, triple, and home run in that order, the homer being a grand slam), Lou Gehrig amazingly hit four home runs and narrowly missed a fifth. On top of that, Babe Ruth launched his 15th home run of the season, second-best in the major leagues. Jimmie Foxx hit his ML-best 19th homer for Philadelphia. Still more headline-worthy, John McGraw announced that he was retiring from baseball after 29 years as manager of the New York Giants because of a two-year battle with a serious sinus condition.

According to the *New York Times*, "Largely because of Gehrig's quartet of tremendous smashes the Yankees outstripped the Athletics in a run-making marathon, winning 20 to 13, after twice losing the lead because of determined rallies by the American League champions."[1] Gehrig joined the Boston Beaneaters' Bobby Lowe (May 30, 1894) and the Philadelphia Phillies' Ed Delahanty (July 13, 1896) as the only players to collect four home runs in a game. In the first and fifth innings, Gehrig hit his bombs beyond the fence in left-center field, and in the fourth and seventh, he cleared the wall in right field. With the home run in the fifth inning, Gehrig became "the first man in baseball history to ever hit three home runs in one game for the fourth time."[2] On top of that, that third home run was a back-to-back-to-back shot, as Earle Combs and Ruth had homered ahead of him.

In the top of the ninth inning, Gehrig "pointed a terrific drive which Simmons captured only a few steps from the furthest corner of the park."[3] Estimates put the drive at 460 feet from home plate. (It was 468 feet from home to the deepest part of the ballpark in center field, near the flagpole.[4])

George Earnshaw started for the Athletics and pitched five innings, allowing seven runs (six earned). His counterpart for the Yankees, Johnny Allen, gave up eight runs (four earned) in 3⅔ innings. Allen was ejected by home-plate umpire Harry Geisel in the fourth inning for "bench jockeying," the usual phrase used when a player argues balls and strikes from the dugout. The Yankees committed five errors in the contest (Ruth, Gehrig, Frank Crosetti with 2, and Allen). The Yankees used five hurlers and Athletics four, and all nine pitchers in the game allowed at least one run. Jumbo Brown picked up his first win of the season in relief, and Lefty Gomez earned his first save. Reliever Roy Mahaffey took the loss for Philadelphia.

Lazzeri stroked five hits in six at-bats. In addition, he stole a base. As of 2018, he was one of only 14 major leaguers to have a natural cycle, and was the only one whose home run was a grand slam.[5] With his five hits, Lazzeri's average jumped to .357, third-best in the American League. Lazzeri and Gehrig each drove in six runs in the Yankees victory. Every starting position player for New York drove in at least one run. Doc Cramer and Ed Coleman led Philadelphia with three RBIs each.

The New Yorkers tied the major league record by hitting seven home runs in the game. (The record was broken on September 14, 1987, when the Toronto Blue Jays hit 10 home runs against the Baltimore Orioles.) The Yankees' 20 runs scored were their highest run total of the season. The 23 hits by New York set a modern record at the time.[6]

The game seesawed back and forth. The Yankees scored twice in the first, highlighted by Gehrig's first home run of the game, a two-run shot. The Athletics responded with two runs in the bottom half of the first, with a Mickey Cochrane home run. Gehrig's second blast, a solo homer, was part of a two-run fourth inning for New York, but then Allen allowed six Philadelphia tallies in the bottom of the fourth, before he was chased from the game. New York seemed to have batting practice, scoring in each of the final six frames, with two runs in the fourth inning, three in the fifth, two in the sixth, three in the seventh, two in the eighth, and six in the ninth inning, capped by Lazzeri's grand slam home run to give him the cycle. Gehrig's missed home run could have meant an even higher score. Philadelphia scored twice in the bottom of the sixth for a short-lived lead, and the A's added two runs in the eighth and a Jimmie Foxx solo home run in the bottom of the ninth. The final score: New York 20, Philadelphia 13.

The next day, the New York Times carried the headline, "Gehrig Ties All-Time Record With Four Straight Home Runs as Yankees Win," across the top of its sports page on June 4, 1932. However, it then only gave the first column to describing the game, and only a small portion was for Gehrig's record-tying feat. Five of the eight columns on the front page of the sports section in the New York Times were devoted to John McGraw, who was only 59 years old when he announced his retirement. Joe McCarthy, manager of the Yankees, told reporters, "McGraw must have been pretty sick, for he is not the kind to give up baseball without a reason."[7] One of Gehrig's finest offensive performances was apparently minimized by the news of McGraw's retirement. Incoming Giants skipper Bill Terry was given close to a full column on the sports pages, and even his wife was given a short article, which stated that "Mrs. Bill Terry was a very, very proud young woman today when she heard of her husband's appointment as manager of the New York Giants."[8]

SOURCES

In addition to the sources cited in the Notes, the author also accessed Retrosheet.org, Baseball-Reference. com, and SABR.org.

NOTES

1   "Gehrig Ties All-Time Record With Four Straight Home Runs as Yankees Win," *New York Times*, June 4, 1932: 10.

2   "Gehrig Ties All-Time Record With Four Straight Home Runs as Yankees Win." Since Gehrig hit these four home runs in the same game, 13 more players have accomplished the feat, for a total of 16. Interestingly, when Philadelphia's Ed Delahanty and Atlanta's Bob Horner (July 6, 1986) hit their four home runs, their teams lost the game.

3   "Gehrig Ties All-Time Record With Four Straight Home Runs as Yankees Win."

4   "Classic Yankees: Tony Lazzeri," http:// bronxbaseballdaily.com/2011/09/classic-yankees-tony-lazzeri/.

5   "Hitting for the Cycle Records," http://baseball-almanac.com/feats/feats16d.shtml.

6   "Gehrig Ties All-Time Record With Four Straight Home Runs as Yankees Win."

7   "McGraw is Lauded by Baseball Men," *New York Times*, June 4, 1932: 10.

8   "Mrs. Terry, in Memphis, is Overjoyed by News; Knows Husband Will Make Good as Manager," *New York Times*, June 4, 1932: 10.

AL SIMMONS BECOMES FIRST ATHLETIC TO HOMER THREE TIMES AT SHIBE PARK

July 15, 1932
Detroit Tigers 11, Philadelphia Athletics 10

By Mike Lynch

From 1929 through 1931, the Philadelphia Athletics claimed one of the most impressive streaks in major-league history, winning at least 100 games in all three seasons and becoming the first team to do so. They won the World Series in 1929 and 1930 before losing to the St. Louis Cardinals in seven games in the 1931 fall classic. They couldn't maintain that level of brilliance in 1932, however, and though they won 94 games, they finished a staggering 13 games behind the pennant-winning New York Yankees.

That would prove to be the end of the Philadelphia Athletics dynasty as team owner-manager Connie Mack systematically dismantled his squad through trades, sales, or both, much as he did after losing the 1914 World Series to the Boston Braves. One of the first casualties of the purge was future Hall of Fame outfielder Al Simmons, who was sold along with outfielder Mule Haas and infielder Jimmy Dykes to the Chicago White Sox for $100,000 only three days after the 1932 season ended. However, before he headed west, he gave Athletics faithful a gift they had never received before – a three-homer game by an Athletics hitter at Shibe Park.

The Athletics' 100-win streak was in jeopardy right out of the gate when they lost 10 of their first 14 games and were already 6½ games out of first by the end of April. They recovered and went 45-27 in their next 72 games, including a 9-2 drubbing of the Detroit Tigers in the first game of a three-game set at Shibe Park on July 14. But the Yankees were making a mockery of the race and though the Athletics had climbed to within a percentage point of the second-place Cleveland Indians, Philadelphia's deficit had grown to 8½ games.

The second game against the Tigers was played on Friday, July 15, and pitted veterans Rube Walberg and George Uhle against each other. Neither was enjoying any success – the soon-to-be-36-year-old, left-handed Walberg was 8-8 with a 4.91 ERA while the 33-year-old, right-handed Uhle was 4-4 with a 4.65 ERA. It's no surprise the game would feature 21 runs on 27 hits, 17 walks, and a hit batter.

The teams wasted little time jumping all over each other. Detroit poured two runs across in the top of the first on a two-run homer by John Stone after a one-out double by Charlie Gehringer. But Simmons quickly tied the game at 2-2 in the bottom of the inning when he deposited a Uhle pitch over the right-field wall after a two-out walk to Mickey Cochrane. Walberg walked Muddy Ruel in the top of the second, but three fly outs set the

One of the best hitters in baseball history, Bucketfoot Al Simmons slashed 23-129-.358 during his nine seasons with the Athletics (1924-1932). He led the AL with a .381 batting average in 1930 and .390 in 1931. (Photo by Mark Rucker/Transcendental Graphics, Getty Images)

Tigers down without further damage. Then the Athletics took the lead in their half of the inning with an unearned run thanks to third baseman Nolen Richardson's error, Walberg's single, a walk to Haas, and a single by Doc Cramer.

Walberg immediately coughed up the lead when Stone smacked his second four-bagger over the right-field fence and onto 20th Street, again scoring Gehringer, who had reached first on a miscue by second baseman Dib Williams. Not to be outdone, Simmons knotted the score again when he belted a shot to the roof above the left-field stands to tie the game at 4-4. The Tigers continued their onslaught in the top of the fourth when they manufactured a run on a walk to Billy Rogell, Richardson's sacrifice, Rogell's steal of third, by Rogell, and a fly ball by Ruel.

The Athletics, sensing that their southpaw needed all the runs he could get, stepped on the gas in the bottom of the frame and plated five to retake the lead at 9-5. Walberg helped himself with another single, which knocked Uhle from the box and brought Chief Hogsett into the fray. The lefty was greeted by Haas's single to left and it was all downhill from there.

Hogsett allowed a run-scoring single by Cochrane, a "robust" double to left by Simmons that scored two, a walk to Jimmie Foxx, and a two-run double by Eric McNair before he was lifted in favor of 22-year-old rookie Buck Marrow, who was making only his third major-league appearance.[1] The North Carolina native didn't seem to have any answers, either, and hit Dykes, then walked Williams to load the bases. But he worked out of the jam by fanning Walberg and getting Haas to pop to shortstop.

However, as James C. Isaminger wrote in the *Philadelphia Inquirer*, "Walberg refused to be comforted by a big lead and constantly sagged."[2] Indeed, he surrendered three more runs in the top of the fifth, all coming with two outs when Stone walked, Earl Webb singled to center, Gee Walker doubled to left to score Stone, and Rogell singled

to left to plate Webb and Walker, and pulled the Tigers to within a run at 9-8.

The dust settled for a couple of innings – Marrow allowed a single to Cramer in the fifth, and issued consecutive walks to Dykes and Williams in the sixth, but no Athletic scored; Walberg was even better, surrendering only a free pass to Stone in the top of the seventh while retiring the other six batters with relative ease.

Marrow couldn't escape harm in the bottom of the seventh, however, and Simmons, the "swashbuckling batsman as of old," made history when he drove the ball to center field on a line and Stone failed to make a shoestring catch. The ball got past him and Simmons rounded the bases for an inside-the-park homer, his third round-tripper of the day.[3] Down 10-8, the Tigers refused to surrender and tied the score in the top of the eighth, thanks in part to Walberg's inability to locate the strike zone and ineffectiveness with two outs.

After retiring Rogell on a grounder to short, Walberg walked Richardson, who was caught stealing second with Ruel at the plate. Ruel walked, then utilityman Billy Rhiel batted for Marrow and singled to left, advancing pinch-runner Bill Lawrence to second.[4] Harry Davis walked to load the bases, and Gehringer tied the score at 10-10 with a two-bagger to right before Davis was thrown out at the plate by Foxx, who took the throw from Haas and fired to Cochrane to end the inning.

The A's had a chance to put the go-ahead run on the board in the bottom of the eighth against 24-year-old rookie hurler Izzy Goldstein, but their two-out rally that had runners at first and third thanks to a Dykes free pass and Walberg's third single of the game fell short when Haas grounded out to Gehringer. Despite having walked eight men against no strikeouts in eight innings, Walberg took the mound for the ninth and issued his ninth walk of the game but got two groundouts to escape unscathed. "He was wilder than a man overboard," wrote Isaminger.[5]

Earl Whitehill, Detroit's fifth pitcher of the contest, retired the side in the bottom of the ninth to send the game into extra frames and Walberg followed suit in the top of the 10th. Philadelphia threatened in the bottom of the inning when McNair doubled to left with one out and Dykes earned an intentional walk to set up a possible double play, but Whitehill struck out Williams and got Bing Miller, who was hitting for Walberg, to pop to third to end the inning.

With Walberg's day finished, Mack called on 20-year-old right-hander Lew Krausse, who entered the game with a 2-0 record and 6.44 ERA, and had only four more major-league appearances ahead of him. Not surprisingly, the youngster couldn't keep the Tigers from scoring and surrendered the eventual winning run when he stole a page from Walberg's script and gave up the tally with two outs.

Whitehill singled to right, but Davis and Gehringer followed with popups to Cochrane and it looked as if the game would go into the bottom of the inning still tied. But singles by Stone and Webb broke the tie and the game ended 11-10 in Detroit's favor when Simmons flied out to center with Cochrane on first in the bottom of the 11th.

SOURCES

In addition to the sources cited in the Notes, the author accessed Retrosheet.org, Baseball-Reference.com, and SABR.org.

NOTES

1   James C. Isaminger, "Simmons Hits Three Homers and Double," *Philadelphia Inquirer*, July 16, 1932: 8.

2   Isaminger.

3   Isaminger.

4   The hit was Rhiel's fourth straight hit as a pinch-hitter and he would slash .481/.500/.593 in that role in 1932.

5   Isaminger.

DOUBLE-X TRIPLE DIPS

June 8, 1933
Philadelphia Athletics 14, New York Yankees 10

By James Forr

It was 92 degrees, with humidity that made it feel like triple digits. The suffocating torpor that hovered over Philadelphia was a metaphor for the Athletics' season and where the franchise was headed.

Two years earlier they had won their third straight American League pennant, but by 1933 the splendid Al Simmons was gone, stalwart pitchers Lefty Grove and George Earnshaw looked like shadows of their former selves, and attendance at Shibe Park was cratering. The future turned out even bleaker than it appeared. It was two cities and almost four decades until the Athletics were relevant again.

But for the moment the A's still clung to a few shreds of their erstwhile glory. For the moment they still had Jimmie Foxx.

Double-X, the 1932 American League Most Valuable Player, got off to a roaring start before slipping into a tailspin in late May and early June. He finally sparked back to life on June 7 with a home run, triple, and five RBIs against Washington, and entered the June 8 game with eight homers, third most in the AL behind New York's Lou Gehrig (10) and Babe Ruth (11).

The first-place Yankees tried to cool Foxx off with one of the league's best pitchers, Lefty Gomez. As it happened, Foxx owned the two-time 20-game winner like almost no one else. Coming into the afternoon, Foxx's career numbers against Gomez included a batting average of .448 with eight home runs and an OPS of 1.219. Gomez once remarked that Foxx probably could hit him blindfolded.[1]

A week earlier the Athletics had visited Yankee Stadium and couldn't get out of their own way. New York swept the series and held Foxx to just two hits in four games. The Yankees made a lot of people look silly early that season. They had won 31 of their first 44 games, including an 8-0 mark against Philadelphia, and held a six-game lead over the White Sox and Senators. The Athletics were next in line, in fourth place, 7½ games back.

The Yankees scored quickly against young lefty Tony Freitas, who was hitting the rocks after a sensational rookie season. Earle Combs scored on Gehrig's fielder's choice and then Ben Chapman singled in Joe Sewell for a 2-0 lead. In the second inning Gomez helped himself with a run-scoring grounder to extend the New York advantage.

In the third, Foxx lined a Gomez pitch into the left-field stands, a ball hit so hard that "it sped as if shot from a gun," according to the *Philadelphia*

Inquirer's James Isaminger.[2] Later in the inning, Dib Williams tripled in Pinky Higgins to draw Philadelphia to within 3-2.

Foxx led off the fourth with a massive solo shot the other way, over the right-field wall and off the awning of a home across 6th Avenue.[3] Then in the fifth inning Foxx ended Gomez's afternoon. With two on and two runs already in, Foxx hammered a ball off the roof of the left-field stands, where it bounced once and then disappeared from sight.[4] That made it 8-3, prompting manager Joe McCarthy to replace Gomez with Wilcy Moore. The home run was Foxx's 11th, tying him with Ruth for the league lead. It also gave him home runs in four consecutive at-bats (he homered in his final plate appearance against the Senators the day before), tying a modern major-league record set by Gehrig against the Athletics a year earlier.

The Yankees, though, wouldn't roll over. They rallied with a pair in the top of the sixth, including a solo shot from Gehrig, which lifted him into a three-way tie for the lead in the AL home-run race. Gehrig doubled in another run off Freitas in the seventh, reducing the gap to 8-6 and ending Freitas's day. Roy Mahaffey stepped into the fire with men at first and third and one out. After Chapman popped up, Tony Lazzeri doubled to right to score Ruth from third and Gehrig from first. Bill Dickey followed that with another double, which plated Lazzeri and gave the Yankees an improbable 9-8 lead.

Moore had kept the A's quiet in the sixth and seventh, but the eighth inning proved to be his downfall – not that it was altogether his fault. Philadelphia had a man on first and one out when Doc Cramer grounded to shortstop Frank Crosetti. It could have been an inning-ending double play, but Crosetti booted it and then the dominos started to fall. After Bob Johnson singled to short left to load the bases, Ed Coleman ripped a bases-clearing double into the left-center-field gap to put the A's back up, 11-9. Foxx and Mickey Cochrane walked to load the bases again. After Higgins struck out, Williams's RBI single scored Coleman and Foxx, and then an infield hit from Lou Finney, who had led off the inning pinch-hitting for Mahaffey, drove in Cochrane. It was 14-9 in favor of Philadelphia. Only two of the six runs off Moore were earned.

Connie Mack called upon Bobby Coombs to mop it up. Coombs, the nephew of the A's 1910 World Series pitching hero Jack Coombs, was making his official professional debut, fresh off the campus of Duke University.[5] The first batter he faced was Ruth, who christened him with a mammoth blast that landed two streets away beyond the right-field wall.[6] Later in life, Coombs liked to joke that it was the longest home run Ruth ever hit.[7]

That cut the lead to 14-10 and put the Babe back in front in the home-run chase. However, if that rude welcome rattled Coombs, he didn't show it, as he retired Gehrig, Chapman, and Lazzeri on routine groundballs to nail down the victory.

(Coombs' career journey was unique. After being hit hard as a rookie he spent nearly a decade in the minor leagues, only to return to the majors in 1943 as a 35-year-old wartime reliever for the New York Giants.)

Foxx homered again the next day. And the next day. And the day after that. It was a streak that propelled him to a second consecutive home-run title and the American League Triple Crown.

Gehrig and Ruth were bigger names and their fame would endure through the ages. But on this afternoon the 12,000 Philadelphia fans in attendance could head home knowing they had just witnessed a bravura performance by a man who was, at that moment, the greatest hitter alive.

One of the strongest players in baseball, Jimmie Foxx led the AL in home runs (58) and RBIs (169) to win the league's MVP award in 1932. The following season he won the Triple Crown (.356-48-163) and was named MVP again. (Photo by George Rinhart/Corbis via Getty Images)

SOURCES

In addition to the newspaper sources cited in the Notes, the author used Baseball-Reference.com and Retrosheet.org for play-by-play and other information:

The author also reviewed the following source for play-by-play and other information:

Drebinger, John. "Athletics' Attack Upsets Yanks, 14-10," *New York Times*, June 9, 1933: 24.

NOTES

1   W. Harrison Daniel, *Jimmie Foxx: The Life and Times of a Baseball Hall of Famer*, 1907-1967 (Jefferson, North Carolina: McFarland & Company, 1996): 114.

2   James C. Isaminger, "A's Crush Yanks as Giants Nip Phillies," *Philadelphia Inquirer*, June 9, 1933: 17.

3   Isaminger.

4   Isaminger.

5   Coombs appeared in the top of the 10th inning in a game against the Senators on the previous day and surrendered a go-ahead run, but the game was interrupted by rain. By rule, the game reverted to a tie and the statistics from the 10th inning were wiped out. See Shirley L. Povich, "Washington Gets One Run in Tenth, Preceding Deluge," *Washington Post*, June 8, 1933: 13.

6   Marshall Hunt, "Foxx Socks 3, Ruth One; A's 14, Yanks 10," *Daily News* (New York), June 9, 1933: 61.

7   Sharon Cummins, "Captain, Baseball Star Called Maxwell House Their Home," Seacoastonline.com, seacoastonline.com/article/20080424/LIFE/804240356 (accessed October 2, 2018).

COLEMAN'S THREE BOMBS HELP A'S OVERCOME WHITE SOX

August 17, 1934
Philadelphia Athletics 9, Chicago White Sox 8
(10 Innings; First Game of a Doubleheader)

By Ken Carrano

Fans of the Philadelphia Athletics could be excused for being confused when they walked into Shibe Park on August 17, 1934, and wondered which team they should support that day. The opponent for the A's this day were the Chicago White Sox, and four of the White Sox had recently been wearing the uniform of Connie Mack's charges. Mack sold Al Simmons, Mule Haas, and Jimmy Dykes to the White Sox after the 1932 season, and one year later he further gutted the recently great A's by trading George Earnshaw to Chicago. All four would feature for the White Sox in game one of a doubleheader this day. (Dykes was the White Sox' player-manager, having succeeded Lew Fonseca early in the season.)

This was the fourth time Earnshaw faced his old mates since he moved to Chicago, and things had gone well so far – he was 2-0 against the A's to that point and had also won all three of his starts in August.[1] Opposing Earnshaw would be A's rookie Al Benton, who had been brilliant in his last start, on August 11, beating the Washington Senators 2-1, allowing only three hits while going the distance. Today would be different.

The White Sox got a runner to second base in the first and second innings on walks but could not advance either runner further. Right fielder Ed Coleman came up second for the A's in the bottom of the second. Coleman, who along with outfielders Bob Johnson and Doc Cramer helped Mack decide to sell off Haas and Simmons to the White Sox,[2] had never really produced with the power that Mack envisioned when the deal was made. He had hit only six home runs in an injury-plagued 1933 season and had 11 coming into the doubleheader. On this day, he found the power he had showed in the minor leagues. After a leadoff walk to Pinky Higgins, Coleman smacked a drive over the right-field wall to give the A's a 2-0 lead.

The advantage lasted two batters into the White Sox third inning. Evar Swanson led off for the White Sox with a walk, giving Haas a chance to torment his former employer – an opportunity he did not waste, following Coleman's homer to right with his own to right field to tie the game. This was the first of 11 times that the game had a lead change or was tied.

In the home half of the fourth inning, after Earnshaw retired Jimmie Foxx and Higgins, Coleman hit his second home run and gave the A's the lead again at 3-2.

The White Sox tied the game in the top of the sixth. With one out, Jackie Hayes doubled to left-center, and after another out, Ed Madjeski singled to left. Johnson's throw from left appeared to be in time to get Hayes at the plate, but catcher Charlie Berry could not handle the throw. The error allowed Hayes to score and tie the game again.

The White Sox took the lead in the seventh, again thanks to the ex-Athletics. With one out, Philadelphia second baseman Dib Williams made an errant throw on Haas's grounder to the hole and Haas got to third base. (He was credited with a single on the play.) Simmons's single to center plated Haas. After Luke Appling lined out to center, Dykes doubled down the left-field line and Simmons scampered home to give the White Sox a 5-3 lead. It quickly disappeared.

Johnny Marcum reached first on an error by first baseman Dykes. Lou Finney pinch-hit for Benton and hit a fielder's choice grounder for the first out, then Cramer doubled to right to put the tying runs in scoring position. Earnshaw struck out Williams for the second out, but Johnson's single to center tied the game, 5-5.

Bill Dietrich relieved Benton in the White Sox' eighth and with two out gave up consecutive singles to Earnshaw and Swanson, then walked Haas to load the bases. Simmons now had the chance to make Mack regret his moves, and he did with a double to right to restore the White Sox' two-run lead.

But Chicago's Earnshaw couldn't hold the lead again. Higgins beat out a grounder to short-stop leading off the bottom of the eighth, bringing up Coleman, who found right field to his liking for a third time, tying the game once again with a home run. With that blast, Coleman became the fifth Athletic to hit three home runs in a game since 1908.[3]

Now it was Dietrich's turn to give up the lead. He started the top of the ninth inning by walking Dykes. Hayes's bunt moved Dykes to second, and he scored on Marty Hopkins's single to center. Earnshaw had a chance to extend the lead to two runs (again) but grounded into a fielder's choice to end the ninth for the visitors.

Manager Dykes might have been inclined to remove Earnshaw who twice was unable to hold a two-run lead, but with the second game of a doubleheader looming and another doubleheader scheduled for the next day, he gave Earnshaw one more chance to close out the game. For the third time in three attempts, Earnshaw failed. Dib Williams led off the bottom of the ninth with a single, and Foxx's walk moved him to second. Higgins followed with a single to tie the game for the fifth time. Coleman came up with a chance to become the second American League player to hit four home runs in a game but flied out to center.[4]

Dietrich finally had a one-two-three inning in the top of the 10th, and the Athletics finally came to bat without chasing the lead. Earnshaw was still in the game, and after striking out Hayes, he walked his counterpart Dietrich to put the winning run on base. Cramer moved that winning run to third with a double, and Williams ended Earnshaw's misery by driving a fly ball to deep center over Haas to score Dietrich with the winning run.

Coleman was the hero of the day, but that status faded quickly. He had four hits in five at-bats four days later in a 12-11 loss to the Cleveland Indians but finished the month of August on a 0-for-23 run and had only two pinch-hitting appearances in September. Despite a solid spring in 1935, he lost his job to the rookie Wally Moses and was traded to the St. Louis Browns. It was later revealed that Coleman was actually five years older than he had claimed and was not the potential young star Mack thought he had.[5]

SOURCES

In addition to the sources cited in the Notes, the author accessed Retrosheet.org, Baseball-Reference.com, SABR's BioProject via SABR.org, *The Sporting News* archive via Paper of Record, and the *Chicago Tribune* and *Philadelphia Inquirer* via Newspapers.com.

NOTES

1   Earnshaw's three wins were also the last three the White Sox had achieved in August, entering the doubleheader on August 17 with a 4-10 record in the month.

2   David Skelton, "Ed Coleman," SABR BioProject, https://sabr.org/bioproj/person/ed-coleman/.

3   This was the sixth time an Athletic had hit three home runs in a game – Jimmie Foxx achieved the feat twice. Three home runs in a game remain the A's record, with it having occurred 28 times, the most recent (as of 2019) by Khris Davis of the Oakland Athletics on May 17, 2017.

4   Lou Gehrig hit four home runs against the A's on June 3, 1932. Three of the home runs were hit off Earnshaw.

5   Skelton.

THINK PINKY:
HIGGINS' AERIAL ASSAULT GROUNDS RED SOX

June 27, 1935
Philadelphia Athletics 14, Boston Red Sox 2

By Andrew Milner

One of just two Philadelphia Athletics to make the 1934 American League All-Star roster, third baseman Mike "Pinky" Higgins was the subject of gossip that offseason that he might be sold to the New York Yankees for as much as $50,000. Owner-manager Connie Mack was peppered with questions about the proposed deal in January 1935 upon returning from an Orient tour, only to reply, "There never was a deal on for Higgins that I know of."[1] The 25-year-old Higgins would not sign a contract for the coming season until February 24.[2]

The A's optimism for 1935 was quashed when Higgins suffered a sprained ankle before the season – not during spring training in Florida, but at the Baker Bowl during the third game of the preseason City Series with the Phillies. As James S. Isaminger of the *Inquirer* related, "Higgins was on second when [pitcher] Fidgety Phil Collins suddenly turned around and zinged the ball to second to catch Mike off base. Higgins regained the bag, but in so doing hurt his ankle."[3] Higgins awoke the next morning with a limp and was out of the starting lineup until May 8. The *Inquirer* lamented, "To be deprived of the services of such a batting and fielding third-sacker as Higgins is nothing short of calamity."[4] Indeed, the A's began the season 2-11.

Higgins entered the lineup lacking his usual power, with Mack even dropping him briefly from fifth to seventh in the batting order. Higgins was batting under .200 as late as June 15. Returning from a three-week road trip that saw Higgins homer only once, the A's opened a homestand against the Boston Red Sox on June 27.

A's starting pitcher Johnny Marcum began the afternoon's offensive assault against Boston starter Wes Ferrell by leading off the third inning with his second home run of the year, to right field. "Johnny's swat landed in 20th St.," reported the *Philadelphia Record*.[5] With one out in the fourth, Higgins, whom Ferrell had struck out in the second, connected for a solo home run to left. "(Higgins) punched the ball completely over the left field roof," the *Bulletin* recounted. "It didn't pause to touch wood on the way over."[6]

The A's drove Ferrell off the mound with a five-run fifth. Catcher Paul Richards led off the inning with a single to left. After a sacrifice and a fly out, Doc Cramer drove in Richards with a single to center, and Bob Johnson homered. Ferrell then walked Jimmie Foxx before Higgins hit his second home run, into the left-field deck. Red Sox player-manager Joe Cronin lifted Ferrell, who had completed his previous four starts, for Henry Johnson.

The A's scored twice more in the sixth on singles by Wally Moses and Cramer. In the seventh, Johnson walked Foxx before surrendering Higgins's third home run of the game, which hit off the roof of the center-field stands.

Philadelphia added three more runs in the bottom of the eighth, scoring in its sixth straight inning, giving Higgins a final turn at bat with Bob Johnson on third, Foxx on first, and none out. Game accounts in the Philadelphia newspapers mentioned the A's fans' excitement at Higgins's chance to equal Lou Gehrig's four-homer performance at Shibe Park three years earlier, but Higgins ended the afternoon as he had begun it, by striking out; adding insult to injury, after the third strike Johnson was tagged out trying to steal home.

Higgins's three home runs equaled his output thus far in 1935, and he was the first big leaguer with a three-homer game since Babe Ruth's swan song a month earlier with the Boston Braves. He was assisted offensively by Doc Cramer's four hits and Bob Johnson, who went 2-for-5 with four RBIs. With such a cushion of runs, Marcum had an easy time dispatching the Red Sox, scattering four hits and four walks en route to his fifth victory of the season.

Most of the game accounts called Higgins, born Michael Franklin Higgins, by a different middle name. "Michael Francis [sic] Higgins, the willowy Texan with the sharpshooter's eyes,

jumped out of his slump in the grand manner at Shibe Park yesterday when, with Joe Louis punches, he bombed three mastodonic home runs in a row to score five of the runs that smeared the Red Sox," Isaminger began his game account in the *Inquirer*.[7] "Sir Michael Francis Higgins walked off with the show," Bill Dooly of the *Record* wrote,[8] while Al Horwits of the *Evening Public Ledger* dubbed Higgins "the Texas Sandow."[9]

The outburst against the Red Sox marked a change in Higgins' fortunes. From June 27 through the end of the season, he hit .331 with a .962 OPS and drove in 72 runs in the final 89 games of the year. His 23 home runs were sixth in the American League. After the AL All-Star selections were made, Isaminger at the *Inquirer* wondered, "Why was Frank Higgins, the beau ideal of third sackers, overlooked? Yes, he started the season in a batting slump because of injuries. So did Simmons, Gehrig, Cronin and Chapman. The difference between Higgins and the other slumpers is that Frank got over his. He is now batting hot and is playing as good ball as he ever did."[10] Henry McCormick of the *Wisconsin State Journal* queried, "And what happened to 'Pinkey' [sic] Higgins of the Athletics, almost anybody's choice for third base?"[11] Pinky was unable, however, to lift the Athletics on his back, as they went 29-52 after the All-Star break to end with a 58-91 record and their first last-place finish since 1921.

SOURCES

In addition to the sources cited in the Notes, the author accessed Retrosheet.org, Baseball-Reference.com, SABR.org, and *The Sporting News* archive via Paper of Record.

NOTES

1   Stan Baumgartner, "Bing Not Out in Cold, Mack Tells Scribes," *Philadelphia Inquirer*, January 10, 1935: 17.

2   "Pinky Higgins Signs," *Hazleton* (Pennsylvania) *Standard-Sentinel*, February 25, 1935: 9.

3   James C. Isaminger, "A's Nail Phillies 16-2 as Foxx Raps Pair," *Philadelphia Inquirer*, April 14, 1935: 27.

4   "Series Slants!" *Philadelphia Inquirer*, April 15, 1935: 17.

5   Bill Dooly, "Mackmen Bomb Boston for Five Circuit Drives; Win Opener, 14-2," *Philadelphia Record*, June 28, 1935: 18.

6   Cy Peterman,"Higgins' Three Homers Pace A's Against Friend Ferrell," *Philadelphia Bulletin*, June 28, 1935: 24.

7   Isaminger, "Macks Win, 14-2; Phils Bow, 11-1, Triumph, 8-7," *Philadelphia Inquirer*, June 28, 1935: 17. On June 25 Joe Louis had defeated Primo Carnera in the sixth round of a bout at Yankee Stadium.

8   Dooly.

9   Al Horwits, "Mack Will Bank on Hurling Staff," *Philadelphia Evening Public Ledger*, June 28, 1935: 27-28. Eugen Sandow (1867-1925) was a well-known German bodybuilder.

10 Isaminger, "Tips from the Sports Ticker," *Philadelphia Inquirer*, July 7, 1935: Sports Section, 6.

11 Henry McCormick, "No Foolin' Now," *Wisconsin State Journal* (Madison), June 30, 1935: 19.

Tony Lazzeri Belts Two Grand Slams and Knocks in 11 Runs

May 24, 1936
New York Yankees 25, Philadelphia Athletics 2

By Mike Huber

Approximately 8,000 fans paid to enter Shibe Park on Sunday, May 24, 1936, to see the seventh-place Philadelphia Athletics take on the first-place New York Yankees. George Turbeville took the mound for Philadelphia against the Yankees' Monte Pearson.

The Athletics scored the first two runs of the game, in the bottom half of the first inning and then were shut out for the rest of the game. New York did the rest, hammering out 19 hits, taking advantage of 16 bases on balls, and scoring 25 runs. The Yankees scored five times in the second and fourth innings and six times in the fifth and eighth innings, adding one run in the sixth and two in the seventh for good measure. The opening sentence of the *New York Times'* account of the game the next day summed up the story: "Tony Lazzeri hammered his way to baseball fame today with an exhibition of batting unparalleled in American League history as he set the pace in the Yankees' crushing 25-2 victory over the Athletics at Shibe Park."[1]

Lazzeri's line in the box score showed a career day: 5 at-bats, 4 runs, 4 hits, 2 putouts, 1 assist, 0 errors. What had to be read under the line scores shows that Lazzeri had a triple and three home runs and he knocked in 11 runs. And he was batting eighth. He bested Jimmie Foxx's previous American League mark of 9 RBIs in a single game. Foxx set that record in 1933 with a double, triple, and home run. The National League record of 12 RBIs in a game was set by St. Louis Cardinals first baseman Jim Bottomley on September 16, 1924. Another Cardinal, Mark Whiten, tied the NL record by knocking in 12 runs on September 7, 1993. Lazzeri's AL record still stood as of 2019.

Lazzeri's Yankee teammates also enjoyed batting success at the hands of the A's hurlers. Joe DiMaggio went 3-for-7, raising his batting average to .396 after 36 games. He had a single, double, and home run with 3 RBIs. DiMaggio was the only New York starter who did not draw a walk. Center fielder Ben Chapman, the Yankees' leadoff batter, had a perfect day at the plate, 2-for-2 (both doubles) and five walks, with four runs scored. He reached base in all seven plate appearances. Catcher Bill Dickey had two triples and a walk, and leadoff hitter Frankie Crosetti had two home runs to go with a walk. First baseman Lou Gehrig went 2-for-4 with two walks, giving the quartet of Gehrig, Chapman, Dickey, and Crosetti a rare team double cycle, as each player collected two hits of one type needed to hit for the cycle.

The A's used five pitchers – George Turbeville, Bill Dietrich, Red Bullock, Herman Fink, and Woody Upchurch. They allowed 5, 5, 5, 2, and 8 runs, respectively. Philadelphia starter Turbeville allowed only one hit in 1⅓ innings, but his five free passes contributed to five earned runs allowed. That one hit was a second-inning grand slam by Lazzeri. Dietrich faced 19 batters in his 2⅔ innings. Bullock faced six batters and retired only one; Fink faced two and retired both. When Upchurch was handed the ball to start the sixth inning, A's manager Connie Mack must have told him he would finish the game. His ERA after pitching four innings and giving up eight runs on eight hits, with two walks and four home runs, ballooned to 9.67. All of New York's 25 runs were earned. The nine-inning contest lasted 2 hours and 34 minutes.

Lazzeri hit a second grand slam in the fifth inning, and he added his third home run in the seventh, giving him two consecutive home runs. *New York Times* writer James P. Dawson wrote, "He missed a fourth by a matter of inches and had to be content with a triple."[2]

With two grand slams in one game Lazzeri "created" a new baseball record; he was the first major leaguer to accomplish the feat. His former teammate Babe Ruth had hit grand slams in consecutive games twice (in 1927 and 1929), but Ruth had never done it in one game. The day before this display of power, on May 23, Lazzeri had hit three home runs in a doubleheader against Philadelphia (in 12-6 and 15-1 victories for the Yankees). And he had gone deep on May 21 against the Detroit Tigers, giving him seven home runs in four games. The Yankees had scored 52 runs in the first three games played against the Athletics. They had 107 total bases and 49 hits. The 16 walks allowed by the five Philadelphia pitchers on May 24 was two short of the all-time mark of 18 allowed in a single game. On this historic day for Lazzeri, the New Yorkers hit six home runs. They had hit five in the second game of the previous day's doubleheader,

for a two-game total of 11 home runs. Dawson also wrote that "Lazzeri was almost mobbed when his triple gave him a new American League mark for runs batted in and at the conclusion of the game he had to fight his way through a cluster of autograph seekers, without police aid by the way."[3]

Against the quintet of Philadelphia pitchers in this game, the Yankees scored in six different innings and left nine men on base. Third baseman Red Rolfe went hitless, the only New York starter without a hit. Even pitcher Monte Pearson had three singles in five at-bats. Pearson struck out three, allowed seven hits and two walks, pitching a complete game and earning his sixth win of the season.

Next to the game story in the *New York Times* was a feature titled "Records Broken, Equaled and Approached By the Yankees in Philadelphia Game."[4] It included five records for Lazzeri: most runs batted in, single game (11); most home runs with bases filled, single game (2); most home runs in four consecutive games (7); most home runs in three consecutive games (6); and most home runs in two consecutive games (5). Tony owned the first four records outright and shared the fifth with Cap Anson and Ty Cobb. With 11 home runs in two consecutive games, the Yankees set a new record. And Ben Chapman's five walks had been exceeded only once, in 1891 by Walter Wilmot of the Chicago Nationals.

Tony Lazzeri was 32 years old when he bashed his way into the record books, in his 11th season as a Yankee. He finished the season with only 14 home runs, meaning he had hit seven in four consecutive games and seven in 146 other games. The future Hall of Famer became the first player to hit two grand slams in one game. Since then, only 12 other players have accomplished the feat (as of 2019).

ACKNOWLEDGMENTS

The author wishes to thank Ms. Rachel Hamelers, science librarian and reference services manager at Trexler Library, Muhlenberg College, for her assistance with obtaining sources.

SOURCES

Dawson, James P., "Yanks Overwhelm Athletics, 25 to 2: Lazzeri Sets American League Record by Driving In Eleven of the Runs," *New York Times*, May 25, 1936, 24.

"Two Grand Slams in One Game," baseball-almanac. com/feats/feats11.shtml.

May 24, 1936, New York Yankees at Philadelphia Athletics Box Score, baseball-reference.com/boxes/PHA/ PHA193605240.shtml.

May 24, 1936, NY (A) vs PHI (A) Box and PBP, retrosheet. org/boxesetc/1936/B05240PHA1936.htm.

NOTES

1   James P. Dawson, "Yanks Overwhelm Athletics, 25 to 2: Lazzeri Sets American League Record by Driving In Eleven of the Runs," *New York Times*, May 25, 1936, 24.

2   Dawson.

3   Dawson.

4   Dawson.

SHACKING UP WITH NEIGHBORS:
THE PHILLIES JOIN THE ATHLETICS AT SHIBE PARK

July 4, 1938
Boston Bees 10, Philadelphia Phillies 5 (Game One);
Philadelphia Phillies 10, Boston Bees 2 (Game Two)

By John Bauer

After 51 seasons and a single pennant at the Baker Bowl, the Philadelphia Phillies moved house. In late June of 1938, Phillies President Gerry Nugent announced that his team would become tenants of the Athletics at Shibe Park. The declining condition of the Baker Bowl motivated the relocation and was probably no surprise to baseball fans. It would not have been a surprise to the late John D. Shibe, the former Athletics vice president who had built a third clubhouse several years before in anticipation of the Phillies' eventual arrival.[1] The Phillies played their final game at the Baker Bowl on Thursday, June 30, a 14-1 drubbing by the league-leading New York Giants witnessed by a mere 1,500. The next day Nugent signed a 10-year lease for Shibe Park and the Phillies were scheduled to debut in their new home with a July 4 doubleheader against the Boston Bees.

The Phillies spent the weekend between home games on a busy road trip. They took two out of three against the Bees in Boston over July 1 and 2 and dropped both games of a July 3 doubleheader against the Dodgers at Ebbets Field. Typical of the

Phillies during this era, they occupied a position at the bottom of the standings. They were in the middle of an era in which they finished seventh or eighth in the NL every season between 1933 and 1945. Independence Day of 1938 found the Phillies dead last: 18-44, and 22 games behind the Giants. The Bees arrived in slightly better condition. Also a regular occupant of the second division, Boston had a 30-31 record and was in fifth place.

The Bees were managed by Casey Stengel, who had led the Dodgers to three second-division finishes between 1934 and 1936. His stint in Brooklyn portended similar results over his time in Boston (although his third big-league managerial job would prove more successful). Jimmie Wilson served as Phillies player-manager, the skipper since 1934 with declining use as a backstop. For the first game of the twin bill, Boston's Johnny Lanning (3-1, 4.34 ERA) opposed Philadelphia's Hugh Mulcahy (5-9, 4.93 ERA) in a matchup of right-handers. Lanning was an occasional starter for the Bees, while Mulcahy served as the Phillies' workhorse. He would pace the 1938 Phillies in starts and innings pitched while leading the league in losses.

Gene Moore led off the first game with a double to left field. After Vince DiMaggio struck out, Gil English was credited with a single on a pop fly lost in the sun by shortstop George Scharein.[2] Max West's grounder to first baseman Buck Jordan started a 3-6-1 double play to end the Bees first. The Phillies went down in order. Boston scored in the top of the second. Mulcahy issued a leadoff walk to Tony Cuccinello and then surrendered a single to Elbie Fletcher. Cuccinello scored from third for the game's first run on a groundout by Ray Mueller. Fletcher took second on the play and also claimed third on Mulcahy's balk. Outs by Rabbit Warstler and Lanning ended the visitors' half of the second.

Tuck Stainback was credited with the Phillies' first hit in their new home when he reached on a one-out bunt single in the bottom of the second. After Pinky Whitney's double advanced him to third, Stainback also scored the first Phillies run at Shibe Park, on Scharein's RBI grounder. Bill Atwood plated Whitney to take the lead, 2-1, before Mulcahy's out ended the inning. The Phillies extended their lead to 3-1 in the third inning when Chuck Klein's two-out double scored Hersh Martin.

Boston regained the lead in the top of the fourth on productive batting and "fiddle-winks outfielding."[3] West led off with a single and, after Cuccinello struck out, Fletcher singled to move West to second. Mueller got his second RBI of the afternoon when his single scored West. Warstler made the inning's second out, but his ball allowed Fletcher to score the game-tying run from third. The rally continued with Lanning's single, bringing Moore to the plate. Stainback played Moore's ball to left field into a triple that scored Mueller and Lanning for a 5-3 Boston lead.

Lanning walked Whitney to start the Philadelphia fourth. Scharein's groundball to second baseman Cuccinello appeared certain to result

in a double play, but after Whitney was forced, Warstler's poor throw to Fletcher missed nailing Scharein at first base.[4] Two batters later, that miss proved costly when Mulcahy doubled to score Scharein. Stengel replaced Lanning with Bobby Reis, but the move did not pay immediate dividends as Mueller's single to center brought home Mulcahy to even the score at 5-5.

The game remained tied for the next few innings. In the top of the eighth, that would change. Fletcher led off with a single to left field, went to second on Mueller's sacrifice, and crossed the plate on Warstler's double to right. Boston now led, 6-5, and the Bees were only getting started. Reis reached safely when Scharein's throw was too low for Jordan to make the play at first.[5] Mulcahy walked Moore to load the bases, and DiMaggio's fly out to left allowed Warstler to cross the plate. With two on and two out, English's smash into the left-field seats gave Boston a 10-5 advantage. The Phillies proved unable to mount much of a rally in the eighth and ninth, allowing Boston to claim victory in the opener.

The second game pitted Philadelphia's 29-year-old right-hander, Claude Passeau (5-8, 4.95 ERA), against Boston's Dick Errickson (0-4, 4.50 ERA). Errickson served as an occasional starter for the Bees, but he had lost his previous two starts. Passeau had pitched well in his last start, in Boston during the weekend road swing to the Northeast; Harl Maggert's pinch-hit eighth-inning homer accounted for the only run in Passeau's complete-game win on July 1. Passeau also looked forward to pitching now at Shibe Park instead of the Baker Bowl. He commented, "This is great stuff. A fellow can pitch naturally and not be afraid of a lucky hit."[6]

After Passeau held the Bees scoreless in the top half of the first, his Phillies teammates got to work atoning for dropping the opener. Mueller led off with a walk and Martin's sacrifice moved him to second. Jordan singled to place runners at the corners, and Klein's walk loaded the bases for

Morrie Arnovich. Described as a "big man with the wagon tongue,"[7] Arnovich doubled to score Mueller and Jordan for a 2-0 Phillies lead. Apparently believing the script was not going to improve, Stengel pulled the plug on Errickson's afternoon five batters into the game. Ira Hutchinson had pitched a complete-game victory over Philadelphia just 48 hours before in Boston. Now, he would be called upon to keep the Bees in this game. Klein scored from third on Whitney's groundout to Warstler for a 3-0 advantage. Arnovich also advanced on the play, but was stranded at third on Scharein's fly out to right fielder Johnny Cooney. In the third, Arnovich "smashed"[8] a run-scoring single that brought Jordan home for a 4-0 lead.

Cooney singled to open the Boston fourth. English flied out to Arnovich in left field, but West smacked a double off the right-field wall. Cooney crossed the plate for the first Bees run. Successive outs by Cuccinello and Fletcher ended the rally. In the bottom half of the inning, Cap Clark led off with a walk and Passeau's sacrifice moved him to second. Mueller's single drove in Clark to score and, just like that, the Phillies had restored their four-run lead. They extended the lead in the fifth. Arnovich hit a leadoff single. Whitney's sacrifice moved him up, and Scharein's single sent him home. Hutchinson walked Clark for the second successive inning and, after Passeau's fly out to DiMaggio in center field, a walk to Mueller loaded the bases. Martin's grounder to Cuccinello seemed likely to end the inning, but the second baseman could not make the play. The error meant that everyone was safe with Scharein scoring for a 7-1 tally.

An extraordinary play by catcher Johnny Riddle in the sixth inning merited special attention from the *Boston Globe*. Reliever Art Kenney issued a leadoff walk to Klein. English,

who had moved to second to replace Cuccinello, then muffed a ground ball from Arnovich. With Klein on second and Arnovich at first, Whitney tried to lay down a bunt. But the ball popped up off his bat, causing Maggert, who had taken over third base from English, to charge in for a diving catch in fair ground between third and home. The ball "slithered through his hands and rolled a foot or so into foul ground."[9] Klein made a break for third, and Riddle rushed over, gathered the ball in stride, and also raced toward third. The catcher won the race, and Klein was out.

In the Phillies' seventh, Bees reliever Art Kenney walked Mueller and Martin, and Jordan's single loaded the bases. Klein's grounder to second was bobbled by Gil English, and Mueller scored. Kenney walked Arnovich and Martin scored. With Whitney at the plate, Jordan scored on a play with runners in motion; Arnovich, however, was out at second. Had everyone stayed put, they would have advanced anyway. Kenney surrendered another walk to Whitney, his fourth pass of the inning and sixth in 1⅓ innings. Stengel ended the walk parade, giving Lanning an encore after his winning performance in the first game. The move worked; Lanning struck out Clark and Passeau to stop the bleeding, but at 10-1, the game was beyond the Bees. Three singles in the top of the eighth resulted in a consolation run by DiMaggio, but Passeau shut the door on Boston as a one-two-three ninth inning ended the game at 10-2, Philadelphia.

Given the state of the Phillies, a split improved their winning percentage but they would remain rooted to the bottom of the league. With their Athletics landlords in similar rough condition, the decision for potential visitors to Shibe Park would be which of Philadelphia's last-place teams they wanted to see in 1938.

SOURCES

In addition to the sources cited in the Notes, the author consulted baseball-reference.com and retrosheet.org.

NOTES

1   James C. Isaminger, "Shibe Park Switch a Break, Say Phils," *The Sporting News*, July 7, 1938: 2.

2   James C. O'Leary, "Bees Triumph, 10-5; Bow to Phils, 10-2," *Boston Globe*, July 5, 1938: 6.

3   Stan Baumgartner, "Phils Wallop Bees in Final, 10-2, But Bow in Opener, 10-5," *Philadelphia Inquirer*, July 5, 1938: 21.

4   O'Leary.

5   O'Leary.

6   Baumgartner.

7   Baumgartner.

8   Baumgartner.

9   "Remarkable Play Is Made by Riddle Forcing Out Klein," *Boston Globe*, July 5, 1938: 6.

PHILLIES' CLAUDE PASSEAU ENDURES MARATHON TO EDGE THE DODGERS

July 9, 1938
Philadelphia Phillies 4, Brooklyn Dodgers 3
(16 Innings)

By Richard Cuicchi

The game between the Philadelphia Phillies and Brooklyn Dodgers on July 9, 1938, may have gone completely unnoticed, except for the fact that Claude Passeau pitched all 16 innings for the Phillies. Only 1,277 fans showed up for the contest between the eighth-place Phillies and seventh-place Dodgers that had little significance for the two second-division teams. When it came to personal-best games, Passeau's impressive complete-game performance in the Phillies' win was surpassed only by his one-hit shutout for the Chicago Cubs in the 1945 World Series.

The contest between the two hapless teams was only the fourth game the Phillies played at Shibe Park. Their former home ballpark, the Baker Bowl which was built in 1887, was closed at the end of June, and the Phillies began sharing Shibe with the Philadelphia A's.

Phillies manager Jimmie Wilson gave Passeau his third start of the month. The Mississippi native, one of the workhorses on the staff of the recurrently weak team, had been the winning pitcher in the Phillies' first win in Shibe Park, the second game of a doubleheader against the Boston Bees[1] on July 4. Passeau had recorded double-digit losses in the two previous seasons.

One of the primary reasons the Phillies were in last place was their woeful offense. They tied the Bees for lowest slugging percentage in the league. They had hit only 28 home runs before this game and would hit only 40 for the season, with Chuck Klein accounting for eight. For the season, the Phillies would score an average of nearly two runs per game less than they allowed.

Brooklyn was managed by former Dodgers pitcher Burleigh Grimes, who was in his second season at the helm. They weren't as terrible as the Phillies, but still occupied seventh place, 16 games behind the league-leading New York Giants.

Grimes gave the starting nod to Freddie Fitzsimmons, a 36-year-old in the twilight of a productive career. He had won three of his last four starts.

The Phillies wasted no time getting on the board when they scored a run in the bottom of the first inning. Buck Jordan singled and Morrie Arnovich doubled him home.

Between the first and second innings, the Dodgers lost the services of manager Grimes, who was ejected from the game by umpire Dolly Stark for arguing a disputed call.[2]

In the third inning, Hersh Martin doubled for the Phillies and advanced to third when Arnovich reached base on an error by Dodgers catcher Merv Shea. Klein's fly ball to center scored Martin.

The Dodgers evened the score in the top of the fourth inning when Cookie Lavagetto's single drove in Buddy Hassett and Dolph Camilli.

The fifth inning saw both teams put up single runs. The Dodgers scored when Goody Rosen singled, Johnny Hudson reached base on an error, and Hassett hit a run-scoring single. The Phillies countered with their run stemming from four singles. After the second single, the Dodgers appeared to have the situation under control when Klein flied out to center and Jordan was called out for leaving second base too soon. But Pinky Whitney followed with the third single of the inning. Grimes replaced Fitzsimmons with Luke Hamlin, who yielded a single to George Scharein, scoring Arnovich. The game was tied again, 3-3.

Except for a threat by the Dodgers in the eighth frame, Passeau and Hamlin settled into a pattern of uncontested innings from the sixth inning through the 11th.

In the top of the 12th inning, the Dodgers mounted another threat to break the tie. Leo Durocher led off with a single, then was forced out at second on Shea's groundball. Hamlin singled, but Passeau managed to get out of the inning without allowing a score.

Both teams had chances to break the deadlock in the 13th inning. In the Dodgers' half, Hassett singled and advanced to third base on Ernie Koy's single. With one out, Lavagetto hit a sharp liner back through the middle, which Passeau speared and doubled off Hassett. After leading off the Phillies' bottom of the inning, Klein doubled. Del Young ran for him. After a walk to Whitney, Scharein's bunt attempt was fielded by third

baseman Lavagetto, who recorded an unassisted out to get Young at third. Bill Atwood grounded out to Lavagetto, with Whitney and Scharein advancing. Passeau, who had already stroked three singles, failed to bring home the winning run as he struck out to end the inning.

Undeterred by their previous attempts to break the tie in the 8th, 12th, and 13th innings, the Dodgers once more got two runners on base in the 14th before Passeau buckled down again to retire them without a run.

Hamlin held the Phillies from scoring in the 15th inning after allowing two runners. Passeau retired the side in the top of the 16th, including the 62nd batter he faced in the game.

Heinie Mueller tripled to lead off the bottom of the 16th inning. After Hamlin loaded the bases with intentional walks to Martin and Phil Weintraub, Arnovich hit a walk-off single to win the game for the Phillies, 4-3.

Passeau, who picked up his third win within the first nine days of July, remarkably didn't serve up any extra-base knocks among the 12 hits he allowed. After he gave up his last run in the fifth inning, he rose to the occasion each time the Dodgers threatened to score. All eight of his strikeouts came after the sixth inning.[3] Only two of the five walks he issued came after the fourth.

Fitzsimmons gave up 10 hits in his 4⅔ innings, while Hamlin gave up nine hits and four walks in his long relief effort of 10⅓ innings.

Arnovich was the hitting star for the Phillies, getting three hits and two RBIs. Passeau didn't do badly at the plate either, with a 3-for-7 game. Hassett's three hits were the most for the Dodgers.

Passeau's 16 innings were the most by a major-league pitcher in 1938. (The Yankees' Spud Chandler had a 15-inning victory on July 31.) Passeau finished the season with his third consecutive losing record (11-18), as the Phillies posted one of the most disastrous seasons in history with only 45 wins. Consequently, attendance at Phillies games for the season was a paltry 166,111, last among National League teams. (The Phillies would repeat their meager 45 wins in 1939.)

Fortunately for Passeau, he was traded to the Chicago Cubs on May 29, 1939, where he enjoyed a significant turnaround in his career. With the Phillies, his ERA was 4.15 and his WHIP was 1.474; with the Cubs he posted an ERA of 2.96 and WHIP of 1.250. His winning percentage increased from .409 to .569, including a 20-win season in 1940. Passeau was one of the Cubs' pitching stars on the 1945 NL pennant-winning team.

Passeau became a dominant pitcher without the use of a true fastball. He was often accused of throwing a spitter and once had to appear before Commissioner Kenesaw Landis to answer questions about claims that he used the illegal pitch.[4]

Durocher took over as Dodgers player-manager in 1939 and helped them become a perennial first-division club, including a National League pennant in 1941, their first since 1920.

The Phillies suffered losing seasons until 1949, when they finished third in the National League. In 1950 they captured their first pennant since 1915.

SOURCES

In addition to the sources cites in the Notes, the author consulted:

baseball-reference.com/boxes/PHI/PHI193807090. shtml.

retrosheet.org/boxesetc/1938/B07090PHI1938.htm.

Westcott, Rich, and Frank Bilovsky. *The New Phillies Encyclopedia* (Philadelphia: Temple University Press, 1993), 311.

"Phillies Nose Out Dodgers in 16th," *Philadelphia Inquirer*, July 10, 1938: S1.

NOTES

1 The Boston Braves were called the Bees from 1936 to 1941.

2 Bill McCullough. "Phillies Down Flock in 16th by 4-3 Count," *Brooklyn Daily Eagle*, July 10, 1938: D1.

3 There is a discrepancy between the *Philadelphia Inquirer* game account and Baseball-Reference box score regarding the number of strikeouts by Passeau in the game. The *Philadelphia Inquirer* box score shows 7 strikeouts, while Baseball-Reference shows 8 strikeouts.

4 Herb Fagen, "Claude Passeau: He Usually Finished What He Started," *Baseball Digest*, December 1995: 84.

First Night Game at Shibe Park

May 16, 1939
Cleveland Indians 8, Philadelphia Athletics 3
(10 Innings)

By Richard Cuicchi

Philadelphia's Shibe Park, opened in 1909, ushered in the modern era of ballpark construction with the first steel-and-concrete stadium in major-league baseball. It was fitting that the elegant ballpark with a French Renaissance-style façade would host the first night game in the American League, on May 16, 1939.

The first night game in the majors was played on May 24, 1935, when the Cincinnati Reds defeated the Philadelphia Phillies 2-1 at Crosley Field.[1]

The A's were the third major-league team to play under the lights, following National League cities Cincinnati and then Brooklyn in 1938 at Ebbets Field. The Phillies, who shared Shibe Park with the A's, followed on June 1, 1939.[2]

The lighting system installed at Shibe Park was said to have enough illumination to light more than 2,000 homes. Huge light standards were erected on the 20th Street side of the park and on top of the left-field stands. In all, 27,080 50-watt lamps were deployed to light the field.[3]

The significance of the game attracted the attendance of many dignitaries from the baseball community, including American League President Will Harridge, Cleveland Indians owner Alva Bradley, Washington Senators President Clark Griffith, and St. Louis Browns President Don Barnes. Commissioner Kenesaw Landis was scheduled to attend the historic game, but canceled because of urgent business in Chicago. The game's pregame festivities included two band concerts.[4]

The game was witnessed by 15,109 shivering fans. Higher attendance was expected, but the low temperature changed some fans' minds. When the game started at 8:55 P.M., the temperature was 54 degrees Fahrenheit and it dropped into the mid-40s by the end of the game at 11:36. The size of the crowd may also have been reduced by an overoptimistic newspaper story earlier in the day predicting that it would be difficult to gain admission because of an expected capacity crowd.[5]

Coming into the game, the Indians had won six of their last seven games. They were in fourth place in the American League, four games behind the New York Yankees, while the A's were in last place, in the middle of a stretch of nine consecutive seasons with a seventh- or eighth-place finish. Owner-manager Connie Mack was in his 39th season as the A's skipper.

Indians manager Ossie Vitt started left-hander Al Milnar, who had posted complete-game wins in his first two starts of the season. Mack countered with Lynn Nelson, who was making his first start of the season after four relief appearances.

Cleveland outfielder Roy Weatherly, who was hitting .414 coming into game, was the first American League player to bat in a game played under the lights. He flied out to center field.

The A's put the first run on the scoreboard in the bottom of the first. After a walk to Joe Gantenbein, a single by Sam Chapman, and a walk to Bob Johnson, Nick Etten drove in Gantenbein with a force out at second base.

The A's scored another run on Frankie Hayes' leadoff home run into the upper deck in the bottom of the second.

The Indians scored in the fourth on team captain Hal Trosky's solo home run. The 26-year-old Trosky suffered from severe headaches that season which limited him to less than 150 games for the first time since he had become the Indians' regular first baseman in 1934.

Neither team threatened to score again until the Athletics' seventh inning. Nelson led off by reaching base on second baseman Jim Shilling's error but was picked off first by catcher Rollie Hemsley. Dee Miles then singled and went to second on Gantenbein's walk. With Chapman batting, Milnar attempted to pick off Miles at second, but the ball was mishandled by Shilling. Runners Miles and Gantenbein both advanced on the error. Chapman's fly ball to right scored Miles and made the score 3-1. Milnar got out of the inning without yielding another run.

The Indians got even in the top of the eighth. Oscar Grimes walked with one out. Nelson struck out Earl Averill, pinch-hitting for Milnar, but he gave up a double to Weatherly, scoring Grimes. Batting for Hemsley, Odell Hale singled in Weatherly to tie the score, 3-3. After a single by Trosky, Roy Parmelee relieved Nelson and retired Jeff Heath.

Philadelphia had an opportunity to break the tie in the home half of the inning. With Johnny Humphries pitching, Billy Nagel began the inning with a double. But Humphries retired the next three batters to squelch the A's go-ahead attempt.

The Indians got a runner to third base in the top of the ninth with one out, but couldn't push across a run against Parmelee. When the Athletics failed to score in the home half, the game went into extra innings.

Parmelee fell apart in the 10th. He gave up three walks, then Heath doubled to score Frankie Pytlak and Weatherly. Bruce Campbell's fielder's-choice groundball to second scored Trosky. Ken Keltner followed with a single that plated Heath, and Campbell scored on Shilling's force-play grounder to short. Parmelee wound up yielding five earned runs on only two hits. Reliever Johnnie Humphreys blanked the Athletics in the bottom of the inning and the Indians were 8-3 winners.

Milnar struck out six before yielding to Humphries, who pitched three efficient innings for his first win of the season. Parmelee suffered his fifth straight loss. Trosky and Heath paced the Indians with two hits apiece.

Cleveland manager Vitt used his reserves extensively throughout the game. By its end, no position players were left on the bench.

After the game American League President Harridge said, "The lights at Shibe Park are wonderful, and I could see details of the game as well as I could if it had been daylight. I can't speak for the league owners as to whether all will go in for lights next year, that's entirely up to them, but there's lots to be said for night baseball. Certainly, I could pick no flaws in this game."[6]

The major leagues had been relatively slow to adopt nighttime baseball. The minors had begun playing under the lights almost 10 years earlier, and virtually every minor-league ballpark had installed lights by the time of Shibe's inaugural night game. Night baseball was considered the salvation of minor-league baseball.

Larry MacPhail, president of the Brooklyn

Dodgers, persuaded Connie Mack to go against the league's owners who opposed night games and install lights at Shibe Park. The Dodgers had attributed their financial turnaround the prior year to night games.[7]

Not yet convinced that night games would be popular among the fans, the A's scheduled only six more night games in Shibe Park in 1939, once for each of the other American League teams. They were all played on weekdays. The next A's game under the lights was played on May 24 against the White Sox in front of a paltry crowd of 1,874. However, their game against the first-place New York Yankees on June 26 drew a near-capacity crowd of 33,074 fans. The Phillies also played eight night games at Shibe Park. American League teams Chicago and Cleveland later played night games in 1939 as well.

Yankees President Ed Barrow still opposed night games at Yankee Stadium. Barrow said, "Just so long as I have anything to do with the Yankees, there will be no night games in our stadium." Nevertheless, he agreed to play in other teams' lighted ballparks, since the Yankees helped pack stadiums in opposing cities.[8] Indeed, Yankee Stadium did not host its first night game until 1946, after Barrow left his job as president.

Of course, major-league teams' apprehensions over night baseball eventually dissipated. Yet it wasn't until August 9, 1988, that the last of the 16 original franchises played its first night game, when the Chicago Cubs played the New York Mets under the lights at Wrigley Field.

SOURCES

In addition to the sources cited in the Notes, the author consulted:

baseball-reference.com/boxes/PHA/PHA193905160.shtml

retrosheet.org/boxesetc/1939/B05160PHA1939.htm

McLinn, Stoney. "Connie Mack, Linking Birth of American with Present, First to Light Up in Loop," *The Sporting News*, May 25, 1939: 2.

NOTES

1   Norm King. "Reds Fans See the Light(s)," *Cincinnati's Crosley Field: A Gem in the Queen City* (Phoenix: Society for American Baseball Research, 2018), 95.

2   baseball-almanac.com/firsts/first10.shtml. Accessed January 11, 2019.

3   James Isaminger, "Nelson Will Hurl Opening Night Tilt Against Indians," *Philadelphia Inquirer*, May 16, 1939: 25.

4   Isaminger, "Nelson Will Hurl Opening Night Tilt Against Indians."

5   "Sidelights on the A.L.'s First Arc-Light Game," *The Sporting News*, May 25, 1939: 4.

6   "Sidelights on the A.L.'s First Arc-Light Game."

7   James Isaminger, "Cleveland Rallies in Tenth to Beat A's in Night Game," *Philadelphia Inquirer*, May 17, 1939: 25.

8   "Yankees Yield on Night Baseball to Aid Other Clubs," *The Sporting News*, May 25, 1939: 1.

A's Suffer Worst Home Loss
in Yankees Beatdown

August 13, 1939
New York Yankees 21, Philadelphia Athletics 0
(8 Innings; Second Game of a Doubleheader)

By Thomas J. Brown Jr.

After streaking out of the gate early in the season, the New York Yankees had cooled off by the time they arrived at Shibe Park on August 11. They won the first two games of the series against the hapless Athletics, including an 18-4 win the previous day. The Athletics' 36-69 record was almost a mirror image of the Yankees' 72-32.

A crowd of 34,570 came to Shibe Park for the doubleheader on the afternoon of August 13 to see if their Athletics might salvage the series against the mighty Yankees. The gates were closed a few innings into the first game and it was estimated that at least 10,000 fans were turned away.[1]

The A's gave the hometown crowd something to cheer about when they won the first game, 12-9. The Athletics scored three runs in bottom of the ninth inning on a walk-off home run by Frankie Hayes to beat the Yankees and break an eight-game losing streak.

Athletics fans were thrilled to see their team finally win a game. It was just the second time they had beaten the Yankees in the 1939 season. They had won on June 26, the last time the Yankees were in town. But the Yankees, in a harbinger of things to come, beat Philadelphia 23-2 the next day.

For the second game of the twin bill, rookie Henry "Cotton" Pippen took the mound for the Athletics. After spending most of the previous seven years in the St. Louis Browns farm system, Pippen had been picked up by the Athletics in the Rule 5 draft the previous fall. Pippen had struggled all season and entered the game with a 2-8 record. Pippen had lost his only start against the Yankees, on May 26 when he pitched a complete game and gave up only one run, the only one the Yankees needed as Oral Hildebrand pitched a shutout.

After Pippen got the Yankees out in order in the first inning, they jumped on him for five runs in the second. Joe DiMaggio singled and ended up on third when Bill Dickey followed with a double. A triple by George Selkirk brought both runners home. Pippen walked the next two batters to load the bases. Pitcher Red Ruffing then singled to bring home two more runners.

After a popup to shortstop got the first out of the inning, Red Rolfe singled in another run. By the time Pippen got the third out, the Athletics were in a 5-0 hole.

In his previous two starts against Philadelphia in 1939, Ruffing had notched two wins behind 18 runs from his teammates. Ruffing walked three batters in the first inning but none of the Athletics reached home. After getting out that jam, Ruffing allowed just three more Athletics hits while striking out five batters.

When Pippen gave up a leadoff single to Dickey in the third, Athletics manager Connie Mack pulled him for Nels Potter. Potter fared no better. After Selkirk singled, an error by third baseman Joe Gantenbein allowed Dickey to score. Ruffing picked up his third RBI of the game when his groundout to the pitcher sent Selkirk home. Potter then walked two batters and surrendered a pair of singles to allow the Yankees to score three more runs. By the time the Athletics got the third out, they were down 10-0.

James Isaminger of the *Philadelphia Inquirer* wrote that "[t]he Athletics were completely smothered in the (game). The Yankees kept up such a steady drumbeat of base blows [that] Pippen was stormed off the tee in the third and Potter merely threw kerosene on the blaze."[2]

The Yankees scored two more runs in the fourth when Babe Dahlgren homered with a runner on base. Even though Potter struggled, Mack kept him in the game. Another run was added to the Yankees' total in the fifth when Charlie Keller singled and later scored. The Yankees' lead now was 13 runs. It was the 12th consecutive game in which Keller hit safely.

As Ruffing kept the Athletics in check, his teammates continued to pound away at Potter. Potter walked Dahlgren and gave up a single to Ruffing to start the sixth. With one out, Rolfe doubled to add another run to the Yankees' total. Two batters later, DiMaggio hit a three-run inside-the-park home run. Potter needed just one more out to get out of the inning but he couldn't get it. Three more singles brought home

the fifth Yankees run of the inning to make the score 18-0.

Potter kept the Yankees from scoring in the seventh but DiMaggio led off the eighth with his second homer, giving him five RBIs for the game. DiMaggio's blast cleared the roof of the left-field stands; Isaminger called it a "masterpiece."[3] After Tommy Henrich reached first on an error, Dahlgren hit the Yankees' second inside-the-park home run of the game. The two-run blast gave the Yankees a 21-0 lead.

As the Yankees scored runs in inning after inning, Ruffing kept the Athletics in check. He gave up just three hits to the Mackmen, the final one a triple by Earle Brucker in the sixth. After Ruffing retired the Athletics on three fly balls in the eighth inning, the game was ended because of Philadelphia's 7 P.M. curfew. It was Ruffing's 17th victory of the season. While Ruffing kept the Athletics off the bases, his teammates battered the A's for 23 hits against Pippen and Potter.

The game was one of five shutouts by Ruffing during his career in which the Yankees scored at least 15 runs. The others were 18-0 (1936), 17-0 (1931), and 15-0 twice (1937 and 1942). Ruffing helped himself in the game by getting four hits and driving in three runs. Ruffing's own powerful bat produced 36 homers and more RBIs than any other modern pitcher.

The *New York Times* made an understated note of the victory, saying "[t]here was nothing to the victory. The Yanks were racing against time in a batting workout, for they had to get in five innings before the 7 o'clock deadline[4] to make it a game." The game was called at 6:49 P.M. to conform with Philadelphia's Sunday baseball law.[5]

The Yankees' victory was the most lopsided shutout since the Detroit Tigers beat the Cleveland Indians 21-0 in 1901. That game was also shortened, because the Indians had to catch a train to Boston.[6]

SOURCES

In addition to the sources cited in the Notes, the author used Baseball-Reference.com and Retrosheet.org for box-score, player, team, and season information as well as pitching and batting game logs, and other pertinent material.

baseball-reference.com/boxes/PHA/PHA193908132.shtml

retrosheet.org/boxesetc/1939/B08132PHA1939.htm

NOTES

1   James Isaminger, "Hayes Ninth Inning Homer Wins Opener," *Philadelphia Inquirer*, August 14, 1939: 17.

2   Isaminger: 18.

3   Isaminger: 17.

4   James Dawson, "Athletics Routed With 23 Hits, 21-0," *New York Times*, August 14, 1939.

5   At the time, Philadelphia's Blue Laws limited what commercial enterprises could take place on Sundays. Sunday baseball began in Philadelphia in 1934 after protracted court battles.

6   Ronald Liebman, "The Most Lopsided Shutouts," *Baseball Research Journal* 5 (1976).

Foxx Finally Hits Number 500

September 24, 1940
Boston Red Sox 16, Philadelphia Athletics 8
(First Game of a Doubleheader)

By Bill Nowlin

In mid-August of 1940, Jimmie Foxx went on a homer-hitting spree, banging out four-base hits five games in a row, hitting seven home runs in a seven-day stretch from August 13 through 19. On August 16 he hit a home run in the first inning and another — a game-winner— in the bottom of the 10th. Those two homers pushed him past Lou Gehrig to second place on the all-time home-run list, second only to Babe Ruth. The run of seven homers in seven days increased his total to 497 homers in the course of his long career. Then he hit only one more in the rest of August (number 498) and another on September 4 (499). He'd hit in 30 games trying to get from 497 to 500, and after number 499 he'd gone 15 games with hitting one out. There were only eight games left on the schedule.

In the first 10 games of September, Foxx's versatility in the field was evident. The team captain caught the first 10 games of the month, then played six games in succession at first base. On September 19 he played third base. On the 22nd he pinch-hit. There was no game on the 23rd. He was back at first base on September 24.

It was perhaps fitting that it was in Philly that Foxx finally hit number 500. He had, after all, begun his big-league career there in 1925. Had there not been a Depression, and had Connie Mack not found the team in desperate straits, he almost certainly would never have dealt one of his biggest stars to wealthy young Boston Red Sox owner Tom Yawkey in December 1935.[1] Foxx had already hit 302 homers and driven in 1,075 runs for the Athletics.

When he stepped into the Shibe Park batter's box shortly after the 1:35 P.M. start on Tuesday afternoon, September 24, he was still stuck on 499. Right-hander Ed Heusser was on the mound for the Athletics. Foxx led off the top of the second inning with a single, then moved to third base on Bobby Doerr's single. The Red Sox loaded the bases and he scored on a sacrifice fly by Johnny Peacock. His was the first of two Red Sox runs scored in the inning.

Next time up, Foxx flied out to the first baseman, but Boston had run its lead up to 5-0. Starting in the fourth, George Caster replaced Heusser on the mound, Heusser having been removed for a pinch-hitter. Even though the pinch-hitter struck out, the Athletics pushed three runs across in the third.

Against Caster, Ted Williams hit a two-out, two-run homer, making it 7-3. Foxx was up next but flied out to left.

Joe Cronin hit a leadoff homer in the fifth.

In the sixth inning, Caster seemed to start grooving them. Dom DiMaggio was up first; he tripled. Doc Cramer flied out to left, and Dom tagged up and scored. 9-3. With the bases empty, Ted Williams hit his second home run of the game, over the right-field fence. 10-3. Foxx, still longing for number 500, stepped up and hit it into the left-field pavilion. Home run 500. 11-3. He had joined Babe Ruth as the only two batters in history to reach the 500 mark, and he was still just 32 years old.

Joe Cronin was next; he homered, too, "bouncing the ball off the leftfield roof."[2] The three consecutive home runs tied the major-league mark at the time. 12-3. Cronin was 4-for-5 in the game.

It was Bobby Doerr's turn next, and he rounded the bases, too – but he'd "only" tripled, off the left-field stands (he hadn't missed another home run by much), coming all the way to score on an errant wild throw by Athletics first baseman Dick Siebert (because of the carom the ball had taken, the Associated Press noted, "observers thought he could have got an inside homer.")[3] 13-3. Next up was Jim Tabor. He homered onto the roof on top of the left-field stands.[4] And Dom DiMaggio doubled in another run. 15-3.

In the sixth inning, Caster had faced seven batters and given up two triples and four solo home runs. That was enough. It was 14-3. Les McCrabb relieved. He finished the game, giving up just one more run. The Athletics scored five times in the bottom of the eighth, off Red Sox starter Joe Heving, who was left in to go the distance, but the final score was 15-8.

Despite a total of 38 base hits (23 by the Red Sox, 6 of them home runs), two walks, and four errors, the game didn't even take two hours to complete. The time of game was 1:55. Foxx was replaced by Tony Lupien, who played first base in the eighth and ninth.

Foxx played the second game of the day's doubleheader, collecting one single in four at-bats and scoring one run. The Red Sox won, 4-3.

There were only an estimated 1,500 fans present.

Foxx played in six more games in 1940, with seven base hits, but none were home runs. He finished the season, satisfied with 36 homers for the season and 500 in his career. His total of 36 home runs in 1940 accomplished something no one had ever done before – including Ruth and Gehrig. Foxx had homered 30 or more times for 12 consecutive seasons.

The five doubles, three triples, and six homers gave the Red Sox 14 extra-base hits in the game, reported by the *Boston Globe* as having set a new major-league record.[5] Their 52 total bases were one shy of the American League mark.

Foxx hit 19 more home runs in 1941, and five more for the 1942 Red Sox before he was placed on waivers and selected on June 1 by the Chicago Cubs. He hit three homers for the Cubs in 1942 and seven more during the war year of 1945 when he was signed as a free agent by the Philadelphia Phillies, for a career total of 534. The Phillies also played their home games at Shibe Park. Home run number 532 was the last one Foxx hit at Shibe, on August 20, 1945. It provided the Phillies their second run in a 4-3 win over the visiting Cincinnati Reds. In all, he hit 181 of his home runs at Shibe Park.

In 1951 Jimmie Foxx was inducted into the National Baseball Hall of Fame. Before the 1953 season, the ballpark he'd called home for most of his career was renamed Connie Mack Stadium.

SOURCES

In addition to the sources cited in the Notes, the author consulted Mark R. Milliken, *Jimmie Foxx: The Pride of Sudlersville* (Lanham, Maryland & London: Scarecrow Press, 1998), Baseball-Reference.com, and Retrosheet.org.

NOTES

1   The trade netted Mack $150,000 in cash.

2   "Red Sox Tie Major Home Run Record," *Boston Globe*, September 25, 1940: 25.

3   "Red Sox Wallop A'S Twice," *San Francisco Chronicle*, September 25, 1940: 22.

4   John Drohan, "Foxx Crashes No. 500, Sox Equal Homer Mark," *Boston Herald*, September 25, 1940: 28.

5   *Boston Globe.*

WITH .400 AT STAKE, WILLIAMS DECIDES TO PLAY

September 28, 1941
Boston Red Sox 12, Philadelphia Athletics 11
(First Game of a Doubleheader)

By Bill Nowlin

The Red Sox split a Sunday doubleheader with Connie Mack's Athletics on the final day of the 1941 season — meaningless games, with the Sox in second place, 17½ games out, and Philadelphia 20 games behind them. But these were professionals. And there was something else at stake.

From May 25 until they arrived in Philadelphia for the final three games of the season, 23-year-old Ted Williams had been above .400 except for a stretch from July 11 through the 24th when he dipped as low as .393.

On Saturday, September 27, Williams was 1-for-4 against 30-year-old rookie Roger Wolff, and his average dropped to .3995535. It would have been rounded up to .400.

There's a long-standing legend that Red Sox manager Joe Cronin had told Ted he could sit out the games to preserve his average. No one would have blamed him if he had. Williams had taken "a special session of batting practice at Shibe Park" during the day on Friday, after the Red Sox arrived in town, and Ted told the *Philadelphia Bulletin's* Frank Yeutter, "I either make it or I don't."

Yeutter mentioned to readers a couple of obstacles Williams would face: "The lengthening shadows of autumn afternoons, and facing strange young pitchers getting the usual end-of-the-season tryouts." The advantage, he said, was in the pitcher's favor.

Naturally, Williams wanted to hit .400. Ty Cobb had done it three times, and so had Rogers Hornsby. (Hornsby could have done it a fourth time, if one applied rounding. Entering the last game of the 1921 season, he had been hitting .39966. Hornsby went hitless and wound up at .397.)

For a retrospective book 50 years later, Williams recalled Cronin telling him, "You don't have to be put in if you don't want to. You're officially .400."[1] Ted reported his reaction: "Well, God, that hit me like a *goddamn lightning bolt*! What do you mean I *don't* have to *play* today?"[2]

Purportedly, Ted had declared, "I want to have more than my toenails on the line."[3]

Truth be told, .39955 is not .400 – as he would have been reminded by Sunday headlines he may have seen. The *Philadelphia Inquirer* was unambiguous: "SOX TOP A's; WILLIAMS FALLS TO .399."

Everyone knew what was on the line. He'd be facing Dick Fowler in the first game – a rookie like Wolff. A's pitcher Porter Vaughan said, "Connie Mack didn't talk to the pitchers but he talked to the catcher, Frank Hayes. Frank was a good catcher. When Ted came to bat, he told Ted that the pitchers had the word from Mr. Mack that they didn't ought to let up at all on Ted, and if they did, they'd have to pay the consequences."[4]

Cronin told the *Boston Globe* before the game: "If there's ever a ballplayer who deserved to hit .400, it's Ted. He's given up plenty of chances to bunt and protect his average in recent weeks. He wouldn't think of getting out of the lineup to keep his average intact. Moreover, most of the other stars who have bettered the mark before were helped by no foul strike rules or sacrifice fly regulations."[5] Had the rule been in effect that does not count a sacrifice fly as an at-bat, Ted would have entered the day hitting comfortably above .400, at .4049773.

Ted himself kept it simple: "'Gee, I only hope I can hit .400,' was all he would say."[6]

The *Philadelphia Bulletin*'s Yeutter reported that "Before the two games started he was nervous and sat on the bench, biting his fingernails. His mammoth hands trembled. He condemned himself for getting only one hit for four times at bat Saturday."

Ted was nervous, and had been since the end of Saturday's game. That evening, he said, he walked the streets of Philadelphia for several hours with Red Sox clubhouse man Johnny Orlando, walking maybe 10 miles.[7]

Williams was batting cleanup and Fowler retired the side in the first, so Ted led off the top of the second. "Bill McGowan was the plate umpire, and I'll never forget it," Ted recalled. "Just as I stepped in, he called time and slowly walked around the plate, bent over and began dusting it off. Without looking up, he said, 'To hit .400 a batter has got to be loose. He has got to be loose.'"[8]

The first pitch was low and outside. The second was low and inside. On the 2-0 count, Ted was ready and he swing at Fowler's pitch. He "singled sharply to right," according to the *Inquirer*'s Stan Baumgartner. Moore of the *Globe*

called it "a sizzling single past first baseman Bob Johnson's right."[9]

After that first hit, Ted's average stood at .4008908. If he'd made an out his second time up, he'd be exactly .400. He had nothing to lose by taking that second at-bat. He led off the fifth inning, still facing Fowler, and homered on a 1-0 pitch driving the ball over the high right-center-field wall, a shot of perhaps 440 feet. It was his 37th homer of the year; he led both leagues in homers. Now he was batting .4022222. He could make outs each of the next *two* times up and still be a little over .400.

He didn't. The Red Sox had taken a 3-2 lead in the top of the fifth, but the A's scored nine times in the bottom of the inning, building up an 11-3 lead. Next time up, in the top of the seventh, Ted was facing reliever Porter Vaughan, who threw two straight curveballs, both of which missed the plate. Vaughan threw another curve, and Ted guessed right. He was waiting for it. "I hit a bullet right through the middle – base hit."[10] It was a single, and the Red Sox scored six runs that inning, closing the gap to 11-10 (they'd scored once in the sixth, too), and Williams singled off Vaughan a second time.

Vaughan told the story: "He got two clean singles off me. On the first one, he hit off a curveball. Our second baseman was Crash Davis. Crash and I had come up at the same time. He played Ted in the hole between second and first. Ted hit the ball to the right of the second baseman. The second one he hit was a fastball. I threw him a fastball. Left fielder Bob Johnson was playing first base. Dick Siebert, our regular first baseman, had gone back to Minnesota; he taught out there. Johnson didn't get to the ball; it was between him and the base. It was close to first base. Ted hit it right down the line. Obviously I didn't fool him at all. He had wonderful eyesight and very quick hands. It was almost impossible to fool him. He really studied pitchers and remembered everything they threw him."[11]

Williams was 4-for-5 in the first game with two RBIs and two runs scored. He might even have been 5-for-5 but for the official scorer. Batting against Newman Shirley, yet another rookie (the hardest pitchers of all for Ted to hit, since they were neither predictable nor necessarily accurate), he grounded to second base and reached base, but with an error charged to second baseman Crash Davis. The Associated Press said that "a very ponderous" scoring decision "robbed" Ted of his fifth consecutive hit, though John Holway has noted that none of the other writers argued the decision.[12]

And even though Boston scored twice in the top of the ninth and won the game, 12-11, the Philly fans were all for Ted all day long. "Each time he came to bat the crowd roared, and when he went back to left field each inning the bleacherites gave him added applause," wrote the *Evening Bulletin*.

By the end of the first game, Williams was batting .4039735. He could have gone 0-for-4 in the second game and still been above .400. He didn't. He went 2-for-3, and was 6-for-8 on the day, and hitting .4057. Or, rounded up: .406.

"There was not a questionable hit among the group," wrote the *Inquirer*. "All were slashing drives that whistled through the infield or fell far out of reach of the outfielders."

After the game Ted said he'd never felt nervous in baseball before. Now, he said, "I was shaking like a leaf when I went to bat the first time. Then when I got that first hit I was all set. I felt good. Gee, there's a lot of luck making that many hits." He turned to Jimmie Foxx and exclaimed, "Just think – hitting .400. What do you think of that, Slug? Just a kid like me hitting that high."

By virtue of reaching base six of the eight times up (not counting reaching on the error), Ted Williams had achieved a season on-base percentage of .553. More than half the times he came to bat in 1941, he got on base. And he struck out only 27 times all season long.

ACKNOWLEDGEMENTS

Thanks to Rock Hoffman for providing photocopies of the Philadelphia newspapers of the day.

NOTES

1   Ted Williams with David Pietrusza, *My Life in Pictures* (Kingston New York: Total Sports Illustrated, 2001), 43.

2   Ted Williams with David Pietrusza, 43.

3   Bill Pennington, "Ted Williams' .406 Is More Than A Number," *New York Times*, September 17, 2011.

4   Porter Vaughan interview with author, July 30, 1997. Williams says Hayes told him, "Ted, Mr. Mack told us if we let up on you he'll run us out of baseball, I wish you all the luck in the world, but we're not giving you a damn thing." Ted Williams, *My Turn at Bat* (New York: Fireside Books, 1969), 90.

5   Gerry Moore, "Williams Hoists Hit Mark to .406 – 37th Homer Caps March to Batting Crown," *Boston Globe*, September 29, 1941: 6.

6   Moore.

7   Williams, 87.

8   Williams, 90.

9   Moore.

10 John B. Holway, *The Last .400 Hitter* (Dubuque, Iowa: Wm. C. Brown Publishers, 1992), 285.

11 Porter Vaughan interview.

12 Holway, 287.

"TEDDY BALLGAME" FINISHES AT .406

September 28, 1941
Philadelphia Athletics 7, Boston Red Sox 1
(Second Game of a Doubleheader)

By Jack Zerby

With their A's once again mired in the American League cellar, an above-season-average 10,268 nonetheless found their way to Philadelphia's Shibe Park on the last day of the 1941 season.[1] A Lefty Grove Day observance celebrating their once-dominating southpaw held a degree of interest as the old-timer returned with the Boston Red Sox. But Ted Williams was also in town, his average at .39955 after months above .400, and not only the fans in Philadelphia but the baseball world wanted to see if The Kid[2] would sit or play. If he played, would the A's pitchers challenge him? If they did, how would Williams do, given the intense pressure he'd been under for weeks and a 1-for-4 game against Philadelphia just the day before?

From September 10 on, Williams had hit .270.[3] "Everyone became a statistics expert," Robert Creamer noted in *Baseball in '41*. Red Sox manager Joe Cronin had gone so far as to mention the idea of Williams' sitting out the final three games in Philadelphia. But "Williams insisted on playing. He'd hang in there. He'd play."[4] That decision had produced Williams's lackluster Saturday performance and the .39955, which would round to .400, as the Sunday doubleheader loomed.

Williams, 22, was in his third Boston season and already beginning to display the pugnacious attitude that led him to joust with writers and fans, especially later in his career.[5] He'd already missed a handful of games with nagging injuries and was firm. "If I'm going to be a .400 hitter, I want more then my toenails on the line."[6] "If I can't hit .400 all the way, I don't deserve it."[7]

The shorter days of autumn heightened the shadows in cavernous Shibe Park and posed problems for hitters, even Williams. Too keyed up about the next day to remain in the team hotel on Saturday night, he recruited Red Sox clubhouse man Johnny Orlando and they embarked on a walking tour of Philadelphia drinking spots that lasted in excess of three hours. "Orlando stopped at bars for occasional sustenance as Williams, who rarely drank alcohol, sipped a soft drink [or maybe partook of some ice cream; vanilla was a favorite of his] outside."[8]

A baseball purist who had observed his share of .400 hitters since debuting in the majors in 1886, Philadelphia manager Connie Mack had instructed his pitchers to pitch to Williams rather than frustrate him with walks. First-game starter Dick Fowler and two relievers did just that.[9] Williams, having been walked repeatedly in recent weeks and relishing a chance to swing, overcame his nerves and the Shibe Park shadows with a home run and three singles. The monkey was off his back; the Red Sox scored two runs in the top of the ninth to pull out a 12-11 win.

Grove, Joe Cronin's pick to start the second game, was feted between games.[10] He had broken in with Mack's A's 16 years before and joined select company on July 25, 1941, when he won his 300th game. Grove was 41 years old, "silver-thatched and portly,"[11] with a tired arm and a sore back, he was 7-6 for the season as he answered the call in his 616th major-league game.

Mack countered with Fred Caligiuri, a 22-year-old rookie right-hander from the wilds of northwestern Pennsylvania. He'd been called up from Class B Wilmington three weeks before and was 1-2.[12]

True to his word, Williams was once again in left field and hitting fourth. Caligiuri summarily retired Dom DiMaggio, Lou Finney, and Al Flair in the top of the first while the A's quickly feasted on Grove in their half, scoring three runs on four hits, a DiMaggio error, and a wild pitch. Grove finally got out of the inning when catcher Johnny Peacock threw out Al Brancato attempting to steal second. When it was over, Cronin sat Grove down in favor of Earl Johnson, who went the rest of the way for Boston, giving up four runs of his own.

Williams faced Caligiuri for the first time leading off the second and raked a single. By the time he came up again in the fourth, the A's had increased their lead to 4-0. Still seeing pitches intended to get him out, Williams lashed a vicious line drive that broke a public-address speaker horn in the farthest reaches of the Shibe Park outfield, then dropped, limiting him to a double. "One writer said it was the hardest Williams had hit a ball in his three seasons with the Red Sox."[13] And it's conceivable the shot inspired a movie scene treasured by many baseball fans.[14]

Caligiuri had notched two outs in the fourth before Williams's double and stranded him, so the epic clout didn't put the Red Sox on the scoreboard. Still nursing a shutout and now with a six-run cushion, Caligiuri won their next encounter, retiring Williams as the leadoff hitter in the Boston seventh.[15]

Frankie Pytlak, who had replaced Peacock behind the plate for Boston, batted for the first time to lead off the eighth and homered to spoil the shutout. Fittingly, with the 7-1, six-hit, win easily standing as the highlight of his month in the majors, Caligiuri made a curtain-call out to end the Philadelphia eighth. That was it – the game was called due to darkness.

As Shibe Park emptied in the dwindling autumn light, Williams was secure at a rounded .406, still, through the 2018 season, the last player to hit .400. Caligiuri could look forward to an offseason warmed by the memory of his last-game success. Grove, knowing the end had come, told Boston owner Tom Yawkey of his decision to retire as the two walked Yawkey's South Carolina hunting preserve in early December.[16]

By 1943 both Williams and Caligiuri[17] were serving in World War II and Grove, too old for service, awaited his inevitable induction to the Hall of Fame.[18] Williams was elected to the Hall in 1966.[19]

SOURCES

In addition to the sources cited in the Notes, I used the Baseball-Reference.com and Retrosheet.org websites for box scores, player, team, and season pages, and day-by-day pitching and hitting logs.

NOTES

1   Stan Baumgartner, "A's, Boston Divide Twin Bill, Williams Ends Year At .406," *Philadelphia Inquirer*, September 29, 1941, 1, 25. The A's averaged 6,868 at home in 1941. They had attracted 11,308 for their opener on April 18 and 28,874 (nearly six percent of the year's total) for a visit by the Yankees two days later.

2   Williams collected several nicknames over his long career: "The Kid," Thumper," The Splendid Splinter," and "Teddy Ballgame." There is no evidence that the latter was in use in 1941, but career profiles of Williams published after his death 2002 featured the nickname. See: Leigh Montville, "Farewell, Teddy Ballgame," *Sports Illustrated*, July 15, 2002, and Ted Williams and David Pietrusza, *Teddy Ballgame: My Life in Pictures* (Toronto: Sport Classic Books, 2002).

3   Williams was hitting .413 on September 10. He had been as low as .308 on May 3.

4   Robert W. Creamer, *Baseball In '41* (New York: Penguin Books, 1991), 268.

5   "The dowagers of local journalism attempted to give elementary deportment lessons to this child who spoke as a god, and to their horror were themselves rebuked. His basic offense against the fans has been to wish that they weren't there," John Updike, "Hub Fans Bid Kid Adieu," *New Yorker*, October 22, 1960.

6   Bill Pennington, "Ted Williams' .406 is More Than a Number," *New York Times*, September 17, 2001.

7   Bill Dwyer, "This Is the Way to Go Out Hitting," *Los Angeles Times*, September 29, 2011.

8   Pennington. Other accounts have Williams opting for ice cream. See: Frank Fitzpatrick, "The Night in Philly Before Ted Williams Hit .406," Philly.com, posted September 27, 2016.

9   Stan Baumgartner noted in his September 29, 1941, game account that "the Athletic pitchers contributed only one thing to Williams' final splurge. They got the ball over the plate."

10 "'Well, he's a better guy now,' said an unnamed Athletic. 'All he used to have was a fastball and a mean disposition.' Connie Mack said, 'I took more from Grove than I would from any man living. He said things and did things – but he's changed. I've seen it year by year. He's got [ten] to be a great fellow.'" Jim Kaplan, "Lefty Grove," SABR Baseball Biography Project, sabr.org.

11 Baumgartner.

12 Caligiuri recalled his first meeting with Connie Mack: "Right after they called me up I was sitting there on the bench. I didn't know anybody and nobody was talking to me. Connie Mack came down the line, tossed me the ball and said, 'You're pitching today.' [September 3, 1941, at Griffith Stadium, Washington]. Two years before I was in Class D, and here I was pitching in the major leagues." Author's telephone conversation with Fred Caligiuri, April 3, 2013.

13 Creamer, 271.

14 Dwyer. "In *The Natural*, the hero, Robert Redford's Roy Hobbs, wore No. 9 and, in his last at-bat, smashed a row of lights with a towering home run. Williams [who wore No. 9] broke a loudspeaker horn with the double on his last day in 1941, and also homered in his last at-bat in 1960."

15 Recollections differ on how the out was made. Some sources recall a fly to right, some, including the Retrosheet play-by-play, a fly to left. Caligiuri himself remembered "a pop-up that carried far enough behind the shortstop that [left fielder] Elmer Valo caught it." Caligiuri conversation, April 3, 2013.

16 Kaplan.

17 Born October 22, 1918, Fred Caligiuri attained age 100 in 2018. He was the oldest living major-league baseball player at the time of his death on November 30, 2018.

18 Grove was elected in 1947, his fourth year of eligibility.

19 Williams's election was in his first year of eligibility.

Fowler Goes Distance in Tough-Luck Marathon

June 5, 1942
St. Louis Browns 1, Philadelphia Athletics 0
(16 Innings)

By Gordon Gattie

The nation's eyes were turned westward on a June Friday morning, toward a small island 1,300 miles northwest of Honolulu, as the Battle of Midway was underway. After attacking Pearl Harbor six months earlier, the Japanese Imperial Fleet dominated the Pacific Ocean with intentions of now destroying the remaining US Pacific Fleet near Midway Island.[1] Front pages across the country carried reports of the initial Japanese air attack on Midway and the American response, which included damaging a Japanese battleship and an aircraft carrier. Light damage was reported on Midway Island with both sides expecting continued attacks in the coming days.[2]

Looking eastward, the Philadelphia Athletics hosted the St. Louis Browns in the first of a four-game series at Shibe Park. Philadelphia was a perennial tail-ender; the team endured a last-place finish in 1941, ending the season with a 64-90 record, 37 games behind the AL pennant-winning New York Yankees. The team finished in the basement in 1940 as well, and had finished either last or next to last every year since 1935. The 1941 Athletics were led by outfielders Sam Chapman (team-high .921 OPS) and four-time AL All-Star Bob Johnson (.863 OPS, team-high 652 plate appearances), and first baseman Dick Siebert (team-high .334 batting average, fifth in the league). The pitching included Phil Marchildon, whose 3.57 ERA in 204⅓ innings led the team, and Jack Knott, who led the A's with 13 wins and had a 4.40 ERA in 194⅓ innings.

The Athletics were not expected to compete for the pennant; *The Sporting News* predicted a last-place finish, just behind the Browns.[3] Although President Franklin D. Roosevelt declared that major-league baseball should continue during wartime, the Athletics lost nine players to the armed services between the 1941 and 1942 seasons,[4] including Chapman, who joined the U.S. Navy in late 1941 and became a flight instructor.[5] Attempting to improve his patchwork infield, legendary Athletics owner Connie Mack promoted 6-foot-3 Jack Wallaesa, who was the tallest shortstop to play major-league ball at the time. Mack commented, "He'll never be a great hitter but he'll do enough with the bat." During spring training, Wallaesa started as a right-handed hitter, then Mack turned him into a switch-hitter.[6]

The Browns finished the 1941 season with a 70-84 record, tied with the Washington Senators and just ahead of Philadelphia. St. Louis started the season solidly, winning the first four games.

After absorbing their first loss to the Detroit Tigers, the Browns rebounded with a 2-1 win in the first game of a doubleheader. St. Louis lost the nightcap, and then lost the next eight games to drop into seventh place. They finished April with a 7-11 record, then improved with a 16-13 May record. Preceding the four-game series with Philadelphia, the Browns won two of three in Washington.

Connie Mack sent 21-year-old rookie Dick Fowler to the hill for the night game. Fowler, who had pitched in four games the prior season, was 1-1 with a 7.18 ERA in 26⅓ innings. He struggled early as his opponents batted .302 against him, and he struck out only eight of the 112 batters he faced. In his most recent appearance, five days earlier, he tossed a scoreless ninth inning against the Yankees, but had been charged with at least four earned runs in each of the three previous appearances. Mack noted in spring training that "Fowler and [Fred] Caligiuri, after showing so much promise last fall, have been hit very hard this spring."[7] Fowler's pitching repertoire included a fastball, change, curve, and fork-slider.[8]

Johnny Niggeling, the Browns' starting pitcher, was a 38-year-old veteran of two nearly full major-league and 10 minor-league seasons. Niggeling toiled in the minors from 1929 with the Waterloo (Iowa) Hawks of the Class D Mississippi Valley League through 1939 with the Indianapolis Indians of the American Association. He made his major-league debut on April 30, 1938, when he pitched ⅓ inning for the Boston Bees. A knuckleballer,[9] Niggeling had started eight games through May, going 5-3 with a 2.69 ERA and 34 strikeouts in 67 innings. He was riding a four-game winning streak, all complete-game victories, heading into the matchup.

St. Louis leadoff hitter Don Gutteridge struck out to start the game, Harlond Clift flied out, and George McQuinn grounded out. Philadelphia leadoff hitter Mike Kreevich struck out, then Pete Suder and Dick Siebert hit popups as Niggeling

matched Fowler's one-two-three inning. In the second and third, both teams placed one runner on base in each frame but posed no scoring threat.

In the fourth inning, McQuinn walked. Wally Judnich grounded out to first and first baseman Siebert attempted to throw out McQuinn at third base. Siebert's throw hit McQuinn squarely in the back,[10] and McQuinn reached third base. He was stranded as the next two batters grounded out. In the bottom half, after Niggeling struck out Suder and Siebert, Johnson walked and Elmer Valo singled, but Bob Swift popped out to the second baseman.

As both starters established their rhythm, the fifth and sixth innings passed quickly. The only runner reaching scoring position was the Browns' Rick Ferrell in the fifth. In the sixth inning, Fowler retired St. Louis in order and Niggeling allowed a harmless walk with two outs.

In the seventh, the Browns' Chet Laabs and rookie Vern Stephens flied out to center. Tony Criscola singled but was caught stealing by Swift. Swift led off the bottom half with a single to left and went to second when left fielder Criscola booted the ball.[11] Buddy Blair walked and Crash Davis' sacrifice moved the runners up. For the first time, Niggeling faced a real threat with runners at second and third base and just one out. But pitcher Fowler grounded to shortstop Stephens, who fired home and caught Swift in a rundown for the second out. Then Kreevich hit a force-play grounder for the third out. Neither team advanced a runner past second base in the eighth or ninth, so the teams ended regulation scoreless. Through nine innings, Fowler had allowed five hits and two walks while Niggeling gave up five hits and four walks. Only four baserunners had reached third base.

Fowler continued his dominance in the 10th inning, allowing a Criscola leadoff single before retiring the side on a bunt groundout, an infield groundout, and a strikeout. In the Athletics' 10th, Kreevich singled to center with one out and

Siebert singled to center with two outs, advancing Kreevich to third. The Athletics again fell short when Johnson grounded out to third base. Each pitcher allowed a baserunner in the 11th and 12th, though no baserunner proceeded into scoring position.

Both teams were now batting around for the sixth time. In the Browns' 13th inning, Fowler allowed a harmless walk. In the bottom of the inning, George Caster was summoned from the Browns' bullpen. The Athletics again threatened with runners at first and second with two outs, but Davis hit a popup. Both teams went one-two-three in the 14th inning. In the 15th, the Browns got two runners on base for the first and only time in the game when Gutteridge and Clift both singled. But with two outs, McQuinn grounded out and stranded the runners. Then Caster set down the Athletics on two groundouts and a fly out.

Judnich, who had reached the outfield once in his previous six appearances,[12] started the 16th inning with a soaring triple off the corrugated right-field wall.[13] Laabs was out on a liner to center field that Kreevich "caught off his shoetops."[14] Judnich tagged up and beat the throw home, scoring the first run of the game. Stephens, who was hitting .300 but went 0-for-7, grounded out and Criscola flied out.

In the bottom of the inning, Caster toughened and retired the Athletics on two foul popouts to Browns catcher Ferrell and an infield groundout to end the marathon game, which lasted 3 hours and 7 minutes.[15]

Fowler, who went all the way for the Athletics, fell to 1-2, though his ERA dropped by 2.50 runs, 7.18 to 4.68. He finished 1942 with a 6-11 record and a 4.95 ERA in 140 innings. By innings played, the game was tied for the longest AL game in 1942 and the majors' longest night game to that point;[16] the Browns defeated the Athletics 5-4 in 16 innings on September 14. The Athletics reached sixth place for one day the following week, but dropped into seventh place the following day and the basement for the remainder of the season on July 23.

SOURCES

Besides the sources cited in the Notes, the author consulted Baseball-Almanac.com, Baseball-Reference.com, and Retrosheet.org.

NOTES

1   Williamson Murray and Allan R. Millet, *A War To Be Won: Fighting the Second World War* (Cambridge, Massachusetts: The Belknap Press of Harvard University Press, 2001), 192-195.

2   United Press, "Jap Battleship, Carrier Smashed as Midway Repulses Air Attack," *Philadelphia Inquirer*, June 5, 1942: 1; Associated Press, "U.S. Forces Battle Strong Jap Fleet After Midway Raid," *St. Louis Post-Dispatch*, June 5, 1942: 1.

3   J.G. Taylor Spink, "Looping the Loops: It's Their Start – And our Finishes," *The Sporting News*, April 9, 1942: 1.

4   United Press, "Athletics Face Tough Summer in Their Loop," *Republican and Herald* (Pottsville, Pennsylvania), April 1, 1942: 8.

5   "Sam Chapman," Gary Bedingfield's Baseball in Wartime, baseballinwartime.com/player_biographies/chapman_sam.htm. Accessed October 17, 2018.

6   Stan Baumgartner, "A's String Along with String-Bean Wallaesa, Longest Player at Short in Majors' History," *The Sporting News*, April 9, 1942: 2.

7   Connie Mack, "Pitching Has Upset Plans for '42 A's, Connie Admits," *Philadelphia Inquirer*, April 8, 1942: 31.

8   Bill James and Rob Neyer, *The Neyer/James Guide to Pitchers: An Historical Compendium of Pitching, Pitchers, and Pitches* (New York: Fireside Books, 2004), 210.

9   James and Neyer, 325.

10   Stan Baumgartner, "Browns Conquer Athletics, 1-0, in 16 Innings," *Philadelphia Inquirer*, June 6, 1942: 25.

11   Stan Baumgartner, "Browns Conquer Athletics," 25.

12   Stan Baumgartner, "Browns Conquer Athletics," 23.

13   Associated Press, "Browns Win in 16th, 1-0," *Pittsburgh Post-Gazette*, June 5, 1942: 13.

14   Stan Baumgartner, "Browns Conquer Athletics," 23.

15   Game summary and Box score, *The Sporting News*, June 11, 1942: 8.

16   Dick Farrington, "Browns Do Tricks at Sewell's Bidding," *The Sporting News*, June 11, 1942: 5.

Tommy Hughes' Marathon

June 28, 1942
Philadelphia Phillies 2, St. Louis Cardinals 1
(15 Innings; First Game of a Doubleheader)

By Courtney Smith

During the 1942 season, the St. Louis Cardinals and the Philadelphia Phillies finished at opposite ends of the National League. The Phillies finished in the basement, while the Cardinals won the pennant on their way to another World Series title. On June 28 the two teams faced off in a doubleheader at Shibe Park. While the Cardinals captured the second game, the Phillies won a memorable opener that featured performances from two young pitchers enjoying the best seasons of their short careers. The Cardinals' Johnny Beazley held the Phillies to one run in his 12 innings of work and showed signs of the pitcher who would slay the New York Yankees in the World Series. The Phillies' Tommy Hughes, however, emerged as the doubleheader's top star. Hughes pitched all 15 innings, held the potent Cardinals lineup to one run, and put his team in position to score the winning run before he left the game for a pinch-runner in the 15th inning.

Heading into the doubleheader, the Phillies and the Cardinals had compiled very different records. The Phillies stood at the bottom of the National League with a paltry record of 18-48. The Cardinals had a more impressive record of 36-26, but it paled in comparison to the 46-17 record of the first-place Brooklyn Dodgers. The

season before, St. Louis had finished in second place behind the Dodgers, and the team had entered the season with aspirations of winning the pennant. The four-game series at Shibe Park ended a 12-game road trip in which the Cardinals had won only one series and four games. Those losses put them a daunting 9½ games behind the Dodgers and seemed to put their goal of the National League pennant out of reach. A four-game series against the lowly Phillies appeared to offer the Cardinals a chance to get their season back on track. Phillies manager Hans Lobert had fined several players for "indifferent work" and had ordered every player to attend morning practice.[1] Lobert also lambasted his players as "'tootsie roll' and 'ice cream cone' warriors" who "lacked fight and dash."[2]

Rain greeted the Cardinals' arrival in Philadelphia and shortened the four-game series to a doubleheader on Sunday, June 28. Despite the postponements, for game one of the twin bill the managers went with the starters they had previously planned to use in the series opener – Beazley and Hughes. At the time, Beazley was in the middle of his first full season with the Cardinals. He had battled through adversity and an elbow injury in the minors before joining the Cardinals in the 1941 season when the rosters expanded in September. He earned his first victory for the Cardinals on the final day of the 1941 season. Heading into game one of the June 28 double-header, Beazley had a 6-4 record; his opponent, Hughes, had a lackluster record of 2-9.

Stan Musial scored the Cardinals' lone run of the marathon opener in the fourth inning. He reached base on a single, moved to third on a single by catcher Ken O'Dea, and scored on a fly ball by first baseman Ray Sanders. After their 15-inning, 2-1 defeat, the Cardinals won game two, 3-1, but the lackluster offensive performance in game one seemed to encapsulate all of the ills facing the club and kept them nine games behind the Dodgers.[3]

In its coverage of the doubleheader's first game, the *Philadelphia Inquirer* focused on the heroics of the pitcher Hughes. Hughes was in his second season with the Phillies; in his rookie campaign, he made 24 starts in 34 games and ended with a record of 9-14.[4] The newspaper called game one "a thriller from the start" and asserted that Hughes had "never pitched with more skill and more poise."[5] Hughes also demonstrated "the fortitude of a Spartan" and pitched "the most spectacular game of his career."[6] Third baseman Danny Murtaugh, who got three hits in the contest, started the game with a single to the center field. Murtaugh did not advance past second base; the next batter, center fielder Lloyd Waner, hit into a fielder's choice that sent Murtaugh back to the dugout. The Phillies scored the game's first run in the first inning and mounted scoring threats in the seventh, 10th, 11th, and 13th innings. They finally broke through in the 15th inning when Stan Benjamin, running for Hughes, crossed the plate after Ernie Koy slapped the game-winning single. Hughes had reached base after reliever Howie Krist hit him with a pitch. Krist (3-1) took the loss for the Cardinals.

Hughes' heroics went beyond pitching 15 innings and getting on base in the 15th inning

after being hit by a pitch; he collapsed in the dugout in the bottom half of the 10th inning. Hughes had beat out a bunt, then reached second base on a wild pitch, and third on an error by catcher Ken O'Dea on a pickoff play. Hughes did not score, and the exertion on the basepath apparently triggered his collapse in the dugout. The *Philadelphia Inquirer* reported that the Phillies' physician revived him, and he then returned to the field to pitch in the top of the 11th inning. He remained in the game until Lobert replaced him with pinch-runner Benjamin in the 15th inning.

Clearly standing out as the game's best performer, Hughes pitched all 15 innings, exerted himself to the point of collapse, and might have scored the winning run if the manager hadn't lifted him for a pinch-runner. Hughes's efforts earned accolades from both the hometown coverage of the game and from the more sedate coverage provided in the St. Louis newspapers. The *St. Louis Post Dispatch* called Hughes "an admirable stripling" and that the Cardinals, aside from Musial, "displayed no inclination to trifle" with the young pitcher.[7] With his victory, Hughes improved his season record to 3-9 on his way to a record of 12-18 and an ERA of 3.06.

Overall, the game offered an interesting prism to analyze each team's 1942 season. Despite the Cardinals' dismal performance in June 1942, they would go on to win the National League pennant and the World Series. Beazley would emerge as one of the Cardinals' stars and finished with a record of 21-6, the best of his short career. He won two games in the World Series, including the final game at Yankee Stadium. World War II interrupted and shortened his promising career. He won only nine games after returning from the war. Like Beazley, Hughes would also enjoy the best season of his short career in 1942 before departing for service in World War II. He appeared in 40 games, started 31 of them, and pitched 19 complete games. His 12 wins were the most wins he had in a single season in his five-year career. Hughes also notched career highs in games started and complete games, and he finished with the lowest single-season ERA of his career. The Phillies, however, went on to their third consecutive last-place finish in the National League. The team's 42 victories left them 62½ games behind the first-place Cardinals, who ended the season with 102 victories.[8] For a brief moment on June 28, 1942, however, a very different outcome to the season seemed possible for both teams. The game, ultimately, showcased how baseball can often be a game of quirks and how one regular-season game often does not define a baseball team's season.

SOURCES

In addition to the sources cited in the Notes, the author accessed Retrosheet.org, Baseball-Reference.com, and SABR.org.

NOTES

1   Steve Grauley, "Cards' Game Again Postponed: Play Phils Twice Tomorrow," *St. Louis Star and Times*, June 27, 1942: 4.

2   Grauley.

3   "Weather Stops the Redbirds," *St. Louis Post Dispatch*, June 27, 1942: 7; Stan Baumgartner, "Rain, Not Brooklyn, Is the Biggest Headache for St. Louis; Pilot Southworth Moans Over Enforced Idleness; Meet Phils Twice Today," *Philadelphia Inquirer*, June 28, 1942: 35; "Cards Split; To Play 22 Home Games," *St. Louis Star and Times*, June 29, 1942: 16; John Fuqua, "Johnny Beazley," SABR BioProject, sabr.org/bioproj/person/82e225d5; "Johnny Beazley," Baseball Reference.com. baseball-reference.com/players/b/beazljo01.shtml.

4   "Tommy Hughes," Baseball Reference, baseball-reference.com/players/h/hugheto04.shtml.

5   Stan Baumgartner, "Phils Win 15-Inning Opener, Drop Second; Hughes Lands Thriller," *Philadelphia Inquirer*, June 19, 1942: 21.

6   Baumgartner.

7   "Cards Won Five, Lost Seven Games on Eastern Trip; Warneke Beats Phils After Redbirds Lose in 15-Inning Battle," *St. Louis Post-Dispatch*, June 29, 1942: 9.

8   Fuqua.

DICK BARRETT HURLS 14-INNING SHUTOUT

July 8, 1943
Philadelphia Phillies 1, Cincinnati Reds 0
(14 Innings; Second Game of a Doubleheader)

By Kevin Larkin

The Thursday afternoon doubleheader between the Philadelphia Phillies and the Cincinnati Reds at Shibe Park featured a little bit of everything for the fans in attendance. The first game was an offensive struggle in which the teams combined for 27 hits and 12 runs. The Reds came away with a 7-5 win as Johnny Vander Meer pitched a complete-game 10-hitter, walking five and striking out four.[1] Every batter in the Reds lineup had at least one hit and the Reds were led by their third baseman, Steve Mesner, who had three hits and scored two runs. Four Philadelphia pitchers allowed 17 hits with Dale Mathewson (no relation to Giants great Christy Mathewson) taking the loss after coming on in relief of School-boy Rowe to begin the seventh inning.

Game two was a pitchers' duel between the Reds' Ray Starr and the Phillies' Dick "Kewpie" Barrett. Starr entered the game with a 7-7 record and a 3.01 ERA. Barrett, a 36-year-old journeyman recently purchased from the Chicago Cubs, was looking for his first win of the season, having lost his first four decisions with the Cubs and his first start with the Phillies, 5-2 to Chicago on July 4. A wartime pitcher, Barrett had debuted for the Philadelphia Athletics in 1933 but spent the bulk of 1933-1943 with Seattle of the Pacific Coast League.

After the offensive explosion in the first contest, the second game unfolded as a pitchers' duel. After two uneventful frames, Barrett had a rocky third inning with all the action occurring after two outs. Lonny Frey reached on an error by Philadelphia shortstop Charlie Brewster. Barrett walked Gee Walker. Bert Haas reached on another error by Brewster, and the bases were loaded. But Barrett got Eric Tipton to ground out to Brewster to end the inning and keep the game scoreless.

In the fourth inning Mesner singled but was erased on a double-play groundball by Eddie Miller. The next batter, Max Marshall, singled but he was caught stealing to end the inning.

From the fourth inning through the sixth, the only scoring opportunity came in the bottom of the sixth when, with two outs, the Phillies loaded the bases with a walk, a single, and an error, but failed to score.

Starr did not allow a Phillies hit until Coaker Triplett singled to left field one out in the fifth inning. However, Triplett was thrown out trying to stretch the single into a double.

In the Reds seventh, Marshall and Al Lakeman singled and Barrett walked Lonny Frey to load the bases with one out. Gee Walker bunted into a force play at the plate, and Barrett got Haas on a comebacker to end the second bases-loaded threat of the game.

The left side of the Phillies infield made five errors in the game. In the eighth inning, Tipton hit a leadoff single, Mesner forced Tipton at second base, and Phillies third baseman Babe Dahlgren made an error on a grounder by Miller. Shortstop Brewster had three errors and was pinch-hit for in the ninth. His replacement, Glen Stewart, also made an error. Barrett got out of the eighth-inning jam with a groundout and a strikeout of Starr.[2]

In turn, the Phillies loaded the bases in the bottom of the eighth but Starr pitched out of it.

The game remained scoreless going into extra innings, with both starters still pitching. Starr came out for a pinch-hitter in the 11th and Joe Beggs relieved him. The last of the six double plays turned in the game was turned by Philadelphia in the top of the 12th.

Barrett set the Reds down in order in the 14th, getting Frey on a groundout and Gee Walker and Haas on fly balls.

Since taking over for Starr in the 11th, Joe Beggs had given up only a single and an intentional walk, both in the 11th. But in the 14th, Coaker Triplett singled with one out and a single by Bob Finley put runners at first and second with two outs. With Pinky May at bat pinch-hitting for Barrett, Triplett stole third base. Then May singled to left field to break up the niftiest pitchers' duel of the season and give the win to the Phillies.[3]

And just in time, as the Phillies fans among the 4,174 spectators discovered. Umpire George Magerkurth had signaled the occupants of the press box that he was going to call the game after the 14th.[4]

Immediately after the game, Bill McKechnie, the Reds manager, lodged a protest with National League President Ford Frick.[5] He asserted that as Barrett, who batted after Finley, approached the plate, Magerkurth told a Phillies player, "I don't think there is a chance of continuing the game"[6] and that it would be called after the 14th. Armed with this knowledge, Phillies manager Bucky Harris sent May up to bat for Barrett.

In 13⅔ innings of work, Starr and Beggs gave up seven hits and seven walks and struck out three. Barrett, getting his first win of the season, allowed nine hits in 14 innings, walked five and struck out six. All of the 18 hits in the game were singles. Steve Mesner and Max Marshall each had three hits in a losing effort while Coaker Triplett of the Phillies had two hits.

The 14-inning outing was the longest of Barrett's career. Later in the season, on September 26, he pitched was an 11-inning complete-game win in a 3-2 Phillies victory over the Cardinals at Sportsman's Park in St. Louis. He also pitched a 10-inning 3-2 win over the Pirates at Shibe Park on July 20, 1944.

SOURCES

In addition to the sources cited in the Notes, the author consulted Baseball-Reference.com and Retrosheet.org.

NOTES

1   "May's Single in the 14th [Gives] Phillies Split," *Louisville Courier Journal*, July 9, 1943: 25.

2   Dahlgren, the man who replaced Lou Gehrig at first base for the New York Yankees, had spent the 1940 season with the Yankees before splitting the 1941 season with the Boston Braves and Chicago Cubs. In 1942 he was with the Cubs, Browns, and Dodgers. He was traded to the Phillies in 1943 for Al Glossop and Lloyd Waner and played in the All-Star Game.

3   "One Run Scored in Game."

4   "One Run Scored in Game."

5   "One Run Scored in Game."

6   "May's Pinch-Hit Wins Second in 14th, 1-0," *Philadelphia Inquirer*, July 9, 1943: 24.

THE STARS COME OUT AT NIGHT

July 13, 1943
American League 5, National League 3

All Star Game

By Lyle Spatz

The 1943 All-Star Game was the first one significantly affected by World War II. Fourteen of the 50 players on the roster for the 1942 game were now serving in the military, including Joe and Dom DiMaggio, Ted Williams, Tommy Henrich, Phil Rizzuto, Pee Wee Reese, Johnny Mize, Pete Reiser, Terry Moore, and Enos Slaughter. They were among servicemen around the world who were able to listen to the game courtesy of the British Broadcasting Company, which was broadcasting it via short-wave radio.

Played at Philadelphia's Shibe Park, this was the first scheduled night game in All-Star history. Although the American League's Athletics and the National League's Phillies shared Shibe Park, the alternating system of home sites made this an AL home game; nevertheless, the cheers from the crowd of 31,938 seemed mostly for the National Leaguers.

A three-run home run by Boston's Bobby Doerr and the pitching of Washington's Dutch Leonard, Detroit's Hal Newhouser, and Boston's Tex Hughson led the American Leaguers to a 5-3 win, their eighth in the 11 games played.

In keeping with the rules of the time, managers Joe McCarthy of the New York Yankees and Billy Southworth of the Cardinals selected the entire 25-man roster. They were required to include at least one player from each team on the final squad.

National Leaguers had attributed the American League's success in these games to the Yankees' dominance. McCarthy, in a slap at the National Leaguers, attempted to demonstrate his league's overall superiority by keeping all of his Yankees players on the bench. Southworth, on the other hand, had five of the eight Cardinals he had chosen in his starting lineup.

Among them were Mort Cooper, again the starting pitcher, and Stan Musial, the league's batting leader at .331. Musial was playing in the first of what would be a record 24 consecutive All-Star Games. One Cardinal selected for the game was absent. Left-handed pitcher Howie Pollet had to report for Army duty, so Giants right-hander Ace Adams, originally scheduled to be the NL's batting-practice pitcher, replaced him on the roster.

The game was scheduled to start at 8:45 P.M., but at the request of the BBC, Leonard didn't make his first pitch until 9:00. Musial's first-inning sacrifice fly gave the Nationals a 1-0 lead, but it was short-lived. Doerr's second-inning home run, which followed walks to Senators catcher

Jake Early and Browns center fielder Chet Laabs, gave the Americans a 3-1 lead, one they would never surrender.

The American Leaguers added a run in the third on doubles by Cleveland third baseman Ken Keltner and rookie sensation Dick Wakefield of Detroit. Wakefield, the first rookie to start an All-Star Game since Joe DiMaggio in 1936, was playing in place of the injured Charlie Keller.

Cincinnati left-hander Johnny Vander Meer, who relieved Cooper in the third, struck out a total of six batters in his 2⅔ innings, tying the mark set by Carl Hubbell in the 1934 game. Vander Meer had now struck out 11 American Leaguers in his 8⅔ innings spread over three All-Star Games. That was the same number as Hubbell, whose 11 strikeouts came in 9⅔ innings over five games. The AL did get its final run against him in the fifth, though it was unearned. Pittsburgh's Rip Sewell and Boston's Al Javery shut them out over the final three innings.

Newhouser pitched the middle three innings for the AL, allowing three hits and a walk, but no runs. The NL scored single runs in the seventh and ninth innings against Hughson. The run in the seventh came on a triple by Pittsburgh's Vince DiMaggio and a sacrifice fly by Brooklyn's Dixie Walker, and the one in the ninth came on a solo home run by DiMaggio, his third hit of the game.

Several National League veterans made memorable appearances in this game. Catcher Ernie Lombardi of the New York Giants, who flied out as a pinch-hitter for Walker Cooper, became the first player to represent three different teams in the All-Star Game. He had previously appeared as a member of the Reds and the Braves. Mel Ott of the Giants and Billy Herman of the Dodgers had now played for the NL in every game since 1934. Ott would play again in 1944, but for Herman this was his final appearance. Herman had been a most effective player for the National League, and his total of 13 hits (in 30 at-bats) was then the All-Star record.

In the home team clubhouse, McCarthy had a simple explanation for not using any Yankee players in the game. "We didn't need them," he said. "We got out there in front early enough. Besides, these other boys deserved a chance to shine. The Yankees have had enough of the limelight. Let some of the other guys get some of it."

The game raised $115,174 for the Army and Navy's Bat and Ball Fund, while each of the selected players received a $50 war bond. In addition to the $65,174 realized in gate receipts, radio rights brought an additional $25,000, Commissioner Kenesaw Landis's office contributed $20,000, and each league contributed $2,500.

SOURCES

The author also accessed Retrosheet.org, Baseball-Reference.com, and SABR.org.

COOPER AND RAFFENSBERGER DUEL

September 24, 1944
St. Louis Cardinals 4, Philadelphia Phillies 3
(16 Innings; First Game of a Doubleheader)

By Paul Hofmann

The late-season doubleheader between the St. Louis Cardinals and homestanding Philadelphia Phillies at Shibe Park was a matchup between two teams at opposite ends of the standings. Entering play, the first-place Cardinals, who had already clinched the National League championship and punched their ticket to the 1944 World Series, had a record of 99-46 and a 12½-game lead over the Pittsburgh Pirates. The last-place Phillies were 58-85, one percentage point behind the seventh-place Brooklyn Dodgers and a discouraging 40 games off the pace.

Both teams entered the day with arm-weary pitching staffs, playing their ninth doubleheader of September. For the Phillies, it was their 17th twin bill since August 6. Given how overworked both pitching corps were, Cardinals manager Billy Southworth and Phillies skipper Freddie Fitzsimmons hoped their starting pitchers would be able to pitch deep. Neither would be disappointed, particularly in the opener, when both starters went the distance in a 16-inning marathon that was the longest game in the National league in 1944.

Ken Raffensberger, who earlier in the summer represented the Phillies and pitched two scoreless innings in the All-Star Game at Forbes Field in Pittsburgh, got the starting assignment for the Phillies. The left-hander entered the game with a 12-19 record and a 3.43 ERA. According to baseball analyst Bill James, Raffensberger was one of the "unluckiest" pitchers in history.[1] He was opposed by right-hander Mort Cooper who entered the game with a record of 21-7, a 2.59 ERA and a league-leading seven shutouts. Cooper, the 1942 National League MVP, was a big, burly pitcher who anchored the Cardinals pitching staff during the war years.[2]

The Sunday afternoon doubleheader drew a crowd of 13,480 to the venerable stadium on Lehigh Avenue. With the temperature in the mid-60s and under partly cloudy skies, Raffensberger delivered the first pitch of the afternoon. The Phillies' southpaw retired the Cardinals in order in the top of the first. Cooper appeared headed to matching the effort when he retired the first two Phillies before Tony Lupien ignited a two-out rally with a single to center. Right fielder Ron Northey followed with a walk and Jimmy Wasdell singled to left to plate the Phillies' first run of the afternoon.

The Phillies extended their lead in the bottom of the third. With two outs, Lupien doubled to left and scored on Northey's single to center. With the score 2-0, the Phillies added another run in the fourth. Johnny Peacock singled to center to lead off the inning and was sacrificed to second by Glen Stewart. Granny Hamner followed with a single to left to advance Peacock to third. After the right-handed-hitting Raffensberger stuck out, second baseman Charlie Letchas singled to center to score Peacock and extend the Phillies lead to 3-0.

The Cardinals started their comeback in the top of the sixth inning. Raffensberger retired the first two hitters before Ray Sanders and Stan Musial both singled to center. Walker Cooper, the younger brother of Mort Cooper, doubled to center to drive in Sanders and Musial and cut the Phillies' lead to 3-2.

The Cardinals tied the score with an unearned run in the top of the seventh inning when left fielder Danny Litwhiler led off with a double to left and took third when Letchas mishandled the throw to third from Wasdell. Marty Marion followed with an infield single to second that scored Litwhiler and tied the game, 3-3. From there, Raffensberger and Cooper settled into a protracted pitchers' duel.

Over the next eight innings, both teams came within 90 feet of either taking the lead or winning the game. The Cardinals had runners at first and third with one out in the top of the eighth, only to see the threat snuffed out when Cardinals third baseman Whitey Kurowski grounded into an inning-ending double play.

Similarly, the Phillies threatened to end the game twice. In the bottom of the 12th inning, they put runners on the corners with two outs before Cooper retired Peacock on a fly ball to right. In the 14th, the Phillies loaded the bases with one out but were turned away. Letchas singled to left to start things off but was thrown out at second when he tried to stretch a single into a double. Buster Adams followed with a single and moved to third when Lupien singled back to the pitcher. Cooper intentionally walked Northey, who was already 3-for-4, to load the bases. The Cardinals hurler escaped the jam when he struck out Wasdell and induced Peacock to hit a grounder to Kurowski, who stepped on the bag at third to end the inning.

Raffensberger kept the Cardinals in check until the top of the 16th inning. After retiring Walker Cooper on a fly ball to center, Kurowski, who was 0-for-6 at that point, stepped to the plate and slammed his 17th home run of the season to give the Cardinals a 4-3 lead.

Clinging to a one-run lead, Cooper returned to the mound for the bottom of the inning. The Phillies refused to go down quietly. Adams led off with a single to shortstop. Lupien was retired on a foul pop fly to Kurowski. With one out, Northey singled to right field, his fourth hit of the day. However, Musial fielded the ball and cut down Adams trying to advance to third. Instead of having runners at first and third with one out, Wasdell came to the plate with Northey on first and two down. The Phillies right fielder hit a fly ball to right that Musial squeezed to end the 16-inning affair in a relatively brief 2 hours and 59 minutes.

The Phillies made four errors in the game as Raffensberger yielded four runs (three earned) on 13 hits. The 16-inning outing was the longest of Raffensberger's 15-year major-league career and the tough-luck loss – one of many in his career – was his National League-leading 20th of the year. On nine other occasions, Raffensberger pitched 10 or more innings and true to the theme of being an unlucky pitcher with little run support, the York, Pennsylvania, native was only 5-5 in games in which he pitched beyond the ninth inning.

The 16-inning outing was also the longest of Cooper's career.[3] Despite giving up 19 hits and being in trouble throughout the game, the Cardinals ace was "tight in the pinches" as he earned his 22nd and last victory of the season – the third year in a row he won 21 or more games.[4] Cooper went on to have two outstanding performances in the World Series against the St. Louis Browns. He was a tough-luck loser himself in a 2-1 Game One loss and came back to shut out the Browns in Game Five.

The victory over the Phillies made the Cardinals the first team in the National League to win 100 or more games in three consecutive seasons.[5] They went on to beat the Browns in six games in the only all-St. Louis World Series.

The nightcap of the doubleheader was an equally as intriguing pitchers' duel. The Cardinals' Ted Wilks (17-3) bested the Phillies' Charley Schanz (13-15), as both went the distance in a 1-0 Cardinals victory. The winning run scored in the top of the ninth inning when Hamner misplayed a potential inning-ending groundball, allowing pinch-runner Pepper Martin to score the winning run. The Phillies went scoreless in the last 21 innings of the double dip that featured one of the greatest pitching duels in Shibe Park history.

SOURCES

In addition to the sources cited in the Notes, the author relied on Baseball-reference.com and Retrosheet.org.

NOTES

1   Warren Corbett, "Ken Raffensberger," SABR Bio Project, sabr.org/bioproj/person/bb62d1a2.

2   Gregory H. Wolf, "Mort Cooooper," SABR Bio Project, sabr.org/bioproj/person/9c707ace.

3   On two other occasions Cooper pitched 14-inning complete games.

4   "Cooper and Wilks Show They Are Ready for Series," *St. Louis Post-Dispatch*, September 25, 1944: 14.

5   Glen Perkins, "Hal Newhouser Gets 27th Win, Yankees Beaten: Cardinals Set Record in National by Getting 100 or More Wins for Third Year," *News-Herald* (Franklin, Pennsylvania), September 25, 1944: 8.

Athletics, Tigers Play to Record Setting 24-Inning Tie

July 21, 1945
Philadelphia Athletics 1, Detroit Tigers 1
(24 Innings)

By Paul Hofmann

The Saturday matinee was a matchup between the first-place Detroit Tigers, who entered play with a three-game lead over the Washington Senators in a tightly contested American League pennant race, and the homestanding Philadelphia Athletics, who were mired in last place, 17½ games behind the Tigers.[1] The 4,526 fans in attendance at Shibe Park that afternoon were treated to both one of the longest games in major-league history and one of the all-time great ironman pitching performances.

Les Mueller, a 26-year-old rookie who had been discharged from the US Army earlier in the year, drew the starting assignment for the visiting Tigers.[2] The right-handed pitcher with a herky-jerky motion and heavy sinkerball was making his ninth start of the season. He entered the game with a 3-4 record and a 4.75 ERA. Russ Christopher, a 27-year-old right-hander took the mound for the Athletics. Christopher, the ace of the Athletics' rotation, was riding a personal four-game losing streak and entered the game with a record of 11-6 and a 3.48 ERA.

The game-time temperature was a steamy 90 degrees when Christopher delivered the first pitch at 3:00 P.M. under clear skies. Moments later, Tigers shortstop Skeeter Webb struck out for the first of 144 outs recorded that afternoon. Christopher held the Tigers hitless for the first four innings while Mueller also cruised through his first three frames, yielding only two singles.

The Athletics scored the game's first run in the bottom of the fourth. With one out, Dick Siebert reached first when Tigers first baseman Rudy York threw wildly to Mueller, who was covering first on Siebert's groundball. Bobby Estalella followed with a double to right field, advancing Siebert to third. Catcher Buddy Rosar singled to left field to plate Siebert with the Athletics' only run of the afternoon. Bill McGhee followed with a walk to load the bases and, with one out and George Kell coming to the plate, the A's had a golden opportunity to add to their lead. Kell sent a grounder to third baseman Bob Maier, who started a 5-4-3 inning-ending double play.[3]

The A's threatened again in the sixth when Hal Peck and Estalella singled to put runners on first and second with one out. Mueller escaped the jam when he fanned Rosar and retired McGhee on a lineout to center field.

The Tigers tied the score in the top of the seventh with "a lucky run."[4] With one out, Roy Cullenbine worked Christopher for a walk and advanced to third when York laced a single to left-center. Doc Cramer then hit a groundball to Siebert that could have started a 3-6-3 double play, but the first baseman hesitated too long before he stepped on first base to get Cramer and threw home too late to get Cullenbine.

After the Tigers tied the score, the A's mustered only one more threat against Mueller. Irv Hall opened the bottom of the 10th inning with a single to center but was erased at second when Peck hit into a fielder's choice. After Siebert flied to right for the second out of the inning, Estalella followed with his fourth hit of the day, a single to left that moved Peck to second.[5] Rosar followed with a sharp single to left, sending Peck around third with what appeared to be the go-ahead run. However, left fielder Jimmy Outlaw came up throwing and threw a perfect strike to Bob Swift to nail Peck at the plate and keep the score deadlocked at 1-1.

The Tigers mounted their own threat in the top of 11th. After they loaded the bases with two outs, York sent a drive to deep center that appeared headed for the bleachers. Estalella got a good jump on the ball and "just as it was about to hit the wall the Cuban jumped, caught the ball in his gloved hand and brought down the house."[6]

The stalemate continued as Mueller and Christopher tossed one-two-three innings over the next 2½ frames. In the top of the 14th inning, the A's 82-year old manager, Connie Mack, summoned 40-year-old right-hander Joe Berry to relieve Christopher, who had given up only five hits and struck out eight in his 13 innings of work. Mueller continued on for the Tigers, who were short of pitchers.

Looking back on the game, Tigers ace Hal Newhouser recalled, "Steve O'Neill would keep saying to (Mueller), 'How are you doing?' 'Can you go another inning?' Les would say he could. He was throwing as hard at the end as he was when he started!"[7]

Years later, Mueller reflectively reminisced on that afternoon. "I always kept hoping we'd get a run, and I'd get a win, but it didn't work out that way," he said.[8] Indeed the Tigers failed to score the winning run while he was on the mound, and after Mueller walked two batters in the bottom of the 20th, the Tigers manager decided that 19⅔ innings were enough. Despite Mueller's pleas to continue, O'Neill lifted him in favor of right-hander Dizzy Trout, who had pitched 4⅔ innings of relief in the first game of a doubleheader against Washington a day earlier.

With Berry tiring and beginning his eighth inning of work in the sweltering heat, the Tigers loaded the bases in the top of the 22nd when Cullenbine hit a one-out double and Berry walked York and Hank Greenberg, who had pinch-hit for Outlaw. "It did not seem that Berry, who was weary, and drenched with perspiration would be even able to get the ball to the plate," observed a sportswriter.[9] However, Berry dug deep and got Maier to fly out to McGhee.

The top of the 24th provided more drama to those fans who stayed for the entire game. A walk to Cullenbine, a single by Cramer, and a walk to 41-year-old Chuck Hostetler loaded the bases with one out.[10] Once again, Berry rose to the occasion when he got Maier to hit a groundball to Busch at short who turned it into a neat 6-4-3 double play to keep the game tied at 1-1. Trout, aided by the twilight conditions, pitched an uneventful bottom of the 24th, wrapping up 4⅓ innings of scoreless relief.

Then, 4 hours and 48 minutes after the start of the game, umpire crew chief Bill Summers halted play as deep shadows engulfed the field. Although lights had been installed at Shibe

Park in 1938, the rules of the day stated that no day game could be continued under the lights.[11] Although the game ended as a 1-1 tie, the fans certainly got their money's worth and "true to baseball traditions, they rose and stretched at the 7th, 14th and 21st innings."[12]

The 24-inning marathon affair is tied for the fourth longest game (by innings) in major-league history and matched the longest game in American League and Philadelphia Athletics history.[13] The time of the game, eclipsed the American League record by one minute.[14]

For Mueller, the game was a defining moment in a relatively short major-league career. While he finished the season with a 6-8 record and a 3.68 ERA in 34 games for the 1945 World Series champion Tigers, it was the 19⅔-inning pitching performance at Shibe Park for which he is best remembered. By 1946 he was back in the minors, never to make it back to the majors.

SOURCES

In addition to the sources cited in the Notes, the author consulted Baseball-Reference.com and Retrosheet.org

NOTES

1 Entering play on July 21, 1945, eight games separated the top seven teams in the American League.

2 Les Mueller appeared in four games with the Tigers in August and September of 1941.

3 Hall of Famer George Kell went 0-for 10 in the game.

4 Stan Baumgartner, "A's Tie Own Mark; Umpire Halts Game," *Philadelphia Inquirer*, July 22, 1945: 21-22.

5 Estalella went 5-for-10 for the Athletics in the game.

6 Baumgartner.

7 Jim Sargent, "Les Mueller," SABR Bioproject, sabr.org/bioproj/person/58f0af66.

8 Sargent.

9 Baumgartner.

10 Chuck Hostetler had entered the game in the top of the 22nd as a pinch-runner for Hank Greenberg. Hostetler stayed in the game, replacing Outlaw in left field.

11 Baumgartner.

12 Baumgartner.

13 The most innings in a major-league game is 26. This happened on May 1, 1920, in a game between the Boston Braves and Brooklyn Robins. The game, like the game between the Tigers and Athletics, was called due to darkness and ended as a 1-1 tie. Almost 14 years earlier, on September 1, 1906, the Philadelphia Athletics beat the Boston Americans 4-1 in 24 innings at Columbia Park in Philadelphia. Jack Coombs pitched the entire 24 innings for the Athletics.

14 James Zerilli, "Trout Goes to Mueller's Aid in 19th," *Detroit Free Press*, July 22, 1945: 29.

Discharged from Canadian Army, Dick Fowler Tosses No-Hitter in First Start in Almost Three Years

September 9, 1945
Philadelphia Athletics 1, St. Louis Browns 0
(Second Game of a Doubleheader)

By Gregory H. Wolf

Dick Fowler, the Philadelphia Athletics right-handed pitcher, had just been discharged from the Canadian Army weeks earlier after serving in World War II for 30 months, and was making his first big-league start in almost three years. So what did he do? Of course, he threw a no-hitter. Here's the story!

The A's, led by owner-manager Connie Mack's since the AL's founding in 1901, were the worst team in the AL (44-88) and headed toward their eighth last-place finish in 11 years. The war and the effort to conserve natural resources, such as gasoline and fuel, played havoc with baseball schedules all season as travel was severely restricted. The club was in the middle of a 28-game homestand and was set to kick off a four-game set with the St. Louis Browns by playing its 12th and 13th doubleheaders since August 19; and 31st and 32nd since June 3. The Browns, normally a brother-in-arms with the A's in the AL cellar, had surprisingly captured the pennant in 1944 for the first time in franchise history. In 1945 manager Luke Sewell's squad (70-63) was in third place, seven games behind the Detroit Tigers, and aimed

for consecutive winning seasons for the first time since 1928-1929. In the middle of a 27-game road swing, the Browns were preparing to play their sixth twin bill in nine days.

After almost four years of war, the mood in America was changing as the 1945 baseball season entered its last few weeks. Germany had surrendered in May, and the recent dropping of atomic bombs in Hiroshima and Nagasaki in August had directly led to Japan's surrender on August 15. Americans turned their attention to the national pastime as a means to come together with a new-found sense of self, pride, and possibility.

On a comfortable Sunday afternoon in the City of Brotherly Love, Shibe Park drew a robust crowd of 16,755 spectators, well above the A's AL-lowest season average of just over 6,000 per game. In the opener of the twin bill, the A's exploded for four runs in the eighth to win 6-2, their fourth victory in succession and their longest winning streak since they took five straight beginning on April 20.

Mack, often called The Tall Tactician, tabbed the 6-foot-4, 215-pound Fowler to start the second game. The 24-year-old from Toronto had debuted with the A's as a mid-September call-up in 1941. In 1942 he served as a swingman, posting a 6-11 slate and logging 140 innings. On June 5 that season he engaged the Browns in a marathon struggle at Shibe Park, tossing a 16-inning, nine-hit complete game, but losing a heartbreaker, 1-0. After serving as a private in the Canadian Army for 30 months, Fowler rejoined the A's after his discharge, and made his season debut on September 1, yielding three runs in a three-inning relief stint. In his last outing, Fowler tossed seven innings of relief in the first game of a doubleheader against the Chicago White Sox and was crushed for 13 hits and eight runs, bloating his ERA to 8.49. His mound opponent on the 9th was John "Ox" Miller, a 30-year-old right-hander making his first big-league start. Miller made five relief appearances for the Washington Senators and Browns in 1943 and spent the entire '44 and most of the '45 campaign with the Toledo Mud Hens in the American Association. It was just his seventh major-league appearance, and his first since May.

The game unfolded as a classic pitchers' duel. The first two frames saw 12 batters up, 12 batters down. That string was broken when Fowler walked Don Gutteridge with one out in the third.

Fowler himself connected for the game's first hit, a two-out double in the third. It was his fourth straight hit; in his last game he went 3-for-3 with a double and an RBI. Dick Siebert collected the A's second hit, a leadoff single in the fifth, but remained stranded on first.

Through six innings, both hurlers were doing their best impressions of Walter Johnson. According to Buddy Rosar, Fowler's batterymate, the Canadian kept the Brownies off-balance with an assortment of curves, changes of pace, fastballs, and a new pitch that he described as "half fork and slider."[1] Quipped the former All-Star catcher with both the New York Yankees and Cleveland Indians,

"I wouldn't have got a good foul if I batted against him."[2]

Fowler issued his second free pass, to Lou Finney to lead off the seventh. He moved up a station on Gene Moore's sacrifice bunt, but died on second.

The A's mounted a mini-rally in the seventh when Irv Hall led off with a walk and moved to second on Siebert's single, but Miller fanned George Kell and induced Rosar to ground out to end the frame.

Sportswriter Stan Baumgartner of the *Philadelphia Inquirer* reported that the Shibe Park crowd was cheering wildly after Fowler's every pitch by the eighth inning, which began with Fowler's third walk, to Vern Stephens.[3] Two batters later, Gutteridge grounded into an inning-ending 4-3 twin killing.

Miller worked around the game's only error, in the eighth, when Mark Christman misplayed Al Brancato's chopper to third to lead off the frame. Two batters later, Mayo Smith grounded into an inning-ending 3-6-3 double play.

Fowler took the mound in the ninth with his no-hitter intact, yet not assured of victory. After Miller popped up to left field, Milt Byrnes drew Fowler's fourth free pass, much to the chagrin of the A's faithful. According to Baumgartner, former A's player Lou Finney smashed a missile over first baseman Siebert's head that seemed like a sure hit. "I held my breath until I saw the ball go foul," said Fowler.[4] On the next pitch, Finney hit a weak grounder to second baseman Irv Hall who initiated a 4-6-3 double play.

There was a loud ovation for Fowler as he walked off the mound and into the dugout, where his teammates congratulated him. Connie Mack, known for his staid demeanor in his customary coat and tie, put his arm around the young hurler. But at 0-0, the game wasn't over yet.

Hal Peck led off the ninth with a smash "against the right-field wall," reported Baumgartner, and slid safely into third.[5] The next batter,

Irv Hall, singled to center to drive in Peck, thus giving the A's the victory and Fowler an improbable no-hitter. The game took just 75 minutes to complete.

Fowler's first victory of the season was his first of 11 eventual shutouts in the big leagues. He fanned six and faced 29 batters. According to Rosar, Fowler didn't shake off his catcher once during the entire game.[6]

"I felt fine from the very first inning," Fowler said. "I knew I had a good start for a no-hitter, but strangely enough I wasn't worrying about it. ... It was a wonderful feeling to get that one run."[7]

It wasn't the first time in Fowler's professional career that he had flirted with a no-hitter. The other time occurred in 1941 when, as a member of the Toronto Maple Leafs in the International League, he held the Baltimore Orioles hitless before yielding two ninth-inning singles.[8]

Fowler's no-hitter was the fourth in A's franchise history. Weldon Henley tossed the first, on July 22, 1905, against the Browns in St. Louis, followed by Chief Bender, whose no-no against the Cleveland Naps on May 12, 1910, was the first at Shibe Park. Bullet Joe Bush had thrown the previous one, on August 26, 1916, against the Cleveland Indians, also at Shibe Park.

Fowler emerged over the next four seasons (1946-1949) as a dependable workhorse, eclipsing 200 innings pitched each season, and winning a career-best 15 in both 1948 and 1949. He posted a 66-79 slate in parts of 10 seasons, all with the A's.

SOURCES

In addition to the sources cited in the Notes, the author accessed Retrosheet.org, Baseball-Reference.com, Newspapers.com, and SABR.org.

NOTES

1   Stan Baumgartner, "A's Fowler Defeats Browns, 1-0," Philadelphia Inquirer, September 10, 1945: 16.

2   Baumgartner.

3   Baumgartner.

4   Hank Littlehales, "Hurler Elated, but Modest of No-Hitter," *Philadelphia Inquirer*, September 10, 1945: 16.

5   Baumgartner.

6   "Athletics' Dick Fowler Hurls No-Hitter Against Browns," *St. Louis Post-Dispatch*, September 10, 1945: 18.

7   Littlehales.

8   Littlehales.

CLEVELAND BUCKEYES DETHRONE
NEGRO LEAGUE CHAMPIONS

September 20, 1945
Cleveland Buckeyes 5, Homestead Grays 0
Game Four of the Negro League World Series

By Bob LeMoine

The Homestead Grays were a dynasty in Negro League baseball in the 1940s. They had won back-to-back world championships in 1943-1944 and seven Negro National League pennants in eight years. Their roster was full of a who's who of Negro League stars, several of whom would one day be recognized for their greatness in the Baseball Hall of Fame. In September of 1945, however, the Grays legends were also up in age: Jud Wilson (49), Cool Papa Bell (42), Buck Leonard (37), Ray Brown (37), Jerry Benjamin (35), Bee Jackson (35), Sam Bankhead (34), and a comparatively "young" Josh Gibson (33). By contrast, the average of the Buckeyes was under 30.

While Negro League records are often incomplete, there was no denying who the Buckeyes hitting star was. Reports listed Sam "The Jet" Jethroe, so-called because of his blazing speed, as batting .393 with 123 total bases, 10 triples, 8 home runs and 21 stolen bases. Jethroe had been involved in a "tryout" at Fenway Park with Jackie Robinson during the season, as white baseball owners were feeling the pressure to integrate the game. The tryout was more of a publicity stunt,

remembered more for a racial slur hurled at them from somebody at the ballpark, but Jethroe was Boston's first black major leaguer when he suited up for the National League's Braves.

The Buckeyes' strength was their pitching. Brothers George and Willie Jefferson had 16-1 and 14-2 seasons, respectively, while Eugene Bremer was 12-5.

Harry Walker, Mo Harris, Jimmy Thompson, and Fred McCleary were the umpiring crew for the series.

The first two games were held in Cleveland; Game One at Cleveland Stadium and Game Two at League Park. Both ballparks were home to the Cleveland Indians, and both teams were forced to suit up in the visitors locker room. The Buckeyes also relied on discarded Indians uniforms, which were a cherished possession since the name "Cleveland" was embroidered across the front. In Game One before a crowd of 6,500, the dominant pitching of Willie Jefferson powered the Buckeyes to a 2-1 victory over the Grays. Game Two saw a wild finish akin to a "story-book thriller" (in the *Call & Post's*[1] description). Cleveland rallied from

2-0 down as over 10,000 shivering fans looked on. The Buckeyes tied the score in the seventh, then Bremer sent them home with jubilation with a bases-loaded walk-off hit to secure a 3-2 win.[2]

After Game Two, the teams boarded the bus and headed south to Pittsburgh. A rainout, however, caused the game to be moved to Griffith Stadium in Washington, where George Jefferson shut out the Grays, 4-0, on three hits.

Game Four was played at Philadelphia's Shibe Park and pitted Big Frank Carswell on the hill for the Bucks against Ray Brown for the Grays. The Buckeyes jumped out on top early. Avelino Canizares, dubbed "the Cuban sensation" by Jimmy Jones of the Call & Post, reached on an infield single.[3] Archie Ware walked, then Jethroe beat out a dribbler to the mound that Brown couldn't secure, and the bases were loaded. Parnell Woods, called "one of the greatest clutch hitters in the game" by Jones, scorched a grounder to second too hot to handle for Bee Jackson, and Canizares and Ware scored. Jackson recovered in time to get Jethroe at second to end the inning.[4]

Only in the third inning did Carswell find trouble. He was helped when Bankhead hit into a double play, erasing Jud Wilson, who had been hit by a pitch. But Ray Brown walked and Benjamin's single put runners at first and third. A walk to Bell loaded the bases, but a grounder by the 19-year-old Dave Hoskins forced Bell at second, and the Grays' best opportunity went by the boards.

The Buckeyes added a run in the fourth when Willie Grace singled and later scored on a long fly ball by Johnnie Cowan, to give the Buckeyes a 3-0 lead.

In the seventh, Cowan singled and Carswell was safe as first baseman Leonard let his roller pass him as he was busy praying for it to spin foul. Cowan snuck all the way to third during the blunder. Canizares bunted Carswell to second, but Cowan had to hold. Ware flied to Bell in left, not deep enough to score a run, and it looked as if the Grays would get out of the inning unscathed.

It was not to be, however, as "the league leading wonder batman," as Jones described Jethroe, came to the plate. His second hit of the game was punched into center field and the Buckeyes added a pair to grab a 5-0 lead.[5]

Carswell continued for the 5-0 shutout, allowing only four hits to the Grays' superstar lineup.

"Nobody gave us a chance," Willie Grace observed over 50 years later. "But we had a great club ourselves. We were fast and we had good pitchers and fielders. I think we surprised them. They thought they were going to sweep us. If we played them a month later, or a week earlier, we probably wouldn't have beaten them. The timing was right."[6]

Bob Williams, sports editor of the Call & Post, recalled the Buckeyes' short history, dating from 1941. Ernie Wright, an Erie, Pennsylvania, businessman, drove up to a shoeshine parlor in Cleveland and made an offer to the man standing there. "Are you Wilbur Hayes?" he asked the local sports promoter. "How'd you like to start up a baseball club, with me as a backer?" The team was born, but its early life wasn't all enjoyable. During its inaugural season, the team had to travel by cars when the team bus broke down. Tragedy struck on September 7, 1942, when one of the cars was in an accident that claimed the lives of two players. The championship was even sweeter considering the Buckeyes' overcoming such sorrow. "At the end of the series," Williams wrote, "we found ourselves staring into the faces of these boys who had been given so little credit as they marched towards their world championship. Yep, we found ourselves staring into the individual faces of these fellows whose united efforts had brought them the highest honor in all Negro baseball."[7]

"They are not individual stars," umpire Harry Walker reflected in his own Call & Post column, "but a star team that plays with a lot of team work, and they have taken the East. They are all a nice group of gentlemen."[8]

A "Cinderella team" is how Wendell Smith of the *Pittsburgh Courier* described the Buckeyes, who, "fired by determination and youth ... pulled one of the biggest surprises in baseball history." While also acknowledging the greatness of the Grays, Smith also noted the passage of time and the Grays "creaking in the joints, in dire need of replacements, and exhausted from that last siege when they had to win nine games in six days to beat out Baltimore and Newark (for the pennant); the Grays just didn't have it in 'em against the inspired, fiery Clevelanders."[9]

A half-century later, Jethroe mentioned a touch of irony. "We beat them in four straight games. Then we continued playing them (in exhibitions) and never won another game."[10]

But they won the games that mattered, through pitching, defense, and a lot of heart, despite being mostly ignored by the white press. Their legacy still stands, as those gathered at Shibe Park that day saw those traits that supersede the color of one's skin. Later that fall, Jackie Robinson signed with the Montreal Royals, a Brooklyn Dodgers farm team. His next step was the major leagues and a newly integrated American pastime.

SOURCES

The author would like to thank Stephanie Liscio, Rick Bush, and the Cleveland Public Library for research assistance. Readers who would like more information on Negro League baseball in Cleveland are referred to Liscio's book, *Integrating Cleveland Baseball: Media Activism, the Integration of the Indians and the Demise of the Negro League Buckeyes* (Jefferson, North Carolina: McFarland, 2010).

"1945 Negro League World Series," baseball-reference.com/bullpen/1945_Negro_World_Series. Retrieved June 1, 2018.

Baseball-Reference.com

"Cleveland Buckeyes." Encyclopedia of Cleveland History. Case Western Reserve University. case.edu/ech/articles/c/cleveland-buckeyes. Retrieved May 31, 2018.

"Here's Buckeye Pitching Staff, Rated Peerless," *Cleveland Call & Post*, September 15, 1945.

Jones, Jimmy. "Buckeyes Grab First Game of Series, 2-1, Carry On in Fight with Mighty Grays," *Call & Post*, September 22, 1945: 6B.

"Sammy Jethroe Again Bucks' Most Valuable Player, League Leader in Almost Every Batting Honor," *Call & Post*, September 15, 1945.

NOTES

1   *The Call & Post*, founded in the late 1920s and based in Cleveland, covers news of interest to the African-American community.

2   "Second Win for Buckeyes Is Like Story-Book Thriller; Bremer Wins Own Game, 3-2," *Call & Post*, September 22, 1945: 6B.

3   Jimmy Jones, "Series Victor of 4-in-Row, Bucks Stand Out as All-Time Greats, Carswell Wins No. 4," *Call & Post*, September 29, 1945: 6B.

4   Jones.

5   Jones.

6   Bob Dolgan, "Championship Memories: The Underdog Cleveland Buckeyes Were Negro League Champs in 1945," *Cleveland Plain Dealer*, February 26, 1996: 1C.

7   Bob Williams, "Sports Rambler," *Call & Post*, September 29, 1945.

8   Harry Walker, "World Series – Dots and Dashes," *Call & Post*, September 29, 1945: 7B.

9   Wendell Smith, "The Sports Beat," *Pittsburgh Courier*, September 29, 1945: 12.

10 Bill Lammers, "The Cleveland Buckeyes: Champions of a Forgotten League," *Cleveland Plain Dealer*, June 14, 1992: 10.

Sam Chapman Wallops Three Homers

August 15, 1946
Philadelphia Athletics 5, Boston Red Sox 3

By Rich Westcott

Of all the games played at Shibe Park, few were more unusual or less predictable than the meeting on August 15, 1946, between the Boston Red Sox and the Philadelphia Athletics. It was a game in which a woeful team beat the best in the league in an upset of mammoth proportions.

The game pitted the American League's first-place Red Sox, at the time the owners of a 79-33 record and a 13½-game lead over the second-place New York Yankees, against the last place Athletics, who took the field with a 32-79 record while trailing Boston by 46½ games. The A's were in the midst of a dreadful period during which they had finished in last place in eight of the previous 11 seasons.

Boston fielded a star-studded lineup that included future Hall of Famers Ted Williams and Bobby Doerr, plus Dom DiMaggio, Johnny Pesky, and Rudy York. Williams would go on to capture the American League's Most Valuable Player Award that season while hitting .342 with 38 home runs, 123 RBIs, and a league-leading 142 runs scored. Pesky would finish with a .335 batting average and DiMaggio hit .316.

The Athletics fielded a team that featured Barney McCosky, Elmer Valo, Sam Chapman, Hank Majeski, Pete Suder, and Buddy Rosar.

None was in quite the same class as the Red Sox stars, although McCosky (.354) and Valo (.307) hit well in 1946 in less than full-time service.

Going into the August 15 game, the Red Sox, who had the best record in baseball, had won nine of their previous 11 outings, including a three-game sweep of the Athletics a week earlier in Boston. The Red Sox had 11 more wins than the next winningest team in the majors (Brooklyn Dodgers). Meanwhile, the Athletics, managed by Connie Mack in his 46th year at the helm and holding the worst record in baseball with 11 fewer wins than the next worst team (Pittsburgh Pirates), entered the three-game series having lost 10 of their last 12 games. Prior to that, the A's had lost nine straight games in late May, and at one point in July lost 13 of 15 games.

Manager Joe Cronin's Red Sox were victorious in the first two games of the series at Shibe Park, 7-5 and 3-1. In the third game, played on a Thursday afternoon, Boston sent to the mound Joe Dobson, one of its top pitchers and the owner of an 11-5 record. Dobson was a right-hander who would go on to post a 13-7 season record during what would become a 14-year big-league career on the mound and a 137-103 won-lost record. His opponent was husky 235-pound Luther "Lou"

Knerr, a highly undistinguished right-handed hurler, who had posted a 2-13 record up to that point after going just 5-11 in his rookie year during a short-term big-league career.

But the A's had Chapman in the lineup. Although he was batting sixth, Chapman would be responsible for giving the game one of the more unexpected outcomes since Shibe Park opened in 1909.

Chapman had been an All-American football player at the University of California, was drafted by the Washington Redskins, and would later be elected to the College Football Hall of Fame. A shortstop and second baseman in high school and college, Chapman decided to pursue a career in baseball rather than football, and had been recommended to Mack by Ty Cobb, who had seen him play as a youth in his native California. Mack then signed Chapman, although other teams had been interested in signing the young player, too.

After his rookie season in 1938, Chapman had been converted to an outfielder, and in 1941 had what would be the best season of his career, hitting .322 with 25 home runs and 106 RBIs. But after the season he had enlisted in the military and would become a Navy pilot during World War II.

Chapman returned to Philadelphia at the end of the 1945 season after spending nearly four years in the service. Like so many other veterans, he was still trying to regain his playing skills in 1946 when he was selected to the American League All-Star team at midseason.

"That year was a very special time," Chapman told this writer many years later. "The fans were great. They were happy to see us back, and they applauded everybody. It took a while to get back into the swing of things, but it was a grand year. It was good to be back."[1]

It was especially good on that quiet afternoon in 1946. With just 5,642 in attendance, Chapman, playing left field, hit a home run with one out in the second inning to give the A's a 1-0 lead.

But with the Athletics' ineptitude clearly on display, Boston stepped out to a 3-1 lead in the third inning. With one out, Roy Partee singled. Then Dobson dropped a bunt, which third baseman Majeski threw wildly to first. When the ball flew into right field, Valo bobbled it, allowing Partee to score and Dobson to reach third base. A single by Tom McBride drove Dobson home. Pesky, and DiMaggio followed with singles with McBride scoring on the latter's hit to put the Red Sox ahead by two runs.

In the bottom of the fourth inning, the Red Sox' lead was erased. With one out Suder, normally a second baseman but playing shortstop in this game, walked. Chapman followed with another home run to tie the score at 3-3.

That twosome was back in business in the eighth inning when they hit back-to-back homers. With one out, Suder, who had a career-high .281 batting average in 1946 but who was typically not a home-run hitter (he hit homers in double figures just once during a 13-year career in the majors), slammed a pitch out of the park. Then Chapman followed with another homer to knock Dobson out of the game and give the A's a 5-3 lead. Chapman's homer was the last of seven hits in the game for the Athletics.

The lead held as Knerr set down the Red Sox in the ninth inning. While allowing just six hits, walking two, and striking out six, the right-handed hurler posted his third and final victory of the season. (He would go on to lose 16.) It would be his last — and only eighth overall — major-league victory in a big-league career that was over early the following year.

Meanwhile, Chapman, who would play in the majors through 1951, finished with a .261 batting average and 67 RBIs for the season. His 20 home runs represented one-half of the Athletics' entire total that year.

"It was a game I'll never forget," he recalled. "Fortunately, Shibe Park was a good hitter's park. It was laid out nicely and small enough that you could get a home run. But it was big enough that you couldn't hit one out all the time."[2]

Only two players in the majors hit three home runs in one game that season. The other was Williams, who was hitless in four trips to the plate in the A's upset victory.

As it turned out, the Athletics posted a 10-7 home record in August, the only month of the season in which they had a winning mark at home. They went on to finish the campaign with a 49-105 record, 55 games out of first place. The Red Sox, who won nine of their next 13 games after the stunning loss to the A's, ended the season with a 104-50 record, 12 games ahead of the second-place Detroit Tigers. That earned the Red Sox a trip to the World Series, which they lost in seven games to the St. Louis Cardinals.

Until that point in the season, though, the most memorable Red Sox loss occurred on that August 15 day when a team that was by far the worst in baseball beat the club with the best regular-season mark in the big leagues. By the way, the time of that game was 1 hour and 37 minutes. That was just as unbelievable as the mind-boggling final score.

SOURCES

In addition to the sources cited in the Notes, the author accessed Retrosheet.org, Baseball-Reference.com, and SABR.org.

NOTES

1   Rich Westcott, *Masters of the Diamond, Interviews with Players Who Began Their Careers More Than 50 Years Ago* (Jefferson, North Carolina: McFarland & Co., 1994), 22.

2   Westcott, 25.

Racial Slurs Won't Stop Jackie Robinson

May 9, 1947
Philadelphia Phillies 6, Brooklyn Dodgers 5
(11 Innings)

By Alan Cohen

"Jackie has been accepted in baseball, and we of the Philadelphia organization have no objection to his playing and wish him all the luck we can. Baseball is an American game, and there are no nationalities, creeds, nor races involved. Jackie Robinson is an American."[1]

This quote, attributed to Philadelphia manager Ben Chapman, was made just before Brooklyn's series at Philadelphia in early May 1947 and was prompted by Chapman's verbal abuse of Robinson, in the form of bench-jockeying, during Philadelphia's visit to Brooklyn earlier in the season. It was, by far, the worst behavior of any of the teams in the league. Chapman maintained that the jockeying was not malicious, saying, "We are not making a target of Robinson. Jockeying from the bench was regular long before I was born."[2] Jack Saunders of the *Pittsburgh Courier* interviewed Chapman in Philadelphia on April 29, and the Philadelphia manager admitted that before the series in Brooklyn, he had instructed his team to give it to Robinson without restraint. He said he told his players to call Robinson everything and anything they wanted to. He assured him that they had his unswerving support.[3]

Chapman's comments appeared in the May 3 issue of the *Pittsburgh Courier*. Earlier, a fan who had been at the games in Brooklyn had contacted the commissioner's office. Criticism of Chapman's Phillies also came from Walter Winchell who commented on their antics during his May 4 radio broadcast. The next day Commissioner Happy Chandler issued an order restraining the Phillies from using "vicious un-American racial remarks" against Robinson.[4]

The order was delivered to the Phillies' general manager, Herb Pennock, by Walter Mulbry, secretary-treasurer in the commissioner's office. Mulbry said that "Mr. Chandler said that no favors should be granted Robinson from the bench, but there is a limit to everything and he thought that hurling racial epithets was beyond that limit."[5] A photographer had Chapman and Robinson pose together, as if there were no tensions, and the photograph appeared in the *Philadelphia Inquirer* on May 10.

Tensions were high in the early weeks of the season. Robinson was receiving a two-man police escort when leaving the ballpark. An article by Stanley Woodward in the *New York Herald Tribune* indicated that the Cardinals had threatened to strike rather than play against Robinson.

Although Cardinals owner Sam Breadon and manager Eddie Dyer denied the claim, they spoke, per orders from National League President Ford Frick, to their ballplayers.[6] Frick said that Robinson had the full backing of the National League and that any unwarranted persecution of him would result in severe disciplinary action against the offenders.[7]

Jackie Robinson had been with the Brooklyn Dodgers for less than a month when the team visited Philadelphia to play the Phillies on May 9, 1947. He was quartered in housing apart from that of his teammates.[8] No sooner had the Dodgers arrived than it was revealed that Robinson had been on the receiving end of poison-pen letters from anonymous sources essentially implying that Robinson should get out of baseball – or else. Two of the letters, each containing a fictitious return address, were turned over to the police by Arthur Mann, assistant to Dodgers President Branch Rickey.

It was Brooklyn's first visit of the season to Philadelphia. The 22,680 fans attending the May 9 contest at Shibe Park applauded Robinson in each of his trips to the plate. They were treated to a close game with the home team winning 6-5 in 11 innings when Emil Verban doubled over the head of Pete Reiser in center field to score Andy Seminick, who had walked and gone to second on a bunt by Lee Handley, with the game-winner. The fans were also treated to Robinson's best game to date.

"There was an inning that should be embalmed in Cooperstown."

– Dick Young, May 10, 1947[9]

The Phillies jumped out to an early lead with five second-inning runs. Wildness by Dodgers starter Hal Gregg was a major factor in the big inning. Walks to Del Ennis and Seminick put runners on first and second with none out. Gregg threw Lee Handley's comebacker into right field

trying for a force at second base. Ennis scored the first run of the game, and Seminick went to third base. Verban followed with a liner off the pitcher's shin that went for an infield hit, scoring Seminick. Philadelphia pitcher Oscar Judd then laid down a perfect bunt that loaded the bases. Skeeter Newsome walked to force Handley home, and Philadelphia had three runs without the benefit of a batted ball having traveled more than 60 feet.

Gregg was replaced by Ralph Branca, who poured gasoline on the fire by walking Harry Walker, forcing in Philadelphia's fourth run. Branca struck out Johnny Wyrostek for the first out of the inning, but walked Nick Etten, bringing home the fifth run. The inning came to an end when Ennis hit into a 6-4-3 double play.

The Dodgers had seven innings in which to close the gap. In the fourth, Brooklyn scored its first run. Robinson doubled to right-center, bringing the crowd to its feet, advanced to third on a fly ball by Reiser and came home on a groundball by Dixie Walker. Branca found his rhythm and retired 15 of the 16 batters he faced in innings three through seven. The score remained 5-1 until the Dodgers came to bat in the eighth inning.

Spider Jorgensen led off the eighth with an infield hit, and Pee Wee Reese walked. Howie Schultz batted for Branca and hit into a double play. Eddie Stanky's hard grounder to third was handled by Handley on a great play, but Handley's throw to first was in the dirt and eluded first baseman Etten. Stanky was awarded a single and Jorgensen crossed the plate with the Dodgers' second run. Robinson's second hit of the game went to center field, and Reiser's double to left-center sent Stanky and Robinson home, making the score 5-4. Philadelphia made a pitching change, bringing in Dutch Leonard to replace Judd. Dixie Walker's single tied the score, but further damage was avoided when Leonard retired Carl Furillo on a groundball.

Hugh Casey succeeded Branca on the mound. He had not been scored upon in six of his seven outings and had two wins and four saves to show for his efforts. Casey retired the Phillies in order in the bottom of the eighth. Leonard mowed down the Dodgers in the ninth, but the Phillies mounted a threat in the home half of the inning. Lee Handley singled to right field to lead off. Emil Verban bunted toward first base and Robinson charged, grabbing the ball before it hit the ground and throwing a bullet to second baseman Ed Stanky covering first, doubling off Handley. Casey struck out Leonard to end the inning, and the game went into extra innings.

There was no scoring in the 10th, and Leonard, in his third inning of relief, put the Dodgers down in order in the 11th inning, setting up the opportunity for Philadelphia to win the game in the bottom of the inning on Verban's double.

The win went to Leonard, bringing his record to 4-1. Casey's record went to 2-1.

Robinson, who had ended April with five hitless games (0-for-18) that saw his batting average plummet from .409 to .225, was rebounding. His 2-for-5 performance on May 9 marked the fifth consecutive game in which he hit safely, and that

streak eventually became 14 consecutive games. He surpassed that streak with a 21-game hitting streak from June 14 through the first game of a July 4 doubleheader. He finished the season with a .297 batting average, led the National League with 29 stolen bases, finished fifth in the MVP balloting, and easily won the Rookie of the Year Award. He played with the Dodgers through 1956, was named National League MVP in 1949, was named to six All-Star teams and entered the Hall of Fame in 1962.

Pitcher Branca, who stopped the bleeding on May 9, went on to have his best season with the Dodgers, finishing at 21-12 with a 2.67 ERA.

Schultz's pinch-hitting appearance in the eighth inning was his last at-bat with the Dodgers. The next day the Dodger first baseman was sold to the Phillies for $50,000.

The loss caused the Dodgers to drop from first to third in the standings, one game behind the Braves and Cubs, who were tied for first. But the Dodgers went on to win the National League pennant before falling to the Yankees in the World Series.

SOURCES

In addition to the sources shown in the Notes, the author used Baseball-Reference.com and the following:

Baumgartner, Stan. "Phils Beat Dodgers in 11th 6-5; 22,680 See Verban's Hit Win," *Philadelphia Inquirer*, May 10, 1947: 14.

Burr, Harold C. "Flock Lose Top Spot, Rickey Wins $50,000," *Brooklyn Daily Eagle*, May 10, 1947: 6.

Brands, Edgar G. "Jackie Will Get Equal Chance, Rest Up to Him," *The Sporting News*, May 21, 1947: 4.

"'Jackie Just Another Player to Us – with No Favors,' Says Chapman," *The Sporting News*, May 7, 1947: 6.

McGowen, Roscoe. "Dodgers Beaten by Phils in 11-Inning Night Contest," *New York Times*, May 10, 1947: 16.

NOTES

1   Hy Turkin, "Police Investigate Poison Pen Threats to Jackie Robinson," *New York Daily News*, May 10, 1947: 25.

2   Turkin.

3   Wendell Smith, "'Stop Race Baiting' – Chandler: Phillies Warned by Baseball Czar Over Robinson Incident," *Pittsburgh Courier*, May 10, 1947: 1, 4.

4   Smith.

5   Smith.

6   Stanley Woodward, "Views of Sport – General Strike Conceived," New York Herald Tribune, May 9, 1947, reprinted in *The Sporting News*, May 21, 1947: 4.

7   "Robinson Reveals Written Threats," *New York Times*, May 10, 1947: 16.

8   "Varied Policies at Hotels Greet Robinson on Trip," *The Sporting News*, May 21, 1947: 8.

9   Dick Young, "Phils Win in Eleventh, Topple Dodgers 6-5," *New York Daily News*, May 10, 1947: 25.

ATHLETICS ROOKIE MCCAHAN
ONE MISCUE AWAY FROM A PERFECT GAME

September 3, 1947
Philadelphia Athletics 3, Washington Senators 0

By David Skelton

"It was all my fault," Philadelphia Athletics first baseman Ferris Fain said in a postgame interview. "I threw the ball while I was still pivoting, and it was five full feet from the bag."[1] The 26-year-old rookie was lamenting his second-inning error on a groundball off the bat of Stan Spence that allowed the Washington Senators center fielder to gain first base. The miscue proved to be the difference between Athletics rookie Bill McCahan and the sixth perfect game in major-league history. Even the opposition took a conciliatory tone afterward. "I'm sorry I had to be the one to spoil [it]," Spence said. "I was just trying to make a base-hit."[2]

When this day started, the chances of such a historic event being played out in Philadelphia's Shibe Park before the tiny crowd of 2,816 seemed most unlikely. Thirty years had passed since the Senators were handcuffed by a no-hitter when Boston Red Sox righty Ernie Shore famously relieved Babe Ruth after just one batter on June 23, 1917. The odds were even greater considering that up until this year only six no-hitters had been twirled by a rookie. The mark is made even more astounding because right-hander McCahan, who two months earlier was on the losing end of Cleveland Indians righty Don Black's gem, remains as of 2016 the only pitcher ever to be on both the winning and losing ends of a no-hitter.

Neither team was in contention for the American League pennant. Entering the day, Philadelphia was at exactly .500 (65-65) and in fifth place, 18 games behind the Yankees. The Senators were seventh, 27½ games back, with a record of 55-74.

It was a close game nonetheless. The game's outcome remained in doubt throughout the entire 1- hour and 26-minute affair as Senators hard-luck hurler Ray Scarborough kept the Athletics popgun offense in check for most of the game. In the second inning, Philadelphia capitalized on two of Scarborough's four walks to take a 1-0 lead before the righty settled down to hold the Athletics scoreless over the next four frames. But a one-out single by McCahan in the seventh ignited a two-run rally with the key blow being a bases-loaded double to right by outfielder Elmer Valo. In the top half of the inning Valo, who was appearing in his first game since an August 9 beaning by Senators right-hander Sid Hudson, had provided the fielding heroics with a spectacular catch against the right-field scoreboard that robbed Senators first baseman Mickey Vernon of a sure extra-base hit. Other fielding gems were recorded by second baseman Pete Suder and center fielder Sam Chapman. But the true hero this day was McCahan, who claimed afterward that he had not given a thought to a no-hitter before the ninth inning. "Then I bore down," the husky hurler said. "[U]ntil that time I was just trying to win a ballgame."[3]

Senators manager Ossie Bluege brought in three consecutive pinch-hitters to face McCahan in the ninth. None of the three got the ball out of the infield. The first flied out to shortstop, the second grounded to second, and McCahan struck out Cecil Travis to win the game. He'd faced 28 batters in all, one over the minimum, Spence reaching on the error in the second inning.

McCahan's journey from a former high-school phenom to a promising major-league hurler began in 1938 when his uncle Izzy Hoffman, a former major-league outfielder, arranged a tryout for his nephew in front of Athletics skipper Connie Mack. Immediately enamored, Mack arranged for McCahan's four-year tuition at Duke University, where the youngster could develop under Blue Devils manager and former Athletics ace Jack Coombs. A successful collegiate career, followed by an equally successful stint pitching for US Army Air Corps clubs during World War II, quickly made McCahan a "can't miss" prospect. The label appeared even more fitting on September 15, 1946, when, in his major-league debut, he outdueled Bob Feller in a 2-0 shutout win.

In 1947 McCahan's path to stardom was slowed by the extraordinarily large number of rainouts he was forced to endure through the first half of the season. In July, when the weather finally began to cooperate, McCahan established himself as one of the Athletics' prized young hurlers as he won seven of nine decisions prior to his historic September performance.

But fate would not shine as brightly throughout the remainder of McCahan's career. An off-season job lifting 100-pound oil drums increased his muscle tone to the point where it adversely affected his delivery. By the following spring he was struggling "like a man pushing a shot instead of [throwing] a baseball."[4] McCahan compiled a record of 5-8, 5.11 over the next two seasons before being demoted to the minor leagues. He never returned.

In the postgame glow of his brilliant September 3, 1947, performance McCahan said, "[s]ome day someone may batter my brains in, and it's possible I'll lose a few."[5] The words proved sadly prophetic following his rookie season as McCahan never attained the stardom that was once predicted for him.

SOURCES

In addition to the Sources cited in the Notes, the author relied on Baseball-Reference.com.

NOTES

1   "Bill Didn't Think About No-Hitter Until Ninth," *The Sporting News*, September 10, 1947: 13.

2   "Bill Didn't Think About No-Hitter Until Ninth."

3   "Bill Didn't Think About No-Hitter Until Ninth."

4   "McCahan Takes Case to Court (Basketball)," *The Sporting News*, November 10, 1948: 7.

5   "McCahan, Prof. Coombs' Diligent Dukester, Makes Varsity Grade on No-Hitter Over Nats," *The Sporting News*, September 10, 1947: 13.

NOBLE'S SLAM GIVES CUBANS 2-1 SERIES LEAD

September 24, 1947
New York Cubans 9, Cleveland Buckeyes 4

Game Three of Negro League World Series

By Mike Lynch

After a regular season in which the Negro American League's Cleveland Buckeyes and Negro National League's New York Cubans dominated their respective competition, they met in a Negro League World Series that proved to be the next to last postseason series in league history. When former Negro League star Jackie Robinson made his groundbreaking major-league debut for the Brooklyn Dodgers on April 15, 1947, it portended the end of the Negro Leagues. Robinson had spent only one season in the NAL, playing shortstop for the Kansas City Monarchs in 1945 and batting .384 with 23 runs batted in 26 games.[1]

After an impressive 1946 season with Montreal of the Triple-A International League, Robinson made the Dodgers' 1947 Opening Day roster and never looked back.[2] Others soon followed. Center fielder Larry Doby debuted for the Cleveland Indians on July 5, 1947; infielder-outfielder Hank Thompson suited up for the St. Louis Browns less than two weeks later; outfielder Willard Brown started in center field for the Browns on July 19; and pitcher Dan Bankhead joined Robinson in Brooklyn in late August.

When catcher Roy Campanella earned a permanent spot on Brooklyn's roster in the summer of 1948, and legendary pitcher Satchel Paige made his first major-league appearance with the Indians on July 9, two days after his 42nd birthday, the writing was on the wall.

Before the 1947 Negro League World Series started, Joe Bostic of the *New York Amsterdam News* gave the Buckeyes a slight edge over the Cubans.[3] The Buckeyes went 42-12 in the NAL and finished five games ahead of the Monarchs; the Cubans went 43-19 in the NNL and finished six games ahead of the Newark Eagles.[4]

They were evenly matched – the Cubans averaged 6.1 runs a game, while allowing 4.0; the Buckeyes averaged 5.8 runs a game, while also allowing 4.0 – but Bostic opined that speedy outfielder Sam Jethroe would be the difference.[5] It made sense. Jethroe was one of the best players in the league and went on to be named the National League's top rookie when he scored 100 runs and paced the NL in stolen bases with 35 for the Boston Braves in 1950.

Cleveland boasted four players who later appeared in the major leagues – Jethroe, catcher-manager Quincy Trouppe, shortstop Al Smith, and pitcher Sam Jones, the first African-American to throw a no-hitter in the big leagues.[6] New York, however, also had major-league talent in third baseman Minnie Miñoso and catcher Ray Noble, who began their major-league careers with the Indians in 1949 and New York Giants in 1951, respectively.

Others of note included shortstop Silvio Garcia, right fielder Claro Duany, and pitcher Luis Tiant, a Cuban and Negro League legend whose son Luis enjoyed a successful major-league career during which he became a Boston icon. Tiant, who turned 41 on August 27, 1947, won all nine of his decisions for the Cubans, pitched to a 2.91 ERA, and led the NNL in strikeout-to-walk ratio at 3.18.[7]

Garcia led the Cubans with 32 RBIs and 9 stolen bases and Dodgers President and general manager Branch Rickey considered him a candidate to break the major leagues' color barrier until Garcia admitted he wouldn't be able to turn the other cheek when subjected to racial insults.[8] Legend has it that Rickey asked Garcia, "What would you do if a white American slapped your face?" García was quick to answer. "I kill him," he replied.[9]

Duany, who at 6-feet-2 and 215 pounds was affectionately nicknamed "El Gigante," had segregationists question whether black and white players could coexist when he collided with former Dodgers catcher Mickey Owen at the Mexican League All-Star game on July 25, 1946. Duany attempted to steal home and when Owen blocked the plate and tagged Duany in the face, El Gigante took offense and decked Owen with one punch, causing the benches to clear and irate fans to climb fences in an effort to join the fray.[10]

Few things could have illuminated how even the Buckeyes and Cubans were than a 5-5 tie in a six-inning rain-shortened game at the Polo Grounds in New York that kicked off the Series on September 19. Game Two was played in front of 9,000 fans at Yankee Stadium on September 21 and once again, the teams were tied, this time at 7-7 through eight innings, before Cleveland scored three in the top of the ninth off starter Lino

Donoso on a walk and four hits. Buckeyes third baseman Leon Kellman had four of Cleveland's 17 hits, including two doubles.

Prior to the third game, to be played at Philadelphia's Shibe Park, Bostic doubled down on his opinion of the Buckeyes. "Now as it turns out, the American League kingpins have an edge in the brains department," he wrote. "Quincy Troups [sic] shapes up as definitely the superior in the matter of strategy and playing the percentages."[11]

He also felt the loss of Cubans center fielder Pedro Pagés would hurt New York and that moving left fielder Cleveland Clark to center would leave a gap in left field "much larger than anyone had ever anticipated." He wasn't high on Rufino Diaz and about Mario Ariosa he wrote, "Ariosa was something less than a ball of fire out there in the pasture."[12]

Cleveland's Game Two win proved to be its only victory in the series. For Game Three, the Buckeyes turned to right-hander Eugene "Flash" Bremer, a New Orleans native who was in his 11th of 12 seasons. Bremer finished his career in 1948 with a 3.13 ERA but posted a career-worst 5.28 ERA in 1947.[13] New York manager José María Fernández countered with 33-year-old North Carolinian Dave Barnhill, a righty in his seventh season who finished his Negro Leagues career in 1948 with a career ERA of 3.08.[14]

The Cubans plated a run in the third to take a 1-0 lead. Barnhill kept the Cleveland offense at bay and the teams went to the bottom of the fifth with the Cubans still holding a slim advantage, but that all changed when Noble hit a bases-loaded bomb that landed on the left-field roof and New York extended its lead to 7-0 with a six-run inning. New York touched Bremer for another run in the bottom of the seventh to go up 8-0 before the Buckeyes showed some life with a four-run eighth.

Cleveland parlayed three singles and two walks to cut New York's lead in half, but the Cubans added insult to injury with a run in the bottom of the eighth and Barnhill shut the Buckeyes down in the top of the ninth to secure a 9-4 win. Noble led the Cubans with three hits and five RBIs, Garcia went 2-for-4 and scored twice, Diaz contributed two hits and a run as did first baseman Lorenzo Cabrera, and Clark scored twice despite going hitless. Jethroe, Bremer, and left fielder Jesse Williams had two hits each for Cleveland, the former two scoring half of the team's runs.

SOURCES

In addition to the sources cited in the Notes, the author accessed Retrosheet.org, Baseball-Reference.com, and SABR.org.

NOTES

1   Seamheads.com Negro Leagues Database, seamheads.com/NegroLgs/player.php?playerID=robin01jac; Baseball-Reference.com lists Robinson as hitting .414 for Kansas City in 58 at-bats, but the Seamheads.com Negro Leagues database has him at .384 in 99 at-bats.

2   Robinson slashed .349/.468/.462 for Montreal in 1946, scored 113 runs, and stole 40 bases in 124 games.

3   Joe Bostic, "Sports Extra," *New York Amsterdam News*, September 27, 1947: 13. Although the article was published after the World Series had already started and the series was tied at a game apiece, Bostic hadn't changed his mind.

4   The Buckeyes and Cubans won-lost records were against teams in their own league. Counting wins and losses vs. all Negro League teams, the Cubans went 46-23-1 while the Buckeyes went 44-25-1.

5   Bostic, "Sports Extra."

6   Pitching for the Chicago Cubs, Jones threw his no-hitter against the Pittsburgh Pirates on May 12, 1955, at Wrigley Field in Chicago. As of 2020 he is the last pitcher to throw a no-hitter in a season in which he lost 20 games.

7   Statistics courtesy of the Seamheads.com Negro Leagues Database.

8   Interview with Negro Leagues expert Gary Ashwill. Statistics courtesy of the Seamheads.com Negro Leagues Database.

9   Joseph Gerard, "Silvio Garcia," sabr.org/bioproj/person/silvio-garcia/.

10 Interview with Negro Leagues expert Gary Ashwill; Gary Joseph Cieradkowski, "Claro Duany: The Giant," studiogaryc.com/2018/04/02/claro-duany-the-giant/, April 2, 2018.

11 Bostic, "Sports Extra."

12 Bostic, "Sports Extra." Bostic referred to Pagés as "Page" and Clark as "Clarke."

13 Statistics courtesy of the Seamheads.com Negro Leagues Database.

14 Statistics courtesy of the Seamheads.com Negro Leagues Database. Barnhill signed with the New York Giants in 1949 and spent three seasons with the Minneapolis Millers of the Triple-A American Association (1949-1951). He finished his career in the Class B Florida International League, pitching for Miami Beach in 1952 and Fort Lauderdale in 1953.

DEL ENNIS TWO-RUN HOMER
CAPS PHILLIES' EXTRA-INNING COMEBACK

April 26, 1949
Philadelphia Phillies 12, New York Giants 11
(11 Innings)

By John J. Burbridge Jr.

Both the Philadelphia Phillies and New York Giants had disappointing 1948 seasons. The Phillies won 66 games and lost 88 while finishing sixth in the National League. This was the 16th consecutive losing season for the Phillies, a streak that began in 1933. The Giants did better, finishing fifth with a 78-76 record.

Still, both teams had high hopes as the 1949 season began. The Phillies had a young nucleus with players like Richie Ashburn, Granny Hamner, Del Ennis and Willie "Puddin Head" Jones, all in their early 20s. Skipper Eddie Sawyer was very familiar with the young talent, having managed several of them in the minor leagues. The Phillies had also made some moves during the offseason, acquiring Eddie Waitkus, Bill Nicholson, Hank Borowy, and Russ Meyer from the Chicago Cubs. Waitkus was penciled in to be the everyday first baseman while Nicholson was a power-hitting outfielder. Borowy and Meyer were dependable starting pitchers. The Giants still had sluggers Johnny Mize, Sid Gordon, and Willard Marshall, who were major contributors in 1947 when the team hit 221 home runs.

In the second week of the 1949 season, the Giants arrived in Philadelphia for a two-game series. The Giants had won three in a row after having lost the first two games of the season to the Brooklyn Dodgers. The Phillies had won only two of their first seven games. In game one of the series, on April 25, the Giants beat the Phillies 6-3 behind pitcher Clint Hartung, while Hank Borowy was the losing pitcher for the Phillies. The second game of the series pitted Russ Meyer against the Giants' best pitcher, Larry Jansen.

The Giants scored first, in the top of the second, on Willard Marshall's fly ball that scored Johnny Mize. The Phillies responded in the bottom of the inning with a bases-empty home run by Willie Jones, who had a hot hand: This was his 10th hit of the season, and eight were for extra bases.[1] However, the Giants came up with three runs in the top of the third on an RBI single by Bobby Thomson and third baseman Jones's wild throw that allowed two runs to score. The Giants added a run in the top of the fifth on Jansen's RBI single.

Jansen was effective for the first five innings and the Giants led 5-1 as the Phillies came to bat in the bottom of the sixth. The Phillies loaded the bases with one out. Light-hitting second baseman Eddie Miller surprised everyone by hitting a grand slam, tying the score, 5-5.

Blix Donnelly, who had relieved Russ Meyer in the top of the sixth inning, got into trouble in the Giants seventh by walking two of the first three hitters. He was replaced by Jim Konstanty, who almost got out of the inning, before an error by shortstop Hamner loaded the bases and Whitey Lockman singled home two runs for a 7-5 Giants lead.

Hank Behrman relieved Larry Jansen to start Phillies seventh. Leading off, Ashburn reached first base on an error by Giants shortstop Buddy Kerr. Ashburn was out at second on Hamner's grounder to the pitcher, but Behrman walked Eddie Waitkus and Del Ennis's single plated Hamner and sent Waitkus to third base. Giants lefty Dave Koslo replaced Behrman. Waitkus scored on Nicholson's force-play grounder to second, again tying the game, 7-7.

With Konstanty still pitching, Johnny Mize led off the top of the eighth with a double and Thomson singled. Both scored when Marshall ripped a single to center field. Ken Trinkle replaced Konstanty and got out of the inning with no further scoring. (Marshall and Pete Milne, who had walked with two outs, were both thrown out trying to steal second.)[2] The Giants now led 9-7. Koslo set down the Phillies in order in the bottom of the eighth. Schoolboy Rowe replaced Trinkle in the top of the ninth and retired all three Giants batters.

With the Giants leading in the bottom of the ninth, the Phillies needed to rally. Koslo was still on the mound for the Giants and gave up a leadoff single to Ashburn and a double to Hamner. Ashburn scored on Waitkus's grounder to first and Hamner took third. Hamner then then scored on a fly ball by Del Ennis. The score was tied again. Nicholson popped out to second and the game went into extra innings.

Both Rowe and Koslo pitched one-two-three 10th innings. In the top of the 11th, Marshall led off with a single. With two outs, Walker Cooper pinch-hit for Koslo and walked. With two runners on base, Jack Lohrke batted for second baseman Bobby Rhawn and responded with a two-run double to right field. The Giants led 11-9 going to the bottom of the 11th.

Giants manager Leo Durocher called upon Andy Hansen to close out the game. The Phillies were probably happy to see Koslo leave; he had a 7-0 record against them.[3] Hansen walked pinch-hitter Bert Haas to begin the inning but retired Ashburn on a force out and Hamner on a fly ball. The Phillies were now down to their last out, but Waitkus got his third hit of the game, a run-scoring single to right field, and Waitkus went to second base when Willard Marshall let the ball roll through his legs for an error. The batter was now Del Ennis, who already had two hits. Ennis hit Hansen's first pitch to him for a home run to deep left field, his third of the season, giving the Phillies a thrilling 12-11 victory before a slim crowd of 3,296. Hansen threw his hat and glove on the mound in disgust as the Phillies stormed out of the dugout, hugged Ennis, and attempted to carry him off the field.[4]

One interesting sidelight was that two days after the game, the Phillies sold Bert Haas to the Giants who apparently wanted to shore up their bench with the versatile infielder/outfielder.

The 1949 Phillies experienced considerable improvement over the 1948 squad, finishing in third place with 81 wins and 73 losses after a late-season surge. The 16-season losing streak had ended. This improvement was just a prelude to the 1950 season when the Whiz Kids won the pennant on the last day of the season in extra innings with Dick Sisler hitting a game-winning home run against the Brooklyn Dodgers. The 1949 season was marred by the shooting of Eddie Waitkus in a Chicago hotel by a deranged young woman. He was unable to finish the season but did return in 1950, playing all 154 games.

The Giants regressed in 1949, finishing sixth with 73 wins and 81 losses. However, two years later Durocher's team would win the pennant on Bobby Thomson's home run. Better times were coming for both teams.

SOURCES

In addition to the sources mentioned in the Notes, a box score and play-by-play account for this game can be seen on Baseball-Reference.com.

NOTES

1   Stan Baumgartner, "Phils' 3 in 11th Tops Giants 12-11," *Philadelphia Inquirer*, April 27, 1949: 37-38.

2   John Drebinger, "Phils Nip Durocher Men, 12-11, on 2 Run Blast by Ennis in 11th," *New York Times*, April 27, 1949: 34.

3   Baumgartner.

4   Baumgartner.

THE PHILLIES SMASH FIVE HOMERS IN ONE INNING TO TIE A MAJOR-LEAGUE RECORD

June 2, 1949
Philadelphia Phillies 12, Cincinnati Reds 3

By C. Paul Rogers III

The 1949 Philadelphia Phillies were in the middle of a youth movement under manager Eddie Sawyer, with uncertain results. The even-keel Sawyer had taken over the reins the previous July from the volatile Ben Chapman and, playing youngsters like Richie Ashburn, Del Ennis, Granny Hamner, Putsy Caballero, Johnny Blatnik, Curt Simmons, and Robin Roberts, had lost 41 of the final 64 games to finish in sixth place, only two games out of the National League cellar.[1]

The team hadn't done much better to start the 1949 season, losing 8 of its first 11 games before starting to show improvement. The Phillies began June 2 in sixth place with a 19-21 won-lost record but stood only 4½ games behind the league-leading Boston Braves. The Phillies had defeated fifth-place Cincinnati, in town for a four-game series, 4-3 in 10 innings the previous evening to close to a game behind the Reds.

The June 2 night game featured two southpaws, the Phillies' 20-year-old bonus baby Simmons versus the Reds' crafty veteran Ken Raffensberger, before a crowd of 10,549. Phillies catcher Andy Seminick led off the bottom of the second with a home run for the game's first run. Meanwhile, Simmons scattered doubles by Jimmy Bloodworth and Bobby Adams in the

first four innings but otherwise kept the Reds in check. In the top of the fifth, however, Simmons allowed consecutive singles to Danny Litwhiler, Ray Mueller, and Johnny Wyrostek with no outs to tie the score. With two outs, Frank Baumholtz singled to left to drive in Wyrostek with the go-ahead run before Simmons retired Virgil Stallcup on a comebacker to end the inning.

The Phillies drew even at 2-2 in the bottom of the sixth on a bunt single by Hamner, a walk to Seminick, and a two-out single to center by Stan Hollmig. But Simmons could not hold the lead in the seventh, allowing doubles to Mueller and his opposite number Raffensberger that put the Reds ahead 3-2.

The Phillies mounted a mild threat in the bottom of the seventh on a walk to Stan Lopata and a single by Hamner but could not score. Heading into the eighth, the Reds' Raffensberger was fairly sailing along and had allowed only four hits and two runs. The wheels suddenly came off, however, and what was a pitchers' duel turned into a rout as the Phillies broke out of a two-week hitting slump with gusto.[2]

It began when Del Ennis greeted Raffensberger's first pitch by hitting a screaming line drive into the upper deck of the left-field stands to tie the score. Seminick followed on the next pitch with an even longer blast that cleared the left-field roof on the fly for one of the longest home runs ever hit at Shibe Park.[3] After just two pitches, Raffensberger found himself down 4-3 and out of the game as manager Bucky Walters brought in right-hander Jess Dobernic in relief.

Dobernic retired Hollmig on a line out to Stallcup at short for the first out of the inning but Puddinhead Jones followed with the third home run of the inning to make the score 5-3. Eddie Miller popped up to Bloodworth at second for the second out to bring up Schoolboy Rowe, who had relieved Simmons on the mound after Lopata had pinch-hit for him in the seventh. Rowe was known as an excellent hitter and promptly deposited a Dobernic pitch into the left-field stands for the fourth circuit blast of the inning.[4]

Walters next tried lefty Kent Peterson, who responded by walking Ashburn and giving up a high drive off the left-field wall to Hamner that missed being another home run by less than a foot. With runners on second and third, Eddie Waitkus grounded to Adams at third for what appeared to be the final out of the inning. First baseman Ted Kluszewski, however, dropped the throw to extend the inning as Ashburn scored to run the score to 7-3. Ennis, up for the second time in the inning as the Phillies had now batted around, singled to center to drive in Hamner and bring Seminick back to the plate.

Seminick struck again, hitting his second home run of the inning and his third of the game, a three-run shot over the fence in left, making the score 11-3. It was the team's fifth home run of the inning, tying a major-league record.[5]

Walters refused to change pitchers again and Peterson proceeded to plunk Hollmig with a pitch. Jones then missed his second home run of the game by two or three inches, ripping a shot off the very top of the wall in left and winding up at third with a triple. Hollmig scored to make it 12-3, but Eddie Miller mercifully struck out to end the inning.[6] The Phillies had scored 10 runs on the five homers, a double, a triple, a single, a walk, and a hit-by-pitch.[7]

Even more remarkable, the Phillies were about 15 inches from clubbing *seven* home runs in the inning. Hamner's blast had missed going out by less than a foot and Jones's triple hit at the very top of the wall.[8]

Rowe retired the Reds without difficulty in the ninth. He was the winning pitcher since he had also pitched a scoreless eighth, entering the game when the Phillies were behind 3-2.[9]

Seminick's three home runs were near the start of a hitting tear. He had homered and doubled two days before and for the week slugged five homers in seven games, driving in an astonishing 14 runs. He continued his hot bat during the following week and in 14 games blasted eight home runs and drove in 22 runs.[10]

Fueled by Seminick's hot hitting, the Phillies' eighth inning June 2 outburst was arguably a turning point for the young team as it won 13 of 17 games to vault into second place. Although the team slumped in July, it caught fire again in August, at one point sweeping the pennant-bound Brooklyn Dodgers at Ebbets Field. The Phillies completed the season in third place, their highest finish in 32 years.

After the final game of the season, manager Sawyer told the team, "We are going to win it all in 1950. Come back next year ready to win."[11] The next year the Phillies would be dubbed "the Whiz Kids" and would do just that, winning the National League pennant on the last day of the season on Dick Sisler's clutch 10th-inning home run for a dramatic victory over the Dodgers in Ebbets Field.[12]

SOURCES

In addition to the sources cited in the Notes, the author accessed Retrosheet.org, Baseball-Reference.com, and SABR.org.

NOTES

1   Sawyer was without big-league experience of any kind but had managed in the minor leagues for Phillies farm teams in Utica and Toronto. With the Utica Blue Sox in particular, Sawyer had managed a number of future Phillies Whiz Kids, including Ashburn, Hamner, Caballero, and Stan Lopata. Robin Roberts and C. Paul Rogers III, *The Whiz Kids and the 1950 Pennant* (Philadelphia: Temple University Press, 1996), 30-32.

2   Stan Baumgartner, "Phils' 5 Homers in Inning on Reds Tie Majors Mark," *Philadelphia Inquirer*, June 3, 1949: 45.

3   Baumgartner. Seminick later said, "It was one of the hardest balls I ever hit." Seminick loved to hit against his former teammate and roommate Raffensberger, saying, "Del Ennis and I, our bats were jumping when he pitched against us." C. Paul Rogers III, "The Day the Phillies Came of Age," *The National Pastime* (1999): 32.

4   The 1949 season was the last in Rowe's 15-year major-league career. He finished with a .263 career batting average and 18 home runs.

5   On June 6, 1939, the New York Giants hit five home runs in the fourth inning of a game against the Reds. The homers were hit by Harry Danning, Frank Demaree, Burgess Whitehead, Manny Salvo, and Joe Moore. Pitcher Salvo's homer was the only one he hit in the big leagues.

6   According to Seminick, Miller was upset at making the second and third outs of the inning, saying, "Hey, maybe I ought to go on home and not come out here." Rogers: 32.

7   Six of the runs were unearned, thanks to Kluszewski's two-out error at first.

8   Jones's triple bounced back toward the infield, leading Seminck to believe that Jones could have had an inside-the-park home run if he had run hard all the way. Instead, he coasted into third standing up. Rogers: 32.

9   It was the next to last victory of the 39-year-old Rowe's outstanding career. He was released by the Phillies before the end of the year, finishing with a 3-7 record. For his career, he won 158 games against 101 losses for a .610 winning percentage.

10 Seminick had hit only .225 in 1948 and had lost the starting catching job in spring training to the rookie Lopata. But with the team's slow start, Sawyer had reinstated him into the starting lineup at the end of April.

11 Roberts and Rogers, 193.

12 Roberts and Rogers. C. Paul Rogers III and Bill Nowlin, eds., *The Whiz Kids Take the Pennant – the 1950 Philadelphia Phillies* (Phoenix: Society for American Baseball Research, 2018); Carson Van Lindt, *Fire and Spirit: The Story of the 1950 Phillies* (Marabou Publishing, 1998); Harry T. Paxton, *The Whiz Kids – The Story of the Fightin' Phillies* (New York: David McKay Company, Inc., 1950).

LATE-GAME HEROICS

April 22, 1950
Philadelphia Athletics 6, Boston Red Sox 5
(15 Innings)

By Alan Cohen

The 1950 season was Connie Mack's 50th year as manager of the Philadelphia Athletics, and before the game against the Boston Red Sox at Shibe Park on Saturday April 22, Mack was honored during a ceremony at home plate.

Much later – 3 hours and 44 minutes later, to be exact – pinch-hitter Paul Lehner ended a long afternoon at the ballpark when he homered off Boston's Ellis Kinder in the 15th inning to give Philadelphia a 6-5 win over Boston before what was left of the 6,977 spectators who had braved the chill of the late April afternoon.

The Red Sox had staked starting pitcher Chuck Stobbs to an early lead. A two-run double by Vern Stephens highlighted a three-run first inning. Philadelphia starter Alex Kellner, in his first start of the young season, didn't help his cause by walking the first two batters he faced – Dominic DiMaggio and Johnny Pesky. The bases were loaded when Billy Goodman beat out a bunt. DiMaggio and Pesky came home on Stephens' double to right field. Kellner's wild pitch allowed Goodman to come home with Boston's third run. Two innings later, Stephens singled and scored on Al Zarilla's double off the right-field wall. Manager Mack was not tempted to remove Kellner, who had won 20 games the season before, and in

time (much time), Mack would be rewarded for keeping Kellner on the mound.

Stobbs weakened in the fourth inning and the A's got back in the game, scoring three runs. A walk to Sam Chapman was followed by a double by Bob Dillinger. On Dillinger's double, Boston's right fielder, Zarilla, attempting a shoestring catch, injured his shoulder. He was tended to by the team trainer and stayed in the game. Elmer Valo's grounder to second baseman Bobby Doerr scored Chapman; a single by Pete Suder scored Dillinger; and singles by Kellner and Eddie Joost moved Suder around the bases to score the third run of the inning.

Ferris Fain of the Athletics tied the game at 4-4 with a fifth-inning solo homer, his first of the season. The Red Sox recaptured the lead in the seventh inning, scoring a run on a single by Tommy O'Brien after two-out walks to Stephens and Doerr.

Stobbs pitched into the eighth inning. After retiring the first two batters, he gave up a single to Mike Guerra. Mack did not opt to pinch hit for Kellner, and Alex singled to left field (his second single of the day), knocking Stobbs out of the game. Walt Masterson took over on the mound and the first batter he faced, Joost, hit his third single of the afternoon to tie the game. Masterson averted further damage when Barney McCosky grounded out to end the inning.

There was no scoring in the ninth inning and the game went into extra innings. Ellis Kinder came into pitch for Boston in the 10th and retired the Athletics in order. He was coming off a 1949 season during which he went a career best 23-6 with six shutouts. The appearance was his second of the season. Three days earlier, he had been hit hard by the Yankees, surrendering eight runs before leaving in the sixth inning. Kellner and Kinder hurled zeros at each other through the 14th inning. Kellner's zeros were with an exclamation point. After walking Tommy O'Brien in the 10th, he retired the next 12 batters. He had strong support in the field from first baseman Ferris Fain, who grabbed a hard liner off the bat of Johnny Pesky in the 11th and ran toward the stands along the right-field line to haul in a foul ball hit by Matt Batts in the 13th. DiMaggio reached on a bad-hop single past shortstop Joost to start the 14th inning but went no farther as Kellner retired Pesky, Goodman, and Stephens.

The home team had chances to win the game in innings 12 through 14, but they were lost opportunities. Fain walked to open the 12th, but was thrown out trying to steal second base. In the 13th, the A's wasted a one-out double by Mike Guerra. And in the 14th, after Kinder walked three batters to load the bases, Guerra's fly ball to center field frustrated the A's chances.

Kellner was ultimately rewarded for his shutout efforts over the last eight innings. As the southpaw returned to the dugout after the 10th and each subsequent inning, manager Mack would say, "How do you feel?" After completing the top of the 14th, Kellner admitted, "I feel a little tired, but I'd like to try it some more." Mack responded, "This will have to be your last inning."[1] In the top of the 15th inning, the Red Sox had runners on the corners after singles by Tommy O'Brien and Matt Batts, but Kellner retired

Kinder on a grounder when Boston manager Joe McCarthy elected not to use a pinch-hitter.

In the bottom of the 15th inning, with not much daylight remaining, manager Connie Mack felt that his pitcher had pitched long enough. Kellner was scheduled to lead off the inning and Mack sent up the lefty-swinging Paul Lehner to bat for the pitcher. Lehner had been acquired along with Bob Dillinger by the A's in an offseason trade with the St. Louis Browns, and his appearance on April 22 was his first at-bat of the season. Kinder began his sixth inning of relief for the Red Sox. Lehner swung wildly and missed Kinder's first offering. He then took a ball before putting a stop to the festivities with a home run over the 50-foot wall in right field.

Kellner, who allowed 12 hits, struck out eight and walked an equal number, was credited with a complete-game win, the first complete game hurled against the Red Sox in 1950. It was his first win of the season and would rank as one of his best efforts in a season in which he went a disappointing 8-20.

The 35-year-old Kinder, with the loss, went to 0-2. He started 23 times and was brought in to relieve on 25 occasions. He went 14-12 with 9 saves.

Red Sox starter Chuck Stobbs had been a football and baseball star in Norfolk, Virginia, before signing with Boston for a bonus in 1947. The bonus rule at the time mandated that he be moved up to the majors after one minor-league season. After spending 1948 on the bench, he went 11-6 in 1949. He would go on to a 12-7 record in 1950.

Lehner's game-winner launched what was to be his best major-league season. He played in 114 games for the Athletics, batting .309 with 9 homers and 52 RBIs.

On this day, part of the story was about someone who didn't play. The Red Sox played the game without Ted Williams. Williams, after playing the first three games of the season, was missing his second straight game. He had taken ill with a severe cold during the Patriots Day double-header on April 19 and missed five games before returning to the lineup on April 26. During the first three games of his absence, Tommy O'Brien, who had two hits on April 22, filled in in left field. The hits on April 22 were O'Brien's last as a member of the Red Sox. On May 8 he was traded to Washington, where his career ended less than a week later.

Both managers were in the last year of their Hall of Fame careers. Boston manager Joe McCarthy was replaced by Steve O'Neill after starting the season 31-28. The Red Sox had been in contention until the final weekend of the 1949 season and, at the time of McCarthy's dismissal in 1950, had lost five games in a row, seen their record slip to 31-28, and dropped to fourth place, 9½ games behind the league-leading Tigers. It would be a frustrating season for Boston. They were without Williams for almost two months after he injured himself running into a wall at the All-Star Game. Nevertheless, the Red Sox mounted a late-season rally and finished in third place, four games behind the Yankees, who repeated as American League champions.

After the April 22 game, the 87-year-old Mack was honored at a formal dinner in Philadelphia. Unfortunately for Mack and the A's, the season would be a year of disappointment: the team finished in the cellar with a 52-102 record. It was 19 years since their last trip to the World Series, and the season was Mack's last as the manager of the team. Jimmy Dykes succeeded him in 1951. Mack stayed on as owner through the 1954 season, after which the team was sold and moved to Kansas City.

SOURCES

In addition to the sources cited in the Notes, the author used Baseball-Reference.com and the following:

Associated Press. "A's Pinch Home Run Beats Red Sox, 6-5," *Palm Beach Post*, April 23, 1950: 19.

Costello, Ed. "A's Triumph 6-5 in 15th; Lehner Hits Pinch Homer to Top Hose," *Boston Sunday Herald*, April 23, 1950: 53-54.

Hurwitz, Hy. "A's Beat Red Sox , 6-5, on Lehner's Pinch Homer in 15th," *Boston Globe*, April 23, 1950: 47.

Morrow, Art. "A's Top Bosox, 6-5, on Lehner's Pinch Homer in 15th," *Philadelphia Inquirer*, April 23, 1950: 1S-2S.

NOTES

1   Roger Birtwell, "Kellner Protected by Connie's Memory," *Boston Globe*, April 23, 1950: 47.

RELENTLESS COMEBACKS FOR THE WHIZ KIDS

September 15-16, 1950
Philadelphia Phillies 8, Cincinnati Reds 7
(19 Innings; Second Game of a Double Header)

By Mark S. Sternman

In one of the most thrilling games of a thrilling season, the Philadelphia Phillies rallied from a 5-0 deficit after five innings and a 7-5 deficit going into the bottom of the 18th to outlast the Cincinnati Reds 8-7 on a walk-off hit by Del Ennis that came just before curfew would have halted the elongated contest. The victory gave the Phillies a sweep of their doubleheader. Ennis's fifth hit of the game gave Philadelphia a dramatic doubleheader sweep and a 7½-game lead in the NL standings.

The starter, Phillies ace Robin Roberts, was seeking his 20th win but struggled, handicapped by a porous Philadelphia defense. With one out in the first, shortstop Granny Hamner, "obviously weary in the field,"[1] made two straight errors. With two Reds on, Roberts got Ted Kluszewski and Joe Adcock to hit two more balls at Hamner, this time for outs.

Cincinnati starter Howie Fox led the National League with 19 losses in 1949, but in 1950 would have the only winning season (11-8) of his nine-year career. Fox also allowed two baserunners in the first, on singles by Richie Ashburn and Ennis, but stranded both by retiring Jackie Mayo on a popup.

After Roberts enjoyed his only 1-2-3 inning in the top of the second, Hamner doubled in the bottom of the inning and Andy Seminick singled him to third base. Fox fanned Mike Goliat and got Roberts to pop to Kluszewski, then walked Eddie Waitkus to load the bases for Ashburn, but the outfielder also popped to Kluszewski to leave the sacks full of Phils.

In the third Fox himself scored the first run. He reached on Hamner's third error of the game (his 44th of the season). A single by Lloyd Merriman pushed Fox to second. After Grady Hatton struck out, Johnny Wyrostek hit one to Waitkus, who erred, allowing Fox to score. With runners on first and second and one out, manager Eddie Sawyer had Roberts walk Kluszewski intentionally, loading the bases for Adcock. His two-run single gave Cincinnati a 3-0 lead. Roberts struck out Connie Ryan with two runners in scoring position (Adcock had advanced to second on the throw to third to try to get Kluszewski), then got Virgil Stallcup on a fly ball to left to keep the score 3-0.

After the Phillies went in order in the bottom of the third, the Reds padded the lead in the top of the fourth thanks to a double by Dixie Howell double and a single by Merriman. Philadelphia mustered just a Seminick walk in the bottom of the fourth and trailed 4-0 after four.

Cincinnati scored again in the top of the fifth on singles by Kluszewski and Adcock and a fly ball by Stallcup. The Phillies wasted a leadoff single by Waitkus in the bottom of the fifth and faced a formidable 5-0 deficit after five innings.

After Seminick grounded out to end the Philadelphia half of the sixth, Sawyer replaced him with Stan Lopata, probably figuring that 15 innings of catching in one day would suffice. But Lopata would end up catching nearly as many innings during the day as Seminick.

Roberts got a 6-4-3 DP to end the top of the seventh, and Philadelphia broke through against Fox in the home half. Goliat doubled and one out later Waitkus reached on an error by Ryan to put runners at the corners. Both scored thanks to Willie Jones's fly ball and a two-out RBI single by Ennis.

Having pinch-hit for Roberts and seeing his team trail 5-2 after seven in the second game of a doubleheader, Sawyer tapped 26-year-old Jack Brittin to make his major-league debut. Brittin pitched an easy eighth inning and even struck out Howell.

The Phillies crept closer in the bottom of the eighth thanks to a walk to Hamner, Goliat's single, and an RBI single by Jimmy Bloodworth, batting for Brittin. After Bloodworth's hit, Fox departed, making way for Ken Raffensberger. The former Phillies pitcher tied Preacher Roe and Johnny Sain with a league-leading 34 home runs given up in 1950, but he escaped the eighth by striking out Waitkus and retiring Ashburn on a groundout to allow Cincinnati to maintain its 5-3 margin.

For the ninth, Sawyer turned to Jim Konstanty, who made his record-setting 66th appearance of the season.[2] After consecutive singles by Merriman and Hatton, Konstanty prevented the Reds from getting a critical insurance run by retiring the heart of the order, Wyrostek, Kluszewski, and Adcock, on two fly balls and a groundout.

The Phillies rallied in the bottom of the ninth after the lefty Raffensberger had fanned Jones. Righty Herm Wehmeier then relieved, and Ennis greeted him with a single. Ignoring the platoon advantage, Sawyer sent right-handed-batting Stan Hollmig up for the left-handed-hitting Mayo. Hollmig doubled to put the tying runs in scoring position. Hamner's double tied the game at 5. Lopata walked, but neither Goliat nor Konstanty could deliver a winning hit.

Konstanty got Cincinnati in order in the top of the 10th. Philadelphia threatened in the bottom of the inning. Waitkus singled. Ashburn forced him at second, then stole second. But Jones and Ennis, the two top RBI men of the 1950 Phillies, could not plate Ashburn.

Neither team had a hitter reach again until Waitkus doubled with two outs in the bottom of the 12th. Wehmeier got Ashburn to fly out.

Konstanty retired 14 Reds in a row before Howell singled with two outs in the top of the 13th, but Wehmeier grounded out to Hamner.

Cincinnati had two baserunners in the 14th on walks to Hatton and Kluszewski (the latter intentionally). The strategy succeeded this time as Adcock popped out to Hamner.

Having failed to win the game with a hit in the ninth, Konstanty singled in the bottom of the 14th but did not score.

The top of the 16th played out similarly to the top of the 14th. With Hatton on second after his single followed by a groundout, Konstanty again passed Kluszewski intentionally and again retired Adcock on an infield grounder to end the inning.

In the bottom of the 17th with one out, Waitkus doubled off Wehmeier for the second time in extra innings but again did not score.

Going into the 18th, the teams had played eight scoreless innings. After fanning Wehmeier to start the top of the inning, Konstanty got tired and wild, walking Merriman, Hatton, and Wryostek to load the bases with one out for Kluszewski. Konstanty came after the slugger and the big man delivered a single that gave the Reds a 7-5 lead. Adcock then bounced into a double play to end the inning. Cincinnati again needed to secure three outs and give up less than two runs to win.

Wehmeier came out for the bottom of the 18th and gave up double to Ennis and a single to Dick Sisler to put the tying runs on the corners with none out. Hamner drove in Ennis with a fly ball, Philadelphia still trailed 7-6 with one out and Sisler on first. Lopata, the fill-in catcher, "then delivered one of his best hits of the year, a resounding triple to right center, scoring Sisler with the tying run."[3] With Lopata on third, Reds shortstop Stallcup "made a nice play on Goliat's grounder"[4] and threw him out at first, holding Lopata at third. Having already used Konstanty for 10 innings, Sawyer pinch-hit with Ken Silvestri, who flied out to end the 18th in a 7-7 deadlock.

Replacement Blix Donnelly yielded a leadoff double to Connie Ryan to start the 19th but retired the next three Reds, finishing with teenager Ted Tappe, who had debuted with a homer against Brooklyn on September 14 but in this game grounded out batting for Wehmeier.

Eddie Erautt came in to pitch for Cincinnati with the 1:00 A.M. curfew looming. Waitkus singled. Ashburn dropped "a beautifully placed bunt down the first base line that stayed fair,"[5] and Jones walked to load the bases with none out for Ennis. "The seconds were ticking off the clock as Ennis batted – the count went to two and two and then Del connected."[6] His drive less than one minute before curfew cashed in Waitkus for the sensational sweep.

NOTES

1 Stan Baumgartner, "Phils' Bench Gets Its Chance, Proves Stouter Than Figured," *The Sporting News*, September 27, 1950: 4.

2 "All-time king of the bullpen, Jim Konstanty ... broke the major league record for most relief appearances in a season when he participated in his sixty-sixth game in the 19-inning nightcap with the Reds, September 15. The old record of 65 games pitched in a season, none started, was been set by Ace Adams of the (New York) Giants in 1945." "Konstanty Breaks Adams' Record With His 66th Stint," *The Sporting News*, September 27, 1950: 32.

3 Stan Baumgartner, "Phils Win, 8-7, in 19th To Take 2; Church Hurt," *Philadelphia Inquirer*, September 16, 1950: 16.

4 Baumgartner.

5 Robin Roberts and C. Paul Rogers III, *The Whiz Kids and the 1950 Pennant* (Philadelphia: Temple University Press, 1996), 293.

6 Associated Press, "Phils Win in 19th after 2-1 Triumph," *New York Times*, September 16, 1950.

Vic Raschi Blanks Phils on Two Hits in World Series Opener

October 4, 1950

New York Yankees 1, Philadelphia Phillies 0

Game One of the World Series

By Greg Erion

Phillies manager Eddie Sawyer faced a dilemma. Who would pitch the first game of the World Series? His ace, Robin Roberts, had started three games in five days, including a 10-inning pennant-clinching effort on the last day of the season. He needed rest. Curt Simmons, whose 17 wins in the league were second only to Roberts, was with his National Guard unit, called to active duty in September. Ken Heintzelman's 3-9 record and Bob Miller's and Bubba Church's ineffectiveness because of injuries hardly inspired Sawyer's sense of confidence.

If he sought guidance in selecting a pitcher, Sawyer needed look no further than his American League counterpart in Philadelphia, Connie Mack. Under slightly similar circumstances, Mack had named little-used Howard Ehmke to pitch the opener for the 1929 World Series, which proved a successful gamble. (Ehmke defeated the Chicago Cubs, 3-1, and struck out a then-record 13 batters.) Sawyer was inspired by this action and decided to call on Jim Konstanty, his top reliever to begin the game. Konstanty had not started in the majors since May 13, 1946.[1]

While giving Roberts rest, Sawyer also felt that Konstanty's off-speed pitching might run counter to the Yankees' preference for fastballers. Ehmke's slow pitching had befuddled the Chicago Cubs 21 years earlier, a factor not lost on Sawyer.[2]

Konstanty had pitched 74 games in relief during the season, setting a major-league record for appearances. Along the way he won 16 games and saved 22 (then an unrecorded statistic).[3] Sawyer's faith in Konstanty was furthered by having managed him in 1948 while both were with the Toronto Maple Leafs of the International League. Konstanty had started 14 games, including many of the seven-inning short games in doubleheaders, and done well. Sawyer intended to just let Konstanty go as long as he was effective.[4]

Konstanty faced a daunting challenge. Odds were heavily stacked against Philadelphia; 2 to 5 in favor of the Yankees.[5] In this, much consideration was based on their records. New York mustered 914 runs scored with 159 home runs; Philadelphia just 722 runs with 125 home runs. New York had won 98 games vs. Philadelphia's 91 victories. These numbers plus the Yankees'

---

postseason experience gave credence to the odds offered.

This was New York's 17th appearance in the World Series and they had won 12 of the previous 16. Of the 18 men on their roster who played in the World Series, 14 had previously appeared in the fall classic. A significant missing face was veteran Tommy Henrich, whose season-long injuries prompted his replacement by late-season waiver pickup Johnny Hopp.[6]

The Phillies had not appeared in a World Series since 1915, when they were defeated in five games by the Boston Red Sox. Of the 19 men on their current roster who would play in the Series, only two, Dick Sisler and Dick Whitman, had appeared previously in a World Series and both only as pinch-hitters.

When told that Konstanty was going to pitch, Yogi Berra in one of the early malapropisms attributed to him, commented, "Yes he probably will, but who's gonna start for the Phils?" As for Konstanty, he observed, "It seemed funny warming up in public."[7]

Sawyer's selection of Konstanty took attention away from his mound opponent, 31-year-old Vic Raschi. Raschi, in his fifth season with New York, had compiled a 21-8 record in 1950 with a league-leading .774 winning percentage. It was his second of three 20-win seasons built on a formidable fastball that gave rise to the West Springfield, Massachusetts, native's nickname, the Springfield Rifle. This was Raschi's third World Series.

Attendance for the first game was 30,746, including Pennsylvania Governor James Duff and Grace Coolidge, widow of the former president. She was a devoted fan of baseball; a serious Red Sox fan who, while first lady, had attended the 1924 World Series between the Washington Senators and the New York Giants. Also on hand at 41-year-old Shibe Park were baseball luminaries Dizzy Dean, Ralph Kiner, and Pie Traynor as well as figures from the entertainment world

including actor William Frawley, soon to gain fame for his role as Fred in the *I Love Lucy* series.[8]

Missing from those in attendance was the Phillies' all-time greatest player, Grover Cleveland "Pete" Alexander. Unlike more contemporary times when retired players are invited to appear at games to honor a team's legacy, Philadelphia gave no thought to inviting the man whose 31 wins were crucial to winning their sole pennant in 1915.

Half-hearted efforts had been made by various entities to bring the ill and impoverished 63-year-old Alexander to the series, but the attempts had fallen through. Last-minute efforts by friends and a Chicago radio station, however, financed his trip back east, one interrupted by illness and delayed flights. As the series began Ol' Pete was on his way.

A vision of what might have been took place before the game started. Simmons had received a last-minute furlough from the service to be at the Series. Despite the opportunity to place him on the roster, Sawyer took a pass. Simmons had not pitched competitively for several weeks and wasn't deemed in shape for the Series. But he did pitch batting practice. Phillies fans could only wonder what if.[9]

Before the game began, all were reminded of life beyond baseball. The World Series began three months after the Korean War commenced. Prior to the first pitch, fans and players stood for a 30-second prayer for peace. The gesture was instigated by Commissioner Happy Chandler, who then threw out the first pitch.

The Series was broadcast nationwide on television to an estimated 35 million viewers, the second year in a row it was shown coast to coast. Radio was still king, however, attracting an estimated 70 million listeners.[10]

Once the game began, it quickly developed into a tight contest with both pitchers in top form. The Yankees started off the first in a promising manner as left fielder Gene Woodling led off with a walk and shortstop Phil Rizzuto singled him to second. Konstanty bore down on the heart of the order to retire Berra, Joe DiMaggio, and Johnny Mize and end the threat. Raschi singled to open the third and Woodling walked, but again Konstanty managed to get out of the inning successfully. Meanwhile Raschi shut down the Phillies in order over the first four innings.

In the top of the fourth, Yankees third baseman Bobby Brown, who had come into the game sporting a .600 batting average in previous Series competition, opened the frame with a double to left, the third time Konstanty had allowed the leadoff batter in an inning to reach base. The Yankees were not to be denied this time as successive fly balls off the bats of Hank Bauer and Jerry

Coleman plated Brown for the first and only score of the game.

The next inning Raschi's string of 13 straight outs ended with third baseman Willie Jones's single. One batter later, catcher Andy Seminick singled Jones to second but Raschi struck out second baseman Mike Goliat to end the threat.

And that was the ballgame. Except for a walk to first baseman Eddie Waitkus in the sixth, no other member of the Phillies reached base. Konstanty held the Yankees scoreless the rest of the way before giving way to Russ Meyer in the ninth, but the damage had been done as New York took the game, 1-0.

It was the third straight year the World Series opened with a 1-0 score. In 1948 Cleveland bested

Game One of the World Series in Shibe Park featured NL MVP Jim Konstanty, making his first start of the season after 74 relief appearances. He tossed a four-hitter over eight innings, but was outdueled by the Yankees' Vic Raschi, who spun a two-hit shutout. (Photo by PhotoQuest/Getty Images)

the Boston Braves by a similar score. The following year the lone tally gave New York a victory over the Brooklyn Dodgers.

Konstanty had pitched well, giving up just four hits. But Raschi, whom Yankees manager Casey Stengel considered the best pitcher he had ever managed, had given up just two. Raschi's pitching was masterful but an emerging presence that would play a large role in the Yankees' continued success also contributed. After the game Raschi told Berra, "Yogi, you called a perfect game. I didn't shake you off once. Thank you." It was the ultimate compliment for the 25-year-old catcher.[11] While Raschi and Berra were a formidable duo, they also benefited from the Phillies' opening game jitters. After the game, Phils shortstop Gran Hamner observed, "We may have been a little nervous and swung at some bad pitches from Raschi."[12]

Stengel's crew won but despite the Yankees being considered heavy favorites, they knew that the Series was going to be harder than forecast. Sawyer's gamble in starting Konstanty had almost paid off. The next day, New York had to face Philadelphia's best pitcher, Robin Roberts, on his home field.

For Raschi the day ended on less than a perfect note. Thieves broke into his hotel room while he was dueling Konstanty. They stole his wife's jewelry and tickets for games at Yankee Stadium being held for friends. He was robbed, but then the Phils could have said the same thing.[13]

NOTES

1   Robin Roberts and C. Paul Rogers III, *The Whiz Kids and the 1950 Pennant* (Philadelphia: Temple University Press, 1996), 340.

2   Sol Gittleman, *Reynolds, Raschi and Lopat: New York's Big Three and the Yankee Dynasty of 1949-1953* (Jefferson, North Carolina: McFarland & Company Publishers, 2007), 86.

3   For his efforts Konstanty would be selected the National League's Most Valuable Player.

4   Roberts and Rogers, 340.

5   Jack Hand, "Yankees as Usual Favored to Win," *Spokane Daily Chronicle*, October 2, 1950: 49.

6   Hopp was obtained from the last-place Pittsburgh Pirates on September 5. He was second in the National League in hitting with a .340 average.

7   "First Game Gossip," *The Sporting News*, October 11, 1950: 10.

8   "Seats Left Empty in Ticket Mix-up," *New York Times*, October 5, 1950: 51.

9   "First Game Gossip."

10 Gittleman, 86.

11 Gittleman, 87.

12 Roscoe McGowen, "Browns Hit Draws Praise from Loser," *New York Times*, October 5, 1950: 51.

13 Dan Daniel, "Raschi Hotel Room rifled of Jewelry, Series Tickets," *The Sporting News*, October 11, 1950: 9.

Joltin' Joe's Jack Sinks Phils

October 5, 1950
New York Yankees 2, Philadelphia Phillies 1
(10 Innings)

Game Two of the World Series

By Greg Erion

The 1949 World Series opened with Allie Reynolds facing Brooklyn's best pitcher, Don Newcombe. Yankees manager Casey Stengel wanted the 1950 World Series to start that way as well. Reynolds against Philadelphia's best pitcher. But it did not work out that way as Jim Konstanty rather than Robin Roberts started Game One. Eddie Sawyer's gambit would not change Stengel's strategy. Reynolds was called on to face Roberts in Game Two.

The 33-year-old Reynolds was not quite as good as Vic Raschi had been in his start. Raschi had given up two hits and no runs. Reynolds allowed seven hits and one run. He also issued four walks to Raschi's one. But it was enough because on this day Joe DiMaggio came through to win the game on the field and at bat.

Reynolds was not the ace of the staff that year; Raschi's 21-8 and Eddie Lopat's 18-8 easily surpassed Reynolds's 16-12 record. While his record did not look impressive, he lost several games by one run, and down the stretch Reynolds was 6-1, which helped make the difference in New York's tight pennant race with Detroit. Stengel

had as much regard for him as he did for Raschi. While a starter, Reynolds could also relieve – a handy option that would prove valuable later in the Series. In his garbled Stengelese syntax, he reflected how he felt about Reynolds, "The greatest two ways, which is starting and relieving, the greatest *ever*. ..."[1]

Roberts, who came up to the Phils in mid-1948, enjoyed the first of six straight 20-win seasons in 1950, going 20-11 in what was to become a Hall of Fame career. With tremendous stamina, the 24-year-old, commanding an overpowering fastball, started a league-leading 39 games and pitched 304⅓ innings.[2]

Attendance for the game was 32,660, up from the 30,746 who attended Game One. Philadelphia, unaccustomed to the ebb and flow of tickets for a World Series, held about 2,000 tickets for baseball groups that were never picked up. By the time the Phils realized they had not been claimed, it was too late to get word out on their availability.[3]

In the first inning, the contest started almost in the same manner as Game One. Two Yankees got on base, via singles by Gene Woodling and Yogi Berra. Roberts managed to end the rally by inducing Johnny Mize to pop up for the third out.

In the second, Roberts ran into trouble again as Jerry Coleman walked with two outs. Reynolds, a .185 hitter during the season, then singled. Woodling hit a high bouncer that Willie Jones could not reach. Granny Hamner grabbed the ball but could not make a play as Coleman scored.[4] Roberts, by his own admission, was not in a groove for the first several innings and continued to work into and out of jams.[5]

Reynolds also faced several scoring threats. In the first Richie Ashburn doubled to right with one out but could get no farther. In the second Hamner tripled with one out but was left stranded. Eddie Waitkus doubled in the third, also with one out, but the threat ended with Ashburn popping up and Dick Sisler grounding out.

Finally in the fifth Philadelphia scored its first run of the Series when second baseman Mike Goliat, a .234 hitter, opened the inning with a single. Roberts bunted, but popped up to the pitcher. Waitkus hit a ball that took a crazy bounce over Coleman's head for his second hit of the game, moving Goliat to third. Ashburn brought Goliat home with a sacrifice fly to Woodling in left to tie the game at 1-1.

The Phillies attempted another rally in the sixth. Leadoff batter Del Ennis, whose 126 RBIs led the National League during the season but who was 0-for-5 to this point, hit a line drive to deep right-center field. DiMaggio, at 35 not fleet of foot any longer, made a dramatic catch over his shoulder right before the 400-foot sign.[6]

Neither team scored over the next three innings. The Yankees put men on in the eighth but they were stranded when Reynolds struck out to end the inning. Hamner doubled with one out in the bottom of the ninth; only DiMaggio's perfect play on the ball in the gap kept it from going for a triple.[7] Reynolds walked pinch-hitter Dick

Whitman, and then induced Goliat to ground into a double play.

The game went into the 10th with Roberts and Reynolds still on the mound. The first batter Roberts faced was DiMaggio. Stepping to the plate, he had not gotten a hit in the Series. Moreover, on each of his previous four at-bats, DiMaggio could not even get the ball out of the infield, popping up each time.

DiMaggio's poor performance in the Series brought back memories of how tough a year this had been for him. Near the end of June he was hitting in unfamiliar .250 territory. He was becoming convinced his skills were eroding: "I haven't got that feeling I used to have that I can walk up there and hit any pitcher who ever lived." He was in a funk, dealing with personal issues, and his frame of mind was not helped by Stengel's starting him at first base in early July.[8] It was the only time in DiMaggio's major-league career that he appeared in a position other than the outfield. He looked distinctly uncomfortable at first. The next day he went back to the outfield. His troubles continued until mid-August, when Stengel announced he was benching DiMaggio for a week. It was what Joe needed.

Upon his return to the lineup on August 18, DiMaggio homered to win a game against the Philadelphia Athletics 3-2. He then went on a tear. In 27 games in September, he drove in 30 runs on the strength of nine home runs, and compiled a .362 batting average. He ended the year at .301 with 32 homers and 122 RBIs and led the league in slugging average with a .585 mark. But now DiMaggio's 0-for-6 over two games without getting the ball out of the infield brought back concerns that he was through.

Roberts worked the count to 2-and-1, then got a ball out over the plate. DiMaggio turned on it and the ball landed in the upper deck in left for a home run, the seventh he hit in World Series competition.[9] After DiMaggio rounded the bases, Roberts retired the side in order.

When DiMaggio went out to play the bottom of the 10th, the fans in center field gave him a loud ovation.[10]

Backup outfielder Jackie Mayo was called on to pinch-hit for Roberts to lead off the bottom of 10th. Mayo had played in only 18 games for the Phils during the season, having been a September callup. He had been added to the roster in place of outfielder Bill Nicholson, whose diabetes had flared up. Mayo worked a walk off Reynolds and advanced to second on a sacrifice by Waitkus. Ashburn popped up for the second out. Dick Sisler, whose three-run homer had won the pennant-clinching game for Philadelphia four days earlier, came to bat.

Reynolds proceeded to fan Sisler to end the game. Working his eighth World Series, umpire Bill McGowan rang up Sisler on a called strike three. Sisler felt he had been robbed. "I shouldn't be complaining about the umpires but I believe McGowan missed that last strike he called on me. It was high and inside and I didn't break my wrist but McGowan said I did – and he has the last word." But Sisler's complaint fell on deaf ears. He acknowledged that he was playing "terrible ball." In that he was right. Through the first two games he was 0-for-9 with four strikeouts.[11] He was not alone in his lack of hitting. For the first two games Philadelphia as a team was batting .145 with nine strikeouts.

After the game Tommy Henrich tried to enter the Yankees clubhouse dressed in street clothes. A policeman barred his way, "Who are you?" "I'm a ballplayer," Henrich replied. Questioning continued until a teammate passing by vouched for him. A year before, Henrich had to be escorted off the field after his home run in the bottom of the ninth gave the Yankees a 1-0 win in the first game of the Series against the Brooklyn Dodgers. The 37-year-old outfielder, ineligible for the Series because of a knee injury, would be released in December.[12]

The Phillies left Shibe Park down two games to none. No team had ever come back from such a deficit to win the World Series. Philadelphia would have to turn things around in Yankee Stadium beginning the next day. And do so with veteran starting pitcher Ken Heintzelman, who had been 3-9 for the season. He would be facing Eddie Lopat, an 18-game winner during the season. The Phillies' challenge was daunting.

Shibe Park had now hosted eight World Series. It was the ballpark's last; Shibe was demolished in 1976 before another Philadelphia team could reach the fall classic.

NOTES

1   Sol Gittleman, *Reynolds, Raschi and Lopat: New York's Big Three and the Yankee Dynasty of 1949-1953* (Jefferson, North Carolina: McFarland & Company Publishers, 2007), 86.

2   Specifically, Roberts tied with Vern Bickford and Warren Spahn of the Braves for the lead at 39 games started.

3   "Second Game Notes," *The Sporting News*, October 11, 1950: 10.

4   "DiMaggio's Homer Wins 10 Rounder," *The Sporting News*, October 11, 1950: 9.

5   Robin Roberts and C. Paul Rogers III, *The Whiz Kids and the 1950 Pennant* (Philadelphia,: Temple University Press, 1996), 340.

6   Richard Whittingham, ed., *The DiMaggio Albums (Vol. 2)* (New York: G.P. Putnam's Sons, 1989), 675.

7   The DiMaggio Albums, 676.

8   DiMaggio's ex-wife was getting a divorce from her second husband, which had the potential for further disrupting his son Joe Jr.'s life. Peter Golenbock, *Dynasty: The New York Yankees, When rooting for the Yankees was like rooting for U.S. Steel* (Englewood Cliffs, New Jersey: Prentice-Hall, Inc., 1975), 36-37.

9   In *The Whiz Kids and the 1950 Pennant*, Roberts has DiMaggio hitting his pitch on a 2-and-0 count. Contemporary news accounts (see "See Second Game Notes," *The Sporting News*, October 11, 1950: 9) describe it as a 2-and-1 pitch.

10   "Second Game Notes."

11   "Second Game Notes."

12   "Second Game Sidelights," *The Sporting News*, October 11, 1950: 9.

DEL WILBER UNLIKELY ONE-MAN SHOW

August 27, 1951
Philadelphia Phillies 3, Cincinnati Reds 0
(Second Game of a Doubleheader)

By Richard Cuicchi

Del Wilber's game on August 27, 1951, could easily rank among the most memorable of his life. After bringing his newborn daughter, Cynthia, home from the hospital earlier in the day, he smacked three solo home runs to account for all of the Phillies' runs in a 3-0 victory over Cincinnati. Batting eighth in the lineup, Wilber was as unlikely a player as anyone to go on a homer spree. A career role player, he hit only 19 home runs during his eight major-league seasons.

Philadelphia claimed Wilber after St. Louis left him unprotected following his 1950 season with Triple-A Rochester. He replaced Stan Lopata as the Phillies backup in 1951. Wilber split time that season with Andy Seminick, and played the most games in one season (84) during his career.

Wilber began his professional career as a 19-year-old in 1938. He missed four full playing seasons (1942-1945) while in the military during World War II. He made his major-league debut on April 21, 1946, with the St. Louis Cardinals. By the time he was acquired by the Phillies in 1951, Wilber had played in only 84 games for the Cardinals, and had never hit a major-league home run.

The Phillies were coming off their pennant-winning season in 1950, when they were known as the Whiz Kids for the improbable championship season by the team that averaged only 26 years of age.

Coming into the doubleheader on August 27 the Phillies were in fourth place, a distant 18 games behind the first-place Brooklyn Dodgers. Seminick was the catcher in the Phillies' win in the first game of the doubleheader, a 2-0 victory on Bill Nicholson majestic homer that exited the stadium in left field and landed on the roof of a house and disappeared down a chimney.[1]

Wilber, 6-feet-3 and 200 pounds, drew the starting assignment behind the plate in the second game. Years later he recalled, "I was sicker than a mule that day. I had a bad, bad cold. I sat in the dugout between innings with a big jacket on and that was August! I never took my chest protector off, I just slipped a jacket on over it and stood there like a guy with malaria or pneumonia or something."[2]

Lefty Ken Johnson was Wilber's batterymate. Johnson, 28, had pitched sparingly during the first half of the season, but had a 4-4 record coming into the game, including two shutouts. The Phillies lineup also included outfielder Tommy Brown, a member of the three-homer club whose feat occurred a year earlier with the Brooklyn Dodgers.

Veteran left-hander Ken Raffensberger, 12-16 for the sixth-place Reds, got the starting nod from manager Luke Sewell.

Neither team generated a threat during the first 2½ innings. Then in the bottom of the third, Wilber led off with his fifth home run of the season and his career.

In the top of the fifth inning, the Reds mounted their best offensive effort of the game, but came up short. With two outs, singles by Bobby Adams and Connie Ryan and a walk to Joe Adcock loaded the bases. However, Johnson retired Ted Kluszewski with a groundout to shortstop Granny Hamner.

Wilber led off the bottom of the fifth with his second home run. It was the only multihomer game of his career.

Aside from Wilber's home runs, the most excitement of the night was provided by the Phillies' Hamner in the bottom of the sixth inning. After Willie Jones doubled with two outs, Hamner hit a slow roller to third baseman Adams, who fielded the ball cleanly but made a low throw to first baseman Kluszewski. Hamner appeared to beat the throw, and Kluszewski was pulled off the bag for good measure. However, umpire Frank Dascoli signaled Hamner out. The ump ejected Hamner for his choice words during the ensuing argument. It was the first career ejection for Hamner.[3]

In the bottom of the seventh, Wilber delivered one more contribution to the excitement of the game when he slammed his third consecutive solo homer of the game. The 400-foot blast landed on the roof in left field. All three were hit off Raffensberger, who served up his 26th, 27th, and 28th circuit blasts of the season. It was the third time in the season he had given up three homers in a game.

Johnson continued to hold the Reds scoreless, and the Phillies wound up with their second victory of the day, 3-0. He pitched his third complete-game shutout of the season in gaining his fifth victory.

The contest was a good indicator of how Raffensberger's season would end up. He took his 17th loss of the season and finished the season tied with teammate Willie Ramsdell and Paul Minner of the Cubs for the most losses in the National League. Raffensberger finished the year with the third-most home runs allowed (29), following Murry Dickson (32) and Preacher Roe (30).

Wilber's explanation for his outstanding performance was simple: "I was loose – in other words I had no tensions that night. I was too sick." He said he didn't really realize what had happened until the game was over. When he got home, his wife said she had heard about it on the radio.[4]

Aware that he had a chance the next day to tie a major-league record of four consecutive home runs, Wilber wasn't originally slated by manager Eddie Sawyer to be in the starting lineup. However, starting catcher Seminick came up sick before the game, and Wilber was inserted into the lineup in his place. In his first time at bat, Wilber struck out. Seminick later acknowledged he faked his illness so that Wilber would have an opportunity to tie the home-run record.[5]

At the time Wilber was only the sixth Phillies player to hit three solo home runs in a game. It was the first time a Phillies batter had hit three home runs in three consecutive at-bats since Johnny Moore accomplished the feat on July 22, 1936. Other Phillies who had slugged three homers in a game were Butch Henline (1922), Cy Williams (1923), and Seminick (1949), while Chuck Klein hit four against Pittsburgh in a 10-inning game on July 10, 1936.[6]

Wilber doesn't hold the record for fewest career home runs by players with three-homer games. That distinction belongs to Merv Connors who hit three on September 17, 1938. Connors managed to hit only eight home runs during his two-year career. Some of baseball's sluggers who never hit as many as three homers in a game include Rafael Palmeiro, Fred McGriff, and Frank Howard.[7]

The 1951 season was the best of Wilber's career. He had career highs in home runs (8), RBIs (34), and batting average (.278). He was traded to the Boston Red Sox the next season, and he finished his major-league playing career in 1954 with the Red Sox.

After his playing days, Wilber spent 15 seasons as a minor-league manager, and was a coach for the Chicago White Sox, Washington Senators, and Texas Rangers.

Wilber was noted for his postgame hobby of painting baseballs for winning pitchers on his team. His artistic handiwork typically captured the game's details, as well as something personal about the player. He would then cover them with fingernail polish, so the balls could be preserved as keepsakes.[8] The three-homer game would have been a great occasion for Wilber to decorate a ball for himself.

SOURCES

In addition to the sources cited in the Notes, the author consulted the following:

baseball-reference.com/boxes/PHI/PHI195108272.shtml.

retrosheet.org/boxesetc/1951/B08272PHI1951.htm.

Smith, Lou. "All Scoring Is on Home Runs," *Cincinnati Enquirer*, August 28, 1951: 18.

NOTES

1   Stan Baumgartner, "Phils Defeat Reds, 2-0, 3-0: Wilber Hits 3 HRs, Nicholson Raps One," *Philadelphia Inquirer*, August 28, 1951: 30.

2   Cynthia Wilber, *For Love of the Game* (New York: William Morrow and Company, 1992), 242.

3   Baumgartner.

4   Baumgartner.

5   Baumgartner.

6   Baumgartner.

7   Olsen, Tim. "King for a Day," *Baseball Digest*, June 2003: 70-74.

8   Frank Yeutter. "Phils' Wilber—Masked Artist," *Baseball Digest*, August, 1951: 89.

A Wet All-Star Game at Shibe

July 8, 1952
National League 3, American League 2

By Paul E. Doutrich

On July 8, 1952, it rained all morning in Philadelphia. It rained the previous night and more rain was predicted for the afternoon. It was not a day for baseball. Commissioner Ford Frick had a dilemma. The 1952 All-Star Game was scheduled for that day. Since the inaugural contest in 1933, no All-Star Game had been canceled for any reason. Fans, media, and sponsors anxiously awaited the 1952 game. And of course, 52 of baseball's best players had assembled in the city. With the rain slowing by late morning, Frick decided that the game would be played.

Because of the weather there was no pregame hitting or fielding. Instead, warming up was limited to stretching in the dugout and a few minutes of catch before the game. Finally, 19 minutes after the scheduled start time, 32,785 patrons watched the American League's leadoff hitter, Dom DiMaggio, step up to the plate. DiMaggio had played in the previous three All-Star Games but this one was different. His brother Joe, who had retired after the 1951 season, was not on the squad. Neither was his Red Sox sidekick, Ted Williams. He was in the Marines flying jet fighter planes in Korea.

On the mound for the National League was hometown favorite Curt Simmons. As a steady drizzle continued to fall, DiMaggio patiently worked the Phillies ace for a walk. Simmons fared better with the next three hitters. He struck out Yankees outfielder Hank Bauer and Cleveland's Dale Mitchell and then got Al Rosen, the Indians third baseman, to roll one to his Phillies teammate Granny Hamner at short.

The American League manager, Casey Stengel, penciled in one of his Yankees hurlers, Vic Raschi, to start the game. For Stengel there was a little extra pressure that came with the 1952 game. He had been the losing manager in the two previous All-Star Games. No manager had ever lost three in a row. Raschi started well, getting New York Giants first baseman Whitey Lockman on a pop to Phil Rizzuto at shortstop. Jackie Robinson followed Lockman. Robinson had three hits in the seven official times he had faced Raschi. This time he smacked Raschi's first pitch to him into the left-field upper deck. Already down a run, Raschi recovered impressively, striking out the National League's batting-average leader, Stan Musial, and home-run leader, Hank Sauer.

The second inning went well for both pitchers. Simmons sandwiched a strikeout of the White Sox first baseman Eddie Robinson between a line out off the bat of catcher Yogi Berra and second baseman Bobby Avila's groundout to Hamner at shortstop. In the bottom half of the inning, catcher Roy Campanella led off for the National League. Campy had been the league's Most Valuable Player the previous season but a series of minor injuries slowed him in 1952. Three times he had been hurt on collisions at the plate, the worst of which kept him out of the starting lineup for 10 days and required a cast on his left thumb. Campanella played through his injuries as much as possible but his hitting had suffered a bit. Facing Raschi, Campanella popped out to third. Veteran Cardinals outfielder Enos Slaughter then struck out and Bobby Thomson flied out to Bauer.

In the third, DiMaggio briefly added a bit of life to the American League attack. Despite some control problems, Simmons continued to mow through opposition hitters. Rizzuto opened the frame with a foul pop to third. Gil McDougald pinch-hit for Raschi. Playing in his first All-Star Game, McDougald grounded out to third. DiMaggio followed with his team's first hit off Simmons, a slicing double into right field. With a runner in scoring position, Hank Bauer fouled out to Campanella, ending the threat.

Bob Lemon, the Cleveland ace, took over for Raschi in the bottom of the third. Leadoff hitter Granny Hamner flied out to Hank Bauer in right field. Stengel then made a surprise maneuver. He attempted to replace Dale Mitchell in left field with Chicago's Minnie Miñoso.[1] Immediately NL manager Leo Durocher challenged the move. He contended that except for pitchers, starting players in All-Star Games were required to play three full innings. Stengel later explained that he made the move because Mitchell had a bad leg and Casey was concerned that he might further aggravate it playing on the rain-soaked outfield. According to the *Philadelphia Inquirer*, Home-plate umpire Al Barlick upheld Durocher's argument.[2] Mitchell returned to left field and Miñoso to the bench. In the bottom of the inning, Durocher sent Pee Wee Reese up to pinch-hit for Simmons. Reese

was playing in his eighth All-Star Game and still looking for his first All-Star base hit. He did not get it this time; he flied to left, pushing his hitless streak to 13. Lockman followed Reese and lifted one that center fielder DiMaggio easily hauled in.

The rain began to fall harder as the game entered the fourth inning. Small puddles were forming in the outfield. The infield, which had been dry until the tarp was removed just before the first pitch, was getting muddy and slippery.

The Cubs' Bob Rush, who took over for Simmons, got into trouble immediately. Now that Dale Mitchell's required playing time was over, Miñoso was sent in to hit for him, and rapped a double into right field. Al Rosen followed with a walk after watching a string of low, outside pitches miss the plate. Yogi Berra stepped into the batter's box. With his team down a run, many expected him to be bunting. Instead Stengel chose to play for a big inning and let his catcher swing away. The strategy failed. Berra popped one to short right field. The next batter, Eddie Robinson, made up for Berra's failure. He sizzled a pitch a couple of steps to the right of Jackie Robinson at second. Normally Jackie would have gobbled the ball up but wading through the infield mud, he slipped and the ball skipped under his glove. Miñoso scored easily. Jackie was part of the American League's second run as well. Bobby Avila bounced a Rush pitch up the middle. Slow getting to the ball, Robinson was able to knock it down but couldn't make a play, and Rosen scored. Phil Rizzuto came to the plate with runners on first and second, two runs in, and one out. Swinging at an inside fastball, he knocked a sharp groundball to his counterpart at shortstop. Hamner handled the ball cleanly and tossed it to second. Robinson got to the ball to force Avila with no problem, but on his double-play pivot he slipped off the bag and made an awkward throw, pulling Lockman at first off the bag a bit. Whitey was able to recover in time to easily get Rizzuto, who was merely jogging down the line. After the game Stengel defended Rizzuto's apparent sloth to critical reporters: "Couldn't you see it? ... He slipped and fell on his hands."[3]

Now with his team down a run, Jackie Robinson came to the plate hoping to atone for his costly error. He did not. Instead he popped to third. Lemon then plunked Stan Musial, putting the tying run on base. Hank Sauer did more than tie the game. He launched a rocket onto what Philadelphia fans sometimes referred to as Foxxville, the left-field pavilion where numerous Jimmie Foxx blasts had landed. The National League now led, 3-2. The home run was especially rewarding for Sauer. Two years earlier, All-Star team manager Burt Shotton had attempted to keep Sauer out of the starting lineup even though fans voted for him to start. Satisfied with his revenge, after the game Sauer said: "I wonder how Shotton feels now."[4]

Lemon's problems didn't end with Sauer's shot. Campanella walked, Slaughter doubled, and after Thompson popped to third, Hamner was intentionally walked, loading the bases. Next up was pitcher Rush. Most expected to see a pinch-hitter but Durocher surprised them. Rush did not. He punched one to third for the final out.

Lemon was scheduled to lead off the American League fifth but after the previous inning's problems and with a crew of heavy hitters on the bench, a pinch-hitter seemed appropriate. Instead Casey let his pitcher hit. Lemon had started his major-league career as a power-hitting third baseman, so Stengel had confidence with him at the plate. After the game Stengel explained: "I wasn't going to use one of my big hitters. ... I might need 'em later. Besides, Lemon's a pretty good hitter."[5] Lemon grounded out to second. Bauer followed with a single off Rush's glove. Then, in another surprising move, Bauer attempted to steal second. Campanella cut him down easily for the final out.

Though he had allowed Lemon to hit in the top of the inning, Stengel pulled him in the bottom of the inning. Little (5-feet-6½, 139 pounds)

Bobby Shantz, another hometown favorite, was sent out to face the heart of the National League lineup. Mixing a sharp curveball with a fastball, Shantz used 13 pitches to strike out the three hitters he faced. Asked after the game if he regretted not having a chance to duplicate or better Carl Hubbell's strikeout feat in the 1934 game, Shantz replied, "No, I was just thinking how awful it would be to get knocked out in the next inning."[6]

Shantz didn't get his chance to better Hubbell. Before he could throw another pitch, the game was halted. Fifty-six minutes later, the umpires deemed the field unplayable and so ended the shortest and wettest All-Star Game ever played, with the National League a 3-2 winner.

SOURCES

In addition to the sources cited in the Notes, the author also consulted Baseball-Reference.com, Retrosheet.com, the *New York Times* and the *St. Louis Post Dispatch*.

NOTES

1   Joe Trimble, "NL Stars Defeat AL in Rain, 3-2," *New York Daily News*, July 9, 1952: 21.

2   Hank Littlehales, "A's Southpaw Fans Side on 13 Pitches," *Philadelphia Inquirer*, July 9, 1952: 45.

3   Gene Ward, "Stengel 'Waited' Too Long," *New York Daily News*, July 9, 1952: 21.

4   "Sauer Recalls Shotton's Snub," *Chicago Tribune*, July 9, 1952: 41.

5   Ward.

6   Littlehales.

ROBERTS TOSSES MARATHON FOR 23RD WIN

September 6, 1952
Philadelphia Phillies 7, Boston Braves 6
(17 Innings, First Game of a Doubleheader)

By Alan Cohen

The annual drive for statistics to validate an otherwise disappointing season brought the Boston Braves to Philadelphia's Shibe Park on September 6, 1952, for a twilight-night doubleheader with the Phillies. The Phillies entered the game in fourth place, but they were 13½ games behind the league-leading Dodgers. The Braves, playing to smallish crowds in Boston, were in sixth place, 27 games behind Brooklyn.

The Phillies won the first game, 7-6, on a game-winning homer by Del Ennis leading off the 17th inning, to give Robin Roberts his 23rd win of the season. A crowd of 12,474 looked on as the Braves took a 6-2 lead, only to see the Phillies come from behind and force extra innings.

Roberts had started the game for Philadelphia against Braves rookie Virgil Jester, a former Colorado sandlot star. Roberts threw the first pitch at 6:00 P.M. The Phillies staked Roberts to an early lead, scoring single runs in the second and third innings. In the second inning, singles by Ennis, Smoky Burgess, and Puddin' Head Jones loaded the bases. Putsy Caballero's double-play ball brought Ennis home. An intentional walk to Eddie Waitkus put runners on the corners, and Phillies manager Steve O'Neill ordered a double steal. The throw from Braves catcher Paul Burris

was cut off by shortstop Johnny Logan. Logan threw to third baseman Eddie Mathews, who tagged Burgess out when he broke for home.[1]

In the third inning Connie Ryan walked with one out and was brought home on singles by Richie Ashburn and Mel Clark. The inning ended when Ashburn tried to score from third on Ennis's foul fly caught by shortstop Logan. Logan's throw to catcher Burris was in plenty of time to nail Ashburn.

The Braves tied the score with two runs in the fourth inning. Singles by Logan and Sid Gordon preceded a game-tying triple by Mathews. In the sixth, two Phillies errors helped the Braves go ahead, 5-2. After a bunt single by Earl Torgeson and a single to center by Gordon, second baseman Ryan's error on a grounder by Mathews allowed Torgeson to score. Third baseman Jones's wild throw on Burris's groundball paved the way for a two-run single by Jack Dittmer. The Braves' sixth run came in the eighth inning on rookie Mathews' 21st homer of the season.

A four-run rally by the Phillies tied the score in the eighth. Clark, whose third-inning single had extended his hitting streak to 14 consecutive games, led off with a double and came home on a single by Burgess. A single by Jones knocked

Jester from the game and the Braves brought in Sheldon Jones, who was not the answer they were looking for. Johnny Wyrostek batted hit for shortstop Caballero and singled Burgess home. Jackie Mayo, who had replaced Waitkus at first base when Waitkus suffered a groin pull, doubled to left, just beating the throw to second by left fielder Gordon as Jones and Wyrostek scored, tying the game at 6-6.

The Braves had a chance to regain the lead in the ninth inning. Logan singled with two outs and Torgeson singled to right. Logan overran third base and was thrown out when catcher Burgess took the throw from the outfield and threw the ball to third baseman Jones, who tagged out Logan. Sheldon Jones retired the Phillies in the ninth as the home team stranded two runners.

The game went into extra innings. When Sheldon Jones came off the field after pitching the 10th inning, he was feeling feverish, and it was determined that Jones was suffering from a virus infection. It was later determined that Jones had been sick the entire day and had not disclosed his illness to the team.[2] Jones was sent back to the team hotel. Bob Chipman came on to pitch for the Braves in the bottom of the 11th.

Chipman subdued the Philadelphia bats from the time he entered the game until he allowed the blast by Ennis. In that time, he allowed only one hit, a single by Willie Jones in the 12th inning. In five of his six innings pitched, Chipman retired the side in order. Roberts, meanwhile, retired the side in order in only four of his 17th innings, yielding 18 hits and walking three batters.

In the 12th, the Braves mounted a threat when Torgeson reached on an infield hit and Gordon bunted for a hit. With runners on first and second, Mathews, who had already tripled and homered in the game, stepped to the plate. Braves manager Charlie Grimm ordered Mathews to bunt. The move backfired as Mathews forced Torgeson at third base. Grimm then outdid

himself sending up pinch-hitter Walker Cooper, who hit into an inning-ending double play. Over the next four innings, Roberts pitched in and out of trouble stranding five batters.

After Roberts retired the side in order in the 17th inning, for the first time since the seventh, Chipman came out for his seventh inning of work. He faced only one batter, Ennis. It was almost 10:00 P.M. when Chipman threw his last pitch, and Ennis lined it to deep left field for a walk-off homer. The longest game of the season in terms of innings was over in 3 hours and 50 minutes.

The hitting star of the game, prior to the Ennis homer, had been Mathews. Mathews went on to hit four more homers in September, including three in one game against the Dodgers on September 27 at Brooklyn, giving him 25 for his rookie year. Among those homers was the game-winning homer in the bottom of the ninth against the Cubs in a 1-0 game at Braves Field in the first game of a doubleheader on September 14. It was the last game the Braves would win at Braves Field.

Chipman was at the end of his major-league career. The loss was the last decision in a 12-year career in which he went 51-46. He appeared in six more games with the Braves in 1952.

Roberts pitched the entire game for the Phillies for his major-league leading 23rd win. It broke a tie between him and Bobby Shantz of the Philadelphia Athletics. Roberts finished the season with a 28-7 record. He finished second in the MVP balloting in 1952. The complete game on September 6 was his third in succession. The streak of complete-game starts extended into the following season and reached 28 in all. Roberts led the National League in complete games in each season from 1952 through 1956. The 1952 season was his third of six in a row with 20 or more wins and the best year of his 19-year Hall of Fame career.

There was a second game that night. It got underway after 10:00 P.M. and was suspended

In one of the most impressive six-year stretches in baseball history (1950-1955), Robin Roberts won 20 or more games each season with the Phillies while leading the NL in wins four times, in games started all six seasons, complete games four times, and in innings pitched five times. (Photo by Kidwiler Collection/Diamond Images/Getty Images)

because of a midnight curfew in the bottom of the eighth inning with the Braves leading 3-1 and the Phillies threatening. With runners at first and second and Mel Clark at the plate, the count went to 2-2. At 11:59 P.M., umpire Frank Dascoli stopped the game. The game was completed without further scoring the next afternoon.

The Phillies, led by Roberts's 28 wins, finished the season at 87-67, 9½ games behind the Dodgers. The loss dropped the Braves to seventh place, and it was there that they would finish the season, their last year in Boston. Their record in their final season as the Boston Braves was 64-89.

SOURCES

In addition to Baseball-Reference.com and the sources shown in the Notes, the author used the following:

Baumgartner, Stan. "Phils Nip Braves in 17th, 7-6; Ennis' Homer Wins; 2nd Suspended," *Philadelphia Inquirer*, September 7, 1952: 1S-2S.

Gillooly, John. "Braves Bow in 17th, 7-6," *Boston Sunday Advertiser*, September 7, 1952: 35.

Mack, Gene Jr. "Ennis Homer Beats Tribe in 17th, 7-6," *Boston Sunday Globe*, September 7, 1952: 47

NOTES

1   Associated Press, "Roberts Goes 17 Innings for 7-6 Phillies Victory," *Tampa Bay Times*, September 7, 1952: S1.

2   "Jones Display of Gameness May Have Cost Braves Game," *The Sporting News*, September 17, 1952: 19.

Athletics Prevail on Final Opening Day in Philadelphia

April 13, 1954
Philadelphia Athletics 6, Boston Red Sox 4

By Nathan Bierma

No one knew it was the Athletics' last home opener in Philadelphia, though if you looked closely you could see the writing on the peeling walls of recently rechristened Connie Mack Stadium. But Opening Day 1954 felt less like the end of an era and more like the beginning of one.

The uniforms were new, after the franchise dropped the block "A" and elephant mascot from their jerseys, replacing them with the scripted "Athletics" in royal blue with red trim – in an attempt to reinforce the use of the team's often-abbreviated full nickname.[1]

The players were new: Only two Opening Day starters returned from the previous year after an offseason roster overhaul.[2] So many starting spots were up for grabs as Philly broke camp that *The Sporting News* calculated the team had 184 potential lineup combinations.[3]

The fans' fervor was new. A crowd of a few hundred surprised the team at the airport when it returned from spring training, and the attendance of 16,331 was the team's best Opening Day showing in five years. Opening Day always brings optimism, but this year the crowd's "air of enthusiasm," *The Sporting News* said, "was in marked contrast to the atmosphere of palled tolerance" during their team's seventh-place finish the previous season.[4]

The invigorated crowd, including Connie Mack Stadium's namesake himself, sitting in box seats on the third-base line, took in the Opening Day pageantry. "The Philadelphia Band played periodically throughout, and Mrs. Dorothy Parker Langdon kept the stadium's new pipe organ singing," reported the *Philadelphia Inquirer*. "Councilman James H.J. Tate did not dislodge a gardenia in presenting Manager [Eddie] Joost with a nine-foot horseshoe of flowers … and Mayor Joseph S. Clark threw out the first ball straight and true."[5]

The A's – or, as the front office now insisted, the Athletics – took command of the game in their first turn at bat against Lou Boudreau's Boston Red Sox and starter Mel Parnell. With two on and two out in the first, Don Bollweg, nursing a broken finger, rammed a line drive up the middle to score Vic Power. Then Bill Renna drove a double down the left-field line that scored Gus Zernial and Bollweg, and Philadelphia was out in front 3-0.

Starting pitcher Bobby Shantz, coming off an injury-shortened season after winning the 1952 American League MVP award, shrugged off one baserunner in each of his first two innings. But Boston broke through in the third on three straight batters, as Billy Consolo singled, Jim Piersall doubled, and Jackie Jensen hit a sacrifice fly to make it 3-1.

In the fourth inning, the Red Sox struck again on a solo home run by Sammy White onto the left-field roof, and the score was 3-2. It was in this inning, Shantz said afterward, that he felt pangs in the shoulder he had injured the previous season against these same Red Sox.[6] The spasms worsened in the fifth, though Shantz escaped a one-out jam with runners at the corners by getting George Kell to hit into a double play.

Zernial did his part to give his starter some pain relief, blasting a two-run homer in the bottom of the fifth to give the Athletics a 5-2 lead. But after just one pitch in the sixth, Shantz "fell back as though struck," the *Inquirer* wrote, and Joost lifted him immediately.[7]

Pressed into emergency service to make his major-league debut, Philadelphia pitcher Ozzie Van Brabant initially faltered. Billy Goodman finished his interrupted at-bat with a single, advanced on Dick Gernert's groundout to the mound, and came home on White's single to left to cut the Philadelphia lead to two runs.

Van Brabant collected himself and notched the next five outs with only one more baserunner. The Athletics loaded the bases in the bottom of the seventh, but when player-manager Joost inserted himself as a pinch-hitter for Van Brabant, he flied out to center off Red Sox reliever Tom Herrin to end the inning.

Joost brought in another rookie, Bill Upton, to start the eighth inning, and watched him load the bases with two outs before getting pinch-hitter Harry Agganis to foul out to right. In the bottom of the eighth, the Athletics loaded the bases again, this time against Joe Dobson. When Boudreau brought in Ellis Kinder, the reliever walked Renna to add another run to Philly's tally and make it 6-3.

Upton came back out for the ninth and allowed a homer to Jensen and a double by Goodman. Down two with two outs, Dick Genert launched a liner to third baseman Pete Suder.

"Suder, the only Mack player except Zernial who was in the A's opening-day lineup last year, executed a high, twisting jump – and came down with the ball for the final out," the *Inquirer* wrote. Philadelphia had won, 6-4.

"For this one day, at least, they are tied for first place in the American League," the *Inquirer* wrote of the victors, unleashing a string of peppy participles to summarize the action: "Big Gus Zernial walloped a two-run homer, darting Spook Jacobs rapped out four hits, raw-boned Bill Renna drove in three runs, bandaged Don Bollweg connected twice at the plate."[8]

The irrepressible optimism of Opening Day would prove fleeting. After a 6-5 record in April, the Athletics tallied 103 losses for the season to finish last in the American League. Shantz made only one more appearance all season. Van Brabant and Upton each made only one more appearance in their careers. The crowds would dwindle again. And the Philadelphia franchise, which proudly opened a then-majestic Shibe Park 45 years earlier, would limp out of town after the season, sold to Arnold Johnson in Kansas City despite a desperate bid by Roy Mack.

Robert Warrington summed up the sunset of the Athletics in Philadelphia for the *Baseball Research Journal*. "A bad team, sparse crowds, burdensome debt, and internal strife all were set against the backdrop of playing in an old ballpark located in a declining neighborhood with limited parking and bad transportation," he wrote.[9]

But on Opening Day, joy chased away all dreariness. As the Philadelphia faithful celebrated their triumphant American League team, the *Inquirer* wrote, "all left with the conviction that pre-season reports of their verve and animation had not been exaggerated."[10]

SOURCES

In addition to the sources cited in the Notes, the author accessed Retrosheet.org, Baseball-Reference.com, SABR.org, and *The Sporting News* archive via Paper of Record.

NOTES

1   Art Morrow, "Athletics Ditch Elephant, Familiar 'A' – Add Color," *The Sporting News,* February 10, 1954: 2.

2   Art Morrow, "Athletics' List Represents Biggest Turnover Since '46," *The Sporting News,* January 13, 1954: 9.

3   Art Morrow, "Vic Power Listed as Triple-Threat Man for Athletics," *The Sporting News,* February 17, 1954: 18.

4   Art Morrow, "Joost's Boys Display Rejuvenated Look to Philly Followers," *The Sporting News,* April 21, 1954: 17.

5   Art Morrow, "Shantz Reinjures Shoulder as A's Top Bosox 6-4," *Philadelphia Inquirer,* April 14, 1954: 47.

6   Morrow, "Shantz Reinjures Shoulder."

7   Morrow, "Shantz Reinjures Shoulder."

8   Morrow, "Shantz Reinjures Shoulder."

9   Robert Warrington, "Departure Without Dignity: The Athletics Leave Philadelphia," *Baseball Research Journal,* Fall 2010. Accessed at sabr. org/research/departure-without-dignity-athletics-leave-philadelphia.

10 Morrow, "Shantz Reinjures Shoulder."

ROBERTS BEING ROBERTS

June 17, 1954
Philadelphia Phillies 3, St. Louis Cardinals 2
(15 Innings)

By Jim Sweetman

In June of 1954, Phillies fans had a good idea of what they were going to see when Robin Roberts was on the mound.

Although Roberts and his remaining Whiz Kids teammates had been unable to repeat their team success in the years after 1950, Roberts was at the top of his game individually. Between 1950 and 1953, he earned four All-Star Game appearances and led the league in starts four times, in innings pitched three times, and in wins and complete games twice. He also earned his first league strikeout crown in 1953.

On the evening of June 17, 1954, Roberts and the Phillies faced the St. Louis Cardinals at Connie Mack Stadium. The visitors trailed the home team by one game in the National League standings. Both teams were already losing ground to New York's powerhouse National League teams, which had started to run away with the pennant race. One silver lining for the Cardinals was that they seemed to have Roberts' number so far in 1954, tagging him for 14 earned runs in four starts (one lasting only two innings). Starting for the visitors was Gerry Staley, an All-Star the previous two seasons and owner of three straight seasons of 17 wins or more. Their silver lining, however, was not as shiny as it could be – Staley

entered the day with a record of 3 wins and 6 losses and an ERA of 6.25.

Roberts' own record stood at a less-than-stellar 7-7, but he had gotten only 10 runs of support in his seven losses and had thrown a couple of gems earlier in the year. In April he one-hit Milwaukee, allowing only a third-inning double to Del Crandall. Facing Cincinnati in May, he gave up a leadoff homer to Bobby Adams, then retired the next 27 batters. Considering these games and his 2.72 ERA, the Phillies faithful might have expected a one-sided affair. Instead, they got more than their money's worth.

The Cardinals struck early, getting a solo home run from catcher Bill Sarni in the second inning. It was the 16th round-tripper yielded by Roberts so far in the season, on his way to a league-leading 35 for the season. Roberts buckled down and retired the next 14 batters in order.

The Phillies responded in the bottom of the fourth without recording a hit. First baseman Earl Torgeson led off the inning with a walk. Left fielder Del Ennis hit a shot to third that was fielded by Ray Jablonski, who made the stop but his throw to first was in the dirt, allowing Ennis to reach and sending Torgeson to third.[1] Second

---

baseman Granny Hamner then flied out to right field, and Torgeson scored.

The two teams traded zeros until the top of the seventh inning, when Red Schoendienst led off with a single to center. Stan Musial followed with another single, sending Schoendienst to third. With Jablonski at bat, Musial tried to swipe second, but he was nabbed by Phillies' backstop Smoky Burgess and Hamner. Jablonski then hit one deep enough to center to score Schoendienst, giving St. Louis the lead.

In the eighth the Phillies had a chance to score but couldn't cash in. With two outs, Staley walked Richie Ashburn, Torgeson, and Ennis. The rally fell short when Hamner topped a ball to Staley, who forced Ashburn at home.[2]

Roberts continued to hold the Cardinals in check, giving his team a chance in the ninth. Staley induced two groundball outs, bringing up shortstop Bobby Morgan. Morgan had just missed a home run when he hit the left-field wall with a blast in the fifth, settling for a double.[3] This time, he hit a 2-and-2 pitch into the left-field seats to tie the game. Staley got the last out of the ninth to send the game to extra innings.[4]

Both pitchers continued to stymie the opposing batters, although the Cardinals got runners into scoring position twice. In the 12th inning, Solly Hemus, who had replaced Jablonski at third base, hit a two-out triple, but ended up stranded. The next inning, Roberts gave up a single to Alex Grammas. With Staley due up, Cardinals manager Eddie Stanky sent up pinch-hitter Joe Frazier. Roberts struck him out, but left fielder Rip Repulski singled to left, sending Grammas

to second. Roberts again neutralized the threat by getting Wally Moon (the 1954 Rookie of the Year) to fly out to left.

To replace Staley on the mound, Stanky called in Joe Presko, a former starter in his first year as a full-time reliever. Despite coming into the game with an ERA above 6.00, Presko threw two clean innings with three strikeouts. Roberts continued to roll as well, allowing only a one-out single to Musial in the 14th inning and retiring the side in the 15th.

It was Roberts who started the winning rally. Leading off the home 15th, he worked a walk. Willie "Puddin' Head" Jones sacrificed him to second. Ashburn followed with a groundout to short that moved Roberts to third. The Cardinals walked the left-handed-hitting Torgeson intentionally to have Presko face a slumping Ennis, who was hitless in five at-bats. The move backfired when Ennis hit a line single to right-center on Presko's first pitch to him, sending Roberts home with the winning run.[5]

Roberts finished the game with 10 hits, 7 strikeouts, and no walks in 15 innings. So far he had allowed only 14 walks in 130⅔ innings.[6] It was the longest Phillies game by innings of 1954, and the second longest in Roberts' career. While Chris Short also went 15 innings in 1965, no Phillies pitcher has thrown more innings in a game as of 2020.

Asked about his complete games, Roberts once said he would happily turn the ball over if the team had someone better, but it didn't.[7] The June 17, 1954, game shows that he was willing to stick to that view no matter how long it took.

SOURCES

In addition to the contemporary news sources listed in the Notes, the author relied on information from Retrosheet, Baseball-reference.com, and *The Sporting News*.

NOTES

1   "Phils Turn Back Cardinals in 15th Behind Roberts," *Camden* (New Jersey) *Courier-Post*, June 18, 1954.

2   Bob Broeg, "Cards, Back to .500 After Roberts Wins, Face Giants Tonight," *St. Louis Post-Dispatch*, June 18, 1954.

3   Broeg.

4   Stan Baumgartner, "Roberts Goes 15, Beats Cards, 3-2 On Ennis' Single," *Philadelphia Inquirer*, June 18, 1954.

5   Broeg.

6   Associated Press, "Roberts Goes 15 Innings to Rack Up Eighth Win," *Jersey Journal* (Jersey City, New Jersey), June 18, 1954.

7   Don Bostrom, "Robin Roberts Epitomized 'Compete Game' in the '50s," *Allentown* (Pennsylvania) *Morning Call*, August 22, 1999.

OUT WITH A WHIMPER:
THE ATHLETICS' FINAL GAME IN PHILADELPHIA

September 19, 1954
New York Yankees 4, Philadelphia Athletics 2

By John Bauer

As their 1954 season staggered toward its conclusion, the Philadelphia Athletics would host the New York Yankees in the home finale at Connie Mack Stadium. The game, however, was bereft of suspense for either team. For the Yankees, winners of the previous five World Series, their dethroning by the Cleveland Indians was complete. The day before, Cleveland clinched the AL pennant with a 3-2 win over the Detroit Tigers. The Yankees beat the Athletics, 6-5, to no avail. Few Philadelphians could be bothered to attend, with a mere 1,834 witnessing that game under overcast conditions. For the Athletics, their record stood at 49-98, an astounding 58 games behind the Indians, and their future in doubt. Reports of their likely relocation occupied almost as many column inches as their on-field activities, the off-field activities providing the only remaining uncertainty to a season of misery.

The Yankees owned a 15-game winning streak over the Athletics, and manager Casey Stengel sent Tom Morgan to the mound to extend it. Morgan had claimed a regular spot in the Yankees rotation over the past two months, and his personal record against Philadelphia included four of his 11 wins so far in the season. Art Ditmar, a 25-year-old right-hander, would see

his first major-league action since June; he had struggled earlier in the season and his 0-4, 7.45 ERA mark awaited his return to the big leagues. Player-manager Eddie Joost had allowed nine players to end their seasons early and depart the team, which may have been responsible for Ditmar seeing some late-season action.

Ditmar opened the game by facing Gil McDougald, and the Yankee slapped the ball into right field for a leadoff single. McDougald's effort came to naught, as Irv Noren's liner to Bill Wilson in center field and routine groundouts by Mickey Mantle and Yogi Berra closed the top of the first. Ditmar allowed back-to-back walks with one out in the second, but Jerry Coleman's double-play ball ended the frame. Morgan led off the Yankees' third with a single to right, but the top of the order went down in order. Mantle's two-out bomb to right field, however, required Vic Power to make a "spectacular jumping catch with his back against the wall."[1] Meanwhile, Morgan did not allow a Philadelphia baserunner during the first pass through the home lineup, and the game remained scoreless through three.

The Athletics ended Morgan's nascent bid for a perfect game when Pete Suder hit a leadoff single in the bottom of the fourth. Lou Limmer followed with a single, and the Athletics appeared to be in business with Jim Finigan up next. A member of the Yankees organization at this time the previous season, Finigan had most productive season of any Philadelphia regular in 1954. Finigan enjoyed a solid rookie season in Philadelphia after injuries to Suder and Joost opened up third base for him. GM and co-owner Earle Mack said of the 26-year-old, "Why, if we wanted to trade or sell him, I'll bet we could write our own ticket."[2] Finigan's season would see him finish runner-up to Yankees pitcher Bob Grim for Rookie of the Year honors. In this at-bat, he lined out to Noren in right field. Gus Zernial's grounder to Coleman at shortstop then triggered an inning-ending double play.

The Yankees almost broke the deadlock in the top of the fifth. Coleman and Morgan popped up for the first two outs, but McDougald and Noren each singled to center. Ditmar walked Mantle to load the bases with cleanup hitter Berra coming to the plate. Berra smacked the ball toward right field, but his line shot ended up in Power's glove. The game was half-over and still scoreless. It seemed likely to stay that way when McDougald snared Power's liner and Morgan struck out Wilson to start the Philadelphia fifth. Jack Littrell drew a walk from Morgan and Jim Robertson singled to keep the inning alive. Ditmar was due up next, but he had yet to collect a hit in his eight prior major-league plate appearances. Joost thus opted for pinch-hitter Don Bollweg, whose hopping groundball was too much for Yankees first baseman Eddie Robinson. Everyone was safe on the error. Suder's single to center field broke the deadlock, with Littrell and Robertson crossing the plate. Limmer lined out to Robinson for the third out, but the Athletics now led, 2-0.

Joost gave the ball to Charlie Bishop to face the Yankees in the sixth. Robinson flied out to Power for the first out. After Bob Cerv and Andy Carey hit back-to-back singles, Stengel called on Enos Slaughter to bat in place of the weak-hitting

Coleman. Slaughter flied out to Zernial in left field, bringing up Morgan. Searching for runs, Stengel selected Joe Collins as a pinch-hitter, but Collins flied out to Wilson for the final out of the New York sixth. Johnny Sain, now 36 and operating as a type of closer before that role was recognized, took the mound in the home half of the inning. The Athletics loaded the bases with one out through a walk to Zernial and singles by Power and Wilson, but the run scorers from the prior inning could not pad the lead. Littrell flied out to Willy Miranda, now playing shortstop in place of Coleman, and Robertson struck out to end the inning.

Bishop walked McDougald and Noren in the top of the seventh, which might have seemed ominous with Mantle and Berra due up. Mantle, however, popped up to first baseman Limmer in foul territory and Berra's line out to Power doubled Noren off first base. In the bottom of the seventh, Berra muffed a two-out popup by Limmer in foul territory. With the reprieve, Limmer singled and stole second base. Finigan's strikeout ended the frame.

Joost brought on Moe Burtschy for Philadelphia in the top of the eighth. The veteran right-hander had pitched commendably in relief during the season, but the Yankees would break through against him. Robinson led off with a single to right, and Stengel replaced the 33-year-old with pinch-running teenager and bonus baby Frank Leja. After Cerv lined out to Wilson, Carey "lashed to left"[3] for a single that advanced Leja to second. Lou Berberet made his first major-league plate appearance hitting in place of Miranda, and the young catcher made the most of his opportunity. Berberet smacked a single to right for his first hit and first RBI, as Leja scored for New York. Rizzuto ran for Berberet, and Moose Skowron batted for Sain. Skowron was out on his grounder back to Burtschy, but the runners advanced to second and third. With the lineup turning over again, McDougald came to the plate. The second baseman "belted the ball"[4] for a home run over the fence in upper left-center. Three runs scored, and the Yankees grabbed the lead, 4-2. Noren's grounder to Suder provided the final out, but the result was academic. The damage was done.

Jim Konstanty had opened the season in Philadelphia with the Phillies. Four years removed from his MVP season with the 1950 pennant-winning Whiz Kids, the Yankees claimed the 37-year-old off waivers in August. Stengel gave Konstanty the assignment of securing the win. Konstanty did not allow a baserunner in the eighth or ninth to earn New York's 100th win of the season, more wins than achieved during the prior five World Series-winning seasons.

The loss was the 99th of the year for the Athletics; they would finish the season with a mark of 51-103. The Sunday afternoon tilt drew a mere 1,715, easily the worst attended major-league game that day. That "crowd" resulted in an aggregate season attendance of 305,362, well below the 600,000 the club stated it needed to break even[5] and less than half of the 738,991 who came out to watch the 75-79 Phillies. It should have been no surprise that stories persisted of the club's impending relocation. Earle Mack would speak optimistically about 1955 despite the last-place finish: "I do not feel we need too much."[6] Days later, though, there were stories of Roy and Earle Mack attending meetings in Chicago with the intent to sell the club to a syndicate led by Arnold Johnson, and AL President Will Harridge signaling his assent to the transaction.[7] Papers would need to be signed and votes would need to be lined up to support the sale to Johnson and relocation to Kansas City, but the Athletics had played their last game as a Philadelphia franchise.

SOURCES

In addition to the articles cited in the Notes, the author consulted baseball-reference.com.

NOTES

1   Art Morrow, "3-Run Clout by Gil Wins 100th Game for New York," *Philadelphia Inquirer*, September 20, 1954: 22.

2   Morrow, "Rookie Jim Finigan Only Bright Spot in 18th Basement Finish by Athletics," *The Sporting News*, September 29, 1954: 30.

3   Morrow, "3-Run Clout": 24.

4   Louis Effrat, "Yanks Register 100th Victory as Rally Beats Athletics, 4-2," *New York Times*, September 20, 1954: 27.

5   "Only 1,715 See A's Finale; 305,362 Attendance for '54," *The Sporting News*, September 29, 1954: 30.

6   "Experience to Aid A's Kids," *The Sporting News*, September 29, 1954: 6.

7   Morrow, "American League Wants Fate of Athletics Settled This Week," *Philadelphia Inquirer*, September 21, 1954: 26.

DEL ENNIS BELTS THREE HOMERS

July 23, 1955
Philadelphia Phillies 7, St. Louis Cardinals 2

By Joseph Wancho

On July 22, 1955, two different scenarios were playing out in the American and National League standings.

In the AL, Chicago (56-35) was mere percentage points ahead of New York (57-36) for first place. Cleveland (55-38) was two games back and Boston (53-40) trailed by four games.

Brooklyn, aided by a 52-19 record from April through June, was alone atop the National League. The Dodgers were not even looking over their shoulder. The Milwaukee Braves provided the closest competition and they were 14½ games in back of Brooklyn with a week to go in July. Brooklyn was rolling toward its fifth pennant in nine years. The rest of the league was playing out the string and offering little resistance thus far.

Two of those teams playing out their schedule were the Philadelphia Phillies and the St. Louis Cardinals. The Phillies won the flag in 1950, but since then were treading in the middle of the pack in the NL. The Cardinals had great success in the previous decade, winning four pennants and three World Series championships. But they had fallen on hard times. After second-place finishes in 1948 and 1949, the Cardinals found themselves much like the Phillies: in the middle of the pack.

St. Louis came a-calling to Connie Mack Stadium on July 22 to begin a five-game set with the Phillies. Philadelphia (47-48) was on a 10-game winning streak, and had risen from seventh place to fourth. The Cardinals were not too shabby themselves, winning 12 of their last 19 games. But they were stymied in sixth place with a 42-46 record.

The series began with a twilight-night doubleheader on Friday evening with each team winning a game. Murry Dickson won the opener, his eighth victory. But the Cardinals bounced back in the nightcap behind Harvey Haddix and pounded Philadelphia, 8-1.

The pitching matchup for the third game of the series was a contrast of experience. St. Louis started Willard Schmidt (1-0, 0.66 ERA), while the Phillies sent the venerable Robin Roberts (15-7, 2.84 ERA) to the hill. Schmidt had made his major-league debut in 1952 with the Cardinals, but often split his seasons between St. Louis and the club's farm teams. The 1955 season was no exception: He began the year at Omaha of the Triple-A American Association, posting a 12-5 record and a 2.56 ERA. Recalled by the Cardinals, he was making his second start for them. (Four days earlier, he had beaten the New York Giants at the Polo Grounds on a four-hitter, pitching his first major-league complete game.)

Roberts was having another masterful season with Philadelphia. His 15 victories were second in the league to Brooklyn's Don Newcombe (16). Roberts led the league in complete games (17) and was second in ERA and strikeouts (109)

It was Ladies Day at the ballpark, with an announced crowd of 16,999 (5,595 paid) at the matinee affair.

The Phillies struck first, in the bottom of the first inning. Richie Ashburn led off with a single to center field. After Bobby Morgan popped out to second and Glen Gorbous flied out to right, Del Ennis stepped to the plate and deposited a Schmidt fastball in the center-field seats. It was Ennis's 17th home run of the season and it gave the Phillies a 2-0 lead.

Roberts protected the lead, blanking the Cardinals for five innings. But St. Louis reached Roberts for a run in the top of the sixth. With two down, Stan Musial singled to left field. Bill Virdon followed with a double to right-center to plate Musial.

The 2-1 lead was short-lived, however, as Gorbous led off the bottom of the inning with a single down the right-field line and scored when Ennis again got hold of a Schmidt fastball and deposited it in the left-field seats for two more runs and a 4-1 advantage.

Brooks Lawrence relieved Schmidt in the bottom of the seventh inning for St. Louis. But Ennis showed that he was not partial about which pitcher was on the mound for the opposition. He came up in the seventh with two men on and sent a slider from Lawrence some 400 feet away as it banged off the façade of the left-field stands and bounded back onto the playing field.

Bill Sarni smacked his third homer of the season, a solo shot, off Roberts in the ninth. That made the final score 7-2, with all the Phillies runs driven in by Ennis.

Roberts raised his record to 16-7 with the win. He scattered nine hits, struck out five, and did not walk a batter. Schmidt took the loss to even his record at 1-1. For the season, Roberts led the league in wins (23), innings pitched (305), and complete games (26). He also surrendered the most home runs (41) and runs (137).

The Phillies swept the Cardinals the next day in a doubleheader to close out the series. The homestand had begun on July 14, and the Phillies had an incredible run in front of the locals. They went 14-2 in that stretch. Ennis went 24-for-57, with six home runs, two doubles, and a .421 batting average. For the season, he raised his batting average to .296 from .261 in 1954, changing boos to cheers from fans in the left-field stands. The three home runs were a career high. He matched his one-game RBI high; he had also driven in seven runs on July 27, 1950.

Philadelphia manager Mayo Smith knew what he had in Ennis. "Don't forget, besides hitting as well as he did, Del played great defensive ball," said Smith of Ennis during their winning streak. "Catches he made saved at least four of those games we won."[1]

Ennis led the Phillies in home runs in eight of his 11 seasons with the team. His 259 homers for the Phillies ranked him third all-time in team history as of 2022, trailing Mike Schmidt (548) and Ryan Howard (382).

Ennis was the first Phillies hitter to smack three home runs in a game since Del Wilber did it on August 27, 1951.

Philadelphia finished the 1955 season in fourth place with a 77-77 record. St. Louis completed its season with a seventh-place finish and a 68-86 record.

SOURCES

The author accessed Baseball-Reference.com for box scores/play-by-play information and other data, as well as Retrosheet.org.

baseball-reference.com/boxes/PHI/PHI195507230. shtml

retrosheet.org/boxesetc/1955/B07230PHI1955.htm

Also accessed were the following:

Baumgartner, Stan. "Ennis Hits 3 HRs, Roberts Wins 16th," *Philadelphia Inquirer*, July 24, 1955: 1-S.

Broeg, Bob. "Ennis's Three Homers, Seven RBI's Beat Cards, 7-2," *St. Louis Post-Dispatch*, July 24, 1955.

NOTES

1   Art Morrow, "Hats Off..." *The Sporting News*, August 3, 1955: 17.

ROBIN ROBERTS WINS 20TH GAME FOR SIXTH STRAIGHT SEASON

August 19, 1955
Philadelphia Phillies 3, Brooklyn Dodgers 2

By Gregory H. Wolf

It was a matchup of the NL's two best pitchers: the Philadelphia Phillies' Robin Roberts and the Brooklyn Dodgers' Don Newcombe. It was also a rematch of the aces' last clash, just five days earlier in the first game of a twin bill at Ebbets Field, when both went the distance, hurling 10 grueling frames, with Roberts emerging victorious, 3-2. Roberts entered this game leading the senior circuit in wins (19), innings (238⅔), and ERA (2.87) while Newk was second in all three categories (18, 196⅓, 2.93).

A 28-year-old right-hander, Roberts was a six-time All-Star, had won 20-plus games in each of the last five seasons, the latter three leading the NL, including a career-best 28 in 1952. While Roberts relied on a moving fastball and an array of breaking balls with pinpoint accuracy, Newcombe was a study in brute strength. He overpowered hitters with his heater and exhibited control as impressive as Roberts, but unlike his counterpart, liked to pitch inside and never shied away from a brushback pitch. A four-time All-Star, Newcombe won 20 in 1951 before missing two complete seasons serving in the military, and had rounded back into form in '55 after an inconsistent campaign (9-8, 4.55 ERA) in '54.

Roberts had the advantage of playing on home turf in the City of Brotherly Love. Skipper Mayo Smith's squad was in fourth place, but a game under .500 (60-61) as they prepared to inaugurate a six-team, 16-game homestand. They trailed "Dem Bums" by a whopping 20 games. Skipper Walter Alston's squad boasted the best record in baseball (78-39), but had lost six of its last 10 games.

While the Dodgers' 14-game lead over the second-place Milwaukee Braves afforded Alston the luxury to contemplate the World Series, Dodgers owner Walter O'Malley had more serious concerns. On the day of the game he met with New York City Mayor Robert F. Wagner and city Parks Commissioner Robert Moses to plead his case for a new taxpayer-funded ballpark in Brooklyn. "The problem is bigger than the Dodgers," he exclaimed, and feared that both the Dodgers and the New York Giants would relocate without new ballparks.[1]

A gorgeous Friday evening with temperatures in the high 80s resulted in the largest crowd of the season (35,444) thus far at Connie Mack Stadium, the steel-and-concrete ballpark that had been known as Shibe Park from its opening in 1909 through the 1952 season, though the Phillies had played there only since 1938.

The story for the first seven innings was Newcombe. He started out "with the determination of a man bent of revenge," gushed sportswriter Art Morrow of the *Philadelphia Inquirer*,[2] while Dick Young of the *New York Daily News* opined that he was "virtually unhittable."[3] The husky, 6-foot-4 former Negro League star yielded just two hits (a first-inning single by Granny Hamner and a double by Andy Seminick in the third). Newcombe was riding a personal two-game losing streak after starting the season on an 18-1 tear, but had won his last eight decisions in Philadelphia.

Compared with Newcombe, Roberts seemed to be "almost in a constant scramble," submitted Morrow.[4] Roberts pitched to contact, and the Dodgers were obliging him. He yielded a single in each of the first four innings, including three times to the leadoff hitter, but was the beneficiary of three double plays.

Roberts' luck finally ran out in the fifth when Gil Hodges lined a leadoff single and then scored on Sandy Amoros's two-out double, which "dented the right-field wall," noted Morrow.[5]

After Roberts enjoyed a one-two-three sixth, Roy Campanella sent his second pitch of the seventh on a line-drive trajectory that smashed "against the left-center balcony girder," reported the *Inquirer*.[6] It was the Philadelphia-native's 27th round-tripper of the season. Roberts worked around a walk to Amoros in the eighth, the sixth time he permitted the leadoff hitter to reach.

The momentum of the game turned in the bottom of the eighth. Eddie Waitkus and Jim Greengrass led off with line-drive singles, drawing Alston to the mound. The Phillies then employed an "unexpected strategy," suggested Roscoe McGowen of the *New York Times*.[7] Seminick faked a bunt and then swung at the first pitch, lining a single to center, to drive in the Phillies' first run of the game. Due to bat was Roberts, a career .143 hitter entering the '55 season.[8] On the other hand, he was baseball's most durable hurler,

and had completed a major-league-most 30, 33, and 29 games the last three seasons, and led the big leagues with 22 (in 29 starts) thus far in '55. So the choice was probably simple for the rookie pilot Smith, though he might have had second thoughts when Roberts grounded back to Newcombe, who initiated a 1-6-3 twin killing. Glenn Gorbous hit an infield popup to end the inning.

Roberts "never looked stronger," cooed Morrow, to begin the ninth.[9] Facing the heart of the Dodgers' thunderous offense which led the majors in runs in 1955, Roberts induced Duke Snider, Campanella, and Hodges to hit three straight infield popups.

Unlike their counterparts, the Phillies were an average offensive team, finishing fifth in runs and seventh in home runs in '55. They caught a break when leadoff hitter Bobby Morgan lined a ball over third baseman Don Hoak's head. According to Morrow, the ball "bounced into foul territory and caromed off the left-field containing screen," enabling Morgan to sprint to second.[10] With the infield drawn in, Hamner singled to right. Cleanup hitter Del Ennis followed with a tailor-made, routine double-play grounder back to the mound. Newcombe "seemed momentarily confused," opined McGowen, and looked initially to third, then threw wildly past a diving Reese at second.[11] Morgan scored to tie the game, and Hamner reached third, Ennis was safe, and there were still no outs. To the plate stepped Willie Jones, the hero in the Roberts-Newcombe matchup five days earlier by virtue of his game-winning two-out single to drive in Richie Ashburn in the 10th. Puddin' Head sent Newk's second pitch into left field to win the game in dramatic fashion. The official game time was 1 hour and 58 minutes.

Roberts was credited with his 20th victory, marking the sixth consecutive season he won at least 20 games. He became just the fifth pitcher in the twentieth century to accomplish that feat, joining Christy Mathewson (12 consecutive seasons, 1903-1914); Walter Johnson (10 times,

1910-1919), Lefty Grove (seven times, 1927-1933), and Mordecai "Three Finger" Brown (six times, 1906-1911). Since Roberts, the exclusive club has welcomed only one additional member, Warren Spahn, who won 20 or more for six straight seasons (1956-1961), from age 35 to 40.

Roberts finished the season with a big-league-most 23 victories and thus concluded one of the most productive six-year stretches in history. He led the NL in starts all six seasons and in innings in the latter five, and in wins and complete games the latter four campaigns. All the innings, though, took their toll on the 6-foot, 190-pound hurler. Beginning in 1956, Roberts experienced a steep drop-off in effectiveness and was never the same kind of hurler he had been. He led the NL in losses in 1956 and 1957, as his ERA soared to over 4.00. From 1956 through the end of his career, he was essentially a league-average pitcher, going 126-143 (3.78 ERA). He retired after the 1966 season with a 286-245 slate, 3.41 ERA, and 4,688⅔ innings, which ranked 11th in big-league history (and 21st as of 2022). In 1976 Roberts was elected to the Baseball Hall of Fame.

SOURCES

In addition to the sources cited in the Notes, the author accessed Retrosheet.org, Baseball-Reference.com, Newspapers.com, and SABR.org.

NOTES

1   Sydney Gruson, "O'Malley Is Fearful of a One-Team Town," *New York Times*, August 20, 1955: 1.

2   Art Morrow, "35,444 See Roberts Win 20th, 3-2, as Phils Top Brooks with 2 in 9th," *Philadelphia Inquirer*, August 20, 1955: 17.

3   Dick Young, "Robin's 20th Nails Newk, 3-2," (New York) *Daily News*, August 20, 1955: 25.

4   Morrow.

5   Morrow.

6   Morrow.

7   Roscoe McGowen, "Phils Triumph Over Dodgers," *New York Times*, August 20, 1955: 12.

8   In 1955 he batted a career-best .252 and drove in a personal-best 13 runs.

9   Morrow.

10 Morrow.

11 McGowen.

ROBIN ROBERTS WINS 200TH GAME

August 1, 1958
Philadelphia Phillies 3, Chicago Cubs 1

By Josh Berk

Phillies pitcher Robin Roberts took the mound of Connie Mack Stadium on August 1, 1958, with 199 career victories under his belt. The weather that night was hot, as were the team and its star hurler. The Phillies had just swept the Cardinals in three straight as they began the series against the Chicago Cubs. Roberts had won three of his last four starts; the sole loss was a 1-0 gem against the Giants and one of the wins was a complete-game victory over the great **Sandy Koufax** of the Dodgers.

Just a year before, Roberts was not sure he'd reach the 200-victory milestone or even play much longer. Pitching for a last-place team with a sore back and arm trouble in 1957, the only thing he led the league in was losses with 22. His earned run average in '57 was over 4.00 for the second straight year after a six-year stretch in which his ERA totaled 2.53 and he won 20 or more games each season. Hand-wringing headlines appeared like "Has Roberts Lost His Fastball?"[1] He even took a pay cut for the 1958 season.[2] But at age 31 the seven-time All-Star wasn't done.

In the offseason Roberts worked with team trainer Frank "Doc" Wiechec to strengthen his arm and refine his pitching motion.[3] The hard-throwing right-hander wasn't duplicating the dominance that made him the finest pitcher in the league for the first half of the decade,[4] but he was having a very good year by any measure. Without much run support, he had a winning record and an ERA of 2.98 through the end of July. Some velocity on the fastball was gone, but Roberts' control remained excellent. At this late point in the season he had given up just 35 walks in 178 innings for a stellar walks-per-9-innings rate of 1.77.

As the sun lowered in Philadelphia, Roberts took his warm-up tosses. His arm felt good, bolstered by an extra day of rest.[5] Both the fastball and curveball were working, popping smoothly off his right hand. The last time Roberts faced the Cubs he lasted only 2⅓ innings, giving up nine hits and four earned runs, including a homer by longtime nemesis **Ernie Banks**.[6] Banks was in the midst of one of the greatest offensive seasons by a shortstop in major-league history and was known for hitting Roberts particularly well.[7] Neutralizing the cleanup hitter known as "Mr. Cub" would be a key to securing the milestone victory.

Roberts was no doubt thankful not to have to face Banks with men on in the first inning as he set down the first three Cubs hitters in order.

Tony Taylor grounded out, Al Dark struck out, and Lou Jackson grounded to first. The Phillies got a run in their half of the first when Solly Hemus walked, Harry Anderson doubled to right, and Willie "Puddin' Head" Jones brought home Hemus with a sacrifice fly to center.

With a record of 46-50, the Phillies were out of the National League pennant race, but the game had some relevance to the standings. They were in sixth place and hoping to leapfrog the Cubs, who stood one rung ahead of them in the National League.[8]

In the top of the second inning, Banks was the leadoff hitter looking to get the offense started. Roberts struck him out. Cubs left fielder Walt Moryn followed with a double to left for a run-scoring opportunity. Roberts rebounded by getting slugger Dale Long on strikes. With two outs, rookie Sammy Taylor hit a grounder to third. Rather than trying to make the throw to nab the speedy catcher at first, Jones charged at the less than fleet-of-foot Moose Moryn. Moryn scrambled back toward second. Jones flipped the ball to Hemus, who applied the tag for the unusual putout. The side was retired.

Roberts cruised through the next two innings and didn't give up another hit until the fifth, when he left a pitch "a little higher" than intended.[9] Long took it deep for a solo home run, tying the score, 1-1. The Cubs' lanky right-hander Dave Hillman was pitching a very good game as well. After the first inning he gave up only a double in the fourth to Dave Philley and a single in the fifth to All-Star center fielder Richie Ashburn, who was locked in a battle with Willie Mays for the National League lead in batting average.[10] Ashburn was stranded, however, and the score remained 1-1 heading to the bottom of the sixth.

It was the Phillies' troubled first baseman Ed Bouchee who got the big hit, driving in Harry Anderson with a two-out single in the sixth on the first pitch of the at-bat.[11] Bouchee then scored on a triple to left by shortstop Chico Hernandez,

giving the Phils a 3-1 lead. It was up to Roberts to make it stick.

To start the seventh, Roberts avoided danger by getting Banks to pop out to third, making the Cubs slugger 0-for-3. Moryn then struck out and Long grounded to second, ending another quiet inning. The Phillies didn't score in the bottom of the frame, and the score remained in their favor at 3-1.

In the Cubs' half of the eighth, Taylor flied to Ashburn for the first out. Bobby Thomson and pinch-hitter Chuck Tanner both grounded to Hemus at second for the second and third outs and another quick one-two-three inning for Roberts, who was only getting stronger as the game went on.

Cubs reliever Glen Hobbie walked two in the bottom of the eighth but pitched around the trouble and kept the Phils off the board. The inning was a costly one for the Cubs, however, as catcher Sammy Taylor was injured on a foul tip. The ring finger on his right hand had the nail torn back and he was taken to a hospital for X-rays.[12]

Roberts would have to face the top of the Cubs order in the ninth. With a two-run lead, cleanup hitter Banks loomed large. If anyone reached, he would be coming up with men on base and the chance to tie or go ahead. To start the inning, Cubs manager Bob Scheffing pulled the slumping Tony Taylor for pinch-hitter Jim Bolger. Bolger couldn't figure Roberts out any better than his teammates on the starting nine. He flied out to Philley in right for the first out. Veteran third baseman and former All-Star Dark was the next hitter. After his first-inning strikeout he hit the ball well twice — a deep flyout in the fourth and a single in the sixth. He hit the ball hard again this time, but right at shortstop Hernandez. Two down. Just one batter remained.

Coming to the plate was 22-year-old rookie Lou Jackson, a big leaguer for all of a week. He was 0-for-3 in the game and it's doubtful he saw pitching anything like the great Roberts while tearing it up for the Class C Magic Valley Cowboys in '57.[13] With the game on the line, he put a good at-bat together and hit the ball hard, but right at shortstop Hernandez. Chico fielded it without trouble and fired to first to get the out. That was it. Banks remained an onlooker in the on-deck circle with his bat on his shoulder as the scoreboard flashed the final score. Philles win 3-1; Robin Roberts gets his 200th win.

"I had a fastball and a hook and it was enough," Roberts said after the game. "I never felt faster."[14] His control was near perfect. He allowed three hits and no walks, going to a three-ball count only once. He recorded six strikeouts. He now had 200 wins in his career, joining Milwaukee's Warren Spahn and the White Sox' Early Wynn as the only active pitchers in the exclusive club. "One extra day's rest helped me a lot," he said.

He gave credit to his catcher as well. **Carl Sawatski** was the backstop for the night, filling in for regular **Stan Lopata**, who was away from the club due to the birth of his daughter.[15] Roberts praised Sawatski, saying, "One thing that helped me was the way Carl Sawatski handled me. He's done a great job." Roberts liked to share the credit, but it was he who was the master all night, pitching "in a manner reminiscent of his greatest years."[16]

During the postgame celebrations, flashbulbs popped as Roberts caroused in the clubhouse. Still damp with sweat from the evening's exertion, Roberts posed with a wicker basket of bright baseballs on his lap, demonstrating the grip on his deadly four-seam fastball to photographer Bill Ingraham's lens. Other images that ran in newspapers across the country showed Roberts grinning with his manager, Eddie Sawyer, laughing and enjoying a well-deserved beer with teammates, and posing under a large banner with broad black numbers simply declaring the number of the day: 200.

SOURCES

I made use of the play-by-play and box-score details accessed through the Baseball-Reference.com website. I consulted various player, team, and season pages at Baseball-Reference.com in addition to those specifically referenced in the Notes.

NOTES

1   Edgar Williams, "Has Roberts Lost His Fastball?" *Baseball Digest*, January-February 1957: 9-10.

2   "Phils Cut Roberts' Salary," *New York Times*, January 22. 1958: 31.

3   Allen Lewis, "Roberts 3-Hits Cubs, 3-1, for 200th Win," *Philadelphia Inquirer*, August 2, 1958: 14-16.

4   "Robin Roberts." National Baseball Hall of Fame, baseballhall.org/hall-of-famers/roberts-robin.

5   Allen Lewis, "Roberts 3-Hits Cubs, 3-1, for 200th Win," *Philadelphia Inquirer*, August 2, 1958: 14-16.

6   Roberts faced the Cubs on June 4.

7   Banks would go on to become the MVP that year, leading the league in home runs and slugging average. In 1957 his 100th career homer came against Roberts and he would hit more (15) off Roberts than off any other pitcher in his career.

8   The Phillies would go 23-35 the rest of the way and finish in last place.

9   Lewis.

10 Ashburn would go on to edge Mays in the last day of the season, finishing with a .350 average for the batting crown.

11 Bouchee, a Rookie of the Year candidate in 1957, had spent much of the 1958 campaign in a psychiatric ward after an offseason arrest for indecent exposure. See J. Price, "Bouchee Dies at 79," *Spokane Spokesman-Review*, January, 25 2013. Retrieved from spokesman.com/stories/2013/jan/25/bouchee-dies-at-79/.

12 Taylor would miss two weeks of the season. Richard Dozer, "Cub Casualty: Phils, Roberts Best Cubs, 3-1 Veteran Wins 200th," *Chicago Tribune*, August 2, 1958: A1.

13 "Lou Jackson Player Page," Baseball-Reference.com. Retrieved from: baseball-reference.com/register/player.fcgi?id=jackso001lou.

14 Joe Reichler (Associated Press), "Robin Roberts Notches 200th Win," *Hagerstown* (Maryland) *Daily Mail*, August 2, 1958: 14.

15 "Phillie Fodder," *Philadelphia Inquirer*, August 2, 1958: 16.

16 "Roberts Pitches 200th Victory, 3-1," *New York Times*, August 2, 1958: 12.

McCormick Yields Single in 6th, Settles for Rain-Shortened No-Hitter

June 12, 1959
San Francisco Giants 3, Philadelphia Phillies 0
(5 Innings)

By Gregory H. Wolf

The Philadelphia Phillies were finally mounting a rally against Mike McCormick and the San Francisco Giants. Trailing 4-0, they had the bases loaded with no outs in the bottom of the sixth with the heart of their order due to bat. Then the rain came. It was a "torrential downpour," accompanied by thunder and lightning, declared Giants beat writer Walter Judge, "almost like a typhoon."[1] After 40 minutes the infield "tarpaulin look[ed] like a lake," he noted, and the umpires called the game. According to baseball rules, the score reverted back to the end of the fifth inning and all statistics accrued since then were erased. The result was "a freakish – but unofficial – no-hit game," opined the *San Francisco Examiner*.[2] "I was lucky," quipped McCormick. "I'll take it."[3]

Skipper Bill Rigney's Giants were in the City of Brotherly Love, their fourth and final stop of a 16-game road swing, during which they had split their first 12 contests. With a record of 32-25, they were in second place, just two games behind the Milwaukee Braves. Manager Eddie Sawyer's Phillies had the worst record (21-33) among the 16 big-league teams and were headed to their second of four consecutive last-place finishes.

Toeing the rubber for the Giants was McCormick, a 20-year-old, highly touted southpaw, who

debuted as a 17-year-old in 1956. Still a teenager, he emerged as a sturdy starter-reliever in 1958, posting an 11-8 slate and logging 178⅓ innings. In his only other start against the Phillies in 1959, he flirted with a no-hitter for 7⅓ frames and settled for a three-hit shutout on May 14 at Seals Stadium. "I've been having some troubles lately," said the hurler, looking forward to ending a slump (15 runs in 11⅓ innings in his last three appearances) against the low-scoring Phillies.[4] Scheduled to be his mound opponent was Ruben Gomez, the former Giant acquired by the Phillies in the offseason, but the Puerto Rican native came down with a sore throat, reported sportswriter Allen Lewis of the *Philadelphia Inquirer*, and was scratched.[5] He was replaced by Jack Meyer, a 27-year-old right-hander, who had made 170 appearances thus far in his five-year big-league career, all but 19 of them in relief.

Rigney was forced to rearrange his outfield with perennial All-Star Willie Mays suffering from a bruised hip. Felipe Alou took over center field, Willie Kirkland occupied the right corner, and Jackie Brandt the left one. He also benched acclaimed shortstop prospect Andre Rodgers, who had committed seven errors in his previous seven games, and inserted Eddie Bressoud.

A robust crowd of 20,595 turned out at Connie Mack Stadium on a warm Friday evening despite the threat of precipitation. Jim Davenport led off with a thunderous line drive off the screen on the lower deck in left field. In a valiant attempt to catch the ball, Harry Anderson "tried to scale the boards to make the catch, failed and fell," reported sportswriter Lewis.[6] With Davenport on third with a triple, Kirkland sent a routine one-out grounder to first, but it dribbled through Ed Bouchee's legs for an error as Davenport scored. (Kirkland was credited with an RBI.) Orlando Cepeda, who entered the game with the NL's fourth-highest batting average (.336), singled sending Kirkland to third where he was called out by veteran umpire Jocko Conlan. An irate Rigney challenged the call vehemently, and after "lots of arm-waving, dirt-kicking and nose-to-nose jawing," noted Walter Judge, was tossed from the game.[7]

McCormick was on cruise control, baffling the listless Phillies with a combination of fastballs, curves, and changeups.[8] He set down the first 10 batters he faced before issuing a one-out walk in the fourth to Gene Freese on a 3-and-2 count.

After holding the Giants hitless since Cepeda's single, Meyer yielded a leadoff double to Bressoud in the fifth. Hobie Landrith then walloped Meyer's first pitch over the right-field fence to give the Giants a 3-0 lead. Davenport laced a one-out single, but was left stranded.

Meyer was back on the mound, following McCormick's one-two-three fifth. Brandt spanked a "dynamic double" off the scoreboard in center to drive in the Giants' fourth run.[9]

Having retired 15 of 16 batters, McCormick began the sixth by issuing consecutive leadoff walks to Valmy Thomas and Jim Bolger, pinch-hitting for Meyer. Richie Ashburn, who entered the game batting just .258 after capturing his second NL batting title in '58 with a .350 average, sent McCormick's first pitch into center field for the Phillies' first hit of the game. The bases were loaded.

McCormick had worked the count to 1-and-2 on Freese when the rain came down, forcing umpires to halt play at 9:45 P.M. Judge wrote that it "appeared to be another quickie" like in the third inning when play was suspended for four or five minutes.[10] But the downpour didn't let up. And after 40 minutes, the umpires called the game. It was declared a 3-0, five-inning victory for the Giants, with an official game time of 1 hour and 35 minutes. It was a "rough break" for the Phillies, lamented Lewis, who added that "little had gone right for them tonight."[11]

McCormick was credited with an unofficial five-inning no-hitter. (Official no-hitters must be complete regulation games of at least nine innings.) He lost his next two starts, but got back on track again against the Phillies, shutting them out on three hits on June 26 in San Francisco. He finished the season with a 12-16 record (3.99 ERA) and surpassed the 200-innings-pitched mark for the first time of five times in his career. An emerging star, McCormick led the NL with a 2.70 ERA in '60, and as SABR member Warren Corbett noted in the player's bio in the BioProject, the left-hander had amassed almost 1,000 innings (970⅓) pitched before his 23rd birthday, a figure only Bob Feller had surpassed in the Live Ball (post-1920) Era. McCormick developed shoulder problems in 1962. He missed large chunks of four seasons (1962-1965) and his career was in jeopardy. He reinvented himself, relying more on breaking balls and off-speed stuff instead of his onetime fastball, and surfaced as one of baseball's feel-good stories in 1967, winning an NL-most 22 games and the Cy Young Award. He finished his 16-year big-league career (1956-1971) with a 134-28 slate and logged 2,380⅓ innings, but never seriously flirted with a no-hitter again in his career after his rain-shortened gem.[12]

SOURCES

In addition to the sources cited in the Notes, the author accessed Retrosheet.org, Baseball-Reference.com, Newspapers.com, and SABR.org.

NOTES

1   Walter Judge, "Rain Gives Mike McCormick 'No-Hit' Win," *San Francisco Examiner*, June 13, 1959: 21.

2   Judge.

3   George Esper (Associated Press), "'I Was Lucky, but I'll Take It' – Mike," *San Francisco Examiner*, June 13, 1959: 21.

4   Esper.

5   Allen Lewis, "Hitless Phils Lose, 3-0, to Giants in 5," *Philadelphia Inquirer*, June 13, 1959: 19.

6   Lewis.

7   Judge.

8   Esper.

9   Judge.

10 Judge. Neither the Philadelphia or San Francisco papers mentioned who scored; however, it was either Cepeda or Daryl Spencer.

11 Lewis.

12 Defined as carrying a no-hitter into the eighth inning or later.

Mahaffey Fans Franchise-High 17

April 23, 1961
Philadelphia Phillies 6, Chicago Cubs 0
(Second Game of a Doubleheader)

By Fran Zimniuch

Part of the beauty of baseball is just how unpredictable the national pastime really is. No matter what the standings show, or what the prospects for a particular team are, on any given day at the ballpark, there is a chance that you might see something you've never seen before.

That was certainly the case when the Philadelphia Phillies hosted the Chicago Cubs on a sunny Sunday at Connie Mack Stadium early in the 1961 season. There was no reason to expect anything spectacular. Long before sabermetrics became part of baseball jargon and thinking, the April 23 doubleheader that pitted the second-place Chicago Cubs (5-4) against the eighth-place Phillies (2-7) didn't appear to be what would ultimately be a memorable day of baseball. But the game is played on the field and the 16,027 fans who turned out saw a day at the ballpark for the ages.

In the opener, veteran Frank Sullivan outdueled young Cubs left-hander Dick Ellsworth, 1-0. Phillies left fielder Bobby Gene Smith smashed a home run to left field to lead of the home half of the ninth inning, ending the game with what would later be called a walk-off home run. But the real fireworks were about to explode in the

nightcap. Not because the Phillies handily beat the Cubs, 6-0, but because the Phillies fireballing right-hander Art Mahaffey fanned 17 Cubs in the process, a new team record. The Cubs and their starter, Bob Anderson, weren't able to put up much of a fight in the record-setting game.

Adding to the improbability of Mahaffey doing anything special that day was the fact that his second start of the season had been delayed a few days after he strained his back running on the previous Tuesday. If other pitchers could be guaranteed the same results, many might have tried to strain their backs as well.

The 23-year-old Mahaffey had electric stuff highlighted by a fastball in the high 90s and a curve that looked as though it could roll off a table, both delivered from a deceptive herky-jerky motion making the hitter's task even more difficult. The game started normally enough. With one out in the top of the first inning, Mahaffey struck out Don Zimmer and Bob Will. They were the first two of what was to be a 17-strikeout performance in a nine-inning game – a Phillies record that still stood in 2020. He blew away the previous Phillies mark of 13 strikeouts held by Earl Moore (September 12, 1910), Ray Benge (June 16, 1929), Robin Roberts (May 2, 1957), and Jack Sanford

(June 7, 1957). Ironically, the opponent in all three of those games was also the Cubs.

Long before pitch counts were relevant in baseball, Mahaffey would throw 146 pitches that day, 98 for strikes. And he could not be accused of bottom feeding, as he fanned future Hall of Famer Ernie Banks as well as Ron Santo, Zimmer, and Frank Thomas each three times. The only starters who did not strike out that day were center fielder Al Heist and first baseman Ed Bouchee.

Mahaffey stuck out at least one Cub in every inning, fanning the side in the second and sixth innings, and punching out two hitters in four frames. Clearly, his strained back was not an issue.

"I never thought about it," he told *Philadelphia Inquirer* sportswriter Allen Lewis. "I wasn't trying to pace myself. I was just trying to get them out. I tired a little around the fifth, but then I got my second wind."[1]

Pitching coach Bob Lemon had a tongue-in-cheek comment. "This ruins all my theories about pitching," he said. "Mahaffey did what he did with a bad back and without doing any running. Funny game, isn't it?"[2]

Phillies hitters wasted little time in giving Mahaffey offensive support, scoring single runs in each of the first two innings. Then in the home half of the fifth inning, Ruben Amaro Sr. led off with a triple. After two infield outs, Anderson walked Tony Taylor. Right fielder Johnny Callison followed with a three-run homer, giving Mahaffey a five-run cushion. By that time, he had amassed 10 strikeouts.

The Phillies were destined to finish in the cellar in the National League with a 47-107 record, 46 games behind the Cincinnati Reds. They would lose 23 straight games from July 29 to the first game of a douleheader on August 20, the most in the major leagues since 1900.

Mahaffey led the staff with 11 wins and 19 losses with a 4.10 ERA. He also was the leader with 12 complete games, three shutouts, 219⅓ innings pitched and 158 strikeouts. Other

starters included Sullivan (3-16), John Buzhardt (6-18), Chris Short (6-12), Robin Roberts (1-10), Don Ferrarese (5-12), and Jim Owens (5-10). The staff as a whole finished last in the league in wins (47), ERA (4.61), complete games (29), earned runs (708), and saves (13).[3]

But still, Mahaffey was an All-Star in 1961 and 1962. In addition to his difficult pitching motion, he also had an outstanding move to first base. He picked off the first three players who got hits against him, Curt Flood and Bill White of the St. Louis Cardinals on July 30, 1960, followed by Jim Marshall of the San Francisco Giants on August 3, 1960.

Against the Cubs, there weren't many opportunities to pick runners off base: Mahaffey scattered four hits and walked just one batter. For most of the game he used all of his pitches, but as the game progressed, he began to concentrate more on his fastball.

"I threw mostly fastballs, particularly in the late innings," he said. "It was working so well, I just kept throwing it. In the last few innings, I didn't throw more than a couple of curves. Earlier, I got maybe five or six strikeouts with my curveball."[4]

Mahaffey continued to cruise through the Cubs lineup with 15 strikeouts through seven innings. The Phillies added one more run in the eighth. Taylor greeted reliever Dick Drott with a single to left. After Callison fanned, Bobby Gene Smith advanced Taylor to second base with a groundout, and Taylor scored on a single by Tony Gonzalez, upping the Phillies' lead to 6-0.

Mahaffey struck out only one Cub in each of the last two innings. Zimmer was his final victim, leading off the top of the ninth inning. Bob Will followed with a single up the middle. Santo flied out to Smith in left field for the second out. While Mahaffey concentrated on getting Banks to be the final out of the game, Will moved to second and base on consecutive calls of defensive indifference, but to no avail, as Banks popped out to Taylor at second base to end the gem.

"Maybe that extra rest helped," Phillies manager Gene Mauch said. "That was the most powerfully pitched game I ever saw and I've been in baseball for 20 years."[5]

Mahaffey fell one whiff short of the major-league record at the time of 18 strikeouts in a nine-inning game held by Bob Feller of the Cleveland Indians in 1938 and Sandy Koufax of the Los Angeles Dodgers in 1959.[6]

"I had two strikes on the last four batters, but only got one strikeout," he said years later. "I came close to having more than 17. With some of the starters the Phillies have had, it's a wonder that it hasn't been broken."[7]

Four Phillies pitchers have come within one strikeout of tying Mahaffey's record: Steve Carlton on June 9, 1982, against the Cubs; Curt Schilling on September 1, 1997, against the New York Yankees; Cliff Lee on May 6, 2011, against the Atlanta Braves, and Vince Velasquez on April 14, 2016, against the San Diego Padres.

Mahaffey once again led the Phillies in victories in 1962 with a 19-14 record, but then shoulder miseries began to nag him and limit his effectiveness. He was 7-10 in 1963 and 12-9 with the ill-fated '64 team. He was a disappointing 2-5 in 1965 and was traded after the season to the St. Louis Cardinals with catcher Pat Corrales and outfielder Alex Johnson for shortstop Dick Groat, catcher Bob Uecker, and first baseman Bill White. His career ended after he went 1-4 for St. Louis in 1966. His career mark was 59-64.

Mahaffey was invited to Citizens Bank Park in Philadelphia on April 20, 2011, to commemorate the 50th anniversary of his 17-strikeout performance by throwing out the first pitch prior to the Phillies game against the Milwaukee Brewers. He threw a perfect strike at the knees.[8]

SOURCES

In addition to the sources cited in the Notes, the author accessed Retrosheet.org, Baseball-Reference.com, and SABR.org.

NOTES

1   Allen Lewis, "Winning Counted, Not That Record," *Philadelphia Inquirer*, April 21, 1961.

2   Lewis.

3   John Thorn and Pete Palmer, eds., *Total Baseball: The Ultimate Encyclopedia of Baseball, Third Edition* (New York: HarperCollins Publishers, 1993).

4   Lewis.

5   Lewis.

6   As of 2020, the record of 18 strikeouts has been eclipsed by Roger Clemens of the Boston Red Sox, Max Scherzer of the Washington Nationals, Randy Johnson of the Arizona Diamondbacks, and Kerry Wood of the Cubs, who all fanned 20 hitters.

7   Larry Shenk, "Mahaffey's 17-Strikeout Gem Stands the Test of Time," mlb.com/news, December 17, 2015.

8   Ralph Berger and Mel Marmer, Art Mahaffey, SABR BioProject, sabr.org.

Sandy Koufax's Third No-Hitter

June 4, 1964
Los Angeles Dodgers 3, Philadelphia Phillies 0

By Marc Z Aaron

The Los Angeles Dodgers (21-25, and in eighth place) came to Philadelphia to play the league-leading Philadelphia Phillies (27-15). It was a great pitching matchup: Sandy Koufax (5-4) and Chris Short (3-2, 0.64 ERA).

Both pitchers set the side down in order in the first inning. In the second inning Tommy Davis singled but was erased on an inning-ending double-play ball. Koufax looked dominant from the beginning of the game, needing only six pitches to set the Phillies down in order in the second and picking up his third strikeout. Johnny Callison, Dick Allen, and Gus Triandos had all gone down swinging.

In the top of the third, Koufax lined a single to center with two out, but Willie Davis fouled out to third baseman Dick Allen. In the bottom half, Tony Taylor went down looking, Ruben Amaro hit a popup to first baseman Ken McMullen, and Chris Short went down swinging.

In the bottom of the fourth with two out, Koufax fell behind in the count 3-and-0 to Dick Allen. Two strikes and one foul ball later, Koufax walked Allen on a fastball that was three inches below the strike zone. Koufax later commented that he shook off the curve to throw the fastball.[1] Allen was erased from the basepaths when he

attempted to steal on a 2-and-2 count with Danny Cater at bat. After the game Koufax said, "(Doug) Camilli had called for a curve, but I shook him off … then right in the middle of my windup I realized I had made a mistake, that Allen would be looking for the fast one. But just like you don't stop a golf shot on the backswing, I kept right on going. There was no doubt about the call. It was a ball."[2]

In the fifth inning Cater went down swinging, Triandos flied to center, and Sievers fouled out to first. In the sixth Taylor hit a grounder back to Koufax, and both Amaro and Short went down swinging at the air.

After six innings there had been only three hits, one error allowing a base, and just the one walk to Allen. A real pitching duel. The Dodgers had not scored a run in 19 straight innings.

In the top of the seventh, Gilliam grounded a ball up the middle and went to third on a line-drive single to right by Tommy Davis. On the next pitch from Chris Short, Frank Howard crushed his 14th home run of the season, the ball taking one hop on the arched roof of the left-field pavilion. Ken McMullen then singled to left but was out trying to stretch it into a double. Doug Camilli hit a fly ball to right for the second out.

Dick Tracewski doubled to left, chasing Short from the mound. Ed Roebuck came in and got Koufax, his former teammate on the Dodgers, to ground out to short.

The Dodgers made some lineup changes in the bottom of the seventh. Wes Parker was now the right fielder and Ron Fairly came in to play first base. They replaced Frank Howard and Ken McMullen. Koufax faced Cookie Rojas and with two strikes Rojas flied out to left. Johnny Callison grounded back to Koufax and Allen hit a high chopper to Gilliam at third. Gilliam came running hard to grab it on the short hop and throw Allen out by three steps.

In the eighth Ray Culp replaced Roebuck. The Dodgers went down in order. In the bottom half of the inning Cater was out on a hard liner to right on the first pitch, and Triandos and Sievers went down swinging.

In the ninth, Tony Taylor struck out. Amaro, swinging at the first pitch, fouled out to first baseman Fairly, who caught the ball about 20 feet behind first. With two outs, Bobby Wine, batting .205 and 1-for-17 against Koufax, batted for Culp. With the count 1-and-2, Wine went down swinging. But not before he had fouled off the second pitch into the dirt. The ball bounced up and hit home-plate umpire Ed Vargo in the throat. Vargo didn't want to hold up the game and allow Koufax to cool off, even though he was having trouble breathing.[3]

Final score: Dodgers 3, Phillies 0. A crowd of 29,704, the biggest of the season so far, witnessed Koufax's third no-hitter. (The crowd for the game against the San Francisco Giants the next night exceeded the Dodgers' crowd by 2,000.) The game took 1 hour 55 minutes to play as Koufax faced the minimum 27 batters. He threw just 97 pitches and the only three-ball count was the one to Allen that resulted in Koufax's lone walk. Koufax struck out 12 Phillies in what was to be the only time he was to shut out the Phillies during his career. It was the 54th time he had struck out 10 or more batters. He joined Bob Feller as the only pitchers to throw three no-hitters in the twentieth century.[4]

Before the no-hitter the Dodgers had been defeated by the Phillies in eight of their nine previous contests.

Koufax remarked after the game, "This was the first time this season that I have been able to put everything together."[5] He was throwing differently than he had earlier in the season. He wasn't stepping as far to the left and not throwing as much across his body. He seemed to have better leverage on his follow-through. He had his old rhythm back. The fastball was overpowering and the curve cut the corners.[6]

Prior to this start, Koufax came across an issue of *Sport* magazine that featured a photo of him during his 1963 no-hitter against the Giants. From the photo angle, Koufax was able to detect a flaw in his stride.[7] He could see that he had to open up a little.[8]

On the bus from the stadium, Koufax remarked to pitcher Joe Moeller, "You know, I got away with a pitch. I hung a curve to Wine."[9] He faced the minimum number of batters and all he could think about was the one pitch that got away. Typical Koufax.

Don Drysdale, who lost 1-0 in 11 innings the night before, was not traveling with the team. When he heard the announcer reporting that Koufax had pitched his third no-hitter, Drysdale asked impatiently, "But did he win?"[10]

SOURCES

In addition to the sources cited in the Notes, the author also consulted Baseball-Reference.com and an article by Bob Hunter in the June 20, 1964, issue of *The Sporting News.*

NOTES

1   John Brogan, "Sandy Shook Off Curve, Fast Ball Walked Allen," *Philadelphia Bulletin*, June 5, 1964.

2   Associated Press, "Koufax Pitches His 3rd No-Hitter," June 4, 1964.

3   Allen Lewis, "Ump Vargo Refused to Leave Contest in spite of Painful Injury From Foul," *The Sporting News*, June 20, 1964. (Vargo would again be behind the plate when Koufax pitched his perfect game against the Cubs in 1965.)

4   Larry Corcoran and Cy Young accomplished the feat in the nineteenth century.

5   Associated Press, "Sandy Found a Flaw, Corrected It, and...," *Los Angeles Times*, June 5, 1964: B1.

6   "Koufax Pitches His 3rd No-Hitter."

7   Jane Leavy, *Sandy Koufax, a Lefty's Legacy* (New York: HarperCollins, 2002), 152.

8   Sandy Koufax with Ed Linn, *Koufax* (New York: Viking Press, 1966), 220.

9   Leavy, 154.

10   Leavy, 154.

A September Afternoon with So Much at Stake

September 10, 1964
Philadelphia Phillies 5, St. Louis Cardinals 1

By John Bauer

Arm's length. The Philadelphia Phillies had held the rest of the NL at arm's length for the better part of two months, maintaining a cushion over their rivals that made clinching the 1964 pennant seem only a matter of time. It wasn't. On Wednesday, September 9, the St. Louis Cardinals rallied for five runs in the top of the 11th to secure a 10-5 win over Philadelphia. Winners of 13 out of their last 16 games, the streaking Cardinals had halved the gap with the Phillies from 10 games to five and now claimed the runner-up spot in the standings. The Phillies had paced the league since mid-July, but three straight defeats at Connie Mack Stadium preceded this game on Thursday, September 10, the final home game before a 10-day road trip.

For the Phillies, there seemed more riding on this afternoon game than the obvious advantage of beating a pennant rival. Management was taking steps to prepare the ballpark for its first World Series since 1950, specifically authorizing construction of a new kitchen behind the current press box so that the current kitchen could be converted into space for the 600 writers expected to attend the fall classic.[1] Also, Philadelphia Mayor James H.J. Tate linked a Phillies pennant with a number of civic improvements before hopefully joyous voters on the November ballot. "It will be a sad blow," said the mayor, should the loss of the pennant also cost sewer, water and subway improvements as well as a $25 million loan for a new ballpark.[2] For now, the fans were reacting enthusiastically to the Phillies season. The team had already broken its single-season attendance record, set during the pennant-winning campaign of 1950, and fans responded to a warm, sunny afternoon with a "surprisingly large mid-week crowd of 14,552."[3]

In addition to World Series and civic expectations, the Phillies were forced to act quickly after first baseman Frank Thomas fractured his thumb sliding into second base during a September 8 loss to the Dodgers. Thomas, just acquired from the New York Mets on August 7, had hit .302 with 7 home runs and 26 RBIs in 33 games for the Phillies. To replace Thomas, Philadelphia quickly acquired 36-year-old Vic Power from the Los Angeles Angels for cash and a player to be named later. Power would make his Phillies debut against the Cardinals.

Chris Short (15-7, 1.94 ERA) took the mound for the Phillies. Curt Flood earned a leadoff single by beating a throw from Ruben Amaro. The Philadelphia shortstop "made a good backhand stop but his throw had no chance."[4] Flood had now hit in 20 of his last 21 games. Lou Brock struck out, then Amaro started an inning-ending double play on a bouncer from Dick Groat. Ray Sadecki (16-9, 3.79 ERA), who won his prior outing against the Phillies on July 26, induced a grounder and popup from Cookie Rojas and Power, respectively, to open his afternoon. Sadecki walked Johnny Callison and shortstop Groat's error allowed Dick Allen to reach first. Third baseman Ken Boyer forced Allen at second base on Alex Johnson's grounder to close the first inning.

The second inning would witness the totality of the afternoon's scoring. The Cardinals struck the first blow, but their half of the inning was a case of "what could have been." With the count full, Short walked Boyer. Charlie James, in the lineup to face the left-handed Short, proved correct his manager's platooning instincts with a drive into right-center field. With runners at the corners, Bill White lined the first pitch into the right-field corner to score Boyer for the game's first run. Short seemed to be wobbling and the Cardinals had an opportunity to extend their lead with no outs and two runners in scoring position. Julian Javier smacked a 2-and-1 offering inside the third-base line, but Allen executed what would prove to be the play of the game. He snared the ball on the foul line 10 feet behind the sack and then delivered a precise throw to Power to catch Javier "by less than half a step."[5] Allen described the play after the game as a mere reaction to a hit ball. He said, "I don't know how I did it. I just did it."[6] The runners held their bases; then, Bob Uecker's strikeout and Sadecki's popup behind the plate ended the half-inning.

The Phillies made the most of their opportunities in the bottom of the second. Tony Taylor singled to left field and Gus Triandos followed with a hard grounder to Boyer that seemed likely to end in a double play. The ball, however, took an awkward bounce and struck Boyer under the chin.[7] Boyer recovered, but the lumbering

Triandos, slower than usual because of a pulled leg muscle, beat the throw at first.[8] Boyer was charged with an error. Boyer would get Triandos in the end: He gathered Amaro's bunt and threw to Groat, who was covering second base on the play. Short brought to the plate a .063 batting average, the product of three singles spread across the 1964 season. The pitcher smacked a "sinking liner down the right field line"[9] into the Phillies bullpen, scoring Taylor and Amaro for a 2-1 lead. The triple, partly the result of James diving but missing the catch, proved to be Short's only extra-base hit of the year. Rojas flied out to Brock in left field for the second out. Power popped up into short left field for what appeared likely to be the inning's final out. Groat waved off Brock, but dropped the ball. The error allowed Short to score and Power to claim second base. Groat said later, "I have no excuses. It was lousy, lousy, lousy – just about as bad a play as you could make. I really fouled it up."[10] The inning thus extended, Callison slugged his team-leading 26th home run over the right-field wall for a 5-1 advantage. Allen almost duplicated Callison's feat, but Flood caught the ball in front of the 430 sign in deep center field for the third out.[11]

The Cardinals opened the third inning with the top of their order due to bat. Short appeared to have settled into the game as Flood, Brock, and Groat went down in order. The Phillies almost added to their advantage in the bottom of the inning. With two outs they loaded the bases on a single by Triandos, another Cardinals error by second baseman Javier on Amaro's grounder, and Short's second hit of the game. Rojas popped up to White in foul ground, though, keeping the score at 5-1. St. Louis got singles by James and Javier in the top of the fourth, but Short otherwise struck out the side with Boyer, White, and Uecker being sent back to the dugout.

Short's pitching now took over the game. The Cardinals were unable to get a baserunner in the fifth, sixth, and seventh innings. Short struck

A five-tool ballplayer, Johnny Callison excelled for the Phillies in the 1960s. In 1964 he hit 31 home runs, knocked in 104 runs, scored 101 runs, and might have been the NL MVP if not for the Phillies' "Phold." (Photo via Mark Rucker archives and SABR)

out four during those frames; he would end the game with a season high of 12. In the fifth inning Sadecki gave way to Mike Cuellar, at that time a 27-year-old enjoying his first extended run in the major leagues. Cuellar used a combination of groundballs and strikeouts to keep the Philadelphia from expanding its lead in the fifth and sixth. Power, who hitherto had spent his entire 11-year big-league career in the AL, stroked his first NL hit, a leadoff single, in the seventh. His glory was short-lived: Cuellar picked him off. Callison singled and, after Allen flied out, Johnson walked. With Taylor at the plate, catcher Uecker's error on a pickoff attempt put Callison and Johnson into scoring position. Taylor, however, struck out looking to end the Phillies seventh.

Short continued to overpower the Cardinals and closed the game strong. Batting for Cuellar to start the eighth, Carl Warwick singled to center; his efforts were quickly erased on a double play ball from Flood. Brock struck out next. In the ninth, Groat grounded out, then Boyer and James both struck out to end the game. Short summarized his outing: "It had to be one of my biggest games with them closing in on us. ... When I started warming up, I knew I had a real good fast ball. So I used it mainly – that and my slider."[12]

Short's excellence over the course of the game could not be ignored. The managers, however, seemed focused on Allen's fielding in the second inning. Phillies manager Gene Mauch called it "the pivotal play of the game."[13] His St. Louis counterpart Johnny Keane agreed that the game turned on that one play. He said, "If the ball got though, we would have won! If Allen doesn't come up with the ball, we've got a 3-0 lead, a man on second, nobody out and Chris Short is probably jerked out of there."[14] With the 5-1 victory, the Phillies appeared back on course for the NL pennant. They departed for the West Coast with a six-game lead in the standings and only 22 games remaining on the schedule. The Cardinals' late-season surge had not ended with this one game, however, and a mammoth losing streak still awaited the Phillies. The 1964 pennant race remained alive and well.

SOURCES

In addition to the articles cited in the Notes, the author consulted Baseball-Reference.com

NOTES

1   "Phils Ready for Writers," *Philadelphia Inquirer*, September 10, 1964: 35.

2   "Phillies Handed Stadium 'Ball,'" *Philadelphia Inquirer*, September 10, 1964: 7.

3   Allen Lewis, "Short Shackles Cards; Phillies Hike Lead to 6," *Philadelphia Inquirer*, September 11, 1964: 1.

4   Neal Russo, "Phils Win; Cards 6 Games Back," *St. Louis Post-Dispatch*, September 10, 1964: 4B.

5   Lewis: 35.

6   John Dell, "Play by Allen Called Pivotal in Phils' Win," *Philadelphia Inquirer*, September 11, 1964: 35.

7   Lewis: 35; Russo, "Phils Win."

8   Lewis: 35.

9   Lewis: 35.

10 Russo, "Kid's Glove Treatment Is Rough," *St. Louis Post-Dispatch*, September 11, 1964: 4C.

11 Russo, "Phils Win."

12 Dell.

13 Dell.

14 Russo, "Gilt-Edge Hurling by Gibson Fuels Redbird Takeoff," *The Sporting News*, September 26, 1964: 4.

THE PHOLD:
PHILLIES' SEVENTH STRAIGHT LOSS DROPS THEM OUT OF FIRST PLACE

September 27, 1964
Milwaukee Braves 14, Philadelphia Phillies 8

By John J. Burbridge Jr.

It had been a terrible week for the Philadelphia Phillies. On Sunday, September 20, after beating the Dodgers in Los Angeles, 3-2, the Phillies had a 6½-game lead over their closest pursuers for the National League pennant, the Cincinnati Reds and the St. Louis Cardinals. After that win, the Phillies returned to Philadelphia and Connie Mack Stadium for a three-game series beginning on Monday, September 21, against the Reds. The Phillies had an opportunity to lengthen their league lead. However, the Reds opened the series with a 1-0 win on Chico Ruiz's steal of home in the sixth inning with Frank Robinson at the plate. The Reds then won the next two games and the Phillies' lead was now 3½ games. The Cardinals lost one of two games against the New York Mets so they were now in third place, five games behind the Phillies.

There was no reason to panic but the Phillies needed to get back to winning against the Milwaukee Braves, who were coming to Philadelphia for a four-game series. The Braves, although not in pennant contention, were a formidable opponent, featuring future Hall of Famers Hank Aaron, Eddie Mathews, Joe Torre, and Warren Spahn.

The Phillies' collapse continued as the Braves won the first three games while the Reds won three in a row against the lowly Mets. As the Phillies prepared for their Sunday game on September 27, their lead, which had looked to be unsurmountable, was down to a half-game over Cincinnati. The day before, they had lost in excruciating fashion as the Braves wiped out a 4-3 Phillies lead with three in the ninth. If the Phillies lost the Sunday game and the Reds won their doubleheader against the Mets, the Reds would be in first place. The Phillies had been in first place since July 21.

For the Sunday contest, the Phillies called upon their ace, Jim Bunning, an 18-game winner so far. This was Bunning's fourth start since September 16. He was pitching on short rest, having started the first game of the series on Thursday night, pitching six innings in a losing effort.

The Braves countered with right-hander Tony Cloninger, who had 17 wins. The Braves scored two runs in the first inning when Felipe Alou and Lee Maye both got hits and Hank Aaron drove them in with a double. The Phillies got on the scoreboard in the bottom of the inning as Tony Gonzalez doubled and scored on a single by Dick Allen.

In the bottom of the second, the Phillies took a 3-2 lead. Clay Dalrymple led off with a double and scored on Tony Taylor's triple. Taylor scored on Bunning's fly out.

The top of the fourth inning proved to be Bunning's undoing: The Braves scored six runs on seven hits. Joe Torre led off the inning with an infield hit. Rico Carty and Denis Menke followed with singles, Menke's driving in Torre. Ty Cline doubled in Carty and Cloninger, a good-hitting pitcher, blooped a single to center field that scored Menke. Manager Gene Mauch replaced Bunning with Dallas Green, who gave up a double to Felipe Alou that scored Cline with the fourth run of the inning. Lee Maye's single drove in Cloninger. Green got Hank Aaron to hit into a double play but Alou scored from third base. The Braves now led 8-3.

The Braves scored four more runs in the fifth. Green retired the first two hitters, but the next six hitters reached base against him, on four singles, a double, a wild throw, and a walk. The big hits were singles by Cloninger and Maye and a two-run double by Felipe Alou. The Braves led 12-3 as Green was replaced by Morrie Steevens.

Johnny Callison led off the bottom of the sixth for the Phillies with a home run. Cloninger had retired eight Phillies in a row. After Callison's home run, Cloninger retired the next three Phillies. The Braves scored a run in the top of the seventh on a wild pitch by Rick Wise. The Phillies threatened in the bottom of the seventh but did not score. Joe Torre led off the top of the eighth with a home run off Jack Baldschun, the Phillies' fifth hurler.

Chi-Chi Olivo replaced Cloninger in the bottom of the eighth and was greeted by Callison's second home run of the game. Tony Taylor

singled in another run, and the score was 14-6 entering the ninth inning. The Phillies scored two runs when Dick Allen doubled and Callison hit his third home run of the game. After Callison's homer, Wes Covington struck out looking and the game was over. When Cincinnati swept its twin bill with the Mets, the Phillies found themselves in second place, a game behind the Reds.

The star of the game for the Braves was Tony Cloninger, who gave up four runs on seven hits in seven innings and got two hits and two RBIs. He was backed by the timely hitting of Lee Maye with five hits. Felipe Alou and Joe Torre also had three hits each. The Braves shelled Phillies hurlers for 22 hits.

Before hitting his first home run, in the sixth inning, Johnny Callison decided to once again stuff a wad of chewing tobacco in his mouth. He had been a user several years before but gave it up at his wife's urging.[1] He was chewing on this same tobacco for both his second and third home runs. His three home runs gave him 31 for the season. Dick Allen also had three hits for the Phillies.

In postgame interviews there was considerable discussion as to the mindset of the Phillies. Catcher Clay Dalrymple raised the issue, saying, "I don't think anybody out there is choking up. I haven't felt any pressure, I mean that."[2] However, manager Mauch seemed to be feeling something as he snapped at reporters, "What do you care how I feel. I'm sick and tired of hearing my own voice. Especially the last seven days."[3] Bobby Bragan, the Braves manager, observed, "There's no question they're feeling the tension. You gotta feel sorry for them."[4] Callison added an optimistic note: "We're going to bounce back. I believe that. I really believe that."[5]

The Cardinals defeated the Pirates and were just a half-game behind the Phillies. The fact that the Phillies lost the National League lead earned a headline on the first page of the *Philadelphia Inquirer* although the release of the Warren Commission report naming Lee Harvey Oswald as the sole assassin of President Kennedy overshadowed the account of the Phillies game.[6]

After the game the Phillies were off to St. Louis for a Monday night game opening a three-game series. They lost all three, and their losing streak was extended to 10 games. Cincinnati lost two of three to the Pittsburgh Pirates, and the Cardinals were now in first place as the teams entered the final weekend. The Phillies still had a shot at tying for the pennant if they won two games in Cincinnati and the Cardinals were swept in a three-game series against the Mets.

Surprisingly, the Phillies were in contention to tie for the pennant as the games began on the final Sunday of the season. The Phillies had come from behind on Friday night to beat Cincinnati while the Mets won the first two games against the Cardinals. While the Phillies won on Sunday, the Cardinals defeated the Mets and won the pennant with the Phillies and Reds tied for second, one game behind. The final two weeks of a bizarre pennant race had finally ended. One that Philadelphians will never forget.

SOURCES

In addition to the sources cited in the Notes, a box score and play-by-play account for this game can be seen on Baseball-Reference.com:

baseball-reference.com/boxes/PHI/PHI196409270.shtml

NOTES

1   Frank Dolson, "Callison Smashes 3 Tobacco 'Belts,'" *Philadelphia Inquirer*, September 28, 1964: 32.

2   Dolson, "Callison Smashes 3 Tobacco 'Belts.'"

3   Frank Dolson, "Phils Don't Want Braves Sympathy," *Philadelphia Inquirer*, September 28, 1964: 35.

4   Dolson, "Phils Don't Want Braves Sympathy."

5   Dolson, "Phils Don't Want Braves Sympathy."

6   "Phils Lose 7th in Row, Drop to 2nd," *Philadelphia Inquirer*, September 28, 1964: 1.

BUNNING WINS EIGHTH STRAIGHT WITH 14-STRIKEOUT, THREE-HIT GEM

June 7, 1966
Philadelphia Phillies 5, Cincinnati Reds 1

By Gregory H. Wolf

"This was the best I've put all my pitches together this season," said Jim Bunning of his overpowering victory over the Cincinnati Reds.[1] In what Philadelphia Phillies beat writer Allen Lewis described as a "dandy display of power pitching," Bunning matched his personal high with 14 strikeouts to win his eighth straight decision, equaling his career-best mark during the club's memorable 1964 pennant race.[2]

The matchup in the City of Brotherly Love featured teams going in the opposite direction. Feisty skipper Gene Mauch's Phillies had won seven of their last eight games to move to 28-21, in fourth place, 3½ games behind the San Francisco Giants. Their opponent for the first game of a three-game tilt as part of a season-long 16-game homestand was the Reds, who had lost 10 of 15 games to drop to 21-25 and sixth place.

One of the reasons for the Phillies' hot start was their 34-year-old right-handed workhorse, Jim Bunning. Acquired in a trade with the Detroit Tigers in December 1963, Bunning had won 19 games in 1964 and 1965 to push his career slate to 156-104 beginning his 12th season. Given his advanced age and hoping to avoid a slump like the one in the previous year when his ERA hovered around 4.00 for the first six weeks of the season,

Bunning asked to pitch more during spring training, and Mauch gladly obliged. "He's a fiercely proud man as I've ever known," said Mauch. "Everything about Jim Bunning is order. ... He never makes a move without thinking about it."[3] The Cincinnati native, who attended that city's Xavier University, entered the game with a stellar 7-1 slate and a 1.66 ERA.

Toeing the rubber for first-year skipper Don Heffner's Reds was Milt Pappas, whose name will be forever linked to one of the most notorious trades in club history. In the offseason, the Reds sent a supposedly over-the-hill 30-year-old former MVP, Frank Robinson, to the Baltimore Orioles in exchange for the crafty right-handed, two-time All-Star with a 110-74 career slate. While fan favorite Robinson subsequently led the Orioles to the World Series title in '66, Papas was coming off a strong campaign in '65 (13-9, tied for fifth-lowest ERA in the AL at 2.60), but got off to a rocky start (4-3, 3.88) with his new team.

The Tuesday evening game with an 8:06 start time drew 12,422 spectators to venerable Connie Mack Stadium, located at 21st Street and Lehigh Avenue on Philadelphia's north side. Baseball's first steel and concrete ballpark was in its 57th year and had been gradually deteriorating for a decade; however, its ornate corner tower and exterior harked back to ballpark's origins.

It was a "weird first inning," quipped sportswriter Bill Conlin in the *Philadelphia Daily News*.[4] Tommy Harper sent Bunning's first pitch to deep left field, where Dick Allen dropped it for a two-base error. Unperturbed by the miscue, Bunning left Harper stranded on the keystone sack, retiring the next three batters, the latter two by strikeout.

Allen's miscue was nothing compared to what happened to Pappas. After Cookie Rojas lined to center, Johnny Callison sent a fly ball to deep left field. According to Conlin, the ball drifted over Deron Johnson's outstretched glove, took one bounce, and caromed off the wall for a double.[5] Allen, who entered the game as one of the hottest hitters in baseball, slashing 8/23/.347 while slugging .716, despite having missed three weeks with a leg injury, smashed the ball on a "half swing" off the left side of the scoreboard in left-center field for a triple, driving in Callison.[6] Bill White followed with a another clout to center field, but it "appeared to be nothing more than a sacrifice fly," thought Allen Lewis.[7] On what "looked like an easy catch," wrote Reds beat writer Lou Smith, center fielder Vada Pinson began waving his hands.[8] He lost the ball in the haze and lights. The ball landed about 30 feet behind Pinson and rolled to the warning track.[9] White scampered around the bases for an inside-the-park home run, his ninth round-tripper of the season, to give the Phillies a 3-0 lead. The first-inning outfield circuit was not yet over. Tony Gonzalez sent another fly to left field, where Johnson dropped it attempting to make a shoestring catch, reported Conlin.[10] Papas retired Dick Groat and Tony Taylor to end the frame.

The Phillies' three first-inning runs were more than they needed the way Bunning pitched. With his sweeping side-arm delivery, he breezed through the next three innings, yielding a bunt single to Johnson in the second, and fanned three

more. In the fifth, Chico Cardenas connected for a one-out home run to deep left field to put the Reds on the board. The hottest player in the league, Cardenas "continued to be the punchless Reds' one-man attack," wrote Smith in the *Cincinnati Enquirer*. It was Cardenas's sixth home run in his last four games and accounted for his ninth run batted in of the last 14 Reds tallies.[11] In the sixth, Pinson blooped a single to shallow center for the Reds' third and final hit.

After his rough first inning, Pappas settled down, allowing only three scattered singles and one walk one in the next five innings. With two outs in the seventh, former Red Cookie Rojas extended his hitting streak to 10 games by walloping his second home run of the season, to deep left field. Callison doubled to left and then scored on Allen's hit to center. Pinson's peg to second baseman Pete Rose erased Allen trying to stretch the hit into a double.

The "Reds were as harmless as a covey of quail before a hard-working Bunning," retorted Lou Smith.[12] Bunning fanned the side in the eighth as the dirt stain on his left thigh grew increasingly larger and more pronounced. "When I'm not getting dirt on my leg," he said, "it means I'm not getting down enough on my follow through."[13] Coming off a career-high 268 strikeouts in 291 innings in '65, Bunning possessed one of baseball's best high heaters, along with Bob Gibson. And like Gibby, Bunning was prone to giving up home runs and lots of fly balls. In this contest, only two balls were hit in the infield: Johnson's bunt and Pete Rose's seventh-inning grounder to Rojas, which accounted for the only assist of the game to equal a major-league record set many times. The key to this game, said Bunning, was his slider, which he tossed with such force from his side-arm delivery that he often careened off the mound and to first base with his gloved hand touching the ground.[14] "When [my slider is] going right, it resembles my fast ball until the last minute, then it moves," said Bunning.[15]

In the years before pitch counts determined how long a pitcher would last, Bunning was concerned that his fatigue might affect his mechanics in the last frame. "When I came in [to the dugout] after striking out those three hitters in the eighth," he disclosed, "I told Gene I was tired and that he better watch me pretty close in the ninth."[16] Tommy Helms led off the ninth by flying out to left. "[He] did me a favor by hitting the first pitch," said Bunning, "and that gave me a lift."[17] Bunning fanned Pinson to rack up his 14th strikeout, matching his career high achieved with the Tigers in 1958. It also tied Chris Short (1963) for the second most by a Phillies pitcher in a nine-inning game, though well off Art Mahaffey's record-setting 17-strikeout performance in 1961. (Short fanned 18 in a 15-inning game on October 2, 1965.) Bunning dispatched Gordy Coleman on yet another outfield fly to end the game in 2 hours and 15 minutes.

Bunning's three-hit gem with no walks was arguably the best game he tossed in a Phillies uniform in his four-year stretch (1964-1967) with the team, during which he averaged 19 wins, 298 innings pitched, and 248 strikeouts, while tossing 23 shutouts. En route to his ninth and final All-Star berth in 1966, Bunning concluded the season by winning 19 games for the third straight season (14 losses), leading the league with 41 starts and 5 shutouts, and setting a personal best with 314 innings pitched.

After pitching for the Pirates and Dodgers from 1968 to 1970, Bunning returned to the Phillies for his final two of 17 big-league seasons (1955-1971), retiring with a 224-184 career slate. He was inducted into the baseball Hall of Fame by the Veterans Committee in 1996. By that time, Bunning was an established Republican politician in the state of Kentucky. He served six terms in the House of Representatives (1987-1999) and two terms in the United States Senate (1999-2011).

SOURCES

In addition to the sources cited in the Notes, the author accessed Retrosheet.org, Baseball-Reference.com, SABR.org, and *The Sporting News* archive via Paper of Record.

NOTES

1   Bill Conlin, "Muddy Bunning Soils Reds with 3-Hitter, Fans 14," *Philadelphia Daily News*, June 8, 1966: 49.

2   Allen Lewis, "Phils Roll, 5-1, Behind Bunning's 3-Hitter," *Philadelphia Inquirer*, June 8, 1966: 45.

3   Bill Conlin, "Muddy Bunning Soils Reds with 3-Hitter, Fans 14."

4   Bill Conlin, "Outfielders Played It by Ear," *Philadelphia Daily News*, June 8, 1966: 49.

5   Bill Conlin, "Outfielders Played It by Ear."

6   Bill Conlin, "Outfielders Played It by Ear."

7   Allen Lewis, "Phils Roll, 5-1, Behind Bunning's 3-Hitter."

8   Lou Smith, "Bunning Baffles Reds on 3 Hits, 5-1," *Cincinnati Enquirer*, June 8, 1966: 41.

9   Bill Conlin, "Outfielders Played It by Ear."

10 Bill Conlin, "Outfielders Played It by Ear."

11 Smith.

12 Smith.

13 Bill Conlin, "Muddy Bunning Soils Reds with 3-Hitter, Fans 14."

14 Frank Dolson, "Jim Bunning: Baseball and Beyond," quoted in Bill James and Rob Neyer, *The Neyer/James Guide to Pitchers* (New York: Fireside, 2004), 150.

15 Bill Conlin, "Muddy Bunning Soils Reds with 3-Hitter, Fans 14,"

16 Allen Lewis, "Bunning Tires in 9th, Gets 'First Pitch' Life," *Philadelphia Inquirer*, June 8, 1966: 45.

17 Allen Lewis, "Bunning Tires in 9th."

Don Lock's Walk-Off Home Run Ends Marathon

May 21, 1967
Philadelphia Phillies 2, Cincinnati Reds 1
(18 Innings)

By Thomas J. Brown Jr.

Cincinnati arrived in Philadelphia on a five-game winning streak. After losing the first game of their four-game series with the Phillies, the Reds had won the next two and were hoping to continue their winning streak in the final game of the series.

The Phillies were already 9½ games behind the Reds and were struggling to stay relevant early in the 1967 season. They had won just two of their previous 10 games. For this game, only 8,641 fans hoped to see their team finally begin to come out of its slump.

Chris Short started for the Phillies. He was one of the anchors of the Philadelphia starting rotation, having led the team in victories the previous year with a 20-10 record. Short pitched well in his two starts before this game, striking out 12 batters and giving up just seven hits in 13⅓ innings. (He did not get a win for his efforts in either game.)

The Phillies wasted no time in giving Short a one run-lead in the bottom of the first. Tony Gonzalez and Dick Allen led off with singles off Reds starter Milt Pappas. Gonzalez moved to third on a fly to right by Johnny Callison and came home on another fly, this one to deep left field, by John Briggs.

Short blanked the Reds through the first eight innings. After getting the side out in order in the first, he gave up two singles in the second but got out of the jam when the next two batters grounded out. When Lee May singled in the fourth, he was caught stealing to end another Reds scoring opportunity.

The same thing happened in the fifth after Chico Ruiz singled. Phillies catcher Clay Dalrymple threw out Ruiz as he tried to steal second. Tommy Harper hit a one-out double in the sixth, but the Reds could not advance him home when Short got the next two outs on a fly ball to center field and a grounder to second. When Tony Perez singled in the seventh, a double play ended the Reds' chance to score.

Phillies manager Gene Mauch "turned the lineup upside down and inside out" to try get some offense. Dick Allen, who hadn't hit a homer in nearly a month, was batting second. "I'm trying find some way to get [other teams] to change their thinking on how to pitch to Allen," Mauch said before the game.[1]

For the first eight innings, it seemed as if that one run would be all Short would need. But he walked leadoff batter Harper in the top of the ninth. Harper stole second and came home with the tying run when Perez banged a groundball cleanly through a hole to left field.

The Phillies faithful hoped their team might score the winning run in the bottom of the ninth. But Ted Abernathy, who had come into the game for Pappas in the eighth, got the Phillies out in order to send the game into extra innings.

Short showed no sign of slowing down. Over the next three innings, he allowed just one baserunner, walking Dick Simpson with one out in the 10th. Short struck out eight batters, walked just two and had lowered his ERA from 2.88 to 2.52 when he was pulled for a pinch-hitter in the bottom of the 12th.

Mel Queen had come in from the bullpen in the 10th for the Reds. He got the side out in order in the 10th and worked out of a jam in the 11th inning after giving up consecutive singles that put a runner on third with two outs.

When Queen returned to the mound in the 12th inning, he surrendered a double to Cookie Rojas, who advanced to third on a relay error by shortstop Leo Cardenas. Queen intentionally walked Gary Sutherland. Reds manager Dave Bristol went to his bullpen and brought in southpaw Billy McCool. Mauch reacted by sending right-handed-batting Jackie Brandt to the plate.

Brandt hit a high chop to third with the infield playing in. He was thrown out at first while Rojas held at third and Sutherland took second. With pinch-hitter Tony Taylor at bat, the Phillies attempted a squeeze play. The Reds guessed what was happening and McCool threw a pitchout. Rojas was caught in a rundown along the third-base line. McCool then got Taylor to fly out, ending another Phillies opportunity to grab a win.

"You know Gene [Mauch] squeezes a lot," Bristol said later. He had signaled his infielders to be ready for the bunt possibility. "They fooled me," Mauch acknowledged. "I never thought that they'd pitch out with Allen coming up next. They showed me something there."[2]

Dick Hall took over the pitching duties for the Phillies in the top of the 13th and pitched five scoreless innings. The Reds put runners in scoring position in the 14th inning when Pete Rose hit a two-out single and went to third when Perez followed with a single to right field. The hit extended Rose's hitting streak to 17 games. Mauch later kidded with reporters about "stopping Rose from getting a hit in the first game of the doubleheader."[3] When Rose hit another single in the 17th, he was the last Red to reach base.

Hall pitched the final six innings. When Mauch asked him if he was all right to continue pitching, Hall told him, "I'm all right. I just had nine days rest."[4]

Meanwhile McCool kept the Phillies in check through the 14th inning. In the 15th he was replaced by Don Nottebart. Nottebart got the Phils out in order in the 15th but had to work himself out of a jam the next inning. In that inning Allen led off with a triple off the scoreboard in right field. Two intentional walks loaded the bases with one out. Dalrymple then hit a groundball to Rose, who had moved to second in the eighth. Rose threw out Allen at the plate, and catcher Johnny Edwards threw to first to get Dalrymple for the double play retiring the side.

The Reds went to their bullpen again in the 17th. Darrell Osteen got the side out in order. When he returned to the mound the next inning, Osteen fanned leadoff batter Dick Hall, then walked Allen, who reached second when Callison grounded out weakly to the right side of the infield. Don Lock, who had entered the game as a substitute for Briggs five innings earlier, hit a single to center field. The speedy Allen did not stop at third and reached home before the throw from Vada Pinson.

The Phillies' 2-1 victory split the series. Bill Ford of the *Cincinnati Enquirer* described the contest as a "titanic struggle that embellished splendid pitching, shrewd strategy and futile frustration."[5]

It took the Phillies 4 hours and 38 minutes to get home the winning run. It tied for the longest game by innings in the majors at that point in the season. (The Red Sox had beat the Yankees, 7-6, on April 16 in a game took 5 hours and 50 minutes to complete, more than an hour longer than it took the Phillies to claim victory.)

Mauch was in a jovial mood after the game, telling reporters, "Every game makes somebody happy." He was asked if he had ever seen a team blow as many chances as his Phillies had in this game. "It happened for us once," he said. "The Giants had the winning run on third twice with none out and one on second – in the 10th, 11th, and 12th. That's the night when Alvin Dark picked up the stool in the clubhouse and tore his finger off when he threw it."[6] Mauch was not throwing any furniture this evening.

The win did not get the Phillies out of their slump. They lost five of their next six games. But they eventually got on track and finished the season in fifth place in the 10-team NL with an 82-80 record. The Reds continued to lead the league but they lost their early-season momentum. After the 18-inning loss in Philadelphia, they lost six of their next 10 games in May. St. Louis eventually overtook the Reds for first place by the end of June and remained there on their way to a World Series championship while the Reds finished in fourth place.

SOURCES

In addition to the sources cited in the Notes, the author used Baseball-Reference.com and Retrosheet.org for box-score, player, team, and season information as well as pitching and batting game logs, and other pertinent material.

baseball-reference.com/boxes/PHI/PHI196705210.shtml

retrosheet.org/boxesetc/1967/B05210PHI1967.htm

NOTES

1 Frank Dolson, "Every Game Has a Happy Side, Mauch Says," *Philadelphia Inquirer*, May 22, 1967: 25.

2 Dolson.

3 Dolson.

4 Dolson.

5 Bill Ford, "Reds Struggle 18 Innings, Then Phils Take 2-1 Decision," *Cincinnati Enquirer*, May 22, 1967: 48.

6 Dolson: 26.

Carlton's 16 Strikeouts Not Enough in Classic Duel with Short

September 20, 1967
Philadelphia Phillies 3, St. Louis Cardinals 1

By Doug Feldmann

The names Ed Spiezio, Steve Huntz, Dave Ricketts, and Eddie Bressoud dotting manager Red Schoendienst's lineup on September 20, 1967, at Connie Mack Stadium were not typical ones for the St. Louis Cardinals. Yet, the men whom the strange platoon was replacing – Brock, Javier, McCarver, Maxvill, and others – had already completed their work. With two weeks to spare, Schoendienst's usual starting nine clinched the National League pennant two nights earlier in Philly as Bob Gibson, rampaging back to form in his third start after being sidelined with a broken leg from a Roberto Clemente line drive in mid-July, registered a 13th victory in his interrupted season. The triumph stretched the Cardinals' lead over the San Francisco Giants to an impassable chasm of 13 games.

That same insurmountable lead stood by the time Steve Carlton (14-8) took the mound on the 20th as the Cardinals (96-56) were looking to complete a perfect six-game road trip. The journey began with Carlton's previous start, on the 15th at Crosley Field in Cincinnati – a 4-0 shutout over the Reds' 19-year-old rookie Gary Nolan, running the left-hander's scoreless-inning streak to 26. The 22-year-old Carlton, in his first year as a full-time starter for the Cardinals, had

struck out 150 entering the game in Philadelphia, second on the team only to fellow youngster Dick Hughes's total of 155. (Hughes had fanned seven Phillies in a 1-0 shutout the previous evening.) As the white-hot southpaw strode to the center of the Philadelphia stadium, the Cardinals' pitching staff had permitted a mere four runs in the team's five contests since leaving St. Louis.

To counter the Cardinals' talented young southpaw, Philadelphia Phillies' manager Gene Mauch "rested Tony Gonzalez, Bill White, and John Callison," Bill Conlin of the *Philadelphia Daily News* reviewed of the Phillies' batting order, "going with an all righthanded hitting lineup for the first time since July."[1]

Taking the hill for the home team was another left-hander in Chris Short. Despite a strong 2.51 ERA, Short held a record of 7-11, had lost his last three starts, and was winless from the Fourth of July until nearly Labor Day (partly due to the Phillies having scored only 14 runs in his 11 defeats). He had been Mauch's choice in the season's home opener on April 14, and was now hurling in the home finale before the Phillies (77-73, sitting in the middle of the NL pack) finished their schedule in Houston and on the West Coast. "In between, there was a lot of blood, sweat, and tears," wrote Conlin regarding Short's 1967 expedition. "In between, Short won only six other games, tore ligaments in his right knee, was divorced in Mexico, suffered muscle spasms in his lower back, was married, and lost a brilliantly pitched game on his wedding night."[2] Also "in between" was a scoreless two-inning performance by Short in the All-Star Game on July 11 – having followed Gibson's own two scoreless innings in the game and four days before Gibson suffered his broken leg.

While the September 20 contest did not impact the pennant race, the mere 8,466 who entered Connie Mack Stadium were treated to perhaps the greatest pitching duel of the season.

Short retired the first nine men he faced, while Carlton struck out the first four Philadelphia batsmen before hits from Bobby Wine, Tony Taylor, and Cookie Rojas plated a run in the third that ended his scoreless inning string at 28⅓. The Phils threatened for more when Rojas and Taylor pulled off a double steal and Don Lock walked to load the bases, but Carlton proceeded to fan Rico Joseph and get Gary Sutherland to loft a fly ball to Curt Flood in center.

The Cardinals answered immediately in the top of fourth as Spiezio broke through against Short with a leadoff home run left field to tie the game, 1-1, a shot that cleared the roof of the ballpark. It would be the only success they mustered against Short all evening.

The Phillies took the lead again with a run in their fourth and added another in the seventh inning for a 3-1 lead. The latter score was aided by a throwing error by Flood, who was firing overhand for the first time in several days, having suffered a sore arm and trying to let the wing heal by throwing side-arm only.

Despite slipping behind, Carlton continued to issue a variety of "stuff" that largely baffled the Phillies. After Sutherland singled to lead off the bottom of the eighth, Carlton fanned Gene Oliver for his 16th strikeout in 7⅓ innings – two shy of the major-league record (shared at the time by Sandy Koufax and Bob Feller) and one short of Dizzy Dean's Cardinals mark set in 1933. "Suddenly, the crowd was rooting for him," sportswriter Conlin noted.[3]

Billy Cowan was next to the plate as Carlton eyed his next strikeout victim. But when he tapped a ball to third baseman Mike Shannon to force Sutherland (and Wine flied out to Alex Johnson in right), the record fell out of Carlton's reach – unless the Cardinals could mount a comeback in the top of the ninth and force the Phillies to bat again.

Short, however, was equal to the task. A single by Flood was all St. Louis could generate as Short finished the evening with a complete-game four-hitter in a 3-1 win in a game that took 2 hours and 21 minutes. "Under ordinary circumstances, Short's pitching would have rated notice strikeout-wise too," noted Allen Lewis in the *Philadelphia Inquirer*. "The Delaware lefty fanned nine, and the two-club total of 25 came within one of the NL record for a nine-inning game."[4]

While Carlton knew he was dominant, he was unaware of his feat "until a fan yelled that I had 15 and I heard Oliver and the umpire talk about the record," he told *St. Louis Post-Dispatch* beat writer Neal Russo in the locker room.[5] Carlton said he had five or six more chances to notch strikeouts on other two-strike counts, "but I made a bunch of mistakes, and that's why I lost."[6] Oliver, who managed two hits in the game, was duly impressed. "He struck me out on a great low curve. He's as good as any lefthander in the league, including Bob Veale and Mike McCormick."[7] Added Lock, "You say he's only 22 years old? I'd like to trade places with him."[8] It was the most strikeouts by any pitcher at Connie Mack Stadium since Art Mahaffey whiffed 17 in the second game of a Sunday doubleheader on April 23, 1961.

Carlton's impressive total, however, was not the most he had achieved in professional baseball, as Russo pointed out. "He struck out 17 when he pitched for the Cardinals' Winnipeg farm club — and he lost the game."[9]

To what did Carlton credit his extra power on this evening in Philadelphia? Reliever Hal Woodeshick, who snapped Lou Brock out of a recent slump by suggesting Brock imbibe in pregame milkshakes, had the answer. "Before the game I took Steve out to dinner," Woodeshick revealed about his hotel roommate, "and I got him to eat cherrystone clams for the first time."[10]

The Cardinals returned home to St. Louis with a hero's welcome at 1:30 the following morning. Hundreds braved an overnight rainstorm to greet the chartered flight of the National League champions as the plane taxied into Lambert Field, while "fans threw fake [World Series] money into the air at Orlando Cepeda, who returned the gesture with a hearty laugh."[11]

Chris Short, meanwhile, used the stellar night to help catapult himself into a 19-win season for the Phillies in 1968 — his last strong campaign in the big leagues.

SOURCES

In addition to the sources listed in the Notes, the author consulted Baseball-Reference.com, Retrosheet.org, and SABR.org

NOTES

1   Bill Conlin, "Lousy Night for Short to Look Brilliant," *Philadelphia Daily News*, September 21, 1967.

2   Conlin.

3   Conlin.

4   Allen Lewis, "Carlton Fans 16, but Phillies' Short Beats Cards, 3-1," *Philadelphia Inquirer*, September 21, 1967.

5   Neal Russo, "Old Story, Same Ending for Carlton," *St. Louis Post-Dispatch*, September 21, 1967.

6   Russo.

7   Russo.

8   Russo.

9   Russo.

10   Russo.

11   Doug Feldmann, *El Birdos: The 1967 and 1968 St. Louis Cardinals* (Jefferson, North Carolina: McFarland and Company, 2007), 157.

27 Outs, 7 Baserunners, and 1 Run:
George Culver Labors Through No-Hitter

July 29, 1968:
Cincinnati Reds 6, Philadelphia Phillies 1
(Second Game of a Doubleheader)

By Gregory H. Wolf

George Culver was feeling sick. "I had an upset stomach," said the 25-year-old right-hander in his first season with the Cincinnati Reds. "I felt lousy, real weak and listless."[1] Not only bothered by nausea and a loss of appetite, the converted reliever suffered from a terribly ingrown toenail. I had to get a shot of Novocain before I could put my shoe on."[2] Culver was scheduled to start the second game of a twin bill against the Philadelphia Phillies, but wasn't sure if he could. "I didn't warm up long," he recalled. "I didn't feel good warming up."[3] The final result was the best game of his career.

Skipper Dave Bristol's Reds were beginning to click on all cylinders as they arrived in the City of Brotherly Love to kick off a three-game, two-day series against the Phillies. The team had won seven of its last nine games to move above .500 (49-47) and into third place, yet trailed the streaking St. Louis Cardinals by 14½ games. After a franchise-record six consecutive winning campaigns, the sixth-place Phillies (48-51) were rapidly sinking into irrelevance. They had won their last two games,

mercifully ending a nine-game losing streak for manager Bob Skinner, the team's third pilot of the season.

Connie Mack Stadium, the deteriorating, one-time jewel and first modern steel-and-concrete ballpark in the US, drew a crowd of 14,083 for a Monday evening doubleheader, considerably more than the Phillies' NL-low season average of 8,204. Skinner's squad showed some resiliency in the first game, overcoming a 6-3 deficit to tie game in the eighth, before Pete Rose tripled and scored the go-ahead run in the ninth. Charlie Hustle, playing right field, ended the game when he fielded Johnny Callison's single and fired a strike to home plate and nailed Dick Allen.

Scheduled to start the second game, Culver arrived during the middle of the first contest and tried to conserve his energy. An offseason acquisition in a multiplayer trade with the Cleveland Indians for Reds speedster Tommy Harper, Culver had appeared in 53 games in 1967, but only once as a starter. He emerged in '68 as one of the Reds' most effective starters, sporting an 8-9 slate (3.02 ERA). His opponent was Chris Short, a 30-year-old southpaw and workhorse who had won 20 games two years earlier. He owned a stellar 2.66 ERA, despite a 9-10 record that pushed his career numbers to 105-93.

After the Reds left two on in the first, a wobbly Culver took the mound. Leadoff hitter Tony Taylor smashed a hard-bouncing grounder that seemed destined to get past shortstop Woody Woodward. The versatile infielder, acquired in early June from the Atlanta Braves, made a quick move to his left, reached the ball, and then made an off-balance throw which, according to sportswriter Allen Lewis of the *Philadelphia Inquirer*, Don Pavletich scooped out of the dirt.[4] That sequence proved to be the defensive gem of the game and one of just two hard-hit balls by the Phillies.

In the bottom of the second, Phillies enigmatic star Dick Allen led off with what Phillies beat reporter Bill Conlin of the *Philadelphia Daily News* described as a "twisting short hop" to third base which Tony Perez fumbled.[5] Woodward snared the carom and threw wildly over Pavletich's head and Allen was standing on second courtesy of the two errors. "It hit the heel of my glove," explained Perez. "It was a tough play, but I am supposed to make tough plays."[6] After Don Lock walked with one out, Cookie Rojas's sacrifice fly drove in Allen.

Rose, who began the day as the NL's second leading hitter (.326), led off the third with a single and tied the game when the league's third-leading batter, Alex Johnson doubled. Consecutive two-out walks to Perez and Pavletich filled the bags. Pat Corrales, promoted from Triple-A Indianapolis about two weeks earlier, hit a grounder that "dribbled off [shortstop Roberto] Pena's outstretched glove," wrote sportswriter Bill Ford of the *Cincinnati Enquirer*, enabling Johnson and Perez to become Corrales' first two RBIs as a Red.[7]

"I was thinking about [a no-hitter] from the third on," admitted Culver. "I looked up and saw the scoreboard with one run and no hits and thought it would be unusual if I could get a no-hitter with run scored."[8] Culver might have also wondered if he would escape the inning when his road roommate Corrales was called for catcher's interference with Short at bat to put the leadoff man on, the Phillies' fourth baserunner. Three straight routine grounders ended the frame.

The Reds were a powerful offensive team in '68, and eventually led the majors in scoring (690 runs) and batting average (.273), and they could see Short didn't have his best stuff. In the fourth, Rose, Tommy Helms, and Johnson strung together one-out singles resulting in another run. After May drew a one-out walk to load the bases, Pavletich sliced a two-run single to give the Reds a 6-1 lead and send Short to the showers.

While Phillies relievers Gary Wagner (4⅓ innings) and Turk Farrell (1 inning) did their part by shutting down the Reds the remainder of the game, yielding just three hits, the Phillies couldn't solve Culver, though he gave them some chances.

Culver had retired 11 straight batters when "the pressure began to mount in the sixth," wrote Ford.[9] The 6-foot-2, 185-pound Californian issued consecutive two-out walks to Callison and Allen, but used his heater to fan five-time St. Louis Cardinals All-Star Bill White to end the threat.

Bill Conlin reported that Culver exhibited "ragged control" and ran deep counts all game.[10] The hurler's wildness flared up again in the eighth; he issued leadoff walks to Gonzalez and Taylor. Skipper Bristol motioned for reliever Clay Carroll to start warming up and made a slow trek to the mound. "I don't really remember what he said other than if I was tired. I said, 'Hell no,'" quipped Culver after the game.[11] "I just tried to calm him down," retorted Bristol, a hothead skipper, just 35 years old. "I didn't know what to tell him. I'm not that smart."[12] Culver retired the next two batters, then got a scare when Allen hit a hard liner, the first ball that remotely resembled a hit since Taylor's leadoff grounder. Two-time All-Star second baseman Tommy Helms knocked it down, scooped it up, and tossed to first to just beat Allen to end the inning.

"I was determined that if they were going to get a hit, it was going to be on a good pitch," said Culver about starting the ninth inning. "I was giving 'em all breaking stuff even though my fastball was working good."[13] Culver and Corrales agreed to go exclusively with sliders and the plan worked to perfection. White swung at the first pitch and grounded to Pavletich, then Lock sent the second pitch back to the mound, a feeble grounder for a 1-3 putout. Culver needed just one more out to complete the Reds first no-hitter since teammate Jim Maloney's 10-inning, 10-walk victory over the Chicago Cubs at Wrigley Field on August 19, 1965, and the first at Connie Mack Stadium since the Los Angeles Dodgers' Sandy Koufax turned the trick on June 4, 1964. To the plate stepped Rojas, the Cuban-born infielder who began the day batting just .239. "I was afraid of [him]," said Culver, perhaps with a flair for the dramatic. "He has hit me pretty well in the winter leagues. As a matter of fact, he once was my manager in Puerto Rico."[14] After swinging and missing on Culver's first pitch, Rojas took a half-swing, according Ford, on the second offering and popped up to Pavletich.[15] The first baseman corralled the ball, ensuring Culver's no-hitter, and ending the game in 2 hours and 43 minutes.

What followed was a "near mob scene," opined Ford. Corrales sprinted to the mound to congratulate his pitcher, while teammates spurted from the dugout for a group celebration.[16] Many Phillies fans, who had been cheering enthusiastically since the eighth inning for Culver to make history, bolted over barriers and rushed on the field.

Culver faced 34 batters, retired 14 of them on groundballs, fanned four, and walked five in what proved to be the best-pitched game of his big-league career. Basking in the afterglow of his accomplishments for a few days, Culver came back down to earth, losing his next three starts and seven of his last nine decisions to finish the season with an 11-16 record and 3.23 ERA in 226 innings. The following season, he served as a swingman, then moved into a full-time relieving role in mid-1970, spending his final five seasons with four different clubs.

SOURCES

In addition to the sources cited in the Notes, the author accessed Retrosheet.org, Baseball-Reference.com, Newspapers.com, and SABR.org.

NOTES

1   Bill Conlin, "'Sick' Culver Staggers to No-Hitter Over Phillies," *Philadelphia Daily News*, July 30, 1968: 49.

2   Ralph Bernstein (Associated Press), "Culver Felt Ill, Also Took Shot for Achy Toe," *Philadelphia Inquirer*, July 30, 1968: 25.

3   Conlin.

4   Allen Lewis, "Culver Hurls No-Hitter, Reds Sweep Phils," *Philadelphia Inquirer*, July 30, 1968: 25.

5   Conlin.

6   Conlin.

7   Bill Ford, "Culver No-Hits Phils, 6-1," *Cincinnati Enquirer*, July 30, 1968: 31.

8   Ford, "Culver No-Hits Phils, 6-1."

9   Bill Ford, "Culver Makes Calls, Gets Calls After No-Hitter," *Cincinnati Enquirer*, July 31, 1968: 22.

10 Conlin.

11 Ford, "Culver Makes Calls, Gets Calls After No-Hitter."

12 Bernstein.

13 Ford, "Culver No-Hits Phils, 6-1."

14 Ford, "Culver Makes Calls, Gets Calls After No-Hitter."

15 Ford, "Culver Makes Calls, Gets Calls After No-Hitter."

16 Ford, "Culver No-Hits Phils, 6-1."

STONEY SETS RECORD FOR FASTEST NO-HITTER BY A FRANCHISE

April 17, 1969
Montreal Expos 7, Philadelphia Phillies 0

By Adam J. Ulrey

It seems that the Expos wanted to give their fans a lifetime of memories as quickly as possible.

As if the inaugural game at Shea Stadium or the first home win at Jarry Park weren't memorable enough, the Expos quickly adopted a flair for the dramatic in just the franchise's ninth game, on April 17, 1969. That night, Bill Stoneman pitched a no-hitter against the Philadelphia Phillies, allowing *Nos Amours*–a French expression meaning Our Loves–to achieve the feat more quickly than any other team.[1]

Montreal came into the game at Connie Mack Stadium with a 3-5 record and was playing its seventh game on the road after two at Jarry Park. What made this game more improbable was Stoneman's career to date. Drafted in 1966 in the 31st round by the Chicago Cubs, he was called up to the big leagues in 1967 and went 2-5 over the next two years, mostly as a reliever. He earned the nickname Toy Tiger as much for his size (5-feet-10), as for his determination. Chicago manager Leo Durocher gave Stoneman only two starts, while using him in relief 44 times. The Expos selected Stoneman with the 10th pick in the 1968 expansion draft, viewing him as a starter even though he had only two starts in his major-league career. Going

into this contest, he had an 0-2 record and a 5.00 ERA.

Stoneman's inexperience showed in his first appearance of the season, when he gave up four earned runs in 1/3 of an inning against the Mets and left the game with a 108.00 ERA. His second outing was slightly better: He pitched 8⅔ innings and gave up all seven runs (but only one earned) in a 7-6 loss to the Cubs. His teammates made three errors behind him.

In this game, though, the defense was excellent from the beginning. Center fielder Don Bosch recovered from a late jump to grab a sinking fly ball by Don Money in the second. In the next inning, Rusty Staub preserved the no-hitter when he snared a liner off the bat of Tony Taylor.

As historic a night as it was for Stoneman, some of his teammates also had noteworthy evenings. In addition to his fielding heroics, Staub put on a batting clinic with four hits, including three doubles and a fourth-inning home run, his third of the season. Staub had 10 total bases in the game and drove in three runs. Le Grand Orange was blossoming.

Also joining the hit parade was rookie Coco Laboy, who rapped out four singles and drove in a run to help the Expos to their fourth win of the year.

Phillies pitchers had forgettable nights. Starter Jerry Johnson went eight innings and gave up four runs (three earned) on 11 hits. The Expos opened the scoring with an unearned run in the third. Laboy singled and went to second when Gary Sutherland reached on an error. After Stoneman struck out, Laboy scored when Tony Taylor made the Phillies' second error of the inning, this time on a Bosch grounder.

Staub homered leading off the fourth inning and with the Expos in front 2-0 in the sixth, run-scoring singles by Ty Cline and Laboy upped the lead to 4-0. In the ninth the Expos put the game away for good with three more runs off Bill Wilson. Staub doubled with the bases loaded, plating Stoneman and Bosch and moving Maury Wills to third. Turk Farrell replaced Wilson and allowed Wills to score on a wild pitch to make the score 7-0.

Stoneman's determination showed in the ninth inning as he finished the game in style, striking out Ron Stone and Johnny Briggs, and then inducing the dangerous Deron Johnson to ground out to Wills. Overall, Stoneman faced 31 batters, struck out eight and walked five. Stoneman later admitted that he wasn't overpowering that night.

"People think that a pitcher who throws a no-hitter totally dominates the game, but that isn't always true," he said. "I had trouble with my control and gave up five walks, which is something that happened a lot in my career."[2]

As sweet as the win was for the players, this game also provided some revenge for Expos manager Gene Mauch, who was fired by the Phillies after 53 games the previous season. Not only did his new team lay a beating on his old one, but he was serenaded by the fans chanting "we want Mauch" from the seventh inning until the end of the game.[3]

The Expos' reaction to the event seems almost quaint by today's standards. Management ripped up Stoneman's contract and gave him a new one with a $2,000 raise. Then, between games of an April 20 doubleheader against the Cubs, public address announcer Claude Mouton asked fans to stay in their seats and then called Stoneman out of the dugout. Team president John McHale pointed to a new Renault car in center field, a gift from the Renault Company. However, the big surprise came when one of the car's doors opened and out stepped Stoneman's mother along with a brother just back from Vietnam.

Nonetheless, Stoneman's first no-hitter was no fluke. He repeated the feat on October 2, 1972, at Montreal's Jarry Park against the Mets, winning by the same 7–0 score. Stoneman struck out nine, but had control problems, walking seven. Ironically, this was the last complete game of his career. He is the only pitcher in major league history to pitch no-hitters in his first and last career complete games.

SOURCES

In addition to the sources listed in the notes, the author consulted:

Ballparks.com

Blackman, Ted. "Stoney Staggered by Montreal Huzzahs Over No-Hitter," *The Sporting News*, May 3, 1969.

Baseball-reference.com.

Conniemackstadium.com.

King, Norman. "Expos get first franchise no-hitter right out of the gate," *Baseball Research Journal*, Spring 2002.

Philadelphia Athletics Historical Society.

NOTES

1   In the expansion era, the California Angels held the previous record, when Bo Belinsky pitched a 2-0 no-hitter against Baltimore on May 5, 1962, in the franchise's 181st game.

2   Al Doyle, "Bill Stoneman: The Game I'll Never Forget: Right-Hander Who Tossed Two No-Hitters During His Career Recalls Victory Over Padres in Which He Fanned 14 Batters," *Baseball Digest*, June 2005.

3   Jacques Doucet and Marc Robitaille, *Il était une fois les Expos*, Volume I (Montreal: Éditions Hurtubise Inc., 2009), 82.

BIRTH OF THE BIG RED MACHINE

August 3, 1969
Cincinnati Reds 19, Philadelphia Phillies 17

By Rich D'Ambrosio

The Philadelphia Phillies could not have picked a better day for a batting-helmet giveaway than Sunday, August 3, 1969. The 13,181 in attendance at Connie Mack Stadium witnessed one of the highest-scoring games in the ballpark's fabled history and, unbeknownst to them, the birth of the Cincinnati Reds' fabled Big Red Machine.

The 1968 season had been regarded as "The Year of the Pitcher," so Major League Baseball made some subtle changes in order to inject more offense into the game in 1969, including as lowering the pitcher's mound from 15 inches to 10 inches. The Phillies moved in the outfield fences at Connie Mack Stadium, shortening the distance from home plate to center field from 447 feet to 410 feet so as to allow for more home runs. As a result of expansion, baseball also welcomed four new teams. Their relatively weak pitching staffs had a propitious effect on batting averages in both leagues.

The August 3 game against Cincinnati came in the middle of a long homestand that began with back-to-back doubleheaders against the Atlanta Braves. The previous week had few dull moments, thanks to an ongoing feud between slugger Dick Allen and manager Bob Skinner. Allen, recently reinstated from a 26-game suspension, had moved

his belongings out of the Phillies' locker room and into a private storage closet and had begun to scrawl messages in the dirt around first base. All of this took attention away from the poor play of the Phillies, who were mired in fifth place in the National League East with a dismal 43-61 record. The Reds (54-44), meanwhile, were in the middle of a tense pennant race in the newly-formed National League West, and trailed the first-place Braves by one game.

The Phillies sent rookie Billy Champion to the mound against veteran Camilo Pascual for the Reds. The Reds opened the scoring with a run in the first, but the Phillies countered with three in their first on three consecutive doubles by Allen, Johnny Callison, and Deron Johnson. That finished Pascual, who lasted one-third of an inning. He was replaced by veteran Jack Fisher.

Each team scored a run in the second, then Cincinnati got three in the third and went ahead 5-4. Champion left the game with a blister on a pitching finger and was relieved by Al Raffo. In the bottom of the third the Phillies erupted for five runs off Fisher and Clay Carroll, highlighted by a bases loaded-triple by Cookie Rojas. At the end of three innings the Phillies led 9-5.

After scratching out a run in the fourth, the Reds rolled out the thunder in the fifth, the inning the Big Red Machine was launched. Chico Ruiz (the bane of the Phillies' existence since his steal of home triggered their ignominious collapse in 1964) began the scoring blitz by reaching base on a bad throw by Phillies' pitcher John Boozer on a comebacker. Carroll singled, and Boozer was relieved by Turk Farrell, who allowed a single to Pete Rose to load the bases. With one out, Alex Johnson hit a two-run single. Tony Perez doubled home another run. With Johnson on third and Perez at second, Lee May blasted a tape measure three-run homer onto the left-field roof, his 30th round-tripper of the season. Johnny Bench followed with a double and scored on a single by Woodie Woodward. Farrell (charged with six runs in a third of an inning pitched) was replaced by Lowell Palmer. Ruiz greeted the rookie pitcher with a single. Two batters later, Rose blasted a three-run homer. The Reds had scored 10 runs and led 16-9. Palmer finally ended the carnage by retiring Bobby Tolan on a fly ball. Cincinnati added two more runs off Palmer in the sixth and increased their lead to a seemingly secure 18-9.

The bizarre game featured another message in the dirt around first base by Dick Allen. He scratched LEE and RICHIE ALLEN NO 15 with his spikes. The LEE was a tribute to first base ump Lee Weyer and Reds first baseman Lee May.

The Phillies mounted a spirited comeback in the bottom of the sixth inning. Larry Hisle led off with a walk. With one out, Callison singled. Johnson drove Hisle home with a single, and Ron Stone singled to load the bases. Reds manager Dave Bristol brought in Pedro Ramos to relieve Carroll. Don Money greeted the veteran right-hander with a single, scoring Callison and Johnson. Pinch-hitter Rich Barry singled, and the bases were loaded again. Tony Taylor unloaded them by belting his first major-league grand slam and making the score a suddenly close 18-16.

Allen hit his 23rd homer of the season, a solo shot into the upper left-field bleachers, off Ramos in the seventh and it was 18-17. The Reds added an insurance run in the eighth on Perez's home run off Billy Wilson. In the bottom of the ninth the Phillies, trailing 19-17, mounted a last-ditch rally. Reds reliever Wayne Granger got two quick outs, but walked Callison and gave up a single to Johnson. With the tying runs on base, Ron Stone worked the count to 2-and-0 before hitting a line drive to right field. Rose lunged and made a shoetop catch to end the game.

There was evidence that the teams used juiced baseballs during the game. The previous afternoon, the Eastern League All-Stars played the Reading Phillies at Connie Mack Stadium after the Phillies-Reds game. The Eastern League president Tommy Richardson said the game was to be played with a ball that was 5 percent livelier. "We're using experimental ball Five Triple X. The players don't know it."[1] During the game, one of the minor-league all-stars hit a home run over the Cadillac sign on the left-field roof, a target that was normally only reached by hitters like Allen and Hank Aaron. Phillies manager Skinner, watching the game from a box seat, turned to GM John Quinn and said, "What kind of ball are they using?"[2] On Sunday, the Reds put on a display in batting practice "that had the crowd buzzing as ball after ball flew out of the park."[3] Bench hit a ball far over the left-field roof and several others that landed in the upper deck.

Reds manager Dave Bristol swore that when he went out to remove a pitcher, he noticed that the ball was lopsided. Losing pitcher Farrell claimed that the ball being used felt like a watermelon. After Taylor's grand slam, Quinn joked, "We may be using the same balls we used in that exhibition game last night. I better check."[4] Bench also complained that despite a good pitch by Ramos, Taylor was able to hit a slam: "It was a curve, low and away. A helluva pitch. ... It's no fun to sit back there and think you called a good pitch and they hit it. You know what? My roomie (Pat Corrales) walked up to me after the last out and said, 'Congratulations. You called a nice game.'"[5]

Despite all of the offense, the game, which took 3 hours and 29 minutes to complete, did not break any National League records. The Reds' victory, their sixth in seven games, moved them past the Braves and into first place in the National League West. When the Reds arrived back in Cincinnati later that evening, they were greeted by a crowd of 500 fans. In his game account in the *Cincinnati Enquirer*, Bob Hertzel referred to the Reds as "The Big Red Machine."

Perhaps the most fitting comment on this game came from Skinner, who said, "Normally, once a season, every team goes crazy with the bat. Today, two teams did it at the same time. When you score 17 runs and lose, something's got to be wrong."[6] Skinner's frustration with the Phillies' losing ways and dealing with Allen would culminate in his resignation four days later.

SOURCES

In addition to the sources cited in the Notes, the author used the Baseball-Reference.com and Retrosheet.org websites.

NOTES

1   Frank Dolson, "Phils, Reds Didn't Use Experimental Ball-Or Did They?" *Philadelphia Inquirer*, August 4, 1969: 19.

2   Dolson.

3   Dolson.

4   Dolson.

5   Dolson.

6   Associated Press, "What's the Name of This Game?" (Cincinnati 19, Philadelphia 17), *Allentown* (Pennsylvania) *Morning Call*, August 4, 1969: 17.

Opening Day Swan Song

April 7, 1970
Philadelphia Phillies 2, Chicago Cubs 0

By Matt Albertson

The Philadelphia Phillies planned to open the 1970 season at the new Veterans Stadium in South Philadelphia but site delays forced the club to open its home schedule at the oldest ballpark in the major leagues, 61-year-old Connie Mack Stadium, on April 6, 1970. A crowd of 15,918 attended the home opener between the Phillies and Cubs and watched as the new-look Phillies, sporting new uniforms designed to usher in a new era in Phillies baseball at Veterans Stadium, shut out the Cubs 2-0. Chris Short pitched a five-hitter against former Phillies prospect Ferguson Jenkins.

In addition to stylish new white and maroon uniforms, the Phillies debuted a new, young lineup that included two flashy rookies, Larry Bowa at shortstop and Denny Doyle at second base. Only two Phillies played the same position on Opening Day 1970 as they did on Opening Day 1969, pitcher Chris Short and Larry Hisle in center field. The new-look Phillies hoped a fresh look and youthful lineup would be the start of a special rebuild in Philadelphia after finishing fifth in the National League East in 1969 with a 63-99 record. The *Philadelphia Evening Bulletin* expressed as much in an April 6, 1970, column: "While Bowa and Doyle may not be aware of it, they are assuming a double burden starting tomorrow – of

putting an untimely end to Philadelphia's reputation as the city of losers and reviving lagging fan interest in the National League Phillies."[1]

The Cubs on the other hand entered 1970 with a strong veteran lineup that finished the 1969 season in second place with a 92-70 record, eight games behind New York's "Miracle Mets." The Cubs' second-place finish was their highest since they won the National League pennant in 1945. The club was expected to compete for the pennant in 1970.

Opening Day 1970 was also Phillies skipper Frank Lucchesi's first game as a major-league manager. He was a veteran manager, having spent 19 years guiding squads in the minor leagues, but was awestruck on this day. "I came to the park early," he told *Evening Bulletin* reporter Ray Kelly, "and went out and looked around the empty stands. Then I stood in the dugout and thought what an honor it was to be in the same place where Mr. Connie Mack managed those great Athletics teams. It made me feel humble."[2] Lucchesi's first Opening Day in the big leagues was the last in history for the aged ballpark but the Philadelphia fans made it a memorable one.

The 15,918 fans made it sound as though the ballpark was filled to capacity when the opening lineups were announced. The famous Philadelphia fans erupted and left an indelible impact on the Phillies players. Veteran pitcher Chris Short simply said, "It was unbelievable." Phillies third-base coach George Myatt said he had never experienced anything like the ovation in his 35 years in baseball. Phillies pitcher Joe Hoerner, acquired from the St. Louis Cardinals in the offseason, said, "I actually got goose pimples. Third baseman Don Money said, "After that kind of reception there was no way we could lose." Lucchesi said he choked up. "I shed a tear or two," he said. "Let's face it, these people gave me, a complete stranger, an ovation and I hadn't even managed a ballgame yet."[3]

Phillies starting pitcher Chris Short was off his mark in the first inning but made it through unscathed. He walked Don Kessinger to open the frame and surrendered a single to center by Glenn Beckert. When Billy Williams grounded out to first, Kessinger and Beckert moved up. Ron Santo popped to second base. Short then walked Ernie Banks to load the bases but got out of the inning when Johnny Callison grounded to first base.

The Phillies' rookie double-play combination led off the home half of the first inning. Larry Bowa popped out to shortstop. Denny Doyle singled to right but was tagged out at second trying to stretch his hit into a double. Next up, Larry Hisle doubled to right field but the scoring threat ended when Deron Johnson popped out to third.

Both Short and Cubs starter Fergie Jenkins set their opponents down in order in the second inning.

Short held the Cubs scoreless in the third inning, then the Phillies broke the ice in the home half of the frame. Don Money led off with a double to left and took third on Short's grounder to second. Money held third as Bowa grounded to second. Then Doyle tripled to center, scoring Money. Larry Hisle grounded out to shortstop to end the inning.

The score remained 1-0 from the fourth through the top of the seventh inning, though

the Phillies threatened in the sixth. With one out, Denny Doyle got his third hit, a single to left, and went to second on Hisle's single. But Doyle was caught attempting to steal third as Deron Johnson struck out, completing an inning-ending double play.

In the bottom of the seventh, Tony Taylor singled through shortstop with one out. After Tim McCarver flied out to left, Money doubled to center, scoring Taylor. Short's groundball ended the frame. Money's RBI gave the Phillies a 2-0 lead going into the eighth inning.

Down two runs, Cubs manager Leo Durocher had Cleo James pinch-hit for Jenkins, who had thrown 94 pitches over seven innings and given up the two runs, eight hits, and one walk. Short retired James on a groundball to shortstop. Kessinger popped out to first and Beckert grounded out to second to end the inning. The Phillies failed to plate a run in the bottom of the inning.

Christ Short made short work of the Cubs' hitters in the top of the ninth inning and sent Williams, Santo, and Banks down in order to cap his shutout, achieved in a brisk 2 hours and 7 minutes. He threw 128 pitches and gave up five hits and two walks. He struck out three.[4]

Little fanfare was made of the final home opener at Connie Mack Stadium. The *Inquirer* and the *Evening Bulletin*, Philadelphia's two largest newspapers, only recapped the game and included short stories about players and coaches. Leading up to the game, more coverage was given to when the new Veterans Stadium in South Philadelphia would open for business. Although the ballpark was behind schedule, it was expected that Phillies games would be played at the Vet as early as May. This didn't happen and the opening was pushed back a year, to April 10, 1971. As the season progressed, a sense of nostalgia built for the old ballpark, culminating in festivities at the final Phillies home game on October 1, 1970.

SOURCES

In addition to the sources cited in the Notes, the author accessed Retrosheet.org, Baseball-Reference.com, Newspapers.com, and SABR.org.

NOTES

1   Ray Kelly, "Bowa, Doyle Key to Phils New Image," *Philadelphia Evening Bulletin*, April 6, 1970: 27.

2   Ray Kelly, "Lucchesi: 'I Shed a Tear,'" *Philadelphia Evening Bulletin*, April 8, 1970: 72.

3   Kelly, "Lucchesi: 'I Shed a Tear,'": 65.

4   Philadelphia Phillies 2, Chicago 0, retrosheet.org/boxesetc/1970/B04070PHI1970.htm.

GIBSON FANS 16 IN
HALL OF FAME MATCHUP WITH BUNNING

May 23, 1970
St. Louis Cardinals 3, Philadelphia Phillies 1

By Doug Feldmann

When would-be saboteurs tried to pull distractions on Bob Gibson, it never seemed to diminish his work. Rather, it merely poked the bear.

Before pitching the seventh game of the 1967 World Series in Boston, Gibson was disturbed in his hotel room three times in the middle of the night by "mistaken" wake-up calls. And when he sat down to his breakfast at the hotel's coffee shop in the morning, he was given burnt toast by his server – twice.

Therefore, in early hours of May 23, 1970, it was little wonder to the star pitcher that the fire alarm in the Sheraton Hotel in Philadelphia had been pulled at 6 o'clock in the morning – as Gibson and his St. Louis Cardinals were slated to face the Phillies that night in Connie Mack Stadium.[1] Rubbing his sleepy eyes inside another room down the hall was Dick Allen, the former Phillies slugger who had spent the past seven seasons in the City of Brotherly Love but was now returning to town as a Cardinal after being part of a multiplayer trade.

To Gibson's surprise, the alarm turned out to be legitimate. A fire had broken out on the 15th floor of the hotel, with the Cardinals staying on the 19th and 20th floors as Jose Cardenal, Mike

Shannon, and Julian Javier banged on doors to wake the inhabitants – but only after Javier struggled to locate his eyeglasses.[2] The groggy Cardinals (19-18, in second place in the National League's Eastern Division and winners of nine of their last 13) readied themselves for manager Frank Lucchesi's struggling Phillies (15-24, in last place in the East and losers of 12 of their last 14).

The tempestuous Allen had been acquired after the 1969 season in a trade involving seven players, including longtime St. Louis catcher Tim McCarver. McCarver had been a mainstay behind the plate for the Cardinals' three pennant-winning teams in the 1960s but would not be facing his old batterymate in Gibson on this particular evening, as he had broken his hand on May 2 and was lost to the Phillies for the next four months. Also shipped out of St. Louis in the transaction was outfielder Curt Flood, who refused to report to Philadelphia when the deal was announced.

Gibson, holding a 19-6 career record against the Phillies entering the game, was set to square off against fellow living legend Jim Bunning, who was 5-9 lifetime against the Cardinals. The two future Hall of Famers had seen better days; Gibson was 2-3, not having won since April 26 and being pounded by the Astros and Pirates in his last two starts with his ERA ballooning to 5.34. Bunning, meanwhile, was 1-5, having suffered from poor run support, evidenced by his 2.45 ERA.

Absent from the leadoff slot for the Cardinals was their customary figure. Yet another future inductee to Cooperstown, Lou Brock, had been out of the St. Louis lineup since he fouled a ball off his instep during batting practice five days before in Houston's Astrodome. "Brock, who has been wearing a sandal on his right foot, was ready to pinch-hit, manager Red Schoendienst said," wrote Neal Russo in the *St. Louis Post-Dispatch*.[3]

In Brock's stead was Cardenal, gazing out at the 13-year veteran Bunnin,g who entered the night with 2,689 career strikeouts –behind only Walter Johnson's distant total of 3,509. The game started an hour and 18 minutes late because of a lingering rainstorm as a sparse crowd of just over 12,000 fans looked on.

After retiring Cardenal on a groundout to rookie shortstop Larry Bowa and striking out Leron Lee for number 2,690, Bunning faced off against Allen. Challenging for the National League lead in hitting at .312, Allen was greeted with "far more boos than cheers," noted Russo.[4] A derisive banner hanging from the ballpark's left-field pavilion read, "How Do You Like Your New Babysitter, Richie?" – invoking a variation of Allen's first name that he did not appreciate.[5]

Waving his big club at Bunning, Allen had already left his mark against his former teammates in 1970, having homered three times against the Phillies – once in the series opener on May 21 off Woodie Fryman, once back in St. Louis off Bunning on May 11 (providing all three runs in a 3-0 Cardinals triumph), and the following night off Lowell Palmer as well.

On a 1-and-2 count, Allen caught hold of a Bunning curveball and sent a drive into the left-center-field gap. At the last second, center fielder Oscar Gamble swooped in and snared the ball.

When it was Gibson's turn to go to work in the bottom of the first, he looked over at first base and saw Allen back at his preferred position. Only in the past week had Dick returned there, having been forced to patrol third base since the start of the season with Shannon's absence due to his frightening battle with nephritis.

After Bunning escaped unharmed in the second when the Cardinals loaded the bases with nobody out, Allen returned for his second chance in the top of third. Stepping into the box with two down, he saw Lee on second base. Lee had singled and stolen second off rookie catcher Mike Compton (during the pregame rain delay, Lee had borrowed Allen's jersey, wrapped a towel around his head, and headed to the Phillies' dugout to say hello – a move that fooled the fans who were watching, but not his former teammates).

On a 2-and-2 count, Allen drove a long home run over the center-field wall to give the Cardinals a 2-0 advantage, "a titanic drive, well beyond the 410-foot marker," marveled Russo.[6]

Gibson, meanwhile, retired the first 10 Phillies he faced, seven on strikeouts. Denny Doyle broke the string with one out in the fourth inning by pushing a single to left field, snapping a personal 0-for-18 stretch. He was quickly erased, however, as Gamble grounded into a double play to Dal Maxvill at short to keep Gibson at the minimum faced.

Allen appeared again in the fifth with two out. He hooked a Bunning pitch just foul to the upper deck, making the count 1-and-2. On the next offering – a curveball low and away – he was able to keep the ball fair this time with "a drive that hit the sign on the roof in left field." Allen was actually fooled on the pitch, but simply "flicked his wrists" and his massive strength sent the sphere off the premises.[7] It was his 16th homer of the season, tying him for the major-league lead with Hank Aaron. "It was difficult to tell which balls were traveling faster – the ones Allen hit or the ones Gibson threw," *Philadelphia Inquirer* writer Allen Lewis concluded at that point.[8]

The minimum for Gibson continued through the Philadelphia fifth and sixth, as six more went down in order. Among them were four more strikeouts, bringing Gibson's total to 11, But Bunning, the fireballer from northern Kentucky, was nearly as good, fanning his counterpart Gibson to start the seventh and getting Cardenal looking on strikes as well. (Cardenal, ejected from the previous night's game for arguing a called third strike, had to then be restrained from home-plate umpire Ken Burkhart.)

Scoring against Gibson appeared hopeless until Larry Hisle walked to lead off the Phillies' eighth and was tripled home by Ron Stone. But Gibson righted himself, striking out Byron Browne in the ninth to end the game for a 3-1 Cardinals win in a mere 2 hours and 8 minutes.

Gibson's 16 strikeouts matched teammate Steve Carlton's total posted two nights earlier in Connie Mack Stadium and were his regular-season career high, topped only by his famous Game One performance (17 K's) in the 1968 World Series against the Detroit Tigers. "That was the hardest I've thrown since '68," Gibson affirmed. "Tonight I had something extra. And I got just about every pitch where I wanted."[9] It was Gibson's final appearance in Connie Mack Stadium with the opening of Veterans Memorial Stadium in the south end of town the following spring.

As for Bunning, his career would slightly outlast the old yard. After joining Cy Young in August 1970 as the only pitchers to record at least 100 victories in each league, Bunning returned to the Phillies for one final season in 1971 and won the first game in their shining new facility.

Allen, meanwhile, seemed to show little sentimentality for Philadelphia. "I just want to hit one more [homer in the series finale the next day] and get out of here," he said after the game.[10]

As the Cardinals headed to New York for the next leg of their road trip, Flood, their former All-Star center fielder, would be there as well — appearing as the plaintiff in his lawsuit against Major League Baseball's reserve clause at the courthouse in Manhattan.

In a gesture of friendship, Gibson left tickets for Flood at Shea Stadium should he wish to attend.[11]

SOURCES

In addition to the sources listed in the Notes, the author consulted Baseball-Reference.com, Retrosheet.org, and SABR.org.Notes

NOTES

1   Neal Russo, "Tired Hoolie Gets Four RBIs," *St. Louis Post-Dispatch*, May 23, 1970: 5A.

2   Doug Feldmann, *Gibson's Last Stand: The Rise, Fall, and Near-Misses of the St. Louis Cardinals, 1969-1975*, 70. (Columbia: University of Missouri Press, 2013).

3   Neal Russo, "Gibson and Allen Overcome Phillies, 3-1," *St. Louis Post-Dispatch*, May 24, 1970: 1E.

4   Russo.

5   Feldmann, 70.

6   Russo.

7   Russo, 4E.

8   Allen Lewis, "Allen's 2 Homers Rock Phils, 3-1," *Philadelphia Inquirer*, May 24, 1970: 16.

9   Lewis.

10 Lewis.

11 Feldmann, 71.

WRECKING BALL

October 1, 1970
Philadelphia Phillies 2, Montreal Expos 1
(10 Innings)

By Ken Carrano

The Philadelphia Phillies had hoped to play their 1970 season at the new Veterans Stadium, but delays in construction meant the 1970 season would at least begin at Connie Mack Stadium. Built in 1909 and originally called Shibe Park, Connie Mack Stadium was the home of the Philadelphia Athletics until 1954 and the Phillies beginning in July 1938. The Phillies vice president of baseball operations, Bill Giles, believed the that the team would move into Veterans Stadium in midsummer, so he celebrated Opening Day as a major event.[1] The game, however, drew only 15,918, and as the season progressed. It became apparent that the Phillies would finish the season at 21st & Lehigh.

Giles and his staff came up with a promotion for the last game that they called "Farewell to Connie Mack Stadium." Employees wore old-fashioned clothes, concessions sold peanuts for a nickel, and an old-time bicycle group performed.[2] Connie Mack Jr. gave some opening remarks before the game. Mack received a typical Philadelphia welcome. "For a while I thought I was dreaming I was in Philadelphia, then I heard the boos and I knew I was back," he told the crowd.[3] Claude Passeau, the pitcher who won the first game for the Phillies at Shibe Park on July 4, 1938, after their move from the Baker Bowl, threw out the first pitch.[4] Giles's plan was to give away several prizes after the game, including a 1970 Mustang, and then a helicopter would transport home plate to its new home. Those plans would need to be altered.

There was trouble before the game even started. Joseph Sohosky of Exton, Pennsylvania, was purchasing a ticket for the game around 7:30 P.M. when he felt a stinging sensation on his back. He turned and saw four youths running away and then saw he was bleeding from a stab wound. He was taken to a local hospital but returned to see the game.[5]

There was not much at stake for this final game of the season between the Phillies and Montreal Expos. Philadelphia entered the day 72-88, 15½ games behind their in-state rival Pittsburgh Pirates in the National League East Division. The Expos, in their second season, were a half-game better at 73-88. The Phillies started Barry Lersch (6-3), who had joined the starting rotation in mid-August. The Expos countered with Carl Morton, easily the best pitcher on their staff, who entered the game with a record of 18-11. Both pitched well but neither factored in the decision.

The Expos threatened in the second inning, when John Bateman reached on an error and

Bobby Wine singled him to third with two out, but Lersch struck out his counterpart Morton to end the threat. The Phillies scored in the third. Lersch led off with a single but was retired on a fielder's choice by Tony Taylor. Taylor scored when catcher Tim McCarver tripled to right. The run would be nearly enough for Lersch. He gave up a single in the fourth to Boots Day and one in the sixth to Ron Fairly, but was otherwise untouched until the eighth inning. In that inning a leadoff walk to Mack Jones was followed by an error by Taylor on a grounder off the bat of Jim Gosger, and the Expos were threatening. Gary Sutherland sacrificed the runners along and Rusty Staub was intentionally walked to load the bases. Fairly had a chance to put the Expos in the lead but struck out, and Lersch escaped the jam by getting Bob Bailey to ground out.

Morton was every bit Lersch's equal. After the run in the third inning, Morton scattered only four more hits through the eighth inning. Lersch, who had thrown three complete games since joining the rotation, was ready to finish off the season and close the curtain on Connie Mack Stadium, but he wouldn't only be playing against the Expos – he would also be competing against some of the some of the 31,822 in attendance. Lersch retired Day on a popup, bringing up Bateman, who lofted a fly ball to left. Ron Stone moved to catch the fly, but he had also brought some baggage. "When Stone broke for the ball, he discovered he was wearing a 130-pound kid, one of many who cavorted across the playing field late in the game."[6] "I couldn't believe it," Stone said. "I felt this kid grab my arm. When I tried to break away Lersch had already thrown the pitch."[7] Wine doubled to right-center to bring in pinch-runner Adolfo Phillips, and the game was tied, 1-1. Phillies manager Frank Lucchesi brought in the closer, Dick Selma, who quickly dispatched the Expos. "The statistics don't begin to tell the kind of year Selma had," McCarver said after the game.

The fan who had interfered with Stone was not the only on-field visitor that day. Two hundred police officers were on hand for the game but made few arrests. There were so many kids running on the field by the 10th inning that the umpiring crew considered forfeiting the game. "I told the umpires, 'Don't you even think about forfeiting. You forfeit and you'll get somebody hurt real bad,'" former Phillies manager Gene Mauch said after the game.[8]

The Expos brought in Howie Reed to pitch the ninth, and he got the Phillies in order to send the game to extra innings. Selma did the same to the Expos in the top of the 10th. After two outs, McCarver singled and stole second base, only his second steal of the year. Oscar Gamble then singled to center, sending McCarver home with what proved to be the last run to be scored at Connie Mack Stadium. "When Tim was on first I was trying to hit the ball a long way," said Gamble. "After the steal, I just wanted to get a hit."[9]

The game might have been over, but the mayhem would continue unabated. Allen Lewis noted for the *Philadelphia Inquirer* that "Lucchesi raced toward first base to congratulate Gamble, then both he and Oscar ran for their lives to the dugout as the fans raced on the field."[10]

The Phillies decided to help "celebrate" the final game at Connie Mack Stadium by passing out artifacts from the park to the crowd, including slats from old seat backs. It must have seemed like a good idea at the time. "The idea was to give away souvenir seat slats to discourage vandalism," Lewis stated.[11] Instead, vandalism is all the fans thought of. "When the fans wearied of using the wooden clubs to bash up the furniture they began throwing them at the players and at each other. Or using them like blackjacks," Bill Conlin in the *Philadelphia Daily News* reported.[12] Lewis reported in *The Sporting News* that "Fans ripped up their seats and ransacked the dugouts. They ripped off railings and billboards, tore up the infield cover, ripped up the coach's box, tore off doors and one fan even carried off one of the toilets."[13]

Joan Rosney, a nurse at the ballpark, treated 25 postgame casualties, nine of them injured badly enough to require hospitalization. An elderly man suffered a stroke after being swept onto the field after the game. "I got hit with a karate chop," coach Billy DeMars said. "They were stealing everything in sight; bats, helmets. It was mob violence. It kind of scares you."[14] The Phillies postponed the postgame giveaway of the prizes until the next day. It seemed that most of the fans had already gotten what they wanted.

SOURCES

In addition to the sources listed in the notes, the author accessed Retrosheet.org, Baseball-Reference.com, SABR's BioProject via SABR.org, *The Sporting News* archive via Paper of Record, the *New York Times* archives, and the *Chicago Tribune*, *Philadelphia Inquirer*, and *Philadelphia Daily News* via newspapers.com.

NOTES

1   Bruce Kuklick, *To Every Thing a Season: Shibe Park and Urban Philadelphia* (Princeton: Princeton University Press, 1991), 179.

2   Kuklick, 180.

3   Bill Conlin, "Connie Mack Stadium Expires with a Smash," *Philadelphia Daily News*, October 2, 1970: 3.

4   Allen Lewis, "Phils Bid Old Park Adieu – Fans Ransack the Place," *The Sporting News*, October 17, 1970: 33.

5   "Gets Stabbed, Still Sees Game," *Philadelphia Daily News*, October 2, 1970: 4.

6   Bill Conlin, "Phils Go Out in Proud, Scuffling Style," *Philadelphia Daily News*, October 2, 1970: 72.

7   Conlin, "Phils Go Out in Proud, Scuffling Style."

8   Conlin, "Phils Go Out in Proud, Scuffling Style."

9   Allen Lewis, "31,822 See Last Game at Stadium," *Philadelphia Inquirer*, October 2, 1970: 27.

10   Lewis, "31,822 See Last Game."

11   Lewis, "31,822 See Last Game."

12   Conlin, "Phils Go Out in Proud, Scuffling Style."

13   Lewis, "Phils Bid Old Park Adieu – Fans Ransack the Place."

14   Conlin, "Phils Go Out in Proud, Scuffling Style."

SHIBE PARK/CONNIE MACK STADIUM
BY THE NUMBERS

By Dan Fields

The ballpark was known as Shibe Park from 1909 through 1952 and as Connie Mack Stadium from 1953 through 1970.

1st

Night game in American League history, on May 16, 1939. The Cleveland Indians beat the Philadelphia Athletics 8-3 in 10 innings.

1st

Black player in Philadelphia Athletics history: Bob Trice, on September 13, 1953. In the first game of a doubleheader against the St. Louis Browns, he gave up five runs in eight innings and took the loss.

1-1

Score of a 24-inning tie between the Philadelphia Athletics and Detroit Tigers on July 21, 1945.

1.48 and 4.62

ERA of Rick Wise of the Philadelphia Phillies at home and on the road, respectively, in 1969.

2

All-Star Games played at Shibe Park. On July 13, 1943, the American League beat the National League 5-3. It was the first All-Star Game to be held at night and the first of 24 consecutive All-Star Games for Stan Musial. On July 8, 1952, the NL beat the AL 3-2 in five innings. It was the first All-Star Game to be cut short by rain.

2

Shutouts by Johnny Marcum of the Philadelphia Athletics in this first two major-league starts, on September 7, 1933, against the Cleveland Indians and on September 11, 1933 (second game of doubleheader), against the Chicago White Sox.

2

Grand slams in one game by Tony Lazzeri of the New York Yankees on May 24, 1936, and by Jim Tabor of the Boston Red Sox on July 4, 1939 (second game of doubleheader). They were the first two major leaguers to accomplish the feat.

2

Triples by Al Zarilla of the St. Louis Browns in the fourth inning on July 13, 1946, against the Philadelphia Athletics. He was the first player in the AL to hit two triples in an inning.

2

Bases-loaded triples hit by Elmer Valo of the Philadelphia Athletics on May 1, 1949, in the first game of a doubleheader against the Washington Senators.

2.49

ERA of the Philadelphia Athletics at home in 1914, the lowest by the team at Shibe Park/Connie Mack Stadium since 1913 (when ERA became an official statistic in the AL).

2.92

ERA of the Philadelphia Phillies at home in 1963, the lowest by the team at Shibe Park/Connie Mack Stadium.

4.54

ERA of the Philadelphia Phillies at home in 1961, the highest by the team at Shibe Park/Connie Mack Stadium.

5

Players who hit for the cycle at Shibe Park: Danny Murphy, Philadelphia Athletics, August 25, 1910; Bob Meusel, New York Yankees, July 3, 1922; Tony Lazzeri, New York Yankees, June 3, 1932; George Kell, Detroit Tigers, June 2, 1950 (second game of doubleheader); and Gus Bell, Pittsburgh Pirates, June 4, 1951.

5

Home runs by the Philadelphia Phillies in the eighth inning on June 2, 1949, against the Cincinnati Reds. Andy Seminick hit two of the home runs.

5.90

ERA of the Philadelphia Athletics at home in 1936, the highest by the team at Shibe Park/Connie Mack Stadium.

7

Consecutive batters struck out by Juan Marichal of the San Francisco Giants on September 6, 1964, against the Philadelphia Phillies.

8

World Series played at Shibe Park. The Philadelphia Athletics played in seven (1910, 1911, 1913, 1914, 1929, 1930, and 1931) and clinched the title at the ballpark in 1911, 1929, and 1930. The Philadelphia Phillies were swept by the New York Yankees in 1950.

9

Nine-inning complete-game no-hitters thrown at Shibe Park/Connie Mack Stadium, by Chief Bender of the Philadelphia Athletics on May 12, 1910; Bullet Joe Bush of the Philadelphia Athletics on August 26, 1916; Sad Sam Jones of the New York Yankees on September 4, 1923; Howard Ehmke of the Boston Red Sox on September 7, 1923; Dick Fowler of the Philadelphia Athletics on September 9, 1945 (second game of doubleheader); Bill McCahan of the Philadelphia Athletics on September 3, 1947; Sandy Koufax of the Los Angeles Dodgers on June 4, 1964; George Culver of the Cincinnati Reds on July 29, 1968 (second game of doubleheader); and Bill Stoneman of the Montreal Expos on April 17, 1969.

9

Runs scored by the Philadelphia Phillies before making an out on August 13, 1948, against the New York Giants. The Phillies scored 10 runs in the first inning and won 12-7.

10

Home runs by Harry Heilmann of the Detroit Tigers in 12 games at Shibe Park in 1922. He hit 11 home runs in the other 106 games he played that season.

10

Runs scored by the Philadelphia Athletics in the seventh inning of Game Four of the 1929 World Series against the Chicago Cubs. The rally erased an eight-run deficit, and the Athletics won 10-8.

11

Consecutive home wins by the Philadelphia Phillies from July 15 to July 22 (first game of doubleheader), 1955.

13

Consecutive home losses by the Philadelphia Athletics from May 27 to July 6 (first game of doubleheader), 1920, and by the Philadelphia Phillies from July 23 (second game of doubleheader) to September 3 (first game of doubleheader), 1944.

13

Runs scored by the Philadelphia Athletics in the eighth inning on June 15, 1925, against the Cleveland Indians. The Athletics overcame a 12-run deficit (during the seventh inning) to win 17-15.

13

Home runs during June 1934 at Shibe Park by Bob Johnson of the Philadelphia Athletics.

13

Home runs by the New York Yankees in a doubleheader against the Philadelphia Athletics on June 28, 1939. The Yankees hit eight in the first game, winning 23-2, and five in the second game, winning 10-0.

19-53-2

Record of Philadelphia Athletics at home in 1915, their worst year at Shibe Park/Connie Mack Stadium.

21-0

Score by which the New York Yankees beat the Philadelphia Athletics in the second game of a doubleheader on August 13, 1939.

22

Consecutive home wins by the Philadelphia Athletics from July 15 (first game of doubleheader) to August 31, 1931.

22-55-0

Record of the Philadelphia Phillies at home in 1945, their worst year at Shibe Park/Connie Mack Stadium. They had a home record of 22-55-1 in 1961.

23rd

And final career grand slam by Lou Gehrig of the New York Yankees, off Buck Ross of the Philadelphia Athletics on August 20, 1938.

24

Consecutive games with a hit at Shibe Park by Al Simmons of the Philadelphia Athletics from July 24 to September 7, 1929. He had 45 hits in 96 at-bats (.469) during the streak.

30-2

Record of Lefty Grove (17-1) and George Earnshaw (13-1) of the Philadelphia Athletics at home in 1931.

44.7

Percentage of home wins by the Philadelphia Athletics in 1922 that were credited to Eddie Rommel. He had 17 of the team's 38 wins at Shibe Park that year.

45⅓

Consecutive scoreless innings pitched at Connie Mack Stadium by Woodie Fryman of the Philadelphia Phillies from April 17 to June 14, 1968.

48-29-1

Record of the Philadelphia Phillies at home in 1950 and 1953, their best years at Shibe Park/ Connie Mack Stadium.

60-15

Record of the Philadelphia Athletics at home in 1931, their best year at Shibe Park/Connie Mack Stadium.

61

Extra-base hits by Al Simmons of the Philadelphia Athletics at home in 1930. He had 25 doubles, 11 triples, and 25 home runs. On the road, he had 32 extra-base hits: 16 doubles, 5 triples, and 11 home runs.

68

Home runs by Babe Ruth at Shibe Park, including 66 with the New York Yankees and two with the Boston Red Sox.

77

Home runs by the Philadelphia Phillies at home in 1965, the most by the team at Shibe Park/ Connie Mack Stadium.

87

Combined age, in years, of the battery comprising pitcher Jack Quinn (46 years, 10 months) and catcher Wally Schang (40 years, 9 months) of the Philadelphia Athletics on May 22, 1930, in the second game of a doubleheader against the New York Yankees.

109

Home runs by the Philadelphia Athletics at home in 1932, the most by the team at Shibe Park/ Connie Mack Stadium.

120-32

Record of Lefty Grove at Shibe Park, including 112-27 with the Philadelphia Athletics from 1925 to 1933 and 8-5 with the Boston Red Sox from 1934 to 1941. During the five-year span from 1929 to 1933, he had a record of 75-11 (.872) at the ballpark.

.233

Batting average of the Philadelphia Phillies at home in 1940 and 1968, the lowest by the team at Shibe Park/Connie Mack Stadium.

.235

Batting average of the Philadelphia Athletics at home in 1915, the lowest by the team at Shibe Park/Connie Mack Stadium.

239

Total bases by Al Simmons of the Philadelphia Athletics at home in 1930. He had 153 total bases on the road.

.275

Batting average of the Philadelphia Phillies at home in 1953, the highest by the team at Shibe Park/Connie Mack Stadium.

.323

Batting average of the Philadelphia Athletics at home in 1925, the highest by the team at Shibe Park/Connie Mack Stadium.

500th

Career home run by Jimmie Foxx of the Boston Red Sox on September 24, 1940 (first game of doubleheader), off George Caster of the Philadelphia Athletics. Foxx became the second player (after Babe Ruth) to reach this milestone. He was 32 years old.

40,952

Attendance at a doubleheader between the Philadelphia Phillies and Brooklyn Dodgers on May 11, 1947, the largest baseball crowd at Shibe Park/Connie Mack Stadium.

1,205-1,340-13

Regular-season record of the Philadelphia Phillies at Shibe Park/Connie Mack Stadium from May 16 to 28, 1927, and from July 4, 1938, to October 1, 1970.

1,598-1,487-27

Regular-season record of Philadelphia Athletics manager Connie Mack at Shibe Park (1909 to 1950).

1,672

Total bases by Al Simmons at Shibe Park.

1,762-1,704-31

Regular-season record of the Philadelphia Athletics at Shibe Park/Connie Mack Stadium from April 12, 1909, to September 19, 1954.

146,223

Regular-season attendance of the Philadelphia Athletics at home in 1915, the lowest for the team at Shibe Park/Connie Mack Stadium.

207,177

Regular-season attendance of the Philadelphia Phillies at home in 1940, the lowest for the team at Shibe Park/Connie Mack Stadium.

945,076

Regular-season attendance of the Philadelphia Athletics at home in 1948, the highest for the team at Shibe Park/Connie Mack Stadium.

1,425,891

Regular-season attendance of the Philadelphia Phillies at home in 1964, the highest for the team at Shibe Park/Connie Mack Stadium.

Part of the Athletics' "$100,000 infield," Hall of Fame second baseman Eddie Collins batted .345 and averaged 110 runs scored and 60 stolen bases per season in his first six full big-league seasons (1909-1914) with Connie Mack's first dynasty.

CAREER LEADERS AT
SHIBE PARK/CONNIE MACK STADIUM

BATTING

GAMES

921	Richie Ashburn
891	Jimmy Dykes
839	Del Ennis
780	Tony Taylor
779	Willie Jones

PLATE APPEARANCES

4140	Richie Ashburn
3598	Jimmy Dykes
3503	Del Ennis
3193	Tony Taylor
3181	Bob Johnson

AT-BATS

3572	Richie Ashburn
3183	Del Ennis
3057	Jimmy Dykes
2903	Tony Taylor
2765	Granny Hamner

RUNS

579	Jimmie Foxx
562	Richie Ashburn
520	Bob Johnson
517	Al Simmons
488	Jimmy Dykes

HITS

1120	Richie Ashburn
1000	Al Simmons
923	Del Ennis
879	Jimmy Dykes
857	Jimmie Foxx

DOUBLES

197	Al Simmons
169	Jimmy Dykes
151	Del Ennis
151	Wally Moses
148	Johnny Callison

TRIPLES

62	Richie Ashburn
54	Johnny Callison
53	Al Simmons
52	Wally Moses
48	Eddie Collins

HOME RUNS

181	Jimmie Foxx
149	Bob Johnson
134	Del Ennis
123	Al Simmons
92	Willie Jones

RBIs

700	Al Simmons
642	Jimmie Foxx
589	Del Ennis
533	Bob Johnson
453	Jimmy Dykes

WALKS

569	Max Bishop
478	Richie Ashburn
471	Jimmie Foxx
425	Bob Johnson
413	Elmer Valo

INTENTIONAL WALKS

55	Del Ennis
47	Dick Allen
39	Clay Dalrymple
38	Jimmie Foxx
35	Johnny Callison

STRIKEOUTS

421	Dick Allen
416	Johnny Callison
410	Tony Taylor
338	Jimmie Foxx
323	Jimmy Dykes

HIT BY PITCH

46	Jimmy Dykes
34	Tony Taylor
28	Bing Miller
27	Wally Schang
23	Richie Ashburn
23	Eddie Collins

BATTING AVERAGE (MIN. 1,400 AT-BATS)

.368	Al Simmons
.353	Jimmie Foxx
.350	Eddie Collins
.332	Mickey Cochrane
.331	Home Run Baker

ON-BASE PERCENTAGE (MIN. 1,400 AT-BATS)

.458	Jimmie Foxx
.456	Max Bishop
.443	Ferris Fain
.440	Eddie Collins
.429	Mickey Cochrane

SLUGGING PERCENTAGE (MIN. 1,400 AT-BATS)

.668	Jimmie Foxx
.616	Al Simmons
.564	Dick Allen
.546	Bob Johnson
.513	Mickey Cochrane

OPS (MIN. 1,400 AT-BATS)

1.126	Jimmie Foxx
1.029	Al Simmons
.947	Dick Allen
.944	Bob Johnson
.942	Mickey Cochrane

STOLEN BASES

207	Eddie Collins
104	Richie Ashburn
92	Home Run Baker
88	Tony Taylor
81	Amos Strunk

PITCHING

ERA
(MIN. 500 INNINGS, STARTING IN 1913)

2.71   Jim Bunning
2.76   Bullet Joe Bush
2.86   Lefty Grove
2.97   Bobo Newsom
3.06   Larry Jackson

For Bullet Joe Bush, eight innings in 1912 (before ERA was an official statistic in the AL) were excluded from the calculation.

WINS

126   Robin Roberts
120   Lefty Grove
94   Eddie Rommel
70   Curt Simmons
70   Rube Walberg

LOSSES

94   Robin Roberts
60   Curt Simmons
57   Chris Short
52   Rube Walberg
51   Eddie Rommel

WINNING PERCENTAGE
(MIN. 40 WINS)

.789   Lefty Grove
.766   Jack Coombs
.740   Chief Bender
.714   George Earnshaw
.648   Eddie Rommel

GAMES PITCHED

271   Robin Roberts
240   Eddie Rommel
211   Lefty Grove
203   Chris Short
202   Turk Farrell

GAMES STARTED

237   Robin Roberts
156   Curt Simmons
152   Lefty Grove
144   Chris Short
130   Eddie Rommel

COMPLETE GAMES

140   Robin Roberts
100   Lefty Grove
77   Eddie Rommel
63   Rube Walberg
59   Eddie Plank

SHUTOUTS

15   Robin Roberts
13   Chief Bender
11   Eddie Plank
11   Curt Simmons
10   Lefty Grove
10   Chris Short

SAVES

28   Turk Farrell
28   Jim Konstanty
22   Lefty Grove
20   Jack Baldschun
16   Ed Roebuck

INNINGS PITCHED

1953	Robin Roberts
1370⅓	Lefty Grove
1284	Eddie Rommel
1136	Curt Simmons
1109	Chris Short

WALKS

449	Curt Simmons
379	Chris Short
377	Rube Walberg
364	Lefty Grove
362	Robin Roberts

INTENTIONAL WALKS

38	Robin Roberts
33	Chris Short
31	Turk Farrell
30	Curt Simmons
27	Jim Bunning

STRIKEOUTS

1052	Robin Roberts
868	Lefty Grove
788	Chris Short
611	Curt Simmons
609	Jim Bunning

HOME RUNS ALLOWED

186	Robin Roberts
89	Eddie Rommel
82	Rube Walberg
78	Chris Short
72	Curt Simmons

HIT BY PITCH

41	Jim Bunning
32	Cy Morgan
24	Chris Short
19	Art Mahaffey
17	Robin Roberts

WILD PITCHES

32	Chris Short
29	Bullet Joe Bush
27	Alex Kellner
22	Phil Marchildon
21	Rube Walberg

SINGLE-SEASON LEADERS AT
SHIBE PARK/CONNIE MACK STADIUM

BATTING

Games: 81 by Dick Allen, Philadelphia Phillies, 1964; Johnny Callison, Philadelphia Phillies, 1964

Plate appearances: 364 by Al Simmons, Philadelphia Athletics, 1932

At-bats: 339 by Al Simmons, Philadelphia Athletics, 1932

Runs: 89 by Al Simmons, Philadelphia Athletics, 1932

Hits: 129 by Al Simmons, Philadelphia Athletics, 1925

Doubles: 31 by Wally Moses, Philadelphia Athletics, 1937

Triples: 13 by Eddie Collins, Philadelphia Athletics, 1910

Home runs: 31 by Jimmie Foxx, Philadelphia Athletics, 1932; Jimmie Foxx, Philadelphia Athletics, 1933

RBIs: 101 by Al Simmons, Philadelphia Athletics, 1930

Walks: 78 by Eddie Joost, Philadelphia Athletics, 1949

Intentional walks: 14 by Dick Allen, Philadelphia Phillies, 1968

Strikeouts: 80 by Larry Hisle, Philadelphia Phillies, 1969

Hit by pitch: 9 by Tony Taylor, Philadelphia Phillies, 1964

Batting average: .411 by Al Simmons, Philadelphia Athletics, 1931

On-base percentage: .544 by Jimmie Foxx, Philadelphia Athletics, 1935

Slugging percentage: .820 by Jimmie Foxx, Philadelphia Athletics, 1932

OPS: 1.332 by Jimmie Foxx, Philadelphia Athletics, 1932

Stolen bases: 38 by Eddie Collins, Philadelphia Athletics, 1910

PITCHING

ERA: 1.30 by Scott Perry, Philadelphia Athletics, 1918

Wins: 19 by Jack Coombs, Philadelphia Athletics, 1910

Losses: 13 by Grant Jackson, Philadelphia Phillies, 1969

Games pitched: 38 by Jim Konstanty, Philadelphia Phillies, 1950

Games started: 22 by Jack Coombs, Philadelphia Athletics, 1911

Complete games: 18 by Jack Coombs, Philadelphia Athletics, 1910; Elmer Myers, Philadelphia Athletics, 1916; Scott Perry, Philadelphia Athletics, 1918; Robin Roberts, Philadelphia Phillies, 1953

Shutouts: 7 by Jack Coombs, Philadelphia Athletics, 1910

Saves: 11 by Dick Selma, Philadelphia Phillies, 1970

Innings pitched: 187⅔ by Jack Coombs, Philadelphia Athletics, 1911

Walks: 83 by Elmer Myers, Philadelphia Athletics, 1916

Intentional walks: 10 by Alex Kellner, Philadelphia Athletics, 1954; Jim Bunning, Philadelphia Phillies, 1967

Strikeouts: 149 by Jim Bunning, Philadelphia Phillies, 1967

Home runs allowed: 22 by George Earnshaw, Philadelphia Athletics, 1932; Robin Roberts, Philadelphia Phillies, 1957

Hit by pitch: 15 by Cy Morgan, Philadelphia Athletics, 1911

Wild pitches: 11 by Jack Hamilton, Philadelphia Phillies, 1962

SINGLE-GAME LEADERS AT SHIBE PARK/CONNIE MACK STADIUM

(* = extra-inning game)

BATTING

Runs: 5 by Jimmy Walsh, Philadelphia Athletics, September 23, 1913; Charlie Jamieson, Cleveland Indians, September 15, 1921 (first game of doubleheader); Lu Blue, Detroit Tigers, August 22, 1922 (second game of doubleheader); Tony Lazzeri, New York Yankees, May 22, 1930 (second game of doubleheader); Al Simmons, Philadelphia Athletics, June 23, 1930 (second game of doubleheader); Jimmie Foxx, Philadelphia Athletics, May 5, 1932; Jim Tabor, Boston Red Sox, July 4, 1939 (second game of doubleheader); Hank Greenberg, Detroit Tigers, July 30, 1939 (first game of doubleheader); Eddie Yost, Washington Senators, September 7, 1953 (first game of doubleheader)

Hits: 6 by Jimmie Foxx, Philadelphia Athletics, May 30, 1930 (first game of doubleheader)*; Bob Johnson, Philadelphia Athletics, June 16, 1934 (second game of doubleheader)*; Doc Cramer, Philadelphia Athletics, July 13, 1935 (first game of doubleheader); Rip Radcliff, Chicago White Sox, July 18, 1936 (second game of doubleheader); Cookie Lavagetto, Brooklyn Dodgers, September 23, 1939 (first game of doubleheader); Jim Fridley, Cleveland Indians, April 29, 1952

Doubles: 3 on 64 occasions

Triples: 3 by Willie Mays, San Francisco Giants, September 15, 1960*

Home runs: 4 by Lou Gehrig, New York Yankees, June 3, 1932; Pat Seerey, Chicago White Sox, July 18, 1948 (first game of doubleheader)*

RBIs: 11 by Tony Lazzeri, New York Yankees, May 24, 1936

Walks: 5 by Roger Peckinpaugh, New York Yankees, June 2, 1919 (first game of doubleheader); Whitey Witt, New York Yankees, July 2, 1924 (second game of doubleheader); Max Bishop, Philadelphia Athletics, April 29, 1929; Max Bishop, Philadelphia Athletics, May 21, 1930 (first game of doubleheader); Ben Chapman, New York Yankees, May 24, 1936; Andy Seminick, Philadelphia Phillies, September 30, 1951*; Dick Allen, Philadelphia Phillies, August 16, 1968

Intentional walks: 3 by Jimmie Foxx, Philadelphia Athletics, September 2, 1933 (first game of doubleheader); Ted Kluszewski, Cincinnati Reds, September 15, 1950 (second game of doubleheader)*; Del Ennis, Philadelphia Phillies, April 24, 1951; Clay Dalrymple, Philadelphia Phillies, June 11, 1965*; John Roseboro, Los Angeles Dodgers, May 5, 1967; Dick Allen, Philadelphia Phillies, June 18, 1968 (second game of doubleheader); Dick Allen, Philadelphia Phillies, August 16, 1968

Strikeouts: 5 by Cy Morgan, Philadelphia Athletics, September 18, 1911 (second game of doubleheader)*; Lefty Grove, Philadelphia Athletics, June 10, 1933 (first game of doubleheader); Ron Kline, Pittsburgh Pirates, September 22, 1958 (first game of doubleheader)*; Dick Allen, St. Louis Cardinals, May 24, 1970*

Stolen bases: 5 by Eddie Collins, Philadelphia Athletics, May 18, 1912

PITCHING

Innings pitched: 19⅔ by Les Mueller, Detroit Tigers, July 21, 1945*

Runs allowed: 24 by Allan Travers, Detroit Tigers, May 18, 1912

Hits allowed: 26 by Allan Travers, Detroit Tigers, May 18, 1912

Walks: 16 by Bruno Haas, Philadelphia Athletics, June 23, 1915 (second game of doubleheader)

Intentional walks: 4 by Jim Konstanty, Philadelphia Phillies, May 5, 1951*; Bunky Stewart, Washington Senators, September 20, 1953 (second game of doubleheader)*; Dave Giusti, Houston Astros, June 11, 1965*; Ron Perranoski, Los Angeles Dodgers, September 16, 1967*

Strikeouts: 17 by Art Mahaffey, Philadelphia Phillies, April 23, 1961 (second game of doubleheader)

Home runs allowed: 6 by George Caster, Philadelphia Athletics, September 24, 1940 (first game of doubleheader)

Hit by pitch: 4 by Byron Houck, Philadelphia Athletics, October 4, 1912

Wild pitches: 4 by Sandy Koufax, Los Angeles Dodgers, September 9, 1958; Jack Hamilton, Philadelphia Phillies, September 20, 1962 (second game of doubleheader)

SOURCES

Society for American Baseball Research. *The SABR Baseball List and Record Book* (New York: Scribner, 2007).

Sugar, Bert Randolph, ed. *The Baseball Maniac's Almanac* (fifth edition) (New York: Sports Publishing, 2019).

Baseball-Reference.com

NationalPastime.com

Retrosheet.org/boxesetc/P/PK_PHI11.htm

CONTRIBUTORS

Matt Albertson resides in Havertown, Pennsylvania, with his wife, Jess, and their young son, Garret. He joined SABR in 2015 and was the 2018 SABR Nineteenth Century Committee's Chairman's Award recipient. In 2017 he dedicated a Pennsylvania Historical Marker to the Jefferson Street Ballparks in Philadelphia. Matt is currently the president of the Athletic Base Ball Club of Philadelphia and is the historical columnist for SportsTalkPhilly.com.

John Bauer resides with his wife and two children in Bedford, New Hampshire. By day, he is an attorney specializing in insurance regulatory law and corporate law. By night, he spends many spring and summer evenings cheering for the San Francisco Giants and many fall and winter evenings reading history. He is a past and ongoing contributor to other SABR projects.

Josh Berk is an author, librarian, and lifelong Phillies fan. His books for young people include the "Lenny and the Mikes" series of baseball mysteries about a group of Phillies-loving kids. He is the co-host of the "This Week in 1920s Baseball" podcast and previously contributed to SABR's *The 100 Greatest Games of Babe Ruth's Career*.

He was happy to have the chance to write about Robin Roberts for this book, as Roberts was one of his dad's favorite players of all time.

Nathan Bierma is president of SABR Southern Michigan. He lives in Grand Rapids. The first two major-league ballparks he set foot in as a kid were Tiger Stadium and Wrigley Field, and they forged a lifelong love of baseball and historic ballparks. His writing has appeared in the *Chicago Tribune, Chicago Sports Review*, and *Detroit Free Press*, and in SABR's recent books on the greatest games at Wrigley Field and Comiskey Park. He is the author of *The Eclectic Encyclopedia of English: Language at Its Most Enigmatic, Ephemeral, and Egregious*. His website is www.nathanbierma.com.

John J. Burbridge Jr. is professor emeritus at Elon University, where he was both a dean and professor. He is also an adjunct at York College of Pennsylvania. While at Elon he introduced and taught the course Baseball and Statistics. He has authored several SABR publications and presented at SABR Conventions, NINE, and the Seymour meetings. He is a lifelong New York Giants baseball fan. The greatest Giants-Dodgers game he attended was a 1-0 Giants victory in Jersey City in 1956. Yes, the Dodgers did play in Jersey City in 1956 and 1957. John can be reached at burbridg@elon.edu.

Thomas J. Brown Jr. is a lifelong Mets fan who became a Durham Bulls fan after moving to North Carolina in the early 1980s. He was a national-board-certified high-school science teacher for 34 years. Tom still volunteers with ELL students, serving as a mentor to those students while they are in school as well as after graduation. He is also a resource for ELL teachers in the local school system. Tom has been a member of SABR since 1995 after learning about the organization during a visit to Cooperstown on his honeymoon. He became active in the organization after his retirement and has written numerous biographies and game stories, mostly about the New York Mets. Tom also enjoys traveling as much as possible with his wife and has visited major-league and minor-league baseball parks across the country on their trips. He loves to cook, making the meals for his family as well as writing about the recipes that he cooks on his blog, Cooking and My Family.

A lifelong White Sox fan surrounded by Cubs fans in the northern suburbs of Chicago, **Ken Carrano** works as a chief financial officer for a large landscaping firm and as a soccer referee. He has been a SABR member since 1992, and has contributed to several SABR publications and the SABR Games Project. Ken and his Brewers' fan wife, Ann, share two children, two golden retrievers, and a mutual distain for the blue side of Chicago.

Alan Cohen has been a SABR member since 2010. He serves as vice president-treasurer of the Connecticut Smoky Joe Wood Chapter, is a datacaster (MiLB First Pitch stringer) for the Hartford Yard Goats, the Double-A affiliate of the Colorado Rockies, and has been serving as

head of SABR's fact-checking committee since December 13, 2020. He attended Franklin and Marshall College and attended Opening Night at Connie Mack Stadium on April 14, 1967. His biographies, game stories, and essays have appeared in more than 60 SABR publications. Since his first *Baseball Research Journal* article appeared in 2013, Alan has continued to expand his research into the Hearst Sandlot Classic (1946-1965), from which 87 players advanced to the major leagues. He has four children, nine grandchildren, and one great-grandchild, and resides in Connecticut with wife Frances, their cats, Morty, Ava, and Zoe, and their dog Buddy.

Richard Cuicchi joined SABR in 1983 and is an active member of the Schott-Pelican Chapter. Since his retirement as an information technology executive, Richard authored Family Ties: A Comprehensive Collection of Facts and Trivia about Baseball's Relatives. He has contributed to numerous SABR BioProject and Games Project publications. He does freelance writing and blogging about a variety of baseball topics on his website, TheTenthInning.com. Richard lives in New Orleans with his wife, Mary.

Rich D'Ambrosio is an ardent Phillies fan who was born and raised in Philadelphia and still lives there. A SABR member since 1997, Rich is the author of the bios on Dick Allen, Larry Bowa, and Pat Burrell. He is a graduate of Temple, La Salle, and St. Joseph's Universities and teaches English at St. Hubert Catholic High School for Girls in Philadelphia. Rich is a serious baseball memorabilia collector and attended his first Phillies game at Connie Mack Stadium in 1970.

Paul E. Doutrich is professor emeritus at York College of Pennsylvania, where he taught American history for 30 years. He now lives in Brewster, Massachusetts. Among the courses he taught was a one entitled Baseball History. He has written scholarly articles and contributed to several anthologies about the Revolutionary era, and has written a book about Jacksonian America. He has also curated several museum exhibits. His recent scholarship has focused on baseball history. He has contributed numerous manuscripts to various SABR publications and is the author of *The Cardinals and the Yankees, 1926: A Classical Season and St. Louis in Seven*.

Greg Erion died in December 2017 after a brief illness. He retired from the railroad industry and taught history part-time at Skyline Community College in San Bruno, California. He wrote several biographies and game articles for SABR. Greg was one of the leaders of SABR's Baseball Games Project. With his wife, Barbara, he was a resident of South San Francisco, California.

Doug Feldmann is a professor in the College of Education at Northern Kentucky University and a former scout for the Cincinnati Reds, Seattle Mariners, and San Diego Padres. He is the author of 12 books on a variety of sports topics, more about which can be learned at dougfeldmannbooks.com.

Scott Ferkovich is a native of Detroit. He is the author of *Motor City Champs: Mickey Cochrane and the 1934-1935 Detroit Tigers*.

Dan Fields has contributed to many SABR books. He is a senior manuscript editor at the *New England Journal of Medicine* and a longtime volunteer with the Grief Support Services program of Samaritans Inc. He lives in Framingham, Massachusetts, and can be reached at dfields820@gmail.com.

James Forr is a recovering Pirates fan in the heart of Cardinals country. His book *Pie Traynor: A Baseball Biography*, co-authored with David Proctor, was a nominee for the 2010 CASEY

Award. He is also a winner of the McFarland-SABR Baseball Research Award and was a speaker at the 2019 Frederick Ivor-Campbell Nineteenth Century Base Ball Conference.

Brian Frank is passionate about documenting the history of major- and minor-league baseball. He is the creator of the website The Herd Chronicles (www.herdchronicles.com), which is dedicated to preserving the history of the Buffalo Bisons and professional baseball in Buffalo. His articles can also be read on the official website of the Bisons. He was an assistant editor of the book *The Seasons of Buffalo Baseball, 1857-2020*, and he's a frequent contributor to SABR publications. Brian and his wife, Jenny, enjoy traveling around the country in their camper to major- and minor-league ballparks and taking an annual trip to Europe. Brian was a history major at Canisius College, where he earned a bachelor of arts. He also received a juris doctor from the University at Buffalo School of Law.

Gordon J. Gattie is a lifelong baseball fan and a SABR member since 1998. Currently a civilian US Navy engineer, he includes among his baseball research interests ballparks, historical trends, and statistical analysis. Gordon earned his Ph.D. from SUNY Buffalo, where he used baseball to investigate judgment performance in complex dynamic environments. Ever the optimist, he dreams of a Cleveland Indians World Series championship. Lisa, his wonderful wife, who roots for the Yankees, and Morrigan, their beloved Labrador retriever, are looking forward to resuming their cross-country travels visiting ballparks and other baseball-related sites. Gordon has contributed to many SABR publications, including several issues of *The National Pastime*, and the Games project.

Mike Huber is professor of mathematics at Muhlenberg College in Allentown, Pennsylvania, which is about an hour north of where Shibe Park/Connie Mack Stadium used to be. Part of his research includes studying rare events in baseball, such as hitting for the cycle. A lifelong Orioles fan, he joined SABR in 1996 and enjoys contributing to the Games project. He routinely teaches a course in sabermetrics.

Lawrence Knorr is the president and CEO of Sunbury Press, Inc., a trade publishing company based in Pennsylvania. He is the author or co-author of numerous books on US history, focusing on the colonial and Revolutionary periods and the Pennsylvania Dutch. A lifelong Philadelphia baseball fan, Lawrence is the author of *Gettysburg Eddie: The Story of Eddie Plank*, which was released in April 2018, and *Wonder Boy: The Story of Carl Scheib*, released in May 2016. He resides in Mechanicsburg, Pennsylvania.

For over 20 years, **Kevin Larkin** patrolled the highways and byways of the roads in his hometown of Great Barrington, Massachusetts. When not at work keeping the citizens of his hometown safe, inevitably Larkin was listening to a baseball game on the radio. He has been going to baseball games since he was five years old. His baseball life is the only thing he loves more than his children and grandchildren. One day while he was browsing in a local bookstore, the owner of the bookstore asked him if he was interested in writing a book about baseball. Larkin's first effort was *Baseball in the Bay State: A History of Baseball in Massachusetts*. He then took quite an interest in the history of the game, authoring a book on one of his heroes, Lou Gehrig called *Gehrig: Game by Game*, a look at every game that the Iron Horse played during his major-league career. He has since written five more books on the sport. He also writes and fact-checks for SABR, an experience he considers the best decision he has ever made.

Bob LeMoine is a librarian and adjunct professor in New Hampshire. A lifelong Red Sox fan, Bob has contributed to several SABR projects and was co-editor of two SABR books: *Boston's First Nine: the 1871-75 Boston Red Stockings* and *The Glorious Beaneaters of the 1890s*.

Len Levin is a longtime newspaper editor in New England, now retired. He lives in Providence with his wife, Linda, and an overachieving orange cat. He now (Len, not the cat) is the grammarian for the Rhode Island Supreme Court and edits its decisions. He also copyedits many SABR books, including this one. He is just down the interstate from Fenway Park, where he has spent many happy hours.

SABR member and Massachusetts native **Mike Lynch** is the founder of Seamheads.com and the author of five books, including *Harry Frazee, Ban Johnson and the Feud That Nearly Destroyed the American League*, which was named a finalist for the 2009 Larry Ritter Award and was nominated for a Seymour Medal. His most recent work includes a three-book series called *Baseball's Untold History* and several articles that have appeared in SABR books. His collaboration with others on Negro Leagues history earned him the 2019 Tweed Webb Lifetime Achievement Award given by SABR's Negro Leagues Research Committee. He lives in the Roslindale section of Boston with Catherine and their cats, Jiggs and Pepper.

Andrew Milner has been a SABR member since 1984. He has given presentations at SABR regionals, written for the *SABR Review of Books*, *The National Pastime* and *Baseball's Biggest Blowout Games*, and was a primary researcher for *The World Series in the Deadball Era*. In addition, he was a copy editor at the Philadelphia sports magazine *The Fan*, regularly reviewed baseball books for the *Philadelphia City Paper* until its closure in 2015 and contributed a Phillies historical entry to the reference serial *Sports in America* (Sharpe Reference, 2011). He lives in suburban Philadelphia.

Bill Nowlin was born and still lives in the Boston area, and admits to a prejudice in favor of Fenway Park. A former professor of political science, and co-founder of Rounder Records back in 1970, he has devoted much of the last 10 years to writing about baseball and helping edit the works of others. A member of the SABR board of directors since 2004, he has worked on several dozen SABR books and contributed over 1,000 articles to SABR's research holdings.

J.G. Preston has written biographies and game stories for several SABR books. He attended his first major-league game at Crosley Field (RIP) in 1966 and sat on Astros first baseman Chuck Harrison's lap on the car ride back to the hotel afterward. In the 1980s he covered the Minnesota Twins as sports director of the Minnesota News Network and later served as editor of the Twins' program magazine. He lives in Santa Fe, New Mexico.

Carl Riechers retired from United Parcel Service in 2012 after 35 years of service. With more free time, he became a SABR member that same year. Born and raised in the suburbs of St. Louis, he became a big fan of the Cardinals. He and his wife, Janet, have three children and he is the proud grandpa of two.

Paul Rogers is a law professor and former dean at Southern Methodist University, where he has served as its faculty athletics representative for 34 years. Although a native of Wyoming, Rogers has been a Phillies fan since he was a boy, suffering through many losing seasons and then the 1964 collapse. He later had the wonderful good fortune to co-author two books with his boyhood hero Robin Roberts and more recently co-edited the

SABR team history on the 1950 Phillies titled *The Whiz Kids Take the Pennant.* He is also the president of the Ernie Banks-Bobby Bragan SABR Chapter in Dallas-Fort Worth.

Harry Schoger is a Hoosier transplanted to the Buckeye state, where he now lives with his wife, Eleanor, of 61 years. In his professional career he worked in management roles in the primary steelmaking industry. His fifth-grade teacher brought in his radio so the class could listen to the 1948 World Series. The experience made him an Indians fan to this day. By coincidence he now lives in Canton, Ohio, home of the Pro Football Hall of Fame, and near Cleveland. He has been a history aficionado all his life and a SABR member for about four years. He has contributed both bios and games to several books.

From an early age **David E. Skelton** developed a love of baseball when the lights from Philadelphia's Connie Mack Stadium shone through his bedroom window. Long removed from Philly, David is retired and has lived in Central Texas with his wife, Susan, since 2007. David is a fierce Tampa Bay Rays fan, a carryover from his years residing in or near Tampa, Florida, in the late 1990s and early 2000s. He is an avid collector of sports memorabilia.

Courtney Michelle Smith is a lifelong resident of Delaware County, Pennsylvania, and is a passionate fan of Philadelphia's professional sports teams. She has belonged to SABR since 2006 and is a member of the Philadelphia-based Connie Mack Chapter. Since 2008 she has worked as a full-time faculty member at Cabrini University in Radnor, Pennsylvania. She is a professor of history and political science, and she incorporates sports history into her courses. She is the author of several books and articles on topics covering baseball, local history, and the American presidency.

Lyle Spatz, a SABR member since 1973, was chairman of the Baseball Records Committee from 1991 to 2016. Among the books he has written is *The Midsummer Classic: The Complete History of Baseball's All-Star Game*, co-authored with David Vincent and Dave Smith.

As a kid growing up in New York who rooted for the Montreal Expos, New York Yankees, and Oklahoma Sooners, **Mark S. Sternman** naturally roots against most Philadelphia teams except when the 76ers play the Celtics in the NBA playoffs and Jalen Hurts plays QB for the Eagles. He never saw a game in Shibe Park but did see games at Veterans Stadium. Having profiled Joe Girardi for *Time for Expansion Baseball* (SABR, 2018), Sternman wished the Phillies well under the tutelage of the former skipper of the Bronx Bombers.

Jim Sweetman's paternal great-grandfather emigrated from Ireland to work in the shipyards in Bristol, Pennsylvania, in the late 1800s, establishing the family's affinity for Philadelphia baseball. He remains a lifelong Phillies fan, despite growing up on the edge of the New York media market in central New Jersey and living for the past 30-plus years just outside Washington, D.C. Since 1994, he's operated www.broadandpattison.com, a website providing daily slices of Phillies history based on extensive reviews of contemporary press accounts.

Joseph Wancho has been a SABR member since 2005. He currently serves as vice chair for the Baseball Index Project.

Rich Westcott is the author of 27 books, mostly about baseball and including ones on Shibe Park/Connie Mack Stadium, Veterans Stadium, and Philadelphia's Old Ballparks. A newspaper and magazine writer and editor for more than 40 years, he has appeared in 10 film documentaries, six produced by MLB. Publisher for 14 years of the esteemed *Phillies Report*, this lifelong Philadelphia-area resident, who played and coached high-school and college baseball, is a former president of the Philadelphia Sports Writers Association, was once an official scorer at Phillies games, and has been inducted into four halls of fame.

Gregory H. Wolf was born in Pittsburgh, but now resides in the Chicagoland area with his wife, Margaret, and daughter, Gabriela. A professor of German studies and holder of the Dennis and Jean Bauman Endowed Chair in the Humanities at North Central College in Naperville, Illinois, he has edited more than a dozen books for SABR. Since January 2017 he has been co-director of SABR's BioProject, which you can follow on Facebook and Twitter.

Jack Zerby, who died in August 2021, was a retired attorney and estates/trust administrator. He grew up in rural western Pennsylvania, far removed from Shibe Park but the home of Fred Caligiuri, who figures prominently in one of the games accounts Jack wrote for this book. A SABR member since 1994, Jack joined the Biography Project at inception. He wrote more than a dozen SABR biographies, including Fred Caligiuri's, and numerous Games Project accounts. After 25 years in Southwest Florida, where he and SABR colleague Mel Poplock founded the Seymour-Mills regional chapter, Jack and his wife, Diana, moved to Brevard, North Carolina.

A lifelong New Jersey resident, **John Zinn** is an independent historian and a longtime member of SABR. He is the chairman of the board of the New Jersey Historical Society. John is the author of five books including three about the Brooklyn Dodgers as well as numerous essays and articles. He also writes a blog on baseball history entitled A Manly Pastime. His biography of Charles Ebbets received the 2019 Ron Gabriel Award for the best research on the Brooklyn Dodgers. He is the scorekeeper for the Flemington Neshanock vintage baseball team. John holds BA and MBA degrees from Rutgers University and is a Vietnam veteran.

Don Zminda has been a White Sox fan since attending his first game at Old Comiskey in August of 1954. As director of publications for STATS, Inc. (now STATS LLC) from 1988 to 2000, he co-authored or edited a dozen annual sports publications. Don's book *The Legendary Harry Caray: Baseball's Greatest Salesman* was a 2019 CASEY Award nominee; his latest offering, *Double Plays and Double Crosses: The Black Sox and Baseball in 1920*, was published by Rowman & Littlefield in March 2021. A SABR member since 1979, he is retired and has lived in Los Angeles with his wife, Sharon, since 2000.

Friends of SABR

You can become a Friend of SABR by giving as little as $10 per month or by making a one-time gift of $1,000 or more. When you do so, you will be inducted into a community of passionate baseball fans dedicated to supporting SABR's work.

Friends of SABR receive the following benefits:
- ✓ Annual Friends of SABR Commemorative Lapel Pin
- ✓ Recognition in This Week in SABR, SABR.org, and the SABR Annual Report
- ✓ Access to the SABR Annual Convention VIP donor event
- ✓ Invitations to exclusive Friends of SABR events

SABR On-Deck Circle - $10/month, $30/month, $50/month

Get in the SABR On-Deck Circle, and help SABR become the essential community for the world of baseball. Your support will build capacity around all things SABR, including publications, website content, podcast development, and community growth.

A monthly gift is deducted from your bank account or charged to a credit card until you tell us to stop. No more email, mail, or phone reminders.

 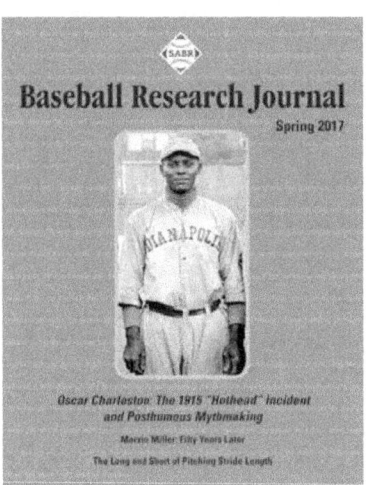 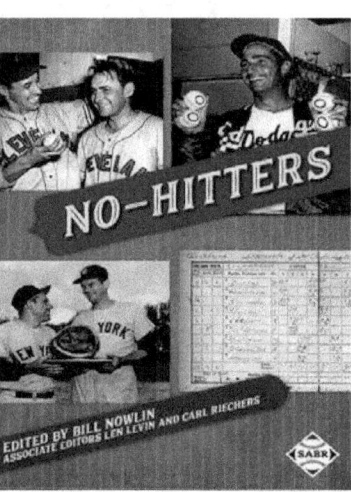

Join the SABR On-Deck Circle

Payment Info: _____Visa _____Mastercard

Name on Card: _____

Card #: _____

Exp. Date: _____ Security Code: _____

Signature: _____

- ○ $10/month
- ○ $30/month
- ○ $50/month
- ○ Other amount _____

Go to sabr.org/donate to make your gift online

NEW BOOKS FROM SABR

Part of the mission of the Society for American Baseball Research has always been to disseminate member research. In addition to the *Baseball Research Journal*, SABR publishes books that include player biographies, historical game recaps, and statistical analysis. All SABR books are available in print and ebook formats. SABR members can access the entire SABR Digital Library for free and purchase print copies at significant member discounts of 40 to 50% off cover price.

JEFF BAGWELL IN CONNECTICUT:
A CONSISTENT LAD IN THE LAND OF STEADY HABITS
This volume of articles, interviews, and essays by members of the Connecticut chapter of SABR chronicles the life and career of Connecticut's favorite baseball son, Hall-of-Famer Jeff Bagwell, with special attention on his high school and college years.
Edited by Karl Cicitto, Bill Nowlin, & Len Levin
$19.95 paperback (ISBN 978-1-943816-97-2)
$9.99 ebook (ISBN 978-1-943816-96-5)
7"x10", 246 pages, 45 photos

1995 CLEVELAND INDIANS:
THE SLEEPING GIANT AWAKENS
After almost 40 years of sub-500 baseball, the Sleeping Giant woke in 1995, the first season in the Indians spent in their new home of Jacob's Field. The biographies of all the players, coaches, and broadcasters from that year are here, sprinkled with personal perspectives, as well as game stories from key matchups during the 1995 season, information about Jacob's Field, and other essays.
Edited by Joseph Wancho
$19.95 paperback (ISBN 978-1-943816-95-8)
$9.99 ebook (ISBN 978-1-943816-94-1)
8.5"X11", 410 pages, 76 photos

TIME FOR EXPANSION BASEBALL
The LA Angels and "new" Washington Senators ushered in MLB expansion in 1960, followed by the Houston Colt .45s and New York Mets. By 1998, 10 additional teams had launched: the Kansas City Royals, Seattle Pilots, Toronto Blue Jays, and Tampa Bay Devil Tays in the AL, and the Montreal Expos, San Diego Padres, Colorado Rockies, Florida Marlins, and Arizona Diamondbacks in the NL. *Time for Expansion Baseball* tells each team's origin and includes biographies of key players.
Edited by Maxwell Kates and Bill Nowlin
$24.95 paperback (ISBN 978-1-933599-89-7)
$9.99 ebook (ISBN 978-1-933599-88-0)
8.5"X11", 430 pages, 150 photos

BASE BALL'S 19TH CENTURY "WINTER" MEETINGS
1857-1900
A look at the business meetings of base ball's earliest days (not all of which were in the winter). As John Thorn writes in his Foreword, "This monumental volume traces the development of the game from its birth as an organized institution to its very near suicide at the dawn of the next century."
Edited by Jeremy K. Hodges and Bill Nowlin
$29.95 paperback (ISBN 978-1-943816-91-0)
$9.99 ebook (ISBN978-1-943816-90-3)
8.5"x11", 390 pages, 50 photos

MET-ROSPECTIVES:
A COLLECTION OF THE GREATEST GAMES IN NEW YORK METS HISTORY
This book's 57 game stories—coinciding with the number of Mets years through 2018—are strictly for the eternal optimist. They include the team's very first victory in April 1962 at Forbes Field, Tom Seaver's "Imperfect Game" in July '69, the unforgettable Game Sixes in October '86, the "Grand Slam Single" in the 1999 NLCS, and concludes with the extra-innings heroics in September 2016 at Citi Field that helped ensure a wild-card berth.
edited by Brian Wright and Bill Nowlin
$14.95 paperback (ISBN 978-1-943816-87-3)
$9.99 ebook (ISBN 978-1-943816-86-6)
8.5"X11", 148 pages, 44 photos

CINCINNATI'S CROSLEY FIELD:
A GEM IN THE QUEEN CITY
This book evokes memories of Crosley Field through detailed summaries of more than 85 historic and monumental games played there, and 10 insightful feature essays about the history of the ballpark. Former Reds players Johnny Edwards and Art Shamsky share their memories of the park in introductions.
Edited by Gregory H. Wolf
$19.95 paperback (ISBN 978-1-943816-75-0)
$9.99 ebook (ISBN 978-1-943816-74-3)
8.5"X11", 320 pages, 43 photos

MOMENTS OF JOY AND HEARTBREAK:
66 SIGNIFICANT EPISODES IN THE HISTORY OF THE PITTSBURGH PIRATES
In this book we relive no-hitters, World Series-winning homers, and the last tripleheader ever played in major-league baseball. Famous Pirates like Honus Wagner and Roberto Clemente—and infamous ones like Dock Ellis—make their appearances, as well as recent stars like Andrew McCutcheon.
Edited by Jorge Iber and Bill Nowlin
$19.95 paperback (ISBN 978-1-943816-73-6)
$9.99 ebook (ISBN 978-1-943816-72-9)
8.5"X11", 208 pages, 36 photos

FROM SPRING TRAINING TO SCREEN TEST:
BASEBALL PLAYERS TURNED ACTORS
SABR"s book of baseball's "matinee stars," a selection of those who crossed the lines between professional sports and popular entertainment. Included are the famous (Gene Autry, Joe DiMaggio, Jim Thorpe, Bernie Williams) and the forgotten (Al Gettel, Lou Stringer, Wally Hebert, Wally Hood), essays on baseball in TV shows and Coca-Cola commercials, and Jim Bouton's casting as "Jim Barton" in the *Ball Four* TV series.
Edited by Rob Edelman and Bill Nowlin
$19.95 paperback (ISBN 978-1-943816-71-2)
$9.99 ebook (ISBN 978-1-943816-70-5)
8.5"X11", 410 pages, 89 photos

To learn more about how to receive these publications for free or at member discount as a member of SABR, visit the website: sabr.org/join